# Introduction to Management Accounting

All Internet Resources are updated every two weeks by Ph.D.-granted professors around the world, as well as a team of full-time technical support staff.

You can always rely on Prentice Hall's PHLIP/CW to provide you and your students with the services you need!

## "Syllabus Manager":

❏ Allows instructors to construct on-line syllabi tailored to assignments and events for their classes, and linked to specific modules on the Web site and other on-line content
❏ Provides students with quick access to course materials by using a calendar feature found on the navigation bar

## "Faculty Resources/Lounge" includes:

❏ Password- protected site
❏ Downloads of on-line supplements
  Archive of teaching resources created by other faculty using this text
❏ Chat room for faculty use only
❏ Teaching tools for the "Current Events"
❏ PHAS General Ledger

## "Study Guide" includes:

❏ Separate multiple choice, fill-in-the-blank, and essay practice tests for each chapter
❏ "Hints" for each problem
❏ Immediate feedback on tests with total score, and an explanation provided for each incorrect answer
❏ Ability to e-mail results to faculty member or other designated individual
❏ All questions created specifically for the Web site; no duplication of questions taken from text, test bank, or print study guide

**Companion Website**

Chapter 1: Introduction to Business in the United States

### Objectives

After studying this chapter, you should be able to:

1. Describe the four factors of production.

2. Explain the basic concepts of capitalism and how they relate to the profit motive.

3. Explain the basic issues in the debate over whether businesses have a social responsibility.

4. Distinguish among the three basic forms of business organization - the proprietorship, the partnership, and the corporation - and describe the advantages and disadvantages of each.

5. Distinguish among the three major types of business activities and define hybrid type businesses.

6. Explain the basic need for international business trade and the complications involved in this activity.

7. Describe the SEC's authority over accounting reporting standards and describe the current standard-setting process in the United States.

8. Explain the purpose of an independent financial audit.

# Introduction to Management Accounting

## A User Perspective

Kumen H. Jones
Arizona State University, Retired

Michael L. Werner
University of Miami

Katherene P. Terrell
University of Central Oklahoma

Robert L. Terrell
University of Central Oklahoma

**Prentice Hall,** Upper Saddle River, New Jersey 07458

We dedicate this book to our siblings—
our first critics and best friends.

To Norma Dee, Peggy, Marrilyn, Gordon and Paul
. . . Kumen Jones

To Margaret, Carol, Cynthia
and my brother-in-law and mentor Lowell Elsea
. . . Michael Werner

To John and Elane
. . . Katherene Terrell

To Janet
. . . Robert Terrell

Special Thanks to
George R. Violette, University of Southern Maine
for his contributions

Executive Editor: Debbie Hoffman
Assistant Editor: Kasey Sheehan
Senior Editorial Assistant: Jane Avery
Editor-in-Chief: PJ Boardman
Executive Marketing Manager: Beth Toland
Production Editor: Marc Oliver
Managing Editor: Sondra Greenfield
Senior Manufacturing Supervisor: Paul Smolenski
Senior Manufacturing/Prepress Manager: Vincent Scelta
Cover Design: Steve Frim
Design Manager: Patricia Smythe
Interior Design: Carlisle Communications
Cover Illustration/Photo: Jerry McDaniel
Composition: Carlisle Communications

**Library of Congress Cataloging-in-Publication Data**

Introduction to management accounting : a user perspective / Kumen H.
  Jones . . . [et al.]. — 1st ed.
      p.    cm.
   Includes bibliographical references and index.
   ISBN 0-13-012553-9
   1.  Managerial accounting.   I.  Jones, Kumen H.
  HF5657.4.I59   2000
  658.15' 11—dc21                                          99–33621
                                                              CIP

Prentice-Hall International (UK) Limited, London
Prentice-Hall of Australia Pty. Limited, Sydney
Prentice-Hall Canada, Inc., Toronto
Prentice-Hall Hispanoamericana, S.A., Mexico
Prentice-Hall of India Private Limited, New Delhi
Prentice-Hall of Japan, Inc., Tokyo
Pearson Education Asia Pte. Ltd., Singapore
Editora Prentice-Hall do Brasil, Ltda., Rio de Janeiro

Printed in the United States of America

10 9 8 7 6 5 4 3 2

# Contents

## CHAPTER    3   *Determining Costs of Products*      *M-69*

## CHAPTER    4   *Cost Behavior*      *M-117*

## CHAPTER 8 *The Operating Budget* M-265

**CHAPTER**   **10**   *Evaluating Performance*      *M-377*

# Preface

As we enter the twenty-first century, we who are involved in accounting education at the collegiate level have reassessed the way we prepare our students for the business world. Technology changes more quickly than most of us can comprehend, complicating accounting education. Yet one constant remains: Business people must be prepared to perform tasks that only people can perform—in particular, communicating, thinking, and making decisions. Decision making is *the* critical skill in today's business world, and *Introduction to Management Accounting: A User Perspective* helps students to better use accounting information and improve their decision-making skills.

This text provides an introduction to accounting within the context of business and business decisions. Readers will explore accounting information's role in the decision-making process, and learn how to use accounting information in a variety of management decision situations. Seeing how accounting information can be used to make better business decisions will benefit all students, regardless of their major course of study or chosen career.

We agree with the recommendations made by the Accounting Education Change Commission in its *Position Statement No. Two: The First Course in Accounting.* We believe the course should be a broad introduction *to* accounting, rather than introductory accounting as it has traditionally been taught, and it should be taught from the perspective of the user, not the preparer. It should emphasize *what* accounting information is, *why* it is important, and *how* it is used by economic decision makers.

*Introduction to Management Accounting: A User Perspective* was written as a companion text to *Introduction to Financial Accounting: A User Perspective,* Second Edition, by the same author team. Obviously, we hope you will adopt and use both texts. We believe strongly, however, that this text can be effectively used in the second course of the introductory accounting sequence irrespective of what financial accounting text you use.

As you work with this text, you will find it focuses heavily on the uses of accounting information rather than the preparation of the information. This, however, is only one characteristic which distinguishes *Introduction to Management Accounting: A User Perspective* from other texts you may have used in the past.

## SUPPORT FOR THE INTERACTIVE CLASSROOM

We believe this text provides tools to actively involve students in their learning processes. The conversational tone of the text, its user perspective, and the logical presentation of topics all contribute to the ability of this text to meet that goal. However, several features are particularly important in developing a classroom atmosphere in which students share ideas, ask questions, and relate their learning to the world around them.

Throughout each chapter of the text, you will find Discussion Questions (DQs) that challenge students to reach beyond the surface of the written text to determine answers. Far from typical review questions, for which the students can scan a few pages of the text to locate an answer, many of the DQs provide relevant learning by relating students' personal experiences to the knowledge they gain through the text.

The DQs provide a variety of classroom experiences:

- Many DQs provide the basis for lively classroom discussions, requiring students to think about issues and formulate or defend their opinions.
- Some DQs are springboards for group assignments (in or out of the classroom) to put cooperative learning into practice.
- DQs may be assigned as individual writing assignments to allow students to practice and develop their writing skills.
- Combining individually written DQ responses with follow-up group discussions leading to group consensus can spark lively debate!
- Having students keep a journal of their responses to all DQs (regardless if they are used in another way) encourages solitary pondering of accounting concepts.

The DQs comprise a critically important part of the text's pedagogy designed to emphasize important points that students may skim across in their initial reading. Even if they are not formally part of the required work for your course, students will gain a greater understanding of the concepts discussed when they take time to consider each question as part of the text.

Students get enthused about accounting when they can relate it to real-world situations. This presents a challenge in presenting management accounting concepts because (a) many companies modify and tailor management accounting concepts to their individual needs, and (b) management accounting concepts often involve proprietary company policies and processes, so many companies guard their application of these concepts. When possible, however, we have tried to include as many real-world examples as we could. In addition to these features which help to foster an open, interactive environment in the classroom, a major distinction of this text is its total separation of the use of accounting and its preparation.

## SEPARATION OF ACCOUNTING AND BOOKKEEPING

This text approaches accounting from the user perspective. The chapters contain no bookkeeping. Although we feel that a knowledge of bookkeeping is valuable, we feel that it is difficult for beginning accounting students to digest the uses of accounting information and the details of bookkeeping simultaneously.

Separating accounting and bookkeeping makes both subjects easier to grasp and more enjoyable to learn. To facilitate the separation of accounting and bookkeeping, accounting procedures are covered in appendices to selected chapters. This approach allows instructors and institutions to determine when and to what degree bookkeeping procedures are covered in their programs. Some schools choose to have all students learn basic recording procedures; others may only require accounting majors to acquire these skills.

Management accounting by its nature has less bookkeeping procedure than financial accounting. However, in Chapters M2, M3, and M9 we have included appendices that cover the bookkeeping procedures required to record the topics presented.

In addition to the decision to focus on the uses of accounting information rather than the details of accounting procedures, in this text we have made several other deliberate and important choices about topical coverage.

## TOPICS COVERED

We carefully considered the inclusion or exclusion of topics from this text consistent with our pedagogical goals of building foundations that support effective student learning. Because our focus introduces students to accounting information and its uses in decision making, we could not simply follow the traditional coverage of topics. As we considered individual topics, we continually explored whether their inclusion would enhance a student's ability to interpret and use accounting information throughout his or her personal and professional life. Based on our own experiences in industry and conversations we have had with both operations and accounting managers from many companies, we believe that *Introduction to Management Accounting: A User Perspective* covers those topics that every introductory accounting student should leave the course understanding well. In short, we sought quality of learning, not quantity of minutiae.

For example, in our coverage of the separation of a mixed cost into its variable and fixed components, we discuss regression analysis, but do not include any calculations using this method. By limiting the coverage of detailed calculations, we have the opportunity to focus on the concept of cost separation without losing students in computations.

Another example of building foundations to learning is the introduction to the operating budget. Instead of sending students straight into the preparation of the budgets included in the operating budget, we present all the budgets conceptually first, and then walk them through budget preparation.

We also include some topics that traditional books omit. Chapter M7 includes not only information on how to budget for capital expenditures, but where capital budgeting fits in a company's overall planning and control process. This chapter also discusses frankly some of the dysfunctional management behavior caused by inappropriate use of the capital budgeting process. Likewise, Chapter M8 includes a forthright discussion of appropriate and inappropriate uses of the operating budget.

From our classroom experience with this text, we believe that the content is appropriate for college sophomores to embrace and take forward to additional courses. The carefully chosen sequence of topics helps to make them more understandable by establishing firm conceptual foundations.

## SEQUENCE OF COVERAGE

To effectively present the user perspective, we developed a logical flow of topics so that each chapter builds on what the student has already learned. Students can easily understand how the topics fit together logically and how they are used together to make good decisions. Moreover, students can see that accounting and the information it provides is not merely something that exists unto itself, but rather it is something developed in response to the needs of economic decision makers.

If you could read the entire text before using it in your classroom, you would have a very clear picture of the experience awaiting your students. However, even a short tour through the material covered in each chapter will show you how we have structured our presentation of the topics to maximize student learning.

**Chapter M1** provides a brief overview of the environment and future of management accounting. We have included not only a description of how management accounting compares and contrasts with financial accounting, but also the historical forces that have led to the development of management accounting techniques. Further, we discuss the state of management accounting today and what kinds of management accounting information will be needed in the future.

**Chapter M2** presents an introduction to various cost classifications used in management accounting situations. We cover the concepts of cost objects, direct and indirect costs, and product and period costs. Students are introduced to the differences in product cost for a merchandiser and a manufacturer and learn the components of the costs included in each of the three types of inventory in a manufacturing operation. Finally, we explore the calculation of cost of goods manufactured and cost of goods sold for a manufacturer and cost of services for a service type firm. The chapter appendix presents the journal entries associated with the information presented in the chapter.

**Chapter M3** introduces students to how manufacturers determine the cost of manufactured product. We present the documents used to help control the costs of manufactured products and cover how overhead costs are allocated to products using both traditional overhead allocation and activity-based costing. We walk students through the steps required to determine the cost of manufactured product using job order and process costing. The chapter appendix presents the journal entries associated with process costing and job order costing.

**Chapter M4** explores the subject of cost behavior. We explain the differences between fixed costs and variable costs, and how to classify costs by cost behavior. We also cover the concept of the relevant range and its effect on cost behavior information. We then present the characteristics of a mixed cost and discuss how to separate a mixed cost into its fixed and variable components using the engineering approach, the scatter graph, the high-low method, and regression analysis.

**Chapter M5** extends the topic introduced in Chapter M4 by using cost behavior information to make business decisions. In this chapter we present the functional income statement and contribution income statement and the differences between them. We cover the calculation of per unit amounts for sales, variable cost, and contribution margin, as well as the contribution margin ratio and its importance as a management tool. We present the contribution margin income statement for a merchandiser and introduce the concept of cost-volume-profit analysis, which we use to determine the amount of sales required to break even or to earn a targeted profit in both single-product and multiple-product situations. Finally, we use CVP to perform sensitivity analysis to changes in selling price, variable cost, and fixed cost.

**Chapter M6** presents the topic of isolating and using relevant cost information in decision making. Included is a discussion of the characteristics of relevant and irrelevant costs, and a consideration of qualitative factors that should be considered when making business decisions. The specific decision situations covered in the chapter are equipment replacement, whether to accept or reject a special order, and the effects of fixed costs and opportunity costs on a make or buy decision.

**Chapter M7** provides an in-depth look at the capital budget. The overall business planning process is discussed and where the capital budget fits in that process. The four shared characteristics of all capital projects are presented, as well as the cost of capital and the concept of scarce resources. Students learn how to identify the information relevant to the capital budgeting decision. We present four techniques used to evaluate proposed capital projects including net present value, internal rate of return, payback, and accounting rate of return. There is an appendix to this chapter which presents the concept of the time value of money and all the calculations students need to compute net present values and internal rates of return.

**Chapter M8** presents the operating budget, its benefits, preparation, and uses. First, we introduce and discuss all the budgets included in the operating budget from a conceptual standpoint. Then we present various approaches to budgeting, including perpetual, incremental, zero-based, top-down, bottom-up, imposed, and participative approaches. Next we discuss and stress the importance of the sales forecast in the budgeting process. Finally, we walk students through the preparation of all the budgets, and then discuss appropriate and inappropriate uses of the operating budget in the management process.

**Chapter M9** presents the procedures involved in standard costing. We explore what standard costing is and why it can be an effective tool for managers. We cover management by exception, ideal and practical standards, and the weaknesses of standard costing. We compare standard costing, actual costing, and normal costing and introduce students to methods used to set standards for a manufacturing company. Finally, we walk students through the calculations of standard cost variances for direct material, direct labor, variable manufacturing overhead, and fixed manufacturing overhead. The chapter appendix presents the journal entries used to record all the procedures described in the chapter.

**Chapter M10** introduces students to various methods of evaluating performance. We discuss centralized and decentralized management styles, business segments, and the problems associated with determining segment costs. We also present the segment income statement and how it is used to evaluate segment performance. We introduce students to return on investment and residual income as methods used to evaluate performance. We also discuss some nonfinancial performance measures including quality, customer satisfaction, employee morale, employee safety, efficiency, and just-in-time.

## Other Important Features of This Text

In addition to the Discussion Questions discussed in detail above, our text offers other features that will enhance the learning process.

- Learning Objectives—Previewing each chapter with these objectives allows students to see what direction the chapter is taking, which makes the journey through the material a bit easier.
- Marginal Glossary—Students often find the process of learning accounting terminology to be a challenge. As each new key word is introduced in the text, it is shown in bold and also defined in the margin. This feature offers students an easy way to review the key terms and locate their introduction in the text.
- Summary—This concise summary of each chapter provides an overview of the main points, but is in no way a substitute for reading the chapter.
- Key Terms—At the end of each chapter, a list of the new key words directs students to the page on which the key word or phrase was introduced.
- Review the Facts—Students can use these basic, definitional questions to review the key points of each chapter. The questions are in a sequence reflecting the coverage of topics in the chapter.
- Apply What You Have Learned—Our end-of-chapter assignment materials include a mix of traditional types of homework problems and innovative assignments requiring critical thinking and writing. Many of the requirements can be used as the basis for classroom discussions. You will find matching problems, short essay questions, and calculations. Assignments dealing directly with the use of financial statements are also included. Many of these applications also work well as group assignments.
- Glossary of Accounting Terms—An alphabetical listing of important accounting terms, including all of the key terms plus additional terms, defines the terms and lists the page on which the term first appears.

## Supplements for Use by the Instructor

Additional support for your efforts in the classroom is provided by our group of supplements.

### Management Instructor's Resource Manual, 0-13-182411-2
This comprehensive resource includes chapter overviews that identify the chapter concepts, explains the chapter rationale and philosophy, and reviews the significant topics and points of the chapter. Also included are chapter outlines organized by objectives, lecture suggestions, teaching tips, various chapter quizzes, transparency masters, group activities derived from the textbook Discussion Questions

(DQs) as well as the Solutions to the DQs, communication exercises, and suggested readings.

### Management Solutions Manual and Transparencies

Management Solutions Manual 0-13-182429-5

Management Transparencies 0-13-961898-8

Solutions are provided for all the end-of-chapter assignments. The Solutions Manual is also available in acetate form and on disk to adopters.

### Management Test Item File, 0-13-182437-6

The Test Item File includes test items that can be used as quiz and/or exam material. Each chapter contains multiple-choice questions (both conceptual and quantitative), problems, exercises, and critical thinking problems. Each question will identify the difficulty level, page reference, the corresponding learning objective(s), and the category classification according to Bloom's Taxonomy.

### Management Prentice Hall Test Manager by
### Engineering Software Associates Inc., 0-13-236480-8

This easy-to-use computerized testing program can create exams, evaluate, and track student results. The PH Test Manager also provides on-line testing capabilities. Test items are drawn from the Test Item File.

### Management PH Professor:
### A Classroom Presentation on PowerPoint, 0-13-014590-4

PowerPoint presentations are available for each chapter of the text. Each presentation allows instructors to offer a more interactive presentation using colorful graphics, outlines of chapter material, additional examples, and graphical explanations of difficult topics. Instructors have the flexibility to add slides and/or modify the existing slides to meet the course needs. Each presentation can also be downloaded from our Web site at *www.prenhall.com/phbusiness.*

**PHLIP/CW** (Prentice Hall's Learning on the Internet Partnership) offers the most expansive internet-based support available. Our Web site provides a wealth of resources for students and faculty, which include:

- Student Study Hall
- Hotlinks to in-text companies
- Learning Assessment sections
- On-line tutorial assistance
- Practice tests with immediate grading and feedback
- Faculty lounge
- On-line study guide
- Downloadable supplement
- Distance Learning capabilities

We believe that the instructor and student can have a rich and wonderful experience as they discover how accounting fits into the big picture of business and relates to their life, regardless of their chosen career. We have devised homework and classroom materials to stimulate robust and invigorating interchanges between instructor and student as together they grapple with accounting issues.

## ACKNOWLEDGMENTS

No project this large takes place in a vacuum. This project would not have happened without the resounding support and encouragement from a number of people, the faith in the concept's value from Prentice Hall, and the suggestions for improvements from our colleagues.

We thank executive editors Annie Todd and Debbie Hoffman for their patience, determination, and faith in the project. They were always there for us. We also thank Prentice Hall team members Jim Boyd, PJ Boardman, Stephen Deitmer, Jane Avery, Elisa Adams, Charlotte Morrissey, Natacha St. Hill Moore, Marc Oliver, Beth Toland, and Kasey Sheehan for their help and contributions.

Our colleagues keep us on our toes, and this book is enriched by their intellectual contributions and friendship. Martha Doran, San Diego State University, good friend and teacher, shared her wisdom with us about learning and teaching, and our students are better off because of it. Many other colleagues tested our ideas, were brave enough to offer constructive criticism, and gave us friendship through the difficult times. They include: Gary J. Weber and Kay C. Carnes, Gonzaga University; Connie D. Weaver, University of Texas-Austin; Juan M. Rodriguez, Elizabeth Dreike Almer, Paul Munter, Frank Collins, Oscar J. Holzmann, Olga Quintana, Thomas R. Robinson, and the other faculty members at the University of Miami; Richard E. Flaherty, Harriet Maccracken, Patrick B. McKenzie, and Karen Gieger, Arizona State University; Lorren H. Beavers, Charles R. Pursifull, Mary F. Sheets, Bambi A. Hora, Thomas K. Miller, Ura Lee Denson, David J. Harris, Joan Stone, Karen Price, and Jane Calvert, University of Central Oklahoma; Alfonso R. Oddo, Niagara University; Marilyn T. Zarzeski, University of Central Florida; Joanne Sheridan, Montana State University-Billings; Ellene Ormiston and Charles Lewis, Mesa Community College; Allison L. Drews-Bryan, Clemson University; and George R. Violette, University of Southern Maine.

We would also like to thank Thomas Greco, Manta Racing; Bruce Perlmuter, The Perlmuter Printing Company; and Cam Matheis, Stephen Speace, Carole Anderson, Jennifer Furman, and Kevin Maupin, Pitman Photo Supply.

Several other groups deserve special thanks and recognition for their valuable work:

### Reviewers for the *Introduction to Management Accounting, A User Perspective:*

| | |
|---|---|
| Jeffrey J. Archambault | Clarkson University |
| Lorren H. Beavers | University of Central Oklahoma |
| Roger K. Doost | Clemson University |
| Cherie L. Francisco | Simpson College |
| Jessica J. Frazier | Eastern Kentucky University |
| Edward S. Goodhart | Shippensburg University |
| Bambi A. Hora | University of Central Oklahoma |
| Steven D. Hunter | Western Baptist College |
| Thomas A. Jones | |
| Raymond L. Larson | Appalachian State University |
| Mary D. Maury | St. John's University |
| Alfonso R. Oddo | Niagara University |
| Charles J. Pineno | Clarion University |
| Joanne Sheridan | Montana State University-Billings |
| Sheldon R. Smith | Brigham Young University-Hawaii |
| Patricia M. Sommerville | Saint Mary's University |
| Caroly Streuly | |
| Marilyn T. Zarzeski | University of Central Florida |

### Supplements Authors:

| | | |
|---|---|---|
| Barry Nab Dahl | Lake Superior College | PowerPoint Presentation |
| Karen P. Schoenebeck | Wichita State University | Companion Web site |
| Diane L. Tanner | University of North Florida | Instructor's Manual |
| Mary F. Sheets | University of Central Oklahoma | Test Item File |
| Bambi A. Hora | University of Central Oklahoma | Test Item File |
| Thomas K. Miller | University of Central Oklahoma | IMA Solutions Manual |

Thanks also for contributions made by Charles R. Pursifull, Lorren H. Beavers, and Ura Lee Denson to the Test Item File and the Solutions Manuals.

Thanks go to our students, who are the reason for the work and who become our living laboratory. Special thanks to Stacie R. Mayes and Jason R. Earhart who critiqued this manuscript from the student's perspective. Finally, we thank our families who abide with us through this process.

Kumen H. Jones
Michael L. Werner
Katherene P. Terrell
Robert L. Terrell

# *Introduction to Management Accounting*
## *A User Perspective*

# *Chapter* 1

# *Management Accounting: Its Environment and Future*

*T*imes have changed! During the 1970s and 1980s the United States saw a serious erosion in its position as the world's business leader. Industry after industry in the United States began to suffer from the effects of significant foreign competition. At the time, experts offered any number of reasons to explain what was happening. Low labor costs in foreign countries, excessively high labor costs at home, too much government regulation of U.S. industries, and too little government regulation of U.S. industries were just a few of the explanations offered.

Because the "reasons" given were simplistic, the "solutions" were simplistic. U.S. industries lobbied Congress for tariffs on imported products (essentially a form of tax) to offset the low labor costs in foreign countries. The issue of excessively high labor rates was used by U.S. companies in negotiating labor costs with their employees, either to hold the line on wage increases, or in some instances to actually negotiate lower wage rates. Throughout the 1970s and 1980s, the U.S. government alternatively deregulated and then reregulated some American industries to try and increase U.S. companies' competitiveness globally.

Eventually, as the quick fix, simplistic approaches did not solve the competitiveness problem, managers in the United States began to see that the problem arose from differences in organizational structure and worker productivity between U.S. businesses and their foreign competitors. Consider the following comparison of U.S. and Japanese auto manufacturers in the mid-1980s.[1]

---

[1]John Lee, *Managerial Accounting Changes for the 1990s (Addison Wesley, 1987),* 14.

### Ford
- Produced an average of two engines a day per employee
- Daily production required 777 square feet of plant space

### Toyota
- Produced an average of nine engines a day per employee
- Daily production required 454 square feet of plant space

### Chrysler
- Had about 500 in-plant classifications

### Toyota
- Had 7 in-plant job classifications

### A Typical U.S. Auto Plant
- A change from metal-stamping one model to another required 6 hours

### Toyota
- The same change required 3–5 minutes

Because of more efficient production techniques, a small Toyota car cost $1,700 less to produce than a comparable U.S. car. This cost difference made it difficult for U.S. automakers to effectively compete against Toyota and the other car companies employing more efficient manufacturing methods.

The automobile industry was by no means alone. By the mid-1980s, U.S. companies in many different industries had realized the need to change business operations to remain competitive. Beginning in the last half of the 1980s and continuing throughout the 1990s, many of those businesses began to take significant steps to increase their competitiveness.

Our focus will be not on the specific changes that managers made but rather on the way these changes have affected their accounting needs and how accounting information has responded. ∎

## LEARNING OBJECTIVES

*After completing your work on this chapter, you should be able to do the following:*

1. Describe management accounting and contrast it with financial accounting.
2. Explain major historical developments that have affected management accounting.
3. Discuss what may have led to the stagnation in the development of management accounting.
4. Describe how changes in management accounting affect today's businesses.
5. Explain how businesspeople use management accounting information and skills.

# WHAT IS MANAGEMENT ACCOUNTING?

**management accounting**
The branch of accounting designed to provide information to internal economic decision makers (managers).

**managerial accounting**
Another name for management accounting.

**cost accounting**   A narrow application of management accounting dealing specifically with procedures designed to determine how much a particular item (usually a unit of manufactured product) costs.

**Management accounting** is the branch of accounting designed to provide information to the firm's internal economic decision makers, or managers. It is also sometimes called **managerial accounting** or **cost accounting.** Because these three terms are often used interchangeably in accounting literature, confusion can result. Management accounting is

> ... the process of identification, measurement, accumulation, analysis, preparation, interpretation, and communication of financial information used by management to plan, evaluate, and control ... an organization ...
>
> Statement on Management Accounting (No.1A. IMA, 1981)

Management accounting and managerial accounting mean exactly the same thing. We will use the term *management accounting* throughout our discussions of the subject. However, in references to other writings you may see the term *managerial accounting.*

The third term, *cost accounting,* is a narrow application of management accounting. Cost accounting deals specifically with procedures designed to determine how much a particular item (usually a unit of manufactured product) costs.

# CONTRASTING FINANCIAL AND MANAGEMENT ACCOUNTING

Financial accounting provides information to external decision makers—to people outside the company. Management accounting, in contrast, provides information to internal decision makers. Exhibit 1–1 lists only some of the many external and internal users of a company's accounting information.

**Exhibit 1–1**
External and Internal Decision Makers

| External | Internal |
|---|---|
| • Stockholders (present and potential) | • Marketing managers |
| • Bankers and other lending institutions | • Salespersons |
| • Bondholders (present and potential) | • Production managers |
| • Suppliers | • Production supervisors |
| • Customers | • Strategic planners |
| • Competitors | • Company president |
| | • Engineers |

## Discussion Questions

**1-1.** For each of the external parties listed in Exhibit 1-1, suggest one economic decision they might make regarding a company.

**1-2.** Name two external parties in addition to those listed in Exhibit 1-1, and provide an example of an economic decision each might make regarding a company.

**1-3.** For each of the internal parties listed in Exhibit 1-1, describe one economic decision they might make regarding their company.

**1–4.** Name two more internal parties in addition to those listed in Exhibit 1–1, and give an example of an economic decision each might make regarding the company.

Discussion Questions 1–1 through 1–4 highlight the different nature of the decisions made by external and internal parties. If you review your answers to these questions, you will discover that the decisions external parties make focus on the company as a whole, whereas the decisions internal parties make usually center on some *part* of the company. Because people use financial accounting information and management accounting information differently, the nature of the two differs.

## Accounting Rules

Financial accounting information must be prepared in accordance with rules known as Generally Accepted Accounting Principles (GAAP). No such rules apply to management accounting. Because management accounting information is prepared for use by those working within the company, its users can question the content, meaning, level of detail, and validity of the accounting information they receive. They can also determine the format of the information. As discussed later, in addition to accountants, managers may also gather and prepare management accounting information. In sum, internal decision makers can generally make certain the information they receive is exactly what they want. External decision makers must accept the financial accounting information they receive, like it or not.

## Level of Detail

In contrast to the general-purpose nature of financial accounting information, firms prepare management accounting information to address specific company issues. Therefore, it is often much more detailed than financial accounting information. For example, it may be fine for a potential investor to know that IBM's sales were $82 billion last year, but this information would be nearly useless to the national sales manager for IBM ThinkPads™, the company's line of notebook computers, who needs to know that product's sales numbers for last year.

# Discussion Question

**1–5.** In addition to sales information, what other accounting information would you want if you were the national sales manager for IBM ThinkPads™?

In addition to preparing general-purpose financial statements for the public, a company's accountants also prepare management accounting information for the managers or employees who need it. For a given internal decision, a user may need specific information from a division, product line, product, or department. The company's accountants should be able to customize information to fit the needs of the user.

For example, Motorola, Inc. has a production facility on 52nd Street and McDowell Road in Phoenix, Arizona. This facility requires various types of maintenance, including mowing the lawn and weeding the flower beds outside the buildings. This maintenance costs money. The amount spent for grounds maintenance at this Phoenix facility is totally irrelevant to external parties. The maintenance supervisor at that facility, however, would find that amount quite relevant. Motorola's accountants should be able to customize a report providing the supervisor with pertinent cost information.

### Timeliness

Timeliness is important to both financial and management accounting information users. Regardless of whether the user is external or internal, accounting information is useful only if it is available in time to help the decision maker.

Because it has become customary, users of financial accounting information expect that financial results will be available quarterly. However, managers making frequent decisions need information much more often. They need information monthly, weekly, or even daily, so they can make informed decisions. Because of the fast pace of business decision making, sometimes it is better to forfeit precision in favor of speed. Management accountants must strike a balance between information accuracy and timeliness to provide managers with information that is accurate enough to make good decisions, and yet timely enough to make a difference.

### Future Orientation

Although financial accounting information should have predictive value, it primarily depicts historical results. In contrast, management accounting has a forward-looking orientation. Management accounting focuses on estimating future revenues, costs, and other measures to forecast future activities and their results. Firms use these forecasts to plan their course of action toward future goals.

As you can see, because of the fundamental differences between the information needs of external and internal parties, financial and management accounting differ. Exhibit 1–2 summarizes the differences we have discussed.

**Exhibit 1–2**
Contrast of Financial and Management Accounting

| Feature | Financial Accounting | Management Accounting |
|---|---|---|
| • Principal users | External parties | Internal parties |
| • Rules and regulations | Governed by GAAP | No rules |
| • Level of detail | Deals with the company as a whole | Deals with various parts of the company |
| • Timeliness | Quarterly and annually | As users need |
| • Orientation | The past | The future |

## WHERE ACCOUNTING FITS IN A COMPANY

**treasurer** The corporate officer who is responsible for cash and credit management and for planning activities, such as investment in long-lived property, plant, and equipment.

Exhibit 1–3 presents a typical corporate organizational structure. Note where financial and management accounting fit within a company.

The accounting function centers around the treasurer and the controller. Generally, the **treasurer** is responsible for managing cash and credit and for planning activities, such as investment in long-lived property, plant, and equipment. The **controller** is a company's chief accountant. This person is responsible for preparing accounting reports for both external and internal decision makers.

**Exhibit 1–3**
Corporate Organization

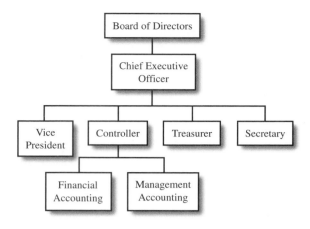

**controller** A company's chief accountant, who is responsible for the preparation of accounting reports for both external and internal decision makers.

In a large company, such as Sara Lee or Rockwell, the treasurer and controller are both likely to have large staffs reporting to them. At a midsized company, one or two people may perform all the duties of the treasurer and controller. In small firms, one person may perform all the functions.

## Discussion Question

1–6. What possible problems may arise when the same accountants prepare reports for both external parties and internal parties?

## THE ORIGIN AND EVOLUTION OF MANAGEMENT ACCOUNTING

Accounting and accounting records have existed since the dawn of civilization. Indeed, formal accounting systems have been in use for thousands of years. The need for accounting information for management decision-making purposes, however, did not exist until the early 19th century. Before that time almost all businesses were proprietorships or small partnerships. Businesses had no permanent employees to speak of and no management as we know it today. Management usually consisted of the proprietor or partners and immediate family members. Because businesses had no management, they had no need for management accounting information. Virtually all transactions were between the company and parties outside the company. Transactions with external parties such as suppliers, contract labor, and customers were easy to measure and evaluate: A company was successful if it collected more cash from its customers than it paid to suppliers and contract laborers.

In the hundred years between 1825 and 1925, however, four significant changes took place in business operation and organization: the emergence of permanent employees, the Industrial Revolution, the rise of scientific management, and diversification. These changes altered the nature of management accounting.

## Emergence of Permanent Employees

For the most part, businesses had no employees before the 1880s. Businesses purchased labor with a piece rate contract and hired independent contractors to complete all their production functions. A chair manufacturer, for example, purchased wood at a certain price per board foot. Then the company contracted someone to turn the wood into legs, arms, seats, and backs at some specified rate per item. When the pieces were produced and paid for, the company contracted someone else to assemble the chairs, and paid that person some specified amount per chair assembled. Determining the cost of a chair produced was very simple—the sum of the wood cost, the amount paid per component piece (arm, leg, and so on), and the cost of assembling it. The company was not terribly interested in how long it took any of these contractors to complete their tasks, so long as they met the needs of the company.

Then companies began hiring permanent employees to fill the role of the independent contractors. Why the switch to permanent employees happened and whether it was positive or negative has been hotly debated by scholars for over 100 years. From the company's standpoint, moving from a contract system to a wage system gave the firm greater control of the production process and, in fact, created what we now know as the factory. From the laborer's standpoint, the change was likely an exchange of freedom for security.

## Discussion Questions

**1-7.** In what ways do you think hiring permanent employees gives a company greater control of the production process?

**1-8.** What kinds of freedom do you think permanent employees exchange for security?

When we see the word *factory*, we tend to think of the huge factories of the 20th century. Actually, early factories were still small businesses. Management accounting did not develop because of the size or complexity of the organization. Rather, it developed because the accounting systems then in existence did not provide business people with enough information to determine the cost of a manufactured product.

## Discussion Question

**1-9.** Why do you think the emergence of the factory (even a small one) made it more difficult to determine the cost of a manufactured product?

## The Industrial Revolution

**Industrial Revolution** A term used to describe the transition in the United States from an agricultural-based economy to a manufacturing-based economy.

The **Industrial Revolution** was the 19th-century transition of the United States from an agricultural-based economy to a manufacturing-based economy. From 1825 to 1925 businesses greatly increased their investment in property, plant, and equipment and began to rely more on machines instead of human labor to produce products. As companies grew in size and complexity, owners found it impossible to be in all places at all times. They were forced to create hierarchical levels of management for their organizations. These managers sought needed information to control costs and production processes. Over time, businesses developed methods to measure the conversion of raw materials into units of finished product. These methods were the foundation for present-day management accounting. Their focus was on the effectiveness and efficiency of various internal processes, rather than on the overall profitability of the company.

## Scientific Management

**scientific management** A management philosophy based on the notion that factories were run by machines—some mechanical and some human. Scientific management experts believed they could improve production efficiency by establishing standards of performance for workers.

The scientific management movement began near the end of the 19th century and had a tremendous influence on business management and management accounting. **Scientific management** was a philosophy based on the notion that factories were run by machines—some mechanical and some human. You may think it insensitive to treat employees as nothing more than machines plugged into the production process. Nonetheless, scientific management took this view. Experts in this area believed they could improve production efficiency by establishing standards of performance for workers. In a tool-manufacturing company, for instance, experts conducted time-and-motion studies to set a standard for the time workers should take to convert a given amount of resources into a finished product, such as a hammer.

These standards of performance were quickly adapted to accounting for the purpose of determining how much it *should* cost to manufacture a product. The experts, often engineers, determined how much material, labor, and other resources a business needed to manufacture a single unit of product. This information served as a yardstick to measure whether resources were used efficiently or squandered during the production process. Such standards were the beginning of what is referred to as *standard costing*, one of the most important developments in management accounting. We will discuss standard costing in greater detail in Chapter 9.

## Discussion Questions

Assume a company manufactures tables. Scientific management studies show that each tabletop requires 4 square feet of wood, and it takes a worker 45 minutes to convert the wood into a tabletop.

**1-10.** If the wood costs the company $2 per square foot and the company's workers are paid $10 per hour, how much does each tabletop cost to produce?

**1-11.** What other costs should be considered in the calculation of the cost to produce the tabletop? Explain.

## Diversification

During the first two decades of the 20th century, companies began to diversify. Before this time, virtually all companies undertook only one activity, for example, railroad companies were strictly in the railroad business and steel companies were strictly in the steel business. The primary investment decision for these single-activity companies was whether to expand. The emergence of diversified, multi-activity companies changed the nature of decision making.

# Discussion Question

**1-12.** Why do you think companies began to diversify in the early years of the 20th century?

Owners of diversified companies could not directly manage all the various business operations. Instead, they relied on others to manage operations that they could not personally oversee; and they obtained additional management accounting information from the various parts of the business so they could plan, control, and evaluate performance. Company accountants tailored reports to meet the needs of managers at each level of the organization. Lower-level managers, such as production supervisors, received reports that focused on production efficiencies. Higher-level managers received reports that focused on product profits.

## Development Stops (or at least dramatically slows)

**Institute of Management Accountants (IMA)** A professional association of management accountants comparable to the professional association of financial accountants (American Institute of Certified Public Accountants).

In 1919, the formation of the **Institute of Management Accountants (IMA)**—formerly the National Association of Accountants—signified that management accounting was a recognized branch of the accounting profession separate and distinct from financial accounting. Among other purposes, the IMA provided the same sort of professional status for management accountants as the American Institute of Certified Public Accountants (AICPA) did for financial accountants.

In approximately 1925, however, something curious occurred. For reasons we will discuss, development of new management accounting techniques virtually ceased. Essentially all management accounting tools in use as late as 1985 were already in place by 1925. Certainly the business environment changed between 1925 and 1985. Why then were so few management accounting techniques developed to respond to those changing needs? This question has been the subject of much analysis and debate over the past decade by both accountants and business leaders. In the following section, we examine possible causes of the stagnation in the development of management accounting techniques.

## Dominance of Financial Accounting

The growth of publicly held corporations, the stock market crash, and the Great Depression led to the establishment of Generally Accepted Accounting Principles (GAAP) and the Securities and Exchange Commission (SEC). The new rules and regulations governed financial reporting to external parties and required that corporations file audited financial statements with the SEC that were prepared in accordance with GAAP. The rules and regulations led to the design of accounting systems that could provide financial information and reports to outsiders. These financial accounting systems, however, ignored (or at least underrepresented) information managers could use to make decisions about the internal processes of their companies.

Companies could have maintained two systems—one that generated and gathered information to meet external reporting requirements, and another that generated the information managers needed to manage and control the operation of the company. Or, a common system could collect data for both purposes and then customize the information to conform to the informational requests and needs of users. The cost of creating and maintaining a dual-purpose system, however, would have been prohibitive before computers, which is when GAAP and the SEC came into being.

Today, a high percentage of management accountants have a financial accounting background. It stands to reason that those who bring that type of background into a management accounting setting will tend to approach management accounting from a financial accounting perspective.

Consider also the legal environment existing in the 1930s after the creation of the SEC. If a company failed to have an accounting system designed to produce financial accounting information for external parties in accordance with GAAP, there would be serious legal consequences. If a company's accounting system did not produce management accounting information, however, there were no legal consequences. Given this situation, it is not surprising that at that time financial accounting requirements drove the creation and use of accounting information.

## Discussion Question

1–13. What possible problems do you think arise when a company's single accounting system is designed to produce financial accounting information? Explain.

## Accounting Education

Prior to 1900, colleges did not teach accounting. As a result, no uniform methods for gathering and distributing management accounting information were developed. Accountants gathered and distributed management accounting information as needed to suit management's needs. After the formation of the SEC and the development of GAAP, companies needed accountants trained to provide financial accounting information. In response, colleges began to offer accounting courses that focused on financial accounting information preparation.

As college-trained accountants became available, businesses began to rely on them for more than their expertise in providing information to outsiders. Managers also began to rely on accountants to specify *what* management accounting information should be gathered and *how* it should be presented. In the late 1800s, for instance, owners and company engineers developed product costing methods to make reasonable product cost estimates and better pricing decisions. In the early 1900s, trained accountants adapted established accounting methods of product costing to provide information to managers. In short, managers began relying on product costing methods their accountants learned in school instead of newly developed techniques tailored specifically to the needs of the company.

## Focus on Financial Profits

Another possible reason for the slowdown in the development of management accounting is that we usually focus on financial profits in the performance evaluation of managers. Virtually all measures used to evaluate managers in U.S. companies are short-term financial accounting measures. Managers are bright people. In no time they determine how to manipulate the financial results of operations to maximize a short-run performance measure. Think about it. It seems reasonable to expect managers to focus on short-term financial accounting measures if their compensation and career advancement rely on these items.

Bonus programs that motivate key managers to perform better seem reasonable, except that most bonuses are heavily weighted in favor of short-term, not long-term, performance. As John Lee noted in his book *Managerial Accounting Changes for the 1990s:*

Since, at most companies, bonuses for short-term performance are larger than the payments from the long-term incentive program, executives tend to stress short-term strategies to maximize their incomes. For example, at Holiday Inns, the chief executive's 1983 short-term bonus was about $600,000, compared to the annual payout from the long-term incentive program of $46,000. In this type of system, executives have relatively little incentive to concentrate on the long-term health of the company.[2]

These incentives encourage managers to focus on improving financial statement measures rather than on improving productivity and efficiency measures. Preoccupation with financial accounting income has diminished their interest in demanding new management accounting techniques.

The problem of the short-term view is compounded by the mobility of management. In the early part of the century, managers stayed in their jobs longer than they do today. It was not uncommon for a manager to occupy the same position for 10 or even 20 years. For such managers, taking actions that would result in an impressive short-term performance at the expense of the long run made no sense. Today, however, many managers believe they will stay in a particular position for only a few years, so their objective is often to maximize short-term measures and not worry about what will happen in 5 or 10 years.

## Lack of Competitive Pressure

Until the 1970s, the lack of competition from outside the country allowed U.S. companies to flourish, despite management's short-run view. Because many industries lacked serious competition, many decisions—even those made without sophisticated accounting information—led to favorable financial results. If satisfactory decisions could be made without sophisticated accounting information, then why would management even recognize that improvements were needed? Even business executives who were aware of the weaknesses in management accounting systems did not believe changes were worth making because they felt they were no worse off than their competition.

By the early 1980s, however, competition from foreign companies with more sophisticated management accounting systems forced U.S. companies to pay more attention to the relevance of the accounting information they were using to make short-term and long-term business decisions.

## Who or What Should We Blame?

Which factor or factors should we blame for the slowdown in the development of management accounting techniques—the preoccupation of accountants with financial accounting, formal accounting education, management focus on financial results, or the lack of competition? It is difficult to say, but even if we cannot determine precisely why management accounting development slowed, business leaders and accounting academics now recognize a need for better management accounting information for today's business leaders. Even if we could determine who or what caused the problem, what would be the point? An old adage applies well to the situation in the United States in the mid-1980s:

LET'S FIX PROBLEMS, NOT BLAME.

---

[2]Lee, *Managerial Accounting Changes for the 1990s,* 10.

The first step in solving a problem is to recognize that you have a problem. By the mid-1980s, U.S. companies had certainly recognized that they had a problem, and since then have made great strides toward solving that problem.

# CHALLENGES AND TRENDS IN MANAGEMENT ACCOUNTING

As we move toward the 21st century, businesses face many challenges. Global competition is one we have discussed already. Another is a basic consideration of what kind of economy is going to exist in the United States in the future. Many business analysts believe that we are moving away from the traditional manufacturing-based economy toward a service-based economy. If so, management accounting techniques must adapt to such a change.

## The Giant Awakes

Although the United States continues to be a world leader in manufacturing, its businesses have lost some of their dominance. The heightened global competition spurred changes in business operations and management accounting in the United States. Like a giant roused from sleep, the United States has fought back to quell competitive threats.

First, businesses began using production and management techniques that were initiated in other countries, most notably Japan and what used to be West Germany. Second, companies became more innovative. Automobile manufacturers in the United States are much more efficient in their production processes than they were a decade ago. In the area of inventory control alone, American auto manufacturers have drastically reduced the level of inventories on hand, thereby reducing their annual inventory holding cost by hundreds of millions of dollars. This reduced cost translates into cars that are cheaper to manufacture.

As businesses examined and reorganized their operations to become more competitive, they also examined the way managers use accounting information to make decisions. Managers and accountants are making or considering many changes in management accounting as a result.

The question really is, what kind of changes must be made in management accounting techniques and procedures to cope with a dynamic business environment? Opinions about which "old" management accounting techniques still apply and what "new" techniques should be developed are sharply divided. Next, we present three alternative perspectives on what is and what should be happening in management accounting to respond to these fundamental changes taking place in business.

## Out with the Old, in with the New

The first perspective contends that virtually all the management accounting techniques and practices used before the mid-1980s are obsolete and do not apply to the new business environment. Advocates of this perspective urge businesses to develop entirely new management accounting techniques and to shed past methods. A few of the techniques they categorize as "new" include Just-in-time (JIT) inventory systems, Activity Based Management (ABM), Activity Based Costing (ABC), design for manufacturing (DFM), and Process Value Added (PVA).

## Keep the Status Quo

The second perspective does not advocate any change in management accounting methods. Supporters of this view perceive business problems as unrelated to accounting. They believe that as new business practices are developed, management accounting methods of the past can and will provide managers with the information they need to operate their companies. Advocates believe that many of the management accounting techniques developed over the past 10 years are simply variations of traditional techniques that have only been renamed.

## Don't Change Just for the Sake of Change

The third perspective lies somewhere between the first two. Those who hold this view believe that there are serious flaws in the management accounting techniques of the past and that some of them probably have no place in the new business environment. They warn, however, not to change just to change. Supporters of this view advocate caution in abandoning old ways and embracing new ones. They believe that many of the techniques developed over the past 15 years lack universal application—they may greatly benefit some companies, some industries, or some circumstances but should not be hailed as cures for all problems facing all businesses.

The debate over the future of management accounting show no signs of waning. No matter what happens over the next several years, you will have begun your business careers before the debate is settled. The majority of firms today still employ traditional management accounting techniques and practices, and they likely will for many years. Some companies, however, have embraced new techniques. We discuss both traditional and new management accounting techniques throughout the following chapters.

# CONSUMERS OF MANAGEMENT ACCOUNTING INFORMATION

To make effective decisions, business managers must understand the firm's management accounting system, know whether the information is reliable, and recognize that no system will provide perfect information. Decision making by its very nature is forward-looking, and the future always contains an element of uncertainty. Managers should look for ways to reduce the amount of that uncertainty.

Every decision results in an outcome, and even good decisions can lead to bad outcomes. For example, say that you are about to get in the checkout line at the grocery store. You evaluate the lines leading to open cash registers and, after counting the number of people in line and eyeballing the amount of groceries each customer is about to buy, you select what appears to be the shortest line. Your decision is sound and based on the information available. Well, just as the person ahead of you is about to pay, shopping disaster strikes. That customer does not have an acceptable check guarantee card. You must now wait for the manager to arrive and resolve the problem (a process that seems to take as long as college registration) before the cashier can help you. Quickly you look to see whether you can jump to another line, but it is too late: The other lines are now too long, and you must wait it out. Did you make a poor decision? No, you made the best decision you could with the available information. Your good decision simply led to a poor outcome.

Regardless of your career, at some point you will probably use accounting information to make a decision. If you are studying marketing, you may start as an assistant who helps prepare and implement marketing programs. As you advance in the firm, you may manage a staff of people who handle marketing programs, so you will need the accounting tools to make well-informed decisions. When you are responsible for the well-being of a company, department, division, or management team, you will face decisions that depend on your using management accounting information. The following chapters will teach you to be a careful consumer of accounting information.

## SUMMARY

Management accounting is the process of identifying, measuring, and communicating financial information used by managers to plan, evaluate, and control their organization.

Financial accounting, which is intended for use by external parties, is subject to Generally Accepted Accounting Principles (GAAP). No such rules apply to management accounting, which is intended for use by internal parties. The general-purpose financial statements produced by financial accounting focus on past results. Reports produced by management accounting are much more detailed and focus on the future of the organization.

Although accounting and accounting records have existed since the dawn of civilization, the need for accounting information for use by management did not exist prior to the early 19th century. The emergence of permanent employees, the Industrial Revolution, scientific management, and the diversification by businesses all contributed to significant development of management accounting techniques between 1825 and 1925.

Around the year 1925, there was a dramatic slowdown in the development of new management accounting techniques. Some of the contributing factors often cited for this slowdown are the dominance of financial accounting, weaknesses in accounting education, a focus by many companies on short-term financial results, and the lack of competitive pressure on U.S. businesses. However, great strides have been made in the past 15 years toward developing improved management accounting techniques.

American companies face significant competitive challenges as we move toward the 21st century, and the role of management accounting information in helping these companies will be critical.

## KEY TERMS

controller   M-8
cost accounting   M-5
Industrial Revolution   M-9
Institute of Management
   Accountants (IMA)   M-11

management accounting   M-5
managerial accounting   M-5
scientific management   M-10
treasurer   M-7

## REVIEW THE FACTS

A. What are the differences among management accounting, managerial accounting, and cost accounting?
B. What is the purpose of management accounting?
C. What are the primary differences between financial accounting and management accounting?

D. Financial accounting information must be prepared in conformity with GAAP. Why are there no such rules for management accounting?

E. List four significant changes in business that led to the development of management accounting.

F. What is the IMA and what is its purpose?

G. Describe four factors that possibly led to the stagnation of management accounting development.

H. Explain the difference between a good decision and a good outcome.

I. Why is an understanding of management accounting an important ingredient of success in your career?

# APPLY WHAT YOU HAVE LEARNED

## LO 1: Contrast Management Accounting and Financial Accounting

**1–14.** Following are certain characteristics of either financial accounting information or management accounting information.

1. __F__ Must conform to GAAP.
2. __M__ Tends to be quite detailed.
3. __F__ Generally limited to presenting historical information.
4. __M__ Need not conform to a formal set of rules and standards.
5. __F__ Information prepared primarily for external users.
6. __F__ Tends to include only a limited amount of detail.
7. __F__ Information prepared on a quarterly or yearly basis.
8. __M__ Information prepared on a monthly, weekly, or daily basis.
9. __M__ Information often includes future projections.
10. __M__ Information prepared for use by internal parties.

**REQUIRED:**

Designate each of the characteristics as pertaining to (a) financial accounting information or (b) management accounting information.

## LO 1: Describe Management Accounting

**1–15.** Is management accounting important for not-for-profit organizations as well as for-profit organizations? Explain.

## LO 1: Describe Management Accounting

**1–16.** If you were the manager of a Blockbuster Entertainment Store, what accounting information would you desire to help you do your job better?

## LO 3: Stagnation in Development of Management Accounting

**1–17.** Explain why managers tend to focus on improving short-term financial results.

## LO 4: Changes in Management Accounting

**1–18.** Explain why there has been a renewed emphasis on the development of management accounting in the United States in the last decade.

## LO 1: Contrast Management Accounting and Financial Accounting

**1–19.** Following are examples of users of financial accounting information and users of management accounting information.

1. ___I___ Sales supervisor
2. ___I___ Salespersons
3. ___E___ Wall Street analyst
4. ___E___ Suppliers
5. ___E___ Current shareholders
6. ___E___ Potential shareholders
7. ___I___ Personnel manager
8. ___I___ Maintenance supervisor
9. ___I___ Maintenance worker
10. ___E___ Loan officer at a company's bank

**REQUIRED:**

Designate each of the users of accounting information as either (a) external party or (b) internal party.

# Chapter 2

## Classifying Costs

*S*uppose for a moment that your boss has asked you to organize a consumer catalog of all the toys in the world. You need to classify the toys in several ways so users of your catalog will be able to find information easily. After thinking about your task for a while, you start a list of toy classifications—toys organized by age or gender of user, by price, or by design. Your initial list of categories may look like the following:

**Classification**

By Age of User:
Toys for infants
Toys for toddlers ages one to three
Toys for children ages three to five
Toys for children ages five to nine
Toys for children ages 10 and older

By Gender of User:
Toys designed for girls
Toys designed for boys
Toys for all children

By Price:
Toys under $10
Toys for $10 to $50
Toys for $51 to $99
Toys over $100

By Design:
Electronic toys vs. nonelectronic toys
Toys with wheels vs. toys without wheels
Breakable vs. unbreakable toys

Your boss now wants you to pick only one or two categories, to make your job easier. You scan your list to see which classifications will be most useful. You realize that the catalog must have each classification to be as useful as possible, because purchasers may need different information for different decisions.

For instance, if purchasers are choosing toys to donate to the annual toy drive for needy children, they may want to focus on price so they can donate several toys. In this case, the price classification would be most helpful. Further, those same purchasers may want to use the gender classification to find toys for all children because they would not know in advance whether the child receiving the toy is a girl or a boy.

If buyers are shopping for a birthday gift intended for a two-year-old relative, they would use the age classification to find appropriate toys. They might also want to use the price category to help them decide how much to spend. As these examples show, even in making just one decision, more than one classification may provide useful information.

Like our hypothetical toy purchasers, managers must have information to make effective planning and controlling decisions. Cost information is one of the key components of financial decision making; but what exactly is a cost? In accounting, a cost is how much we have to give up to get something. Put more formally, a **cost** is the resources forfeited to receive some goods or services. Note that cost is different from price. Price is what we charge; cost is what we pay.

**cost** The resources forfeited to receive some goods or services.

Business managers classify costs in many different ways because, just like the vast array of toys, there are many types of costs. Each classification can provide managers with useful information. In this chapter, we explore several different cost classifications that managers use to make decisions. ■

## LEARNING OBJECTIVES

*After completing your work on this chapter, you should be able to do the following:*

1. Classify costs by cost objects, and distinguish between direct and indirect costs.
2. Distinguish between product costs and period costs, and contrast their accounting treatment.
3. Explain the differences between product cost for a merchandiser and for a manufacturer.
4. Describe the components of the costs included in each of the three types of inventory in a manufacturing operation.
5. Calculate cost of goods manufactured and cost of goods sold.
6. Describe the components of the cost of services provided by a service firm.

## MAJOR COST CLASSIFICATIONS

Businesses incur many different costs as they operate and there are many useful ways to classify these costs. As managers make each internal business decision, they must determine what cost classifications will help them most. We will first identify important cost terms and investigate several cost classifications.

**Exhibit 2–1**
Common Cost Object Designations

| Cost Object | Examples |
|---|---|
| • Activity | • Repairing equipment, testing manufactured products for quality |
| • Product | • Paper towels, personal computers, automobiles (These can be either purchased or manufactured products.) |
| • Service | • Performing surgery, accounting work, legal work |
| • Project | • Constructing a bridge, designing a house |
| • Geographic region | • A state, a city, a county |
| • Department | • Marketing department, accounting department |

## Assigning Costs to Cost Objects

**cost object** Any activity or item for which a separate cost measurement is desired.

One of the most useful classifications of cost is by cost object. A **cost object** is any activity or item for which we desire a separate cost measurement. Think of any noun associated with business and you have a potential cost object. Exhibit 2–1 lists some cost objects commonly used by companies.

We identify a cost object to determine the cost of that particular object. Such classification can provide useful information. For example, a manufacturer may need information about the cost of the products it manufactures. In this case, the individual products are the cost objects. All costs associated with a particular product are grouped to determine the full cost of that product. Managers may also want to determine the cost associated with a group of products, such as a fleet of delivery trucks. When we assign costs to cost objects, we classify costs as direct or indirect.

**direct cost** A cost that can be easily traced to an individual cost object.

**indirect cost** A cost that supports more than one cost object.

**common cost** Another name for *indirect cost.*

A cost that is easily traced to individual cost objects is a **direct cost.** Many times, however, a cost may benefit more than one cost object, so tracing that cost to individual cost objects becomes difficult or even impossible. A cost that supports more than one cost object is an **indirect cost.** An indirect cost may also be called a **common cost,** because it is common to more than one cost object.

To illustrate the difference between direct and indirect costs, consider 12 Sears stores in Alabama. Each store has a manager who is responsible for the day-to-day operation of that store. Sears also has a general manager who is responsible for the operation of all stores in the state. If we define each of the 12 stores as cost objects, the salary of each store manager would be considered a direct cost to his or her store. The salary of the general manager is not incurred to support any one of the 12 stores. Rather, it supports all 12 stores. Therefore, the general manager's salary would be considered an indirect cost of each cost object (the individual stores).

## Discussion Questions

Assume that instead of defining each individual Sears store as a cost object, we define the entire Sears operation in Alabama as a cost object.

2–1. In this case, would the salaries of the 12 store managers be considered direct or indirect costs? Explain your reasoning.

2–2. Would the salary of the general manager be considered a direct or an indirect cost? Explain your reasoning.

2–3. Why do you think managers at various levels in a company would find it useful to classify costs as direct or indirect?

## Product Cost

**product cost** The cost of the various products a company sells.

When you see inventory on store shelves, you know the store did not get the inventory for free. Rather, each unit of product had some cost. The cost of the various products that a company sells is called **product cost.** More specifically, product costs are the costs associated with making the products available and ready to sell. For a bookstore, such as B. Dalton Booksellers or WaldenBooks, product cost is the cost of the books purchased for resale, the freight to get the books to the store (also known as freight-in), and other costs involved in getting the books ready to sell.

**inventoriable cost** Another name for *product cost.*

Product costs are also known as **inventoriable costs**—product costs become part of a company's inventory until the goods associated with the costs are sold. Because product held for sale is considered an asset, its cost is shown on the balance sheet (inventory) until the product is actually sold. When the goods are sold, the product cost is converted from an asset on the balance sheet to an expense (cost of goods sold) on the income statement.

For example, when Payless Shoe Source buys shoes to sell, the cost of the shoes is a product cost and is added to inventory on the balance sheet. The cost remains in inventory on the balance sheet until the shoes are sold. When the shoes are sold, the reality of the reduced inventory caused by the sale is reflected in the company's accounting records by reducing inventory on the balance sheet and increasing cost of goods sold on the income statement.

## Period Cost

**period cost** All costs incurred by a company that are not considered product cost. Includes selling and administrative cost.

**Period costs** are all the costs that a company incurs which are not considered product costs. They include selling and administrative expenses, but not any costs associated with acquiring product or getting it ready to sell.

**selling cost** The cost of locating customers, attracting customers, convincing customers to buy, and the cost of necessary paperwork to document and record sales.

***Selling Cost*** Selling cost includes the cost of locating customers, attracting them, convincing them to buy, and the cost of necessary paperwork to document and record sales. Examples of selling cost include salaries paid to members of the sales force, sales commissions, and advertising.

Two selling costs are less obvious: the cost of delivering product to customers (also known as freight-out) and the cost of storing merchandise inventory. The reason delivery cost is considered a selling cost is that companies probably would not provide delivery unless it helped sell more product. If customers would buy with or without free delivery, the seller would probably not offer it.

Do not confuse freight-out (period cost) with freight-in (product cost). The key to keeping the two straight is to think about when they are incurred. Freight-in is a cost incurred before the product is ready to sell and is therefore considered a product cost. Freight-out is incurred after the product is ready for sale and is therefore classified as a period cost.

The cost of storing merchandise inventory is also classified as a selling cost, because merchandise in stock enhances its sales potential. Businesses cannot easily sell what they do not have. For example, if you went to your local music shop to buy a compact disc and the salesperson told you, "We don't keep that CD in stock, but we'll be glad to order it for you," then you would probably walk out and find another store that carries a better-stocked inventory of compact discs rather than wait. Because both delivery and merchandise inventory enhance sales, these items are considered selling costs.

**administrative cost** All costs incurred by a company that are not product costs or selling costs. Includes the cost of accounting, finance, employee relations, and executive functions.

***Administrative Cost*** Administrative cost includes all costs that are not product or selling cost. These costs are typically associated with support functions—areas that offer support to the product and selling areas, such as accounting, finance, human resources, and executive functions.

Generally, period costs are shown as operating expenses (selling and administrative expenses) on the income statement. Most period costs—administrators' salaries, for example—are presented as expenses when the expenditure is made. When long-lived assets that will be used for selling or administrative functions are purchased, a slightly different treatment is necessary. At the time they are purchased, the cost of long-lived assets is shown on the balance sheet. As time passes, the depreciation expense associated with these assets becomes part of selling and administrative expense.

## Discussion Questions

Assume that you are using a felt-tip highlighter to mark this book as you read it. Assume further that you purchased the marker at the college bookstore.

2–4. What costs associated with the marker do you think the bookstore would consider to be product costs? Explain your reasoning for each cost you included.

2–5. What costs associated with operating the bookstore do you think would be considered period costs (selling and administrative)? Explain your reasoning for each cost you included.

### Comparing Product and Period Costs

The distinction between product cost and period cost is based on whether the cost in question benefits the process of getting products ready for sale (product cost), or the selling and administrative functions (period cost). Let us look at some examples to make sure you understand the distinction. The cost of a factory security guard is a product cost because it benefits the plant. Conversely, the cost of a security guard in the sales office is a selling expense, which is a period cost. Note that the classification depends on the company function that benefits from the cost.

What about the salary of the vice president of manufacturing? Even though vice president of manufacturing may sound like an administrative position, the cost of it benefits the manufacturing function, so it is a product cost. Further, all costs associated with that position, including the depreciation on the vice president's desk, the cost of his or her support personnel, travel costs, and all other costs associated with this position, would be classified as a product cost. Likewise, the vice president of marketing would be an example of selling expense, which is a period cost. The depreciation on a company sales representative's car would be a selling expense, because it benefits the sales area of the company.

Next, we examine how manufacturing, merchandising, and service firms identify their product costs.

## PRODUCT COST IDENTIFICATION FOR MERCHANDISING FIRMS

Merchandising firms, whether wholesale or retail, purchase products ready to sell, add a markup, and resell the goods. They generate profits by selling merchandise for a price that is higher than their cost. Wholesalers generally buy products from manufacturers (or other wholesalers) and then sell them to retailers. Retailers buy from manufacturers or the wholesalers and sell their products to the final consumers.

In this section we explore how a merchandising company identifies product costs and how those product costs flow through the balance sheet and income statement.

For a merchandising firm, product cost includes the cost of the merchandise itself, freight costs to obtain the merchandise, and any other costs incurred to get the product ready to sell. Because merchandisers buy goods for resale, often the cost of getting products ready to sell is minor or nonexistent. Product cost does not include any cost incurred after the product is in place and ready to sell.

Product cost is often the most significant of all costs for a merchandiser. It is not uncommon for merchandising companies to have cost of goods sold as high as 80 percent of the selling price of the product sold, indicating of course that they have a gross profit as low as 20 percent. Besides increasing sales, managers are always interested in reducing expenses, which is impossible without an understanding of what items are included in product cost. Efforts to reduce total cost of goods sold may focus on any component of that expense, that is, any component of product cost.

## The Flow of Product Cost—Merchandising Company

If you were responsible for the profitability of a product or group of products, not only would you want to know total product cost, but you would also want to know and understand the various components of each product's cost. With this understanding, you could analyze reports detailing these products' cost components and work to isolate costs that could be reduced or eliminated. The diagram in Exhibit 2–2 illustrates the flow of costs in a merchandising operation.

**Exhibit 2–2**
Flow of Product Costs—
Merchandising
Company

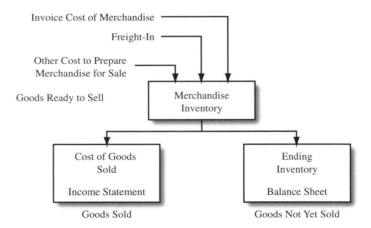

Exhibit 2–2 indicates that as goods are purchased, their cost is classified as merchandise inventory. In fact, all product costs are originally shown like those in Exhibit 2–2, as an asset on the balance sheet. Typically, a merchandising firm has only one inventory classification, which is usually referred to as *merchandise inventory* or, simply, *inventory*. As the units of product are sold, their cost is converted to an expense and shown on the income statement as the cost of goods sold.

## Cost of Goods Sold

Exhibit 2–3 is a cost of goods sold schedule for Jason's Supply Company. As the exhibit shows, we add purchases to the inventory on hand at the beginning of the period to arrive at the goods available for sale. Generally, one of two things can

**Exhibit 2–3**
Cost of Goods Sold
Schedule

**JASON'S SUPPLY COMPANY**
**Cost of Goods Sold Schedule**
**For the Year Ending December 31, 1998**

|   | | |
|---|---|---|
| | Beginning Inventory at January 1, 1998 | $ 23,000 |
| + | Purchases during 1998 | 300,000 |
| = | Goods Available for Sale in 1998 | $323,000 |
| − | Ending Inventory at December 31, 1998 | (30,000) |
| = | Cost of Goods Sold for 1998 | $293,000 |

happen to the goods available for sale: They are either sold or remain on hand at the end of the period and are reflected as ending inventory. Thus, when ending inventory is subtracted from the goods available for sale, we can determine the cost associated with the products that have been sold—that is, we can determine the cost of goods sold.

The January 1, 1998, beginning inventory amount shown in Exhibit 2–3 is actually the ending inventory from Jason's balance sheet at December 31, 1997, and the ending inventory amount shown is from Jason's balance sheet at December 31, 1998. The cost of goods sold amount is included as an expense item on the company's income statement for the year ending December 31, 1998.

## Discussion Question

**2-6.** Accounting for the flow of product cost for a merchandiser seems to be a lot of bother. If all merchandise inventory will eventually be sold anyway, why not just record it as an expense (cost of goods sold) on the income statement when it is purchased?

Any company that sells tangible, physical product must sell its product for more than the product costs or it will eventually go bankrupt. This may seem very obvious, and in fact, good business managers are well aware of this necessity. Understanding the need is one thing; making sure it happens is another. Competitive pressures exist in most industries that cause companies to sell their products for less than desired. Managers of these businesses must have a solid understanding of the relationship between the selling price of their products and the cost of those products, or they may actually sell product for less than it costs.

It's like the two guys who bought watermelons for $1 each and were selling them for $0.90 each. Business was certainly brisk because they were underselling all their competition. Finally, one guy turned to the other and said, "Harry, we need to get a bigger truck." Well, a bigger truck would not help. They could never sell enough watermelons to be profitable because they were selling each melon for less than it cost. Without a thorough understanding of the relationship between the cost of a product and the selling price of that product, managers cannot hope to make prudent business decisions.

Virtually all the products that consumers purchase have undergone some manufacturing process. In this section we explore how a manufacturing company identifies product costs and how those product costs flow through the balance sheet and income statement. As in merchandising firms, product cost for a manufacturer includes all costs associated with acquiring the product and getting it ready to sell. For manufacturers, however, getting the product ready to sell is usually an extensive process requiring the use of factory facilities such as production machinery and factory workers.

For a manufacturer, units of product are normally considered cost objects and their cost encompasses three distinct elements. We will introduce them briefly here and then discuss each of them in more detail a bit later. As we present each of the elements, think back to our discussion earlier in the chapter about cost objects and direct versus indirect costs.

**direct materials cost** The cost of all raw materials that can be traced directly to a unit of manufactured product.

1. **Direct materials cost.** Direct materials cost is the cost of all raw materials that can be traced directly to a single unit of manufactured product, or the cost incurred for only one cost object. Note that direct materials cost is not the cost of all materials used in the manufacture of the product. In most manufacturing operations some materials costs are incurred for multiple cost objects. These costs are indirect materials cost, which we consider a part of manufacturing overhead.

**direct labor cost** The cost of all production labor that can be traced directly to a unit of manufactured product.

2. **Direct labor cost.** Direct labor cost is the cost of all production labor that can be traced directly to a unit of manufactured product. Note that direct labor cost is not the cost of all labor incurred in the manufacture of product. In most manufacturing operations some labor costs are incurred for multiple cost objects. That type of cost is indirect labor cost, which we consider a part of manufacturing overhead, discussed next.

**manufacturing overhead cost** All costs associated with the operation of the manufacturing facility besides direct materials cost and direct labor cost. It is composed entirely of indirect manufacturing cost incurred to support multiple cost objects.

3. **Manufacturing overhead cost.** Manufacturing overhead is all the costs associated with the operation of the manufacturing facility other than direct materials cost and direct labor cost. It is composed entirely of indirect manufacturing cost—that is, manufacturing cost incurred to support multiple cost objects. Among others, manufacturing overhead includes indirect materials and indirect labor as discussed in items 1 and 2.

## Inventory Classifications

As with merchandising firms, product costs for a manufacturer are inventoriable costs. However, manufacturing companies have not just one, but three types of inventory: raw materials, work in process, and finished goods. Note that these three types of inventory are not the same as the three elements of manufactured product we just introduced. Rather, these inventory classifications specify where manufactured product is at any given time in the production process.

As we discuss the three inventory classifications used by manufacturers, consider the following thoughts. First, our discussion in this chapter is intended to serve only as a broad introduction to the flow of product cost through a manufacturing company. The following chapter deals with specific methods used to accumulate product cost for a manufacturer. Second, there is a difference between reality and the measurement of reality. Reality is physical units of product moving through the production process, separate from our attempt to measure that reality.

**raw materials inventory** Materials that have been purchased but have not yet entered the production process.

**material stores** Another name for *raw materials inventory.*

**Raw materials inventory,** sometimes called **material stores,** consists of materials that have been purchased but have not yet entered the production process. Included in raw materials inventory are those that will eventually be accounted for as either direct or indirect materials. For example, Steelcase, Inc. manufactures metal desks, filing cabinets, and other metal office furniture. Raw materials inventory for Steelcase would consist of the sheet metal, screws, paint, and glue it has on hand with which to make metal office furniture. It would not include any of the material in the office furniture the company has begun to manufacture but has not yet finished, nor would it include the material in the office furniture that has been completed. Until raw materials actually enter the production process, the cost associated with those materials is classified as raw materials inventory on the balance sheet.

**work-in-process inventory**
Products that have entered the production process but have not yet been completed.

**Work-in-process inventory** consists of products that have entered the production process but have not yet been completed—those units currently on the production line or in the production process. In our Steelcase example, work-in-process inventory at any given time would consist of the desks, filing cabinets, and other metal office furniture that have been started but are not yet finished. The reality is partially completed desks, filing cabinets, and other metal office furniture. The measurement of reality counts the costs associated with these partially completed units of product and classifies them as work-in-process inventory on the balance sheet. These costs include the cost of the materials associated with these units, the labor cost incurred so far in the production process, and some amount of manufacturing overhead applied to each of the partially completed units of product.

Work-in-process inventory does not include the cost of raw materials that have not yet entered the production process, nor does it include the cost associated with products that have been completed.

**finished goods inventory**
Products that have been completed and are ready to sell.

As you might imagine, **finished goods inventory** consists of products that have been completed and are ready to sell. With respect to Steelcase, finished goods inventory would be the pieces of metal office furniture completed but not yet sold. Remember, these are real units of finished product: They are reality. They have completed the production process and are sitting in a warehouse somewhere waiting to be sold. The measurement of that reality is a classification of inventory on the balance sheet called finished goods inventory. Included in that amount are all the materials, labor, and manufacturing overhead costs accumulated for those units completed, but not yet sold.

## Discussion Question

2–7. Why do you think managers of a manufacturing firm would find it beneficial to separate the amount and cost of inventory items into raw materials, work in process, and finished goods?

If managers in manufacturing businesses are to make prudent production decisions, they must have relevant information. The decisions they must make include how much and what type of materials they need to purchase, how many production workers are needed, what skill level these workers must possess, and whether production capacity is sufficient to produce the product required. The information that managers need to help them make these and many other production decisions includes the amount and cost of raw materials on hand, the composition of the labor force, the capacity and cost of production facilities, and the amount and cost of both work-in-process and finished goods inventory.

Although much of the relevant information managers need to make these decisions is provided by nonaccountants, such as marketing and sales personnel, accountants provide vital information concerning the cost of raw materials, work in process, and finished goods. All three classifications of inventory have one or more of the product cost elements introduced earlier: direct material, direct labor, and manufacturing overhead. We will now discuss each of those elements in more detail.

## Direct Material

**direct material** The raw material that becomes a part of the final product and can be easily traced to the individual units produced.

**Direct material** is the raw material that becomes part of the final product and can be easily traced to the individual units produced. Obviously, direct materials cost is the cost of these raw materials. Examples of direct materials used in the manufacture of automobiles are sheet metal, plastic, and window glass. In the manufacture of computers, direct materials include circuit boards, cathode ray tubes, and other items. At Steelcase, Inc., direct materials would include the sheet metal used to manufacture the desks, filing cabinets, and other metal office furniture.

Often, the final product of one company is purchased by another to be used as part of its raw material in the manufacturing process. For example, direct materials used in the manufacture of Cessna aircraft include aluminum, wheels, tires, cables, and engines. The tires that Cessna uses as raw materials in the manufacture of its aircraft are the finished product of one of the company's suppliers, Goodyear Tire and Rubber Company.

## Discussion Questions

2–8. In addition to the tires supplied by Goodyear, what other finished products do you think Cessna uses in its production of small aircraft? What companies might produce these products?

2–9. Name three additional pairs of manufacturing companies that have a supplier-buyer relationship—that is, the finished product of one company becomes the raw material of another company.

When materials are purchased for use in the manufacture of products, their cost at first is added to raw materials inventory. Once the material has entered the production process (reality), its cost is removed from raw materials inventory and added to work-in-process inventory (measurement of reality). Thus, in our Steelcase example, as sheet metal is purchased, its cost is added to raw materials. Once the metal has been used to make a desk or other piece of office furniture, its cost is removed from raw materials inventory and becomes part of work-in-process inventory.

## Direct Labor

**direct labor hours** The time spent by production workers as they transform raw materials into units of finished products.

**Direct labor hours** are defined as the time spent by production workers as they transform raw materials into units of finished products. Direct labor costs are the salaries and wages paid to these workers, which can be easily traced to the products the workers produce.

Think about some article of clothing, say a pair of pants, you are wearing at this moment. Certainly there is material in the pants. But how did the pants become pants? Well, you may not know all the steps, but you do know that somewhere, someone sat at a sewing machine and stitched the cut material into a pair of pants. The money paid to that person, whether in Taiwan, Korea, or New Jersey, is considered direct labor, because her or his efforts (and therefore cost) can easily be traced to that single cost object (the pair of pants).

The accounting treatment of direct labor cost may surprise you. In prior chapters, employees' wages were classified as wage expense, salaries expense, or some similar expense. However, direct labor needed to get products ready to sell is a product cost that enhances the value of direct material. Because product costs are inventoriable costs, direct labor cost is added to the value of work-in-process inventory, along with direct material. Why? Because the work of production-line personnel increases the value of material as it is fabricated, assembled, painted, or processed. As a result, the cost of production-line labor should increase the value of inventory, shown as an asset on the balance sheet and ultimately as cost of goods sold on the income statement. In our Steelcase example, then, wages paid to workers who actually make the desks, filing cabinets, and other metal office furniture would be considered direct labor and added to work-in-process inventory.

Thus far we have explored two elements of product costs for a manufacturing firm: direct material and direct labor. Next, we consider the third and last element of manufacturers' product costs—manufacturing overhead.

## Manufacturing Overhead

**manufacturing overhead**
All activities involved in the manufacture of products besides direct materials or direct labor.

**Manufacturing overhead** is defined as all activities involved in the manufacture of products besides direct materials or direct labor. Manufacturing overhead cost, then, is the cost of these indirect manufacturing activities. It is also referred to as **factory overhead, factory burden,** or simply **overhead.** In recent years, manufacturing companies have begun to call the cost of manufacturing overhead *indirect manufacturing cost,* which is certainly more descriptive than any of its other names. Old habits die hard, however, so we will call it manufacturing overhead because this term has been and remains universally understood in business.

**factory overhead** Another name for *manufacturing overhead cost.*

**factory burden** Another name for *manufacturing overhead cost.*

**overhead** In a manufacturing company, another name for manufacturing overhead cost; in a service type business, the indirect service cost.

To be considered part of manufacturing overhead, the cost must be associated with the manufacturing facility, not some other aspect of the company such as selling or administrative functions. Manufacturing overhead includes three groups of costs: indirect materials, indirect labor, and other indirect manufacturing costs.

**indirect materials**
Materials consumed in support of multiple cost objects.

***Indirect Material*** **Indirect materials** are those consumed in a manufacturing facility in support of multiple cost objects. There are two types of indirect material costs in manufacturing. The first is the cost of raw materials so insignificant that the added benefit of physically tracing these materials to individual products is not worth the effort. Examples include glue, rivets, solder, small nails, and caulking. In fact, businesses could physically trace all material cost to their products, but in the case of indirect materials, the effort required to trace the cost outweighs the benefit of the additional information. The second type of indirect material is factory supplies. These are materials used in the manufacturing facility but not incorporated into the product. Examples include paper towels, janitorial supplies, and lubricants for production machinery. The cost of all indirect materials, whether the materials actually become part of manufactured product, is added to the cost of the product as part of manufacturing overhead.

**indirect labor** The labor incurred in support of multiple cost objects.

***Indirect Labor*** **Indirect labor** is labor incurred in a manufacturing facility in support of multiple cost objects. As was the case with indirect material costs, there are two types of indirect labor in manufacturing. The first is the cost associated with factory workers who are neither on the production line nor directly involved in the manufacturing process. Examples include the cost of materials handlers, production supervisors, plant security personnel, plant janitorial personnel, factory secretarial and clerical personnel, and the vice president of manufacturing. Although the effort of these workers is important to the production process, their labor costs are not easily traceable to products. They are therefore classified as indirect labor.

The second type of indirect labor is the cost of wages paid to direct labor employees when they are doing something other than working on the product they produce. These activities might include setting up equipment for production runs or sweeping up at the end of a shift. The idea is that direct labor should include only the cost of direct labor personnel when they are actually working on the product. The cost of all indirect labor is added to the cost of the product as part of manufacturing overhead.

Some manufacturers in the United States now consider *all* labor as indirect labor. In some types of operations, the direct labor element of a manufactured product is as low as four percent of the total manufacturing cost. If managers believe labor cost is insignificant, they may choose not to separate it into direct and indirect labor cost and may instead classify all labor costs as indirect.

**Other Overhead Costs**   In addition to indirect material and indirect labor, manufacturing overhead includes other costs associated with the production facility. Examples include depreciation on the factory building, rent paid for production equipment, factory insurance, property taxes for the factory, and telephone service for the factory. All the costs in this category are associated with the operation of the production facility.

We have seen that manufacturing overhead is the sum of all indirect material, indirect labor, and other overhead costs. Manufacturing overhead costs are necessary costs to produce products and enhance the value of the goods being manufactured. Accordingly, as products are being manufactured, manufacturing overhead costs are added to work-in-process inventory.

## Discussion Question

2-10. The textbook you are reading was published (manufactured) by Prentice Hall. What costs of manufacturing this book do you think Prentice Hall would include as

**a.** direct materials?

**b.** direct labor?

**c.** manufacturing overhead?

## The Flow of Product Cost—Manufacturing Company

In a manufacturing environment, just as in merchandising operations, managers must understand the flow of product costs to successfully control and plan for them. Product cost information is also an essential element of the information needed when making pricing and sales decisions. How could a business price a product if none of its managers knew how much the product cost to produce? Having the information is not enough, though. Managers must also understand the components of product cost and the way these costs will affect the company's assets as reported on the balance sheet and the profits as on the income statement. Exhibit 2–4 shows the flow of product costs through a manufacturing operation.

**Exhibit 2–4**
The Flow of Product Costs—Manufacturing Company

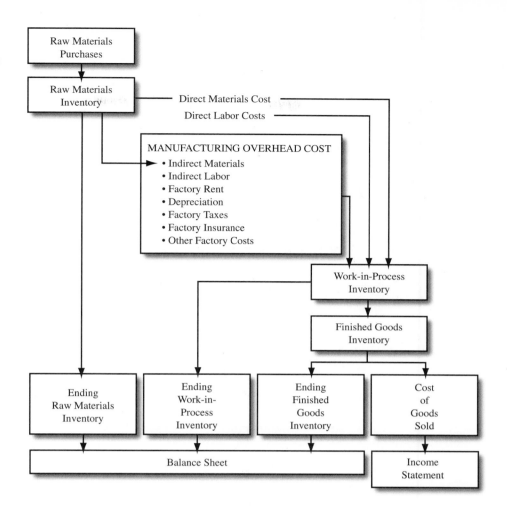

Exhibit 2–4 looks more complicated than it really is. In fact, this exhibit summarizes our entire discussion of product cost identification for a manufacturer. Let us take some time to walk through the diagram.

As raw materials are purchased, they become part of raw materials inventory (a).

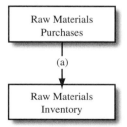

When materials actually enter the production process, their cost is classified as either direct materials (b) or indirect materials (c) depending on the type of material. The cost of any raw materials still on hand at the end of the production period is classified as ending raw materials inventory on the balance sheet at the end of the period (d).

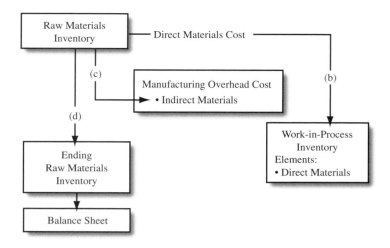

Note that the cost of direct materials is added to work-in-process inventory at this point, whereas the cost of indirect materials is classified as manufacturing overhead. We will return to manufacturing overhead in a moment.

We now have one of the three elements of product cost in work-in-process inventory (direct materials). The next element added is labor. Note that direct labor (e) is added directly to work-in-process inventory, whereas indirect labor (f) is classified as manufacturing overhead.

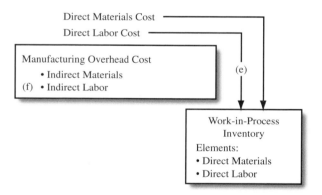

We now have two of the three elements of product cost in work-in-process inventory (direct materials and direct labor). The last element added is manufacturing overhead. In addition to indirect materials and indirect labor (which we classified as manufacturing overhead earlier), all other indirect manufacturing costs are classified as manufacturing overhead (g). The ones we have provided in Exhibit 2–4 are representative only. In reality, the list is almost endless.

Once the manufacturing overhead items and amounts have been accumulated, the cost of manufacturing overhead is added to work in process (h).

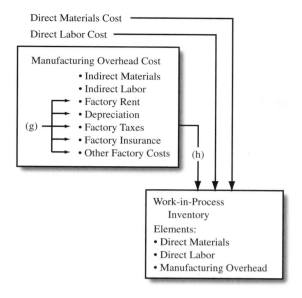

Work-in-process inventory, then, consists of the direct material, direct labor, and manufacturing overhead cost associated with goods that are currently in production. As units are completed, the cost associated with these units is transferred from work-in-process inventory to finished goods inventory (i). The cost of product still in production at the end of the production period is classified as ending work-in-process inventory on the balance sheet at the end of the period (j).

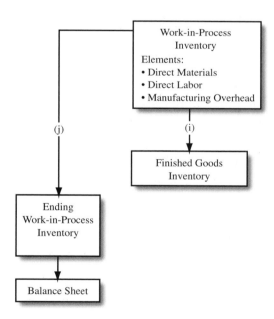

Once finished units of product (and their cost) have been transferred to finished goods inventory, usually only one of two things will happen to the actual units: Either they will be sold by the end of the accounting period or they will not be sold. If they are sold, we transfer the cost associated with them to cost of goods sold (k). We classify the cost of finished product still on hand at the end of the accounting period as ending finished goods inventory on the balance sheet at the end of the period (l).

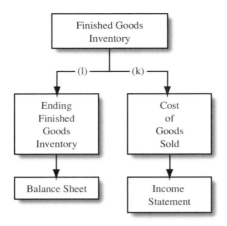

For most manufacturers, inventory is a sizeable asset requiring considerable financial resources. A walk through a manufacturing facility would make you aware of the significance of inventory, because you would be able to see stacks of it sitting there. Raw materials, work in process, and finished goods are all important assets of a manufacturer. Proper measurement of these assets is crucial if managers are to make good decisions about inventory management. For this reason, business people should understand the component costs of each type of inventory.

## Cost of Goods Manufactured

We have seen that a manufacturer's product cost consists of direct material, direct labor, and manufacturing overhead. These three product classifications are summarized on the cost of goods manufactured schedule. You will find a typical presentation of this schedule for Lowell Manufacturing, Inc. in Exhibit 2–5.

**Exhibit 2–5**
Cost of Goods
Manufactured Schedule

### LOWELL MANUFACTURING, INC.
### Cost of Goods Manufactured Schedule
### For the Year Ending December 31, 1998

| | | |
|---|---:|---:|
| Direct Materials: | | |
|     Beginning Direct Material Inventory | $ 13,000 | |
| + Purchases during 1998 | 400,000 | |
| = Materials Available during 1998 | $413,000 | |
| − Ending Direct Material Inventory | (20,000) | |
| = Direct Materials Used during 1998 | | $ 393,000 |
|     Direct Labor during 1998 | | 220,000 |
|     Manufacturing Overhead Cost: | | |
| Indirect Materials | $ 5,000 | |
| Indirect Labor | 20,000 | |
| Factory Rent | 144,000 | |
| Depreciation of Equipment | 250,000 | |
| Repairs and Maintenance on Equipment | 40,000 | |
| Utilities | 39,000 | |
| Property Taxes | 15,000 | |
|     Total Manufacturing Overhead Cost during 1998 | | 513,000 |
|     Manufacturing Cost for Current Period | | $1,126,000 |
| + Beginning Work-in-Process Inventory (1/1/98) | | 41,000 |
| = Cost of Goods Available to be Finished in 1998 | | $1,167,000 |
| − Ending Work-in-Process Inventory (12/31/98) | | (65,000) |
| = Cost of Goods Manufactured during 1998 | | $1,102,000 |

Although this schedule looks quite involved, it consists of four relatively simple parts.

1. Direct Materials Section. This section is similar in format to the cost of goods sold section of the income statement. In both cases, we deal with costs stored in inventory to determine the cost of the inventory that has been used.

**LOWELL MANUFACTURING, INC.**
**Cost of Goods Manufactured Schedule**
**Direct Materials Section**
**For the Year Ending December 31, 1998**

| | | |
|---|---|---|
| Direct Materials: | | |
|     Beginning Direct Material Inventory | $ 13,000 | |
| +   Purchases during 1998 | 400,000 | |
| =   Materials Available during 1998 | $413,000 | |
| −   Ending Direct Material Inventory | ( 20,000) | |
| =   Direct Materials Used during 1998 | | $393,000 |

2. Direct Labor Section. We see that the direct labor section of Lowell Manufacturing's cost of goods manufactured schedule consists of only one line, which is a common way to present this information. Remember, direct labor represents the cost of employees directly involved in the production process.

**LOWELL MANUFACTURING, INC.**
**Cost of Goods Manufactured Schedule**
**Direct Labor Section**
**For the Year Ending December 31, 1998**

| | |
|---|---|
| Direct Labor during 1998 | $220,000 |

3. The Manufacturing Overhead Section. This section lists manufacturing overhead costs by functional description. Depending on the level of detail desired, this section can be as short as one line, which depicts total manufacturing overhead. Lowell's cost of goods manufactured schedule provides several lines detailing the various components of manufacturing overhead.

**LOWELL MANUFACTURING, INC.**
**Cost of Goods Manufactured Schedule**
**Manufacturing Overhead Section**
**For the Year Ending December 31, 1998**

| | | |
|---|---|---|
| Manufacturing Overhead Cost: | | |
|   Indirect Materials | $ 5,000 | |
|   Indirect Labor | 20,000 | |
|   Factory Rent | 144,000 | |
|   Depreciation of Equipment | 250,000 | |
|   Repairs and Maintenance on Equipment | 40,000 | |
|   Utilities | 39,000 | |
|   Property Taxes | 15,000 | |
|   Total Manufacturing Overhead Cost during 1998 | | $513,000 |

4. Cost Summary and Work-in-Process Section. The last section of the cost of goods manufactured schedule summarizes the current period's product cost and incorporates the beginning and ending work-in-process inventory balances. Note that as in a cost of goods sold schedule, beginning inventory is added and ending inventory is subtracted to arrive at inventory used.

**LOWELL MANUFACTURING, INC.**
**Cost of Goods Manufactured Schedule**
**Cost Summary and Work-in-Process Section**
**For the Year Ending December 31, 1998**

|   | | |
|---|---|---|
|   | Manufacturing Cost for Current Period | $1,126,000 |
| + | Beginning Work-in-Process Inventory (1/1/98) | 41,000 |
| = | Cost of Goods Available to be Finished during 1998 | $1,167,000 |
| − | Ending Work-in-Process Inventory (12/31/98) | ( 65,000) |
| = | Cost of Goods Manufactured during 1998 | $1,102,000 |

Using the information from the cost of goods manufactured schedule, we can prepare a cost of goods sold schedule, such as the one for Lowell Manufacturing, Inc. shown in Exhibit 2–6.

**Exhibit 2–6**
Cost of Goods Sold
Schedule

**LOWELL MANUFACTURING, INC.**
**Cost of Goods Sold Schedule**
**For the Year Ending December 31, 1998**

|   | | |
|---|---|---|
|   | Beginning Finished Goods Inventory | $ 70,000 |
| + | Cost of Goods Manufactured during 1998 | 1,102,000 |
| = | Goods Available for Sale in 1998 | $1,172,000 |
| − | Ending Finished Goods Inventory | (28,000) |
| = | Cost of Goods Sold for 1998 | $1,144,000 |

# PRODUCT COST IDENTIFICATION FOR SERVICE FIRMS

In contrast to both merchandisers and manufacturers, service type businesses such as law firms, health care providers, airlines, and accounting firms do not sell tangible, physical products. Many service firms are huge. For example, Hilton Hotels Corporation is a diversified service company in the hospitality industry. The company reported revenues from hotel and casino services of over $1.6 billion for 1996.

Service companies offer their customers a product just as real as those sold by merchandisers and manufacturers, but service products lack physical substance. Determining the cost of its product is as important for a service company as it is for merchandisers and manufacturers, but the procedures differ because service type businesses have no inventory.

Costs can be accumulated for almost any facet of a service company's operation. To illustrate, let us consider the Marston Medical Clinic. The three doctors at the clinic (Dr. Helen Marston and two of her medical school classmates) perform routine physical exams, examinations in response to specific patient symptoms, immunizations, and minor surgery. Major surgery is performed by the doctors at a local hospital. Any one of these services could be designated as a cost object, and cost could be accumulated for a particular service provided to an individual patient. Likewise, costs can be accumulated for a particular category of procedure, for a department or a particular area of the medical practice, or for each of the three doctors or the five nurses.

The three broad cost classifications included in the cost of services provided are materials, labor, and indirect service cost (sometimes called overhead). The cost classifications for a service firm look almost exactly like the classifications used in costing manufactured products, with some important differences.

## Materials

The materials used in performing services are normally incidental supplies. The cost of these materials is relatively insignificant compared to the direct materials used in the production of manufactured products. In the case of Marston Medical Clinic, materials would include items such as tongue depressors, the needles and serum used for immunizations, bandages, and so forth.

Some service companies separate material that is significant enough to trace to individual cost objects from insignificant material that is simply treated as indirect overhead cost. In many cases, however, the materials used in performing a service are actually more like the indirect materials used by a manufacturer. Whereas a manufacturer such as Steelcase might consider glue and screws to be indirect materials, a legal firm would probably consider legal pads, computer discs, and pens as indirect materials, and all costs of materials are treated as indirect (overhead) cost.

## Labor

Generally, service businesses are labor intensive, meaning that the largest component of product cost for service organizations is often labor cost. It includes costs of those people who perform part or all the service. In the case of Marston Medical Clinic, labor cost would certainly include the salaries of the three doctors and the five nurses. It would not, however, include the amount paid to the receptionist or bookkeeper. Even though their work is important, these employees do not perform the health care services provided by the clinic. The labor cost of the receptionist and bookkeeper, then, would be considered a period cost.

## Overhead or Indirect Service Costs

The overhead costs in a service business are similar to those for a manufacturer. They are costs that are associated specifically with performing the services provided but that cannot easily be traced to one specific cost object. In the case of the Marston Clinic, rent on the clinic building is an indirect cost of providing health care—the building is necessary to provide patient services. However, its cost is hard to trace to one cost object, so it is considered an overhead cost.

# Discussion Question

**2-11.** Airline companies, such as United Airlines, often define the routes they fly as cost objects. Given that definition, consider a specific route from New York to Los Angeles and describe the costs you believe United Airlines would include as

**a.** materials

**b.** labor

**c.** overhead

## The Flow of Service Cost—Service Company

Just as managers in manufacturing and merchandising operations must understand the flow of costs associated with products they sell, managers of service type businesses must understand the flow of service costs if they are to control and plan for them. Also, service cost information is an essential element of the information needed when making pricing and sales decisions. Having the information is not enough though. Managers must also understand how these costs will affect the company's assets reported on the balance sheet and profits on the income statement. The flow of costs through a typical service firm is shown in Exhibit 2–7.

**Exhibit 2–7**
The Flow of Service Costs—Service Company

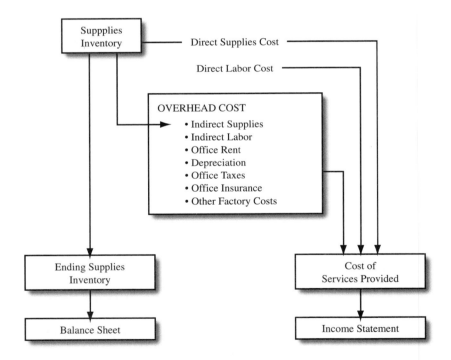

## Cost of Services

As Exhibit 2–7 indicates, cost of services has three parts: direct labor, overhead, and supplies. With this in mind, we can easily create a schedule computing the cost of service products. As an example, the schedule in Exhibit 2–8 shows the computation of cost of medical services for Marston Medical Clinic.

**Exhibit 2–8**
Cost of Services
Schedule

| MARSTON MEDICAL CLINIC | | |
|---|---|---|
| **Cost of Services Schedule** | | |
| **For the Year Ending December 31, 1998** | | |
| Direct Labor Cost | | $ 940,000 |
| Overhead Cost: | | |
|    Indirect Supplies | $12,000 | |
|    Office Rent | 24,000 | |
|    Depreciation | 18,000 | |
|    Office Taxes | 2,000 | |
|    Office Insurance | 8,000 | |
|    Other Indirect Costs | 6,000 | |
| Total Overhead Cost | | 70,000 |
| Direct Supplies Cost | | $ 20,000 |
| Cost of Services Provided | | $1,030,000 |

Exhibit 2–8 shows that the cost of services for Marston Medical Clinic was $1,030,000 for the year ended December 31, 1998. The total cost included the three components of service product cost: direct labor, overhead, and direct supplies.

We have examined how service firms identify product costs and how those costs flow through the firm. We now turn briefly to hybrid firms, which produce both goods and services.

# HYBRID FIRMS

**hybrid firms** Companies that generate revenue from both providing services and selling products.

Some companies, called **hybrid firms,** generate revenue from both providing services and selling products. For example, although the majority of Blockbuster Entertainment's revenue comes from its videotape rental service, the company also generates significant revenue from videotape product sales. In accounting for an operation that combines service and products, companies such as Blockbuster must incorporate techniques used by both service and merchandising firms. A single company, such as General Motors, might actually be a manufacturer (making cars and trucks), a merchandiser (selling floor mats and other accessories to GM dealers), and a service type business (offering GMAC Financing).

# MERCHANDISING, MANUFACTURING, AND SERVICE— A COMPARISON

Now that we have explored how merchandising, manufacturing, and service businesses identify their product costs and how those costs flow through each type of operation, we can see how merchandisers, manufacturers, and service businesses present product costs and period costs on their income statements. We begin with a merchandising operation, then we look at a manufacturer and a service business.

**Exhibit 2–9**
Product Costs and
Period Costs on the
Income Statement—
Merchandiser

---

**JASON'S SUPPLY COMPANY**
**Cost of Goods Sold Schedule**
**For the Year Ending December 31, 1998**

|   |   |   |
|---|---|---|
| | Beginning Inventory at January 1, 1998 | $ 23,000 |
| + | Purchases during 1998 | 300,000 |
| = | Goods Available for Sale in 1998 | $323,000 |
| − | Ending Inventory at December 31, 1998 | (30,000) |
| = | Cost of Goods Sold for 1998 | $293,000 |

**JASON'S SUPPLY COMPANY**
**Income Statement**
**For the Year Ending December 31, 1998**

| | | |
|---|---|---|
| Sales | | $673,000 |
| Cost of Goods Sold | | 293,000 |
| Gross Profit | | $380,000 |
| Operating Expenses: | | |
|   Selling Expense | $120,000 | |
|   Administrative Expense | 80,000 | |
| Total Operating Expenses | | 200,000 |
| Operating Income | | $180,000 |

---

Exhibit 2–9 illustrates how a merchandiser reports its product costs and period costs on an income statement. This exhibit shows the 1998 income statement for Jason's Supply Company and includes the cost of goods sold schedule we developed for Jason earlier in the chapter (presented as Exhibit 2–3).

As Exhibit 2–9 indicates, the amount of product cost recognized as expense (cost of goods sold) on Jason's 1998 income statement ($293,000) is calculated in the cost of goods sold schedule. The period cost recognized is the total of the operating expenses ($200,000).

Exhibit 2–10 illustrates how a manufacturer reports its product costs and period costs on an income statement. This exhibit shows the 1998 income statement for Lowell Manufacturing, Inc. and includes the cost of goods manufactured schedule (presented as Exhibit 2–5) and cost of goods sold schedule (presented as Exhibit 2–6) we developed for Lowell earlier in the chapter.

As Exhibit 2–10 indicates, the amount of product cost recognized as expense (cost of goods sold) on Lowell's 1998 income statement ($1,144,000) is calculated in the cost of goods manufactured schedule and the cost of goods sold schedule. The period cost recognized is the total of the operating expenses ($430,000).

Exhibit 2–11 illustrates how a service type company reports its cost of services and period costs on an income statement. This exhibit shows the 1998 income statement for Marston Medical Clinic and includes the cost of services schedule we developed for Marston earlier in the chapter (presented as Exhibit 2–8).

As Exhibit 2–11 indicates, the amount of services cost recognized as expense (cost of services) on Marston's 1998 income statement ($1,030,000) is calculated in the cost of services schedule. The period cost recognized is the total of the operating expenses ($175,000).

Whether the costs are related to products purchased for sale, products manufactured for sale, or services provided, cost information is an important input in the

### LOWELL MANUFACTURING, INC.
### Cost of Goods Manufactured Schedule
### For the Year Ending December 31, 1998

| | | |
|---|---:|---:|
| Direct Materials: | | |
|   Beginning Direct Material Inventory | $ 13,000 | |
| + Purchases during 1998 | 400,000 | |
| = Materials Available during 1998 | $413,000 | |
| − Ending Direct Material Inventory | ( 20,000) | |
| = Direct Materials Used during 1998 | | $393,000 |
| + Direct Labor during 1998 | | 220,000 |
| + Manufacturing Overhead Cost: | | |
|   Indirect Materials | $ 5,000 | |
|   Indirect Labor | 20,000 | |
|   Factory Rent | 144,000 | |
|   Depreciation of Equipment | 250,000 | |
|   Repairs and Maintenance on Equipment | 40,000 | |
|   Utilities | 39,000 | |
|   Property Taxes | 15,000 | |
|     Total Manufacturing Overhead Cost during 1998 | | 513,000 |
| = Manufacturing Cost for Current Period | | $1,126,000 |
| + Beginning Work-in-Process Inventory (1/1/98) | | 41,000 |
| = Cost of Goods Available to be Finished | | $1,167,000 |
| − Ending Work-in-Process Inventory (12/31/98) | | ( 65,000) |
| = Cost of Goods Manufactured during 1998 | | $1,102,000 |

### Cost of Goods Sold Schedule
### For the Year Ending December 31, 1998

| | | |
|---|---:|---:|
|   Beginning Finished Goods Inventory | | $ 70,000 |
| + Cost of Goods Manufactured during 1998 | | 1,102,000 |
| = Goods Available for Sale in 1998 | | $1,172,000 |
| − Ending Finished Goods Inventory | | ( 28,000) |
| = Cost of Goods Sold for 1998 | | $1,144,000 |

### Income Statement
### For the Year Ending December 31, 1998

| | | |
|---|---:|---:|
| Sales | | $1,884,000 |
| Cost of Goods Sold | | 1,144,000 |
| Gross Profit | | $ 740,000 |
| Operating Expenses: | | |
|   Selling Expense | $250,000 | |
|   Administrative Expense | 180,000 | |
| Total Operating Expenses | | 430,000 |
| Operating Income | | $ 310,000 |

decision-making process. Remember that management accounting information helps internal decision makers plan and control the firm's future. In the chapters that follow, you will see how the cost classifications and cost flows you learned about in this chapter will help you understand and apply management accounting decision-making techniques.

**Exhibit 2–11**
Cost of Services and
Period Costs on the
Income Statement—
Service Type Company

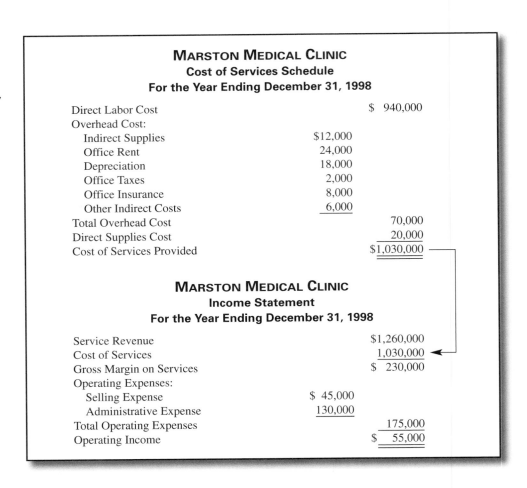

**MARSTON MEDICAL CLINIC**
**Cost of Services Schedule**
**For the Year Ending December 31, 1998**

| | | |
|---|---|---|
| Direct Labor Cost | | $ 940,000 |
| Overhead Cost: | | |
|    Indirect Supplies | $12,000 | |
|    Office Rent | 24,000 | |
|    Depreciation | 18,000 | |
|    Office Taxes | 2,000 | |
|    Office Insurance | 8,000 | |
|    Other Indirect Costs | 6,000 | |
| Total Overhead Cost | | 70,000 |
| Direct Supplies Cost | | 20,000 |
| Cost of Services Provided | | $1,030,000 |

**MARSTON MEDICAL CLINIC**
**Income Statement**
**For the Year Ending December 31, 1998**

| | | |
|---|---|---|
| Service Revenue | | $1,260,000 |
| Cost of Services | | 1,030,000 |
| Gross Margin on Services | | $ 230,000 |
| Operating Expenses: | | |
|    Selling Expense | $ 45,000 | |
|    Administrative Expense | 130,000 | |
| Total Operating Expenses | | 175,000 |
| Operating Income | | $ 55,000 |

# SUMMARY

Businesses incur many different costs as they operate in the modern business world. These costs can be classified in many different ways and managers must determine what cost classifications will be most helpful if they are to make effective planning and control decisions.

Costs can be accumulated by cost object, which is any activity or item for which we desire a separate cost measurement. Some of the costs associated with a cost object can be traced directly to that cost object. These are called direct costs. Other costs incurred to support multiple cost objects are known as indirect costs.

The classification of costs as either product cost or period cost is very important because it determines how costs are reported on a company's income statement. Product cost is the sum of all costs required to make the products available and ready to sell and is reported on the income statement as cost of goods sold. Period costs are all costs a company incurs that are not classified as product cost. Period costs are divided into selling and administrative costs and are reported on the income statement as expenses.

There are significant differences in the way product cost is determined for merchandising companies and for manufacturing companies. For a merchandiser, product cost includes the cost of the merchandise itself and freight costs to obtain the merchandise. For a manufacturer, product cost includes the direct materials, direct labor, and manufacturing overhead required to produce finished units of product.

Manufacturing companies have additional cost classification challenges because they have three distinct types of inventory: raw materials that have been purchased but have not yet entered the production process, work-in-process units that have begun the production process but are not yet complete, and units that have been completed and are ready for sale.

Cost of services performed for a service type business is similar in many ways to product cost for a manufacturer. It includes the cost of materials, labor, and overhead required to perform services.

# APPENDIX—RECORDING BASIC MANUFACTURING COSTS

This appendix is intended to provide a basic overview of how costs are accumulated in the accounting records of a manufacturer. To keep the example simple, we assume that the factory makes only one product and manufacturing overhead is attributed directly to work in process. The technical aspects of the application of manufacturing overhead to production will be covered in the next chapter.

After completing your work in this appendix, you should be able to record the following types of entries:

1. The purchase of raw material
2. The three main components of manufacturing cost
   a. Direct material
   b. Direct labor
   c. Manufacturing overhead
3. The transfer of the cost of completed units from work in process to finished goods
4. The sale of completed units

The following accounts will be used for the entries in this appendix:

1. Cash
2. Accounts receivable
3. Raw materials inventory
4. Work-in-process inventory
5. Finished goods inventory
6. Accounts payable
7. Sales
8. Cost of goods sold

Recall that debits increase assets, expenses, and losses, while credits increase liabilities, equity, revenues, and gains. The dollar amount of the debits must equal that of the credits in each journal entry.

1. $90,000 of raw material was purchased on account on January 2, 2000:

   *2000*
   *Jan. 2*     Raw material inventory                      95,000
                    Accounts payable                                      95,000
                To record the purchase of raw material.

2. a. $70,000 of direct material was transferred to production on January 3, 2000:

   *2000*
   *Jan. 3*     Work-in-process inventory                   70,000
                    Raw material inventory                               70,000
                To record the transfer of direct material
                to production.

**2. b.** $80,000 of direct labor cost was incurred during January 2000.

| 2000 | | | |
|------|------|------|------|
| Jan. 31 | Work-in-process inventory | 80,000 | |
| | Cash | | 70,000 |
| | To record wages paid for direct | | |
| | labor in January. | | |

**2. c.** Paid for various factory overhead items totaling $110,000 during January 2000. To keep the example simple, manufacturing overhead is attributed directly to production. As you will see in the next chapter, manufacturing overhead is generally allocated to production which necessitates the use of more complicated accounting procedures.

| 2000 | | | |
|------|------|------|------|
| Jan. 31 | Work-in-process inventory | 110,000 | |
| | Cash | | 110,000 |
| | To record manufacturing overhead | | |
| | for January. | | |

After the above entries have been posted, the balance in the work-in-process account is $260,000 as shown in the t-account below.

**Work-in-Process**

| | |
|------|------|
| 70,000 | |
| 80,000 | |
| 110,000 | |
| 260,000 | |

**3.** At January 31, a physical count of the goods in production revealed that $230,000 or all but $30,000 of the goods were completed and transferred to finished goods inventory. The amount transferred from work-in-process to finished must equal the cost of goods manufactured.

| 2000 | | | |
|------|------|------|------|
| Jan. 31 | Finished goods inventory | 230,000 | |
| | Work-in-process inventory | | 230,000 |
| | To transfer completed goods from | | |
| | production to finished goods. | | |

After the $230,000 is transferred to finished goods, the work-in-process account and finished goods have balances of $30,000 and $260,000, respectively, as shown below.

**Work-in-Process**

| | |
|------|------|
| 70,000 | 230,000 |
| 80,000 | |
| 110,000 | |
| 260,000 | 230,000 |
| 30,000 | |

**Finished Goods**

| | |
|------|------|
| 230,000 | |

**4.** Goods that cost $210,000 to manufacture were sold on account for $300,000. This transaction is recorded in two parts. First the sale on account is recorded:

| 2000 | | | |
|------|------|------|------|
| Jan. 31 | Accounts receivable | 300,000 | |
| | Sales | | 300,000 |

Next the reduction in finished goods inventory and increase in cost of goods sold is recorded:

*2000*
*Jan. 31*  Cost of goods sold          210,000

         Finished goods                 210,000

The following t-accounts depict balances after recording the $300,000 sale.

**Work-in-Process**

| | |
|---|---|
| 70,000 | 230,000 |
| 80,000 | |
| 110,000 | |
| 260,000 | 230,000 |
| 30,000 | |

**Finished Goods**

| | |
|---|---|
| 230,000 | 210,000 |
| 20,000 | |

**Accounts Receivable**

| | |
|---|---|
| 300,000 | |

**Sales**

| | |
|---|---|
| | 300,000 |

**Cost of Goods Sold**

| | |
|---|---|
| 210,000 | |

# APPENDIX SUMMARY

Recording basic manufacturing entries involves eight accounts: cash, accounts receivable, accounts payable, raw material, work in process, finished goods, cost of goods sold, and sales. The basic flow through the accounts is depicted in Exhibit 2–A1. The purchase of raw material is recorded with a debit to raw material. Work in process is debited to record the transfer of direct material to production and the incurrence of direct labor and manufacturing overhead costs. When goods are completed, work in process is credited and finished goods is debited for the amount of the cost of the goods manufactured. When the finished goods are sold, separate entries are made to reflect the sale and to reflect the decrease in inventory and increase in cost of goods sold.

# KEY TERMS

administrative cost   M-22
common cost   M-21
cost   M-20
cost object   M-21
direct cost   M-21
direct material   M-28
direct materials cost   M-26

direct labor cost   M-26
direct labor hours   M-28
factory burden   M-29
factory overhead   M-29
finished goods inventory   M-27
hybrid firms   M-39
indirect cost   M-21

## Exhibit 2–A1
Basic Flow of Costs Through Manufacturing Accounts

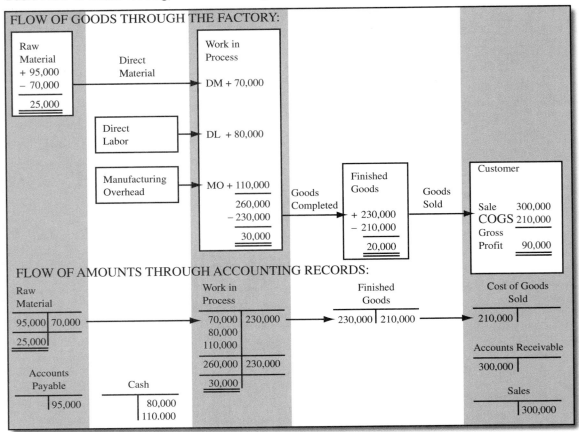

indirect labor   M-29
indirect materials   M-29
inventoriable cost   M-22
manufacturing overhead   M-29
manufacturing overhead cost   M-26
material stores   M-26

overhead   M-29
period cost   M-22
product cost   M-22
raw materials inventory   M-26
selling cost   M-22
work-in-process inventory   M-27

## REVIEW THE FACTS

A. What is a cost object?
B. What is the difference between a direct cost and an indirect cost?
C. What is product cost?
D. What is period cost?
E. Why is the cost of delivering merchandise to customers included in selling expense?
F. Why is the cost of storing inventory that is ready to sell included in selling expense?
G. What classification includes costs that are neither product costs nor costs directly associated with selling activities?
H. Why are product costs called inventoriable costs?

I. Describe the difference between the accounting treatment for product costs and period costs.

J. Describe the flow of inventory costs for a merchandising operation as goods are bought and then sold.

K. What are the inventory classifications for a manufacturing type firm?

L. What are the three main cost components included in product cost for a manufacturing type firm?

M. What is the difference between direct material and indirect material?

N. What is the difference between direct labor and indirect labor?

O. In which product cost classification would you most likely find indirect material and indirect labor?

P. With respect to the cost of goods sold section of an income statement, what is the similarity between purchases for a merchandising type company and cost of goods manufactured for a manufacturing type company?

Q. What is included in the cost of services provided for a service type firm?

# APPLY WHAT YOU HAVE LEARNED

## LO 1: Distinguish between Direct and Indirect Costs

**2–12.** Brittany operates a small chain of five children's shoe stores called Baby Feet. She employs a store manager and two sales clerks for each store. In addition, she rents office space which houses her office, the personnel department, and the bookkeeping department for the chain.

Brittany has collected the following information regarding the stores and has asked you to determine which costs are direct and which are indirect costs.

**REQUIRED:**

For each of the following items, indicate which would describe a direct cost (D) for the store at the corner of Elm Street and Main and which would describe an indirect cost (I) for an individual store.

| | |
|---|---|
| I | 1. Rent for the office space |
| D | 2. Rent for the store |
| I | 3. Brittany's salary |
| D | 4. The store manager's salary |
| I | 5. The company personnel manager's salary |
| I | 6. Bookkeeper's salary |
| D | 7. Maintenance cost for the store |
| D | 8. Depreciation on sales equipment |
| I | 9. Depreciation on bookkeeping computer |
| D | 10. Sales clerks' salaries |
| D | 11. Cost of shoes |
| I | 12. Advertising cost for the chain |

## LO 1: Distinguish between Direct and Indirect Costs

**2–13.** Sue Lee is the president of Baby Care. The company operates a chain of four child care centers in southern Florida. In addition to the four Baby Care locations, the company rents office space which is used by the company's bookkeeper and Sue Lee.

**REQUIRED:**

a. List four costs that would be considered direct costs of one of the four child care centers.

b. List four costs that would be considered indirect costs of one of the four child care centers.

## LO 1: Distinguish between Direct and Indirect Costs

**2–14.** Blue Water Travel operates a chain of travel agent offices in the eastern United States. Blue Water Travel's home office is in New York. There are six sales offices and a district office located in Florida.

**REQUIRED:**

If the cost object is one of the sales offices in Florida, indicate which of the following would describe a direct cost (D) and which would describe an indirect cost (I).

1. _____ Rent for the Florida district office building
2. _____ Rent for the home office building in New York
3. _____ Rent for the sales office
4. _____ The company president's salary
5. _____ The salary of the vice president in charge of the Florida division
6. _____ The salary of a sales office manager
7. _____ The salary of a sales associate

## LO 2: Types of Cost for a Manufacturer

**2–15.** Following are several representative costs incurred in a typical manufacturing company. For each of the costs, indicate in the space provided whether the cost is a direct material (DM), direct labor (DL), manufacturing overhead (MO), selling (S), or administrative (A) cost.

1. _DM_ Material incorporated into products
2. _S_ Sales supplies
3. _MO_ Supplies used in the factory
4. _MO_ Wages of plant security guard
5. _S_ Wages of security guard for the sales office
6. _MO_ Depreciation on a file cabinet used in the factory
7. _A_ Depreciation on a file cabinet used in the general accounting office
8. _A_ President's salary
9. _A_ President's secretary's salary
10. _MO_ Manufacturing vice president's salary
11. _MO_ Salary of the manufacturing vice president's secretary
12. _DL_ Wages paid to production-line workers
13. _MO_ Factory rent
14. _A_ Accounting office rent
15. _S_ Depreciation on a copy machine used in the sales department
16. _MO_ Depreciation on a copy machine used to copy work orders in the factory
17. _MO_ Salary of plant supervisor

## LO 2: Types of Cost for a Manufacturer

**2–16.** Following are several representative costs incurred in a typical manufacturing company. For each of the costs, indicate in the space provided whether the cost is a product cost (PR) or a period cost (PE).

1. _____ Material incorporated into products
2. _____ Sales supplies
3. _____ Supplies used in the factory
4. _____ Wages of plant security guard
5. _____ Wages of security guard for the sales office
6. _____ Depreciation on a file cabinet used in the factory
7. _____ Depreciation on a file cabinet used in the general accounting office
8. _____ President's salary
9. _____ President's secretary's salary
10. _____ Manufacturing vice president's salary
11. _____ Salary of the manufacturing vice president's secretary
12. _____ Wages paid to production-line workers
13. _____ Factory rent
14. _____ Accounting office rent
15. _____ Depreciation on a copy machine used in the sales department
16. _____ Depreciation on a copy machine used to copy work orders in the factory
17. _____ Salary of plant supervisor

## LO 5: Calculate Costs for a Manufacturer, No Inventories

**2–17.** The following data pertain to the Anderson Table Manufacturing Company for January 1997. The company made 1,000 tables during January, and there are no beginning or ending inventories.

| | |
|---|---|
| Wood used in production | $25,000 |
| Cleaning supplies used in the factory | 300 |
| Machine lubricants used in the factory | 100 |
| Factory rent | 2,000 |
| Rent on the sales office | 3,000 |
| Sales salaries | 20,000 |
| Production-line labor cost | 50,000 |
| Plant security guard cost | 1,200 |
| Plant supervision | 2,500 |
| Office supervision | 3,000 |
| Depreciation on production equipment | 4,000 |
| Depreciation on office equipment | 1,000 |

**REQUIRED:**

a. What is the cost of direct material used in production during January 1997?
b. What is the cost of direct labor for January 1997?
c. What is the cost of manufacturing overhead for January 1997?
d. What is the total cost of tables manufactured in January 1997?
e. What is the cost of each table manufactured in January 1997?
f. Do you think the cost per table is valuable information for Carole Anderson, the company's owner? How might she use this information?

## LO 5: Calculate Ending Inventory

**2–18.** Steinmann Window Company makes aluminum window units. At the beginning of November, the company's direct material inventory included 900 square feet of window glass. During November Steinmann purchased another 12,000 square feet of glass. Each completed window unit requires 9 square feet of glass. During November, 9,900 square feet of glass was transferred to the production line.

**REQUIRED:**

How many square feet of glass remain in the ending direct material inventory?

## LO 4: Analyzing Inventory

**2–19.** Van Kirk Manufacturing Company has been in business for many years. Dottie Van Kirk, the company president, is concerned that the cost of raw material is skyrocketing. The production foreman assured Van Kirk that the use of direct material actually dropped in 2001.

Van Kirk has engaged your services to provide insight into what she thinks may be a sizable problem. Not only does it seem that the cost of direct material is increasing, but it also seems that her production foreman is being less than honest with her.

The following information is available:

### VAN KIRK MANUFACTURING COMPANY
#### Direct Materials Schedule
#### For the Year Ending December 31, 2000

| | |
|---|---:|
| Beginning Direct Material Inventory | $ 25,000 |
| Purchases during 2000 | 435,000 |
| Materials Available during 2000 | $460,000 |
| Ending Direct Material Inventory | (30,000) |
| Direct Materials Used during 2000 | 430,000 |

### VAN KIRK MANUFACTURING COMPANY
#### Direct Materials Schedule
#### For the Year Ending December 31, 2001

| | |
|---|---:|
| Beginning Direct Material Inventory | $ 30,000 |
| Purchases during 2001 | 501,000 |
| Materials Available during 2001 | $531,000 |
| Ending Direct Material Inventory | (103,000) |
| Direct Materials Used during 2001 | 428,000 |

**REQUIRED:**

Examine the information presented and write a brief report to Dottie Van Kirk detailing your findings relative to her concerns.

## LO 3: Analyze Costs of a Merchandiser

**2–20.** Ralph Brito opened Brito Auto Sales several years ago. Since then, the company has grown and sales have steadily increased. In the last year, however, income has declined despite successful efforts to increase sales. In addition, the company is forced to borrow more and more money from the bank to finance the operation.

The following information is available:

**BRITO AUTO SALES**
**Income Statement**
**For the Year Ending December 31, 2001**

| | | |
|---|---|---|
| Sales | | $758,000 |
| Cost of Goods Sold | | |
| Beginning Inventory | $ 66,000 | |
| + Cost of Goods Purchased | 639,000 | |
| = Goods Available for Sale | $705,000 | |
| − Ending Inventory | 85,000 | |
| = Cost of Goods Sold | | 620,000 |
| Gross Profit | | 138,000 |
| Operating Expense: | | |
| Selling Expense | $ 55,000 | |
| Administrative Expense | 60,000 | (115,000) |
| Operating Income | | $ 23,000 |

**BRITO AUTO SALES**
**Income Statement**
**For the Year Ending December 31, 2002**

| | | |
|---|---|---|
| Sales | | $890,000 |
| Cost of Goods Sold | | |
| Beginning Inventory | $ 85,000 | |
| + Cost of Goods Purchased | 799,000 | |
| = Goods Available for Sale | $884,000 | |
| − Ending Inventory | 123,000 | |
| = Cost of Goods Sold | | 761,000 |
| Gross Profit | | 129,000 |
| Operating Expense: | | |
| Selling Expense | $ 66,000 | |
| Administrative Expense | 60,000 | (126,000) |
| Operating Income | | $ 3,000 |

**REQUIRED:**

Assume that you are hired by Mr. Brito as a consultant. Review the Brito income statement and write a report to Mr. Brito that addresses his concerns.

## LO 4: Calculate Ending Direct Material Inventory for a Manufacturer

**2–21.** Matheis Designs, Inc. manufactures swimming suits. At the beginning of October 1999, the company had $1,450 worth of cloth on hand which was included in its direct material inventory. During October, Matheis purchased cloth costing $12,360 and used material costing $12,750 in production.

**REQUIRED:**

What is the cost of the ending direct material inventory of cloth for Matheis Designs, Inc.?

## LO 4: Calculate Direct Material Used

**2–22.** The following information relates to the Penny Manufacturing Company.

| | |
|---|---|
| Beginning direct material inventory | $ 540,000 |
| Ending direct material inventory | $ 480,000 |
| Direct material purchased | $4,680,000 |

**REQUIRED:**

a. Compute the cost of direct material used in production.
b. Appendix: Prepare a journal entry to record the use of direct material in production.

## LO 4: Calculate Direct Material Used

**2–23.** The following information relates to the Montoya Manufacturing Company.

| | |
|---|---|
| Beginning direct material inventory | $ 40,000 |
| Ending direct material inventory | $ 48,000 |
| Direct material purchased | $437,000 |

**REQUIRED:**

a. Compute the cost of direct material used in production.
b. Appendix: Prepare a journal entry to record the use of direct material used in production.

## LO 4: Calculate the Cost of Supplies Used

**2–24.** The following information relates to Pons Maintenance Service.

| | |
|---|---|
| Maintenance supplies at January 1, 2000 | $ 4,210 |
| Maintenance supplies at December 31, 2000 | $ 3,840 |
| Maintenance supplies purchased during 2000 | $27,530 |

**REQUIRED:**

What was the cost of maintenance supplies consumed by Pons Maintenance Service during 2000?

## LO 6: Calculate Cost of Materials Used by a Service Company

**2–25.** On January 1, 1999, Bowden Auto Repair had $3,560 worth of auto parts on hand. During the year, Bowden purchased auto parts costing $286,000. At the end of 1999, the company had parts on hand amounting to $4,260.

**REQUIRED:**

What was the cost of the auto parts used by Bowden Auto Repair during 1999.

## LO 3: Calculate the Cost of Goods Sold for a Merchandiser

**2–26.** On January 1, 1997, the cost of merchandise on hand at Margaret's Fashions was $56,530. Purchases during the month amounted to $488,668 and the cost of merchandise on hand at the end of January was $52,849.

**REQUIRED:**

Determine January's cost of goods sold for Margaret's Fashions.

## LO 5: Inventory and Production Costs for a Manufacturer

**2–27.** The following data pertain to the Hudik Manufacturing Company for the year ended December 31, 2000. The company made 115,000 light fixtures during 2000. There are no beginning or ending inventories.

| | |
|---|---:|
| Metal used in production | $750,000 |
| Wire used in production | 40,000 |
| Factory supplies | 5,200 |
| Depreciation on the factory | 48,000 |
| Depreciation on the sales office | 3,000 |
| Sales salaries | 90,000 |
| Assembly-line labor cost | 960,000 |
| Factory security guard cost | 8,200 |
| Factory supervision | 62,500 |
| General accounting cost | 43,000 |
| Depreciation on production equipment | 454,850 |
| Depreciation on office equipment | 9,200 |

### REQUIRED:

a. What is the cost of direct material used during 2000?
b. What is the cost of direct labor during 2000?
c. What is the cost of manufacturing overhead during 2000?
d. What is the total product cost for 2000 production?
e. What is the cost per light fixture for 2000?

## LO 5: Inventory and Production Costs Including Cost of Goods Manufactured and Cost of Goods Sold, No Inventories

**2–28.** The following data pertain to the Elsea Manufacturing Company for the year ended December 31, 2000. The company made 60,000 SW20 switching units during 2000.

| | | |
|---|---|---:|
| DM | Beginning direct material inventory | $ 42,000 |
| | Ending direct material inventory | 48,000 |
| | Beginning work-in-process inventory ✕ | 84,000 |
| | Ending work-in-process inventory | 93,000 |
| | Beginning finished goods inventory | 124,000 |
| | Ending finished goods inventory | 133,000 |
| DM | Direct material purchased | 850,000 |
| MO/H | Indirect material used in production | 4,000 |
| MO/H | Factory supplies | 6,200 |
| M O/H | Depreciation on the factory | 60,000 |
| | Depreciation on the sales office | 4,000 |
| | Depreciation on the administrative office | 3,000 |
| | Sales salaries | 120,000 |
| DL | Assembly-line labor cost | 820,000 |
| M O/H | Factory security guard cost | 12,000 |
| M O/H | Factory supervision | 82,600 |
| M O/H | Depreciation on production equipment | 560,000 |
| | Depreciation on office equipment | 22,200 |

### REQUIRED:

a. What is the cost of direct material used during 2000?
b. What is the cost of direct labor during 2000?
c. What is the cost of manufacturing overhead for 2000?

d. What is total manufacturing cost incurred during 2000?
e. What is the cost of goods manufactured for 2000?
f. What is the cost of goods sold for 2000?

## LO 5: Inventory and Production Costs Including Cost of Goods Manufactured and Cost of Goods Sold

**2–29.** The following data pertain to the Miami Manufacturing Company for the year ended December 31, 2000.

| | |
|---|---:|
| Beginning finished goods inventory | $ 255,000 |
| Ending finished goods inventory | 270,000 |
| Beginning direct material inventory | 82,000 |
| Ending direct material inventory | 98,000 |
| Beginning work-in-process inventory | 164,000 |
| Ending work-in-process inventory | 184,000 |
| Direct material purchased | 1,740,000 |
| Indirect material used in production | 3,000 |
| Factory supplies | 12,500 |
| Depreciation on the factory | 134,000 |
| Depreciation on the sales office | 14,000 |
| Depreciation on the administrative office | 9,000 |
| Sales salaries | 350,000 |
| Assembly-line labor cost | 2,120,000 |
| Factory security guard cost | 22,000 |
| Factory supervision | 183,500 |
| Depreciation on production equipment | 1,340,000 |
| Depreciation on office equipment | 52,200 |

### REQUIRED:
a. What is the cost of direct material used during 2000?
b. What is the cost of direct labor during 2000?
c. What is the cost of manufacturing overhead for 2000?
d. What is total manufacturing cost incurred during 2000?
e. What is the cost of goods manufactured for 2000?
f. What is the cost of goods sold for 2000?

## LO 5: Inventory and Production Costs Including Cost of Goods Manufactured and Cost of Goods Sold

**2–30.** The following data pertain to the Mini Manufacturing Company for the year ended December 31, 2000.

| | |
|---|---:|
| Beginning direct material inventory | $ 2,000 |
| Ending direct material inventory | 3,000 |
| Beginning work-in-process inventory | 4,000 |
| Ending work-in-process inventory | 5,000 |
| Beginning finished goods inventory | 9,500 |
| Ending finished goods inventory | 8,000 |
| Direct material purchased | 22,000 |
| Factory supplies | 12,500 |
| Depreciation on the factory | 34,000 |
| Assembly-line labor cost | 120,000 |
| Depreciation on production equipment | 42,000 |
| Other indirect factory costs | 12,000 |

**REQUIRED:**

a. What is the cost of direct material used during 2000?
b. What is the cost of direct labor during 2000?
c. What is the cost of manufacturing overhead for 2000?
d. What is total manufacturing cost incurred during 2000?
e. What is the cost of goods manufactured for 2000?
f. What is the cost of goods sold for 2000?

## LO 5: Inventory and Production Costs Including Cost of Goods Manufactured and Cost of Goods Sold

**2–31.** The following data pertain to the Ace Manufacturing Company for the year ended December 31, 2001.

| | |
|---|---:|
| Beginning direct material inventory | $ 22,000 |
| Ending direct material inventory | 28,000 |
| Beginning finished goods inventory | 30,000 |
| Ending finished goods inventory | 28,000 |
| Beginning work-in-process inventory | 16,000 |
| Ending work-in-process inventory | 15,000 |
| Direct material purchased | 280,000 |
| Production worker labor cost | 290,000 |
| Depreciation on production equipment | 80,000 |
| Factory rent | 24,000 |
| Other indirect factory costs | 36,000 |

**REQUIRED:**

a. What is the cost of direct material used during 2001?
b. What is the cost of direct labor during 2001?
c. What is the cost of manufacturing overhead for 2001?
d. What is total manufacturing cost incurred during 2001?
e. What is the cost of goods manufactured for 2001?
f. What is the cost of goods sold for 2001?

## LO 5: Preparation of Cost of Goods Manufactured and Cost of Goods Sold Schedules

**2–32.** The following data pertain to the Adler Manufacturing Company for the year ended December 31, 2001.

| | |
|---|---:|
| Beginning direct material inventory | $ 12,000 |
| Ending direct material inventory | 13,000 |
| Beginning work-in-process inventory | 24,000 |
| Ending work-in-process inventory | 25,000 |
| Beginning finished goods inventory | 29,500 |
| Ending finished goods inventory | 28,000 |
| Direct material purchased | 122,000 |
| Factory utilities | 2,500 |
| Rent on the factory | 64,000 |
| Assembly worker labor cost | 86,000 |
| Depreciation on production equipment | 92,000 |
| Other indirect factory costs | 22,000 |

**REQUIRED:**

**a.** Prepare a cost of goods manufactured schedule for 2001.
**b.** Prepare a cost of goods sold schedule for 2001.

## LO 5: Preparation of Cost of Goods Manufactured and Cost of Goods Sold Schedules

**2–33.** The following data pertain to the Clifford Manufacturing Company for the year ended December 31, 2001.

| | |
|---|---:|
| Beginning direct material inventory | $ 2,300 |
| Ending direct material inventory | 3,400 |
| Beginning work-in-process inventory | 5,500 |
| Ending work-in-process inventory | 4,100 |
| Beginning finished goods inventory | 6,500 |
| Ending finished goods inventory | 5,100 |
| Direct material purchased | 12,300 |
| Factory supplies used | 500 |
| Depreciation on the factory | 22,000 |
| Assembly-line labor cost | 48,600 |
| Depreciation on production equipment | 12,000 |
| Other indirect factory costs | 4,700 |

**REQUIRED:**

**a.** Prepare a cost of goods manufactured schedule for 2001.
**b.** Prepare a cost of goods sold schedule for 2001.

## LO 5: Preparation of Cost of Goods Manufactured Schedule, Cost of Goods Sold Schedule, and Multistep Income Statement

**2–34.** The following data pertain to the Lowell Manufacturing Company for the year ended December 31, 2001.

| | |
|---|---:|
| Sales | $1,267,000 |
| Beginning direct material inventory | 40,000 |
| Ending direct material inventory | 50,000 |
| Beginning work-in-process inventory | 70,000 |
| Ending work-in-process inventory | 60,000 |
| Beginning finished goods inventory | 90,000 |
| Ending finished goods inventory | 80,000 |
| Direct material purchased | 350,000 |
| Indirect material used in production | 24,000 |
| Factory supplies used | 6,000 |
| Depreciation on the factory | 90,000 |
| Depreciation on the sales office | 24,000 |
| Depreciation on the administrative office | 36,000 |
| Sales salaries | 110,000 |
| Assembly-line labor cost | 220,000 |
| Factory security guard cost | 22,000 |
| Factory supervision | 42,000 |
| Depreciation on production equipment | 160,000 |
| Depreciation on office equipment | 16,000 |

**REQUIRED:**

  **a.** Prepare a cost of goods manufactured schedule for 2001.
  **b.** Prepare a cost of goods sold schedule for 2001.
  **c.** Prepare a multistep income statement for 2001.

## LO 5: Preparation of Cost of Goods Manufactured Schedule, Cost of Goods Sold Schedule, and Multistep Income Statement

**2–35.** The following data pertain to the Quintana Manufacturing Company for the year ended December 31, 2001.

| | |
|---|---:|
| Sales | $1,302,000 |
| Beginning finished goods inventory | 93,000 |
| Ending finished goods inventory | 86,000 |
| Beginning direct material inventory | 45,000 |
| Ending direct material inventory | 56,000 |
| Beginning work-in-process inventory | 72,000 |
| Ending work-in-process inventory | 77,000 |
| Direct material purchased | 370,000 |
| Indirect material used in production   M o/H | 34,000 |
| Depreciation on production equipment M O/H | 145,000 |
| Depreciation on office equipment | 19,000 |
| Factory supplies used   M O/H | 8,000 |
| Depreciation on the factory M O/H | 96,000 |
| Depreciation on the sales office | 34,000 |
| Depreciation on the administrative office | 30,000 |
| Sales salaries | 122,000 |
| Assembly-line labor cost | 240,000 |
| Factory security guard cost   M O/H | 32,000 |
| Factory supervision   M O/H | 48,000 |

**REQUIRED:**

  **a.** Prepare a cost of goods manufactured schedule for 2001.
  **b.** Prepare a cost of goods sold schedule for 2001.
  **c.** Prepare a multistep income statement for 2001.

## LO 5: Preparation of Cost of Goods Manufactured Schedule, Cost of Goods Sold Schedule, and Multistep Income Statement

**2–36.** The following data pertain to the Rodriguez Manufacturing Company for the year ended December 31, 2000.

| | |
|---|---:|
| Sales | $1,124,000 |
| Beginning direct material inventory | 55,000 |
| Ending direct material inventory | 56,000 |
| Beginning finished goods inventory | 83,000 |
| Ending finished goods inventory | 96,000 |
| Beginning work-in-process inventory | 62,000 |
| Ending work-in-process inventory | 67,000 |
| Direct material purchased | 290,000 |
| Direct labor cost | 220,000 |
| Manufacturing overhead | 286,000 |
| Selling expense | 122,000 |
| Administrative expense | 140,000 |

**REQUIRED:**

a. Prepare a cost of goods manufactured schedule for 2000.
b. Prepare a cost of goods sold schedule for 2000.
c. Prepare a multistep income statement for 2000.

## LO 5: Preparation of Cost of Goods Manufactured Schedule, Cost of Goods Sold Schedule, and Multistep Income Statement

**2–37.** The following data pertain to the Avener Manufacturing Company for the year ended December 31, 2000.

| | |
|---|---:|
| Sales | $333,000 |
| Beginning direct material inventory | 5,000 |
| Ending direct material inventory | 4,000 |
| Beginning work-in-process inventory | 6,000 |
| Ending work-in-process inventory | 7,000 |
| Beginning finished goods inventory | 8,000 |
| Ending finished goods inventory | 10,000 |
| Direct material purchased | 56,000 |
| Direct labor cost | 96,000 |
| Manufacturing overhead | 86,000 |
| Selling expense | 46,000 |
| Administrative expense | 34,000 |

**REQUIRED:**

a. Prepare a cost of goods manufactured schedule for 2000.
b. Prepare a cost of goods sold schedule for 2000.
c. Prepare a multistep income statement for 2000.

## LO 5: Preparation of Cost of Goods Manufactured Schedule

**2–38.** The following information is for Megan Hat Manufacturing Company.

**Inventory information:**

| | January 1, 2001 | December 31, 2001 |
|---|---:|---:|
| Raw materials inventory | $ 9,000 | $11,000 |
| Work-in-process inventory | 22,000 | 18,000 |
| Finished goods inventory | 42,000 | 38,000 |

**Other information:**

| | |
|---|---:|
| Direct materials purchases | $120,000 |
| Direct labor cost | 250,000 |
| Manufacturing overhead | 140,000 |

**REQUIRED:**

a. What is the cost of direct material used in production?
b. Prepare a cost of goods manufactured schedule in good form.
c. Prepare a cost of goods sold schedule.
d. Appendix: Prepare journal entries to record the following:
    1. The purchase of direct material
    2. The use of direct material in production
    3. Direct labor cost
    4. Manufacturing overhead cost (Use "various accounts" for the credit side of the entry.)
    5. The cost of goods manufactured
    6. The sale of finished goods assuming the sale price was $600,000

## LO 5: Preparation of Cost of Goods Manufactured Schedule

**2–39.** The following information is for Friedman Shelving Manufacturing Company.

### Inventory information:

| | January 1, 2001 | December 31, 2001 |
|---|---|---|
| Raw materials inventory | $22,000 | $24,000 |
| Work-in-process inventory | 42,000 | 43,000 |
| Finished goods inventory | 82,000 | 78,000 |

### Other information:

| | |
|---|---|
| Direct materials purchases | $280,000 |
| Direct labor cost | 540,000 |
| Manufacturing overhead | 240,000 |

### REQUIRED:

**a.** What is the cost of direct material used in production?
**b.** Prepare a cost of goods manufactured schedule in good form.
**c.** Prepare a cost of goods sold schedule.
**d.** Appendix: Prepare journal entries to record the following:
   **1.** The purchase of direct material
   **2.** The use of direct material in production
   **3.** Direct labor cost
   **4.** Manufacturing overhead cost (Use "various accounts" for the credit side of the entry.)
   **5.** The cost of goods manufactured
   **6.** The sale of finished goods assuming the sale price was $1,400,000


## LO 5: Preparation of Cost of Goods Manufactured Schedule

**2–40.** The following information is for Tatum Manufacturing Company.

### Inventory information:

| | January 1, 2001 | December 31, 2001 |
|---|---|---|
| Raw materials inventory | $2,000 | $4,000 |
| Work-in-process inventory | 4,000 | 3,000 |
| Finished goods inventory | 8,000 | 6,000 |

### Other information:

| | |
|---|---|
| Direct materials purchases | $ 8,000 |
| Direct labor cost | 12,000 |
| Manufacturing overhead | 9,000 |

### REQUIRED:

**a.** Prepare a cost of goods manufactured schedule in good form.
**b.** Appendix: Prepare journal entries to record the following:
   **1.** The purchase of direct material
   **2.** The use of direct material in production
   **3.** Direct labor cost
   **4.** Manufacturing overhead cost (Use "various accounts" for the credit side of the entry.)
   **5.** The cost of goods manufactured
   **6.** The sale of finished goods assuming the sale price was $40,000

## LO 5: Preparation of Cost of Goods Manufactured Schedule

**2–41.** The following information is for Munter Manufacturing Company.

### Inventory information:

| | January 1, 2001 | December 31, 2001 |
|---|---|---|
| Raw materials inventory | $6,000 | $5,000 |
| Work-in-process inventory | 3,000 | 4,000 |
| Finished goods inventory | 7,000 | 9,000 |

### Other information:

| | |
|---|---|
| Direct materials purchases | $ 9,000 |
| Direct labor cost | 10,000 |
| Manufacturing overhead | 11,000 |

### REQUIRED:
a. Prepare a cost of goods manufactured schedule in good form.
b. Appendix: Prepare journal entries to record the following:
   1. The purchase of direct material
   2. The use of direct material in production
   3. Direct labor cost
   4. Manufacturing overhead cost (Use "various accounts" for the credit side of the entry.)
   5. The cost of goods manufactured
   6. The sale of finished goods assuming the sale price was $39,000

## LO 5: Preparation of Cost of Goods Manufactured Schedule and Multistep Income Statement

**2–42.** The following information is for Collins Manufacturing Company.

### Inventory information:

| | January 1, 2001 | December 31, 2001 |
|---|---|---|
| Raw materials inventory | $16,000 | $14,000 |
| Work-in-process inventory | 23,000 | 25,000 |
| Finished goods inventory | 33,000 | 36,000 |

### Other information:

| | |
|---|---|
| Sales | $760,000 |
| Direct materials purchases | 159,000 |
| Direct labor cost | 110,000 |
| Manufacturing overhead | 221,000 |
| Selling expense | 62,000 |
| Administrative expense | 47,000 |

### REQUIRED:
a. Prepare a cost of goods manufactured schedule in good form.
b. Prepare a multistep income statement in good form.

## LO 5: Preparation of Cost of Goods Manufactured Schedule and Multistep Income Statement

**2–43.** The following information is for Richard Manufacturing Company.

## Inventory information:

| | January 1, 2001 | December 31, 2001 |
|---|---|---|
| Raw materials inventory | $14,000 | $16,000 |
| Work-in-process inventory | 25,000 | 28,000 |
| Finished goods inventory | 32,000 | 36,000 |

### Other information:

| | |
|---|---|
| Sales | $790,000 |
| Direct materials purchases | 162,000 |
| Direct labor cost | 140,000 |
| Manufacturing overhead | 234,000 |
| Selling expense | 72,000 |
| Administrative expense | 57,000 |

**REQUIRED:**

**a.** Prepare a cost of goods manufactured schedule in good form.
**b.** Prepare a multistep income statement in good form.

## LO 3: Preparation of a Multistep Income Statement for a Merchandiser

**2–44.** Bonnie's Pet Cage Company has the following information for 2000:

| | |
|---|---|
| Sales | $300,000 |
| Cost of goods manufactured | 200,000 |
| Selling expense | 30,000 |
| Administrative expense | 25,000 |
| Beginning finished goods inventory | 21,000 |
| Ending finished goods inventory | 28,000 |

**REQUIRED:**

Prepare a multistep income statement for Bonnie's Pet Cage Company.

## LO 3: Preparation of a Multistep Income Statement for a Manufacturer

**2–45.** Albert's Manufacturing Company has the following information for 2000:

| | |
|---|---|
| Beginning finished goods inventory | $ 41,000 |
| Ending finished goods inventory | 58,000 |
| Sales | 600,000 |
| Cost of goods manufactured | 400,000 |
| Selling expense | 90,000 |
| Administrative expense | 60,000 |

**REQUIRED:**

Prepare a multistep income statement for Albert's Manufacturing Company for 2000.

## LO 5: Preparation of cost of a Multistep Income Statement for a Merchandiser

**2–46.** Phillips Merchandising Company has the following information for 2000:

| | |
|---|---|
| Sales | $400,000 |
| Cost of merchandise purchased | 300,000 |
| Selling expense | 30,000 |
| Administrative expense | 20,000 |
| Beginning finished goods inventory | 40,000 |
| Ending finished goods inventory | 50,000 |

**REQUIRED:**
Prepare a multistep income statement for Phillips Merchandising Company for 2000.

## LO 5: Preparation of Cost of a Multistep Income Statement for a Merchandiser

**2–47.** Robinson Merchandising Company has the following information for 2001:

| | |
|---|---|
| Beginning finished goods inventory | $ 60,000 |
| Ending finished goods inventory | 50,000 |
| Sales | 840,000 |
| Cost of merchandise purchased | 630,000 |
| Selling expense | 90,000 |
| Administrative expense | 40,000 |

**REQUIRED:**
Prepare a multistep income statement for Robinson Merchandising Company for 2001.

## LO 6: Determine the Cost of Services Provided and Preparation of a Single-Step Income Statement for a Service Company

**2–48.** Butterfield's Bookkeeping Service began operations on January 1, 2001. The following information is taken from its accounting records as of December 31, 2001.

| | |
|---|---|
| Bookkeeping service revenue | $80,000 |
| Bookkeeping salaries | 42,000 |
| Bookkeeping office rent | 12,000 |
| Depreciation on bookkeeping equipment | 2,000 |
| Bookkeeping supplies used | 700 |
| Advertising | 800 |

**REQUIRED:**
  **a.** What is the cost of services provided?
  **b.** Prepare a single-step income statement for Butterfield's Bookkeeping Service.

## LO 6: Determine the Cost of Services Provided and Preparation of a Single-Step Income Statement for a Service Company

**2–49.** Tony's Film Delivery Service began operations on January 1, 2001. The following information is taken from its accounting records as of December 31, 2001.

| | |
|---|---|
| Delivery revenue | $40,000 |
| Driver wages | 22,000 |
| Depreciation on truck | 4,000 |

| | |
|---|---:|
| Fuel cost | 2,700 |
| Advertising | 800 |
| Bookkeeping cost | 240 |

**REQUIRED:**
a. What is the cost of services provided?
b. Prepare a single-step income statement for Tony's Film Delivery Service.

## LO 3: Preparation of a Multistep Income Statement for a Merchandiser

**2–50.** Cam's Swimsuit Shop provided the following information for 2001.

| | |
|---|---:|
| Merchandise inventory, January 1, 2001 | $ 16,000 |
| Merchandise inventory, December 31, 2001 | 19,000 |
| Sales | 190,000 |
| Advertising | 1,200 |
| Store rent | 2,400 |
| Purchases of merchandise | 82,000 |
| Sales salaries | 22,000 |
| Store utilities | 3,600 |
| Sales supplies used during 2001 | 1,000 |
| Sales supplies on hand, December 31, 2001 | 500 |
| Office rent | 800 |
| Administrative salaries | 18,000 |

**REQUIRED:**
Prepare a multistep income statement for Cam's Swimsuit Shop for 2001.

## LO 3: Preparation of a Multistep Income Statement for a Merchandiser

**2–51.** Leroy's Auto Parts provided the following information for 2001.

| | |
|---|---:|
| Merchandise inventory, January 1, 2001 | $ 19,000 |
| Merchandise inventory, December 31, 2001 | 21,000 |
| Sales | 280,000 |
| Advertising | 2,200 |
| Depreciation on the store | 18,000 |
| Purchases of merchandise | 182,000 |
| Sales salaries | 21,000 |
| Store utilities | 1,200 |
| Depreciation on office building | 4,000 |
| Administrative salaries | 15,000 |
| Office utilities | 600 |

**REQUIRED:**
Prepare a multistep income statement for Leroy's Auto Parts for 2001.

## LO 6: Preparation of a Single-Step Income Statement for a Service Company

**2–52.** Dan's Security Service provided the following information for 2001.

| | |
|---|---:|
| Security revenue | $480,000 |
| Advertising | 12,000 |

| | |
|---|---:|
| Depreciation on the home office building | 12,000 |
| Security guard wages | 362,000 |
| Administrative salaries | 21,000 |
| Sales salaries | 24,000 |
| Utilities | 1,200 |

**REQUIRED:**
Prepare a single-step income statement for Dan's Security Service for 2001.

## LO 3: Preparation of a Multistep Income Statement for a Merchandiser

**2–53.** Margaret's Flower Shop provided the following information for 2001.

| | |
|---|---:|
| Merchandise inventory, January 1, 2001 | $ 1,000 |
| Merchandise inventory, December 31, 2001 | 1,200 |
| Sales | 42,400 |
| Advertising | 3,200 |
| Store rent | 1,200 |
| Purchases of merchandise | 18,000 |
| Sales salaries | 21,000 |
| Utilities | 1,300 |
| Sales supplies used during 2001 | 9,000 |
| Sales supplies on hand, December 31, 2001 | 300 |

**REQUIRED:**
Prepare a multistep income statement for Margaret's Flower Shop for 2001.

## LO 2, 3, & 4: Understanding Cost of Goods Sold

**2–54.** The management of Diversified Incorporated is concerned that few of its employees understand cost of goods sold. The company president has decided that a series of presentations will be made focusing on cost of goods sold.

Assume that the company has formed two teams, Team A and Team B. You and several of your classmates have been assigned to Team B.

Team A is given the responsibility of preparing a presentation detailing the cost of goods sold pertaining to a subsidiary that operates a chain of hardware stores. Team B, your team, has been given the responsibility of preparing a presentation detailing the cost of goods sold of a subsidiary that manufactures electronic calculators.

In short order, Team A has completed its assignment and is ready to make its presentation. Your team, however, is still working. Company executives question why Team A is so far ahead of your team's progress.

**REQUIRED:**
Working as a group, develop a response to the concerns relating to your teams slow progress. Explain why Team A could complete their assignment so quickly, and why your team will have to work longer.

## LO 6: Understanding Service Company Costs

**2–55.** Assume that you are the manager of an accounting practice. You are concerned about billing your clients so that the company covers all costs and makes a reasonable profit.

## REQUIRED:

**a.** What information might you desire to help develop a method of billing clients?

**b.** How would you use the information to ensure that costs are covered and profits result?

## LO 1, 2, & 4:   Understanding Inventory Cost Classifications

**2–56.** The inventory of a manufacturer is typically grouped into one of three classifications—raw material inventory, work-in-process inventory, and finished goods inventory.

## REQUIRED:

Discuss why it provides more useful information to use three classifications of inventory rather than one for a manufacturer.

## LO 1, 2, & 4:   Understanding Inventory Costs

**2–57.** Assume that you work for the Acme Wire Manufacturing Company. Some employees in the company are unsure of which costs should be included in inventories and which costs should not. There is also some confusion regarding the logic of including some items while excluding others.

 You have been assigned to a group that is responsible for making a presentation on which of Acme's costs would properly be classified as inventory costs and which would not.

## REQUIRED:

Prepare a presentation describing the type of items that would be included in inventories and those that would not. Comment on the logic of including some cost items in inventory while excluding others.

## LO 1, 2, & 3:   General Inventory and Cost Analysis

**2–58.** One year ago, Herb Smith quit his job at Adcox Medical where he earned $28,000 a year as a health care technician to start the Super CD Store. He invested almost his entire life's savings in the venture and is now concerned. He notes that, when his money was in the bank, he earned about 4% interest. Now, when he compares his company profits to the amount invested in the store, the profits seem lower than what he could have earned if he had simply left the money in the bank. The following information is available for the company's first year of business:

| | |
|---|---|
| Annual sales | $600,000 |
| Cost of goods sold | 450,000 |
| Selling expense | 90,000 |
| Administrative expense | 50,000 |
| Inventory | 300,000 |
| Other assets | 30,000 |
| Total liabilities | 50,000 |

The administrative expense includes $30,000 received by Herb in the form of salary. Herb's friend Bill has suggested that a simple $5,000 computer might help with company record keeping and ordering inventory. Herb has indicated that he does not mind the added work or ordering the merchandise without a computer. In fact, when it comes to ordering product, he seems quite proud of the job he is doing as he almost always has the CDs his customers want.

Herb has engaged your services as a consultant to determine whether his feelings are correct about the low earnings of the company and to suggest some possibilities to improve the situation. Also, Herb would like some input regarding the computer.

**REQUIRED:**

Prepare a report for Herb addressing each of his concerns.

## LO 1, 2, & 3:   General Inventory and Cost Analysis

**2–59.** Alberto Manufacturing Company has been in business for many years. Toward the end of 2000, management began to notice that the company had to rely more and more on borrowing to support the cash flow needs of the operation. Although sales increased in 2001, profits declined and the cash flow problem worsened. The company president is very concerned that the cash shortfall is caused by mismanagement of the daily operation of the factory. Managers argue that the company's operations are quite satisfactory. They cite that expenses have increased only slightly as sales have risen, and that production levels have been dictated by customer demand.

The president has hired your team of consultants to review the situation and comment on the possible problems that exist. The following information is available for 2000 and 2001.

### ALBERTO MANUFACTURING COMPANY
**Schedule of Cost of Goods Manufactured**
**For the Year Ending December 31, 2000**

| | | |
|---|---:|---:|
| Direct Materials: | | |
| Beginning Direct Material Inventory | $ 15,000 | |
| Purchases during 2000 | 420,000 | |
| Materials Available during 2000 | $435,000 | |
| Ending Direct Material Inventory | (45,000) | |
| Direct Materials Used during 2000 | | $ 390,000 |
| Direct Labor during 2000 | | 225,000 |
| Total Manufacturing Overhead Cost during 2000 | | 415,000 |
| Manufacturing Cost for Current Period | | $1,030,000 |
| Beginning Work-in-Process Inventory 1/1/00 | | 40,000 |
| Cost of Goods Available to be Finished | | $1,070,000 |
| Ending Work-in-Process Inventory 12/31/00 | | ( 82,000) |
| Cost of Goods Manufactured during 2000 | | $ 988,000 |

### ALBERTO MANUFACTURING COMPANY
**Income Statement**
**For the Year Ending December 31, 2000**

| | | |
|---|---:|---:|
| Sales | | $1,758,000 |
| Cost of Goods Sold | | |
| Beginning Finished Goods Inventory | $ 65,000 | |
| + Cost of Goods Manufactured | 988,000 | |
| = Goods Available for Sale in 2000 | $1,053,000 | |
| − Ending Finished Goods Inventory | (75,000) | |
| = Cost of Goods Sold for 2000 | | 978,000 |
| Gross Profit | | 780,000 |

Operating Expense:
| | | |
|---|---|---|
| Selling Expense | $ 355,000 | |
| Administrative Expense | 190,000 | (545,000) |
| Operating Income | | $ 235,000 |

## ALBERTO MANUFACTURING COMPANY
### Schedule of Cost of Goods Manufactured
### For the Year Ending December 31, 2001

Direct Materials:

| | | |
|---|---|---|
| Beginning Direct Material Inventory | $ 45,000 | |
| Purchases during 2001 | 457,000 | |
| Materials Available during 2001 | $502,000 | |
| Ending Direct Material Inventory | ( 73,000) | |
| Direct Materials Used during 2001 | | $ 429,000 |
| Direct Labor during 2001 | | 263,000 |
| Total Manufacturing Overhead Cost during 2001 | | 450,000 |
| Manufacturing Cost for Current Period | | $1,142,000 |
| Beginning Work-in-Process Inventory 1/1/01 | | 82,000 |
| Cost of Goods Available to be Finished | | $1,224,000 |
| Ending Work-in-Process Inventory 12/31/01 | | (154,000) |
| Cost of Goods Manufactured during 2001 | | $1,070,000 |

## ALBERTO MANUFACTURING COMPANY
### Income Statement
### For the Year Ending December 31, 2001

| | | |
|---|---|---|
| Sales | | $1,772,000 |
| Cost of Goods Sold | | |
| Beginning Finished Goods Inventory | $ 75,000 | |
| + Cost of Goods Manufactured during 2001 | 1,070,000 | |
| = Goods Available for Sale in 2001 | $1,143,000 | |
| − Ending Finished Goods Inventory | (93,000) | |
| = Cost of Goods Sold for 2001 | | $1,052,000 |
| Gross Profit | | 720,000 |
| Operating Expense: | | |
| Selling Expense | $ 365,000 | |
| Administrative Expense | 228,000 | (593,000) |
| Operating Income | | $ 127,000 |

## REQUIRED:

Your team should review the provided information and comment on problems that exist. It may help to segment the statements into sections and assign group members to a particular area. For example, a group member might be assigned to review the purchase and use of direct material, another member might be assigned the direct labor and manufacturing overhead areas, and so forth. Each group member should comment on his or her assigned area as it pertains to cash flow and income.

# Chapter 3

## Determining Costs of Products

*E*very year *Fortune* magazine compiles a list of the top 500 publicly traded companies in the United States. This prestigious list is called the Fortune 500. Of the top 25 Fortune 500 companies, most are manufacturing companies demonstrating that manufacturing continues to play a pivotal role in our economy.

In recent years, however, manufacturing companies from outside the United States have begun to exert significant competitive pressure on U.S. manufacturers. The new global marketplace has forced U.S. manufacturers to take a hard look at both the way they operate and the way the results of their operations are measured and evaluated.

One area of vital importance to manufacturing companies is determining the cost of the products they manufacture. If you are the sales manager for IBM's laptop computer division, for example, you must be sure that the selling price you establish is high enough to earn a profit. To ensure that the selling price of each computer exceeds its cost, you need accurate product cost information.

Besides the product pricing decision are several other applications of information about product cost. First, a company must determine the cost of products to compute cost of goods sold on its income statement for a particular period. Second, a company must have product cost information to determine the value of inventories shown on its balance sheet. Third, product cost information helps managers evaluate the efficiency and productivity of a company's manufacturing facility.

In Chapter 2 we stated that the three elements of product cost for a manufacturer are direct material, direct labor, and manufacturing overhead. We also presented an overview of the product costing process. In this chapter we will delve more deeply into the methods that manufacturers use to determine the cost of the individual units of product they produce. ∎

*After completing your work on this chapter, you should be able to do the following:*

1. Compare and contrast process costing with job order costing.
2. Describe how process costing and job order costing work.
3. Describe the documents used to help control the costs of manufacturing products.
4. Describe how overhead costs are allocated to products.
5. Determine the cost of products using job order costing.
6. Determine the cost of products using process costing.

# ACCUMULATING PRODUCT COST—COST ACCOUNTING

The process of assigning manufacturing costs to manufactured products is called *cost accounting*. When we first introduced this term in Chapter 1, we said that it is often used interchangeably with the terms *management accounting* and *managerial accounting*, but that cost accounting is a narrow application of management accounting dealing with costing products. Cost accounting information can help managers plan and control their operations; make decisions about investments in property, plant, and equipment; establish selling prices; and determine the value of inventories on the balance sheet. Cost accounting information also affects reported net income on the income statement, because the cost of the products sold during the income statement period is reported as cost of goods sold.

# UNITS OF PRODUCT AS COST OBJECTS

Recall from Chapter 2 that a cost object is any activity or item for which a separate cost measurement is desired. For our purposes in this chapter, we will consider a unit of manufactured product as the cost object. As we said earlier, the cost of a unit of manufactured product includes the cost of the direct material, direct labor, and manufacturing overhead required to produce that unit of product. The amount of direct material included in each unit of production can actually be traced to finished products. Assigning the cost of direct material to production is relatively simple, as long as the company keeps track of the amount of material used to produce each unit of product. Similarly, if a company keeps track of the amount of direct labor used to produce each unit of product, it can readily assess the cost of direct labor used to produce each unit. Unlike direct material and direct labor, however, the amount of manufacturing overhead cost associated with particular units of production is quite abstract.

Manufacturing overhead cost includes all manufacturing cost except direct material or direct labor costs. Accordingly, it includes a wide assortment of factory-related items. Some examples are production design setup, plant security, supervisory salaries, raw materials storage, building maintenance, and factory supplies.

Even though their cost cannot easily be traced to individual units of production, the manufacturing overhead activities mentioned (and many others) are all necessary to produce products, and their cost should be included in the cost of products produced. The problem, of course, is that the cost of these activities cannot be traced directly to the units of product produced. Their cost, therefore, must be allocated to the units. Consider the cost of factory lighting, for example. The production facility has lights turned on so that those who are working on the product can see what they are doing. As units of product make their way through the production process the lights shine on them and lighting cost is incurred. Because the purpose of the lights is to enhance the production process, a certain amount of the cost of lighting should be included in the cost of each unit of product manufactured. Unfortunately, when the power company sends the bill at the end of the month, there is no breakdown as to how much lighting cost is to be included in each unit. The bill only shows the total cost of electricity used, say $10,000. The manufacturer has to determine how to assign some portion of the lighting cost to each unit produced. **Manufacturing overhead allocation** is a process of assigning or allotting an amount of manufacturing overhead cost to each unit of product produced based on some reasonable basis of distribution. This allocation has traditionally been a two-stage process.

**manufacturing overhead allocation** The process of assigning or allotting an amount of manufacturing overhead cost to each unit of product produced based on some reasonable basis of distribution.

## TRADITIONAL MANUFACTURING OVERHEAD ALLOCATION

**cost pool** An accumulation of the costs associated with a specific cost object.

The first stage in the process of assigning manufacturing overhead costs to products is to gather overhead cost into a cost pool. A **cost pool** is an accumulation of the costs associated with a specific cost object. Traditionally, the cost of manufacturing overhead was gathered into one large cost pool, including all manufacturing costs except for direct material and direct labor.

The second stage is to assign the manufacturing overhead cost gathered in the pool to units of product manufactured. Manufacturers attempt to allocate the amount of manufacturing overhead cost that corresponds to the overhead resources consumed to make the product. In other words, if it seems likely that $1,000 worth of manufacturing overhead resources were consumed to manufacture a pool table, then $1,000 should be allocated to that pool table for overhead. Because it is impractical if not impossible for managers to estimate the amount of overhead associated with each unit of individual product produced, an equitable basis for cost allocation must be determined.

**allocation base** An amount associated with cost objects that can be used to proportionately distribute manufacturing overhead costs to each cost object.

An **allocation base** is an amount associated with cost objects that can be used to proportionately distribute manufacturing overhead costs to each cost object. The traditional approach to allocating manufacturing overhead cost to units produced is to identify some other cost or item to serve as an indicator of the relative amounts of indirect factory resources used to make each unit of production. This other cost or item is then used as the allocation base. Direct labor hours, direct labor cost, and machine hours are common traditional allocation bases.

It seems logical that a larger unit of production would require the use of more factory resources than a smaller unit of production, which may mean more direct labor, direct materials, machine time, or some combination of these. The idea behind using an allocation base such as direct labor dollars is that if a unit of product requires a large amount of direct labor cost, it follows that its manufacture would also consume a large amount of overhead resources.

As an example, assume Buck Slade Company uses direct labor cost as the allocation base for manufacturing overhead. Assume manufacturing overhead was $1,000,000 and direct labor cost totaled $100,000 for July 2000. Slade can express the relationship between these two costs by dividing the $1,000,000 manufacturing overhead by the $100,000 direct labor cost. Notice that we are dividing the cost we wish to allocate (the $1,000,000 manufacturing overhead) by the allocation base (the $100,000 direct labor cost). The result is the company's overhead application rate. Slade will allocate overhead cost to the units of manufactured product at a rate of $10 per direct labor dollar.

What this means is that every time $1 of direct labor cost is added to a unit of product, $10 of manufacturing overhead cost will be added to the product's cost, as well. A product that requires little direct labor will receive a small allocation for manufacturing overhead. The total direct material cost, direct labor cost, and the total allocated manufacturing overhead cost are then added together to determine the cost of the manufactured product.

For example, assume that Buck Slade Company produces a batch of 15,000 precision cutters. If 15,000 cutters required a total of 80 direct labor hours at $10 per hour, the manufacturing overhead allocation would be $8,000, calculated as follows:

| Direct Labor Hours | × | Direct Labor Rate | = | Direct Labor Cost |
|---|---|---|---|---|
| 80 | × | $10 | = | $800 |

| Direct Labor Cost | × | Overhead Allocation Rate | = | Total Overhead Allocation |
|---|---|---|---|---|
| $800 | × | $10 | = | $8,000 |

This method uses a single manufacturing overhead cost pool and a single, plant-wide application rate. Virtually all manufacturers in the United States used this method until the mid-1980s, and many still do today.

During the mid-1980s, some companies realized that a plant-wide application rate has significant weaknesses. Whereas some manufacturing overhead costs may relate to the allocation base, many others do not. Manufacturing overhead costs are typically caused by (or related to) many different activities—the activity that drives one cost may be totally different from the activity that drives another cost. To use one activity (such as direct labor) as the allocation base for applying all manufacturing overhead cost to product will likely cause some products to be overcosted and others to be undercosted. For example, assume that a company uses direct labor hours to allocate all manufacturing overhead cost, and its factory has five machines, two of which use significant amounts of water for cooling. In this situation, the overhead cost per direct labor hour will include an amount for cooling water. The amount will be allocated to products whether they are produced on a machine that requires cooling water or not. Therefore, products that are produced on machines that do not require cooling water will be overcosted and, because some of the cost of cooling water is allocated to products produced on machines that do not require cooling water, products produced on machines that do require cooling water will be undercosted.

In the past decade, many companies have begun to study the cost incurred in their operations and are attempting to determine the activities that cause those costs. Great strides have been made and the result has been the development of a new costing method that provides more realistic and reasonable cost for units of manufactured product. This new method is activity-based costing.

# MANUFACTURING OVERHEAD ALLOCATION USING ACTIVITY-BASED COSTING

**activity-based costing**
Allocating cost to products based on the activities that caused the cost to happen.

One way to increase the accuracy of product cost is to trace the cost of overhead activities to products based on activities that cause the cost. Allocating cost to products based on the activities that cause the cost is called **activity-based costing.**

This allocation process improves on traditional overhead allocation in two ways. First, an analysis of what causes cost to happen may result in the reclassification of certain costs from manufacturing overhead to direct material, direct labor, or some other direct cost classification. That is, some costs traditionally viewed as indirect can actually be traced directly to units of product and need not be allocated. This in and of itself contributes to a more accurate unit cost because less cost remains to be allocated.

Second, rather than using one giant cost pool and a single allocation base resulting in one plant-wide application rate, activity-based costing uses multiple cost pools to develop multiple application rates. Adding manufacturing overhead cost to the units of production based on the various activities that drive the costs leads to more accurate unit product cost.

For example, say Buck Slade Company has analyzed its $1,000,000 of manufacturing overhead cost and has classified the activities that cause that cost to happen. This analysis has led the company to reclassify $220,000 from manufacturing overhead to direct cost because it found that, using modern technology, it could readily trace those costs directly into units of product as they are produced. The remaining $780,000 manufacturing overhead cost consists of the items listed in Exhibit 3–1.

**Exhibit 3–1**
Remaining Overhead for Buck Slade Company

| | |
|---|---|
| Materials purchasing and handling cost | $ 75,000 |
| Production engineering and design | 60,000 |
| Production machine setup | 40,000 |
| Production machine depreciation | 300,000 |
| Production machine maintenance | 50,000 |
| Quality testing | 100,000 |
| Plant security | 25,000 |
| Plant supervision | 70,000 |
| Building maintenance | 10,000 |
| Factory supplies | 20,000 |
| Factory insurance | 30,000 |
| Total manufacturing overhead | $780,000 |

To implement activity-based costing, we begin by reviewing overhead to identify specific overhead activities and their cost. Once identified, the costs of a given overhead activity are removed from the general overhead pool and grouped together in a separate pool. This action results in costs being accumulated in several small cost pools within practical limits instead of a single large pool. For example, separate pools might be established for the cost of setup, materials handling, quality inspection, and so forth.

The second stage of manufacturing overhead allocation is to assign the cost accumulated in the pool to products. Manufacturers hope to find an activity associated with products that causes the cost and that can also be used as an allocation base. This cause is a **cost driver.** It differs from a traditional allocation base in that it actually *causes* the cost. Traditional allocation bases such as direct labor hours, direct labor cost, and machine hours do not cause cost. Rather, they are cost correlates that have historically been viewed as good indicators of the amount of overhead associated with particular products. The lack of a causal relationship between the cost and the allocation base is a significant weakness of traditional overhead allocation.

**cost driver** A cost cause that is used as a cost allocation base.

The estimated activities for the Buck Slade Company are listed in Exhibit 3–2.

Slade has separated the large $780,000 pool into various small pools and used cost drivers to allocate the manufacturing overhead to products. In other words, Slade allocates manufacturing overhead cost to products based on activities that cause the cost.

**Exhibit 3–2**
Estimated Activities for
the Buck Slade
Company

| | |
|---|---|
| Number of parts | 750,000 |
| Number of production runs | 25 |
| Number of machine hours | 2,000 |
| Number of components tested | 25,000 |
| Number of direct labor hours | 10,000 |

Slade has separated the $780,000 manufacturing overhead pool into five smaller pools to be allocated as follows:

Pool 1—Materials purchasing and handling, allocated using the number of parts as the cost driver.

Pool 2—Production engineering and design cost, and production machine setup cost, allocated using the number of production runs as the cost driver.

Pool 3—Production machine depreciation and production machine maintenance, allocated using the number of machine hours as the cost driver.

Pool 4—Quality testing, allocated using the number of components tested as the cost driver.

Pool 5—Remaining manufacturing overhead costs. Because Slade is unable to determine cost drivers, or because it is impractical to determine cost drivers for these remaining costs, a traditional allocation base—direct labor hours—will be used.

To calculate the application rate, we divide the estimated cost from the cost pool by the estimated number of occurrences of the cost driver.

$$\frac{\text{Estimated Overhead Cost}}{\text{Cost Driver}} = \text{Overhead Application Rate}$$

Slade has developed the following applications rates:

| Manufacturing Overhead Pool | Cost Driver (Allocation Base) | Application Based on Occurrence of the Cost Driver |
|---|---|---|
| **Pool 1** | | |
| • Materials purchasing and handling cost | Number of parts | $75,000 ÷ 750,000= $0.10 per part |
| **Pool 2** | | |
| • Production engineering and design | Number of production runs | $100,000 ÷ 25 = $4,000 per prod. run |
| • Production machine setup | | |
| **Pool 3** | | |
| • Production machine depreciation | Number of machine hours | $350,000 ÷ 2,000 = $175 per machine hour |
| • Production machine maintenance | | |
| **Pool 4** | | |
| • Quality testing | Number of components tested | $100,000 ÷ 25,000 = $4 per comp. tested |
| **Pool 5** | | |
| • Plant security | Number of direct labor hours | $155,000 ÷ 10,000 = $15.50 per direct labor hour |
| • Plant supervision | | |
| • Building maintenance | | |
| • Factory supplies | | |
| • Factory insurance | | |

For every part added to a unit of product, $0.10 of manufacturing overhead cost is added to the product as well (Pool 1). Every time a production run is made, $4,000 is added to the cost of the products in that production run (Pool 2). For every machine hour devoted to the unit of product, $175 of manufacturing overhead is added; and for every component tested, $4 of manufacturing overhead is added (Pools 3 and 4). For every hour of direct labor, $15.50 of manufacturing overhead is added to the cost of the product (Pool 5). The total direct material cost, direct labor cost, and total allocated manufacturing overhead cost are then added together to determine the cost of the product.

As an example, take another look at Slade's production run of 15,000 precision cutters. Each cutter is made of three parts. In addition, it takes 16 machine hours and 80 direct labor hours to produce the 15,000 cutters. Finally, during production, samples totaling 1,000 cutters are tested for sharpness. The manufacturing overhead cost for the cutters is calculated as follows:

| Manufacturing Overhead Pool | Cost Allocation |
|---|---|
| **Pool 1** | |
| • Materials purchasing and handling cost | 15,000 × 3 × $0.10 = $ 4,500 |
| **Pool 2** | |
| • Production engineering and design | 1 × $4,000 = $ 4,000 |
| • Production machine setup | |
| **Pool 3** | |
| • Production machine depreciation | 16 × $175 = $ 2,800 |
| • Production machine maintenance | |
| **Pool 4** | |
| • Quality testing | 1,000 × $4 = $ 4,000 |
| **Pool 5** | |
| • Plant security | 80 × $15.50 = $ 1,240 |
| • Plant supervision | |
| • Building maintenance | |
| • Factory supplies | |
| • Factory insurance | |
| Total manufacturing overhead for the 15,000 cutters | $16,540 |
| Manufacturing overhead per cutter ($16,540 ÷ 15,000) | $ 1.103 |

Notice that the $16,540 of overhead allocated to the precision cutters when activity-based costing is used is more than double the $8,000 allocated when a traditional allocation method is used. The cutters are not more expensive to make when activity-based costing is used; rather, the amount of overhead allocated to the cutters under activity-based costing is a more accurate representation of the cost attributable to the products produced.

# PRODUCT COSTING METHODS

To make informed decisions about which products should be produced and what selling price should be charged, managers need accurate product cost information.

Users of accounting information generally rely on one of two methods for determining the cost of products, the job order cost method and the process cost method. Although both methods are used, they are not interchangeable. A company must select the method best suited to the type of products being made and to the manufacturing process itself.

## Job Order Costing Basics

**job order costing** A costing method that accumulates cost by a single unit, or batch of units.

**Job order costing** is a method that accumulates the cost of production for each job, each individual unit of production, each order, or each product. This method is used to accumulate the cost of one-of-a-kind and custom-made goods such as custom furniture or custom cabinets, ships, airplanes, bridges, buildings, and advertising posters. For instance, when Boeing manufactured the five Boeing 777-200 passenger jets ordered by Air China in 1997, the airplane manufacturer used job order costing to determine how much each plane costs.

The key consideration for choosing between process costing and job order costing is whether the goods produced consumed similar enough amounts of factory resources (direct material, direct labor, and manufacturing overhead) that an average cost per unit would be an accurate reflection of the product's cost. If the units consumed very different amounts of factory resources, an average cost per unit is meaningless, and job order costing should be used.

Under job order costing, managers keep close track of the material and labor associated with each job. The "job" may consist of a single unit or a batch of units. For example, a job for Boeing would consist of a single airplane. For Perlmuter Printing, however, a job would consist of a batch of 20,000 advertising posters. In either case, the cost of direct material, direct labor, and overhead are accumulated and totaled for each job.

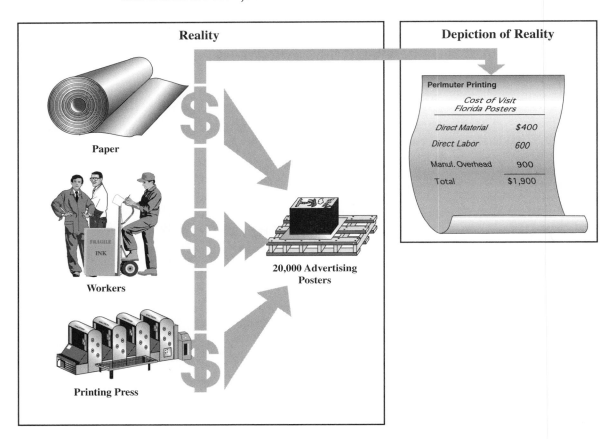

## Process Costing Basics

**process costing** A method of allocating manufacturing cost to products to determine an average cost per unit.

**Process costing** is a method of allocating manufacturing cost to products to determine an average cost per unit. Process costing is used when units of production are identical, or nearly so, and each unit of production receives the same manufacturing input as the next. Examples of such products are milk, soda, canned goods, breakfast cereal, household cleaners, motor oil, and gasoline. For example, Eastman Kodak uses process costing to determine the cost of the color film it produces.

When process costing is used, total manufacturing cost is divided by the number of units produced to arrive at a per unit cost. For example, if a toothbrush factory makes 2 million toothbrushes and the total production cost is $400,000, then the cost per tooth brush is $0.20, computed as follows:

$$\frac{\text{Total Production Cost}}{\text{Number of Units Produced}} = \text{Cost Per Unit}$$

$$\frac{\$400,000}{2,000,000 \text{ Units Produced}} = \$0.20 \text{ Per Unit}$$

The reason this simple method is adequate for a product such as toothbrushes is that each toothbrush is identical to, and consumes the same amount of resources as, the next. Accordingly, an average cost per toothbrush provides an accurate indication of each unit's cost.

## Discussion Questions

**3–1.** Name four products (other than those mentioned in the text) for which process costing would be appropriate.

**3–2.** Name four products (other than those mentioned in the text) for which job order costing would be appropriate.

**3–3.** Are any products difficult to classify? List some and explain the difficulty.

The first product costing method we will explore in detail is job order costing. As we cover job order costing, we will also look at the documents manufacturers use to control factory resources and accumulate the cost of products.

## JOB ORDER COSTING

We have seen that in job order costing the job may be the production of a single unit, or a batch of units. The key is that the units produced for one job are dissimilar from the units produced for another job, and that cost information is gathered for each individual production job.

Keeping track of product cost is not as challenging as it may seem. Particular documents help keep track of the direct material, direct labor, and manufacturing overhead associated with each production job.

For example, a company that makes custom boats would keep a list of the direct material cost, direct labor hours, and direct labor cost used to make a boat. It would also need to keep track of the manufacturing overhead associated with each boat made. The firm would total the direct material, direct labor, and manufacturing overhead to determine the boat's cost.

Managers use a system of documents to track the cost of units produced and to control the costs incurred in the factory. We will review these documents—a critical part of a job order cost method—and explore the process of job order costing in the following sections.

The manufacturer in our example, Manta Power Boats, is a top-quality, custom boat manufacturer located in Hollywood, Florida. In contrast to production-line boats—boats made in large quantities that are nearly identical—Manta's boats are manufactured to the specifications of each customer. Customers select the boat style, interior, engines, construction material, and paint scheme they want. No two boats are alike. Let us look at how Manta calculates the cost of one power boat.

## Documentation Relating to Job Order Costing

**job cost sheet** A document that tracks the costs of products and organizes and summarizes the cost information for each job.

When job order costing is used, a document called a **job cost sheet** simplifies tracking the costs of products because it organizes and summarizes the cost information for each job. An example of a job cost sheet is shown in Exhibit 3–3.

**Exhibit 3–3**
Job Cost Sheet for Manta Power Boats

### Job Cost Sheet

Job #: 97384    Date Promised: 7-11-99

Customer: Bill Hudik    Date Started: 6-2-99

Product Description: 38 Open Fisherman

| Direct Materials | | | Direct Labor | | Manufacturing Overhead | | | Total |
|---|---|---|---|---|---|---|---|---|
| Date | Req # | Amount | Date | Amount | Base | Rate | Amount | Total |
| | | $ | | $ | | | $ | $ |
| | | | | | | | | |
| | | | | | | | | |
| | | | | | | | | |
| | | | | | | | | |
| | | | | | | | | |
| Total | | $ | | $ | | | $ | $ |

Date Completed: _____

The job cost sheet in Exhibit 3–3 will list the manufacturing costs for job 97384. An entry will be made on the job cost sheet each time direct material, direct labor, and manufacturing overhead costs are incurred in connection with the job. Managers can refer to a job cost sheet any time they need information about the cost of producing a particular boat.

A job cost sheet is prepared for each individual unit produced. In Manta's case, the costs for each boat are placed on a separate job cost sheet. In Exhibit 3–3, job 97384 is for a 38-foot Open Fisherman. At any time, Tom Greco, owner of Manta Power Boats, can review the job cost sheet for job 97384 to determine its cost.

Job cost sheets not only help managers keep track of the costs of current production, but they also provide historical information that can help managers estimate the cost of future production. For example, if an order is received for a boat similar to one that Manta has made in the past, Tom Greco can look at the first boat's job cost sheet to help estimate how much the next boat will cost.

Let us now look at how these costs are monitored and measured. We begin with an analysis of direct material.

**Cost Information for Raw Material** Manufacturers such as Manta generally keep close track of raw material costs because it is such an expensive part of the manufacturing process. The raw materials needed at Manta to build power boats include fiberglass cloth, polyester resin, wood, plastic, aluminum, engines, and much more. Because these materials are so costly, Manta, like other manufacturers, does not allow just any employee to buy raw material on behalf of the company. An unqualified employee might buy too much or too little, or they may buy the wrong raw material altogether. In most manufacturing companies, a request for material is made by the employee in charge of monitoring the raw material inventory levels. This person may be in charge of the materials store room or perhaps is the production supervisor. At Manta, Carl Bevans monitors the amount of material on hand, and when polyester resin is needed, Carl requests that more be purchased. This purchase request comes in the form of a purchase requisition.

A **purchase requisition** is a request form that lists the quantity and description of the materials needed. This form helps to control and monitor all material requested to ensure that the company secures the right amount and quality. Copies of the completed purchase requisition are forwarded to Manta's purchasing department and to the accounts payable clerk in charge of paying the company's bills. Exhibit 3–4 shows the completed materials requisition for Manta Power Boats.

**purchase requisition**
A request form that lists the quantity and description of the materials needed.

**Exhibit 3–4**
Purchase Requisition for Manta Power Boats

| Manta Power Boats Purchase Requisition | |
|---|---|
| | Number: 1001 |

Date: _6-4-99_

Name: _Carl Bevans_

Department: _Production Material Stores_

| Quantity | Description |
|---|---|
| 110 gal. | Polyester Resin |
| | |
| | |
| | |
| | |

Signature: _Carl Bevans_

**purchasing department**
A specialized department that purchases all the goods required by a company.

**purchase order** A formal document used to order material from a vendor.

The **purchasing department** is a specialized department that purchases all the goods required by the company. In the purchasing department, trained individuals called purchasing agents contact several competing vendors or suppliers to obtain the highest-quality material at the lowest price.

Once the purchasing agent has selected a vendor, the agent issues a **purchase order,** a formal document created to order material from a vendor. The purchase order specifies the quantity, type, and cost of the materials, payment terms, and method of delivery. Copies of the purchase order are distributed to the receiving department, the accounts payable department, and the vendor. A sample purchase order for Manta Power Boats is shown in Exhibit 3–5.

**Exhibit 3–5**
Purchase Order for
Manta Power Boats

| Purchase Order | | | |
|---|---|---|---|
| PO #: 06059702 | | | |

**Vendor:** Pitman Sales Company   **Order Date:** 6-5-99

**Address:** 8650 SW 132 Street   **Delivery Date:** 6-7-99

Miami, FL 33156

**Phone:** 305 – 555 – 9558

**Purchase Requisition #:** 1001   **Department:** Prod. Mat. Stores

| Quantity | Description | Unit Cost | Total Cost |
|---|---|---|---|
| 110 gal. | Polyester Resin | 6.00 | 660.00 |
| | | | |
| | | | |
| | | | |
| | | | |
| | | | |
| | | | |
| | | | |
| | | | |
| | | | |
| | | | |
| | | | |

**Purchasing Agent:** Bob Pass

**receiving report** A document that indicates the quantity of each item received.

When Manta's receiving department receives the material from the supplier, the receiving clerk compares the material received to the purchase order and completes a receiving report. The **receiving report** is a document that indicates the quantity of each item received. It is used to note any differences between the goods ordered and the goods received. Lauren Elsea, Manta's receiving clerk, completes a receiving report for each delivery received as shown in Exhibit 3–6.

A copy of the receiving report is sent to the accounts payable department. Manta's accounts payable clerk now has three documents related to the purchase: (1) the purchase requisition, (2) the purchase order, and (3) the receiving report. When the accounts payable clerk receives the vendor's invoice for the materials, information on the invoice is matched to the other three documents. If everything is correct, the invoice is paid according to the payment terms.

**Exhibit 3–6**
Receiving Report for
Manta Power Boats

| Receiving Report | | |
|---|---|---|
| **Vendor:** _Pitman Sales Company_ | | |
| **Purchase Order #:** _06059702_ | | **Date Received:** _6–7–99_ |

| Quantity | Description |
|---|---|
| 110 gal. | Polyester Resin |
| | |
| | |
| | |
| | |
| | |
| | |
| | |
| | |

**Receiving Clerk:** _Lauren Elsea_

# Discussion Question

**3–4.** The accounts payable department verifies that the information on the vendor's invoice matches the purchase requisition, the purchase order, and the receiving report. What would a discrepancy show if the information on the following documents conflicted?

a. The receiving report conflicts with the vendor's invoice.

b. The purchase order conflicts with the receiving report.

c. The purchase requisition conflicts with the purchase order.

Once the materials have been checked in, they are stored in the materials stores warehouse until they are needed for production. Generally, such storage space is quite secure to protect the raw material from damage and theft.

When the material is needed for production, Manta's production manager, Kevin Dunn, completes a materials requisition. The **materials requisition** is a formal request for material to be transferred from the raw materials storage area to production. The document lists the type of material and the quantity needed. To begin work on the 38-foot Open Fisherman boat for job 97384, fiberglass and polyester resin are needed, so Kevin Dunn has prepared the materials requisition shown in Exhibit 3–7 to transfer this material into production.

**materials requisition**   A formal request for material to be transferred from the raw materials storage area to production.

**Exhibit 3–7**
Materials Requisition
for Manta Power Boats

| Materials Requisition | | | | |
|---|---|---|---|---|
| | | | | Req #: 2002 |

Job #:  97384

Date:  6-16-99

| Quantity | Item # | Description | Unit Cost | Total Cost |
|---|---|---|---|---|
| 55 gal. | PR55X | Polyester Resin | 6.00 | 330.00 |
| | | | | |
| | | | | |
| | | | | |
| | | | | |
| | | | | |
| | | | | |

Issued By:  Carl Bevans

Received By:  Kevin Dunn

Keep in mind that a materials requisition is different from a purchase requisition. The purchase requisition is a request to purchase material, whereas the materials requisition is a request by manufacturing personnel to transfer previously purchased material from the materials stores warehouse to production.

The materials requisition is a useful tool for accumulating the cost of products. Materials requisitions show how much material is being used, for what purpose, and at what cost. The information from the materials requisitions is transferred to the job cost sheets to show the quantity and cost of material used for each job.

For instance, Exhibit 3–8 shows how the accounting department at Manta Power Boats transfers information from the materials requisition to the job cost sheet for job 97384.

Materials requisitions are also valuable tools for controlling the movement of materials in the factory. Because the movement is documented, it is easier to monitor employees' use of material. This record helps prevent theft, waste, or other inappropriate use of material.

***Cost Information for Direct Labor***   Once raw material enters the production process, factory workers begin working with it, converting the material into finished product. Remember from Chapter 2 that the value of the goods in work-in-process inventory is enhanced by the cost of the raw material incorporated into the product *and* by the labor of production workers. Therefore, in accounting records, work-in-process inventory is increased not only by the cost of direct material, but also by the cost of direct labor.

## Exhibit 3-8
Transfer of Information from a Materials Requisition Form to a Job Cost Sheet

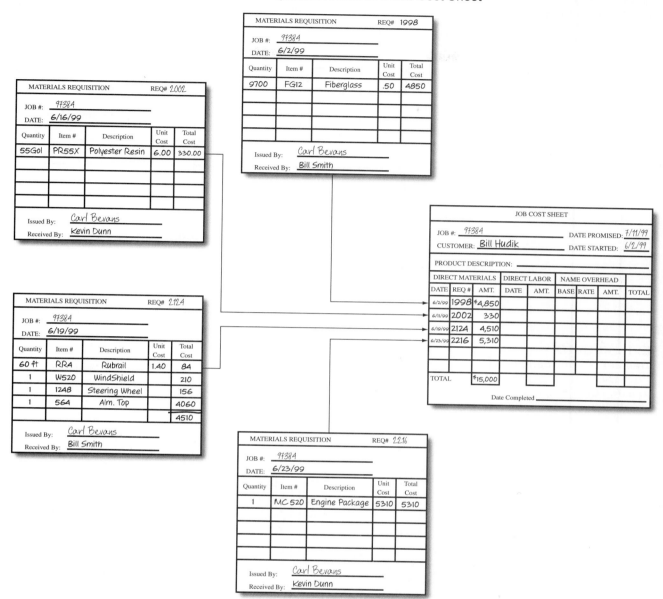

A **labor time ticket** is used to track the amount of time each employee works on a particular production job or a particular task in the factory. Exhibit 3–9 shows a sample labor time ticket for Manta Power Boats.

Labor time tickets include a wealth of information regarding the amount of direct labor associated with each production job. As was the case with the materials requisitions, cost information is transferred from the labor time tickets to the job cost sheet for each job. Exhibit 3–10 shows how information is transferred from the labor time tickets to the job cost sheet for job number 97384 at Manta Power Boats.

Most companies now use computer technology to make entries on labor time tickets. Employees are issued identification cards that are scanned by a card

**labor time ticket** A document used to track the amount of time each employee works on a particular production job or a particular task in the factory.

## Exhibit 3–9
Labor Time Ticket for Manta Power Boats

### Labor Time Ticket

Employee: _Edward Clark_

Employee Number: _127_                    Week Ending: _6-8-99_

| Job # | M | T | W | T | F | S | S | Total |
|-------|---|---|---|---|---|---|---|-------|
| 97384 | 8 | 8 | 4 |   | 8 |   |   | 28 |
| 97383 |   |   | 4 | 8 |   |   |   | 12 |
|       |   |   |   |   |   |   |   |   |
|       |   |   |   |   |   |   |   |   |
|       |   |   |   |   |   |   |   |   |

Supervisor: _MLW_                    Receiving Clerk: _E.C._

## Exhibit 3–10
Transfer of Information from Labor Time Tickets to a Job Cost Sheet at Manta Power Boats

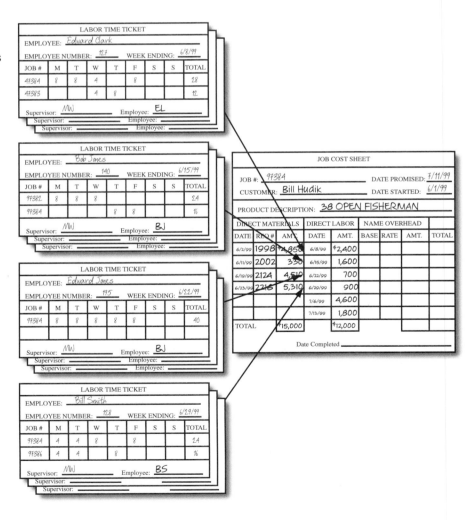

reader. The employee then enters codes to indicate the duties they are performing and the job to which these duties relate. Information from the electronic labor time tickets is stored in a computer file and transferred electronically to electronic job cost sheets.

## Manufacturing Overhead

The information from the materials requisitions and labor time tickets makes it easy to trace direct material cost and direct labor cost to individual jobs. Tracing manufacturing overhead is not quite as straightforward.

As discussed, the cost of manufacturing overhead must be allocated to production. Accurate allocation is often difficult to achieve because the benefit of manufacturing overhead expenditures is difficult to trace to individual jobs or units of production. Manufacturing overhead generally benefits the factory as a whole and therefore all units produced. Because it cannot be traced to individual units, manufacturing overhead must be allocated to the individual units produced. As seen in Exhibit 3–11, generally the cost to be allocated is divided by the total allocation base to determine the amount to allocate per occurrence of the allocation base.

**Exhibit 3–11**
General Formula to Allocate a Cost

$$\frac{\text{Cost to Be Allocated}}{\text{Total Occurences of the Allocation Base}} = \text{Cost Per Occurrence of the Allocation Base}$$

When manufacturing overhead is allocated to production, the first step in the process is selecting an allocation base. One alternative is to use the number of units produced as the allocation base.

If we use the number of units produced as an allocation base, we divide the manufacturing overhead by the number of units to arrive at an amount of overhead per unit. This method of allocation provides an equal amount of manufacturing overhead cost for each unit of production. When the products produced are different from one another, such as Manta's, a uniform cost per unit is generally inadequate for job order costing.

For instance, if the overhead for Manta Power Boats is $75,000, and the company makes five boats, the overhead per boat would be $15,000 for each boat produced, as calculated in Exhibit 3–12.

However, this allocation of $15,000 per boat seems unfair because the boats are so different from one another. It stands to reason that a large boat would consume more factory resources and should receive a higher overhead cost allocation than a small boat. It would be more accurate to allocate according to the resources consumed instead of allocating the exact same manufacturing overhead cost to each boat produced.

In selecting an allocation base, we should strive to find one that will distribute cost fairly. The best allocation base would be one that causes the cost which is to be allocated; but, when a single cost pool is used for manufacturing overhead, it is impossible to find a single allocation base that causes all the cost in the pool. Instead, we attempt to find an allocation base that has the second-best attribute for cost allocation, an allocation base that is correlated to the incurrence of cost. Thus, we should try to find an allocation base that is correlated to the amount of manufacturing overhead resources consumed by each unit produced.

**Exhibit 3–12**
Allocating
Manufacturing
Overhead Based on
the Number of Units
Produced

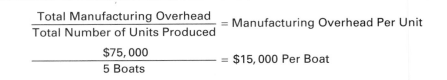

$$\frac{\text{Total Manufacturing Overhead}}{\text{Total Number of Units Produced}} = \text{Manufacturing Overhead Per Unit}$$

$$\frac{\$75,000}{5 \text{ Boats}} = \$15,000 \text{ Per Boat}$$

Manufacturing overhead cost

$15,000

$15,000

$15,000

$15,000

$15,000

Taking a closer look at our boat company example, we note that no two boats are identical, and manufacturing a larger or more complicated boat would, in all likelihood, consume more overhead than a smaller or less complicated boat. As a start, we should find an allocation base that would apportion more overhead to a larger or more complicated boat and less to a smaller, less complicated boat. To do this, the allocation base must increase as boat size or complexity increases.

It seems logical that the amount of factory resources consumed to make a large boat would be more than those consumed to make a small boat. It also seems reasonable that a correlation exists between the number of direct labor hours and the amount of manufacturing overhead resources consumed to make each boat.

As an example, let us use direct labor cost for Manta Power Boats as the allocation base for manufacturing overhead.

When we calculate product cost using actual amounts for direct material, direct labor, and manufacturing overhead, the system is called an actual cost system. Manufacturing overhead is allocated to production based on actual manufacturing overhead cost and the actual amount of the allocation base. For example, we use actual direct labor to allocate actual manufacturing overhead.

Unfortunately, when we do this, several problems emerge. First, managers must wait until the end of the accounting period for actual cost information to be known. Another problem with using actual amounts to allocate overhead is that the overhead application rate fluctuates as actual overhead and direct labor fluctuate.

The overhead application rate will be different for each period if it is calculated using these fluctuating actual amounts. This will result in identical products having different cost amounts unless they were made during the same months.

To eliminate these problems, we estimated annual amounts. In this approach, called a **normal cost system,** product cost reflects actual direct material cost, actual direct labor cost, and estimated overhead costs. Estimated annual manufacturing overhead cost and the annual estimated amount for the allocation base are used to calculate a **predetermined overhead application rate.**

Manta Power Boats allocates overhead using a normal cost system. Suppose, for example, that the estimated annual overhead for Manta Power Boats is $1,000,000 and estimated annual direct labor cost is $1,250,000. In this case, the predetermined overhead application rate is 80 percent ($1,000,000/$1,200,000) of direct labor cost. To determine the overhead cost for the 38-foot Open Fisherman boat for job 97384, we must know the direct labor cost. According to the job cost sheet in Exhibit 3–11, the direct labor cost for this job is $12,000. Using the predetermined overhead application rate of 80 percent of direct labor cost, we calculate the manufacturing overhead associated with job 97384 as follows: $12,000 × 80% = $9,600.

The total cost for job 97384 is $15,000 for direct material, $12,000 for direct labor, and $9,600 for manufacturing overhead. These costs are summarized in the job cost sheet in Exhibit 3–13.

**normal cost system**
System in which product cost reflects actual direct material cost, actual direct labor cost, and estimated overhead costs.

**predetermined overhead application rate** An overhead allocation rate calculated using estimated annual manufacturing overhead cost and the annual estimated amount for the allocation base.

**Exhibit 3–13**
Completed Job Cost Sheet for Job 97384

### Job Cost Sheet

Job #: 97384

Date Promised: 7–11–99

Customer: Bill Hudik

Date Started: 6–2–99

Product Description: 38 Open Fisherman

| Direct Materials | | | Direct Labor | | Manufacturing Overhead | | | |
|---|---|---|---|---|---|---|---|---|
| Date | Req # | Amount | Date | Amount | Base | Rate | Amount | Total |
| 6–2–99 | 1998 | $ 4,850 | 6–8–99 | $ 2,400 | DL$ | 80% | $ 1,920 | $ |
| 6–16–99 | 2002 | 330 | 6–15–99 | 1,600 | DL$ | 80% | 1,280 | |
| 6–19–99 | 2124 | 4,510 | 6–22–99 | 700 | DL$ | 80% | 560 | |
| 6–23–99 | 2216 | 5,310 | 6–29–99 | 900 | DL$ | 80% | 720 | |
| | | | 7–6–99 | 4,600 | DL$ | 80% | 3,680 | |
| | | | 7–13–99 | 1,800 | DL$ | 80% | 1,440 | |
| Total | | $ 15,000 | | $ 12,000 | | | $ 9,600 | $ 36,600 |

Date Completed: 7–11–99

A normal cost system generally is superior to an actual cost system because it smoothes out the fluctuations in product cost due to monthly differences in overhead cost and the allocation base. In addition, because the predetermined application rate is calculated at the very beginning of the year, there is no need to wait until month's end when actual overhead cost information is available to determine product cost.

W.P INV.          15,000
                            15,000
     RAW MATL

W.P INV        12,000
                         12,000
   CASH

            9600      9600
W.P INV
Mfg. O/H Applied

Finished Good  36,600
                         36,600
   W.P INV

***Activity-Based Costing in Job Order Costing***   Let us explore how activity-based costing works by revisiting our Manta Boats example. Manta boats are made of fiberglass and plastic resin formed in molds. A series of molds is used to make the necessary components of each boat. Before a mold can be used, it must be cleaned and waxed to keep the fiberglass and plastic resin from sticking. The process of preparing production equipment to produce a particular product, in this case preparing molds to make a boat, is called setup.

When activity-based costing is used, the cost of each manufacturing activity is accumulated in a dedicated cost pool. In the case of Manta Power Boats, overhead costs are examined and all costs associated with setup are separated out and grouped in a cost pool. Now setup cost can be allocated to products separately from other overhead costs. Assume the annual setup cost at Manta is $117,000.

Next a cost driver must be selected to allocate setup cost. Assume that Manta has decided to use the number of molds used as the cost driver. Preparing a single mold for use causes additional setup cost to occur. The number of molds required to make a single boat varies depending on each boat design. As shown in Exhibit 3–14, a basic Open Fisherman boat requires the use of 10 molds, but a basic sport boat requires the use of only five molds. The actual number of molds used to make a boat varies depending on the customer's specifications.

**Exhibit 3–14**
Number of Molds Used
for Each Basic Boat
Design

Number of Molds Used

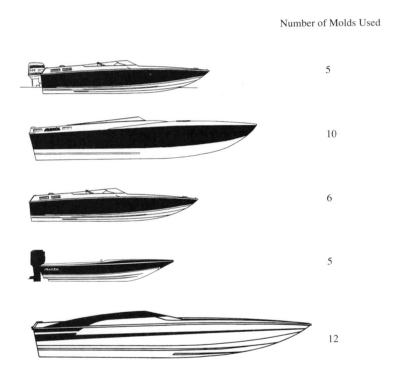

5

10

6

5

12

The effort and cost of setup varies from boat to boat depending on the number of molds required. By using the number of molds as the cost driver, we can reflect the differing amounts of setup effort in the costs of each boat produced. For example, the setup cost for a boat that requires 12 molds will be twice as much as the setup cost for a boat that requires six molds.

The calculations for allocating an overhead cost pool using a cost driver are similar to the calculations using a traditional allocation base. The total estimated annual cost for the cost pool is divided by the estimated annual activity of the cost driver to arrive at an application rate per occurrence of the cost driver. The general formula is as follows:

$$\frac{\text{Total Cost to Be Allocated}}{\text{Total Occurrences of the Cost Driver}} = \text{Cost Per Occurrence of the Cost Driver}$$

Based on past experience, Manta estimates that it will need 360 mold preparations this year to produce 45 boats. Recall that Manta's estimated total annual setup cost is $117,000. With those two numbers, we can find Manta's application rate for setup. Manta divides the estimated total setup cost by the estimated number of mold preparations for the year to determine the application rate for setup cost.

$$\frac{\text{Total Setup Cost}}{\text{Total Number of Mold Preparations}} = \text{Cost Per Mold Preparation}$$

$$\frac{\$117,000}{360 \text{ Mold Preparations}} = \$325 \text{ Per Mold Preparation}$$

We find that with an estimated annual setup cost of $117,000 and a total number of mold preparations of 360, the application rate is $325 per mold used.

## Discussion Questions

3-5. If you owned a factory, would you prefer that employees spend time setting up production equipment or producing product?

3-6. If the production manager was able to use one less mold when making a boat, would the cost allocated to that boat be less? Is it likely that the company's actual setup cost would also be less?

Using the activity-based costing application rate, we can now allocate setup cost to each boat based on the number of molds required. For example, boat 1 requires the use of five molds, so its setup cost would be $1,625 (5 × $325 = $1,625). The setup cost allocated to boat 2 would be $3,250 based on the use of 10 molds (10 × $325 = $3,250). The more molds required to make a boat, the higher the allocation for setup cost.

In a traditional cost system, a manager can reduce manufacturing overhead cost associated with a given product by reducing the allocation base used to allocate the cost. For example, if manufacturing overhead is allocated using machine hours, a manager could reduce the overhead allocated to his or her product by reducing the amount of machine time it takes to make the product. This process would reduce the manufacturing overhead cost allocated to the given product, but it would generally not affect the various overhead costs actually incurred by the company. Reducing machine hours has no significant effect on the amount the company spends for manufacturing overhead items such as property taxes, plant insurance, plant security, indirect material, indirect labor, and so forth. Even though accounting records would indicate a lower cost for that product's manufacturing overhead, the reduced machine hours would have little effect on the dollars the company spent for manufacturing overhead.

When activity-based costing is used to reduce the setup cost of a particular boat, a manager would try to decrease the number of molds used. For instance, if the number of molds used to make boat 2 were reduced by one mold, the cost allocated to that boat would be reduced by $325. With this cost reduction technique, the decrease in the allocation base (the cost driver) actually reduces the amount of cost incurred by the company. That is, reducing the number of molds used actually reduces the amount of work that must be done to make a boat. In general, this reduction in work contributes to true cost savings for the company.

We have seen how well job order costing works for custom-made, one-of-a-kind products, but tracking the cost of each unit would be impractical if hundreds or thousands of identical products are made on a dedicated production line. In such a case, a process costing method is preferred.

# PROCESS COSTING

Recall that with process costing we allocate cost to products by dividing the total manufacturing cost of the period by the number of units produced to arrive at an average per unit cost. The basic method is simple—just total direct materials, direct labor, and manufacturing overhead; then divide by the number of units produced.

For example, to determine the cost of each tube of toothpaste made in a toothpaste factory, we first determine the total manufacturing cost and divide it by the number of units produced. Assume that the total manufacturing cost for toothpaste is $100,000 and the total number of units produced is 1 million. The cost per tube is 10 cents per tube ($100,000 / 1,000,000 = $0.10). Because each tube of toothpaste is identical to the next, the 10 cents per unit would be a reasonably accurate measure of the cost of each unit. This method only works well if all the units produced are the same—if each unit of production is identical to the next, with the exception of minor variations such as color.

Process costing presents some challenges, however, because some units are only partially completed at the end of the accounting period. To reflect reasonably accurate cost amounts, process costing calculations must accommodate situations when some units are only partially completed.

Like job order costing, process costing is simply a method to help managers determine the cost of products. It provides several key items of information:

1. The number of equivalent units of production
2. The cost per unit
3. The cost of the completed units
4. The cost of the units that remain in ending work-in-process inventory

An understanding of the basics of process costing is a necessary foundation to using product cost information wisely. Let us take a closer look at process costing and the complexities related to beginning and ending work-in-process inventories.

Assume that a company makes decorative pink flamingos. The process to make the decoration is simple. A two-part mold is pressed together and the inside coated with hot plastic. After the plastic has cooled and hardened, the mold is pulled apart and the animal figure drops out. It is finished except for painting the eyes and beaks and adding the legs.

## Equivalent Units

The number of units produced must be established before a cost per unit can be determined. In our example, assume that 10,000 flamingos were completed and another 1,000 are still in production. The 1,000 units in production comprise the work-in-process inventory. Obviously the 10,000 units completed should be included in the number of units produced, but what about the other 1,000 units? By definition, units in ending work-in-process inventory are incomplete. Thus, it would be inaccurate to assign the same cost per unit to these units as to the completed units. However, they required expenditures for direct material, direct labor, and manufacturing overhead to bring them to their present state of completion. Thus, some cost should be assigned to these units. Let us see how we arrive at a cost.

The 1,000 flamingos in work-in-process inventory are at various stages of completion. It would be impractical to determine the percentage of completeness for each individual unit of production, so we use an average. In our example, on average, the flamingos in work-in-process inventory are approximately 40 percent complete.

Because the flamingos are only 40 percent complete, we should not include the entire 1,000 units in the number of units produced. Instead, we proportion the number of units by multiplying the number of units by their average completion percentage. Because the 1,000 flamingos are on average 40 percent complete, they are the equivalent of 400 completed flamingos (1,000 × 40% = 400 equivalent units).

Theoretically, if we had started only 400 flamingos into the production process, we could have concentrated our efforts on those 400 units and possibly completed them. However, we started 1,000 units into the production, and we ended up with 1,000 units that were 40 percent complete, which is equivalent to 400 completed units.

**equivalent units** The number of units that would have been completed if all production efforts resulted in only completed units.

In process costing, **equivalent units** are the number of units that would have been completed if all production efforts resulted in only completed units. The number of equivalent units is calculated by adding the number of completed units to the number of units in ending work-in-process inventory times their percentage complete. In our example the calculations for the number of equivalent units of production—10,400 units—is as follows:

|  | Number of Raw Units | | Percent Complete | | Equivalent Units |
|---|---|---|---|---|---|
| Units completed | 10,000 | × | 100% | = | 10,000 |
| Ending work in process | 1,000 | × | 40% | = | 400 |
| Total equivalent units | | | | | 10,400 |

It is likely that the percentage of completion for direct material is different from that of direct labor or manufacturing overhead. Product costs would be more accurate if we used separate completion percentages for direct material, direct labor, and manufacturing overhead. Although necessary in practice, such precise calculations greatly complicate process costing. To keep our example simple and understandable, we will use a single percentage to represent the degree of completion for direct material, direct labor, and manufacturing overhead.

## Cost Per Equivalent Unit

In our example, we also assume that the manufacturer uses the average inventory cost flow method. Generally acceptable accounting principals allow companies to use the first in first out (FIFO), last in first out (LIFO), or the average cost flow method. In process costing, the FIFO and average cost flow methods are popular.

The FIFO cost flow method assumes that the cost of the first units added to inventory is the first cost removed from inventory. Thus, the cost of units must be tracked through the inventory records so the first cost in is the first cost out. As you might expect, this complicates process costing calculations. To keep our example simple, we assume the average cost flow method is used.

Now let us examine the cost associated with producing the 10,400 equivalent units in our flamingo factory. Assume the production costs are $5,400 as summarized in Exhibit 3–15.

**Exhibit 3–15**
Summary of
Production Cost

| | |
|---|---|
| Cost of beginning work in process | $  500 |
| Current month's cost | 4,908 |
| Total | $5,408 |

To compute cost per unit when the average cost flow method is used in process costing, we divide the total production cost by the number of equivalent units as follows:

$$\frac{\text{Total Production Cost}}{\text{Equivalent Units}} = \text{Cost Per Equivalent Unit}$$

$$\frac{\$5,408}{10,400 \text{ Equivalent Units}} = \$0.52 \text{ Per Equivalent Unit}$$

In our example we see that the cost per flamingo is $0.52. Now that we know the cost of each unit produced, we can determine the cost of the ending work-in-process inventory and the cost of the units completed. Barring theft or other losses, units of production are either completed and transferred to finished goods inventory, or they remain in ending work-in-process inventory. Therefore, it stands to reason that production costs are associated either with completed units or with units in ending work-in-process inventory.

## Cost of Ending Work-in-Process Inventory

The cost of ending work-in-process inventory is shown as an asset on manufacturers' balance sheets. To determine this cost, the number of equivalent units (not raw units) in ending work-in-process inventory is multiplied by the cost per unit. For our flamingo example, 400 equivalent units are in ending work-in-process inventory and the cost per unit is $0.52. Therefore, the cost of the ending work-in-process inventory is $208 as follows:

| Number of Equivalent Units | | Cost Per Unit | | Cost of Ending Work-in-Process Inventory |
|:---:|:---:|:---:|:---:|:---:|
| | × | | = | |
| 400 | × | $0.52 | = | $208 |

## Cost of Completed Units

To determine the cost of completed units, we multiply the number of completed units by the cost per unit. For our flamingo example, 10,000 completed units is multiplied by the $0.52 cost per unit. The cost of the completed units then is $5,200, calculated as follows:

| Number of Units | | Per Unit Cost | | Cost of Units Completed and Transferred to Finished Goods Inventory |
|:---:|:---:|:---:|:---:|:---:|
| 10,000 | × | $0.52 | = | $5,200 |

The cost of completed units is important because initially it becomes part of finished goods inventory. Then, as products are sold, the cost of sold units becomes part of cost of goods sold on the income statement.

Assuming no units are spoiled, stolen, or otherwise lost, the cost of production is either transferred to finished goods inventory or remains as the cost of ending work-in-process inventory. In our example the total manufacturing cost was $5,408. If no units are lost or spoiled during production, the actual units are either completed and physically transferred to finished goods or they remain in ending work-in-process inventory. As we see in Exhibit 3–16, part of the $5,408 total manufacturing cost is transferred to finished goods inventory, and the remainder reflects the cost of the units that remain in ending work-in-process inventory.

**Exhibit 3–16**
Flow of
Manufacturing Cost

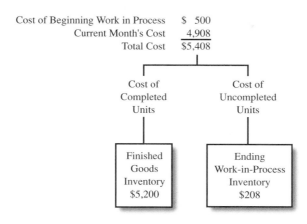

As stated at the beginning of this chapter, it is important for managers, such as the sales manager for IBM's lap top computer division, to know how much products cost. Otherwise, how could managers know which products are profitable and which are not? Whether it is being used to determine the company's cost of goods sold, the cost of inventories shown on the balance sheet, or to help set selling prices and determine the profitability of individual products, accurate product cost information is essential.

## SUMMARY

As American manufacturing companies experience increasing competition, both domestic and foreign, accurate costing of the products they produce becomes ever more important. Information about the cost of manufactured product is useful in establishing a selling price for the products, determining cost of goods sold on the income statement, and valuing of inventories on the balance sheet.

The cost of a manufactured product is composed of the cost of direct materials, direct labor, and manufacturing overhead associated with the units of product produced. Although accounting for the cost of direct materials and direct labor is relatively straightforward, determining the amount of manufacturing overhead that should be included in a unit of manufactured product is more difficult because these costs must be allocated to the units of product produced.

The traditional method of allocating manufacturing overhead to product uses a plant-wide application rate based on a single allocation base. Manufacturing overhead allocation using activity-based costing uses multiple application rates based on the various activities that cause costs to be incurred.

Job order costing is one of two main methods used to accumulate product costs and is most appropriate when units or batches of production are unique. Under this method, cost information is gathered for each production job. The second of the two main product costing methods is called process costing and is most appropriate when units of production are identical and each unit of production receives the same manufacturing input as the next.

Regardless of whether the job order costing method or the process costing method is used, the overall purpose of accumulating product costs is to provide managers with the information they need to make many of the decisions necessary to plan and control their operations.

# APPENDIX—RECORDING MANUFACTURING COST AND THE ALLOCATION OF MANUFACTURING OVERHEAD

This appendix is intended to provide a basic overview of how costs are recorded for manufactured products.

After completing your work in this appendix, you should be able to record the following types of entries:

1. The use of direct material in production
2. The use of direct labor for production
3. The accumulation of manufacturing overhead
4. The allocation of manufacturing overhead to production
5. The transfer of the cost of a completed job to finished goods
6. The entry to close over or under applied manufacturing overhead
7. The transfer of the cost of completed products to finished goods when process costing is used

The following accounts will be used for the entries in this appendix:

1. Cash
2. Raw materials inventory
3. Work-in-process inventory
4. Manufacturing overhead incurred
5. Manufacturing overhead applied
6. Finished goods inventory
7. Accumulated depreciation
8. Utilities payable
9. Cost of goods sold

Recall that debits increase assets, expenses, and losses, while credits increase liabilities, equity, revenues, and gains. The dollar amount of the debits must equal that of the credits in each journal entry.

We will use the job cost sheet in Exhibit 3–13 for the 38 Open Fisherman job 97384 to provide information for the entries that follow. In practice, separate entries are made for each transfer of material, each payment of wages, and each application of manufacturing overhead. To simplify our example, we will make entries that summarize the amounts for each cost category.

1. The following entry records the $15,000 of direct material used to manufacture job 97384.

| | | |
|---|---|---|
| Work-in-process inventory | 15,000 | |
| Raw material inventory | | 15,000 |
| To record the transfer of direct material to production for job 97384. | | |

2. The following entry records the $12,000 of direct labor cost incurred to manufacture job 97384.

| | | |
|---|---|---|
| Work-in-process inventory | 12,000 | |
| Cash | | 12,000 |
| To record direct labor for job 97384. | | |

3. The Manta Power Boats example indicates that the actual manufacturing overhead for the month is $75,000. We will assume that the manufacturing overhead is composed of the following items:

| | |
|---|---|
| Factory rent | $33,000 |
| Factory utilities | 11,000 |
| Factory supervision | 23,000 |
| Depreciation for production equipment | 8,000 |
| Total | $75,000 |

We will record the actual manufacturing overhead costs listed above in an account called manufacturing overhead incurred. Sometimes this account is called actual manufacturing overhead or simply manufacturing overhead.

The following entries would be made to record the actual overhead costs listed previously:

| | | |
|---|---|---|
| Manufacturing overhead incurred | 33,000 | |
|    Cash | | 33,000 |
| To record factory rent for June 1999. | | |

| | | |
|---|---|---|
| Manufacturing overhead incurred | 11,000 | |
|    Cash (or utilities payable) | | 11,000 |
| To record factory utilities for June 1999. | | |

| | | |
|---|---|---|
| Manufacturing overhead incurred | 23,000 | |
|    Cash | | 23,000 |
| To record factory supervision for June 1999. | | |

| | | |
|---|---|---|
| Manufacturing overhead incurred | 8,000 | |
|    Accumulated depreciation | | 8,000 |
| To record depreciation of production equipment June 1999. | | |

After the above entries have been posted, the manufacturing overhead incurred account has a balance of 75,000 as shown in the following T-account:

**Manufacturing Overhead Incurred**

| | |
|---|---|
| 33,000 | |
| 11,000 | |
| 23,000 | |
| 8,000 | |
| 75,000 | |

4. As you recall from the chapter, the actual costs of manufacturing overhead items is not generally assigned directly to particular products being manufactured. Rather, a predetermined overhead application rate is used to allocate manufacturing overhead to production. In our example, the overhead is allocated at 80 percent of direct labor cost. Therefore job 97384 was allocated overhead of $9,600.

| | | |
|---|---|---|
| Work in process | 9,600 | |
|    Manufacturing overhead applied | | 9,600 |
| To apply manufacturing overhead to job 97384. | | |

Note that the account used to record the application of manufacturing overhead to production is different from the one used to record the actual manufacturing overhead costs itself. The use of different accounts allows managers and accountants to keep track of both the actual overhead costs incurred and the overhead applied to production.

5. When job 97384 is completed, its cost is transferred to finished goods as follows:

| | | |
|---|---|---|
| Finished goods inventory | 36,600 | |
|   Work-in-process inventory | | 36,600 |
|     To transfer the completed job from production | | |
|     to finished goods. | | |

6. As you might imagine, the actual amount of manufacturing overhead cost incurred will be different than the amount applied to production. In a given month, the actual amount of overhead may be more than the amount applied and in another month it may be less. The hope is that the differences will nearly balance out during the year. If the amount applied to production exceeds the actual overhead amount, overhead is over applied. If the amount applied to production is less than the actual overhead amount, overhead is under applied. The under or over application of overhead is monitored during the year but generally no accounting entries are made to dispense with the amount until the end of the year. In most cases, an accounting entry is made at year end to close the manufacturing overhead incurred, and manufacturing overhead is applied to cost of goods sold. Because the amount of under or over applied overhead is generally relatively small, and most product cost ends up in cost of goods sold by year end, closing the overhead accounts to cost of goods sold is adequate for most companies.

    Assume that the year end balances in the manufacturing overhead incurred and manufacturing overhead applied accounts are as follows:

**Manufacturing
Overhead
Incurred**

| | |
|---|---|
| 1,091,000 | |

**Manufacturing
Overhead
Applied**

| | |
|---|---|
| | 1,072,000 |

In this case, manufacturing overhead is $19,000 under applied. The following entry closes the manufacturing overhead accounts to cost of goods sold.

| | | |
|---|---|---|
| Cost of goods sold | 1,091,000 | |
|   Manufacturing overhead incurred | | 1,091,000 |
| To close manufacturing overhead incurred to | | |
| cost of goods sold. | | |
| | | |
| Manufacturing overhead applied | 1,072,000 | |
|   Cost of goods sold | | 1,072,000 |
| To close manufacturing overhead applied to cost | | |
| of goods sold. | | |

7. The next entry is to transfer of the cost of completed products to finished goods when process costing is used.

    You have already learned to record direct material, direct labor, and manufacturing overhead in the work-in-process account. Those entries are basically the same for job order and process costing. The purpose of the next section is to emphasize the fact that the cost calculated for the units completed in process costing is the same amount transferred from work in process to finished goods.

According to the information presented in the flamingo example, goods costing $5,200 were completed and transferred to finished goods. The entry to record this transaction is as follows:

| | | |
|---|---|---|
| Finished goods inventory | 5,200 | |
|    Work-in-process inventory | | 5,200 |
| To transfer completed goods from production to finished goods. | | |

The above entry is significant in arriving at appropriate ending balances in the inventory accounts. After the $5,200 is transferred to finished goods, the work-in-process account and finished goods have balances of $208 and $5,200, respectively, as shown below.

**Work in Process**

| | |
|---|---|
| 500 | 5,200 |
| 4,908 | |
| 5,408 | 5,208 |
| 208 | |

**Finished Goods**

| | |
|---|---|
| 5,200 | |

## APPENDIX SUMMARY

Work-in-process is debited to record the transfer of direct material to production and the incurrence of direct labor. Manufacturing overhead incurred is debited to record the actual amount of manufacturing overhead cost incurred. To apply manufacturing overhead to production, work-in-process inventory is debited and manufacturing overhead applied is credited. If the amount applied to production exceeds the actual overhead amount, overhead is over applied. If the amount applied to production is less than the actual overhead amount, overhead is under applied. Manufacturers generally make an accounting entry at year end to close the manufacturing overhead incurred and manufacturing overhead applied accounts to cost of goods sold. When products are completed, finished goods is debited and work in process is credited for the cost of those products.

## KEY TERMS

activity-based costing   M-72
allocation base   M-71
cost driver   M-73
cost pool   M-71
equivalent units   M-91
job cost sheet   M-78
job order costing   M-76
labor time ticket   M-83
manufacturing overhead
  allocation   M-71

materials requisition   M-81
normal cost system   M-87
predetermined overhead
  application rate   M-87
process costing   M-76
purchase order   M-79
purchase requisition   M-79
purchasing department   M-79
receiving report   M-80

# REVIEW THE FACTS

**A.** Describe a manufacturing overhead cost pool.

**B.** What are the two stages of assigning manufacturing overhead cost to products?

**C.** List three traditional manufacturing overhead allocation bases.

**D.** What is the significant weakness of a plant-wide allocation base?

**E.** What is activity-based costing?

**F.** In what two ways does activity-based costing improve upon the traditional approach to manufacturing overhead allocation?

**G.** Describe a cost driver.

**H.** What are the general characteristics of products for which process costing would be used?

**I.** What are the general characteristics of products for which job order costing would be used?

**J.** What is the purpose of a job cost sheet?

**K.** Which form is sent to a vendor to order materials and supplies?

**L.** What is the purpose of a receiving report?

**M.** What is the difference between a purchase requisition and a materials requisition?

**N.** Which type of form is used to track the amount of labor associated with various jobs?

**O.** List the four key items of information provided by process costing.

**P.** Define the term *equivalent units* as used in process costing.

# APPLY WHAT YOU HAVE LEARNED

## LO 1: Compare Process Costing with Job Order Costing

**3–7.** Following is a list of several products.

1. __J__ Commercial jetliners
2. __P__ Hair spray
3. __J__ Oil tankers
4. __P__ Breakfast cereal
5. __J__ Office buildings
6. __P__ Aspirin
7. __P__ Dog food
8. __P__ Advertising posters
9. __J__ Custom kitchen cabinets
10. __P__ Gasoline

**REQUIRED:**
For each item, indicate whether job order costing (J) or process costing (P) would be the preferred costing method.

## LO 4: Calculate and Describe How Overhead Costs Are Allocated to Products

**3–8.** The Jessie Lynne Company manufactures playground equipment. For 2000, budgeted manufacturing overhead is $240,000. Budgeted direct labor is 30,000 hours at a cost of $384,000. Budgeted machine hours are 12,500.

## REQUIRED:

**a.** When production begins on January 1, 2000, would it be a good idea for the managers to determine the cost of the manufacturing overhead associated with each swing set produced, or should managers wait for this information until actual overhead cost amounts are available at the end of the year?

**b.** If we assume that managers need to know the manufacturing overhead cost associated with the playground equipment as soon as the equipment is manufactured, would *actual* overhead cost information be available when the first few swing sets are made in January?

**c.** If we assume managers need to know the overhead cost associated with the playground equipment as soon as the equipment is made, and it is too early in the year to have actual overhead cost information, what overhead cost information must be used to allocate overhead cost to playground equipment produced by the company?

**d.** Determine the overhead application rates based on the following:
   **(1)** Direct labor hours
   **(2)** Direct labor cost
   **(3)** Machine hours

**e.** If you were asked to help select an allocation base for the Jessie Lynne Company, which of the three used in (d) would you recommend? Which would you not recommend? Why?

## LO 4: Calculate Traditional Overhead Allocation

**3–9.** The Griswald Company allocates manufacturing overhead to production based on direct labor hours. The following information is available for Griswald:

| | |
|---|---:|
| Estimated manufacturing overhead | $403,200 |
| Actual manufacturing overhead | $378,000 |
| Estimated direct labor hours | 21,000 |
| Actual direct labor hours | 20,000 |

## REQUIRED:

**a.** Compute Griswald's overhead application rate.

**b.** Assuming that Griswald's overhead application rate is $19, calculate the amount of overhead that should be allocated to production.

**c.** Appendix: Prepare the following journal entries:
   **(1)** Record the actual manufacturing overhead. (Use "various accounts" for the credit side of the entry.)
   **(2)** Assuming that Griswald's overhead application rate is $19, record the overhead allocated to production.
   **(3)** Close the over or under application of overhead.

## LO 4: Calculate Traditional Overhead Allocation

**3–10.** The Anderson Company allocates manufacturing overhead to production based on machine hours. The following information is available for Anderson:

| | |
|---|---:|
| Estimated manufacturing overhead | $2,000,000 |
| Actual manufacturing overhead | $2,100,000 |
| Estimated machine hours | 125,000 |
| Actual machine hours | 140,000 |

**REQUIRED:**

a. Compute Anderson's overhead application rate.

b. Assume that Anderson's overhead application rate is $18. Calculate the amount of overhead that should be allocated to production.

c. Appendix: Prepare the following journal entries:

(1) Record the actual manufacturing overhead. (Use "various accounts" for the credit side of the entry.)

(2) Assuming that Anderson's overhead application rate is $18, record the overhead allocated to production.

(3) Close the over or under application of overhead.

## LO 4: Calculate Traditional and ABC Overhead Allocation

**3–11.** The president of Simple Products, Inc. is attending a management seminar and has just heard about activity-based costing. He wonders whether it would help his company.

Simple Products, Inc. uses common machinery to manufacture two simple products. Each year, there are two production runs for each product requiring similar setup effort. Manufacturing overhead includes setup cost of $50,400 per year. Total overhead for the company including the setup cost is $198,000 annually and direct labor hours are expected to total 18,000 for the year.

The following information is available for products A and B.

|                               | Product A | Product B |
|-------------------------------|-----------|-----------|
| Units produced                | 1,000     | 8,000     |
| Direct material cost per unit | $14       | $14       |
| Direct labor cost per unit    | $24       | $24       |
| Machine hours per unit        | 1         | 1         |
| Direct labor hours per unit   | 2         | 2         |

**REQUIRED:**

a. Calculate the cost per unit for each product using traditional overhead allocation.

b. Calculate the cost per unit for each product using activity-based costing.

c. Do you believe activity-based costing would benefit Simple Products, Inc.? Explain your answer.

## LO 4: Calculate Traditional and ABC Overhead Allocation

**3–12.** The president of Complex Products, Inc. is attending a management seminar and has just heard about activity-based costing. She wonders whether it would help her company.

Complex Products, Inc. uses common machinery to manufacture two complex products. Each year, there are two production runs for each product requiring similar setup effort. Manufacturing overhead includes setup cost totaling $52,000. To maintain a competitive edge, these products are updated periodically to conform to the latest technological advancements. These engineering changes are considered part of manufacturing overhead and cost $26,000 per year. Total overhead for the company including the cost of setup and engineering changes is $175,000 per year. Direct labor hours total 7,000 for the year.

The following information is available for products C and D.

|  | Product C | Product D |
|---|---|---|
| Units produced | 1,000 | 1,000 |
| Direct material cost per unit | $24 | $24 |
| Direct labor cost per unit | $36 | $48 |
| Machine hours per unit | 6 | 8 |
| Direct labor hours | 3 | 4 |
| Engineering changes per year | 6 | 2 |

## REQUIRED:

a. Calculate the cost per unit for each product using traditional overhead allocation.

b. Calculate the cost per unit for each product using activity-based costing.

c. Do you believe activity-based costing would benefit Complex Products, Inc.? Explain your answer.

## LO 4: Calculate Traditional and ABC Overhead Allocation

**3–13.** The following estimates are available for Violette Manufacturing for 2000.

### VIOLETTE MANUFACTURING
### Estimated Manufacturing Overhead
### For the Year Ended December 31, 2000

| | |
|---|---|
| Materials handling cost | $ 50,000 |
| Product engineering | 110,000 |
| Production machine setup | 200,000 |
| Production machine depreciation | 450,000 |
| Quality testing | 100,000 |
| Other overhead cost | 250,000 |
| Total manufacturing overhead | $1,160,000 |

### VIOLETTE MANUFACTURING
### Estimated Overhead Activities
### For the Year Ended December 31, 2000

| | |
|---|---|
| Number of material movements | 200,000 |
| Number of product engineering hours | 4,400 |
| Number of machine setups | 100 |
| Number of machine hours | 18,000 |
| Number of tests performed | 125,000 |
| Number of direct labor hours | 25,000 |

The following information is available for production runs of two products, the FP111 and the FP222:

|  | FP111 | FP222 |
|---|---|---|
| Selling price | $ 23 | $ 26 |
| Number of units produced | 5000 | 500 |
| Direct material cost | $60,000 | $6,000 |
| Direct labor cost | $14,400 | $1,440 |
| Number of material movements | 10,000 | 1,000 |
| Number of product engineering hours | 100 | 100 |
| Number of machine setups | 1 | 1 |
| Number of machine hours | 200 | 20 |
| Number of tests performed | 1,250 | 125 |
| Number of direct labor hours | 800 | 80 |

Violette Manufacturing uses a traditional overhead allocation system. Manufacturing overhead is allocated based on direct labor hours.

Violette Manufacturing's sales manager has submitted a proposal that would shift the marketing focus to low-volume products such as the FP222. The proposal is prompted by the higher markups that can be charged for these products without customer complaint. The company president is concerned that the company's cost per unit may be sending the wrong message. He recently learned of activity-based costing and wonders if it might help.

Assume that you are part of a group that has been assigned to review the situation.

**REQUIRED:**

a. Determine the per unit cost for FP111 and FP222 using direct labor hours as the allocation base for all manufacturing overhead cost.
b. Determine the per unit cost for FP111 and FP222 using activity-based costing to allocate manufacturing overhead cost. (Note: Allocate other overhead cost based on direct labor hours.)
c. Discuss the marketing manager's proposal in light of your findings. Discuss what would happen if the marketing manager's sales strategy was adopted.

## LO 4: Calculate Traditional and ABC Overhead Allocation

**3–14.** The following estimates are available for George Manufacturing for 2000.

**GEORGE MANUFACTURING**
**Estimated Manufacturing Overhead**
**For the Year Ended December 31, 2000**

| | |
|---|---|
| Production machine setup | $ 75,000 *750* |
| Production machine depreciation | 240,000 *75* |
| Quality testing | 25,000 *.5* |
| Other overhead cost | 150,000 *9.38* |
| Total manufacturing overhead | $490,000 |

**GEORGE MANUFACTURING**
**Estimated Overhead Activities**
**For the Year Ended December 31, 2000**

| | |
|---|---|
| Number of machine setups | 100 |
| Number of machine hours | 3,200 |
| Number of tests performed | 50,000 |
| Number of direct labor hours | 16,000 |

The following information is available for production of two products, the AA1 and the BB2:

| | AA1 | BB2 |
|---|---|---|
| Selling price | $ 2.40 | $3.25 |
| Number of units produced | 10,000 | 500 |
| Direct material cost | $ 5,000 | $ 250 |
| Direct labor cost | $ 6,400 | $ 320 |
| Number of machine setups | 1 | 1 |
| Number of machine hours | 100 | 5 |
| Number of tests performed | 100 | 50 |
| Number of direct labor hours | 400 | 20 |

George Manufacturing uses a traditional overhead allocation system. Manufacturing overhead is allocated based on direct labor hours. George Manufacturing's sales manager has submitted a proposal that would shift the marketing focus to low-volume products such as the BB2. The proposal is prompted by the higher markups and lack of competition, even at high selling prices.

The company president is concerned that the company's cost per unit may be sending the wrong message. He recently learned of activity-based costing and wonders if it might help.

Assume that you are a member of a work team that has been assigned to review the situation.

**REQUIRED:**
a. Determine the per unit cost for AA1 and BB2 using direct labor hours as the allocation base for all manufacturing overhead cost.
b. Determine the per unit cost for AA1 and BB2 using activity-based costing to allocate manufacturing overhead cost. (Note: Allocate other overhead cost based on direct labor hours.)
c. Discuss the marketing manager's proposal in light of your findings. Discuss what would happen if the marketing manager's sales strategy was adopted.

## LO 4: Calculate Traditional Overhead Allocation

**3–15.** The Nunez Company allocates manufacturing overhead to production based on cost of direct labor. The following information is available for Nunez:

| | |
|---|---|
| Estimated manufacturing overhead | $3,500,000 |
| Actual manufacturing overhead | 3,485,000 |
| Estimated cost of direct labor | 1,750,000 |
| Actual cost of direct labor | 1,700,000 |

**REQUIRED:**
a. Compute the overhead application rate for the Nunez Company.
b. Assume that the overhead application rate for Nunez is 190%. Calculate the amount of overhead that should be allocated to production.

## LO 4 & 5: Calculate Traditional Overhead Allocation and Determine the Cost of Products Using Job Order Costing

**3–16.** LHE Custom Truck Bodies makes aluminum truck bodies for medium and large trucks. The estimated manufacturing overhead for 2001 is $40,000, and the estimated direct labor cost is $60,000. Manufacturing overhead is applied to production based on direct labor cost.

The following information pertains to truck bodies manufactured during February 2001.

**Beginning work-in-process inventory:**

| | | |
|---|---|---|
| Job 101 | Direct material | $1,000 |
| | Direct labor | 2,000 |
| Job 102 | Direct material | 750 |
| | Direct labor | 1,200 |

**Cost for current month:**

| | | |
|---|---|---|
| Direct material | Job 101 | $ 500 |
| | Job 102 | 1,100 |
| | Job 103 | 2,300 |

| Direct labor | Job 101 | $ 800 |
| | Job 102 | 1,300 |
| | Job 103 | 3,200 |

Job 101 was completed and sold in February and job 102 was completed, but has not been sold. Job 103 remains in production.

**REQUIRED:**

a. What is the cost of LHE's beginning work-in-process inventory for February 2001?

b. What is the cost of LHE's ending work-in-process inventory for February 2001?

c. (1) What is the cost of job 101?

(2) How would job 101 appear on LHE's financial statements?

d. (1) What is the cost of job 102?

(2) How would job 102 appear on LHE's financial statements?

## LO 4 & 5: Calculate Traditional Overhead Allocation and Determine the Cost of Products Using Job Order Costing

**3–17.** Williams Company began operations in June 2001. During that month, two jobs were started. The following costs were incurred:

| | Job 101 | Job 202 |
|---|---|---|
| Direct material | $3,000 | $4,000 |
| Direct labor | 6,000 | 7,000 |

Factory overhead is applied at 60% of direct labor cost. During the month, job 101 was completed but not sold. Job 202 is yet to be completed.

**REQUIRED:**

a. Calculate the cost of the ending work-in-process inventory as of June 30, 2001.

b. Calculate the cost of the finished goods inventory as of June 30, 2001.

## LO 4 & 5: Calculate Traditional Overhead Allocation and Determine the Cost of Products Using Job Order Costing

**3–18.** Masa Manufacturing began operations in August 2001. During that month, two jobs were started. The following costs were incurred:

| | Job 1 | Job 2 |
|---|---|---|
| Direct material | $5,400 | $8,900 |
| Direct labor | 6,500 | 9,000 |

Factory overhead is applied at 50% of direct labor cost. During the month, job 1 was completed but not sold. Job 2 has not been completed.

**REQUIRED:**

a. Calculate the cost of the ending work-in-process inventory as of August 31, 2001.

b. Calculate the cost of the finished goods inventory as of August 31, 2001.

## LO 4 & 5: Calculate Traditional Overhead Allocation and Determine the Cost of Products Using Job Order Costing

**3–19.** Northern Manufacturing began operations in September 2001. During that month, two jobs were started. The following costs were incurred:

|  | Job A | Job B |
|---|---|---|
| Direct material | $2,500 | $5,000 |
| Direct labor | 7,000 | 9,500 |

Factory overhead is applied at 120% of direct labor cost. During the month, job A was completed but not sold. Job B has not been completed.

**REQUIRED:**

a. Calculate the cost of the ending work-in-process inventory as of September 30, 2001.
b. Calculate the cost of the finished goods inventory as of September 30, 2001.
c. Appendix: Prepare the following journal entries:
   (1) Record direct materials for each job.
   (2) Record direct labor for each job.
   (3) Record the allocation of manufacturing overhead for each job.
   (4) Record the transfer to finished goods of job A.

## LO 4 & 5:  Calculate Traditional Overhead Allocation and Determine the Cost of Products Using Job Order Costing

**3–20.** Southern Manufacturing began two jobs during the month of January 2001. There was no beginning inventory. The following costs were incurred:

|  | Job A | Job B |
|---|---|---|
| Direct material | $2,000 | $3,000 |
| Direct labor | 4,000 | 5,000 |

Southern's estimated manufacturing overhead for 2001 is $117,000, and the estimated direct labor cost is $90,000. Southern applies overhead to production based on direct labor cost. During the month, job A was completed but not sold. Job B has not been completed.

**REQUIRED:**

a. Calculate the cost of the ending work-in-process inventory as of January 31, 2001.
b. Calculate the cost of the finished goods inventory as of January 31, 2001.
c. Appendix: Prepare the following journal entries:
   (1) Record direct materials for each job.
   (2) Record direct labor for each job.
   (3) Record the allocation of manufacturing overhead for each job.
   (4) Record the transfer to finished goods of job A.

## LO 4 & 5:  Calculate Traditional Overhead Allocation and Determine the Cost of Products Using Job Order Costing

**3–21.** Slater Industries makes custom optical glass equipment. The company began two jobs during January 2001. There was no beginning inventory. The following information is available:

|  | Job 7 | Job 8 |
|---|---|---|
| Direct material | $7,250 | $3,640 |
| Direct labor | $4,251 | $5,125 |
| Direct labor hours | 212 | 234 |

Slater's estimated manufacturing overhead for 2001 is $110,400, and the company estimates that labor force will work 9,200 direct labor hours. Slater applies overhead to production based on direct labor hours.

**REQUIRED:**
a. Calculate the cost of job 7.
b. Calculate the cost of job 8.

## LO 4 & 5: Calculate Traditional Overhead Allocation and Determine the Cost of Products Using Job Order Costing

**3-22.** Willig-Davis Cleaning Equipment began two jobs during March 2001. There was no beginning inventory. The following information is available:

| | Job 10 | Job 15 |
|---|---|---|
| Direct material | $14,350 | $23,530 |
| Direct labor | $ 7,231 | $15,125 |
| Machine hours | 124 | 236 |

The company estimated manufacturing overhead for 2001 is $307,200, and the company estimates that 4,800 machine hours will be used during the year. Willig-Davis applies overhead to production based on machine hours.

**REQUIRED:**
a. Calculate the cost of job 10.
b. Calculate the cost of job 15.

## LO 5: Determine the Cost of Products Using Job Order Costing

**3-23.** Speace Automotive Security converts regular automobiles to armored cars. Each car is custom made to conform to the needs of each individual customer. Modifications may be as minor as the addition of bullet-resistant windows or as extravagant as full armor. The following information is presented for March 2001.

**Beginning work-in-process inventory:**

| Job 2727 | Direct material | $24,000 |
|---|---|---|
| | Direct labor | 9,000 |
| | Manufacturing overhead | 5,400 |

**Cost for current month:**

| | Direct Material | Direct Labor | Manufacturing Overhead |
|---|---|---|---|
| Job 2727 | $ 8,000 | $4,000 | $2,400 |
| Job 2728 | 11,000 | 6,000 | 3,600 |

Job 2727 was completed and sold in March, and job 2728 was not complete as of March 31.

**REQUIRED:**
a. What is the cost of the beginning work-in-process inventory for March 2001?
b. What is the cost of the ending work-in-process inventory for March 2001?
c. (1) What is the cost of job 2727?
   (2) How would job 2727 appear on the financial statements?

## LO 4 & 5: Calculate Traditional Overhead Allocation and Determine the Cost of Products Using Job Order Costing

**3-24.** Crespin Brothers Equipment Company began two jobs during March 2001. At the beginning of March, job 303 was the only job in work-in-process inventory. There was no finished goods inventory. The cost in beginning work-in-process inventory for job 303 consisted of $5,450 in direct material cost, $8,825 in direct labor cost, and manufacturing overhead cost of $7,354. The following information is available for costs added during March:

| | Job 303 | Job 304 | Job 305 |
|---|---|---|---|
| Direct material | $ 4,350 | $12,650 | $11,300 |
| Direct labor | $ 8,400 | $ 8,125 | $ 6,750 |
| Direct labor hours | 560 | 520 | 480 |

Job 303 was completed and sold during March. Job 304 was completed but has yet to be sold, and job 305 remains in production.

Crespin's estimated manufacturing overhead for 2001 is $225,000, and the company estimates that the labor force will work 18,000 hours during the year. Crespin applies overhead to production based on direct labor hours.

**REQUIRED:**

a. Calculate the cost of the ending work-in-process inventory as of March 31, 2001.

b. Calculate the cost of the finished goods inventory as of March 31, 2001.

c. Calculate the cost of goods sold for March.

## LO 4 & 5: Calculate Traditional Overhead Allocation and Determine the Cost of Products Using Job Order Costing

**3–25.** Greenberg and Son Manufacturing began two jobs during July 2001. At the beginning of July, job 227 was the only job in work-in-process inventory. There was no finished goods inventory. The cost in beginning work-in-process inventory for job 227 consisted of $1,500 in direct material cost, $2,000 in direct labor cost, and manufacturing overhead cost of $4,500. Total manufacturing overhead for the month was $16,054. The following information is available for costs added during July:

| | Job 227 | Job 228 | Job 229 |
|---|---|---|---|
| Direct material | $ 935 | $ 2,850 | $ 1,300 |
| Direct labor | $ 1,840 | $ 3,225 | $ 1,975 |
| Direct labor hours | 184 | 310 | 204 |

Job 227 was completed and sold during July. Job 228 was completed but has yet to be sold, and job 229 remains in production.

Greenberg's estimated manufacturing overhead for 2001 is $180,000, and the company estimates that the labor force will work 8,000 hours during the year. Greenberg applies overhead to production based on direct labor hours.

**REQUIRED:**

a. Calculate the cost of the ending work-in-process inventory as of July 31, 2001.

b. Calculate the cost of the finished goods inventory as of July 31, 2001.

c. Calculate the cost of goods sold for July.

## LO 4 & 5: Calculate Traditional Overhead Allocation and Determine the Cost of Products Using Job Order Costing

**3–26.** Baillie Manufacturing began two jobs during May 2001. At the beginning of May, job 411 was the only job in work-in-process inventory. There was no finished goods inventory. The cost in beginning work-in-process inventory for job 411 consisted of $4,000 in direct material cost, $6,000 in direct labor cost, and manufacturing overhead cost of $8,000. Total manufacturing overhead for the month was $22,050. The following information is available for costs added during May:

| | Job 411 | Job 412 | Job 413 |
|---|---|---|---|
| Direct material | $ 2,000 | $ 4,000 | $ 6,000 |
| Direct labor | $ 2,500 | $ 6,500 | $ 8,500 |
| Direct labor hours | 225 | 570 | 780 |

Job 411 was completed and sold during May. Job 412 was completed but has yet to be sold, and job 413 remains in production.

Baillie's estimated manufacturing overhead for 2001 is $277,875, and the company estimates that the labor force will work 19,500 hours during the year. Baillie applies overhead to production based on direct labor hours.

### REQUIRED:

a. Calculate the cost of the ending work-in-process inventory as of May 31, 2001.
b. Calculate the cost of the finished goods inventory as of May 31, 2001.
c. Calculate the cost of goods sold for May.

## LO 4 & 5: Calculate Traditional and ABC Overhead Allocation and Determine the Cost of Products Using Job Order Costing

**3–27.** Salter Equipment Company began the following jobs during March 2001:

| | Job 303 | Job 304 |
|---|---|---|
| Direct material | $2,000 | $2,000 |
| Direct labor | $3,120 | $6,240 |
| Direct labor hours | 260 | 520 |
| Machine hours machine A | 5 | 30 |
| Machine hours machine B | 20 | 0 |
| Machine setups | 2 | 1 |
| Engineering changes | 22 | 9 |

**Estimated overhead cost for 2001:**

| | |
|---|---|
| Depreciation machine A | $ 100,000 |
| Depreciation machine B | 500,000 |
| Machine setup cost | 50,000 |
| Engineering cost | 200,000 |
| Other overhead cost | 150,000 |
| Total | $1,000,000 |

**Estimated activities for 2001:**

| | |
|---|---|
| Machine hours machine A | 1,000 |
| Machine hours machine B | 1,000 |
| Number of setups | 80 |
| Number of engineering changes | 800 |
| Number of direct labor hours | 20,000 |

### REQUIRED:

a. Calculate the cost of each job using direct labor hours as the allocation base for all overhead.
b. Calculate the cost of each job using activity-based costing. Use direct labor hours as the allocation base for "other overhead cost."

## LO 4 & 5: Calculate Traditional and ABC Overhead Allocation and Determine the Cost of Products Using Job Order Costing

**3–28.** Duskin Equipment Company began the following jobs during August 2001:

|  | Job 500 | Job 600 |
|---|---|---|
| Direct material | $1,000 | $1,000 |
| Direct labor | $1,800 | $3,000 |
| Direct labor hours | 120 | 200 |
| Machine hours machine A | 10 | 50 |
| Machine hours machine B | 50 | 0 |
| Machine setups | 2 | 1 |
| Material movements | 200 | 75 |

**Estimated overhead cost for 2001:**

| | |
|---|---|
| Depreciation machine A | $ 50,000 |
| Depreciation machine B | 300,000 |
| Machine setup cost | 75,000 |
| Material handling cost | 100,000 |
| Other overhead cost | 80,000 |
| Total | $605,000 |

**Estimated activities for 2001:**

| | |
|---|---|
| Machine hours machine A | 500 |
| Machine hours machine B | 500 |
| Number of setups | 75 |
| Number of material movements | 5,000 |
| Number of direct labor hours | 10,000 |

### REQUIRED:

a. Calculate the cost of each job using direct labor hours as the allocation base for all overhead.

b. Calculate the cost of each job using activity-based costing. Use direct labor hours as the allocation base for "other overhead cost."

## LO 4 & 5: Calculate Traditional and ABC Overhead Allocation and Determine the Cost of Products Using Job Order Costing

**3–29.** Vazquez Manufacturing Company began the following jobs during July 2001:

|  | Job 901 | Job 922 |
|---|---|---|
| Direct material | $3,000 | $3,000 |
| Direct labor | $1,800 | $3,000 |
| Direct labor hours | 250 | 100 |
| Machine hours machine A | 20 | 12 |
| Machine hours machine B | 0 | 8 |
| Machine setups | 1 | 2 |
| Material movements | 90 | 300 |

**Estimated overhead cost for 2001:**

| | |
|---|---|
| Depreciation machine A | $ 150,000 |
| Depreciation machine B | 600,000 |
| Machine setup cost | 175,000 |
| Material handling cost | 150,000 |
| Other overhead cost | 180,000 |
| Total | $1,255,000 |

**Estimated activities for 2001:**

| | |
|---|---|
| Machine hours machine A | 700 |
| Machine hours machine B | 700 |
| Number of setups | 100 |
| Number of material movements | 5,000 |
| Number of direct labor hours | 10,000 |

### REQUIRED:

a. Calculate the cost of each job using direct labor hours as the allocation base for all overhead.
b. Calculate the cost of each job using activity-based costing. Use direct labor hours as the allocation base for "other overhead cost."

## LO 6: Determine the Cost of Products Using Process Costing—No Beginning or Ending Inventory

**3–30.** Daysi's Specialty Food Company makes canned chili. The following cost information is available for March 2001:

| | |
|---|---|
| Units produced | 25,000 units |
| Direct material cost | $8,000 |
| Direct labor cost | $3,000 |
| Manufacturing overhead costs | $2,000 |

There were no beginning or ending inventories.

### REQUIRED:

a. What is the total production cost for Daysi's Specialty Food Company?
b. What is the cost per unit?
c. If the chili sold for $0.82 per can, what is the gross profit for the company?

## LO 6: Determine the Cost of Products Using Process Costing—With Beginning Inventory

**3–31.** Dunn Electronic Manufacturing Company makes low-cost calculators. The following information is available for January 2001:

| | Units | Percent Complete | Cost |
|---|---|---|---|
| Beginning work-in-process inventory | 700 | 40% | $224 |
| Ending work-in-process inventory | 900 | 60% | ? |
| Units completed | 12,000 | calculators | |

Manufacturing cost for January 2001 is $10,659.

### REQUIRED:

a. What is the number of equivalent units of production for January 2001?
b. What is the cost per equivalent unit?
c. What is the cost of the 900 calculators in the ending work-in-process inventory?
d. What is the cost of the calculators that were completed during January?
e. If 11,000 of the completed calculators were sold for $1.12 each, what is the gross profit for the Dunn Electronic Manufacturing Company?
f. (1) Do you think there is a benefit for Dunn's managers to know the cost of the calculators that are in ending work-in-process inventory? Explain.
  (2) Where would the cost of the ending inventory appear on the financial statements?

(3) Do you think there is a benefit for Dunn's managers to know the cost of the calculators completed during January? Explain.

(4) Where would the cost of the 11,000 sold calculators be found on the financial statements?

(5) Where would the cost of the calculators that were completed, but not yet sold be found on the financial statements?

## LO 6: Determine the Cost of Products Using Process Costing—With Beginning Inventory

**3–32.** The following information is for Suzanne's Volleyball Manufacturing Company for February 2001:

|  | Units | Percent Complete | Cost |
|---|---|---|---|
| Beginning work-in-process inventory | 2,400 | 80% | $2,304 |
| Ending work-in-process inventory | 3,200 | 50% | |

64,000 volleyballs were completed in February. Manufacturing cost for February is $86,256.

### REQUIRED:

a. What is the number of equivalent units of production for February?

b. What is the cost per equivalent unit for February?

c. What is the cost of the 3,200 volleyballs in the ending work-in-process inventory for February?

d. What is the cost of the volleyballs that were completed during February?

e. If 50,000 of the completed volleyballs were sold for $1.80 each, what is the gross profit for Suzanne's Volleyball Manufacturing Company?

## LO 6: Determine the Cost of Products Using Process Costing—No Beginning Inventory

**3–33.** Valentine's Manufacturing makes candy. During 2001, the company's first year of operations, the company completed 200,000 boxes of candy and incurred direct material cost of $160,800, direct labor cost of $40,200, and manufacturing overhead cost of $60,300. There were 2,000 boxes of candy that were 50% in the production process at the end of the year.

### REQUIRED:

a. What is the number of equivalent units of production for 2001?

b. What is the cost per equivalent unit of production for 2001?

c. What is the cost of the 2001 ending work-in-process inventory?

d. What is the cost of the boxes of candy that were completed in 2001?

## LO 6: Determine the Number of Equivalent Units

**3–34.** The following information relates to the Collins Company for 2001:

|  | Units | Percent Complete |
|---|---|---|
| Work in process at January 1 | 10,000 | 75% |
| Units started into production | 145,000 | |
| Units completed | 138,000 | |
| Work in process at December 31 | 17,000 | 50% |

**REQUIRED:**
Calculate the number of equivalent units of production.

## LO 6: Determine the Number of Equivalent Units

**3–35.** The following information relates to the Munter Company for June 2001:

| | Units | Percent Complete |
|---|---|---|
| Work-in-process at June 1 | 115,000 | 60% |
| Units started into production | 1,800,000 | |
| Units completed | 1,850,000 | |
| Work-in-process at June 30 | 65,000 | 30% |

**REQUIRED:**
Calculate the number of equivalent units of production.

## LO 6: Determine the Number of Equivalent Units

**3–36.** The following information relates to the Holder Company for July 2001:

| | Units | Percent Complete |
|---|---|---|
| Work-in-process at July 1 | 5,000 | 90% |
| Units started into production | 70,000 | |
| Units completed | 72,000 | |
| Work-in-process at July 31 | 3,000 | 20% |

**REQUIRED:**
Calculate the number of equivalent units of production.

## LO 6: Determine the Number of Equivalent Units with Missing Information

**3–37.** The following information relates to the Mayber Company for May 2001:

| | Units | Percent Complete |
|---|---|---|
| Work-in-process at May 1 | 5,000 | 45% |
| Units started into production | 77,000 | |
| Work-in-process at May 31 | 12,000 | 35% |

**REQUIRED:**
a. Assuming no units of production were lost or spoiled, how many units were completed during May?
b. Calculate the number of equivalent units of production.

## LO 6: Determine the Number of Equivalent Units with Missing Information

**3–38.** The following information relates to the Strayform Company for August 2001:

|  | Units | Percent Complete |
|---|---|---|
| Work-in-process at August 1 | 7,000 | 95% |
| Units started into production | 87,000 | |
| Work-in-process at August 31 | 6,500 | 25% |

**REQUIRED:**

a. Assuming no units of production were lost or spoiled, how many units were completed during August?

b. Calculate the number of equivalent units of production.

## LO 6: Determine the Number of Equivalent Units with Missing Information

**3–39.** The following information relates to the Golden Company for February 2001:

|  | Units | Percent Complete |
|---|---|---|
| Work-in-process at February 1 | 22,500 | 80% |
| Units started into production | 185,000 | |
| Work-in-process at February 28 | 14,500 | 25% |

**REQUIRED:**

a. Assuming no units of production were lost or spoiled, how many units were completed during February?

b. Calculate the number of equivalent units of production.

## LO 6: Determine the Cost of Products Using Process Costing— With Beginning Inventory

**3–40.** The following information relates to the Smithfield Company for July 2001:

|  | Units | Percent Complete |
|---|---|---|
| Work-in-process at July 1 | 19,500 | 50% |
| Units started into production | 220,000 | |
| Units completed in July | 231,000 | |
| Work-in-process at July 31 | 8,500 | 40% |
| Cost of the beginning work in process | $ 7,020 | |
| Current month's production cost | 166,436 | |

**REQUIRED:**

a. Calculate the number of equivalent units of production.

b. Calculate the cost per equivalent unit of production.

c. Calculate the cost of the ending work-in-process inventory.

d. Calculate the cost of the completed units.

## LO 6: Determine the Cost of Products Using Process Costing— With Beginning Inventory

**3–41.** The following information relates to the Richard Renick Company for 2001:

|  | Units | Percent Complete |
|---|---|---|
| Work-in-process at January 1 | 42,000 | 50% |
| Units started into production | 420,000 | |
| Units completed in 2001 | 390,000 | |
| Work-in-process at December 31 | 72,000 | 20% |
| Cost of the beginning work in process | | $ 14,280 |
| Current year's production cost | | 248,580 |

**REQUIRED:**
a. Calculate the number of equivalent units of production.
b. Calculate the cost per equivalent unit of production.
c. Calculate the cost of the ending work-in-process inventory.
d. Calculate the cost of the completed units.

## LO 6: Determine the Cost of Products Using Process Costing— With Beginning Inventory

**3–42.** The following information relates to the Robert Lewis Manufacturing Company for 2001:

|  | Units | Percent Complete |
|---|---|---|
| Work-in-process at January 1 | 120,000 | 25% |
| Units started into production | 1,300,000 | |
| Units completed in 2001 | 1,290,000 | |
| Work-in-process at December 31 | 130,000 | 70% |
| Cost of the beginning work in process | | $ 40,200 |
| Current year's production cost | | 1,768,910 |

**REQUIRED:**
a. Calculate the number of equivalent units of production.
b. Calculate the cost per equivalent unit of production.
c. Calculate the cost of the ending work-in-process inventory.
d. Calculate the cost of the completed units.

## LO 6: Determine the Cost of Products Using Process Costing— With Beginning Inventory

**3–43.** The cost of the work-in-process inventory at January 1 for Ralph Robinson Manufacturing was $7,420, consisting of 10,000 units that were 35% complete. An additional 130,000 units were started into production during the year. The cost of material, labor, and overhead added during the year amounted to $280,680. The units completed and transferred to finished goods totaled 125,000. The ending work-in-process inventory consisted of 15,000 units which were 60% complete.

**REQUIRED:**
a. Calculate the number of equivalent units of production.
b. Calculate the cost per equivalent unit of production.
c. Calculate the cost of the ending work-in-process inventory.
d. Calculate the cost of the completed units.

## LO 6: Determine the Cost of Products Using Process Costing— With Beginning Inventory

**3–44.** The cost of the work-in-process inventory at January 1 for Jim Mays Manufacturing was $61,875, consisting of 11,000 units that were 45% complete. An additional 150,000 units were started into production during the year. The cost of material, labor, and overhead added during the year amounted to $1,872,855. The units completed and transferred to finished goods totaled 145,000. The ending work-in-process inventory consisted of 16,000 units which were 65% complete.

### REQUIRED:
a. Calculate the number of equivalent units of production.
b. Calculate the cost per equivalent unit of production.
c. Calculate the cost of the ending work-in-process inventory.
d. Calculate the cost of the completed units.

## LO 6: Determine the Cost of Products Using Process Costing— With Beginning Inventory

**3–45.** The cost of the work-in-process inventory at January 1 for Hanamura Manufacturing was $119,805, consisting of 122,500 units that were 30% complete. An additional 750,000 units were started into production during the year. The cost of material, labor, and overhead added during the year amounted to $2,627,820. The units completed and transferred to finished goods totaled 790,000. The ending work-in-process inventory consisted of 72,500 units which were 25% complete.

### REQUIRED:
a. Calculate the number of equivalent units of production.
b. Calculate the cost per equivalent unit of production.
c. Calculate the cost of the ending work-in-process inventory.
d. Calculate the cost of the completed units.
e. Appendix: Prepare a journal entry to transfer the cost of completed goods from work in process.

## LO 6: Determine the Cost of Products Using Process Costing— With Beginning Inventory and Missing Information

**3–46.** The following information relates to the Robert Lewis Manufacturing Company for 2001:

|  | Units | Cost |
|---|---|---|
| Work-in-process at January 1 | 18,500 | $ 35,668 |
| Units started into production | 190,000 | |
| Units completed in 2001 | 187,000 | |
| Current production cost | | 1,873,052 |

The beginning work-in-process inventory is 20% complete and the ending work-in-process inventory is 55% complete.

### REQUIRED:
a. Calculate the number of equivalent units of production.
b. Calculate the cost per equivalent unit of production.
c. Calculate the cost of the ending work-in-process inventory.

d. Calculate the cost of the completed units.

e. Appendix: Prepare a journal entry to transfer the cost of completed goods from work in process.

## LO 6: Determine the Cost of Products Using Process Costing—With Beginning Inventory and Missing Information

**3–47.** The following information relates to the Mathias Manufacturing Company for 2001:

|  | Units | Cost |
|---|---|---|
| Work-in-process at January 1 | 77,000 | $ 107,415 |
| Units started into production | 602,500 | |
| Work-in-process at December 31 | 92,000 | |
| Current production cost | | $2,979,922 |

The beginning work-in-process inventory is 30% complete and the ending work-in-process inventory is 80% complete.

### REQUIRED:
a. Calculate the number of equivalent units of production.
b. Calculate the cost per equivalent unit of production.
c. Calculate the cost of the ending work-in-process inventory.
d. Calculate the cost of the completed units.
e. Appendix: Prepare a journal entry to transfer the cost of completed goods from work in process.

## LO 6: Determine the Cost of Products Using Process Costing—With Beginning Inventory and Missing Information

**3–48.** The following information relates to the Heromi Manufacturing Company for 2001:

|  | Units | Cost |
|---|---|---|
| Work-in-process at January 1 | 13,000 | $ 4,368 |
| Units started into production | 83,500 | |
| Work-in-process at December 31 | 7,500 | |
| Current production cost | | $37,262 |

The beginning work-in-process inventory is 70% complete and the ending work-in-process inventory is 20% complete.

### REQUIRED:
a. Calculate the number of equivalent units of production.
b. Calculate the cost per equivalent unit of production.
c. Calculate the cost of the ending work-in-process inventory.
d. Calculate the cost of the completed units.
e. Appendix: Prepare a journal entry to transfer the cost of completed goods from work in process.

# Chapter 4

## Cost Behavior

$L$aura Jorgensen is the newly elected social chairperson of her mountain climbing club. Her first duty is to plan the club's big kickoff party for the upcoming year. Of course funds are limited, so she must plan well and estimate costs carefully.

Laura's first step in estimating the total cost of the party is to identify the individual costs involved. As she begins the planning process, she identifies two major costs:

1. Entertainment—A live band is a must.
2. Food and drinks—Large amounts are essential.

When Laura checks the records of last year's social chairperson, she discovers he spent $3,650 on these two items for last year's party ($525 for entertainment and $3,125 for food and drinks). Assuming the prices for entertainment and food and drinks have remained the same, the club should be able to have this year's party for $3,650. In fact, Laura has money to spare because the spending limit for this year's event is $5,500.

But wait. . . . The mountain climbing club has grown, so about 175 guests are expected to attend this year's party, compared to 125 last year. Laura must estimate the party's cost for 175 guests, not 125. How should she begin?

To determine the total expected cost of the party, Laura needs to know which costs are and which costs are not affected by the number of guests attending. Let us examine Laura's two major costs for the party:

1. Entertainment:     Will the band charge more if more guests attend? No.
2. Food and drinks:     Will the caterer charge more if the number of guests increases? Yes.

How should Laura determine the cost of this year's party when the number of people attending is 175 rather than 125? Clearly, she knows her cost for the item that is unaffected by the activity level (the band), but what about the cost that is affected by a change in activity level (food and drinks)? This chapter will demonstrate how to determine these amounts.

As managers plan for business success, they must know which costs will vary with changes in business activity and which will remain constant. That is, managers must determine cost behavior. **Cost behavior** is the reaction of costs to changes in levels of business activity. ■

**cost behavior**   The reaction of costs to changes in levels of business activity.

## LEARNING OBJECTIVES

*After completing your work on this chapter, you should be able to do the following:*

1. Describe the differences between fixed costs and variable costs.
2. Classify costs by cost behavior.
3. Explain the concept of relevant range and its effect on cost behavior information.
4. Describe the characteristics of a mixed cost and the four basic approaches to separating a mixed cost into its fixed and variable components.
5. Determine the fixed and variable components of a mixed cost using scatter graphs and the high-low method.

# COMMON COST BEHAVIOR PATTERNS

Costs may react in various ways to changes in activity levels, creating many different cost behavior patterns. In this chapter we describe and compare the two most common patterns: fixed and variable.

## Fixed Costs

**fixed cost**   A cost that remains constant in total regardless of the level of activity.

**Fixed costs** are costs that remain constant *in total* regardless of the level of activity. In our chapter-opening example, the entertainment cost is a fixed cost. As the number of guests increases, this cost does not change. The band will cost $525 for the night, regardless of how many guests attend the club's party.

Suppose Laura is interested in determining the fixed cost *per guest*. Would the fixed cost amount change per guest as the number of guests changes? Let us take a look.

|                   | 125 Guests            | 175 Guests            |
| ----------------- | --------------------- | --------------------- |
| Total fixed cost  | $525                  | $525                  |
| Cost per guest    | $525 ÷ 125 = $4.20    | $525 ÷ 175 = $3.00    |

As you can see, the fixed cost *per unit* (in this case, the entertainment cost per guest) changes as the activity level changes. A fixed cost, then, is a cost that remains constant in total, but changes per unit as the activity level changes. Fixed cost per unit decreases as activity increases.

## Discussion Question

**4–1.** Consider the costs involved in operating a fast-food restaurant such as McDonald's. What are three examples of fixed costs?

### Variable Costs

**variable cost** A cost that changes in total proportionately with changes in the level of activity.

**Variable costs** are costs that change *in total* proportionately with changes in the level of activity. As activity increases, total variable cost also increases. In our party example, the variable cost is the catering cost of $25 per guest. We know this because the total cost for food and drinks last year was $3,125 for 125 guests, and $3,125 / 125 = $25. For each additional guest added to the party, the total cost for food and drinks will increase by $25.

If 175 guests attend, the total catering cost is as follows:

$$175 \text{ guests} \times \$25 = \$4,375$$

Variable cost per unit stays the same as activity changes. In our example, the catering cost per guest remains constant. Variable cost is a cost that increases in total, but remains constant per unit as activity increases.

## Discussion Question

**4–2.** Consider the costs involved in operating a fast-food restaurant such as McDonald's. What are three examples of variable costs and the activity or activities that cause them to change?

### Comparison of Cost Behaviors

Cost and activity can be plotted on a graph to yield a visual representation of cost behavior. When doing so, the activity is plotted on the horizontal axis (called the x-axis). The type of cost is plotted on the vertical axis (called the y-axis). You may recall from past math classes that $x$ is the independent variable, and $y$ is the dependent variable, which means that the item depicted on the x-axis (activity) affects the item shown on the y-axis (cost).

A graphical representation of a fixed cost is as follows:

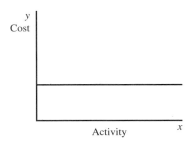

Examples of activities and fixed costs are shown in Exhibit 4–1. Notice that each example in Exhibit 4–1 suggests a cost that remains constant even if the level of the activity changes.

**Exhibit 4–1**
Examples of Fixed
Costs

| Activity | Fixed Cost |
|---|---|
| Production | Rent on the factory building |
| Production | Depreciation on production equipment |
| Sales | Salary of vice president of sales |
| Delivery | Vehicle insurance |

From our party example, we can graph the cost of the band as an example of a fixed cost, as shown in Exhibit 4–2.

**Exhibit 4–2**
Graph of Fixed Cost
Behavior Pattern of
Entertainment at the
Climbing Club Party

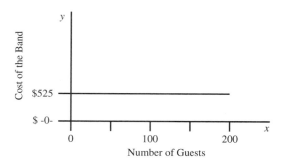

The horizontal line on the graph in Exhibit 4–2 shows that the fixed cost of entertainment stays constant no matter how the number of guests changes.

A graphical representation of variable cost is as follows:

Examples of activities and variable costs are shown in Exhibit 4–3. Notice that for each example in Exhibit 4–3, a change in the level of the activity results in a change in the total cost.

The cost of catering is a variable cost and can be graphically depicted as shown in Exhibit 4–4. The upward sloping line in Exhibit 4–4 shows us that as the number of guests increases from 125 to 175, the catering cost increases proportionately.

**Exhibit 4–3**
Examples of Variable
Costs

| Activity | Variable Cost |
|---|---|
| Production | Direct material |
| Production | Direct labor |
| Sales | Sales commissions |
| Delivery | Gasoline |

**Exhibit 4–4**
Graph of Variable Cost
Behavior Pattern for
Catering Cost at the
Climbing Club Party

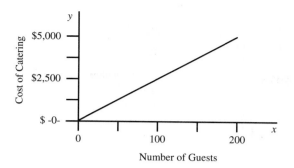

# Discussion Question

**4–3.** Identify four additional costs of hosting the mountain climbing club party and describe the cost behavior of each if the number of guests changes.

In this section, we defined and compared the two most common types of cost behavior. Next, we see how to estimate the total cost of an activity.

### Determining Total Cost

Once managers classify costs according to cost behavior, they can determine the total cost of an activity. The formula for finding total cost is as follows:

TOTAL COST = FIXED COST + VARIABLE COST

Recall from our example that we have $525 of fixed cost for the band, and $4,375 of variable cost for the food and drinks (based on 175 guests). Using this information, Laura can calculate the total cost of the party as $4,900, as follows:

$4,900 = $525 + $4,375

The total cost of the party is shown on the graph in Exhibit 4–5.

The graph in Exhibit 4–5 shows both the horizontal line depicting the fixed cost of the band and the upward sloping line representing the fixed cost plus the variable

**Exhibit 4–5**
Graph of Total Climbing
Party Cost

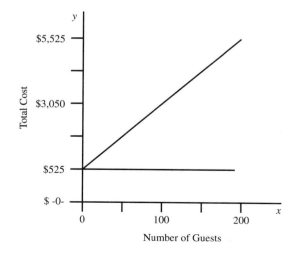

cost of the food and drinks. Exhibit 4–5, then, is actually a combination of the graphs in Exhibits 4–2 and 4–4. These graphs are consistent with the statement that total cost is equal to fixed cost plus variable cost.

Since the budget for the event was $5,500, and Laura plans to spend only $4,900, she must have planned well, right? Not necessarily. Keep in mind that the numbers only tell part of the story. As a decision maker, Laura must not be lulled into thinking that she has made the most effective spending choices just because she failed to spend every budgeted dollar. Is it wise to spend nearly $5,000 on one event? Could some costs be reduced? To make strong decisions, managers must consider all issues—not just whether the budget has been met. In this chapter, we examine cost behaviors to equip you with a cost estimation tool. Remember, however, that when making decisions the numbers tell part, not all, of a story.

## Discussion Question

**4–4.** The total cost of $4,900 covers the cost of 175 guests. Based on the cost behavior information available, what is the largest possible number of guests that could attend the party within the $5,500 budget?

## RELEVANT RANGE

Are there any situations when a cost behavior might change? Let us reexamine the cost of entertainment in the party example to answer this question. We assumed the cost of the band would remain fixed if the number of guests attending the party increased; however, if the number of guests increased well outside normal expectations to 500 or 1,000, the guests could not be entertained with a single band. At least two bands would be needed. Once the number of guests exceeds a certain range, the entertainment cost does not remain fixed at $525.

**relevant range** The range of activity within which cost behavior assumptions are valid.

The range of activity within which cost behavior assumptions are valid is the **relevant range.** In the party example, the relevant range might be up to 250 guests. If more than 250 guests attend, another band will be needed. For a business, relevant range is usually considered to be the normal range of activity for the company.

Activity that is outside the relevant range can affect costs in a business setting. For example, in Exhibit 4–1, we described rent for a factory building as a fixed cost relative to production. This fixed cost behavior holds true only within the relevant range. On the one hand, if production dropped to two units there would be no point in having a factory. Work could be contracted to an outside party. Conversely, if the factory building provided just enough space to produce 1,000 units per month, and production requirements increased to 1,500 units per month, a second factory would be needed. If the activity level were higher than the relevant range, factory rent would no longer be fixed at the original cost level.

Variable costs also have a relevant range. To illustrate, we return to the catering costs for the party example. The caterer charged the club $25 per guest for food and drinks for a party with 125 to 175 guests. Would the caterer offer the same service for $25 per guest if the event were a private evening with only six people attending? Probably not. The caterer's fee is based on a relatively large number of guests. Conversely, the caterer might be willing to provide food and drinks for a cost of less than $25 per guest if the crowd were significantly larger. For example, the caterer might offer a $25 per guest charge for groups of 50 to 200, and a $20 per guest charge for groups of more than 200. In such a case, the relevant range of the variable cost behavior would be from 50 to 200 guests.

In business settings, similar types of quantity discounts exist. For example, if IBM were to purchase just enough electrical wire to manufacture one computer, it would likely pay a higher price for the wire than if it were buying enough to make 1,000 computers. Buying enough electrical wire to make 1,000 computers allows IBM to get quantity discounts that would be unavailable otherwise. At the other extreme, if IBM were to make such a large number of computers that it outstripped its normal source for wire and had to resort to secondary, more expensive suppliers, the cost for electrical wire per computer could actually increase as production increased.

With these examples in mind, how can fixed cost be described as a cost that remains constant in total, and variable cost be described as cost that remains constant per unit regardless of activity? For most decision situations, the fixed and variable cost information provided to managers assumes activity will be within the relevant range, that is, the normal operating range for the company. The relevant range can be depicted graphically as shown in Exhibit 4–6.

**Exhibit 4–6**
Relevant Ranges of Fixed and Variable Costs

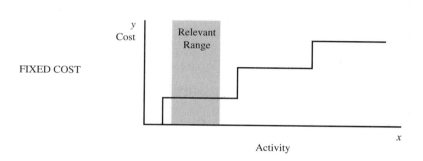

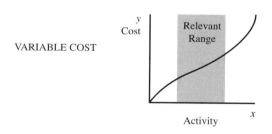

As shown in Exhibit 4–6, the fixed cost remains constant in total and the variable cost is constant per unit within the relevant range.

Decision makers usually assume activity levels will be within a company's relevant range. Activity levels may exceed or fall below the relevant range, such as when growth in production activity is significant. However, unless some evidence suggests the contrary, you should assume in our text discussion that the activity levels will be within the relevant range.

## MIXED COSTS

The costs we have looked at thus far have been either completely fixed (the cost of entertainment at the party) or completely variable (the cost of food and drinks at the party). Some costs, however, are actually a combination of fixed and variable

**mixed cost** An individual cost that has both a fixed cost and a variable cost component. It also describes a company's total cost structure.

cost, and are known as mixed costs. A **mixed cost** is an individual cost that has elements of both fixed and variable costs.

For decision-making purposes, it is useful to identify the fixed and variable components of a mixed cost. For example, consider the cost of electricity consumed in a manufacturing facility. When production lines are completely shut down on weekends, production is zero. Even without any production, however, the facility will still require minimal electricity to operate water heaters, refrigerators, and security lighting. This minimum cost of keeping the factory ready for use is the fixed portion of electricity cost. When production begins and production machinery cranks up, much more electric power is used. This incremental cost, which is driven by the actual use of the manufacturing facility, is the variable portion of electricity cost. Exhibit 4–7 shows a graph of a mixed cost.

**Exhibit 4–7**
Graph of a Mixed Cost

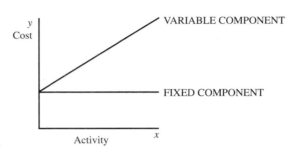

Exhibit 4–7 shows that even when the activity level is at zero (the intercept of the x-axis and the y-axis), cost is incurred. This cost is the fixed element of the mixed cost. As activity increases, the cost rises from that initial point. This cost is the variable component of the mixed cost.

You may have observed that the graph in Exhibit 4–7 is quite similar to that in Exhibit 4–5 depicting the total cost of the climbing club party. This similarity occurs because total cost (which is composed of its fixed costs and its variable costs) could be described as one giant mixed cost.

# Discussion Questions

**4-5.** Consider the costs involved in operating a fast-food restaurant such as McDonald's. What are three examples of activities that would have mixed costs?

Assume you are the sales manager for the Hinds Wholesale Supply Company, and you are trying to estimate the cost of operating the fleet of delivery vehicles for the coming year. The only information you have is that $110,000 was spent last year to operate the fleet.

**4-6.** Would it help you to know which delivery vehicle costs are fixed and which are variable? Why?

**4-7.** What other information would you need to gather before being able to estimate next year's costs?

**4-8.** Why would the sales manager at Hinds Wholesale Supply Company be concerned about the cost of delivery vehicles?

# IDENTIFYING THE FIXED AND VARIABLE ELEMENTS OF A MIXED COST

We often know that a cost has behavioral characteristics of both fixed and variable costs, but we have no information to tell us how much of the cost is unaffected by the level of activity (fixed) and how much of it will increase as activity increases (variable). Mixed cost information is much more useful for cost control, planning, and decision-making purposes if the manager can determine which part of the mixed cost is fixed and which is variable. In this section we will discuss four methods commonly used to identify the fixed and variable elements of a mixed cost: the engineering approach, scatter graphing, the high-low method, and regression analysis.

## The Engineering Approach

**engineering approach**
A method used to separate a mixed cost into its fixed and variable components using experts who are familiar with the technical aspects of the activity and associated cost.

The **engineering approach** relies on engineers or other professionals who are familiar with the technical aspect of the activity and the associated cost to analyze the situation and determine which costs are fixed and which are variable. This approach may employ time-and-motion studies or other aspects of scientific management.

For example, experts in the field of aviation and aircraft operations could analyze the cost of operating a corporate aircraft to determine which portion of the operating cost increases as aircraft usage increases and which portion of the cost remains constant. Based on the experts' industry experience and evaluations, they would then separate the fixed and variable components of this mixed cost.

Analysts would be likely to use flying time as the activity level base because hours of use will affect costs. They would then classify the cost of insurance and of renting hangar space in which to store the plane as fixed costs. Why? The insurance and rental costs are unaffected by the number of hours the plane may be flown. The cost of the airplane's battery will likely be classified as a fixed cost because the deterioration of this item and the need for replacement are affected more by the passing of time and very little by the number of flight hours.

Aviation experts would probably classify fuel costs and expected maintenance and repair costs as variable costs, as both depend on usage. For example, experts may estimate that a plane's engines require an overhaul every 2,000 hours of flight time.

## Discussion Questions

Again assume you are a sales manager for the Hinds Wholesale Supply Company trying to estimate the cost of operating the fleet of delivery vehicles for the coming year.

**4–9.** Would you engage the services of an automotive expert to help separate costs into fixed and variable? Why or why not?

**4–10.** List four costs you (or the automotive expert) would identify as part of the cost of operating the fleet of delivery trucks. Classify each by its cost behavior and the activity to which it relates.

**4-11.** If an expert determined that the fixed cost of operating each vehicle is $3,000 per year and the variable cost is $0.10 per mile, what would be the expected cost of operating the fleet? (Assume there are eight trucks, and they are driven an average of 25,000 miles each.)

The engineering approach to separating mixed cost relies on an expert's experience and judgment to classify costs as fixed or variable. It is often used when the company has no past experience concerning a cost's reaction to activity. In contrast, the other three methods we examine use historical data and mathematical computations to approximate the fixed and variable components of mixed cost.

## Scatter Graphing

**scatter graphing** A method used to separate a mixed cost into its fixed and variable components by plotting historical activity and cost data to see how a cost relates to various levels of activity.

**Scatter graphing** plots historical activity and cost data on a graph to see how a cost relates to various levels of activity. The analyst places a straight line through the *visual center* of the points plotted on the graph, so roughly half the dots are above the line and half are below the line, as shown in Exhibit 4–8.

With some simple calculations, an analyst can now approximate the fixed and variable elements of the cost being analyzed.

**Exhibit 4–8**
A Scatter Graph

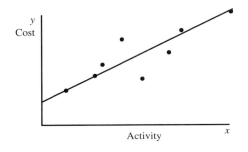

To demonstrate how scatter graphing is used, imagine you are again the sales manager for the Hinds Wholesale Supply Company with the task of estimating the expected delivery vehicle maintenance cost for 2001. Your first step is to obtain relevant historical cost data. At your request, the accounting department provides you with the following maintenance cost information about the company's delivery vehicles for 2000:

| Truck Number | Maintenance Cost |
| --- | --- |
| 202 | $2,000 |
| 204 | 1,600 |
| 205 | 2,200 |
| 301 | 2,400 |
| 422 | 2,600 |
| 460 | 2,200 |
| 520 | 2,000 |

You now ask yourself a couple of questions. First, is vehicle maintenance cost a fixed cost? Clearly it is not a fixed cost, because the cost is not the same for all trucks. Second, is this cost a variable cost? Well, if it is a variable cost, it varies based on some activity. After careful consideration, you determine that activity might be either (1) the number of miles driven or (2) the number of packages delivered. On request, the accounting department provides you with the following expanded data for 2000:

| Truck Number | Maintenance Cost | Miles Driven | Packages Delivered |
|---|---|---|---|
| 202 | $2,000 | 15,000 | 1,200 |
| 204 | 1,600 | 11,000 | 1,000 |
| 205 | 2,200 | 24,000 | 1,500 |
| 301 | 2,400 | 30,000 | 1,500 |
| 422 | 2,600 | 31,000 | 500 |
| 460 | 2,200 | 26,000 | 1,000 |
| 520 | 2,000 | 20,000 | 2,000 |

Remember, if a cost is truly variable, it changes proportionately as activity changes. Let us consider miles driven first and see whether there is a proportional change in total vehicle maintenance cost as activity changes. Compare trucks 202 and 301. The miles driven for truck 301 are exactly twice as many as for truck 202. If vehicle maintenance cost is variable based on miles driven, then the cost for truck 301 should be twice the cost for truck 202, but it is not.

Now we look at packages delivered as the activity. Compare truck 204 with truck 422. Truck 204 delivered twice as many packages as truck 422. If vehicle maintenance cost is variable based on the number of packages delivered, the cost for truck 204 should be exactly twice the cost for truck 422. Again, it is not.

If a cost is neither fixed nor variable, then it is mixed, meaning it has both a fixed element and a variable element. This is the case with Hinds' delivery vehicle maintenance cost. Therefore, you must find a way to estimate the amount of fixed and variable costs associated with the maintenance cost if you are to reasonably predict the vehicle maintenance cost for 2001.

You have decided to use the scatter graph method to determine the fixed and variable elements of the vehicle maintenance cost. The first step is to plot the information for each observation (in this case, each delivery vehicle) on a graph. Remember, the vertical axis on a graph is the y-axis (total cost), and the horizontal axis is the x-axis (activity). Recall also that the independent variable, shown as the x-axis, is not affected by a change in y. However, the dependent variable value, shown on the y-axis, depends on the numerical value of the x variable. The assumption is that a change in x will lead to a change in y.

If a truck driver travels 1,000 miles, for example, Hinds must spend money on gasoline. In our case, driving is the independent (x) variable and the company's gasoline cost is the dependent (y) variable. Driving affects the company's gasoline cost; however, the reverse does not hold true. The mere purchase of gasoline, which increases the dependent (y) variable, will not cause a change in the number of miles driven.

For mixed cost calculations, the y variable is the cost affected by the activity and it is the cost you are trying to estimate. The x variable represents the activity you believe will affect the cost behavior. Do not fall into the trap of thinking that the dependent variable (y) will be measured in dollars and the independent variable (x) will not. It is possible to predict a cost such as sales commissions, expressed in dollars, based on an activity such as sales, also expressed in dollars.

Recall the Hinds Wholesale Supply Company example. The data provided by the company's accounting department show two possible activity-cost pairs. The first pair is the number of miles driven and vehicle maintenance cost. The second pair is the number of packages delivered and vehicle maintenance cost.

We begin by graphing maintenance cost and miles driven. When we plot the data on a graph, we plot each observation as a pair of values. The maintenance cost for a particular vehicle, the dependent variable, is plotted using the index on the y-axis. The miles driven for the same vehicle, the independent variable, are plotted using the index on the x-axis. The position on the graph occupied by the plotted pair of numbers is called a *coordinate*. As the graph in Exhibit 4–9 indicates, each observation is represented by a dot.

**Exhibit 4–9**
Partial Scatter Graph for Hinds Company Vehicle Maintenance Cost and Miles Driven

DATA:

| Truck Number | Maintenance Cost | Miles Driven |
|---|---|---|
| 202 | $2,000 | 15,000 |
| 204 | 1,600 | 11,000 |
| 205 | 2,200 | 24,000 |
| 301 | 2,400 | 30,000 |
| 422 | 2,600 | 31,000 |
| 460 | 2,200 | 26,000 |
| 520 | 2,000 | 20,000 |

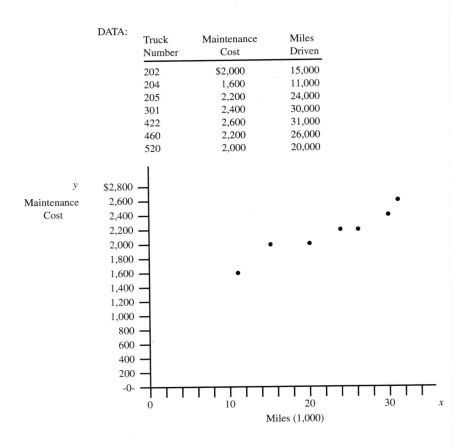

The next step is to place a straight line through the visual center of the plotted coordinates, which we have done in Exhibit 4–10.

In Exhibit 4–10 it is easy to place the straight line through the points on the graph because they seem to line up in a nearly straight line on their own. This straight line

**Exhibit 4–10**
Completed Scatter Graph for Vehicle Maintenance Cost and Miles Driven

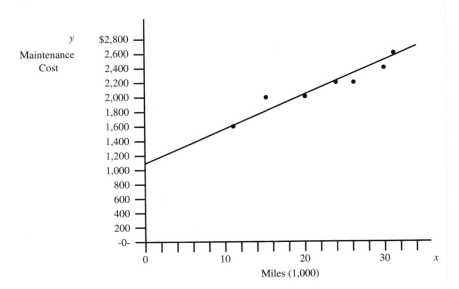

effect occurs when the relationship of the two variables is relatively constant, or linear. The graph in Exhibit 4–10 suggests a relatively constant relationship between the miles driven (x) and maintenance cost (y). The straight line represents the behavior of maintenance cost as it relates to the number of miles driven.

Now that we have a completed scatter graph for Hinds's vehicle maintenance cost, we can employ some simple calculations to approximate the fixed and variable portion of that cost. As you recall from earlier in the chapter:

$$\text{Total Cost} = \text{Fixed Cost} + \text{Variable Cost}$$

For total mixed costs we can modify the equation slightly as follows:

$$\text{Total Mixed Cost} = \text{Fixed Cost Element} + \text{Variable Cost Element}$$

When using the scatter graph method, we identify the fixed element of the maintenance cost first. Note that in Exhibit 4–10 the straight line that indicates the relationship of miles driven and maintenance cost intercepts the y-axis at $1,100. At this point, the x variable (miles) is zero, which suggests that when activity is zero, maintenance cost will still be $1,100. That $1,100 represents fixed cost. In the scatter graph method, fixed cost is determined simply by noting where the straight line intercepts the y-axis. Thus, in our example we now know the following information:

$$\text{Total Mixed Cost} = \$1,100 + \text{Variable Cost Element}$$

Next, we find the variable cost per mile using simple mathematics. First we choose two points along the scatter graph line to determine the effect of the x variable on the y variable. Note: We select two points on the *scatter graph line,* not two points as plotted to represent our original data. Any two positions on the line are fine, but it is better to select points that are somewhat separated. That way, the error caused by our visual estimation in reading the graph will be small relative to the numerical difference between the two points selected.

As one coordinate for our variable cost per unit calculations, we select the point at which activity is zero and cost is $1,100. We then choose as our second point the coordinate at which the activity level is 34,000 miles and cost is $2,700. As the graph in Exhibit 4–11 indicates, we determined that coordinate by choosing a position on the line and following the lines to the x-axis and the y-axis. The locations on these axes indicate the cost and activity level represented by that position on the line.

**Exhibit 4–11**
Scatter Graph with
Activity Points Selected

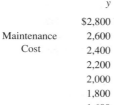

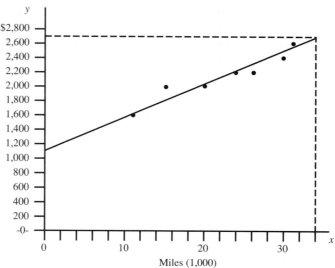

Miles (1,000)

The next step is to determine the mathematical difference between the two coordinates.

| Miles | Cost |
|---|---|
| 34,000 | $2,700 |
| ( -0- ) | (1,100) |
| 34,000 | $1,600 |

We can see from our calculations that the maintenance cost at 34,000 miles is $1,600 higher than it is for zero miles. What do you think caused the $1,600 difference? We assume it is the change in the activity level that causes changes in the cost. That is, it cost an additional $1,600 in maintenance cost to drive the 34,000 extra miles.

Now we can calculate the average amount of maintenance cost per mile caused by the additional activity. We do this by dividing the 34,000 mileage difference into the $1,600 increased maintenance cost:

$$\$1,600 \div 34,000 = \$0.047059, \text{ or about 4.7 cents per mile}$$

The calculations show that each additional mile of driving causes maintenance cost to rise by $0.047. If we add this information to the fixed cost information determined earlier, we can create a cost formula for vehicle maintenance cost:

$$\text{Vehicle Maintenance Cost} = \$1,100 + (\$0.047 \text{ per mile driven})$$

We have now used scatter graphing to separate maintenance cost into its fixed and variable components. With this information, we can project maintenance cost at any level of activity. To do this, we add the fixed cost to the activity multiplied by the cost per unit of activity. For example, the estimated maintenance cost for a single delivery truck that is to be driven 28,000 miles is $2,416, calculated as follows:

$$\$1,100 + (\$0.047 \times 28,000) = \$2,416$$

## Discussion Questions

**4-12.** Based on the information obtained from the scatter graph, what would be the maintenance cost of operating one delivery truck if we expected the truck to be driven 25,000 miles next year?

**4-13.** Based on the information obtained from the scatter graph, what would be the maintenance cost of operating a fleet of delivery trucks? (Assume there are eight trucks, and they are driven an average of 25,000 miles each.)

Now we turn to the information the accounting department provided about the number of packages delivered. Then we use the scatter graphing method to plot maintenance cost as the dependent ($y$) variable and packages delivered as the independent ($x$) variable. Exhibit 4–12 shows a partial scatter graph of the maintenance cost and packages delivered.

We draw a straight line through the points depicted by the observations, as in Exhibit 4–13.

Note in Exhibit 4–13 that placing a straight line through the points on this graph is considerably more challenging than in the previous scatter graph. This is because a straight line could take any one of several paths through the points on the graph. Each of the lines seems to depict the relationship between maintenance cost and packages delivered, but none does a very good job. The reason for the difficulty is

**Exhibit 4–12**
Partial Scatter Graph
for Vehicle
Maintenance Cost and
Packages Delivered

DATA:

| Truck Number | Maintenance Cost | Packages Delivered |
| --- | --- | --- |
| 202 | $2,000 | 1,200 |
| 204 | 1,600 | 1,000 |
| 205 | 2,200 | 1,500 |
| 301 | 2,400 | 1,500 |
| 422 | 2,600 | 500 |
| 460 | 2,200 | 1,000 |
| 520 | 2,000 | 2,000 |

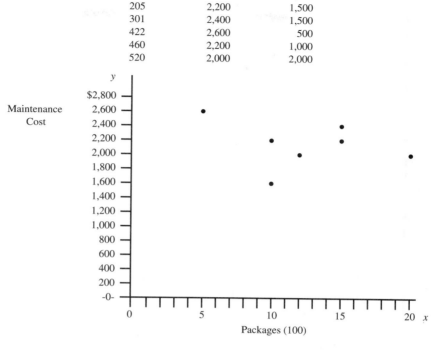

**Exhibit 4–13**
Completed Scatter
Graph for Vehicle
Maintenance Cost and
Packages Delivered

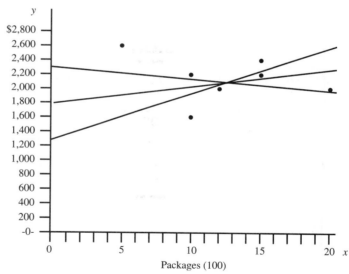

that the relationship between the variables is not linear. The question is, how do we use this method if the data do not have a clear linear relationship? The answer is, we don't. Before we employ the scatter graph method, we must be sure the activity we have chosen has a relatively linear relationship with the cost in question. If we plot points on a graph and the coordinates resemble a random pattern with little linearity, the data do not indicate a constant relationship between the activity and the cost. In the case of a random pattern, any conclusions drawn from the data will be useless for predicting future cost, and may cause trouble if used. Once we see that random pattern, then, we should not use the packages delivered data to estimate the fixed and variable elements of vehicle maintenance cost.

Even if a scatter graph appears to represent a linear relationship between an activity and a cost, we must be cautious to not imply relationships that do not exist. For instance, if we tried to determine cost behavior of vehicle maintenance cost by relating it to an activity such as the number of direct labor hours worked, we might possibly get mathematically reasonable results. However, common sense tells us that no relationship exists between direct labor hours and vehicle maintenance cost, so the results would be meaningless. A random guess would provide as good or better information. The activity and cost should have a clear, common sense relationship.

## The High-Low Method

**high-low method**  A method used to separate a mixed cost into its fixed and variable components using the mathematical differences between the highest and lowest levels of activity and cost.

Like the scatter graph approach, the **high-low method** uses historical data and mathematical computations to approximate the fixed and variable components of mixed cost. To illustrate the steps required by the high-low method, we review the following vehicle maintenance cost and activity data gathered for the Hinds Wholesale Supply Company:

| Truck Number | Maintenance Cost | Miles Driven | |
|---|---|---|---|
| 202 | $2,000 | 15,000 | |
| 204 | 1,600 | 11,000 | Low |
| 205 | 2,200 | 24,000 | |
| 301 | 2,400 | 30,000 | |
| 422 | 2,600 | 31,000 | High |
| 460 | 2,200 | 26,000 | |
| 520 | 2,000 | 20,000 | |

The high-low method focuses on the mathematical differences between the highest and lowest observations. If we examine the data list, we see that the highest observation is 31,000 miles with a maintenance cost of $2,600. The lowest observation is 11,000 miles with a maintenance cost of $1,600.

Remember, our purpose is to find the amount of the fixed and variable elements of a mixed cost. With the high-low method, we focus on determining the variable component of the cost first. The calculations to determine variable cost per unit are similar to those used in scatter graphing. By comparing the differences in activity and cost between the highest observation and the lowest observation, we can calculate a per unit cost that describes the relationship shown by these differences as follows:

| | Miles | Cost |
|---|---|---|
| High | 31,000 | $2,600 |
| Low | (11,000) | (1,600) |
| Difference | 20,000 | $1,000 |

Notice the mileage difference of 20,000 miles is accompanied by a cost difference of $1,000. So, to drive the extra 20,000 miles, the company spent $1,000 more in maintenance cost. We assume that the $1,000 increase in maintenance cost was caused exclusively by the increase in the number of miles from 11,000 to 31,000 miles. The cost per mile, then, is simply the $1,000 increased cost divided by the 20,000 additional miles as shown here:

$$\$1,000 \div 20,000 = \$0.05, \text{ or 5 cents per mile}$$

Before we calculate the fixed cost element, recall that total mixed cost is total fixed cost plus total variable cost (Total Mixed Cost = Fixed Cost Element +

Variable Cost Element). The variable cost element can be calculated by multiplying the variable cost per unit by the activity. In this case we multiply the variable cost per mile by the number of miles. With what we have determined thus far, we can begin to construct a cost formula for vehicle maintenance cost as follows:

Total Mixed Cost = Fixed Cost Element + ($0.05 per mile driven)

For each of our observations (high and low), we know the total mixed cost and variable cost element. Therefore, we can easily determine the fixed cost element with simple calculations. Let us determine the fixed cost element associated with the high observation used in our example.

Total Mixed Cost = Fixed Cost Element + ($0.05 per mile driven)
$2,600 = ? + ($0.05 × 31,000)
$2,600 = ? + $1,550

To solve the equation, the fixed cost element must be $2,600–$1,550, or $1,050, shown as follows:

Total Mixed Cost = Fixed Cost Element + ($0.05 per mile driven)
$2,600 = $1,050 + $1,550

We now know both the variable cost per mile and the total fixed cost of operating one of the delivery vehicles. To check our math, we can do the same calculation for the low observation, as follows:

Total Mixed Cost = Fixed Cost Element + ($0.05 per mile driven)
$1,600 = ? + ($0.05 × 11,000)
$1,600 = ? + $550

For the low observation, to solve the equation, fixed cost must be $1,600–$550, or $1,050, as we see next.

Total Mixed Cost = Fixed Cost Element + ($0.05 per mile driven)
$1,600 = $1,050 + $550

The high-low method yields a fixed cost for maintenance of $1,050, and a variable cost of 5 cents per mile. As with scatter graphing, to estimate the mixed cost at a particular level of activity, we add the fixed cost to the activity multiplied by the cost per unit of activity. For example, the estimated maintenance cost for a single delivery truck that is to be driven 28,000 miles is $2,450, calculated as follows:

$1,050 + ($0.05 × 28,000) = $2,450

## Discussion Questions

4-14. Using the high-low method and the data from our example, what would be the maintenance cost for operating one of the delivery trucks if we expected the truck to be driven 25,000 miles next year?

4-15. Using the high-low method and the information from our Hinds Company example, what would be the maintenance cost for operating the fleet of eight trucks, if each is to be driven 25,000 miles on average?

When we compare the scatter graph method with the high-low method, we find that the fixed and variable cost results are somewhat different. If you were going to present your cost estimates to the vice president of marketing, which method would you use? Which provides the most dependable information? The scatter graph method is based on visual estimation whereas the high-low method is based on hard mathematics with no visual estimation. Does that make the high-low method better? No, because the high-low method considers only two observations. What if these two observations are not representative of the data in general? Then the cost behavior conclusions will be flawed and possibly misleading.

Another drawback to the high-low method is that users cannot assess whether the data items have a linear relationship, which is necessary to find meaningful results. Because the scatter graph method considers all observations and indicates whether the data items have a linear relationship, practitioners regard it as superior to the high-low method, despite the fact that it is more time consuming to use and it is based on visual estimation.

## Regression Analysis

**regression analysis**  A method used to separate a mixed cost into its fixed and variable components using complex mathematical formulas.

**least-squares method** Another name for *regression analysis.*

**linear regression analysis** Another name for *regression analysis.*

**Regression analysis,** also called the **least-squares method** or **linear regression analysis,** is a mathematical approach to determining fixed and variable cost with statistical accuracy. The mathematical computations are complex and beyond the scope of this text; however, it is important to note that regression is a more reliable estimation technique than either the scatter graph method or the high-low method. Regression analysis uses the information contained in all the observations in a data set. That thoroughness makes it superior to the high-low method. Because it considers all these points of observation mathematically, rather than visually, regression analysis is also superior to the scatter graph method.

The basic mathematical equation for regression analysis follows:

$$Y = a + bX$$

When applying regression analysis to find the fixed and variable elements of a mixed cost, the variables in the regression equation are defined as follows:

$$Y = \text{total cost}$$
$$a = \text{fixed cost}$$
$$b = \text{unit variable cost}$$
$$X = \text{activity level}$$

Results of regression analysis would provide answers to the same questions that we posed for the scatter graph and the high-low methods. In fact, the results of regression analysis allow us to determine total cost, Y, for any given level of activity, X. Reexamine the basic regression analysis formula and compare it with the total cost equation.

$$Y = a + bX$$

Where:    $Y = \text{total cost}$
$a = \text{fixed cost}$
$b = \text{unit variable cost}$
$X = \text{activity level}$

When we rewrite the equation, we see that it translates directly to our earlier total cost equation, as follows:

Total Cost = Fixed Cost + (Unit Variable Cost × Activity Level)

Although regression analysis is difficult to compute manually, most spreadsheet software packages provide easy-to-use regression functions. Also, almost all business calculators, such as the Hewlett-Packard 12c, are programmed to compute linear regression problems. By reading your calculator's instruction manual, and practicing a little, you can easily determine fixed and variable cost components of a mixed cost using linear regression.

No matter which of the methods a company uses to separate mixed costs into fixed and variable elements, the outcome of the mixed cost analysis is useful information for controlling costs, setting prices, and assessing profitability. Indeed, a variety of internal users of accounting information, from marketing managers to production managers, will want access to such cost behavior information.

Whether large or small, simple or complex, managers of all companies must understand cost behavior. Production managers at companies as diverse as Caterpillar Tractor and Campbell Soup Company need this information to plan and control their operations. Marketing managers at companies as different as General Motors and Gerber Baby Foods must know how costs react to activity if they are to do their jobs properly.

Once a determination has been made as to a cost's behavior, an appropriate notation can be made in the accounting records to designate it as fixed, variable, or mixed. Then, the accounting system can produce reports sorted by cost behavior. Internal reports providing cost behavior information are valuable in a variety of decision-making settings. We will explore several of these settings in more detail in the next chapter.

## SUMMARY

If managers are to plan and control their operations effectively, they must understand cost behavior. Cost behavior is the reaction of costs to changes in levels of business activity.

The most common cost behavior patterns are fixed cost, variable cost, and mixed cost. A fixed cost is a cost that remains constant in total regardless of the level of activity within the relevant range. A variable cost is a cost that changes in total proportionately with changes in the level of activity within the relevant range. The relevant range is the range of activity within which fixed and variable cost assumptions are valid. A mixed cost is a cost that has both a fixed cost element and a variable cost element.

Over the years, several methods have been developed to separate a mixed cost into its fixed and variable components. The most commonly used methods are the engineering approach, scatter graphing, the high-low method, and regression analysis.

The engineering approach to separating a mixed cost into its fixed and variable components uses experts who are familiar with the technical aspects of the activity and associated cost. Scatter graphing separates a mixed cost into its fixed and variable components by plotting historical activity and cost data to see how a cost relates to various levels of activity. The high-low method uses the mathematical differences between the highest and lowest levels of activity and cost. Regression analysis uses complex mathematical formulas, but the results are more mathematically precise than those of the scatter graph or high-low method.

Regardless of the method that managers choose to separate mixed costs into fixed and variable elements, the analysis provides useful information for a myriad of business decisions.

## KEY TERMS

cost behavior    M-120
engineering approach    M-127
fixed cost    M-120
high-low method    M-134
least-squares method    M-136
linear regression analysis    M-136

mixed cost    M-125
regression analysis    M-136
relevant range    M-124
scatter graphing    M-128
variable cost    M-121

# REVIEW THE FACTS

A. What is cost behavior?
B. For fixed costs, what happens to total cost as activity increases?
C. For fixed costs, what happens to the cost per unit as activity increases?
D. For variable cost, what happens to total cost as activity increases?
E. For variable cost, what happens to the cost per unit as activity increases?
F. With respect to cost behavior, what is the relevant range?
G. Does the relevant range pertain to fixed costs, variable costs, or both fixed and variable costs?
H. What are the two elements of a mixed cost?
I. What are the four methods of separating a mixed cost into its two cost components?
J. Compare the high-low method to the scatter graph method. Which provides the more dependable information?
K. What is the major limitation of the high-low method?
L. What is another name for regression analysis?
M. If you desired the reliability of the regression analysis method but did not want to suffer through the difficulty of doing the mathematics manually, what would you do?

# APPLY WHAT YOU HAVE LEARNED

## LO 2: Classifying Cost by Cost Behavior

4–16. Indicate whether the following costs are more likely to be fixed (F), variable (V), or mixed (M) with respect to the number of units produced.

1. __V__ Direct material
2. __V__ Direct labor
3. __F__ Cost of plant security guard
4. __F__ Straight line depreciation on production equipment
5. __M__ Maintenance on production equipment
6. __M__ Maintenance on factory building
7. __V__ Cost of cleaning supplies used in the factory
8. __F__ Rent on the factory building
9. __F__ Salary for the two factory supervisors
10. __F__ Vice president of manufacturing's salary
11. __M__ Cost of electricity used in the factory
12. __VM__ Cost of production machine lubricants

## LO 2: Classifying Cost by Cost Behavior

4–17. Assume that you are trying to analyze the costs associated with driving your car. Indicate whether the following costs are more likely to be fixed (F), variable (V), or mixed (M) with respect to the number of miles driven.

1. _____ Cost of the car
2. _____ Insurance cost
3. _____ Maintenance cost
4. _____ Cost of gasoline
5. _____ The cost of a college parking permit
6. _____ AAA membership

## LO 2: Classifying Cost by Cost Behavior

**4–18.** Assume that you are planning a large party. As you are trying to figure out how much the party will cost, you decide to separate the costs according to cost behavior. Indicate whether the following costs are more likely to be fixed (F), variable (V), or mixed (M) with respect to the number of guests attending the party.

1. _____ Rent for the party hall
2. _____ Cost of the band
3. _____ Cost of cold drinks
4. _____ Cost of food
5. _____ Cost of party decorations
6. _____ Cost of renting tables and chairs

## LO 2: Classifying Cost by Cost Behavior

**4–19.** Assume that you have been assigned to analyze the costs associated with operating the law firm of Moore & Moore and Company. The law firm just moved into a new, large office building that it purchased last year. Indicate whether the following costs are more likely to be fixed (F), variable (V), or mixed (M) with respect to the number of attorneys working for the firm.

1. _____ Cost of the new office building
2. _____ Basic telephone service
3. _____ Cost of attorney salaries
4. _____ Cost of the receptionist's wages

## LO 2: Classifying Cost by Cost Behavior

**4–20.** Assume that you have been assigned to analyze the costs of a retail merchandiser, Auto Parts City. Indicate whether the following costs are more likely fixed (F), variable (V), or mixed (M) with respect to the dollar amount of sales.

1. _____ Cost of store rent
2. _____ Basic telephone service
3. _____ Cost of salaries for the two salespeople
4. _____ Cost of advertising
5. _____ Cost of store displays
6. _____ Cost of electricity
7. _____ Cost of merchandise sold

## LO 4: Evaluating a Mixed Cost Situation

**4–21.** Assume that you work for Wilma Manufacturing Company and have been asked to review the cost of delivery truck maintenance. The company president, Wilma Hudik, is dissatisfied with the accounting department's reluctance to calculate the fixed and variable cost of truck maintenance as it pertains to the number of units produced in the factory.

The accounting department prepared the following scatter graph:

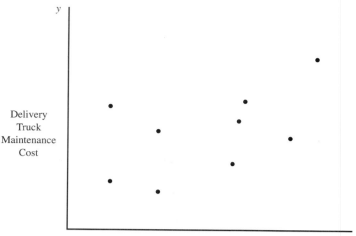

The accounting department personnel seem unable to use the graph to determine fixed and variable cost. The company president knows that regression analysis will provide mathematically accurate amounts for the fixed and variable truck maintenance cost, but no one in the accounting department seems to know how to do it.

**REQUIRED:**
Prepare a short memo to the president that details the feasibility of using the scatter graph and regression analysis to determine the fixed and variable components of delivery truck maintenance relative to the amount of factory production. In addition, your memo should recommend an alternative approach that could be used to evaluate the cost and cost behavior of truck maintenance.

## LO 5:  Use of a Scatter Graph for Separating Mixed Cost

**4–22.** Consider the following scatter graphs:

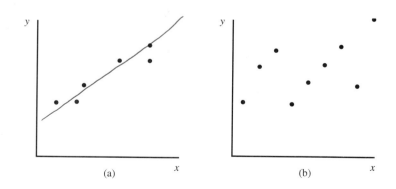

(a)     (b)

**REQUIRED:**
Which of the scatter graphs (a or b) do you think would be more appropriate for determining the fixed and variable portions of a mixed cost? Explain your reasoning.

## LO 5: Separating Mixed Cost Using the High-Low Method

**4–23.** The following information pertains to Jacobs Incorporated:

| 2000 | Information: | |
|---|---|---|
| | Sales | $2,300,000 |
| | Selling expense | 347,000 |

| 2001 | Information: | |
|---|---|---|
| | Sales | $2,860,000 |
| | Selling expense | 369,400 |

**REQUIRED:**
Using the high-low method, determine the following:
a. The variable cost element for selling expense
b. The fixed selling expense
c. The selling expense that can be expected if sales are $2,500,000

## LO 5: Separating Mixed Cost Using the High-Low Method

**4–24.** The following information pertains to the Robin Rappaport Company:

| 2000 | Information: | |
|---|---|---|
| | Units packaged | 14,500 |
| | Packaging cost | $32,567 |

| 2001 | Information: | |
|---|---|---|
| | Units packaged | 15,300 |
| | Packaging cost | $33,191 |

**REQUIRED:**
Using the high-low method, determine the following:
a. The variable cost element for packaging cost
b. The fixed packaging cost
c. The packaging cost that can be expected if 15,000 units are packaged

## LO 5: Separating Mixed Cost Using the High-Low Method

**4–25.** The inspection department at the Rose Spiegel Company inspects every third unit produced. The following information is available for the inspection department:

| 2000 | Information: | |
|---|---|---|
| | Number of inspections | 41,950 |
| | Inspection cost | $77,273 |

| 2001 | Information: | |
|---|---|---|
| | Number of inspections | 48,600 |
| | Inspection cost | $83,790 |

**REQUIRED:**
Using the high-low method, determine the following:
a. The variable cost element for inspection cost
b. The fixed inspection cost
c. The inspection cost that can be expected if 45,000 units are inspected

## LO 5: Separating Mixed Cost Using the High-Low Method

**4–26.** The plant manager has asked you to analyze the cost of electricity used in the manufacturing facility. Information for 2000 and 2001 follows:

|  | 2000 | 2001 |
|---|---|---|
| Machine hours | 100,000 | 120,000 |
| Cost of electricity | $188,000 | $221,600 |

### REQUIRED:
a. Determine the variable rate for electricity per machine hour.
b. Determine the total fixed cost of electricity.
c. Determine the estimated cost of electricity for next year if machine hours are expected to be 122,500.

## LO 5: Separating Mixed Cost Using the High-Low Method

**4–27.** The office manager has asked you to analyze the cost of service and supplies for the office copy machines. Information for 2000 and 2001 follows:

|  | 2000 | 2001 |
|---|---|---|
| Number of copies produced | 52,550 | 77,800 |
| Cost of service and supplies | $1,961.57 | $2,592.82 |

### REQUIRED:
a. Determine the variable cost per copy.
b. Determine the total fixed cost for service and supplies for the copy machines.
c. Determine the estimated cost of service and supplies for next year if 75,000 copies are made.

## LO 5: Separating Mixed Cost Using the High-Low Method

**4–28.** The production manager has asked you to analyze the cost of materials handling. Information for 2000 and 2001 follows:

|  | 2000 | 2001 |
|---|---|---|
| Number of parts handled | 154,300 | 185,400 |
| Materials handling cost | $9,244.77 | $10,675.37 |

### REQUIRED:
a. Determine the variable cost per part handled.
b. Determine the total fixed cost for materials handling.
c. Determine the estimated cost of materials handling if 160,000 parts are handled next year.

## LO 5: Separating Mixed Cost Using the High-Low Method

**4–29.** The sales manager has asked you to estimate the shipping cost that can be expected for 2002. Following is information for 2000 and 2001:

|  | 2000 | 2001 |
|---|---|---|
| Sales in units | 15,000 | 18,000 |
| Shipping cost | $30,000 | $35,400 |

### REQUIRED:
Estimate 2002 shipping cost assuming sales of 16,500 units.

## LO 5:   Separating Mixed Cost Using the High-Low Method

**4–30.** The transportation manager has asked you to estimate the operating cost that can be expected for the company jet for 2002. Following is information for 2000 and 2001:

|  | 2000 | 2001 |
|---|---|---|
| Flight time in hours | 1,250 | 1,875 |
| Aircraft operating cost | $1,563,750 | $2,148,125 |

**REQUIRED:**

Estimate the cost of operating the company jet for 2002 assuming that flight time will be 1,500 hours.

## LO 5:   Separating Mixed Cost Using the High-Low Method

**4–31.** Tom Robinson is the owner of Robinson Fishing Guide Service. He is trying to estimate the cost of operating his fishing service next year. He expects to have 185 charters during 2002. The following information is available:

|  | 2000 | 2001 |
|---|---|---|
| Number of charters | 150 | 190 |
| Operating cost | $7,741 | $8,601 |

**REQUIRED:**

Determine the estimated operating cost for 2002.

## LO 5:   Separating Mixed Cost Using the High-Low Method

**4–32.** The following information pertains to Picon Manufacturing for 2000:

|  | Number of Purchase Orders Issued | Cost of Operating the Purchasing Department |
|---|---|---|
| Fourth quarter of 1999 | 2,500 | $130,000 |
| First quarter of 2000 | 1,000 | 80,000 |
| Second quarter of 2000 | 1,500 | 110,000 |
| Third quarter of 2000 | 2,000 | 115,000 |
| Fourth quarter of 2000 | 3,000 | 140,000 |

**REQUIRED:**

Using the high-low method, determine the following:
 a. The variable cost per purchase order
 b. The fixed cost of operating the purchasing department for one quarter
 c. The estimated cost of operating the purchasing department in 2001 assuming that 7,000 purchase orders will be issued. (Hint: Remember that the fixed cost for one year is four times the amount of fixed cost for one quarter.)

## LO 5:   Separating Mixed Cost Using the Scatter Graph Method

**4–33.** Refer to the information from problem 4–32.

**REQUIRED:**

Using the scatter graph method, determine the following:
 a. The variable cost per purchase order
 b. The fixed cost of operating the purchasing department for one quarter

c. The estimated cost of operating the purchasing department in 2001 assuming that 7,000 purchase orders will be issued. (Hint: Remember that the fixed cost for one year is four times the amount of fixed cost for one quarter.)

## LO 5: Separating Mixed Cost Using the High-Low Method

**4-34.** The following information pertains to Blue Glass Bottled Spring Water:

|  | Number of Sales Invoices Processed | Cost of Operating the Invoicing Department |
|---|---|---|
| Fourth quarter of 1999 | 10,500 | $50,574.65 |
| First quarter of 2000 | 11,000 | 52,711.12 |
| Second quarter of 2000 | -15,000 | 58,231.51 |
| Third quarter of 2000 | 12,000 | -59,439.73 |
| Fourth quarter of 2000 | - 9,000 | - 46,299.73 |

### REQUIRED:
Using the high-low method, determine the following:
a. The variable cost per invoice processed
b. The fixed cost of operating the invoicing department for one quarter
c. The estimated cost of operating the invoicing department in 2001 assuming that 45,000 invoices will be processed. (Hint: Remember that the fixed cost for one year is four times the amount of fixed cost for one quarter.)

## LO 5: Separating Mixed Cost Using the High-Low Method

**4-35.** The following information pertains to Jillian Munter & Associates:

|  | Number of Computers Repaired | Cost of Operating the Repair Department |
|---|---|---|
| Fourth quarter of 1999 | 125 | $26,100.91 |
| First quarter of 2000 | 130 | 26,529.16 |
| Second quarter of 2000 | 110 | 25,400.65 |
| Third quarter of 2000 | 105 | 25,212.91 |
| Fourth quarter of 2000 | 115 | 25,799.88 |

### REQUIRED:
Using the high-low method, determine the following:
a. The variable cost per computer repair
b. The fixed cost of operating the repair department for one quarter
c. The estimated cost of operating the repair department in 2001 assuming that 450 invoices will be processed. (Hint: Remember that the fixed cost for one year is four times the amount of fixed cost for one quarter.)

## LO 5: Separating Mixed Cost Using the High-Low Method

**4-36.** The following information is taken from Sweepy Broom Manufacturing Company:

|  | Number of Brooms Produced | Total Production Cost |
|---|---|---|
| January | 9,800 | $17,100 |
| February | 7,000 | 15,000 |

| | | |
|---|---|---|
| March | 8,000 | 16,000 |
| April | 7,500 | 15,500 |
| May | 10,100 | 17,200 |
| June | 9,000 | 17,000 |
| July | 10,500 | 19,000 |
| August | 11,600 | 20,000 |
| September | 10,600 | 18,200 |
| October | 8,500 | 16,800 |
| November | 12,100 | 20,500 |
| December | 11,000 | 18,000 |

**REQUIRED:**
Using the high-low method, determine the following:
 a. The variable production cost per unit
 b. The total fixed production cost
 c. The expected production cost to produce 12,000 brooms

## LO 5: Separating Mixed Cost Using the Scatter Graph Method

**4–37.** Refer to the information in problem 4–36.

**REQUIRED:**
Using the scatter graph method, determine the following:
 a. The variable production cost per unit
 b. The total fixed production cost
 c. The expected production cost to produce 12,000 brooms

## LO 5: Separating Mixed Cost Using the High-Low Method

**4–38.** Ace Computer Training offers short computer courses. The number of course sessions offered depends on student demand. The following information pertains to 2001:

| | Number of Sessions | Cost |
|---|---|---|
| First quarter | 30 | $ 75,000 |
| Second quarter | 35 | 78,000 |
| Third quarter | 15 | 42,000 |
| Fourth quarter | 20 | 48,000 |
| Total | 100 | $243,000 |

**REQUIRED:**
Using the high-low method, determine the following:
 a. The variable cost per session
 b. The total fixed cost of operating the company
 c. The expected cost for a quarter if 25 sessions are offered

## LO 5: Separating Mixed Cost Using the Scatter Graph Method

**4–39.** Refer to the information in problem 4–38.

**REQUIRED:**
Using the scatter graph method, determine the following:
 a. The variable cost per session
 b. The total fixed cost of operating the company
 c. The expected cost for a quarter if 25 sessions are offered

## LO 5:  Separating Mixed Cost Using the High-Low Method

**4–40.** The following information is taken from Miami Avionics Testing Service:

|           | Number of Tests Performed | Total Cost of Testing |
|-----------|---------------------------|------------------------|
| January   | 61,000                    | $1,420,000             |
| February  | 55,000                    | 1,340,000              |
| March     | 50,000                    | 1,290,000              |
| April     | 72,000                    | 1,430,000              |
| May       | 78,000                    | 1,440,000              |
| June      | 81,000                    | 1,540,000              |
| July      | 90,000                    | 1,590,000              |
| August    | 108,000                   | 1,610,000              |
| September | 111,000                   | 1,700,000              |
| October   | 128,000                   | 1,720,000              |
| November  | 140,000                   | 1,860,000              |
| December  | 132,000                   | 1,810,000              |

### REQUIRED:
Using the high-low method, determine the following:
a. The variable cost per test
b. The total fixed cost of operating the testing facility
c. The expected cost for a month if 125,000 tests are performed

## LO 5:  Separating Mixed Cost Using the Scatter Graph Method

**4–41.** Refer to the information in problem 4–40.

### REQUIRED:
Using the scatter graph method, determine the following:
a. The variable cost per test
b. The total fixed cost of operating the testing facility
c. The expected cost for a month if 125,000 tests are performed

## LO 5:  Separating Mixed Cost Using the High-Low Method

**4–42.** The following information is for the Valdez Supply Company:

|                     | 2001        | 2002        |
|---------------------|-------------|-------------|
| Sales               | $1,000,000  | $1,150,000  |
| COSTS:              |             |             |
| Cost of goods sold  | $ 800,000   | $ 920,000   |
| Sales commissions   | 15,000      | 17,250      |
| Store rent          | 3,000       | 3,000       |
| Depreciation        | 20,000      | 20,000      |
| Maintenance cost    | 3,800       | 4,100       |
| Office salaries     | 34,000      | 35,500      |

### REQUIRED:
Assuming sales is the activity base, use the high-low method to determine the variable cost element and the fixed cost component of each of the costs just listed.

## LO 5:  Separating Mixed Cost Using the High-Low Method

**4–43.** The following information is for the General Production Company:

|                        | 2001       | 2002       |
|------------------------|------------|------------|
| Units produced         | 257,000    | 326,000    |
| COSTS:                 |            |            |
| Direct material        | $ 611,660  | $ 775,880  |
| Direct labor           | 1,662,790  | 2,109,220  |
| Manufacturing overhead | 1,781,820  | 1,868,760  |

**REQUIRED:**

Assuming units produced is the activity base, use the high-low method to determine the variable cost element and fixed cost component of each of the costs just listed.

## LO 5:  Separating Mixed Cost Using the High-Low Method

**4–44.** The following information is for the Maupin Gift Shop:

|                     | 2001      | 2002      |
|---------------------|-----------|-----------|
| Sales               | $100,000  | $150,000  |
| COSTS:              |           |           |
| Cost of goods sold  | $ 75,000  | $112,500  |
| Sales commissions   | 5,000     | 7,500     |
| Store rent          | 1,000     | 1,000     |
| Depreciation        | 500       | 500       |
| Maintenance cost    | 200       | 250       |
| Office salaries     | 5,000     | 6,000     |

**REQUIRED:**

a. Assuming sales is the activity base, use the high-low method to determine the variable cost element and the fixed cost component of each of the costs just listed.

b. Why is it useful to know the information requested in requirement a?

## LO 4:  Components of Mixed Cost

**4–45.** Consider the following mathematical formula:

$$Y = a + bX$$

**REQUIRED:**

Match the variables to the correct descriptions. Some variables have two correct matches.

1. Y _f._     a. Independent variable
              b. Variable cost per unit
2. a _d  a_   c. Dependent variable
              d. Total fixed cost
3. b _b  c_   e. Activity
              f. Total cost
4. X _e_

## LO 4:  Describing the Methods of Separating Mixed Cost

**4–46.** Besides the engineering approach, this chapter discussed three methods of separating a mixed cost into its variable and fixed components.

**REQUIRED:**

Write a brief memo outlining the relative advantages and disadvantages of the high-low method, the scatter graph method, and regression analysis in estimating the variable and fixed portions of a mixed cost.

## LO 4: Describing the Methods of Separating Mixed Cost

**4–47.** Mr. Robinson, the director of Medical Diagnostics Clinic, is preparing a presentation to the clinic's board of directors about the fee charged for thallium stress tests. Part of the presentation will include information about the variable cost element and fixed costs associated with the tests. The accounting department has provided the director with a report which details the monthly costs associated with the thallium stress tests and the number of tests performed each month. Mr. Robinson is contemplating whether to use the scatter graph method, the high-low method, or regression analysis to separate the cost into its variable cost element and fixed cost. The director has asked your help in choosing an appropriate method.

**REQUIRED:**

Prepare a short report to Mr. Robinson providing insight into the strengths and weaknesses of the scatter graph method, the high-low method, and regression analysis. Your report should conclude with support for a final recommendation of one of the methods of separating mixed cost.

## LO 1, 2, 4, and 5: Analyzing a Situation Using Cost Behavior

**4–48.** Accents Furniture Company has been in business for two years. When the business began, Accents established a delivery department with a small fleet of trucks. The delivery department was designed to be able to handle the substantial future growth of the company. As expected, sales for the first two years of business were low and activity in the delivery department was minimal.

In an effort to control costs, Accents Furniture Company's store manager is considering a proposal from a delivery company to deliver the furniture sold by Accents for a flat fee of $30 per delivery.

The following information is available regarding the cost of operating Accents's delivery department during its first two years of business.

|                                    | 2000    | 2001    |
|------------------------------------|---------|---------|
| Number of deliveries               | 600     | 700     |
| Cost of operating the delivery department | $25,480 | $26,480 |

Sales and the number of deliveries are expected to increase greatly in the coming years. For example, sales next year will require an estimated 1,250 deliveries, while in 1999, it is expected that 1,775 deliveries will be required.

Due to the high growth rate, the store manager is concerned that the delivery cost will grow out of hand unless the proposal is accepted. He states that the cost per delivery was about $42.47 ($25,480/600) in 2000 and $37.83 ($26,480/700) in 2001. Even at the lower cost of $37.83, it seems the company can save about $7.83 ($30.00 - $37.83) per delivery. For 1999, the store manager believes the proposal can save the company about $13,898.25 (1,775 × $7.83).

**REQUIRED:**

Assume that you have been assigned to a group which has been formed to analyze the delivery cost of Accents Furniture Company. Your group should prepare a report and presentation that indicates the advantage or disadvantage of accepting the proposed delivery contract. Your report and presentation should not only include calculations to support your recommended course of action, but should also address the nonmonetary considerations of contracting with an outside source for delivery services.

### LO 1, 2, 3, and 4:  Addressing a Situation Using Cost Behavior Concepts

**4–49.** Mr. Reed is considering starting his own business. He has worked for a large corporation all his life and desires a change of pace. He is most interested in retail merchandising, but does not know what products his new business should sell. Mr. Reed is unsure about how to proceed with this major change in his life and has hired a consulting firm to help.

Assume that you have been assigned to the consulting group that will advise Mr. Reed.

**REQUIRED:**

Your group is to prepare a report that recommends a particular product line for Mr. Reed's new retail merchandising business. In addition, your report should recommend ways for Mr. Reed to gather information about the various costs associated with the merchandising business you have recommended. Finally, your report should explain how costs are classified as variable, fixed, and mixed costs, and why such classification by cost behavior is important.

### LO 1, 2, and 4:  Analyzing a Situation Using Cost Behavior

**4–50.** The Bowl-O-Mat operates a small chain of bowling alleys in southern Florida. Bowl-O-Mat's president, Al Palmer, is considering adding a supervised playground facility to each of the bowling alley properties. The playgrounds would require that a small addition be built onto each of the bowling alley buildings. Each playground would include a swing, a slide, climbing bars, and some other small-scale playground equipment. Each child would be charged an admission fee to use the facility. It is expected that parents will stay at the bowling alleys longer while their children are occupied in the playground area.

Mr. Palmer is interested in obtaining cost information relative to the proposed playground project. He understands that the more hours each playground area is open for business, the higher the cost of operating the playground will be. Beyond that, he knows nothing of cost behavior patterns.

**REQUIRED:**

Prepare a memorandum to Mr. Palmer that describes the following:
  **a.** The various variable, fixed, and mixed costs that are likely to be associated with the new playground facilities
  **b.** The concept of fixed costs, variable costs, and mixed costs
  **c.** Why an understanding of the methods available for estimating cost behavior patterns will help him to better plan and control his operations

# Chapter 5

## Business Decisions Using Cost Behavior

$C$ laudia June is the owner of Upstart T-Shirt Shop, one of many souvenir shops located on Highway A1A in Daytona Beach, Florida. Upstart sold 3,000 T-shirts during 1997 (the company's first year of operation), and Claudia's accountant prepared the following multistep income statement for the year.

### UPSTART T-SHIRT SHOP
#### Income Statement
#### For the Year Ended December 31, 1997

| | | |
|---|---:|---:|
| Sales | | $36,000 |
| Cost of Goods Sold | | 21,600 |
| Gross Profit | | $14,400 |
| Operating Expense: | | |
|   Selling Expense | $9,500 | |
|   Administrative Expense | 7,900 | (17,400) |
| Operating Loss | | $(3,000) |

Frankly, Claudia was quite pleased with the results for 1997 because she did not expect the store to be profitable in its first year. As Claudia planned for 1998, she figured she needed to increase sales by only 625 T-shirts to break even for the year. Her reasoning was based on the fact that each T-shirt cost $7.20 and sold for $12, resulting in $4.80 gross profit on each T-shirt ($12.00 − $7.20 = $4.80). If the shop sold 3,625 T-shirts, it would earn a gross profit of $17,400 (3,625 × $4.80), which would be exactly enough to cover the selling and administrative expenses of $17,400. If Claudia met her sales goal, the store would break even in only its second year of operation.

As luck would have it, Upstart T-Shirt Shop sold exactly 3,625 T-shirts during the year ended December 31, 1998. Each T-shirt sold for exactly $12 and cost the company exactly

$7.20. Confident that the shop had broken even for the year, Claudia excitedly opened the envelope from her accountant and found the following multistep income statement for 1998.

**UPSTART T-SHIRT SHOP**
**Income Statement**
**For the Year Ended December 31, 1998**

| | | |
|---|---:|---:|
| Sales | | $43,500 |
| Cost of Goods Sold | | 26,100 |
| Gross Profit | | $17,400 |
| Operating Expense: | | |
|   Selling Expense | $10,438 | |
|    Administrative Expense | 8,897 | (19,335) |
| Operating Loss | | $(1,935) |

Claudia was disappointed and discouraged when she saw an operating loss of $1,935 for the year. She rechecked the arithmetic and her assumptions about what it would take to break even for 1998 and could not understand why the store had an operating loss.

Claudia may not understand what happened, but after having studied Chapter 4 and its discussion of cost behavior, you should understand the problem. Claudia failed to consider that some costs are affected by changes in activity level and others are not. In this chapter, we explore cost-volume-profit analysis and see how business people use an understanding of this analytical technique to predict financial performance effectively. ■

**LEARNING OBJECTIVES**

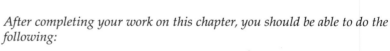

*After completing your work on this chapter, you should be able to do the following:*

1. Describe the differences between a functional income statement and a contribution income statement.
2. Determine per unit amounts for sales, variable cost, and the contribution margin.
3. Determine the contribution margin ratio and explain its importance as a management tool.
4. Prepare and analyze a contribution income statement for a merchandising firm.
5. Describe cost-volume-profit (CVP) analysis and explain its importance as a management tool.
6. Use CVP analysis to determine the amount of sales required to break even or to earn a targeted profit.
7. Use CVP to perform sensitivity analysis.

# THE CONTRIBUTION INCOME STATEMENT

As discussed in Chapter 4, separating costs by means of cost behavior provides managers insight about forecasting cost at different levels of business activity. This valuable cost behavior information, however, is not presented in either the multi-step or the single-step income statement used for financial reporting. The traditional income statement prepared for external parties separates costs (expenses) as either product costs or period costs.

**functional income statement** An income statement that classifies cost by function (product cost and period cost).

An income statement that separates product and period costs is called a **functional income statement.** Management accountants have developed a special income statement format for internal use that categorizes costs by behavior (fixed cost and variable cost) rather than by function (product cost and period cost). An income statement that classifies costs by behavior is a **contribution income statement.** Now, do not be alarmed, as this new format is no more complicated than the income statements you studied in earlier chapters. The main difference between the two is that the contribution income statements list variable costs first, followed by fixed costs. Note that the contribution income statement cannot be used for financial accounting information prepared for external decision makers; it is only used for internal decision-making purposes.

**contribution income statement** An income statement that classifies cost by behavior (fixed cost and variable cost).

## Purpose of the Contribution Income Statement

Let us return to the Upstart T-Shirt Shop example to see how a contribution income statement could have helped Claudia better predict the future profitability of her merchandising company. The two income statements presented for Upstart (1997 and 1998) were functional income statements. Upstart's 1997 functional income statement is reproduced as Exhibit 5–1.

**Exhibit 5–1**
Upstart's 1997 Functional Income Statement

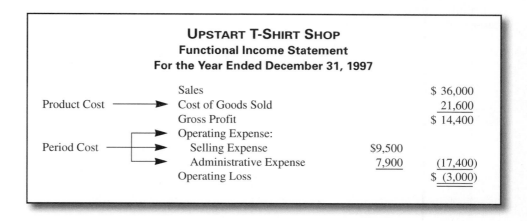

**UPSTART T-SHIRT SHOP**
**Functional Income Statement**
**For the Year Ended December 31, 1997**

| | | | |
|---|---|---|---|
| | Sales | | $ 36,000 |
| Product Cost → | Cost of Goods Sold | | 21,600 |
| | Gross Profit | | $ 14,400 |
| | Operating Expense: | | |
| Period Cost → | Selling Expense | $9,500 | |
| | Administrative Expense | 7,900 | (17,400) |
| | Operating Loss | | $ (3,000) |

We see that the cost information in Exhibit 5–1 is separated into product cost (cost of goods sold) and period cost (selling expenses and administrative expenses). Next we will examine how Claudia can convert her functional income statement into a contribution income statement.

First, Claudia needs additional information about the cost behavior of the expenses in Upstart's 1997 functional income statement. On request, Claudia's accountant provides the following information:

| | |
|---|---|
| Cost of goods sold | All variable |
| Selling expense | 40% variable, so 60% must be fixed |
| Administrative expense | $6,300 Fixed, so $1,600 must be variable |

# Discussion Question

**5–1.** With the cost behavior information just presented, can you help Claudia determine how much her profit will change if she sells 5,000 shirts in 1999? (Remember to look at the 1998 income statement shown at the beginning of the chapter.)

Now that she has Upstart's cost behavior information, Claudia can prepare a contribution income statement for 1997. The contribution income statement lists sales first, as does the functional income statement, with variable costs listed next. These costs are subtracted from sales to arrive at the contribution margin. **Contribution margin** is defined as the amount remaining after all variable costs have been deducted from sales revenue. The contribution margin is an important piece of information for managers, because it tells them how much of their company's original sales dollars remain after deduction of variable costs. This remaining portion of the sales dollars contributes to fixed costs and, once fixed costs have been covered, to profit. The contribution margin, then, is the amount available to contribute to covering fixed costs and ultimately toward profits for the income statement period.

Upstart's 1997 contribution income statement (through the contribution margin) is presented as Exhibit 5–2.

**contribution margin** The amount remaining after all variable costs have been deducted from sales revenue.

**Exhibit 5–2**
Upstart's Partial 1997 Contribution Income Statement

| UPSTART T-SHIRT SHOP | | |
|---|---|---|
| **Partial Contribution Income Statement** | | |
| **For the Year Ended December 31, 1997** | | |
| Sales | | $36,000 |
| Variable Cost: | | |
| Cost of Goods Sold | $21,600 | |
| Variable Selling Expense ($9,500 × 40%) | 3,800 | |
| Variable Administrative | | |
| Expense ($7,900 – $6,300) | 1,600 | |
| Total Variable Cost | | (27,000) |
| Contribution Margin (Sales Less Total Variable Cost) | | $ 9,000 |

Finally, fixed costs are listed and subtracted from the contribution margin to arrive at operating income, as shown in Exhibit 5–3.

Like a functional income statement, the contribution income statement can be detailed or condensed depending on the needs of the information users. It can also be prepared showing the per unit costs and percentage of sales calculations. A condensed version of Upstart's 1997 contribution income statement, including per unit and percentage of sales figures, is presented as Exhibit 5–4.

Throughout the rest of the chapter we will use a condensed version of the contribution income statement.

# Discussion Questions

**5-2.** Why is the gross margin found on the functional income statement different from the contribution margin found on the contribution income statement?

**5-3.** Why is the operating loss shown on Upstart's 1997 contribution income statement exactly the same as the operating loss shown on the company's 1997 functional income statement?

Looking at the per unit column in Exhibit 5–4, we note that the contribution margin per unit is $3. We calculate this by dividing the total contribution margin of $9,000 by the number of units sold—in this case 3,000 ($9,000 / 3,000 = $3). The $3 per unit contribution margin means that for every T-shirt sold, the sale generates $3 to contribute toward fixed costs. Then, once fixed costs have been covered, $3 per T-shirt sold contributes to profit. That is, if Upstart sells one more shirt for $12, then the $12 selling price less the $9 variable cost leaves $3. The contribution margin contributes toward fixed cost first, then to profits.

**Exhibit 5–3**
Upstart's Completed 1997 Contribution Income Statement

UPSTART T-SHIRT SHOP
Contribution Income Statement
For the Year Ended December 31, 1997

| | | |
|---|---:|---:|
| Sales | | $36,000 |
| Variable Cost: | | |
| Cost of Goods Sold | $21,600 | |
| Variable Selling Expense ($9,500 × 40%) | 3,800 | |
| Variable Administrative | | |
| Expense ($7,900 – $6,300) | 1,600 | |
| Total Variable Cost | | (27,000) |
| Contribution Margin (Sales Less Total Variable Cost) | | $ 9,000 |
| Fixed Cost: | | |
| Fixed Selling Expense ($9,500 × 60%) | $ 5,700 | |
| Fixed Administrative | | |
| Expense | 6,300 | |
| Total Fixed Cost | | (12,000) |
| Operating Loss | | $ (3,000) |

**Exhibit 5–4**
Upstart's Condensed 1997 Contribution Income Statement

UPSTART T-SHIRT SHOP
Contribution Income Statement
For the Year Ended December 31, 1997

| | Total | Per Unit | Sales (%) |
|---|---:|---:|---:|
| Sales in Units | 3,000 | 1 | |
| Sales | $36,000 | $12.00 | 100 |
| Variable Cost | (27,000) | (9.00) | (75) |
| Contribution Margin | $9,000 | $ 3.00 | 25 |
| Fixed Cost | (12,000) | | |
| Operating Loss | $ (3,000) | | |

**contribution margin ratio**
The contribution margin expressed as a percentage of sales.

Note in the percentage column of Exhibit 5–4 that the contribution margin is 25 percent of sales. When the contribution margin is expressed as a percentage of sales, it is called the **contribution margin ratio.**

The contribution margin ratio is calculated by dividing the total contribution margin by total sales, or by dividing the per unit contribution margin by per unit selling price, as follows:

$$\frac{\text{Total Contribution Margin}}{\text{Total Sales}} = \text{Contribution Margin Ratio}$$

or

$$\frac{\text{Per Unit Contribution Margin}}{\text{Per Unit Selling Price}} = \text{Contribution Margin Ratio}$$

In the case of Upstart T-Shirt Shop, the calculations are as follows:

$$\frac{\$9,000}{\$36,000} = 25\%$$

or

$$\frac{\$3}{\$12} = 25\%$$

The contribution margin ratio is the same whether it is computed using total figures or per unit figures, because the contribution margin is based on sales minus only variable costs. Thus, the variable costs and contribution margin change in direct proportion to sales. This proportional relationship holds true whether we are using per unit amounts or amounts in total.

In our example, the 25 percent contribution margin ratio means that, of each sales dollar, 25 percent (or 25 cents) is available to contribute toward fixed cost and then toward profit.

## Discussion Question

**5–4.** If Upstart's sales increase by $20,000, and the contribution margin ratio is 25%, by how much will profits increase?

The contribution income statement is a wonderful management tool because it allows managers to see clearly the amounts of fixed and variable costs incurred by the company. Understanding which costs are variable and which are fixed is essential if managers are to reasonably predict future costs. More importantly, a solid understanding of the contribution income statement approach and the concept of the contribution margin and contribution margin ratio is the backbone of another important decision-making tool: cost-volume-profit analysis.

## COST-VOLUME-PROFIT ANALYSIS

**cost-volume-profit (CVP) analysis** The analysis of the relationship between cost and volume and the effect of these relationships on profit.

As its name implies, **cost-volume-profit (CVP) analysis** is the analysis of the relationships between cost and volume (the level of sales), and the effect of those relationships on profit. In this section, we examine how managers can use CVP concepts to predict sales levels at which a firm will break even or attain target profits. CVP analysis is a useful tool for managers, business owners, and potential business owners for determining the profit potential of a new company or the profit impact of changes in selling price, cost, or volume on current businesses.

Thousands of businesses are started every day. Unfortunately, most of them fail a short time later, and the people who start these businesses suffer significant financial and emotional hardship. Such hardships might be avoided if new business owners used CVP analysis to evaluate the potential profit of their business ventures. With CVP analysis, a new business owner can discover potential disaster before starting the business, thereby preserving savings that could be used more productively elsewhere.

## Breakeven

**breakeven** Occurs when a company generates neither a profit nor a loss.

**break-even point** The sales required to achieve breakeven. This can be expressed either in sales dollars or in the number of units sold.

We begin our coverage of CVP analysis with a discussion of breakeven. **Breakeven** occurs when a company generates neither a profit nor a loss. The sales volume required to achieve breakeven is called the **break-even point.** Because most businesses exist to earn a profit, why would managers be interested in calculating a break-even point? In at least two situations this kind of information is valuable. First, the break-even point will show a company how far product sales can decline before the company will incur a loss. This information could provide the encouragement to continue in business, or may provide an early warning of impending business failure. Second, owners and managers may use break-even analysis when starting a business, just as Claudia did with the Upstart T-Shirt Shop. Recall that Upstart experienced a $3,000 operating loss in its first year of operation, but Claudia expected the loss because she understood most businesses are not profitable in their first year. Her break-even prediction for Upstart's second year, however, failed to allow for certain cost increases as sales increased.

With our understanding of cost behavior and the contribution income statement, we can predict the level of sales that Upstart will need to break even for the year.

Let us look again at the 1997 contribution income statement for Upstart T-Shirt Shop, reproduced in Exhibit 5–5.

**Exhibit 5–5**
Upstart's Condensed 1997 Contribution Income Statement

### UPSTART T-SHIRT SHOP
#### Contribution Income Statement
#### For the Year Ended December 31, 1997

|                      | Total      | Per Unit  | Sales (%) |
|----------------------|-----------:|----------:|----------:|
| Sales in Units       | 3,000      | 1         |           |
| Sales                | $36,000    | $12.00    | 100       |
| Variable Cost        | (27,000)   | (9.00)    | (75)      |
| Contribution Margin  | $9,000     | $ 3.00    | 25        |
| Fixed Cost           | (12,000)   |           |           |
| Operating Loss       | $ (3,000)  |           |           |

Managers who use CVP analysis must apply simple formulas to obtain useful information. Understanding and applying these formulas during this course should be relatively simple, but remembering them when you are actually working as a manager may be difficult. To make these formulas easier to remember, we will relate them to the most basic math used in an income statement, beginning with sales minus cost equals profit. Next, recall that cost can be broken down into variable and fixed cost. We use this information to derive a basic CVP equation, as shown in Exhibit 5–6.

**Exhibit 5–6**
Basic CVP Equation

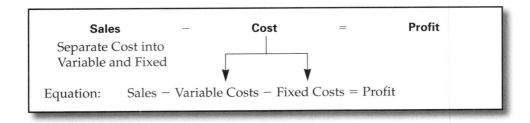

The basic equation for CVP analysis in Exhibit 5–6 requires that the costs be identified as fixed or variable, and that any mixed cost be separated into its fixed and variable components. In the examples that follow, we assume costs have been properly classified as fixed or variable.

Managers can calculate the break-even point based either on units or on sales dollars. We will demonstrate the process in units first, and then in sales dollars.

***Break-Even Point in Units*** To illustrate how to find the break-even point in units, we examine the Upstart T-Shirt Shop example. As shown in Exhibit 5–5, the selling price per T-shirt is $12, the variable cost is $9 per shirt, the contribution margin is $3 per T-shirt, and fixed costs total $12,000 per year. With this information, we can determine the number of T-shirts Upstart must sell to achieve a break-even point by dividing the contribution margin per unit into the total fixed cost, as shown in the following CVP formula:

***CVP Formula 1—Break-Even Point in Units***

$$\frac{\text{Total Fixed Cost}}{\text{Contribution Margin Per Unit}} = \text{Break-Even Point in Units}$$

Using the information from Upstart, we calculate the following:

$$\frac{\$12,000}{\$3} = 4,000 \text{ T-shirts}$$

By using this simple formula (and our knowledge of the cost behavior patterns associated with Upstart T-Shirt Shop), we see that if Upstart had sold exactly 4,000 T-shirts in 1998, the company would have broken even for the year. We can prove this fact if we use the equation from Exhibit 5–6 and the information from Upstart as follows:

| Sales | – | Variable Costs | – | Fixed Costs | = | Profit |
|---|---|---|---|---|---|---|
| (4,000 × $12) | – | (4,000 × $9) | – | $12,000 | = | Profit |
| $48,000 | – | $36,000 | – | $12,000 | = | $ 0 |

We can also prove it by preparing a contribution income statement based on the results of our calculation, as shown in Exhibit 5–7.

***Break-Even Point in Sales Dollars*** Because business performance is measured in total dollar sales and in the number of units of product sold, managers also find it useful to have breakeven presented in both sales dollars and unit sales. To demonstrate the calculation of the break-even point in sales dollars, we once again use the information provided by Upstart T-Shirt Shop's contribution income statement in Exhibit 5–5.

When calculating the break-even point in sales dollars, we divide the contribution margin ratio into total fixed cost, as shown in the second of the CVP formulas.

**Exhibit 5–7**
Upstart's Condensed
1998 Contribution
Income Statement

**UPSTART T-SHIRT SHOP**
**Projected Contribution Income Statement**
**For the Year Ended December 31, 1998**

|  | Total | Per Unit | Sales (%) |
|---|---|---|---|
| Sales in Units | 4,000 | 1 | |
| Sales | $ 48,000 | $12.00 | 100 |
| Variable Cost | (36,000) | (9.00) | (75) |
| Contribution Margin | $ 12,000 | $ 3.00 | 25 |
| Fixed Cost | (12,000) | | |
| Operating Income | $ -0- | | |

### CVP Formula 2—Break-Even Point in Sales Dollars

$$\frac{\text{Total Fixed Cost}}{\text{Contribution Margin Ratio}} = \text{Break-Even Point in Sales Dollars}$$

Using the information from Upstart's contribution income statement, we know that total fixed cost is $12,000 and the contribution margin ratio is 25 percent. The break-even point calculation is

$$\frac{\$12,000}{25\%} = \$48,000 \text{ Sales Dollars}$$

A quick review of the contribution income statement in Exhibit 5–7 shows that our calculation of $48,000 sales at the break-even point is correct.

We have examined the calculation of a break-even point in required units and in sales dollars. As stated earlier, however, companies are not in business to break even. Rather, they are usually interested in earning profits. In the next section, we discuss how the break-even calculations are modified to predict a company's profitability.

## Predicting Profits Using CVP Analysis

Claudia June now knows that her T-shirt business must sell 4,000 T-shirts to break even, assuming of course that the T-shirt selling price and the variable and fixed costs remain unchanged. Claudia can also use CVP analysis to predict Upstart's profit for any given level of sales above the break-even point. Assume, for example, that Upstart expects to sell 7,500 shirts in 1999. Claudia can quickly predict the expected profit at that sales level by preparing a contribution income statement, such as that in Exhibit 5–8.

**UPSTART T-SHIRT SHOP**
**Projected Contribution Income Statement**
**For the Year Ended December 31, 1999**

|  | Total | Per Unit | Sales (%) |
|---|---|---|---|
| Sales in Units | 7,500 | 1 | |
| Sales | $ 90,000 | $12.00 | 100 |
| Variable Cost | (67,500) | (9.00) | (75) |
| Contribution Margin | $ 22,500 | $ 3.00 | 25 |
| Fixed Cost | (12,000) | | |
| Operating Income | $ 10,500 | | |

If we did not want to take the time required to construct an actual contribution income statement, we could calculate the same operating income using the following basic CVP equation shown in Exhibit 5–6.

| Sales | – | Variable Costs | – | Fixed Costs | = | Profit |
|---|---|---|---|---|---|---|
| (7,500 × $12) | – | (7,500 × $9) | – | $12,000 | = | Profit |
| $90,000 | – | $67,500 | – | $12,000 | = | $10,500 |

The sales figure in this calculation is the number of T-shirts multiplied by the selling price per unit (7,500 × $12 = $90,000). Variable cost is the number of T-shirts sold multiplied by the variable cost per unit (7,500 × $9 = $67,500). The fixed cost of $12,000 remains the same in total. With these three figures in place, simple arithmetic gave us the expected profit of $10,500 if 7,500 T-shirts are sold.

## Projecting Sales Needed to Meet Target Profits Using CVP Analysis

Using CVP analysis to project profits at a given level of sales is only one application of this technique. Next we explore how to use CVP analysis when price and cost information are known, and a manager wants to determine the sales required to meet a specific target profit objective. As with the break-even point, we can apply CVP analysis to determine the sales needed to meet target profits in either units or sales dollars.

***Projecting Required Sales in Units*** Assume Claudia targets $27,000 as Upstart's profit for 1999. By making a simple addition to the formula we used to calculate the break-even point, Claudia can determine how many T-shirts Upstart must sell to earn that target profit. The modified formula is as follows:

### *CVP Formula 3—Unit Sales Required to Achieve Target Profits*

$$\frac{\left(\text{Total Fixed Cost + Target Profit}\right)}{\text{Contribution Margin Per Unit}} = \text{Required Unit Sales}$$

Recall that the contribution margin is the amount available to contribute to covering fixed cost first, and then profits. When considering the break-even point, we calculated the number of units required simply to cover the fixed cost. In our present discussion, we are looking for the number of units required not only to cover the fixed cost, but also to achieve a specific target profit. As shown in CVP formula 3, we simply add the target profit to the total fixed cost and then divide the sum by the contribution margin per unit. This equation will tell us how many units must be sold to cover all the fixed cost and to attain the target profit. Using the information from Upstart, the calculation is as follows:

$$\frac{\left(\$12,000 + \$27,000\right)}{\$3} = \text{Required Unit Sales}$$

or

$$\frac{\$39,000}{3} = 13,000 \text{ T-Shirts}$$

We see, then, that with a fixed cost of $12,000 and a contribution margin per unit of $3, Upstart will need to sell 13,000 T-shirts to earn $27,000 profit.

## Discussion Question

**5-5.** How would you prove to Claudia that 13,000 T-shirts must be sold to earn a $27,000 profit?

***Projecting Required Sales in Dollars*** To demonstrate the calculation of the sales dollars required to attain target profits, we once again use the information provided by Upstart T-Shirt Shop's contribution income statement in Exhibit 5–5.

We use the contribution margin ratio as the denominator in the CVP formula, instead of the unit contribution margin, as follows:

### CVP Formula 4—Sales Dollars Required to Achieve Target Profits

$$\frac{(\text{Total Fixed Cost} + \text{Target Profit})}{\text{Contribution Margin Ratio}} = \text{Required Sales Dollars}$$

With the information from Upstart, the calculation is as follows:

$$\frac{(\$12,000 + \$27,000)}{25\%} = \text{Required Sales Dollars}$$

or

$$\frac{\$39,000}{25\%} = \$156,000 \text{ in Sales}$$

## Discussion Question

**5-6.** How would you prove to Claudia that sales must total $156,000 to earn a $27,000 profit?

In this section we introduced you to four cost-volume-profit formulas, as summarized in Exhibit 5–9.

**Exhibit 5–9**
Cost-Volume-Profit Formulas

| Formula | Calculation | Purpose |
|---|---|---|
| CVP Formula 1 | $\dfrac{\text{Total Fixed Cost}}{\text{Contribution Margin Per Unit}}$ | To determine the break-even point in units |
| CVP Formula 2 | $\dfrac{\text{Total Fixed Cost}}{\text{Contribution Margin Ratio}}$ | To determine the break-even point in sales dollars |
| CVP Formula 3 | $\dfrac{(\text{Total Fixed Cost} + \text{Target Profit})}{\text{Contribution Margin Per Unit}}$ | To determine the unit sales required to achieve a target profit |
| CVP Formula 4 | $\dfrac{(\text{Total Fixed Cost} + \text{Target Profit})}{\text{Contribution Margin Ratio}}$ | To determine the sales dollars required to achieve a target profit |

These formulas are used daily by managers of manufacturing, merchandising, and service type companies as they attempt to predict the future performance of their firms. Regardless of the career you choose, if it involves business you will see these formulas again and will be using them much sooner than you might think.

## Cost-Volume-Profit Graph

In addition to the calculations we have been studying, CVP analysis can also be depicted graphically. The graph used to present CVP analysis is similar to those used in the discussion of cost behavior in Chapter 4. A CVP graph for Upstart T-Shirt Shop is presented as Exhibit 5–10.

**Exhibit 5–10**
CVP Graph—Upstart
T-Shirt Shop

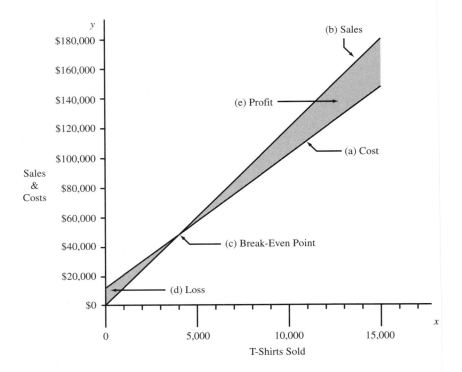

The main difference between the graph in Exhibit 5–10 and those in Chapter 4 is the graph in Exhibit 5–10 shows sales in addition to variable and fixed costs. The cost line (a) on the graph is exactly like those in Chapter 4. Note that this line intercepts the $y$-axis at $12,000, the total fixed cost for Upstart T-Shirt Shop. Thus, Upstart incurs $12,000 fixed cost even if the company sells no T-shirts. The cost line slopes upward at $9 for each T-shirt sold (variable cost).

Now consider the sales line (b) on the graph. If Upstart sells no T-shirts, there would obviously be no sales dollars, which explains why the sales line intercepts the $y$-axis at zero. The line slopes upward at $12 for every T-shirt sold. The point at which the cost line and the sales line cross (c) is Upstart's break-even point, which we know from our calculations in this chapter to be 4,000 T-shirts, or $48,000 in sales revenue. The loss area (d) on the graph and the profit area (e) represent a loss and profit, respectively, for Upstart. Thus, if Upstart sells fewer than 4,000 T-shirts, the company will experience a loss. If it sells more than 4,000 T-shirts, the company will earn a profit.

# Discussion Question

**5-7.** Using the CVP graph in Exhibit 5–10, can you plot the level of sales (in units and dollars) where Upstart will earn a profit of

    **a.** $10,500?

    **b.** $27,000?

The CVP graph is a useful management tool. Although it should not take the place of the calculations we have demonstrated thus far in this chapter, it has a distinct advantage over the calculations in that it allows managers to view the entire cost-volume-profit picture. Claudia June can, for example, assess Upstart's profit potential at any level of business within the relevant range of activity.

# Discussion Question

**5-8.** If Claudia is faced with competition from a new T-shirt shop in town, and is forced to lower her selling price to $11 per T-shirt, how much profit can she expect in 1998? (Assume that Claudia expects to sell 13,000 shirts and the cost information stays the same.)

To demonstrate the basics of CVP analysis, we have assumed that the selling price per unit, variable costs per unit, and total fixed cost all remained unchanged. Businesses, however, experience daily pressures that can cause each of these items to change. CVP analysis can adapt to any such change.

Now that we have covered the basics, we are ready to put CVP to perhaps its greatest use: sensitivity analysis.

## Sensitivity Analysis—What If?

**sensitivity analysis** A technique used to determine the effect on cost-volume-profit when changes are made in the selling price, cost structure (variable and/or fixed), and volume used in the CVP calculations. Also called "what if" analysis.

**Sensitivity analysis** is a technique used to determine the effect on CVP when changes are made in the selling price, cost structure (variable and/or fixed), and volume used in the calculations. Sensitivity analysis is also called "what if?" analysis. Managers are often looking for answers to the following types of questions, in terms of the effect on projected profits: "What if we raised (or lowered) the selling price per unit?" "What if variable cost per unit increased (or decreased)?" and "What if fixed cost increased (or decreased)?" Sensitivity analysis can provide those answers.

One other item to note before we proceed with the discussion of sensitivity analysis is that we will be using only CVP formula 3 and CVP formula 4. Although sensitivity analysis can certainly be used to assess the effect of changes in selling price, variable cost, and fixed cost on breakeven, all our examples will include target profits.

To demonstrate how sensitivity analysis is used, we return to Claudia June and the Upstart T-Shirt Shop. Assume 1999 has now ended. Upstart's contribution income statement for the year is presented as Exhibit 5–11.

**Exhibit 5–11**
Upstart's Condensed
1999 Contribution
Income Statement

## UPSTART T-SHIRT SHOP
### Contribution Income Statement
### For the Year Ended December 31, 1999

| | Total | Per Unit | Sales (%) |
|---|---|---|---|
| Sales in Units | 11,286 | 1 | |
| Sales | $135,432 | $12.00 | 100 |
| Variable Cost | (101,574) | (9.00) | (75) |
| Contribution Margin | $ 33,858 | $ 3.00 | 25 |
| Fixed Cost | (12,000) | | |
| Operating Income | $ 21,858 | | |

Claudia is quite pleased with the $21,858 profit Upstart earned in 1999 and is aiming for a target profit of $27,000 in 2000 (the same target profit as 1999). The problem is that a new T-shirt shop just opened three doors from Upstart. Claudia feels she must lower her selling price to $11 due to competitive pressure and wants to know how many T-shirts Upstart must now sell to attain the $27,000 target profit. Claudia can use CVP analysis to determine the required sales level to achieve a targeted profit even if she changes her selling price.

## Change in Selling Price

If the selling price changes but variable cost does not, the number of units required to attain a target profit is determined using CVP formula 3 and a recalculated contribution margin based on the new selling price. In the case of Upstart T-Shirt Shop, the new contribution margin is $2 (new selling price of $11 − variable cost of $9). We now apply this contribution margin to the formula. (Remember, the fixed cost is unchanged.)

$$\frac{\left(\$12,000 + \$27,000\right)}{\$2} = \text{Required Unit Sales}$$

or

$$\frac{\$39,000}{\$2} = 19,500 \text{ T-shirts}$$

Our calculations show that with a lower selling price, as reflected in the revised contribution margin per unit, Upstart must sell 19,500 T-shirts to attain the target profit of $27,000.

# Discussion Question

**5-9.** How would you prove to Claudia that 19,500 T-shirts must be sold to earn a $27,000 profit if she reduces the selling price per T-shirt from $12 to $11?

We can also calculate the sales dollars required to attain the target profit of $27,000. To do this, we first calculate a new contribution margin ratio and then use CVP formula 4 to determine the sales dollars needed to earn the target profit. The new contribution margin ratio is 18.182 percent (rounded), which is calculated by dividing the new selling price ($11) into the new contribution margin ($2). We now apply this new information to CVP formula 4.

$$\frac{\left(\$12,000 + \$27,000\right)}{18.182\% \text{ (rounded)}} = \text{Required Sales Dollars}$$

or

$$\frac{\$39,000}{18.182\% \text{ (rounded)}} = \$214,498 \text{ Sales Dollars (rounded)}$$

By applying the revised contribution margin ratio to CVP formula 4, we see that Upstart will need $214,498 in sales to achieve the target profit of $27,000.

## Discussion Questions

**5–10.** How would you prove to Claudia that sales must total $214,498 to earn a $27,000 profit if she reduces the selling price per T-shirt from $12 to $11?

**5–11.** Why must we calculate a new contribution margin ratio when the per unit selling price changes?

**5–12.** Under what other circumstances must we calculate a new contribution margin ratio?

If Claudia reduces her selling price to $11, then Upstart must sell 19,500 T-shirts in 2000 to earn the target profit of $27,000. Claudia believes it would be impossible to sell that many shirts, so she begins to consider alternative ways to earn a $27,000 profit in a competitive environment.

Notice that Claudia was able to determine by CVP analysis that her business may be in trouble. The analysis itself, however, does nothing whatever to solve the problem—that is up to Claudia. Management accounting can provide the informational tools to help managers and business owners spot problems, but it is ultimately up to the manager or owner to make the decisions and solve the problems.

## Discussion Question

**5–13.** If Claudia must lower her selling price to $11 per shirt to be competitive, and it would be impossible to sell 19,500 T-shirts, what are some of the alternatives she might consider to attain the $27,000 profit?

### Change in Variable Cost and Fixed Cost

Alternatives to changing the selling price include changing variable cost or fixed cost. Because Claudia believes the selling price per T-shirt must be $11, either the variable cost per unit or the total fixed cost must be reduced. We start with an analysis of possible changes in variable cost.

First, we must analyze how Upstart determined its original variable cost. We determine per unit variable cost by dividing the total variable cost by the number of units sold. Recall from the earlier discussion and Exhibit 5–4 that Upstart sold 3,000 T-shirts during 1997, and total variable cost was $27,000. Therefore, the variable cost per unit was calculated as $9 ($27,000 variable cost / 3,000 units sold).

**Exhibit 5–12**
Analysis of Upstart's
Variable Cost
Components

| | Total Cost | | Units Sold | | Unit Cost |
|---|---|---|---|---|---|
| Cost of Goods Sold (T-shirts) | $21,600 | ÷ | 3,000 | = | $7.20 |
| Variable Selling Expenses | 3,800 | ÷ | 3,000 | = | 1.27 |
| Variable Administrative Expenses | 1,600 | ÷ | 3,000 | = | .53 |
| Variable Cost | $27,000 Total | | | | $9.00 Per Unit |

To analyze how a change in variable cost will affect the variable cost per unit of $9, we must look at the three components of per unit variable cost: the cost of each T-shirt, the variable selling expenses, and the variable administrative expenses. We need to know what portion of the $9 variable unit cost relates to each component. We can determine these portions by dividing the 3,000 units sold into each of the three cost components. We use 3,000 because that number of units caused these costs to be incurred. We find the cost of each variable cost component in the contribution income statement presented in Exhibit 5–3. The cost and per unit calculation for each component are presented in Exhibit 5–12.

Claudia does not believe any change can be made in either the variable selling expenses or the variable administrative expenses. Any possible reduction in variable cost, then, must be in the cost of the T-shirts. Our calculations in Exhibit 5–12 show that the per unit cost of each T-shirt is $7.20.

Assume Claudia has contacted her shirt supplier which has agreed to lower its price from $7.20 to $6 per T-shirt. This reduction of $1.20 ($7.20 − $6.00 = $1.20) will reduce Upstart's variable cost from $9 per shirt to $7.80 per shirt ($9.00 − $1.20 = $7.80). The new contribution margin is $3.20 ($11 selling price − $7.80 variable cost = $3.20), and the new contribution margin ratio is 29.091 percent ($3.20 contribution margin / $11 selling price = 0.29091 or 29.091 percent rounded).

Now consider a change in Upstart's fixed cost. Recall that Upstart's total fixed cost is $12,000. Assume that Claudia has agreed to provide fellow businesswoman Susan Williams with space in her shop to sell bathing suits to Claudia's customers. Susan has agreed to pay Claudia $250 per month as rent on the space she will use. The $250 per month works out to be $3,000 per year ($250 per month × 12 months = $3,000). Thus, Upstart's total fixed cost decreases from $12,000 to $9,000.

With these proposed changes in Upstart T-Shirt Shop's variable cost and fixed cost, we can now do sensitivity analysis. Let us see what effect these changes would have on Claudia's company. To do this, again, we will use CVP formulas 3 and 4. We simply need to plug the new cost structures (variable and fixed) into the formulas as follows:

### CVP Formula 3—Unit Sales Required to Achieve Target Profits

$$\frac{\left(\text{Total Fixed Cost} + \text{Target Profit}\right)}{\text{Contribution Margin Per Unit}} = \text{Required Unit Sales}$$

$$\frac{\left(\$9,000 + \$27,000\right)}{\$3.20} = 11,250 \text{ T-shirts}$$

By using CVP formula 3 (and Upstart's new variable and fixed cost structure), we found that if Upstart sells 11,250 T-shirts in 2000, the company will earn a profit of $27,000.

To calculate the sales dollars required to attain Upstart's target profit of $27,000, we use the company's new contribution ratio and CVP formula 4:

## CVP Formula 4—Sales Dollars Required to Achieve Target Profits

$$\frac{\left(\text{Total Fixed Cost} + \text{Target Profit}\right)}{\text{Contribution Margin Ratio}} = \text{Required Sales Dollars}$$

$$\frac{\left(\$9,000 + \$27,000\right)}{29.091\% \text{ (rounded)}} = \$123,750 \text{ in Sales (rounded)}$$

With the changes in cost structure Claudia has negotiated, she will be able to earn $27,000 profit in 2000 even if her sales drop from 11,286 T-shirts (the 1999 sales level) to 11,250 T-shirts.

## Discussion Questions

**5–14.** How would you prove to Claudia that sales must total $123,750 (11,250 T-shirts) to earn a $27,000 profit if she reduces the cost per T-shirt from $7.20 to $6 and reduces total fixed cost from $12,000 to $9,000?

**5–15.** If Claudia is more successful than anticipated in 2000 and sells 13,000 T-shirts by reducing her selling price to $11, and she also implements the variable and fixed cost changes described earlier, what will be Upstart's profits for 2000?

**5–16.** What complications do you foresee in using CVP analysis if Claudia begins selling a deluxe line of T-shirts that cost $11.50 each and sell for $17?

## Multiple Products and CVP

In reality, most companies sell more than one product. Companies that sell multiple products often have information about total variable cost and total sales for a given income statement period, but have no one variable cost and selling price that can be easily determined and used for CVP.

When a company sells multiple products, managers may still use CVP analysis, but they must apply CVP formula 2 for break-even analysis and CVP formula 4 to determine the required level of sales to attain target profits. CVP formulas 1 and 3 are useless in a multiproduct situation if the various products sold have different unit contribution margins.

To demonstrate how managers use CVP analysis in a multiproduct situation when per unit information is unavailable, let us consider the example of Margaret's Frame Factory.

Margaret's Frame Factory makes and sells picture frames of various size and quality. Exhibit 5–13 presents Margaret's condensed contribution income statement for 1997.

There is a per unit variable cost and selling price for each of the frame models Margaret's manufactures and sells, but they are not included in Exhibit 5–13. All we have are the totals. The $185,000 contribution margin comes from the sale of several different products, each with its own contribution margin. The 37 percent contribution margin ratio, then, is an average contribution margin ratio based on the sales mix of these different products. Even with this limited information, however, we can use CVP analysis to both calculate a break-even point and predict target profits.

**Exhibit 5–13**
Margaret's Condensed
1997 Contribution
Income Statement

| | **MARGARET'S FRAME FACTORY** | |
|---|---|---|
| | **Contribution Income Statement** | |
| | **For the Year Ended December 31, 1997** | |
| | **Total** | **% of Sales** |
| Sales | $ 500,000 | 100% |
| Variable Cost | (315,000) | (63%) |
| Contribution Margin | $ 185,000 | 37% |
| Fixed Cost | (143,000) | |
| Operating Income | $ 42,000 | |

## Break-Even Point in a Multiproduct Situation

To calculate the break-even point in a multiproduct situation, we use CVP formula 2.

### CVP Formula 2—Break-Even Point in Sales Dollars

$$\frac{\text{Total Fixed Cost}}{\text{Contribution Margin Ratio}} = \text{Break-Even in Sales Dollars}$$

Using the information from Margaret's, the calculation is as follows:

$$\frac{\$143,000}{37\%} = \$386,486 \text{ Sales Dollars (rounded)}$$

We know that Margaret's is well above the break-even point because the company earned a profit of $42,000 in 1997. The break-even calculation is still valuable to company management because it reveals how far sales could decline before the company would experience a loss. In this example, sales could decline by $113,514 ($500,000 1997 sales − $386,486 break-even point = $113,514 decline) before Margaret's would experience a loss.

## Projecting Required Sales in a Multiproduct Situation

Assume that Margaret's is interested in increasing profits to $80,000 in 1998. Based on the information contained in the 1997 contribution income statement presented in Exhibit 5–13, what would be the required sales to earn this target profit of $80,000? To find out, we use CVP formula 4:

### CVP Formula 4—Sales Dollars Required to Achieve Target Profits

$$\frac{\left(\text{Total Fixed Cost} + \text{Target Profit}\right)}{\text{Contribution Margin Ratio}} = \text{Required Sales Dollars}$$

Using the information from Margaret's Frame Factory's contribution income statement, we know that total fixed cost is $143,000, the target profit is $80,000, and the contribution margin ratio is 37 percent. The calculation of the required sales dollars is as follows:

$$\frac{\$143,000 + \$80,000}{37\%} = \$602,703 \text{ in Sales (rounded)}$$

Our calculations indicate that Margaret's Frame Factory will need $602,703 in sales to attain a target profit of $80,000.

# Discussion Question

**5-17.** How would you prove to Margaret's that sales must total $602,703 to earn an $80,000 profit?

We have demonstrated how CVP analysis can provide useful information about how changes in selling price, variable cost, and fixed cost affect a company's break-even point. Managers can also use CVP analysis to see what sales (in either units or dollars) the company needs to attain target profits.

CVP analysis is highly adaptable. It works equally well when managers are trying to determine profit potential, whether of a small segment of a large business or of an entire company. Before a company expands an existing business market or makes the decision to enter new markets, management should invest some time in gathering revenue and cost data, separating the cost-by-cost behavior, developing a contribution income statement, and applying these simple CVP procedures.

## CVP Assumptions

CVP analysis is a great "what if?" management tool because it is used by managers to estimate a company's profit performance under a variety of different scenarios. It is, however, an estimation technique only, and the following assumptions are made when this type of analysis is used.

1. All costs can be classified as either fixed or variable. Implicit in this assumption is that a mixed cost can be separated into its fixed and variable components.
2. Fixed costs remain fixed throughout the range of activity.
3. Variable cost per unit remains the same throughout the range of activity.
4. Selling price per unit remains the same throughout the range of activity.
5. The average contribution margin ratio in a multiproduct company remains the same throughout the range of activity.

These assumptions rarely, if ever, match reality. Market pressures, inflation, and a myriad of other factors cause revenue and cost structures to change in ways that place limitations on CVP analysis. Notwithstanding these limitations, however, CVP helps managers make more realistic estimates of future profit potential. It is a technique used every day by managers of large and small companies worldwide as they attempt to better manage their businesses.

## SUMMARY

The functional income statement, which separates the costs shown into product cost and period cost, is limited in its usefulness to managers as they attempt to plan and control their operations. It does not take into account that some costs change as volume changes, and some do not. The contribution income statement is more useful to managers as a planning tool because it separates the costs presented into fixed costs and variable costs rather than into product costs and period costs.

An integral part of the contribution income statement is the contribution margin, which is the amount remaining after all variable costs have been deducted from sales revenue. When the contribution margin is presented as a percentage of sales, it is called the contribution margin ratio. Both the contribution margin and the contribution margin ratio are used in cost-volume-profit analysis.

Cost-volume-profit (CVP) analysis is the analysis of the relationships between cost and volume, and the effect of those relationships on profit. The first application of CVP analysis is the calculation of breakeven, which is the sales level resulting in neither a profit nor a loss. Breakeven can be calculated either in sales dollars or in the number of units of product that must be sold.

Cost-volume-profit analysis can also be used to calculate the sales level required to achieve a target profit. As was the case with breakeven, the sales level required to achieve a target profit can be calculated in both sales dollars and the number of units of product that must be sold.

Cost-volume-profit analysis can also be used to perform sensitivity analysis, which is a technique used to determine the effect on CVP when changes are made in the selling price, cost structure (variable and/or fixed), and volume used in the calculations.

Although CVP analysis is easier to perform in a single-product situation, it can also be used to calculate breakeven and sales required to achieve target profits in a multiple product situation.

## KEY TERMS

| | |
|---|---|
| breakeven   M-155 | cost-volume-profit (CVP) |
| break-even point   M-155 | analysis   M-154 |
| contribution income statement   M-151 | functional income statement   M-151 |
| contribution margin   M-152 | sensitivity analysis   M-161 |
| contribution margin ratio   M-154 | |

## REVIEW THE FACTS

**A.** What is the difference between a contribution income statement and a functional income statement?

**B.** What is the contribution margin?

**C.** What does the contribution margin "contribute toward"?

**D.** How does total contribution margin differ from contribution margin per unit?

**E.** What is the contribution margin ratio and how does it differ from the contribution margin?

**F.** What is cost-volume-profit (CVP) analysis?

**G.** What does the term *break-even point* mean?

**H.** In what ways does the calculation of the break-even point in units differ from the calculation of the break-even point in sales dollars?

**I.** How would you calculate the required sales in units to attain a target profit?

**J.** How would you calculate the required sales in dollars to attain a target profit?

**K.** What does the term *sensitivity analysis* mean in the context of CVP analysis?

**L.** What does the term *average contribution margin ratio* mean for a company that sells multiple products?

**M.** Which two of the four CVP formulas are used to calculate breakeven and sales required to attain target profits for a multiproduct company?

**N.** Why are two of the CVP formulas useless in a multiproduct situation when contribution margins for individual products are unknown?

# APPLY WHAT YOU HAVE LEARNED

## LO 4:   Prepare a Contribution Income Statement

**5–18.** Fresh Baked Cookie Company sells cookies in a large shopping mall. The following multistep income statement was prepared for the year ending December 31, 2000.

**FRESH BAKED COOKIE COMPANY**
**Income Statement**
**For the Year Ended December 31, 2000**

| | | |
|---|---:|---:|
| Sales | | $36,000 |
| Cost of Goods Sold | | 4,000 |
| Gross Profit | | $32,000 |
| Operating Expense: | | |
|   Selling Expense | $18,000 | |
|    Administrative Expense | 10,000 | 28,000 |
| Operating Income | | $ 4,000 |

Cost of goods sold is a variable cost. Selling expense is 20% variable and 80% fixed, and administrative expense is 5% variable and 95% fixed.

**REQUIRED:**
Prepare a contribution income statement for the Fresh Baked Cookie Company.

## LO 4:   Prepare a Contribution Income Statement

**5–19.** The following multistep income statement was prepared for Steinmann's Bait Shop for the year ending December 31, 2000.

**STEINMANN'S BAIT SHOP**
**Income Statement**
**For the Year Ended December 31, 2000**

| | | |
|---|---:|---:|
| Sales | | $98,000 |
| Cost of Goods Sold | | 22,000 |
| Gross Profit | | $76,000 |
| Operating Expense: | | |
|   Selling Expense | $27,000 | |
|    Administrative Expense | 36,000 | 63,000 |
| Operating Income | | $13,000 |

Cost of goods sold is a variable cost. Selling expense is 30% variable and 70% fixed, and administrative expense is 10% variable and 90% fixed.

**REQUIRED:**
Prepare a contribution income statement for Steinmann's Bait Shop.

## LO 4:   Prepare a Contribution Income Statement

**5–20.** Quality Fishing Gear Company sells high-quality fiberglass fishing rods to retailers. The following multistep income statement was prepared for the year ending December 31, 2000.

**QUALITY FISHING GEAR COMPANY**
**Income Statement**
**For the Year Ended December 31, 2000**

| | | |
|---|---:|---:|
| Sales | | $540,000 |
| Cost of Goods Sold | | 360,000 |
| Gross Profit | | $180,000 |
| Operating Expense: | | |
|   Selling Expense | $88,000 | |
|   Administrative Expense | 72,000 | 160,000 |
| Operating Income | | $ 20,000 |

Cost of goods sold is a variable cost. Selling expense is 65% variable and 35% fixed, and administrative expense is 25% variable and 75% fixed.

**REQUIRED:**

Prepare a contribution income statement for Quality Fishing Gear Company.

## LO 4: Prepare a Contribution Income Statement

**5–21.** Ray Placid is considering opening a greeting card shop in a local mall. Ray contacted the mall manager and determined that the store rent will be $550 per month. In addition, he called the telephone company and based on the information from the telephone company representative, he estimates that the cost of telephone service will be about $95 per month. Based on the size of the store, Ray believes that cost of electricity will average about $200 per month. Ray will be able to buy the greeting cards for $0.50 each and plans to sell them for $2 each. Salaries are expected to be $1,200 per month regardless of the number of cards sold. Ray estimates that other miscellaneous fixed costs will total $150 per month and miscellaneous variable cost will be $0.10 per card. Ray anticipates that he will be able to sell about 3,000 greeting cards per month. If Ray opens the store, his first month of business will be November 2001.

**REQUIRED:**

Prepare a projected contribution approach income statement for November 2001.

## LO 4: Prepare a Contribution Income Statement

**5–22.** Joe's Pretzel Stand is located in the Orange Bowl stadium and sells pretzels during sporting events. The following information is available:

- Selling price per pretzel      $2.00
- Cost of each pretzel      $0.25
- Cost of renting the pretzel stand is $12,000 per year.
- Instead of an hourly wage, Joe pays college students $0.20 per pretzel sold to run the pretzel stand.

**REQUIRED:**

Prepare a contribution income statement for 2000 assuming that 8,000 pretzels are sold.

## LO 4: Prepare a Contribution Income Statement

**5–23.** The following information is available for Blaire's Snow Cone Stand:

- Selling price per snow cone      $1.25
- Cost of each snow cone      $0.30

- Rent paid for the stand, at a local flea market is $2,400 per year.
- Instead of an hourly wage, Blaire's pays high school students $0.40 per snow cone sold.

**REQUIRED:**
Prepare a contribution income statement for 2000 assuming that 6,000 snow cones are sold.

## LO 4:   Prepare a Condensed Contribution Income Statement

**5–24.** The following is the contribution income statement for The Bevens Company:

### THE BEVENS COMPANY
#### Contribution Income Statement
#### For the Year Ended December 31, 2001

| | | |
|---|---:|---:|
| Sales | | $800,000 |
| Variable Cost: | | |
| Cost of Goods Sold | $420,000 | |
| Variable Selling Expense | 75,000 | |
| Variable Administrative Expense | 33,000 | |
| Total Variable Cost | | 528,000 |
| Contribution Margin | | $272,000 |
| Fixed Cost: | | |
| Fixed Selling Expense | $128,000 | |
| Fixed Administrative Expense | 53,000 | |
| Total Fixed Cost | | 181,000 |
| Operating Income | | $ 91,000 |

**REQUIRED:**
Based on the contribution income statement for The Bevens Company, prepare a condensed contribution income statement.

## LO 1:   Prepare a Multistep Income Statement

**5–25.** Refer to the information presented in problem 5–24.

**REQUIRED:**
Prepare a multi-step income statement for the Bevens Company.

## LO 4:   Prepare a Condensed Contribution Income Statement

**5–26.** Following is the contribution income statement for The Lauren Company:

### THE LAUREN COMPANY
#### Contribution Income Statement
#### For the Year Ended December 31, 2001

| | | |
|---|---:|---:|
| Sales | | $4,800,000 |
| Variable Cost: | | |
| Cost of Goods Sold | $2,320,000 | |
| Variable Selling Expense | 265,000 | |
| Variable Administrative Expense | 484,000 | |
| Total Variable Cost | | 3,069,000 |
| Contribution Margin | | $1,731,000 |
| Fixed Cost: | | |
| Fixed Selling Expense | $ 648,000 | |
| Fixed Administrative Expense | 973,000 | |
| Total Fixed Cost | | 1,621,000 |
| Operating Income | | $ 110,000 |

**REQUIRED:**
Based on The Lauren Company's contribution income statement, prepare a condensed contribution income statement.

## LO 1: Prepare a Multistep Income Statement

**5–27.** Refer to the information presented in problem 5–26.

**REQUIRED:**
Prepare a multi-step income statement for The Lauren Company.

## LO 4: Prepare a Condensed Contribution Income Statement

**5–28.** The following is the contribution income statement for Carl's Athletic Shop:

**CARL'S ATHLETIC SHOP**
**Contribution Income Statement**
**For the Year Ended December 31, 2001**

| | | |
|---|---:|---:|
| Sales | | $422,000 |
| Variable Cost: | | |
|   Cost of Goods Sold | $205,000 | |
|   Variable Selling Expense | 55,000 | |
|   Variable Administrative Expense | 22,000 | |
|     Total Variable Cost | | 282,000 |
| Contribution Margin | | $140,000 |
| Fixed Cost: | | |
|   Fixed Selling Expense | $ 75,000 | |
|   Fixed Administrative Expense | 34,000 | |
|     Total Fixed Cost | | 109,000 |
| Operating Income | | $ 31,000 |

**REQUIRED:**
Based on this contribution income statement, prepare a condensed contribution income statement for Carl's Athletic Shop.

## LO 1: Prepare a Multistep Income Statement

**5–29.** Refer to the information presented in problem 5–28.

**REQUIRED:**
Prepare a multi-step income statement for Carl's Athletic Shop.

## LO 4: Prepare a Contribution Income Statement

**5–30.** Paradise Manufacturing makes weight-lifting equipment. During 2000, the following costs were incurred:

| | Amount | Percent Fixed | Percent Variable |
|---|---:|---:|---:|
| Direct material | $680,000 | – | 100 |
| Direct labor | 420,000 | – | 100 |
| Variable manufacturing overhead | 130,000 | – | 100 |
| Fixed manufacturing overhead | 900,000 | 100 | – |
| Selling cost | 300,000 | 20 | 80 |
| Administrative cost | 220,000 | 10 | 90 |

Sales for 2000 totaled $2,780,000 and there were no beginning or ending inventories.

**REQUIRED:**
Prepare a contribution income statement for the year ended December 31, 2000.

## LO 4: Prepare a Contribution Income Statement

**5–31.** The following information is available for Nicole's Toy Manufacturing Company for 2000:

|  | Amount | Percent Fixed | Percent Variable |
|---|---|---|---|
| Direct material | $440,000 | – | 100 |
| Direct labor | 90,000 | – | 100 |
| Variable manufacturing overhead | 70,000 | – | 100 |
| Fixed manufacturing overhead | 800,000 | 100 | – |
| Selling cost | 950,000 | 45 | 55 |
| Administrative cost | 570,000 | 85 | 15 |

Sales for 2000 totaled $3,164,000 and there were no beginning or ending inventories.

**REQUIRED:**
Prepare a contribution income statement for the year ended December 31, 2000.

## LO 4: Prepare a Contribution Income Statement

**5–32.** The following information is available for Rick's Watch Company for 2000:

|  | Amount | Percent Fixed | Percent Variable |
|---|---|---|---|
| Direct material | $534,000 | – | 100 |
| Direct labor | 129,000 | – | 100 |
| Variable manufacturing overhead | 397,000 | – | 100 |
| Fixed manufacturing overhead | 998,000 | 100 | – |
| Selling cost | 196,000 | 33 | 67 |
| Administrative cost | 243,000 | 78 | 22 |

Sales for 2000 totaled $2,745,000 and there were no beginning or ending inventories.

**REQUIRED:**
Prepare a contribution income statement for the year ended December 31, 2000.

## LO 4: Prepare a Contribution Income Statement

**5–33.** Alumacraft Manufacturing makes aluminum serving carts for use in commercial jetliners. During 2001, the following costs were incurred:

|  | Amount | Percent Fixed | Percent Variable |
|---|---|---|---|
| Direct material | $2,600,000 | – | 100 |
| Direct labor | 1,820,000 | – | 100 |
| Variable manufacturing overhead | 540,000 | – | 100 |
| Fixed manufacturing overhead | 1,900,000 | 100 | – |
| Selling cost | 380,000 | 15 | 85 |
| Administrative cost | 230,000 | 5 | 95 |

Sales for 2001 totaled $7,900,000 and there were no beginning or ending inventories.

**REQUIRED:**

Prepare a contribution income statement for the year ended December 31, 2001.

## LO 6: Determine Breakeven and Sales Required to Earn Target Profit Using Per Unit Amounts

**5–34.** The following information is available for Medical Testing Corporation.

| | |
|---|---|
| Amount charged for each test performed | $ 90 |
| Annual fixed cost | 200,000 |
| Variable cost per test | 25 |

**REQUIRED:**

**a.** Calculate how many tests Medical Testing Corporation must perform each year to break even.

**b.** Calculate how many tests Medical Testing Corporation must perform each year to earn a profit of $25,000.

## LO 6: Determine Breakeven and Sales Required to Earn Target Profit Using Per Unit Amounts

**5–35.** The following information is available for Dottie's Donut Shop.

| | |
|---|---|
| Amount charged per dozen doughnuts | $ 0.99 |
| Annual fixed cost | 385,000.00 |
| Variable cost per dozen doughnuts | 0.22 |

**REQUIRED:**

**a.** Calculate how many dozen doughnuts Dottie must sell each year to break even.

**b.** Calculate how many dozen doughnuts Dottie must sell each year to earn a profit of $35,000.

## LO 6: Determine Breakeven and Sales Required to Earn Target Profit Using Per Unit Amounts

**5–36.** Jim is considering starting a small company to paint driveways. The following information is available.

| | |
|---|---|
| Amount charged per square yard painted | $ 5 |
| Annual fixed cost | 3,000 |
| Variable cost per square yard painted | 2 |

**REQUIRED:**

**a.** Calculate how many square yards of driveway Jim must paint each year to break even.

**b.** Calculate how many square yards of driveway Jim must paint each year to earn a profit of $5,000.

## LO 6: Determine Breakeven and Sales Required to Earn Target Profit Using Per Unit Amounts

**5–37.** Carbonnel Calendar Company is considering adding a new calendar design to their line. The following information is available.

| | |
|---|---|
| Selling price | $ 3.97 |
| Additional annual fixed cost | 4,558.00 |
| Variable cost per calendar | 3.11 |

**REQUIRED:**

a. Calculate how many calendars must be sold each year to break even.

b. Calculate how many calendars must be sold each year to earn a profit of $2,580.

## LO 3 & 6:   Use Ratios to Determine Breakeven and Sales Required to Earn Target Profit

5–38. Melissa Valdez is planning to expand her clothing business by opening another store. In planning for the new store, Melissa believes that selling prices and costs of the various merchandise sold will be similar to that of the existing store. In fact, she thinks that variable and fixed costs for the new store will be similar to that of the existing store, except that rent for the new store will be $300 per month more than the rent paid for the existing store.

The following information is available for the existing store for the year ended December 31, 2000:

| | |
|---|---|
| Sales | $200,000 |
| Variable cost | 130,000 |
| Fixed cost | 48,000 |

**REQUIRED:**

a. Determine the sales required for the new store to break even.

b. Determine the sales required for the new store to earn a profit of $20,000 per year. (Hint: Keep in mind that the $300 increase in rent is a monthly amount and the fixed cost of $48,000 is an annual amount.)

## LO 3 & 6:   Use Ratios to Determine Breakeven and Sales Required to Earn Target Profit

5–39. Emergency Medical, Inc. is considering opening a new emergency care facility. The fees charged and costs of the new facility will be similar to that of the existing facility. The only exception is that the annual fixed cost for the new facility is expected to be $75,000 more than that of the existing facility.

The following information is available for Emergency Medical's existing facility for 2000:

| | |
|---|---|
| Revenue | $1,250,000 |
| Variable cost | 600,000 |
| Fixed cost | 420,000  + 75,000 = 495,000 |

**REQUIRED:**

a. Determine the revenues required for the new emergency care facility to break even.

b. Determine the revenues required for the new emergency care facility to earn a profit of $120,000 per year.

## LO 3 & 6:   Use Ratios to Determine Breakeven and Sales Required to Earn Target Profit

5–40. Wendt Industries is considering opening a second school supply store. The annual fixed cost of the new store is expected to be $225,000 per year. The following information is available for Wendt's first school supply store for 2000.

| | |
|---|---|
| Revenue | $3,650,000 |
| Variable cost | 1,387,000 |

**REQUIRED:**

a. Based on this information, what is the required revenue for the second store to break even?

b. Based on this information, what is the required revenue for the second store to earn a profit of $125,000?

## LO 2, 4, & 6: Use Per Unit Amounts to Determine Breakeven and Sales Required to Earn Target Profit and Prepare a Contribution Income Statement

**5–41.** Richard Davenport owns a clothing store and is considering renting a soda vending machine for his store. He can rent the soda machine for $125 per month. Richard would supply the soda for the machine which he can buy for $3 per twelve pack. Richard plans to charge $0.75 per can.

**REQUIRED:**

a. List the fixed costs for renting and stocking the soda machine.

b. List the variable costs for renting and stocking the soda machine.

c. Calculate the contribution margin per can of soda.

d. (1) Calculate how many cans of soda Richard must sell each month to break even.

    (2) Prepare a contribution income statement that proves the answer you just calculated.

e. (1) Calculate how many cans of soda Richard must sell each month to earn a profit of $50.

    (2) Prepare a contribution income statement that proves your answer to the previous requirement.

## LO 2, 4, & 6: Use Per Unit Amounts to Determine Breakeven and Sales Required to Earn Target Profit and Prepare a Contribution Income Statement

**5–42.** Erich Traebeecke owns the Kenpo Karate School in Miami. He is considering renting a candy vending machine for his school lobby. He can rent the candy machine for $90 per month. Erich would supply the candy bars for the machine. He can buy a box of eight candy bars for $1 per box. Erich plans to sell each candy bar for $0.35.

**REQUIRED:**

a. List the fixed costs of renting and stocking the candy machine.

b. List the variable costs of renting and stocking the candy machine.

c. Calculate the contribution margin per candy bar.

d. (1) Calculate how many candy bars must be sold each month to break even.

    (2) Prepare a contribution income statement that proves the answer you just calculated.

e. (1) Calculate how many candy bars must be sold each month to earn a profit of $180.

    (2) Prepare a contribution income statement that proves your answer to the previous requirement.

## LO 2, 4, and 6: Use Per Unit Amounts to Determine Breakeven and Sales Required to Earn Target Profit and Prepare a Contribution Income Statement

**5–43.** Monica Llobet owns Monica's School of Dance. She is considering installing a cappuccino machine in the school's dance studio. Monica can rent the cappuccino machine for $48.88 per month. Coffee and supplies would cost about $.12 per cup of cappuccino. Monica plans to sell each cup of cappuccino for $2.

**REQUIRED:**
a. List the fixed costs of renting and stocking the cappuccino machine.
b. List the variable costs of renting and stocking the cappuccino machine.
c. Calculate the contribution margin per cup of cappuccino.
d. **(1)** Calculate how many cups of cappuccino must be sold each month to break even.
   **(2)** Prepare a contribution income statement that proves the answer you just calculated.
e. **(1)** Calculate how many cups of cappuccino must be sold each month to earn a profit of $100. (Round your answer to the nearest unit.)
   **(2)** Prepare a contribution income statement that proves your answer to the previous requirement.

## LO 2 & 6: Use Per Unit Amounts to Determine Breakeven and Sales Required to Earn Target Profit

**5–44.** Alberto Pons is interested in selling pin-on buttons at school pep rallies. The button machine will cost $200, and the material to produce each button costs $0.15. In exchange for the right to sell the buttons, Alberto has agreed to donate $300 per year and $0.20 per button to the school's booster club. Alberto plans to sell the buttons for $1 each and to operate the service for four years. By then it will be time to graduate, and the button machine will be worn out.

**REQUIRED:**
a. Assuming the button machine will be able to produce buttons for four years, calculate the cost per year for the button machine.
b. Calculate the total fixed cost per year for Alberto's button business.
c. Calculate the variable cost per button.
d. Calculate the annual break-even point
   **(1)** in units.
   **(2)** in dollars.
e. Calculate how many buttons must be sold to earn an annual profit of $800.
f. Calculate the sales in dollars required to earn an annual profit of $800.

## LO 2 & 6: Use Per Unit Amounts to Determine Breakeven and Sales Required to Earn Target Profit

**5–45.** Betty Lopez is interested in setting up a stand to sell mylar helium balloons at a local roller rink. The stand would cost $250, and the material for each balloon would cost $0.75. In exchange for the right to sell the balloons, Betty has agreed to pay $500 per year and $0.50 per balloon to the roller rink's owner. Betty plans to sell the balloons $3 each. Betty thinks the stand will last four years.

**REQUIRED:**

a. Assuming the balloon stand has an estimated useful life of four years, with no salvage value, calculate the cost per year for the balloon stand.
b. Calculate the total fixed cost per year for Betty's balloon business.
c. Calculate the variable cost per balloon.
d. Calculate the annual break-even point
    (1) in units.
    (2) in dollars.
e. Calculate how many balloons must be sold to earn an annual profit of $2,000.
f. Calculate the sales in dollars required to earn an annual profit of $2,000.

## LO 2 & 6:  Use Per Unit Amounts to Determine Breakeven and Sales Required to Earn Target Profit

**5–46.** Bill Smith is interested in selling ice cream bars at school events. The vendor stand will cost $800, and the ice cream bars cost $0.65. In exchange for the right to sell the ice cream bars, Bill has agreed to donate $600 per year and $0.25 per ice cream bar to the school's booster club. Bill plans to sell the ice cream bars for $1.50 each. Bill intends to sell the ice cream bars and run the stand for four years. By then it will be time to graduate, and the vendor stand will be worn out.

**REQUIRED:**

a. Assuming the vendor stand can be used for four years, calculate the cost per year for the vendor stand.
b. Calculate the total fixed cost per year for Bill's ice cream business.
c. Calculate the variable cost per ice cream bar.
d. Calculate the annual break-even point.
    (1) in units.
    (2) in dollars.
e. Calculate how many ice cream bars must be sold to earn an annual profit of $3,000.
f. Calculate the sales in dollars required to earn an annual profit of $3,000.
g. Calculate Bill's profit if sales were $8,000 for this year.

## LO 3 & 6:  Determine the Contribution Margin Ratio and Determine Breakeven and Sales Required to Earn Target Profit

**5–47.** Amanda is considering opening a gift shop. She has collected the following information:

| | |
|---|---|
| Monthly rent | $2,800 |
| Monthly sales salaries | 1,200 |

In addition to the sales salaries, Amanda intends to pay sales commissions of 5% of sales to her sales staff. The cost of the merchandise sold is expected to be 40% of sales.

**REQUIRED:**

a. Determine the following:
    (1) Amanda's break-even point in monthly sales dollars
    (2) The monthly sales dollars required to earn a profit of $2,000 per month
    (3) Amanda's break-even point if she is able to reduce rent by $200
b. Assume that Amanda has negotiated a 10% discount on all merchandise purchases. The new cost of merchandise will not change the selling price of product. Determine the following:

**(1)** The new contribution margin ratio

**(2)** The new break-even point in monthly sales dollars

## LO 3 & 6:   Determine the Contribution Margin Ratio and Determine Breakeven and Sales Required to Earn Target Profit

**5–48.** Noelle is considering opening a bookstore. She has collected the following information:

| | |
|---|---|
| Monthly rent | $3,286 |
| Monthly sales salaries | 4,200 |

In addition to the sales salaries, Noelle intends to pay sales commissions of 10% of sales to her sales staff. The cost of the merchandise sold is expected to be 30% of sales.

**REQUIRED:**

**a.** Determine the following:
  **(1)** Noelle's break-even point in monthly sales dollars
  **(2)** The monthly sales dollars required to earn a profit of $1,500 per month
  **(3)** Noelle's break-even point if she is able to reduce rent by $300
**b.** Assume that Noelle has negotiated a 5% discount on all merchandise purchases. The new cost of merchandise will not change the selling price of product. Determine the following:
  **(1)** The new contribution margin ratio
  **(2)** The new break-even point in monthly sales dollars

## LO 2 & 6:   Use Per Unit Amounts to Determine Breakeven and Sales Required to Earn Target Profit

**5–49.** Clarice is considering buying a video rental business. If she finances the entire purchase price, the payments will be $2,900 per month. Store rent would be $2,000 per month and cost of sales clerks, replacement tapes, and other expenses would be $1,200 per month. Clarice plans to rent the tapes for $2 each.

**REQUIRED:**

**a.** Calculate the variable cost (if any) per tape rental.
**b.** Calculate the total fixed cost per month.
**c.** Determine how many tapes Clarice must rent each month to break even.
**d.** Determine how many tapes Clarice must rent each month to earn a profit of $1,000 per month.

## LO 3 & 6:   Determine the Contribution Margin Ratio and Determine Breakeven and Sales Required to Earn Target Profit

**5–50.** Margaret Pitman is considering opening a gift shop. She has collected the following information:

| | |
|---|---|
| Monthly rent | $1,800 |
| Monthly sales salaries | 1,200 |

The cost of the merchandise sold is expected to be 55% of sales.

**REQUIRED:**

**a.** What is the annual rent cost?
**b.** What is the annual sales salaries cost?

c. What is the contribution margin ratio?
d. What is the break-even point in dollars?
e. Determine the amount of sales needed to earn a profit of $12,000 for the year.

## LO 3 & 6:   Determine the Contribution Margin Ratio and Determine Breakeven and Sales Required to Earn Target Profit

**5–51.** Carol Jean is considering opening a frame shop. She has collected the following information:

| | |
|---|---|
| Monthly rent | $ 600 |
| Monthly sales salaries | 1,100 |

The cost of the merchandise sold is expected to be 45% of sales.

### REQUIRED:
a. What is the annual rent cost?
b. What is the annual sales salaries cost?
c. What is the contribution margin ratio?
d. What is the break-even point in dollars?
e. Determine the amount of sales needed to earn a profit of $18,000 for the year.

## LO 3 & 6:   Determine the Contribution Margin Ratio and Determine Breakeven and Sales Required to Earn Target Profit

**5–52.** Birdie Musicus is considering opening a beauty supply store. She has collected the following information:

| | |
|---|---|
| Monthly rent | $3,400 |
| Monthly sales salaries | 2,800 |

The cost of the merchandise sold is expected to be 68% of sales.

### REQUIRED:
a. What is the annual rent cost?
b. What is the annual sales salaries cost?
c. What is the contribution margin ratio?
d. What is the break-even point in dollars?
e. Determine the amount of sales needed to earn a profit of $36,000 for the year.

## LO 3 & 6:   Determine the Contribution Margin Ratio and Determine Breakeven and Sales Required to Earn Target Profit

**5–53.** Vivian Farias is considering opening a music store. She has collected the following information:

| | |
|---|---|
| Monthly rent | $1,400 |
| Monthly sales salaries | 1,700 |

The cost of the merchandise sold is expected to be 52% of sales.

### REQUIRED:
a. What is the annual rent cost?
b. What is the annual sales salaries cost?
c. What is the contribution margin ratio?
d. What is the break-even point in dollars?
e. Determine the amount of sales needed to earn a profit of $36,000 for the year.

## LO 2, 3, 4, & 5:   Analyze a Situation Using CVP

**5–54.** Quality Instrument Company manufactures various industrial thermometers. Last year the company sold 600 model QI-22 thermometers for $129 each. Managers are concerned that the profits from the QI-22 were only $7,740 last year. Fixed costs for this product are $50,000 per year. In an effort to increase profits, the company raised the price of the QI-22 to $148. Based on annual sales of 600 units, managers are confident that profits from the QI-22 will be increased to $19,140 next year.

The sales manager is concerned about the price increase. He believes the company should move a little slower in making the pricing decision and has suggested that a group be formed to explore the ramifications of such a pricing move.

### REQUIRED:

Assume that you have been assigned to the group who will evaluate the proposed price change. The group is to create a report discussing the various ramifications of the price increase including its effect on projected sales and profits. Your report should make recommendations that are supported by calculations similar to those found in this chapter.

## LO 2, 3, 4, & 5:   Analyze a Situation Using CVP

**5–55.** Reuben Steinman's Sliding Glass Door Company manufactured and sold 1,000 model SD4896 doors for $88 each. Managers are concerned that the profits from the SD4896 doors were only $8,000 last year. In an effort to increase profits, the company raised the price of the SD4896 to $106. Based on annual sales of 1,000 units, managers are confident that profits from the SD4896 will increase to $26,000 next year. Fixed costs of $40,000 are allocated to the SD4896 based on the number of units produced.

The sales manager is concerned about the price increase. He believes the company should move a little slower in making the pricing decision and has suggested that a group be formed to explore the ramifications of such a pricing move.

### REQUIRED:

Assume that you have been assigned to the group who will evaluate the proposed price change. The group is to create a report discussing the various ramifications of the price increase including its effect on projected sales and profits. Your report should make recommendations that are supported by calculations similar to those found in this chapter.

## LO 2, 3, 4, & 5:   Analyze a Situation Using CVP

**5–56.** Carol Juriet is considering the purchase of a hot dog vending cart to sell hot dogs in a busy parking lot. The city of Daytona Beach requires that the cart be licensed at a cost of $500 per year.

### REQUIRED:

a. (1) How would Carol determine the cost to rent a small space in the parking lot to operate the hot dog cart?

(2) How much do you think the monthly rent would be?

(3) How much do you think the hourly wage would be for an employee to operate the stand?

(4) How many hours per day do you think the stand should be open?

- **(5)** Based on your answers to 3 and 4, what would you estimate monthly wage cost to be for the hot dog stand?
- **(6)** How much do you think Carol should charge for each hot dog?
- **b.** Answer the following questions using your answers to question 1.
  - **(1)** What is the variable cost per hot dog?
  - **(2)** What is the monthly fixed cost for operating the hot dog stand?
  - **(3)** What is the contribution margin per hot dog?
  - **(4)** What is the contribution ratio?
  - **(5)** What is the variable cost ratio?
  - **(6) a)** How many hot dogs must Carol sell each month to break even?
    - **b)** Prepare a contribution income statement which proves your answer.
  - **(7) a)** How many hot dogs must Carol sell each month to earn a profit of $300?
    - **b)** Prepare a contribution income statement that proves your answer.

# Chapter 6

## Making Decisions Using Relevant Information

Financial accounting information provided to external decision makers must be relevant to be useful. Not surprisingly, management accounting information provided to internal decision makers must also possess the characteristic of relevance. It is critically important that managers make their decisions based on relevant information and that they disregard all irrelevant information. To be relevant, the information must be pertinent to the decision at hand. In accounting, **relevant costing** is the process of determining which dollar inflows and outflows pertain to a particular management decision.

Determining which costs are relevant is not always an easy job. For instance, consider an actual example about a couple that went to Disney World with their three-year-old daughter, Jessica. The family stayed at a Disney hotel to be close to the Disney attractions, and to take advantage of the hotel's staff of baby-sitters. The baby-sitting service required payment of a 4-hour minimum at $11 per hour, or $44. Users must cancel 3 hours in advance to avoid the $44 minimum fee. Jessica's parents planned to take her to the Magic Kingdom early in the day and then leave her with a sitter in the late afternoon while they visited EPCOT on their own.

Jessica and her parents went to Disney's Magic Kingdom as they had planned and were having a wonderful time. As the day progressed, Jessica enjoyed the amusement park so much that Jessica's parents were having second thoughts about leaving her with the sitter. They had to make a decision: Should they take Jessica to EPCOT or leave her with the sitter as planned?

**relevant costing** The process of determining which dollar inflows and outflows pertain to a particular management decision.

Because the family's admission tickets permitted them to enter all the Disney parks, the main issue was the minimum $44 charge for the sitter, because it was too late to cancel. As Jessica's parents discussed the pros and cons of each alternative, they realized the $44 charge would have to be paid whether they took Jessica to EPCOT or not. The baby-sitter's fee, then, was an irrelevant cost in this decision, because Jessica's parents would have to pay the baby-sitting fee no matter which alternative they chose. Once Jessica's parents determined that the fee was irrelevant, they dismissed the sitter and Jessica was off to EPCOT with them.

In business, the issue of what is relevant often confuses even the most seasoned business executive. To make the best possible decisions, decision makers must learn to consider only relevant information. ■

## LEARNING OBJECTIVES

*After completing your work on this chapter, you should be able to do the following:*

1. Identify the characteristics of a relevant cost.
2. Explain why sunk costs and costs that do not differ between alternatives are irrelevant costs.
3. Describe the qualitative factors that should be considered when making a business decision.
4. Use accounting information and determine the relevant cost of various decisions.
5. Explain the effects of fixed costs and opportunity costs on outsourcing decisions.

## RELEVANT COSTS

You may wonder why an entire chapter of this text is devoted to determining which costs are relevant. Isn't it understood that decision makers should disregard superfluous information and concentrate on the facts that relate to the decision at hand? Yes, but with so many cost considerations to muddy the water, determining what information is relevant is not always as easy as it might seem.

**relevant cost** A dollar inflow or outflow that pertains to a particular management decision in that it has a bearing on which decision alternative is preferable.

A **relevant cost** is a cost that is pertinent to a particular decision in that it has a bearing on which decision alternative is preferable. A relevant cost possesses two important characteristics: (1) The cost must be a future cost, and (2) the cost must differ between decision alternatives.

A relevant cost must be a future cost because current decisions can have no effect on past expenditures. Expenditures that have already occurred are called **sunk costs** and they cannot be changed by current or future actions. Because sunk costs are unaffected by current decisions, they are irrelevant and should not be considered when evaluating current decision alternatives. For example, if your firm was deciding whether to replace an old printing press with a new, labor-saving model, the cost of the old press would be irrelevant. Why? The firm already bought the old

**sunk cost** A past cost that cannot be changed by current or future actions.

press. The purchase of the new printing press would not lessen or change the amount paid for the old press. Whether the company purchases the new press or not, the cost of the old press is a sunk cost: Nothing we can do now can change it. Sunk costs include both amounts paid in the past and past commitments to pay. That is, once there is a binding commitment to pay cash or otherwise transfer resources, the cost associated with that commitment is a sunk cost.

A relevant cost must differ between decision alternatives. If a cost remains the same regardless of the alternative we choose, it is irrelevant. Again, focus on the decision to buy a new printing press or to keep the old one. If the new printing press will use the same quantity and type of ink as the old one, the cost of ink is irrelevant no matter how large the dollar figure.

## Discussion Questions

**6-1.** Refer back to the decision faced by Jessica's parents in Disney World. Which criteria of relevance did the $44 baby-sitting cost fail to meet? Explain your reasoning.

**6-2.** Have you ever made a decision and later found that you mistakenly let irrelevant factors sway your choice? Explain.

**quantitative factors** Factors that can be measured by numbers.

**qualitative factors** Factors that cannot be measured by numbers—they must be described in words.

The term *relevant cost* is something of a misnomer. Perhaps a better description of this topic would be *relevant factors*. The reason for this is that the term relevant cost is used to describe not only changes in cost, but also changes in revenue. These cost and revenue changes often result in inflows of resources rather than outflows.

**Quantitative factors** are those that can be represented by numbers. Almost all accounting information is quantitative, including relevant cost. However, managers often consider additional factors that cannot be quantified. **Qualitative factors** are factors that cannot be measured numerically—they must be described in words. Examples include customer satisfaction, product quality, employee morale, and customer perceptions.

In addition to their financial impact, business decisions affect a multitude of nonfinancial areas. For example, closing an outdated factory may reduce production cost, but it will also adversely impact employee moral. The employees that remain after the plant closing may believe that the company's loyalty is to profits, not their well-being. Lower employee moral is likely to lead to less productivity. Qualitative factors should also be considered in smaller, routine decisions. For example, a furniture store manager considering a proposal to switch from company owned and operated delivery trucks to a delivery service should consider her lack of control if the delivery service is used. Even though it may be less expensive to use a delivery service, the furniture store's manager may not want to lose the ability to select the most responsible truck drivers and to schedule deliveries exactly as desired. When making a decision, managers should evaluate all relevant quantitative and qualitative factors.

## Discussion Questions

Assume you are planning a trip from Miami to Texas to visit some friends. You have a job, but your boss will let you take off as many days as you wish for the trip. Your car is unreliable, so you compare two alternatives—take a bus or take an airplane.

**6-3.** What are the relevant quantitative factors you should consider in making your decision?

**6-4.** What are the relevant qualitative factors you should consider in making your decision?

Decision makers must question the relevance of accounting information. As discussed in Chapter 1, managers and engineers no longer specify accounting information requirements. Instead, accountants provide information to managers based on accepted accounting techniques, so its relevance to management decision makers has diminished. Although some businesses have taken steps to make management accounting information more relevant to internal decision makers, managers should be able to determine for themselves what is relevant so they can make sound, well-informed decisions (see Exhibit 6–1).

**Exhibit 6–1**
Determining
Relevant Cost

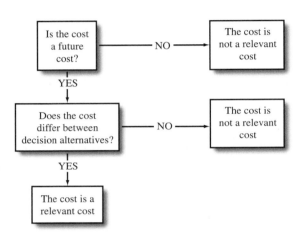

Throughout the remainder of this chapter, we will explore several common business situations to demonstrate how to determine relevant cost and its importance to good decision making. For each example, we will gather all costs associated with the decision. Next, we will determine the relevant cost of each decision alternative. Finally, we will compare the relevant costs of the alternative and determine the preferred alternative. The first example we will explore is an equipment replacement decision.

## EQUIPMENT REPLACEMENT

To apply the concepts of relevant costing, we examine a proposed equipment replacement project. Our example highlights the treatment of depreciation, sunk costs, and costs that do not differ between alternatives.

Bill Smith & Partners, a local law firm, purchased and installed a sophisticated computer system two weeks ago at a cost of $35,500. Bill's brother, John, stops by the law office to say hello. While there, he notices the new system. He remarks that it is too bad the system is not the latest and quickest because, if it were, the data input time could be cut in half. John suggests that Bill consider updating. Bill responds, "I can't buy a new system. I just bought this one two weeks ago." John advises Bill to take a closer look before deciding.

## Gather All Costs Associated with the Decision

Bill turns to you for advice. He explains that the recently installed computer system cost $35,500 to purchase, has an estimated useful life of five years, with a residual value of $500. He notes that the firm plans to use straight-line depreciation, so it will recognize $7,000 depreciation per year. The cost of operating the recently installed system, which we will call the "old" system, includes two operators at $18,000 per year, and a maintenance contract at $1,000 per year. The maintenance agreement, however, can be canceled at any time. After calling around, Bill informs you that he can sell the old system now, but he will get only $10,000 for it (everyone wants the new model). The new model would cost $76,000 and also has an estimated useful life of five years with a $1,000 residual value. Using the straight-line method, annual depreciation would be $15,000. Because data entry is twice as fast, the new computer system would require only one operator at $18,000 per year. The maintenance contract on the new machine would cost $1,000 per year and would be cancelable at any time.

A summary of the cost of each system is shown in Exhibit 6–2. These costs are generally classified as start-up costs, operating costs, and shutdown costs.

**Exhibit 6–2**
Computer System
Replacement
Cost Summary

| | Old System | Replacement System |
|---|---|---|
| **Start-up costs:** | | |
| Cost of system | $ 35,500 | $76,000 |
| **Operating costs:** | | |
| Annual depreciation | $ 7,000 | $15,000 |
| Total depreciation | 35,000 | 75,000 |
| Annual labor cost | 36,000 | 18,000 |
| Total labor cost | 180,000 | 90,000 |
| Annual maintenance cost | 1,000 | 1,000 |
| Total maintenance cost | 5,000 | 5,000 |
| **Shutdown costs:** | | |
| Residual value of system | $ 500 | $ 1,000 |
| Current sale price of old system | 10,000 | |

To help Bill make a wise decision about the new computer system, you must first look at each cost and determine whether it is relevant. To make an informed decision, a manager must consider the total cost of each alternative, including all the costs incurred over the life of the alternative. For our computer replacement decision, the annual costs associated with each system are multiplied by the number of years the system will be used to determine the total cost of the system over its lifetime.

## Determine the Relevant Cost of Each Alternative

Next we determine the relevant cost of each decision alternative. As you consider each cost, try to determine whether it is relevant to the equipment replacement decision. Ask yourself the following two questions: (1) Is the cost a future cost? and (2) Does the cost differ between alternatives? We will examine the cost associated with the old computer system first.

***Relevant Cost of the Old Computer System*** The $35,500 cost of the old system is not relevant because it is a sunk cost. Bill's decision to purchase or not to purchase the new computer system cannot change the past expenditure for the old one.

Although it may appear that depreciation is a future cost, it is nothing more than an allocation of an asset's original cost. The cost of an asset purchased in the past is a sunk cost, and, therefore, depreciation simply allocates this sunk cost. If depreciation expense relates to an asset purchased in the past, it is irrelevant. In this situation, the depreciation for the old computer system is not relevant because the depreciation is an allocation of the purchase price, which is a sunk cost.

The total cost of $180,000 to pay for two operators is relevant, because it is a future cost and it differs between alternatives. The old system requires two operators, each costing $18,000 per year. Over the five-year expected life of the old system, that totals $180,000 (2 operators × $18,000 × 5 years).

The $5,000 total cost of the maintenance contract for the old system is irrelevant, because it does not differ between decision alternatives. The cost of the maintenance contract for the old system is the same as that for the new one. Therefore, although this is a future cost, it is irrelevant because it does not differ between alternatives.

The $500 residual value of the old system is relevant because it is a future cost and it differs between alternatives. If Bill stays with the old computer system, he will be able to sell it at the end of its useful life for $500. If, however, he buys the new one, he will sell the old one now for $10,000, and therefore he will be unable to sell it for its residual value in five years.

The $10,000 that Bill could get if he sells the old system now is a future cost that differs between alternatives, and therefore it is relevant. If Bill buys the new computer system, he can sell the old one for $10,000, but if he does not buy the new system, he will need the old one so he would not sell it.

***Relevant Costs of the Replacement System***   Next, we will analyze the start-up, operating, and shutdown costs of the replacement computer system. The only start-up cost for the replacement system is the $76,000 to purchase and install it. This cost is relevant because it is a future cost and it differs between alternatives.

The $75,000 in total depreciation on the new computer system is an allocation of the replacement system's cost. Because we have already considered the cost of the new computer system, we avoid double-counting by excluding its depreciation expense from our analysis of relevant costs.

The $90,000 ($18,000 × 5 years) total labor cost for the replacement system's one operator is relevant because it is a future cost that differs between alternatives. The labor cost for the old system is $180,000, whereas the labor cost for the replacement system is $90,000.

The total cost of the maintenance contract on the replacement system is $5,000. As it happens, the maintenance cost of the old system is also $5,000. In this situation, although maintenance cost is a future cost, it is irrelevant because it does not differ between alternatives.

The $1,000 residual value for the new computer system is relevant because it is a future cost that differs between alternatives. If Bill replaces his current system with a new one, then he can sell the new system for $1,000 at the end of its useful life (in the future). If he does not buy the new one, he obviously cannot sell it.

## Compare the Relevant Costs and Select an Alternative

Now that you have determined which costs are relevant, you compare them to see which alternative is best for Bill's firm. It is important to differentiate between inflows and outflows. In Exhibit 6–3 we use parentheses to identify outflows.

As this analysis shows, Bill would save $24,500 over the next five years by buying the new computer system. So he should buy the new system to save money,

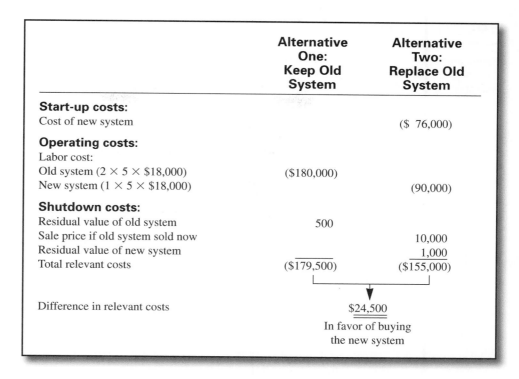

**Exhibit 6–3**
Relevant Cost Comparison for Bill Smith & Partners

| | Alternative One: Keep Old System | Alternative Two: Replace Old System |
|---|---|---|
| **Start-up costs:** | | |
| Cost of new system | | ($ 76,000) |
| **Operating costs:** | | |
| Labor cost: | | |
| Old system (2 × 5 × $18,000) | ($180,000) | |
| New system (1 × 5 × $18,000) | | (90,000) |
| **Shutdown costs:** | | |
| Residual value of old system | 500 | |
| Sale price if old system sold now | | 10,000 |
| Residual value of new system | | 1,000 |
| Total relevant costs | ($179,500) | ($155,000) |
| | | |
| Difference in relevant costs | $24,500 | |
| | In favor of buying the new system | |

right? From a purely monetary point of view, he should. However, can he? The replacement system is not cheap. Often business decision makers determine the best alternative, only to learn the business does not have enough available cash to take advantage of a course of action that would save money in the long run. Considering only relevant costs in decision making will lead to better business decisions, but it will not necessarily enable a company to take advantage of what can be learned in the process.

## Discussion Questions

6–5. Assuming all purchases and sales of computer systems are cash transactions, how much cash would Bill need to buy the new system?

6–6. Now that we know the relevant cost associated with the computer replacement, what qualitative factors should Bill consider before he makes his final decision?

### Interest—The Time Value of Money

New equipment purchase decisions generally have long-term effects. Because of the long life of the equipment, the associated cash inflows and outflows will occur for many years. Therefore, decision makers should consider the interest-earning potential of the cash flows associated with equipment acquisitions. The interest earning potential of cash is sometimes called the **time value of money.** Chapter 7 covers special techniques developed to incorporate the effect of interest and the timing of cash flows.

**time value of money** The interest earning potential of cash.

# SPECIAL ORDERS

**special order** An order that is outside a company's normal scope of business activity.

Manufacturing businesses must often consider whether to accept a **special order**—an order that is outside its normal scope of business activity. As we will see, proper treatment of fixed cost is critical in making sound special order decisions.

Assume that your company, Alumafloat, makes small aluminum boats. Alumafloat has been in operation for almost 10 years and sells boats to marine supply stores in southern Florida. One day, a Sears Roebuck and Company representative approaches you with an interesting proposition. Sears is interested in purchasing 1,000 of your boats for $125 each. The largest order your company has received to date was for 100 boats, so obviously, this huge order requires special consideration.

## Gather All Costs Associated with the Decision

The $125 offer from Sears is considerably less than Alumafloat's normal selling price of $160 per boat. In fact, the boats cost $130 each to produce, so the company would lose $5 per boat if it accepts Sears's $125 offer.

As you discuss the order with the representative from Sears, you tell her that you would be willing to sell the boats to Sears at a discounted price of $140 each because of the large quantity of boats they need. Sears refuses your offer. The store will only pay $125 per boat, and the representative expects you to accept or reject the order within five days.

You gather all the information necessary to make a wise decision. First, you meet with your company's cost accountant, who confirms that your cost per unit is $130. You also request a report detailing production cost so you can see how the cost per unit figure was calculated. Using expected total sales (excluding the special order from Sears) and production costs for the year, the cost accountant prepares the report shown in Exhibit 6–4.

**Exhibit 6–4**
Per Unit Cost Report for Alumafloat

| | | |
|---|---|---|
| Expected sales (5,500 units at $160 each) | | $880,000 |
| Less: Cost of goods sold (see detail below) | | (715,000) |
| Expected gross margin | | $165,000 |

**Detailed calculation for cost of goods sold:**

| | Per Unit | Total |
|---|---|---|
| Number of units | 1 | 5,500 |
| | | |
| Direct material costs | $ 50 | $275,000 |
| Direct labor costs | 55 | 302,500 |
| Variable production costs | 10 | 55,000 |
| Fixed production costs | 15 | 82,500 |
| Total cost of goods sold | $130 | $715,000 |

We must determine the potential effect on Alumafloat's revenues and expenses of accepting the order. Which costs shown in Exhibit 6–4 would be affected by the decision to accept the special order from Sears? To determine which costs are relevant, we will again ask the following two questions: (1) Is the cost a future cost? and (2) Does the cost differ between alternatives?

## Determine the Relevant Cost of Each Alternative

Next you must determine which costs are relevant. In this situation, the alternatives are to accept the order or reject it. Generally speaking, because no cost is associated with rejecting the order, our analysis focuses on the alternative to accept.

If the order is accepted, sales will increase by $125,000 (1,000 boats × $125 per boat). The increase in sales due to the special order is relevant, because it is something that will happen in the future and it differs between alternatives.

All variable costs are relevant because they are future costs that differ between alternatives. If the special order is accepted, variable costs will be incurred to produce the 1,000 boats. In this example, variable cost includes direct material, direct labor, and variable production costs.

Depending on the decision situation, fixed cost may or may not be relevant. Often fixed production costs are not relevant costs because total fixed cost for the company will be unaffected by the increase in production volume. This fact holds true unless specific fixed cost increases occur due to the special order, or the order is so substantial that production would exceed the relevant range if the company accepts the order. As the report in Exhibit 6–4 indicates, the company expects total fixed costs to be $82,500. Assume in our example that the decision to accept or reject the special order from Sears would not affect total fixed cost. Therefore, in this case, fixed cost does not differ between alternatives and is irrelevant to the special order decision.

## Compare the Relevant Costs and Select an Alternative

Armed with information about relevant cost, you can make an informed decision about the Sears order. Exhibit 6–5 presents a schedule of relevant costs for this special order. The schedule excludes fixed costs because they are irrelevant.

**Exhibit 6–5**
Relevant Costs for Special Order of 1,000 Boats

|  | Per Unit | Total |
|---|---|---|
| Sales from special order | $125 | $125,000 |
| Direct material costs | (50) | (50,000) |
| Direct labor costs | (55) | (55,000) |
| Variable production costs | (10) | (10,000) |
| Total relevant production costs | (115) | (115,000) |
| Total increase in income | $ 10 | $ 10,000 |

Alumafloat's income would increase by $10,000 if it accepted the special order.

The reasoning in the Alumafloat example may seem logical, but companies often reject special orders that would increase profits, because managers do not understand the concept of relevant cost as it pertains to fixed cost. To avoid making poor decisions, managers must carefully consider how a special order will affect fixed cost.

An accountant for a Fortune 500 manufacturing company once remarked, "I can't believe that the product sales manager is selling below cost. He is disregarding fixed cost as he sets prices to move old stock." In fact, the manager may have made a good decision about the price of the product, depending on whether the fixed costs are relevant to the pricing decision. As a manager, you should know that routinely prepared accounting information cannot be relevant to every decision. Accounting information must be tailored, sometimes by the information user, to provide information that is relevant to the decision at hand.

# Discussion Questions

**6-7.** What would happen if you treated every order as a special order and routinely disregarded fixed cost considerations from your pricing decisions?

**6-8.** Assume that the production manager at Alumafloat reminds you that four years ago sales skyrocketed for a while. Demand was so great that production increased to the limit of the company's capacity. Alumafloat produced 6,950 boats in a 12-month period. What implications does this information have on your decision to accept the special order from Sears?

**6-9.** What qualitative factors should you consider regarding accepting an order to sell Sears the boats for less than the price you charge your regular customers? For example, what would your regular customers think if they found that Sears was selling the same style boat they buy from you?

# OUTSOURCING: THE MAKE OR BUY DECISION

**outsourcing** Buying services, products, or components of products instead of producing them.

Often companies purchase subcomponents used to manufacture their products instead of making them in their in-house manufacturing facilities. Buying services, products, or components of products from outside vendors instead of producing them is called **outsourcing**. Decision makers considering a make or buy decision must pay close attention to fixed costs and opportunity costs.

Assume you are a product manager at Microbake, a plant that manufactures microwave ovens. A vendor has approached you about supplying the timer assemblies for your ovens for $12 each. Currently, Microbake makes the timers in its own subassembly department. The subassembly department makes many of the small component parts for the various products manufactured at the plant. When you review the cost sheets for the timers, you discover that the company uses 80,000 timers each year and they cost $14 each to produce in-house.

## Gather All Costs Associated with the Decision

You call a meeting with Microbake's cost accounting department to discuss the situation and confirm that the $14 in-house manufacturing cost is correct. Even when pressed, the cost accountants are confident their cost figures are carefully prepared and accurate. In fact, they are surprised the company can buy the timers from the outside vendor for only $12 each. At your request, the cost accounting department prepares the cost breakdown for the timers shown in Exhibit 6-6.

**Exhibit 6-6**
Cost of Producing Oven Timers In-House

| Number of timers produced each year | | 80,000 |
|---|---|---|
| | **Per Unit** | **Total** |
| Direct material | $ 5 | $ 400,000 |
| Direct labor | 4 | 320,000 |
| Variable manufacturing overhead | 1 | 80,000 |
| Fixed manufacturing overhead | 4 | 320,000 |
| Total | $14 | $1,120,000 |

**Exhibit 6–7**
Selecting Relevant
Costs of Producing
Oven Timers

|  | Future? | Differs? | Relevant? |
|---|---|---|---|
| Direct material: | yes | yes | yes |
| Direct labor: | yes | yes | yes |
| Variable manufacturing overhead: | yes | yes | yes |
| Fixed manufacturing overhead: | yes | **no** | **no** |

## Determine the Relevant Cost of Each Alternative

Once again we assess whether each cost is relevant by asking the following questions: (1) Is the cost a future cost? and (2) Does the cost differ between alternatives? The answers follow in Exhibit 6–7.

By definition, *fixed* manufacturing overhead remains constant in total regardless of the level of activity (in this case "activity" is the number of units produced). The fixed cost presented by the cost accountants is an allocation of the total fixed overhead cost of the whole factory, or possibly of the subassembly department. If the company stops making the timers, the subassembly department will not go away and neither will its fixed cost, because the company needs the subassembly department to produce other components. Unless fixed cost changes based on management's decision to buy the timers, it is irrelevant.

## Compare the Relevant Costs and Select an Alternative

We compare the relevant costs of the make or buy decision in Exhibit 6–8.

**Exhibit 6–8**
Relevant Cost of Make
or Buy Decision for
Oven Timers

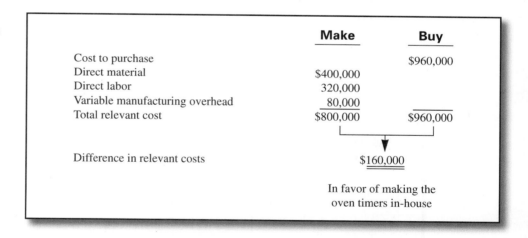

As Exhibit 6–8 indicates, once we have screened out the irrelevant fixed costs it becomes apparent that Microbake can save $160,000 per year by making the timers rather than buying them. Based on this relevant cost comparison, you decide to not purchase the timer assemblies from the outside vendor.

In a final effort to get the sale, the vendor contacts several people at Microbake informing them that you are squandering your company's money. The vendor points out to other Microbake managers that its price is $2 per unit less than your in-house production cost as determined by Microbake's highly trained cost accountants. Other managers are pressing to accept the outside vendor's proposal.

To settle the issue, you call a meeting of the managers and present your relevant cost findings. Several managers comment that your information disregards fixed manufacturing overhead. You explain that the fixed manufacturing overhead is irrelevant. The other managers argue that fixed manufacturing overhead is a very real part of business cost and that it should be included in your presentation. As it happens, this presents little problem. Including fixed manufacturing overhead, although irrelevant, may highlight how fixed costs are affected (or in this case, unaffected) by changes in production. You must demonstrate, however, that if the units are manufactured in-house, fixed manufacturing overhead cost will happen; and that if the units are purchased from the outside vendor, the fixed manufacturing overhead will still occur. The relevant cost comparison can include the irrelevant fixed cost as shown in Exhibit 6–9.

**Exhibit 6–9**
Relevant Cost of Make or Buy Decision for Oven Timers with Fixed Costs Shown

|  | Make | Buy |
|---|---|---|
| Cost to purchase |  | $ 960,000 |
| Direct material | $ 400,000 |  |
| Direct labor | 320,000 |  |
| Variable manufacturing overhead | 80,000 |  |
| Fixed manufacturing overhead | 320,000 | 320,000 |
| Total cost | $1,120,000 | $1,280,000 |

Difference in total costs $160,000
In favor of making the
oven timers in-house

As Exhibit 6–9 shows, because fixed manufacturing overhead is the same for the two alternatives, the outcome of the comparison is the same as that in Exhibit 6–8. Microbake can save $160,000 by making the timers instead of buying them.

## Discussion Question

**6–10.** What will happen to the cost of producing other Microbake products if your decision is overturned and the company outsources the timer assemblies?

### Special Relevant Cost Considerations for Fixed Costs

In some situations, fixed costs are affected by the alternative selected. For example, suppose Microbake could eliminate an entire 8-hour production shift if it no longer made the timers. Eliminating that shift thus eliminates one line supervisor whose annual salary is $45,000 per year and reduces other fixed costs by $150,000. Therefore, fixed manufacturing overhead would decrease by 195,000 ($45,000 + $150,000). Exhibit 6–10 shows the relevant cost of the make or buy decision when the alternative to buy the timers enables the company to eliminate a production shift.

**Exhibit 6–10**
Relevant Cost of the
Make or Buy Decision
for Oven Timers with
Relevant Fixed Costs

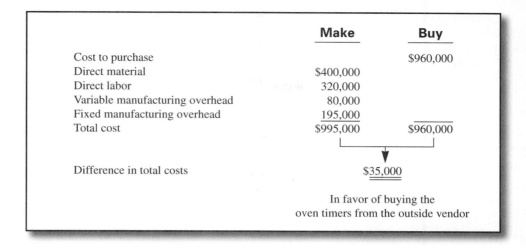

|  | Make | Buy |
|---|---|---|
| Cost to purchase |  | $960,000 |
| Direct material | $400,000 |  |
| Direct labor | 320,000 |  |
| Variable manufacturing overhead | 80,000 |  |
| Fixed manufacturing overhead | 195,000 |  |
| Total cost | $995,000 | $960,000 |
| Difference in total costs | $35,000 | |

In favor of buying the
oven timers from the outside vendor

Exhibit 6–10 shows that the savings in fixed manufacturing overhead alters the cost comparison such that Microbake should opt to buy the timers. If the $195,000 reduction in fixed costs were realized, Microbake would save $35,000 by purchasing the timer assemblies from the vendor instead of making them.

## Discussion Question

6-11. What qualitative factors should managers at Microbake consider with respect to their outsourcing decision?

### Considering Opportunity Costs

**opportunity cost** The benefit foregone (given up) because one alternative is chosen over another.

Recall that an **opportunity cost** is the value of what is foregone (given up) because one alternative is chosen over another. For example, the opportunity cost of attending college rather than working full time is what you could have earned by working instead of going to college.

If Microbake buys the timer assemblies from an outside vendor, it may have an alternate use for the production capacity or assets used to make the timers—it may have an opportunity to enhance its earnings through an alternate use of the facilities. Assume that Microbake can use the production capacity freed up by purchasing the timers to make electronic alarm clocks. Assume further that the electronic alarm clocks would provide an annual contribution margin of $200,000 with no significant changes to fixed cost. If Microbake continues to make the timer assembles, it would forego the opportunity to earn the $200,000. The foregone $200,000 contribution margin on the electronic alarm clocks is an opportunity cost.

Because opportunity cost is the cost of *not* doing something, it is not reflected in the accounting records of a business and is not reported in the company's external financial statements or internal management reports. This does not mean an opportunity cost is not real—remember, reality and the measurement of reality are not the same thing. Opportunity cost is an economic reality. Although it is not generally part of financial accounting measures, opportunity cost is a relevant consideration in business decisions.

Returning to the Microbake timer example, the relevant costs of making or buying the 80,000 timers, including the $200,000 opportunity, is presented in Exhibit 6–11.

**Exhibit 6–11**
Relevant Cost of Make
or Buy Decision for
Oven Timers with
Opportunity Cost

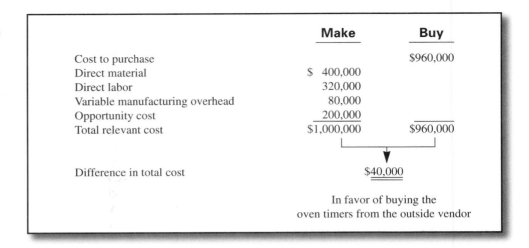

|  | Make | Buy |
|---|---|---|
| Cost to purchase |  | $960,000 |
| Direct material | $ 400,000 |  |
| Direct labor | 320,000 |  |
| Variable manufacturing overhead | 80,000 |  |
| Opportunity cost | 200,000 |  |
| Total relevant cost | $1,000,000 | $960,000 |
| Difference in total cost | $40,000 | |

In favor of buying the
oven timers from the outside vendor

Exhibit 6–11 suggests that if the $200,000 contribution margin from the production of alarm clocks could be realized, Microbake should buy the timer assemblies from the outside vendor. The production capacity no longer needed to produce the timers could then be used to produce the alarm clocks, resulting in a $40,000 difference in the relevant cost in favor of buying the timers.

Microbake's outsourcing problem is an example of a very real business dilemma. Managers cannot rely solely on the cost information from accountants. They themselves must have enough accounting knowledge to determine the relevant cost of each decision alternative.

A few years ago, an accounting instructor overheard some graduate students talking among themselves during a make or buy lecture. The students were engineers at a manufacturing plant that made sophisticated health care products. After some time, the instructor's curiosity prompted him to ask the students what they were discussing. They explained how their company had been outsourcing more and more components, and profits were declining. The problem had snowballed and production costs on the remaining in-house components seemed to rise as more components were outsourced. It seemed that outsiders found it progressively easier to sell components to the company for less than the in-house production cost. During the lecture, the students figured out that their company was treating fixed costs improperly in make or buy decisions. Oddly enough, the students had questioned company cost accountants, only to be told the product cost information provided was correct. Indeed, the product cost information probably was correct; however, was it all relevant? Probably not. The moral of the story: You cannot always rely on accountants to determine exactly what information is most useful to you in a given decision situation. As an economic decision maker, you need to be able to evaluate accounting information for yourself.

Although we have explored relevant cost using only three examples, you should understand that relevant cost concepts apply to almost every business decision. Relevant costing is even helpful with personal decisions such as whether to attend summer school at a local university or enroll in a student exchange program and study abroad. Business situations and life in general provide an array of quantitative and qualitative considerations for every decision alternative. As a decision maker, you must be able to seek out the relevant considerations and disregard the irrelevant ones.

# SUMMARY

All management decision making entails choosing between or among alternatives. If managers are to have any chance of making the best decision in a given situation, they must attempt to consider only relevant information.

A relevant cost is a cost that makes a difference in a given decision situation. What is relevant in one situation may not be relevant in another. Relevant costs are also always future costs, because past costs cannot be changed by any current or future actions. Further, a future cost must differ between or among the alternatives to be considered relevant. Opportunity costs are often relevant and should be considered by managers making decisions. An opportunity cost is the value of benefits foregone because one alternative is chosen over another.

In addition to the quantitative information managers must consider in making decisions, qualitative information such as customer satisfaction, product quality, and employee morale must also be considered. Oftentimes the qualitative considerations should outweigh purely quantitative considerations.

There are many applications of relevant costing in management decision making. Careful application of relevant costing techniques can help managers to make appropriate decisions in various business situations.

# KEY TERMS

opportunity cost   M-195
outsourcing   M-192
qualitative factors   M-185
quantitative factors   M-185
relevant cost   M-184

relevant costing   M-184
special order   M-190
sunk cost   M-184
time value of money    M-189

# REVIEW THE FACTS

A. What is relevant costing?
B. What is a relevant cost?
C. What two important characteristics do all relevant costs possess?
D. What is a sunk cost?
E. Describe the difference between qualitative and quantitative factors.
F. When trying to determine whether a cost is relevant, what are the two questions the decision maker should ask?
G. Why is the depreciation for existing assets considered irrelevant for equipment replacement decisions?
H. What is the time value of money?
I. Why is the time value of money important for decisions involving the purchase of long-lived assets?
J. What would cause a fixed cost to be relevant for a special order decision?
K. What is outsourcing?
L. Define opportunity cost.
M. The concepts of relevant costing apply to what types of decisions?

## LO 1: Determine Which Costs Are Relevant

**6–12.** The production manager at Ace Manufacturing is contemplating whether he should upgrade some old production equipment. He is considering the following factors:

1. _I_ The cost of the old equipment
2. _R_ The cost of the new equipment
3. _I_ Depreciation on the old equipment
4. _RI_ Depreciation on the new equipment
5. _R_ Trade-in value of the old equipment
6. _R_ Salvage value of the old equipment
7. _R_ Salvage value of the new equipment

**REQUIRED:**

For each item listed, indicate whether it is relevant (R) or irrelevant (I).

## LO 3: Quantitative and Qualitative Considerations

**6–13.** Tom Robinson is thinking about buying a portable computer. He has a computer at home, but the portable computer would allow him to work during his frequent business trips. Tom is trying to convince his boss that the computer would save the company some money. Tom hopes that his company will pay at least part of the computer's purchase price and the monthly fee for an e-mail service.

Tom has asked a group of friends to help him think of all the advantages of buying the computer. Assume you are part of the group.

**GROUP REQUIREMENTS:**

a. Prepare an informal schedule of the costs associated with the computer purchase.

b. List as many quantitative benefits as you can that the company will gain if Tom buys the portable computer.

c. List as many quantitative benefits as you can that Tom will gain if he buys the portable computer.

d. List as many qualitative benefits as you can that the company will gain if Tom buys the portable computer.

e. List as many qualitative benefits as you can that Tom will gain if he buys the portable computer.

f. How much of the computer's cost do you think Tom should pay? How much should Tom's employer pay?

## LO 3 & 4: Determine Relevant Cost Schedule and Qualitative Factors

**6–14.** Tina Alberts is thinking about trading her car for a new one. Her present car is only three years old, completely paid for, but out of warranty. The car's original cost was $22,000. Lately, the car has been somewhat undependable and the repair bills have been quite high. In the last three months, Tina paid over $1,200 for repairs. Tina intends to use her trade-in as the down payment and then finance the balance. She is looking at a new Nissan which she can get for about $23,000, less her trade.

Tina has asked a group of close friends to help her think of all the relevant advantages and disadvantages of getting the new car. Assume you are part of this group.

## GROUP REQUIREMENTS:

a. Prepare an informal schedule listing the relevant quantitative factors that Tina should consider. Do not limit your answer to the items found in the problem. Include all the factors you can think of. When possible, try to include estimated dollar amounts in your schedule.
b. Prepare an informal schedule listing the relevant qualitative factors that Tina should consider.
c. From a quantitative point of view, do you think Tina should buy the new car?
d. Considering both quantitative and qualitative factors, do you think Tina should buy the new car?

## LO 1: Determine Which Costs Are Relevant

**6–15.** Jean Parks is a salesperson for Quality Food Products, Inc. She is considering a 250-mile trip to visit a potential customer, ByLots. Following are factors she is pondering.

1. __R__ The cost of traveling the 250 miles to ByLots
2. __R__ The time she will spend on the road
3. __R__ The time she will spend visiting with ByLots's executives
4. __I__ The amount of time already devoted to ByLots
5. __R__ The revenue potential from ByLots
6. __I__ The cost of her last visit to ByLots
7. __R__ The probability that her visit will result in new sales
8. __I__ The cost of lunch for herself if she visits ByLots
9. __R__ The cost of the lunch she would buy for ByLots's executives

**REQUIRED:**
For each item listed, indicate whether it is relevant (R) or irrelevant (I).

## LO 3: Determine Quantitative and Qualitative Factors

**6–16.** This question is based on the same situation as 6–15. Jean Parks is a salesperson for Quality Food Products, Inc. She is considering a 250-mile trip to visit a potential customer, ByLots. Following are factors she is pondering.

1. __A__ The cost of traveling the 250 miles to ByLots
2. __B__ The time she will spend on the road
3. __B__ The time she will spend visiting with ByLots's executives
4. __B__ The amount of time already devoted to ByLots
5. __A__ The revenue potential from ByLots
6. __A__ The cost of her last visit to ByLots
7. __B__ The probability that her visit will result in new sales
8. __A__ The cost of lunch for herself if she visits ByLots
9. __A__ The cost of the lunch she would buy for ByLots's executives

**REQUIRED:**
For each item listed, indicate whether it is quantitative (A) or qualitative (B).

## LO 3: Determine Quantitative and Qualitative Factors

**6–17.** Managers at Ace Manufacturing are considering upgrading some production equipment. They are considering the following factors:

1. __A__ Maintenance cost
2. __B__ Changes in product quality

3. __A__ Salvage value of the old equipment
4. __A__ Cost of new equipment
5. __B__ Difficulty of training employees to use new equipment
6. __A__ Salvage value of the new equipment
7. __B__ The ill feelings due to the possible reduction in the labor force

**REQUIRED:**
For each item listed, indicate whether it is quantitative (A) or qualitative (B).

## LO 1, 2, 3, & 5: List All Costs, Indicate Relevant Costs, Indicate Qualitative Factors

**6–18.** Assume that you are deciding whether to live in a campus dormitory room or an off-campus apartment.

**REQUIRED:**
a. List all the costs that come to mind as you think about this decision.
b. Review your list and indicate which costs are relevant and which are irrelevant to the decision.
c. What are some qualitative factors that you should consider when making this decision?

## LO 1, 2, 3, & 5: List Costs, Indicate Relevant Costs, Indicate Qualitative Factors

**6–19.** Assume that you are deciding what to do next summer. You are considering two alternatives: Go to summer school, or tour Europe.

**REQUIRED:**
a. List all the costs that come to mind as you think about this decision.
b. Review your list and indicate which costs are relevant and which are irrelevant to your decision.
c. What are some qualitative factors that you should consider when making this decision?

## LO 1, 2, 3, & 5: List Costs, Indicate Relevant Costs, Indicate Qualitative Factors

**6–20.** George Binkley's car is seven years old. The car is no longer under warranty and requires frequent repairs. George is trying to decide whether to buy a new car. He has asked you what you think about his idea.

**REQUIRED:**
a. List all the costs that come to mind as you think about his decision.
b. Review your list and indicate which costs are relevant and which are irrelevant to the decision.
c. What are some qualitative factors that he should consider when making this decision?

## LO 4: Determine Relevant Cost for Equipment Replacement

**6–21.** The managers at Miami Manufacturing Company are considering replacing the industrial mixer used in the company's factory.

### Information about the old mixer:

| | |
|---|---|
| Cost | $28,000 |
| Estimated useful life | 10 years |
| Estimated salvage value | $0 |
| Current age | 5 years |
| Estimated current fair value | $8,000 |
| Annual operating cost | $15,000 |

### Information about the new mixer:

| | |
|---|---|
| Cost | $34,000 |
| Estimated useful life | 5 years |
| Estimated salvage value | $0 |
| Annual operating cost | $12,000 |

**REQUIRED:**

Prepare a relevant cost schedule showing the benefit of keeping the old mixer or buying the new one.

## LO 4:   Determine Relevant Cost for Equipment Replacement

**6–22.** The managers at General Manufacturing Company are considering replacing the industrial lathe used in the company's factory.

### Information about the old lathe:

| | |
|---|---|
| Cost | $57,000 |
| Estimated useful life | 8 years |
| Estimated salvage value | $0 |
| Current age | 2 years |
| Estimated current fair value | $32,000 |
| Annual operating cost | $32,000 |

### Information about the new lathe:

| | |
|---|---|
| Cost | $61,000 |
| Estimated useful life | 6 years |
| Estimated salvage value | $0 |
| Annual operating cost | $24,000 |

**REQUIRED:**

Prepare a relevant cost schedule showing the benefit of keeping the old lathe or buying the new one.

## LO 4:   Determine Relevant Cost for Equipment Replacement

**6–23.** John Paul Hudik, president of J. P. Hudik Boat Hauling, is considering replacing the company's industrial lift used to haul boats. The new lift would allow the company to lift larger boats out of the water.

### Information about the old lift:

| | |
|---|---|
| Cost | $94,000 |
| Estimated useful life | 12 years |
| Estimated salvage value | $10,000 |
| Current age | 4 years |
| Estimated current fair value | $48,000 |
| Annual contribution margin | $50,000 |

### Information about the new lift:

| | |
|---|---|
| Cost | $128,000 |
| Estimated useful life | 8 years |
| Estimated salvage value | $ 25,000 |
| Annual contribution margin | $ 65,000 |

**REQUIRED:**

Prepare a relevant cost schedule showing the benefit of keeping the old lift or buying the new one.

## LO 4: Determine Relevant Cost for Equipment Replacement

**6–24.** The managers at Wilma Manufacturing are considering replacing a printing press with a new, high-speed model.

### Information about the old printing press:

| | |
|---|---|
| Cost | $255,000 |
| Estimated useful life | 10 years |
| Estimated salvage value | $ 25,000 |
| Annual depreciation | $ 23,000 |
| Current age | 3 years |
| Accumulated depreciation to date | $184,000 |
| Estimated current fair value | $150,000 |
| Annual contribution margin | $110,000 |

### Information about the new printing press:

| | |
|---|---|
| Cost | $535,000 |
| Estimated useful life | 7 years |
| Estimated salvage value | $ 45,000 |
| Annual depreciation | $ 70,000 |
| Annual contribution margin | $150,000 |

**REQUIRED:**

Prepare a relevant cost schedule showing the benefit of keeping the old printing press or buying the new one.

## LO 4: Determine Relevant Cost for New Business Segment

**6–25.** Photo Express operates a small camera store in Ft. Lauderdale, Florida. The store has two departments, camera sales and photo finishing. Rent, utilities, and other operating expenses are allocated to the departments based on the square footage occupied by the department. Currently, the camera sales department occupies 3,000 square feet and the photo finishing department occupies 2,000 square feet.

Photo Express president, Billy Clifford, is thinking about buying a computer system to produce poster prints. The poster print system would occupy 200 square feet of the store's floor space.

### Budgeted monthly information for the store:

| | |
|---|---|
| Store rent | $ 5,000 |
| Salaries and wages | 10,500 |
| Utilities | 750 |
| Other operating expenses | 3,000 |
| Sales | 125,000 |
| Cost of goods sold | 95,000 |

### Information about the poster print system:

| | |
|---|---|
| Cost of the poster system | $25,700 |
| Estimated useful life | 5 years |
| Estimated salvage value | $ 500 |
| Floor space required | 200 square feet |
| Monthly cost of electricity used by poster system | $ 50 |
| Budgeted monthly amounts: | |
| Poster sales revenue | $ 1,200 |

| | |
|---|---:|
| Poster supplies | 200 |
| Wages for poster operation | 250 |
| Store rent | 200 |
| Utilities | 32 |
| Other operating expenses | 120 |

Clifford believes the company should not buy the poster system because it will show a loss every month. Because he is not sure, he has contacted a small consulting group to seek advice. Assume you are part of the consulting group.

**REQUIRED:**

a. Would the poster system show a loss every month as Clifford suggests? Prepare a schedule to substantiate your answer.

b. Would the company's overall monthly profits increase or decrease as a result of buying the poster system? Prepare a schedule to substantiate your answer.

c. Prepare a relevant cost schedule showing the advantage or disadvantage of buying the poster system.

## LO 4:   Determine Relevant Cost for New Business Segment

**6–26.** The Largo Gift Hut operates a small souvenir shop in Key Largo, Florida. The shop has two departments, retail sales and mail order. Rent, utilities, and other operating expenses are allocated to the departments based on the square footage occupied by the department. Currently, the retail sales department occupies 5,000 square feet and the mail order department occupies 1,000 square feet.

Largo's president, Bobbye Kenyon, is thinking about buying a silk screen machine to make souvenir T-shirts. The silk screen machine would occupy 500 square feet of the souvenir shop's floor space.

**Budgeted monthly information for the store:**

| | |
|---|---:|
| Store rent | $ 5,100 |
| Salaries and wages | 8,500 |
| Utilities | 1,000 |
| Other operating expenses | 3,000 |
| Sales | 80,000 |
| Cost of goods sold | 57,000 |

**Information about the silk screen machine:**

| | |
|---|---:|
| Cost of the silk screen machine | $9,640 |
| Estimated useful life | 5 years |
| Estimated salvage value | $ 400 |
| Floor space required | 500 square feet |
| Monthly cost of electricity used by silk screen machine | $ 20 |
| Budgeted monthly amounts: | |
| T-shirt sales revenue | $1,700 |
| Cost of T-shirts | 450 |
| Cost of T-shirt supplies | 100 |
| Wages for the T-shirt operation | 250 |
| Store rent | 425 |
| Utilities | 85 |
| Other operating expenses | 250 |

Kenyon believes she should not buy the silk screen machine because it will show a loss every month. Because she is not sure, she has contacted a small consulting group to seek advice. Assume you are part of the consulting group.

**REQUIRED:**

    **a.** Would the silk screen machine show a loss every month as Kenyon suggests? Prepare a schedule to substantiate your answer.

    **b.** Would the company's overall monthly profits increase or decrease as a result of buying the silk screen machine? Prepare a schedule to substantiate your answer.

    **c.** Prepare a relevant cost schedule showing the advantage or disadvantage of buying the silk screen machine.

## LO 4: Determine Relevant Cost for Equipment Replacement

**6–27.** Frank's Marine Service purchased a forklift five years ago for $16,000. When it was purchased the forklift had an estimated useful life of 10 years and a salvage value of $4,000. The forklift can be sold now for $6,000. The operating cost for the forklift is $4,500 per year.

    Frank is thinking about buying a newer forklift for $17,000. The newer model would have an estimated useful life of five years and a salvage value of $7,000. The operating cost for the newer forklift would be $3,000 per year.

**REQUIRED:**

    **a.** What are the relevant costs associated with the decision to replace the forklift?

    **b.** Prepare a relevant cost schedule showing the advantage or disadvantage of buying the forklift.

## LO 4: Determine Relevant Cost for Equipment Replacement

**6–28.** Al Hart of Hart Engineering is considering whether to purchase a new copy machine. He purchased the old machine two years ago for $8,500. When purchased, the old machine had an estimated useful life of eight years and a salvage value of $500. The operating cost of the old machine is $3,000 per year. The old machine can be sold today for $2,000. A new machine can be bought today for $10,000 and would have an estimated useful life of six years with a salvage value of $1,000. The operating cost of the new copy machine is expected to be $1,500 per year.

**REQUIRED:**

    **a.** Prepare a schedule showing all the costs associated with the current copy machine.

    **b.** Prepare a schedule showing all the costs associated with the new copy machine.

    **c.** Prepare a schedule showing the relevant cost of the copy machine replacement decision and the favored alternative.

    **d.** Discuss the qualitative factors that Hart should consider.

    **e.** Would you buy the newer copy machine?

## LO 4: Determine Relevant Cost for Equipment Replacement

**6–29.** Mike Thomlinson is considering whether to replace one of his delivery trucks. He purchased the current delivery truck four years ago for $24,000, and it came with a three-year, 75,000-mile warranty. When purchased, the current truck had an estimated useful life of five years and a salvage value of $2,000. Thomlinson uses the straight-line method for depreciation. The new truck would be identical to the current truck, except it would be new and would have the new truck warranty. The operating cost for the current truck is $4,000 for fuel, $23,200 for the driver's salary, and maintenance cost is about $5,000 per year. If Thomlinson keeps the old truck, it will last another five years, but would require the $5,000 in maintenance each year. The current truck can be sold now for $4,000, or it can be sold in five years for $1,000. The new truck would cost $25,500, has an estimated useful life of five years, and can be sold at the end of the five years for $4,000. At the end of the warranty period, the new truck will require maintenance of $5,000 per year.

### REQUIRED:
a. Prepare a schedule showing all the costs associated with the current truck.
b. Prepare a schedule showing all the costs associated with the new truck.
c. Prepare a schedule showing the relevant cost of the truck replacement decision and the favored alternative.
d. Discuss the qualitative factors that Thomlinson should consider.
e. If the old truck had an estimated useful life of five years when it was purchased, and it has already been used for four years, discuss the ramifications of using the truck for another five years.
f. Would you buy the new truck? Why or why not?

## LO 4:   Determine Relevant Cost for Equipment Replacement

**6–30.** Jack Owens is considering whether to replace a piece of production equipment with a new model. The new machine would cost $170,000, have an eight-year life, and have no salvage value. The variable cost of operating the machine would be $180,000 per year. The present machine was purchased one year ago, and could be used for the next eight years. When it was purchased, the present machine had an estimated useful life of nine years and a salvage value of zero. The present machine can be sold now for $28,000, but will have no salvage value in eight years. The variable cost of operating the present machine is $200,000 per year.

### REQUIRED:
a. Prepare a schedule showing the costs associated with the present machine.
b. Prepare a schedule showing the costs associated with the new machine.
c. Prepare a schedule showing the relevant cost of the equipment replacement decision and the favored alternative.
d. Discuss the qualitative factors that Owens should consider.

## LO 3 & 4:   Determine the Relevant Cost of Buying a House and List Qualitative Factors

**6–31.** Lowell Elsea is in the process of buying a house. He is interested in two houses. One house is two miles from his work, the other is on the outskirts of town, 34 miles from work. Surprisingly, the two houses are nearly identical, except the closer house is much more expensive. The house that is two miles from Lowell's work is $127,000, whereas the other house is only $109,000. Maintenance, taxes, insurance, and other costs would be the same for both houses.

Lowell goes to work about 250 days each year. Lowell has just traded his old car for a new one. Each time his car reaches 80,000 miles, Lowell trades it for a new model. Generally, he expects to pay about $20,000 when he trades for a new car. His cars usually get about 20 miles per gallon of regular, $1.25-per-gallon gasoline. Maintenance on his car runs about 5 cents per mile on average. Other than driving to and from work,

Lowell drives about 15,000 miles each year.

Regardless of which house Lowell buys, he expects to be transferred to another area of the country in five years.

Lowell is about to buy the less expensive house when he asks your advice.

**REQUIRED:**
a. Which house should Lowell buy?
b. How much will Lowell save if he follows your advice? (Disregard the time value of money.)
c. What qualitative factors should Lowell consider?

## LO 4:   Relevant Cost of a Make or Buy Decision

**6–32.** Microline is considering buying computer cabinets from an outside vendor. Currently, Microline makes the cabinets in its own manufacturing facility. Microline can buy the cabinets for $15 each. The company uses 15,000 cabinets each year. Information about Microline's cost to manufacture the 15,000 cabinets follows:

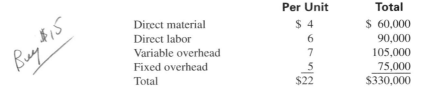

|  | Per Unit | Total |
|---|---|---|
| Direct material | $ 4 | $ 60,000 |
| Direct labor | 6 | 90,000 |
| Variable overhead | 7 | 105,000 |
| Fixed overhead | 5 | 75,000 |
| Total | $22 | $330,000 |

Fixed cost for Microline would not change if the company stopped making the cabinets.

**REQUIRED:**
Prepare a relevant cost schedule that indicates whether Microline should buy the cabinets or continue to make them.

## LO 4:   Relevant Cost of a Make or Buy Decision

**6–33.** Gem Products is considering buying the casters it uses in the manufacture of office chairs from an outside vendor. Currently, Gem Products makes the casters in its own manufacturing facility. Gem Products can buy the casters for $1.15 each. The company uses 450,000 casters each year.

Information about Gem Products' cost to manufacture the 450,000 casters follows:

|  | Per Unit | Total |
|---|---|---|
| Direct material | $ .50 | $225,000 |
| Direct labor | .10 | 45,000 |
| Variable overhead | .40 | 180,000 |
| Fixed overhead | .25 | 112,500 |
| Total | $1.25 | $562,500 |

Fixed cost for Gem Products would not change if the company stopped making the casters.

**REQUIRED:**
Prepare a relevant cost schedule that indicates whether Gem Products should buy the casters or continue to make them.

## LO 4:   Relevant Cost of a Make or Buy Decision

**6–34.** RJ Manufacturing is considering buying the mounting brackets it uses to make its fire extinguishers from an outside supplier. Currently, RJ Manufacturing makes the brackets in its own manufacturing facility. RJ Manufacturing can buy the brackets for $0.75 each. The company uses 700,000 brackets each year.

Information about RJ Manufacturing's cost to manufacture the 700,000 brackets follows:

|  | Per Unit | Total |
|---|---|---|
| Direct material | $.30 | $210,000 |
| Direct labor | .10 | 70,000 |
| Variable overhead | .40 | 280,000 |
| Fixed overhead | .14 | 98,000 |
| Total | $.94 | $658,000 |

Fixed cost for RJ Manufacturing would not change if the company stopped making the brackets.

**REQUIRED:**

Prepare a relevant cost schedule that indicates whether RJ Manufacturing should buy the brackets or continue to make them.

## LO 4:   Relevant Cost of an Outsourcing Decision

**6–35.** Jumbo Chinese Restaurant operates a small laundry facility to launder the uniforms, tablecloths, and other linens used by its restaurant chain. Jumbo's laundry operation occupies space in an industrial area close to the company's home office and its largest restaurant. Jumbo is considering using a laundry service to perform the laundering needed by the company.

Jumbo's $180,000 administrative expense is allocated based on the number of employees. Jumbo employs 90 people.

Information about the laundry facilities follows:

| Direct cost information: | |
|---|---|
| Wages for two employees | $38,000 |
| Cost of equipment | $ 7,500 |
| Original estimated useful life of equipment | 5  years |
| Estimated remaining useful life of equipment | 1  year |
| Building rent per year | $ 3,000 |
| Utilities | $ 2,000 |
| Miscellaneous cost | $ 1,500 |
| Indirect cost information: | |
| Administrative expense | $ 4,000 |

An outside laundry service has offered to provide Jumbo's laundering services for $50,000 per year. The fee is guaranteed for one year. If the offer is accepted, Jumbo will scrap the laundry equipment and close down its laundry operation completely.

**REQUIRED:**

The president of Jumbo has asked you to prepare a report that details the qualitative and quantitative factors that should be considered in making the decision about whether to close the laundry operation. Your report should discuss the relevant qualitative and quantitative factors for each alternative and include a relevant cost schedule. Your report should conclude with a well-supported recommended course of action.

## LO 4: Relevant Cost of an Outsourcing Decision

**6–36.** Fast Track Delivery Service operates a small auto repair facility to service its fleet of 35 delivery vehicles. Fast Track's repair facility occupies space in an industrial area close to the company's home office. Fast Track is considering using a local repair shop to service its vehicles. Fast Track's $120,000 administrative expense is allocated based on the number of employees. Fast Track employs 50 people.

Information about the repair facility follows:

| | |
|---|---|
| Direct cost information: | |
| Wages for three employees | $64,000 |
| Cost of equipment used | $33,500 |
| Original estimated useful life of equipment | 12 years |
| Estimated remaining useful life of equipment | 9 years |
| Building rent per year | $ 6,000 |
| Utilities | $ 2,000 |
| Cost of automobile parts | $30,000 |
| Miscellaneous cost | $ 1,500 |
| Indirect cost information: | |
| Administrative expense | $ 7,200 |

A dependable automotive service center has offered to provide maintenance contracts of each vehicle for $3,000 per vehicle. If Fast Track accepts the offer it would close the maintenance facility. The company estimates that it can sell the maintenance equipment for $10,000.

**REQUIRED:**

The president of Fast Track has asked you to prepare a report that details the qualitative and quantitative factors that should be considered in making the decision about whether to close the maintenance facility. Your report should discuss the relevant qualitative and quantitative factors for each alternative and include a relevant cost schedule. Your report should conclude with a well-supported recommendation.

## LO 3 & 4: Relevant Cost and Qualitative Factors of a Special Order Decision

**6–37.** Abraham Manufacturing produces 22,000 rubber engine mounts each year for use in its electric cart manufacturing plant. Abraham's engine mounts have an excellent reputation for strength and durability. At a production level of 22,000, the cost per unit is as follows:

| | |
|---|---|
| Direct material | $ .53 |
| Direct labor | 1.45 |
| Variable overhead | .92 |
| Fixed overhead | 1.27 |
| Total | $4.17 |

A competitor, Jenkins Cart Company, is interested in purchasing 14,000 rubber engine mounts from Abraham. Jenkins has offered to pay $4.17 each for the engine mounts. Abraham Manufacturing has the capacity and can easily manufacture the engine mounts for Jenkins.

Several managers at Abraham are concerned that there would be no financial benefit whatsoever for Abraham if the engine mounts are sold at cost.

**REQUIRED:**

a. Prepare a schedule that details the advantage or disadvantage of selling the 14,000 engine mounts to Jenkins.

b. Discuss the qualitative aspects of selling the parts to Jenkins.

## LO 3 & 4: Relevant Cost and Qualitative Factors of a Special Order Decision

**6–38.** Kelly Gas Grill Company produces 200,000 RV22 propane gas regulator and valve assemblies each year for use in its gas grill factory. Kelly's gas grills are known for quality and have a reputation of lasting a lifetime.

At 200,000 units per year, the cost per unit is as follows:

| | |
|---|---|
| Direct material | $ 3.02 |
| Direct labor | 2.44 |
| Variable overhead | 1.20 |
| Fixed overhead | 5.60 |
| Total | $12.26 |

A competitor, Econo Grill, is interested in purchasing 80,000 RV22 assemblies from Kelly. Econo Grill has offered to pay $12.30 per unit. Kelly has the capacity and can easily manufacture the parts for Econo Grill.

Several managers at Kelly are concerned that there would be almost no financial benefit if the RV22 assemblies are sold for $12.30 each.

**REQUIRED:**

a. Prepare a schedule that details the advantage or disadvantage of selling the 80,000 RV22 assemblies to Econo Grill.

b. Discuss the qualitative aspects of selling the parts to Econo Grill.

## LO 3 & 4: Relevant Cost and Qualitative Factors of a Special Order Decision

**6–39.** Eiroa Marine Cable Company produces 400,000 feet of SS316 cable each year. At 400,000 feet per year, the cost per foot is as follows:

| | |
|---|---|
| Direct material | $.32 |
| Direct labor | .14 |
| Variable overhead | .08 |
| Fixed overhead | .73 |
| Total | $1.27 |

A competitor, Garcia Marine, is interested in purchasing 175,000 feet of SS316 cable from Eiroa. Garcia has offered to pay $0.92 per foot for the cable. Eiroa has the capacity and can easily manufacture the cable for Garcia Marine.

Frank Eiroa, president of Eiroa Marine Cable, is concerned that there is no financial benefit for the company if it sells the cable for only $0.92 per foot.

**REQUIRED:**

a. Prepare a schedule that details the advantage or disadvantage of selling the 175,000 feet of cable to Garcia Marine.

b. Discuss the qualitative aspects of selling the cable to Garcia.

## LO 3 & 4: Relevant Cost and Qualitative Factors of a Special Order Decision

**6–40.** Gator Corporation manufactures camping equipment. One of the Gator's most popular product is its T1012 tent which the company sells for $28 each. Gator sells about 9,000 T1012 tents each year through its mail-order business. Another camping equipment company, TreeClimb Corporation has approached Gator about purchasing 2,000 T1012 tents. The tents would be the same as the T1012 except they would bear the TreeClimb brand. TreeClimb is willing to pay $20 per tent. Although Gator has plenty of plant capacity to produce the additional 2,000 tents, the company's manufacturing cost is $23 per unit, or $3 more per tent than TreeClimb is willing to pay.

The following per unit information pertains to Gator's cost to produce 9,000 T1012 tents.

| | |
|---|---|
| Direct material | $ 9 |
| Direct labor | 4 |
| Variable manufacturing overhead | 2 |
| Fixed manufacturing overhead | 5 |
| Total | $20 |

### REQUIRED:
a. By what amount would Gator's operating income increase or decrease if the company accepts the special order?
b. Discuss the qualitative aspects of this special order decision.

## LO 3 & 4: Relevant Cost and Qualitative Factors of a Special Order Decision

**6–41.** Refer to problem 6–40. Assume that Gator Corporation would have to purchase an additional sewing machine to accept the special order from TreeClimb. The cost of the new sewing machine is $2,500.

### REQUIRED:
a. By what amount would Gator's operating income increase or decrease if the company accepts the special order under these circumstances?
b. Discuss the qualitative aspects of this special order decision.

## LO 4: Relevant Cost of a Special Order Decision

**6–42.** Hi-Cast Corporation manufactures fishing rods. Part of Hi-Cast's sales success comes from a patented material, tuflex, used to make the fishing rods. Tuflex allows the fishing rods to be very flexible, yet nearly unbreakable. Hi-Cast sells about 150,000 fishing rods annually to wholesalers for $18 each. A major department store chain, Sale-Mart, is interested in purchasing 30,000 fishing rods that would bear the Sale-Mart's brand name. Sale-Mart is willing to pay only $9 per fishing rod, considerably less than Hi-Cast's normal selling price. Although Hi-Cast has plenty of plant capacity available to make the additional 30,000 fishing rods, the company's manufacturing cost is $11 per fishing rod, or $2 more per rod than Sale-Mart is willing to pay. Sale-Mart has indicated that the 30,000 fishing rods do not have to be as flexible and tough as the regular Hi-Cast rods.

The following per unit information pertains to Hi-Cast's cost to produce 150,000 fishing rods.

| | |
|---|---|
| Direct material: | |
| Tuflex | $4 |
| Other material | 1 |
| Direct labor | 3 |
| Variable manufacturing overhead | 1 |
| Fixed manufacturing overhead | 2 |
| Total | $11 |

If fiberglass is used in place of tuflex, the direct material cost can be reduced by $2 per rod.

**REQUIRED:**

By what amount would Hi-Cast's operating income increase or decrease if the company accepts the special order?

## LO 3 & 4: Relevant Cost and Qualitative Factors of an Outsourcing Decision

**6–43.** Ace Equipment Company makes high-pressure pumps. Ace makes 10,000 V1 valve assembles per year for use in production. The manufacturing facilities used to make the V1 valves are also used to produce a variety of other subassemblies and products. Accordingly, no special production equipment is needed to make the V1 valves.

The production cost for V1 valve assembles is as follows:

| | |
|---|---|
| Direct material | $ 55,000 |
| Direct labor | 140,000 |
| Variable manufacturing overhead | 70,000 |
| Fixed manufacturing overhead | 210,000 |
| Total | $475,000 |

Sure Flow Valve Company has offered to supply the V1 valve assemblies to Ace for $32 each.

**REQUIRED:**
a. Prepare a schedule that shows whether Ace should buy the valves from Sure Flow or continue to make them.
b. Discuss the qualitative factors that Ace should consider in this make or buy decision.

## LO 3 & 4: Relevant Cost and Qualitative Factors of an Outsourcing Decision

**6–44.** Refer to problem 6–43. Assume Ace could use the manufacturing facilities which are no longer needed to make the V1 valves to produce a new line of small pumps. The small pumps would provide a contribution margin of $60,000.

**REQUIRED:**
a. Prepare a schedule that shows whether Ace should buy the valves from Sure Flow or continue to make them.
b. Discuss the qualitative factors that Ace should consider in this make or buy decision.

## LO 3 & 4: Relevant Cost and Qualitative Factors of an Outsourcing Decision

**6–45.** General Manufacturing Company makes residential aluminum windows. A company has offered to supply General with the window crank assembly it needs for $3.50 each. General uses 50,000 crank assemblies each year. The machinery used to make the window cranks is used to produce a variety of other subassemblies and products.

The production cost for the window crank assemblies is as follows:

| | |
|---|---|
| Direct material | $ 70,000 |
| Direct labor | 40,000 |
| Variable manufacturing overhead | 55,000 |
| Fixed manufacturing overhead | 35,000 |
| Total | $200,000 |

**REQUIRED:**

a. Prepare a schedule that shows the relevant cost and the preferred alternative of this make or buy decision.

b. Discuss the qualitative factors that General should consider when deciding whether to buy the window cranks from the outside supplier.

## LO 3 & 4: Relevant Cost and Qualitative Factors of an Outsourcing Decision

**6–46.** Hutchens Electric produces electric fans. Hutchens manufactures 19,000 small electric fan motors each year. Dalta Motor Company has offered to supply Hutchens with the small electric motors for $12.50 each. The facilities that Hutchens uses to make the small motors is used to make larger motors and other components.

Hutchens's production cost for the small electric fan motors is as follows:

| | |
|---|---|
| Direct material | $132,000 |
| Direct labor | 26,500 |
| Variable manufacturing overhead | 43,500 |
| Fixed manufacturing overhead | 77,500 |
| Total | $279,500 |

**REQUIRED:**

a. Prepare a schedule that shows whether Hutchens Electric should buy the electric fans or continue to make them.

b. Discuss the qualitative factors that Hutchens should consider when making this make or buy decision.

## LO 3 & 4: Relevant Cost and Qualitative Factors of an Outsourcing Decision

**6–47.** Refer to problem 6–46. Assume that Hutchens Electric can use the facilities freed up by purchasing the electric motors from Dalta Motor Company to produce a new model fan that would have a contribution margin of $95,000.

**REQUIRED:**

a. Prepare a relevant cost schedule that shows whether Hutchens Electric should buy the electric fans or continue to make them.

**b.** Discuss the qualitative factors that Hutchens should consider when making this make or buy decision.

## LO 3 & 4: Relevant Cost and Qualitative Factors of an Outsourcing Decision

**6–48.** Nunez Inc. requires 12,000 units of part X45 per year. At the current level of production, the cost per unit is as follows:

| | |
|---|---|
| Direct material | $ 3 |
| Direct labor | 1 |
| Variable overhead | 2 |
| Fixed overhead | 4 |
| Total | $10 |

JLW Inc. has offered to sell Nunez 12,000 units of X45 for $8 each. If Nunez is no longer required to produce the X45s, a supervisor can be eliminated. The supervisor's salary of $24,000 is part of fixed overhead cost. Other fixed overhead costs would remain the same.

**REQUIRED:**
**a.** Prepare a schedule that details the advantage or disadvantage of buying the 12,000 units of X45 from JLW Inc.
**b.** Discuss the qualitative aspects of purchasing the parts from JLW Inc.

## LO 3 & 4: Relevant Cost and Qualitative Factors of an Outsourcing Decision

**6–49.** Cox Inc. requires 3,000 spindles per year. At the current level of production, the cost per unit is as follows:

| | |
|---|---|
| Direct material | $ 38 |
| Direct labor | 12 |
| Variable overhead | 14 |
| Fixed overhead | 44 |
| Total | $108 |

AMW Inc. has offered to sell Cox the 3,000 spindles for $100 each. If Cox is no longer required to produce the spindles, a supervisor can be eliminated. The supervisor's salary of $36,000 is part of fixed overhead cost. Other fixed overhead costs would remain the same.

**REQUIRED:**
**a.** Prepare a schedule that details the advantage or disadvantage of buying the 300 spindles from AMW Inc.
**b.** Discuss the qualitative aspects of purchasing the parts from AMW Inc.

## LO 3 & 4: Relevant Cost and Qualitative Factors of an Outsourcing Decision

**6–50.** Adcox Inc. requires 4,000 switch assemblies per year. At the current level of production, the cost per unit is as follows:

| | |
|---|---|
| Direct material | $ 3 |
| Direct labor | 3 |
| Variable overhead | 2 |
| Fixed overhead | 2 |
| Total | $10 |

Camron Inc. has offered to sell Adcox Inc. the 4,000 switch assemblies for $9 each. If Adcox is no longer required to produce the switch assemblies, part of the building can be leased to another company for $10,000 per year. Other fixed overhead costs would remain the same.

**REQUIRED:**
a. Prepare a schedule that details the advantage or disadvantage of buying the 4,000 switch assemblies from Camron Inc.
b. Discuss the qualitative aspects of purchasing the parts from Camron Inc.

## LO 1, 2, & 4:   Prepare a Report for an Equipment Replacement Decision

6–51. The Sakura Company operates a chain of Japanese restaurants. Restaurant managers are paid bonuses based on the financial profits of their restaurants.

Last year, the manager of the South Miami Sakura Restaurant installed a new oven that cost $5,000. At the time, the oven had an estimated useful life of five years with no salvage value. Annual repair and maintenance on the oven is $900, and the cost of electricity used by the oven is $3,400 per year. The old oven can be sold now for $1,500.

A salesperson is trying to convince the store manager to replace the oven purchased last year with a new, energy-efficient model. The salesperson says the new oven will increase company profits. The new oven can be purchased for $6,000, and has an estimated useful life of four years with a salvage value of $1,000. The annual repair and maintenance would be the same as the old oven, or $900 per year, but the annual cost of electricity used by the oven would drop to $1,800.

The manager is not convinced by the salesperson. "If I buy this new oven, my financial income will drop and I'll never get my bonus. The loss in the first year will make me look like a fool!"

**REQUIRED:**
a. Prepare a report showing the relevant cost of keeping the old oven versus buying the new one.
b. Based on your report, what do you think of the restaurant manager's comments?

# Chapter 7

## The Capital Budget: Evaluating Capital Expenditures

*S*uppose for a moment that you are contemplating two very different kinds of purchases: a compact disc and a new automobile. You would probably devote different amounts of time and effort to each purchase. You probably would not spend time reviewing your long-term goals and annual budget for the compact disc purchase. Nor would you be likely to create a list of costs and benefits to decide which compact disc to buy. If you were in the market for a new car, however, you might spend considerable time deciding whether you needed a new car, and if you did, which car to buy. The purchase of an expensive item that will be used for a long time, such as a car, warrants careful planning. Such planning is needed because once you have bought the expensive item, it is usually costly to change your mind—in our example, you would have to sell or trade the new car, probably at a substantial discount.

What is true in your personal financial decisions is also true in business. Unlike personal expenditures made for comfort or convenience, business expenditures (large and small) are made to further the goals of the business. In fact, most business expenditures are made to increase a company's profits. For this reason, business expenditures are really investments, by which the company hopes to earn both a return *of* the investment and a return *on* the investment.

Business expenditures for acquiring expensive assets that will be used for more than one year are called **capital investments.** Because of the cost and extended useful life of these assets, companies devote tremendous time and energy to evaluating potential capital investments. For example, according to

**capital investments**
Business expenditures in acquiring expensive assets that will be used for more than one year.

**capital projects** Another name for *capital investments*.

**capital budgeting** The planning and decision process for making investments in capital projects.

information in its annual report, Motorola, Inc. invested more than $4.5 billion in capital expenditures during 1995. Certainly, this magnitude of investment required serious analysis on the part of this company before it committed to the various projects represented by those dollars.

Generally, capital investments, also known as **capital projects,** are investments in property, plant, and equipment. Examples include investments in computer equipment, production equipment, another factory, a new wing of a hospital, or a new campus dormitory. **Capital budgeting** is the planning and decision process for making investments in capital projects. Although we focus on business firms in our discussion, all types of organizations can use capital budgeting techniques: for-profit, nonprofit, and social organizations.

In this chapter, we explain how firms make capital budgeting decisions. Capital budgeting, however, is only part of a much more involved planning process, which we also discuss in this chapter.

Two of the evaluation techniques used to evaluate potential capital projects rely heavily on a knowledge of the time value of money. For this reason, we have included an appendix to the chapter that details the time value of money. ■

## LEARNING OBJECTIVES

*After completing your work on this chapter, you should be able to do the following:*

1. Describe the overall business planning process and where the capital budget fits in that process.
2. Explain in your own words the process of capital budgeting.
3. Discuss the four shared characteristics of all capital projects.
4. Describe the cost of capital and the concept of scarce resources.
5. Determine the information relevant to the capital budgeting decision.
6. Evaluate potential capital investments using four capital budgeting decision models: net present value, internal rate of return, payback period method, and accounting rate of return.
7. Determine present and future values using present value tables and future value tables (chapter appendix).

## THE BUSINESS PLANNING PROCESS

Managers use accounting information for two main types of business decisions, planning and control. In this section, we give an overview of how organizations plan for the future. We discuss the *why,* the *what,* the *how,* and the *who* of business planning. Though management accounting information is used in all steps in the planning process, it is especially important to the *what, how,* and *who* decisions.

## Company Goals: The Why

**organizational goals** The core beliefs and values of the company. They outline why the organization exists and are a combination of financial and nonfinancial goals.

People form an organization to accomplish a purpose or purposes—the organization's goals. These goals define why the organization exists. Setting goals, then, is the *why* of the business.

**Organizational goals** constitute the core beliefs and values of the company, so those goals should not be subject to short-term economic pressures. Examples of some organizational goals might be to earn money, to save lives, or to improve communication among employees. Most companies' goals are stated in general terms that are not easily quantified, which means that although progress toward fulfillment can be measured, it is not really possible to determine when the goals have been attained. For instance, a firm with the goal of earning money usually does not specify exactly how much money it must earn to meet its goal.

The goals of a business organization are usually a combination of nonfinancial and financial aspirations. Whether nonfinancial or financial, however, almost all goals have either a direct or indirect effect on the company's financial well-being. Does this sound strange? The next section explains why almost all goals can affect the financial health of a business.

### Nonfinancial Goals

Typically, nonfinancial goals do not mention money. Rather, they refer to activities that may or may not result in profits. A hospital's nonfinancial goals, for instance, might be to provide the best health care possible to its patients; to recruit and employ highly qualified workers; to provide a safe, pleasant environment for its employees and patients; and to create an atmosphere of caring for both the physical and the emotional concerns of its patients.

## Discussion Questions

**7-1.** Consider the hospital's nonfinancial goals. What financial effect will occur if the hospital *does* work toward those goals?

**7-2.** What financial effect will result if the hospital *does not* work toward those goals?

**7-3.** Review the hospital's nonfinancial goals. How would you determine when those goals have been reached?

Note that the nonfinancial goals for the hospital are stated in very general language. More than specific results, these goals represent standards of conduct and performance toward which the hospital should always be striving. They are stated in such a way that it is very difficult, if not impossible, to determine when the goals have been attained.

### Financial Goals

For most business organizations, the primary financial goal is to earn a profit. What this really means, of course, is that the goal is to earn a return on investment for the business owner or owners. This goal may be worded as "achieving superior financial performance," "earning a reasonable return for the stockholders," "maximizing shareholder value," or similar language. As was the case with the nonfinancial goals, it is difficult to determine when these financial goals have been attained.

## Goal Awareness

Once goals have been set, the company should communicate them to every person in the organization. This communication maximizes the likelihood that a business will achieve its goals. Many companies use a **mission statement**—a summary of the main goals of the organization—to communicate the firm's goals to all employees. Exhibit 7–1 is a sample mission statement from Johnson & Johnson. This mission statement is representative of those of many large companies.

The goals in the Johnson & Johnson mission statement address the concerns of all parties who have a stake in how the company conducts its business. For instance, Johnson & Johnson's stakeholders include health care providers, consumers, suppliers, employees, the community, and stockholders. Johnson & Johnson's mission statement communicates the firm's goals and presents the image of a responsible, ethical business.

**Exhibit 7–1**
Johnson & Johnson Mission Statement. Copyright © Johnson & Johnson, Inc.

### Our Credo

We believe our first responsibility is to the doctors, nurses and patients, to mothers and fathers and all others who use our products and services. In meeting their needs everything we do must be of high quality. We must constantly strive to reduce our costs in order to maintain reasonable prices. Customers' orders must be serviced promptly and accurately. Our suppliers and distributors must have an opportunity to make a fair profit.

We are responsible to our employees, the men and women who work with us throughout the world. Everyone must be considered as an individual. We must respect their dignity and recognize their merit. They must have a sense of security in their jobs. Compensation must be fair and adequate, and working conditions clean, orderly and safe. We must be mindful of ways to help our employees fulfill their family responsibilities. Employees must feel free to make suggestions and complaints. There must be equal opportunity for employment, development and advancement for those qualified. We must provide competent management, and their actions must be just and ethical.

We are responsible to the communities in which we live and work and to the world community as well. We must be good citizens—support good works and charities and bear our fair share of taxes. We must encourage civic improvements and better health and education. We must maintain in good order the property we are privileged to use, protecting the environment and natural resources.

Our final responsibility is to our stockholders. Business must make a sound profit. We must experiment with new ideas. Research must be carried on, innovative programs developed and mistakes paid for. New equipment must be purchased, new facilities provided and new products launched. Reserves must be created to provide for adverse times. When we operate according to these principles, the stockholders should realize a fair return.

Johnson & Johnson

Merely stating lofty goals in a mission statement is not enough to reach the goals. Businesses must act consistently with their goals to ensure progress. Consider the following two examples. In 1982 Johnson & Johnson demonstrated the company's commitment to its goals after two fatalities occurred in the Chicago area when someone injected cyanide into six bottles of Tylenol. Once aware of these events, Johnson & Johnson immediately responded by recalling all Tylenol bottles. The company also instituted a nationwide advertising campaign advising consumers *not* to use Tylenol and provided full disclosure about the situation. In short, the company responded in a manner consistent with its goals.

Compare Johnson & Johnson's actions to Ford Motor Company's response to faulty ignition systems in some of its cars. These faulty ignition systems caught fire without warning and created a dangerous and potentially fatal situation. Ford's response was to wait for the federal government to tell the company which cars it had to recall. Legal? Certainly. A smart way to conduct business? In the short run, it cost Ford less than a total recall of the affected vehicles. In the long run, however, the company may not be conducting its business in a way consistent with its stated goal of total quality.

**strategic plan** A long-range plan that sets forth the actions a company will take to attain its organizational goals.

Once a business has set its goals, the firm must then create a **strategic plan**—a long-range plan that sets forth the actions the firm will take to attain its goals. In the following section, we explore briefly how firms develop strategic plans.

## Strategic Plan: The What

The steps outlined in the strategic plan, sometimes referred to as a long-range budget, are the *what* of doing business. The actions specified in the strategic plan describe what actions a business must take to implement its goals. To be effective, then, strategic plans should support—not conflict with—the company's goals.

Companies make long-range plans so they are well positioned to reach their goals and benefit as the future unfolds. For example, it can take Dow Chemical Company five years or longer to build a production facility, so Dow managers must anticipate product demand accurately in advance, in order to build a plant of the appropriate size in time to produce enough to meet consumer demand.

A company's strategic plan tends to have objectives that are quantifiable, and a time frame for attainment of the objectives. A company might specify, for instance, that it plans to replace its four least-efficient production facilities over the next five years, reduce customer complaints by 20 percent over the next three years, or increase market share for its newest product by 25 percent within 10 years. As you can readily see, a firm can determine exactly when it has met all these objectives.

After an organization has developed a strategic plan that specifies the actions it will take to reach its goals, the company then decides how to allocate its monetary resources to implement its strategies, and who will be responsible for the day-to-day activities of the business. This step in the planning process is the preparation of budgets.

## Preparation of the Capital Budget: The How

**capital budget** The budget that outlines how a company intends to allocate its scarce resources over a five-year, 10-year, or even longer time period.

The capital budget is the *how* of the planning process. The **capital budget** is the budget that outlines how a firm intends to allocate its scarce resources over a five-year, 10-year, or even longer time period.

The capital budget lays out plans for the acquisition and replacement of long-lived expensive assets such as land, buildings, machinery, and equipment. During the capital budgeting process, companies decide whether and what items should be purchased, how much should be spent, and how much profit can be generated from the items. In sum, capital budgeting decisions should further the strategic plan and goals of the business.

## Operating Budget: The Who

**operating budget** The budget that plans a company's routine day-to-day business activities for one to five years.

Companies not only must budget for long-term activities, they also must plan and budget for day-to-day business activities. The budget that pertains to routine company operations for one to five years in the future is called the **operating budget.** The operating budget establishes who is responsible for the day-to-day operation of the organization, so we refer to it as the *who* of the planning process. The operating budget will be our focus in Chapter 8.

An important thing to understand about the planning process is the interrelationship among goals, strategic plan, capital budget, and operating budget. Exhibit 7–2 demonstrates that interrelationship.

**Exhibit 7–2**
Interrelationship among the Planning Elements

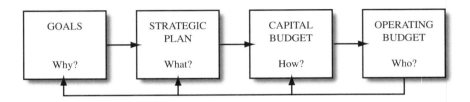

The overall function of management accounting is to provide a substantial portion of the information that company management needs not only to achieve the *what*, the *how*, and the *who*, but also to ensure that these functions are achieved within the context of the *why*.

# THE CAPITAL BUDGET: WHAT IS IT?

**capital assets** Long-lived expensive items such as land, buildings, machinery, and equipment.

The capital budget plans for the acquisition and replacement of long-lived expensive items such as land, buildings, machinery, and equipment. These long-lived items are called **capital assets.** The capital budget focuses on the long-term operations of the company to determine how an organization intends to allocate its scarce resources over the next five, 10, or even 20 years. Thus, we refer to this part of the planning process as the *how* of being in business and doing business.

During the capital budgeting process, companies decide whether items should be purchased, how much should be spent, and how much profit the items promise to generate. No decisions made in the capital budgeting process, however, should conflict with the company's strategic plan or organizational goals.

## Capitalizing Assets

Capital budgeting deals with decisions regarding investments that will benefit the company for many years, so most companies do not use capital budgeting techniques for small purchases or those that provide benefits for only the current year.

When an expenditure is made, the cost of the item purchased will be reflected either as an expense on the company's income statement for the year of purchase, or as an increase in the company's assets on its balance sheet. Theoretically, the distinction lies in whether the item purchased will provide economic value to the company beyond the year of purchase. If a purchased item is expected to provide economic benefits beyond the year in which it was purchased, it should be capitalized, which means that its cost has been recorded as an increase in long-term assets and will be depreciated (converted from asset to expense) over the item's estimated useful life. Conversely, if a purchased item is not expected to provide economic benefit to the company beyond the year of purchase, its cost should be reflected as an expense on the income statement for that year.

To illustrate, the cost of a delivery truck should be reflected as an increase in assets because the truck will likely be used for several years. In contrast, the cost of last month's lawn service does not provide any future value and therefore should be reflected as an expense immediately.

Judgment plays an important role in determining whether a purchased item should be capitalized or expensed. For example, how should the cost of a $3 wastebasket with an estimated useful life of three years be recorded? Because the wastebasket will be used for several years, the item should theoretically be capitalized—its cost should be added to long-term assets and depreciated over the wastebasket's estimated useful life.

From a practical standpoint, it is senseless to expend the additional accounting effort to capitalize and then depreciate the wastebasket. Why? Because, whether the wastebasket is capitalized and depreciated over its estimated useful life or expensed immediately, the effect on a company's financial statements would be so minimal that no economic decision maker will be influenced by the alternative selected. Thus, the cost of the wastebasket is immaterial, so due to the modifying convention of materiality discussed in financial accounting, the wastebasket is expensed when purchased.

## Capitalization Amount

Generally, companies set a cost threshold that helps determine the appropriate accounting treatment for capitalizing long-lived items. For example, a company might say that any long-lived item costing less than $3,000 will be expensed when purchased, while those costing $3,000 or more will be capitalized. There are no hard and fast rules for setting the capitalization threshold, but most businesses choose an amount between $500 and $5,000 as their capitalization amount.

## Characteristics of Capital Projects

Capital budgeting deals with planning for purchases of items that will be capitalized, meaning they will be classified as assets when purchased and then depreciated over their estimated useful lives. While the capitalization amount and the evaluation process for capital projects vary from company to company, all capital projects share certain characteristics. The four main shared characteristics include

1. *Long lives.* Capital projects are expected to benefit the company for at least two years, which is the whole idea behind capitalizing the cost of a purchased item. As discussed in the previous section, if a purchased item will benefit the company only in the year of purchase, the cost of the item is expensed immediately. If the item purchased is likely to benefit a company in years beyond the year of purchase, the cost of that item is capitalized. Usually the kinds of purchases we are discussing in this chapter benefit the company longer than two years, perhaps five, 10, or an even greater number of years.

2. *High cost.* Technically, the purchase of any long-lived item for which the cost exceeds a company's capitalization amount is considered a capital project. As stated earlier, this may be as low as $500 for some firms. As a practical matter, however, the capital budgeting techniques we consider in this chapter are used to evaluate high-cost projects. A good example is the cost of a new factory built by

Motorola or Intel. Such a factory may cost $500 million or more. Another example is the decision by Wal-Mart or KMart to open a new store in a particular location. Many millions of dollars are involved in opening a store for these companies.

**3.** *Quickly sunk costs.* Costs that cannot be recovered are called sunk costs. A capital project usually requires a firm to incur substantial cost in the early stages of the project. As new information about market size, technology, and so on becomes available, the company's management may decide the project should be abandoned. Unfortunately, much of the cost already incurred may not be able to be recouped. For example, consider the case of a manufacturer that begins construction on a new factory with an estimated cost of $500 million. After spending $200 million on construction, the company decides the new factory is not needed because the product it planned to manufacture in the facility has become obsolete. The company cannot sell the partially completed factory and has no other use for it. The $200 million is a sunk cost because it cannot be recovered.

**4.** *High degree of risk.* Capital projects have a high degree of business risk because they involve the future, which always entails uncertainty. Because of the long lives, high costs, and sunk costs of capital projects, companies must try to estimate the returns from those projects in future years. These characteristics increase the likelihood of erroneous estimates. The uncertainty of the future coupled with the high initial investment make capital projects quite risky.

## Discussion Question

Consider these questions: "Will I be paid?" "How much will I be paid?" and "When will I be paid?"

> **7-4.** Why do you think these questions were extremely difficult for Microsoft to answer as the company considered the development of Windows 98 as a potential capital project?

## THE COST OF CAPITAL AND THE CONCEPT OF SCARCE RESOURCES

**cost of capital** The cost of obtaining financing from all available financing sources.

**cost of capital rate** Another name for *cost of capital.*

**required rate of return** Another name for *cost of capital.*

**hurdle rate** Another name for *cost of capital.*

When you put money into a savings account, you expect to earn interest. This interest is the return on your investment. Like most people, you would like the return to be as high as possible. If you were going to deposit $5,000 in a savings account, you would probably shop for a secure bank, with a return as high as or higher than that of competing banks.

Businesses shop for capital projects the same way you would shop for a bank in which to deposit your $5,000. If it appears that a capital project will be profitable, how does a company determine whether it will be profitable enough to warrant investing its money? A proposed project should promise a return that is equal to or exceeds the firm's cost of capital.

In evaluating potential capital projects, a company must determine a benchmark rate of return to help select which capital project or projects it will undertake. The benchmark return rate for selecting projects is usually the company's **cost of capital,** which is the cost of obtaining financing from all available financing sources. Cost of capital is also referred to as the **cost of capital rate,** the **required rate of return,** or the **hurdle rate.** For the sake of consistency, we use cost of capital throughout all our discussions in this chapter.

As you may recall from financial accounting, companies can obtain financing from two sources, borrowing from creditors (debt financing) and investments by owners (equity financing). When a company invests in a capital project, the money must come from one or both of these sources. Both creditors and owners require a return on the funding they provide to the company, and the company must seek investments that provide a return at least equal to the cost of obtaining funding from debt and equity sources. If a company borrows funds at an interest rate of 9 percent, then the expected return on a capital project must be at least 9 percent. Similarly, if a company's owners provide the financing and expect a return of 20 percent on their investment, then the expected return from a capital project should be at least 20 percent to be acceptable.

## Blended Cost of Capital

**blended cost of capital**
The combined cost of debt financing and equity financing.

**cost of debt capital** The interest a company pays to its creditors.

**cost of equity capital**
What equity investors give up when they invest in one company rather than another.

The funding for a company's capital projects usually comes from a combination of debt and equity financing. The combined cost of debt and equity financing is called the **blended cost of capital.** The rate for the blended cost of capital represents the combined rate of the cost of both debt and equity financing.

The **cost of debt capital** is the interest a company pays to its creditors. The interest rate, say 8 percent, is agreed upon when a company borrows from either the bank or the bond market. The amount of interest a company pays is easy to determine because it is reported on the company's income statement as interest expense.

The cost of a company's equity financing is more challenging to determine than the cost of its debt financing, because the **cost of equity capital** is what equity investors relinquish when they invest in one company rather than another. To illustrate, assume Elizabeth Todd has $5,000 to invest and she is considering the purchase of either Boardman Company stock or Emry Company stock. The question is, what does Elizabeth give up if she invests her $5,000 in Boardman? She relinquishes what she would have earned had she invested in Emry. That is, she lost the opportunity to earn whatever she would have earned had she purchased Emry's stock rather than Boardman's.

The amount an equity investor earns is a combination of dividends received and the appreciation in the market value of the stock the investor owns. In Elizabeth's case, the amount earned if she buys the Boardman Company stock is a combination of the dividends she receives from Boardman, plus any increase in the market value of the Boardman stock she owns.

## Discussion Question

Assume Elizabeth buys the Boardman stock and consistently earns an 8% return on her investment (dividends plus appreciation of the Boardman stock).

7-5. If Elizabeth could earn a 17% return on an investment in Emry Company stock (or some other company), what would you advise her to do? Explain your reasoning.

It's all well and good for us to discuss this topic from the investor's point of view (in this case Elizabeth Todd), but what has this to do with the cost of equity capital for Boardman Company? Well, if Boardman wants to keep Elizabeth as a stockholder, it must return to her an amount at least as great as she could earn by investing her money somewhere else. If Elizabeth can earn 17 percent from an investment in Emry, Boardman must give her that kind of return or she may sell her Boardman stock and invest in Emry (or some other company). Boardman, then, would use 17 percent as the cost of the equity capital it received from Elizabeth, because that is what she could earn elsewhere. In other words, that is what she gave up by investing in Boardman.

In a real-world situation, Boardman Company would not know about the alternatives being considered by Elizabeth Todd and her $5,000. Therefore, the company cannot determine the specific percentage return Elizabeth must earn to keep her happy. What Boardman must do is try to determine what percentage return equity investors can generally expect on their investments and use that percentage as the cost of equity capital.

Unlike debt financing costs (interest expense), the cost of equity financing is not reported in financial statements in its entirety. Firms do report profit distributions to stockholders in the form of dividends, but the larger part of the cost of equity capital is the appreciation in the market value of stockholders' ownership interest. This market value is not reported on financial statements.

To determine the full cost of equity capital, we must examine how stocks appreciate in value. We assume first that rational investors would desire a return on an investment in an individual company at least equal to the return they could receive from investing in other, similar publicly traded companies.

If all companies whose stocks are traded on recognized stock markets (NYSE, AMEX, NASDAQ, and so on) were separated based on the percentage return they provide their stockholders, the breakdown would appear as shown in Exhibit 7–3.

**Exhibit 7–3**
Returns Provided by the Stock Market

```
┌──────────────────────────────────┐
│                                    │
│      HIGH RETURN COMPANIES         │
│         25% of Firms               │
│                                    │
├──────────────────────────────────┤
│                                    │
│                                    │
│     MEDIUM RETURN COMPANIES        │
│         50% of Firms               │
│                                    │
│                                    │
├──────────────────────────────────┤
│                                    │
│      LOW RETURN COMPANIES          │
│         25% of Firms               │
│                                    │
└──────────────────────────────────┘
```

The high return companies in Exhibit 7–3 represent one-fourth of all the companies whose stock is publicly traded. The medium return companies comprise one-half of the companies, and the low return companies represent one-fourth of the total.

## Discussion Question

**7-6.** If you owned stock in a publicly traded company, in which group of companies in Exhibit 7–3 would you want your company to be?

Most equity investors desire to own stock in high return companies because they naturally want their investment to earn the highest possible return. Many high return companies in the stock market yield as high as 17 percent to 20 percent annually to their stockholders in the form of dividends and appreciation in stock value.

## Discussion Questions

Assume you own stock in a publicly traded company and you consistently earn an 8% return on your investment (dividends plus appreciation of the company's stock).

**7-7.** If you are certain you could earn a 20% return on an investment in some other company's stock, what would you do? Explain your reasoning.

**7-8.** Because a publicly traded company receives money only when its stock is originally issued, why do you think it would care about the stock's market value in the stock market?

It is important to note here that the issue is not whether investors can, in fact, earn a 20 percent return by selling their stock in one company and investing in another. They only need to *think* they can earn the higher return.

If enough of a company's stockholders begin selling their stock, the market price of the stock will drop—the economic law of supply and demand at work. As the stock price drops, more stockholders may decide to sell their stock before the price drops even lower. This, of course, makes the stock price drop further.

## Discussion Question

**7-9.** What would you think about a company whose stock was selling for $50 a share in January and $12 a share in December?

Stock analysts, customers, suppliers, and many other parties have a tendency to gauge a company's health by the market value of its stock. For this reason, companies have a vested interest in making sure the market value of their stock does not begin a downward spiral.

Because the investors in the stock market think they can earn a 17 to 20 percent return by investing in the top performing companies, a company must return 17 to 20 percent annual return to its stockholders to be considered one of the high performing companies. Publicly traded companies usually consider their cost of equity financing to be as high as 20 percent. This percentage is commonly used to compute the company's blended cost of capital.

To illustrate the calculation of the blended cost of capital, we consider the case of Adler Enterprises, which has $2,000,000 in assets. A total of $1,200,000 (60 percent) of these assets were obtained using debt financing with an interest rate of 7.5 percent. The remaining $800,000 (40 percent) was financed through equity capital and the company uses a 20 percent cost of equity financing. We find the blended cost of capital for Adler Enterprises using the following calculation.

| Method of Financing | Proportion of Financing Provided | | Cost of Financing | | Weighted Cost of Financing |
|---|---|---|---|---|---|
| Debt | 60% | × | 7.5% | = | 4.5% |
| Equity | 40% | × | 20.0% | = | 8.0% |
| | | Blended Cost of Capital | | | 12.5% |

We see that Adler's weighted cost of debt financing is the proportion of debt financing (60 percent) multiplied by the cost of that financing (7.5 percent). The company's weighted cost of equity financing is the proportion of equity financing (40 percent) times the cost of the equity financing (20 percent). Its blended cost of capital is the sum of the weighted cost of each type of financing—12.5 percent.

Firms use their blended cost of capital as a benchmark rate of return to evaluate capital projects. For example, suppose Adler Enterprises is considering a capital project that requires an investment of $200,000. If Adler decides to undertake this project, it must obtain $200,000 to fund it. Recall that Adler's blended cost of capital is 12.5 percent. Unless the expected rate of return on the project is 12.5 percent or higher, Adler's management will probably reject the project. Otherwise, it would cost more to fund the project than the project could earn.

## Discussion Questions

**7-10.** When you consider that companies are generally in business to earn a profit, why might it be acceptable to select a capital project that promises a return that is just equal to the blended cost of capital?

**7-11.** Under what circumstances do you think a company might accept one capital project over another even though the project selected promises a lower return?

**7-12.** Do you think there would ever be a situation when a company should proceed with a capital project even though the project promises a return lower than the cost of capital? Explain your reasoning.

**7-13.** What do you think might cause a company to reject a proposed capital project even though it promises a return significantly higher than the cost of capital?

### Scarce Resources

*I'm so broke that if they was selling steamboats for a dime apiece, I could run up and down the bank saying 'ain't that cheap'.*

—Roy Clark

In our personal lives, what we buy is usually not limited by how much we want, but rather by how much money we have available to spend. Well, what is true for individuals is also true for businesses. The number and size of capital projects a company undertakes is not limited by a lack of viable alternative projects. What limits companies is that they simply do not have access to enough money to take advantage of all the opportunities available to them. This limitation on the amount available to spend is commonly called **scarce resources.** Even huge multinational companies must select only investments they consider most favorable from a virtually unlimited pool of possible investment opportunities, because firms do not have access to enough money to invest in every good project that comes along. Managers must carefully evaluate the alternative capital projects available to their companies so they can select the projects that promise the highest return (as long as the projects are consistent with the company's goals and strategies).

**scarce resources** A term describing the limited amount of money a company has to invest in capital projects.

# EVALUATING POTENTIAL CAPITAL PROJECTS

Because capital projects are usually long lived, costly, and high risk, managers must carefully evaluate capital expenditure decisions, especially in light of their financial limitations. The evaluation process generally includes the following four steps.

1. Identifying possible capital projects
2. Determining the relevant cash flows for alternative projects
3. Selecting a method of evaluating the alternatives
4. Evaluating the alternatives and selecting the capital project or projects to be funded

Let us investigate each of these steps from the manager's point of view.

## Identifying Possible Capital Projects

Businesses usually make capital expenditures to maximize profits by either increasing revenue, reducing costs, or a combination of the two. A project that satisfies the company's desire to maximize profits will be identified as a potential capital expenditure.

Firms often generate revenue increases by investing in projects that increase capacity or draw more customers. For a hotel chain, an increase in available rooms might increase revenue. For a restaurant, revenue might be enhanced by investing in cooking equipment that prepares food more rapidly. For a hospital, the ability to provide additional services or an increased number of beds might be the key to added revenue.

To reduce operating costs a manufacturer might upgrade production equipment so less direct labor or less electricity is required. An airline catering company could invest in more energy-efficient ovens to reduce food preparation cost. Reducing cost has exactly the same effect as increasing revenue. As Benjamin Franklin said, "A penny saved is a penny earned." If you think about it, this really makes sense. If a company saves $1 by reducing costs by $1, the cost reduction has the same impact on profits as increasing selling price to increase revenue by $1.

Although the majority of potential capital projects are intended to either increase revenue or reduce costs, in certain instances a company must make a capital expenditure that will result in neither. These projects are usually concerned with safety or environmental issues and may come as a result of governmental regulation requirements; or, a company may simply determine such an expenditure is necessary given its goal of worker safety or good corporate citizenship.

In any event, capital projects that are deemed necessary but do not promise either to increase revenue or reduce costs are usually not evaluated using the same criteria as those projects that do promise increased profits. In this chapter, we restrict ourselves to the evaluation of potential capital projects that promise to either increase revenue or reduce costs.

As the need for increasing revenue or reducing costs presents itself, all alternative courses of action should be explored. Brainstorming sessions and input from multiple sources both within and outside a firm can help generate ideas for alternative options.

## Determining Relevant Cash Flows for Alternative Projects

Throughout our discussion of capital budgeting, we have discussed capital projects that promise to increase a company's profits by either increasing revenue or reducing costs (expenses). Recall, however, that under accrual accounting, revenue is not the same as cash inflow and expense is not the same as cash outflow in the short run. Recall also that in the long run, revenue and expenses measured using accrual accounting *are* the same as cash inflow and cash outflow.

**net cash flows**  Cash inflow less cash outflow.

Because capital projects usually are long lived, most business managers believe it is appropriate to analyze an alternative using cash inflow and cash outflow over the life of the project. They do this by determining the **net cash flow** of a project—the project's expected cash inflows minus its cash outflows for a specific time period. For example, if a manager estimates that investing in a new production machine will yield $40,000 in cash inflows during the useful life of the machine but will require spending $30,000 for the same period, the net cash flow would be $10,000 ($40,000 − $30,000).

**relevant net cash flows**  Future net cash flows that differ between or among the alternatives being considered.

Only relevant net cash flows should be considered in a capital budgeting decision. **Relevant net cash flows** are future cash flows that differ between or among alternatives. Thus, a relevant cash flow must be one that will occur in the future, not one that has already occurred, and it must be affected by the investment decision. Past cash flows, or cash flows that will not change as a result of the investment decision, are irrelevant and should not be considered in the decision process. This concept should seem familiar because it follows the same reasoning as our discussion of relevant costs, the subject of Chapter 6.

Once a company obtains and assesses the relevant cash flows for each alternative project, the next step is to choose a method to measure the value of each project.

## Selecting a Method of Evaluating the Alternatives

Over time, many capital budgeting decision methods have been developed to evaluate potential capital projects. In this chapter, we present four methods:

- Net present value
- Internal rate of return
- Payback period method
- Accounting rate of return

Each of these methods offers a different way to measure a project's value, and sometimes the different methods render conflicting rankings. In such a case, managers should be aware of the strengths and weaknesses of each capital budgeting method. In the next section we discuss each of the four methods and the advantages and disadvantages of each.

## Selecting Capital Budgeting Projects

To select a capital budgeting project, firms decide first whether to accept or reject a project using one or more capital budgeting techniques to measure the project's value. If the project does not generate an acceptable rate of return, it will probably be rejected. Furthermore, any proposed capital project that is inconsistent with a company's goals and strategic plan should be rejected, even if the promised return on that project is higher than some other potential project.

Once a project has been accepted as viable, the project can then be ranked with other acceptable projects based on expected performance.

# CAPITAL BUDGETING DECISION METHODS

In this section, we explain four capital budgeting methods: net present value, internal rate of return, payback period method, and accounting rate of return. The first two methods, which are discounted cash flow methods, are used more frequently in business because they include the concept of the time value of money.

A dollar received at some point in the future does not have the same value as a dollar received today. The reason for the difference in value is that if cash is available now, it can be invested now and earn a return as time passes. This increase in the value of cash over time due to investment income is referred to as the **time value of money.** The concept of the time value of money is used to determine either the future value of money invested today or the present value of money to be received at some point in the future.

In the following discussion of net present value and internal rate of return, we assume you have a working knowledge of the time value of money, discussed in detail in the appendix to this chapter. Refer to it now if you need to refresh your understanding.

Capital projects deal with cash flows that begin in the present and extend into the future, sometimes for many years. Therefore, the evaluation of these kinds of projects uses the concept of present value. Determining the present value of cash to be received in future periods is called **discounting cash flows.**

## Discounted Cash Flow Methods

Business managers use two discounted cash flow methods to evaluate potential capital projects: net present value and internal rate of return.

***Net Present Value*** The **net present value (NPV)** of a proposed capital project is the present value of cash inflows minus the present value of cash outflows associated with a capital budgeting project. Note that the net present value is different from the present value. The former is the difference between the present value of a capital project's net cash flows. The latter is the amount a future payment or series of payments is in today's dollars evaluated at the appropriate discount rate. The net present value method is used to determine whether a proposed capital project's return is higher or lower than the blended cost of capital.

A company calculates the NPV of a capital project by discounting the net cash flows for all years of the project using the company's blended cost of capital as the discount rate. A positive net present value indicates that the expected return on a proposed project is higher than the company's cost of capital. A negative net present value indicates that the expected return on a proposed project is lower than the company's cost of capital. A net present value of zero shows that the expected return on a project is exactly equal to the company's cost of capital.

To illustrate the net present value calculations, assume the Juan Rodriguez Company is considering a computer hardware upgrade that would require an investment of $100,000. Assume further that the enhanced speed of the computer is expected to save $31,000 annually in operator salaries. Remember, this reduction

**time value of money** The increase in the value of cash over time due to investment income.

**discounting cash flows** Determining the present value of cash to be received in the future.

**net present value (NPV)** The present value of all cash inflows associated with a proposed capital project minus the present value of all cash outflows associated with the proposed capital project.

of cash outflow is a cash inflow in net present value analysis. The computer has an estimated useful life of five years with no residual value.

The cash flows associated with the computer upgrade are shown in Exhibit 7–4.

**Exhibit 7–4**
Expected Cash Flows for Juan Rodriguez Company Computer Upgrade

Notice in Exhibit 7–4 that the initial cash outlay of $100,000 occurs at "time 0." When working with present values, time 0 is considered today, or the present. Unless otherwise specified, we assume all other cash flows for this project will occur at the end of each period.[1]

Juan Rodriguez Company has a 14 percent blended cost of capital, so we use 14 percent as the discount rate to evaluate whether the company should accept the computer upgrade project; that is, we use a 14 percent discount rate to calculate the present value of the project's cash outflows and cash inflows. In this case, the project's $100,000 cash outflow occurs today (time 0), so that amount is already stated in present value terms.

Next, we must find the present value of the project's cash inflows, which occur at the end of each of the next five years. Because the stream of $31,000 positive cash flows constitutes an annuity, we use the *Present Value of an Annuity of $1 Table*, found in the chapter appendix in Exhibit A7–10, to find the present value factor of a five-year annuity, with a discount rate of 14 percent. We have reproduced a portion of the table as Exhibit 7–5. As you can see from the highlighted portion in this exhibit, the factor for five years with a discount rate of 14 percent is 3.433.

**Exhibit 7–5**

### Present Value of Annuity of $1

| Period | 4% | 5% | 6% | 7% | 8% | 10% | 12% | 14% | 16% |
|---|---|---|---|---|---|---|---|---|---|
| 1 | .962 | 0.952 | 0.943 | .935 | 0.926 | 0.909 | 0.893 | 0.877 | 0.862 |
| 2 | 1.886 | 1.859 | 1.833 | 1.808 | 1.783 | 1.736 | 1.690 | 1.647 | 1.605 |
| 3 | 2.775 | 2.723 | 2.673 | 2.624 | 2.577 | 2.487 | 2.402 | 2.322 | 2.246 |
| 4 | 3.630 | 3.546 | 3.465 | 3.387 | 3.312 | 3.170 | 3.037 | 2.914 | 2.798 |
| 5 | 4.452 | 4.629 | 4.212 | 4.100 | 3.993 | 3.791 | 3.605 | 3.433 | 3.274 |
| 6 | 5.242 | 5.076 | 4.917 | 4.767 | 4.623 | 4.355 | 4.111 | 3.889 | 3.685 |
| 7 | 6.002 | 5.786 | 5.582 | 5.389 | 5.206 | 4.868 | 4.564 | 4.288 | 4.039 |

---

[1]We also ignore depreciation in our analysis because depreciation is a noncash expense under accrual accounting and the NPV method focuses on cash flow rather than accrual operating income.

We multiply $31,000, the amount of the annuity, by the 3.433 present value factor and find that the present value of the annuity is $106,423 ($31,000 × 3.433 = $106,423). Finally, we find the net present value of the project by subtracting the present value of cash outflows from the present value of cash inflows. In our example, the net present value calculations are presented in Exhibit 7–6.

**Exhibit 7–6**
Net Present
Value Calculations

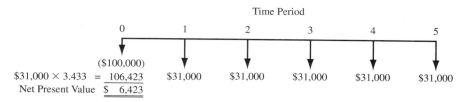

NPV = PV of project's expected returns - initial cash outlay

NPV = $106,423 - $100,000

NPV = $6,423

As Exhibit 7–6 shows, the positive net present value of $6,423 indicates that the project's expected return exceeds Juan Rodriguez Company's 14 percent blended cost of capital.

A word of caution here. A net present value of $6,423 does not mean that the project's return is only $6,423. Rather, it means that the project's return *exceeds* the company's 14 percent cost of capital by $6,423.

## Discussion Questions

**7-14.** How would you explain the difference between present value and net present value?

**7-15.** Should a business accept or reject a project with an NPV of zero? Explain your reasoning.

The Juan Rodriguez Company example was relatively easy to calculate because the project's expected cash flows were the same each year (an annuity). When the expected cash flows are uneven, we find the present value of each year's cash flow and then add those amounts. To demonstrate, assume that the Juan Rodriguez Company's computer upgrade has expected annual returns of $31,000, but in year 3 the computer system will require $12,000 in maintenance fees (a cash outflow), and at the end of year 5, the system can be sold for $6,000 (a cash inflow). A time line depicting these additional cash flows is shown in Exhibit 7–7.

**Exhibit 7–7**
Uneven Expected Cash
Flows for Juan
Rodriguez Company
Computer Upgrade

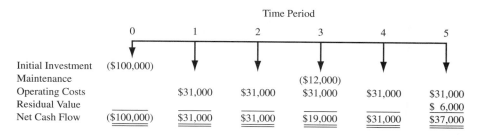

Each of the amounts for the five years shown in Exhibit 7–7 can be discounted to present value using the *Present Value of $1 Table*, found in the chapter appendix in Exhibit A7–5, a portion of which is reproduced as Exhibit 7–8.

## Exhibit 7–8

**Present Value of $1**

| Period | 4% | 5% | 6% | 7% | 8% | 10% | 12% | 14% | 16% |
|--------|------|------|------|------|------|------|------|------|------|
| 1 | 0.962 | 0.952 | 0.943 | 0.935 | 0.926 | 0.909 | 0.893 | 0.877 | 0.862 |
| 2 | 0.925 | 0.907 | 0.890 | 0.873 | 0.857 | 0.826 | 0.797 | 0.769 | 0.743 |
| 3 | 0.889 | 0.864 | 0.840 | 0.816 | 0.794 | 0.751 | 0.712 | 0.675 | 0.641 |
| 4 | 0.855 | 0.823 | 0.792 | 0.763 | 0.735 | 0.683 | 0.636 | 0.592 | 0.552 |
| 5 | 0.882 | 0.784 | 0.747 | 0.713 | 0.681 | 0.621 | 0.567 | 0.519 | 0.476 |
| 6 | 0.790 | 0.746 | 0.705 | 0.666 | 0.630 | 0.564 | 0.507 | 0.456 | 0.410 |
| 7 | 0.760 | 0.711 | 0.665 | 0.623 | 0.583 | 0.513 | 0.452 | 0.400 | 0.354 |

The calculation of the present values, using the highlighted factors in the 14 percent discount rate column, are shown in Exhibit 7–9.

## Exhibit 7–9
Net Present Value Calculations with Uneven Cash Flows

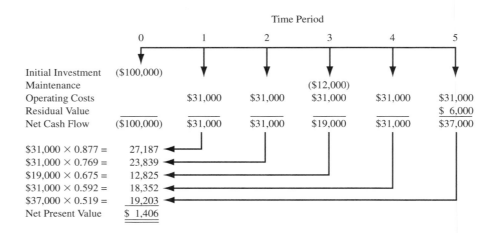

As Exhibit 7–9 demonstrates, the positive $1,406 net present value indicates that the computer upgrade exceeds the 14 percent blended cost of capital for the Juan Rodriguez Company. This positive NPV indicates that the project is acceptable for the company.

Although the net present value method indicates whether a proposed capital project is acceptable, it does have limitations as a ranking method to compare competing projects. A direct comparison of the net present values of various projects may lead to poor decisions regarding project selection, because NPV is measured in dollars rather than percentages. For example, assume that management intends to select one of two projects, Project A and Project B. Calculations indicate that the NPV of Project A is $5,000, whereas the NPV of Project B is $6,000.

Although choosing the project with the higher NPV seems wise, this is not always a good choice because NPV analysis does not consider the relative investments required by the projects. In our example, for instance, say the present value of Project A's cash inflows was $105,000 and the present value of its cash outflows was $100,000. Then suppose that the present value of Project B's cash inflows was

$206,000 and the present value of its cash outflows was $200,000. We see that Project A requires an investment of $100,000, whereas Project B requires double that investment amount. In firms with scarce funds, the relatively small increase in the NPV from $5,000 to $6,000 may not justify selecting a project that requires double the amount of investment. How then can the net present value method be used when ranking various projects? The problem of selecting among projects is solved by using a profitability index.

### Profitability Index

The **profitability index** is an index of the values of alternative but acceptable capital budgeting projects, whose index values are calculated by dividing the present value of the project's cash inflows by the present value of its cash outflows. To illustrate, we return to our example. We know that both Projects A and B have positive NPVs and are acceptable projects. Suppose, however, we want to rank the projects in order of preference.

We find that the profitability index for Project A is 1.05 ($105,000/$100,000 = 1.05). The profitability index for Project B is 1.03 ($206,000/$200,000 = 1.03). We would rank Project A higher than Project B because Project A's index value is 1.05 compared to Project B's lower index value of 1.03. We see, then, how the profitability index is a tool that allows firms to rank competing projects.

Although the NPV method indicates whether a project's return is lower or higher than the required rate of return, it does not show the project's expected percentage return. Many managers find it helpful to know the expected rate of return of projects when making capital budgeting decisions. The internal rate of return method, discussed in the following section, is a capital budgeting method that provides this information.

### Internal Rate of Return

The **internal rate of return (IRR)** of a proposed capital project is the calculated expected percentage return promised by the project. Just like the net present value method, the internal rate of return method considers all cash flows for a proposed project and adjusts for the time value of money. However, the IRR results are expressed as a percentage, not a dollar amount. This method, also known as the **real rate of return,** or the **time-adjusted rate of return,** determines the discount rate that makes the present value of a project's cash inflows and the present value of a project's outflows exactly the same.

To calculate a project's IRR, we use the same present value tables we use to calculate net present value, but we interpret them differently. In this application, we consult the tables to determine a discount rate (a percentage), rather than present value amounts (expressed in dollars).

As an example, assume that Project C requires an initial investment of $300,000 and will provide cash inflows of $56,232 per year for eight years. Because this project is an annuity, to determine the IRR we use the *Present Value of an Annuity of $1 Table* found in the chapter appendix in Exhibit A7–10, a portion of which is reproduced as Exhibit 7–10.

First we calculate the present value factor for the project as follows:

$$\frac{\text{Initial Investment}}{\text{Expected Annual Return}} = \text{Present Value Factor}$$

In the case of Project C, the present value factor is

$$\frac{\$300,000 \text{ Initial Investment}}{\$56,232 \text{ Expected Annual Return}} = 5.335 \text{ Present Value Factor}$$

Now that we know the present value factor, we can find Project C's internal rate of return by moving down the time period column on the table in Exhibit 7–10 to eight periods, as that is the life of the project. Next we follow across the row corresponding to eight periods until we find a factor that is close to the one we calculated (5.335). As we follow across the row for eight periods, we find a factor that is not just close but matches exactly. The factor of 5.335 is in the 10 percent column, which indicates the internal rate of return for Project C is 10 percent. Thus, the actual rate of return promised by Project C is 10 percent.

**Exhibit 7–10**
Partial Present Value of an Annuity of $1 Table

### Present Value of Annuity of $1

| Period | 4% | 5% | 6% | 7% | 8% | 10% | 12% |
|---|---|---|---|---|---|---|---|
| 1 | 0.962 | 0.952 | 0.943 | .935 | 0.926 | 0.909 | 0.893 |
| 2 | 1.886 | 1.859 | 1.833 | 1.808 | 1.783 | 1.736 | 1.690 |
| 3 | 2.775 | 2.723 | 2.673 | 2.624 | 2.577 | 2.487 | 2.402 |
| 4 | 3.630 | 3.546 | 3.465 | 3.387 | 3.312 | 3.170 | 3.037 |
| 5 | 4.452 | 4.629 | 4.212 | 4.100 | 3.993 | 3.791 | 3.605 |
| 6 | 5.242 | 5.076 | 4.917 | 4.767 | 4.623 | 4.355 | 4.111 |
| 7 | 6.002 | 5.786 | 5.582 | 5.389 | 5.206 | 4.868 | 4.564 |
| 8 | 6.733 | 6.463 | 6.210 | 5.971 | 5.747 | 5.335 | 4.968 |
| 9 | 7.435 | 7.108 | 6.802 | 6.515 | 6.247 | 5.759 | 5.328 |
| 10 | 8.111 | 7.722 | 7.360 | 7.024 | 6.710 | 6.145 | 5.650 |
| 11 | 8.760 | 8.306 | 7.877 | 7.499 | 7.139 | 6.495 | 5.938 |
| 12 | 9.382 | 8.863 | 8.384 | 7.943 | 7.536 | 6.814 | 6.194 |

Once determined, the internal rate of return is compared to the cost of capital to gauge the project's acceptability. An internal rate of return that exceeds the firm's cost of capital indicates an acceptable project. For example, if the company's cost of capital is nine percent, Project C's 10 percent internal rate of return shows that the firm would find the project acceptable.

In the example for Project C, we contrived the dollar amounts so that the factor we calculated exactly equaled one of the factors in the present value table. In a real-life situation, the calculated factor will usually fall between two factors on the present value table. For example, assume Project D would require an investment of $330,000 and would generate estimated annual returns of $64,900 for eight years. The present value factor for this project is 5.085, determined as follows:

$$\frac{\$330,000 \text{ Initial Investment}}{\$64,900 \text{ Annual Returns}} = 5.085 \text{ Present Value Factor}$$

Returning to the table in Exhibit 7–10 and following across the year 8 row, we find that our calculated 5.085 factor is between the factors 5.335 (the 10 percent column) and 4.968 (the 12 percent column), but is much closer to 4.968. Therefore, the project's return would fall between 10 and 12 percent, but would be much closer to 12 percent. We then estimate that the internal rate of return for Project D is slightly less than 12 percent.

***Comparing Projects Using the IRR Method***   Managers can use the internal rate of return method to rank projects. For example, the internal rate of return of Project C (10 percent), can be compared to the approximate internal rate of return of Project D (almost 12 percent). Assuming both projects were acceptable, Project D would be ranked higher than Project C because it promises a higher IRR.

***Comparing the NPV and IRR Methods***   Both the net present value method and the internal rate of return method are well-respected techniques used to determine the acceptability of a proposed capital project for two reasons. First, they are based on cash flows, not accounting income. Second, both methods consider the time value of money.

The net present value method is used to determine whether the promised return from a proposed capital project meets the minimum acceptable return requirements (cost of capital). A drawback of this method is that the calculated net present value is stated in dollars rather than percentages. Thus, comparison between projects is difficult. The profitability index overcomes this difficulty.

The internal rate of return method is used to calculate a proposed capital project's actual expected rate of return. Because this method is calculated using percentages rather than dollars, it can be used as a direct comparison of various proposed projects.

## Nondiscounted Cash Flow Methods

The net present value and internal rate of return methods are generally considered the most reliable techniques available because they utilize the time value of money in their evaluation of potential capital projects. Other methods that ignore the time value of money exist, however, and are used to some degree by many companies. We now discuss two of them—the payback period method and the accounting rate of return method.

**payback period method**
A capital budgeting technique that measures the length of time a capital project must generate positive cash flows that equal the original investment in the project.

***Payback Period Method***   As its name implies, the **payback period method** is a capital budgeting technique that measures the length of time a capital project must generate positive net cash flows that equal, or "pay back," the original investment in the project. For instance, assume that a project's estimated initial outlay is $40,000. Assume further that the project is expected to generate a net cash inflow of $12,500 per year. When net cash inflows are equal from one year to the next, we determine the payback period by dividing the required initial investment by the annual cash inflows. In our example, we find that the payback period is 3.2 years. The calculations follow:

$$\frac{\text{Required Initial Investment}}{\text{Annual Net Cash Inflow}} = \text{Payback Period in Years}$$

$$\frac{\$40,000}{\$12,500} = 3.2 \text{ Years}$$

If a project has uneven cash flows, we can determine the payback period by adding the cash inflows year by year until the total equals the required initial investment. For example, suppose a project requires an initial investment of $50,000 and is expected to generate the following net cash inflows:

| | |
|---|---|
| 2001 | $12,000 |
| 2002 | $15,000 |
| 2003 | $18,000 |
| 2004 | $15,000 |
| 2005 | $12,000 |

We find the payback period by totaling the net cash inflows until we reach $50,000 as shown in Exhibit 7–11.

**Exhibit 7–11**
Payback Period with Uneven Cash Flows

| Year | Cash Received in Prior Years | | Cash Received in Current Year | | Accumulated Cash Received |
|------|------------------------------|---|-------------------------------|---|---------------------------|
| 1 | 0 | + | $12,000 | = | $12,000 |
| 2 | $12,000 | + | $15,000 | = | $27,000 |
| 3 | $27,000 | + | $18,000 | = | $45,000 |
| 4 | $45,000 | + | $15,000 | = | $60,000 |
| 5 | $60,000 | + | $12,000 | = | $72,000 |

As Exhibit 7–11 shows, the initial investment will be "paid back" after the third year, but before the end of the fourth year. At the end of the third year, it is anticipated that $45,000, or all but $5,000 of the initial $50,000 investment will be recouped. The remaining $5,000 will be received during the fourth year as part of the $15,000 net cash inflows anticipated for that year. It will take about 1/3 ($5,000/$15,000) of the fourth year to collect the final $5,000 to make up the $50,000 needed to payback the initial investment. Therefore the payback period is 3 1/3 years.

The payback period method highlights the liquidity of an investment and can be used as a screening device to reject projects with unreasonably low cash flow expectations. This method is simple to use, is easily understood, and offers some limited insight into a project's liquidity.

The payback period method is not often used to make final capital investment decisions because it does not consider three crucial elements: (1) the expected returns of a project after the payback period, (2) how the returns will compare to the firm's cost of capital, or (3) the time value of money.

Because the payback method ignores the firm's cost of capital, total cash flow, and time value of money concerns, managers do not normally accept or reject a project based solely on the payback period method. If used at all, the payback period method is usually a screening device only to eliminate potential projects from further evaluation. Companies often establish a maximum payback period for potential projects. If a proposed capital project promises a payback of longer than the established maximum period, that project would be eliminated from further consideration. For example, assume a company has established a maximum payback period of three years. Using this standard, the project presented in Exhibit 7–11 would be rejected because its payback period is longer than three years.

***Accounting Rate of Return Method*** In our discussion so far, we have emphasized that the focus in capital budgeting decisions should be on cash flows. Over time, however, the net cash flow associated with a capital project should approximate operating income as determined using accrual accounting revenue and expense recognition. The accounting rate of return method uses accrual accounting operating income, rather than net cash flow, as the basis for evaluating alternative capital budgeting projects.

The **accounting rate of return** is the rate of return for a capital project based on the anticipated increase in accounting operating income due to the project, relative to the amount of capital investment required.

**accounting rate of return**
The rate of return for a capital project based on the anticipated increase in accounting operating income due to the project, relative to the amount of capital investment required.

This method focuses on how the project changes a company's operating income and the company's required investment. As an example, we reexamine the computer hardware upgrade project for the Juan Rodriguez Company discussed earlier in the chapter. As you recall, the computer hardware upgrade required an initial investment of $100,000. Additionally, the upgrade would reduce operating expenses by $31,000 per year for five years. The computer has an estimated useful life of five years with no residual value. Accounting operating income would be affected in two ways by the computer upgrade. First, the reduced operating expenses would increase operating income by $31,000 each year. Second, depreciation for the computer upgrade would decrease operating income by $20,000 each year ($100,000/5 years). With this information, we can calculate the accounting rate of return as follows:

$$\frac{\text{Increase in Operating Income}}{\text{Required Investment}} = \text{Accounting Rate of Return}$$

$$\frac{\$31,000 - 20,000}{\$100,000} = 11\% \text{ Accounting Rate of Return}$$

The accounting rate of return is simple to calculate and provides some measure of a project's profitability; however, it has two major drawbacks. First, the accounting rate of return method focuses on accounting income rather than cash flow. In capital budgeting it is generally believed that a focus on cash flow is preferred to a focus on accounting income. Second, like the payback method, the accounting rate of return does not consider the time value of money.

The accounting rate of return method is generally considered to be superior to the payback period method because it offers at least a limited measure of a proposed capital project's rate of return. As with the payback period method, however, managers should not accept or reject a project based solely on the accounting rate of return. Both of these methods should be used only as screening devices or in conjunction with discounted cash flow methods of evaluating capital project alternatives.

# FACTORS LEADING TO POOR CAPITAL PROJECT SELECTION

The process of determining which capital projects to select is serious business for any company. We mentioned earlier in the chapter that Motorola reported investment in capital projects of over $4.5 billion in 1995. If managers do not treat capital budgeting with the seriousness it deserves, they run the risk of making poor decisions as to the capital projects selected. At the very least, selecting the wrong capital projects is enormously costly. At worst, investing in the wrong projects can lead to financial ruin for any company, regardless of its size or past performance. The two main factors leading to poor capital project selection are natural optimism on the part of managers and the tendency of some managers to turn the capital project evaluation process into a game.

## Natural Optimism

Human beings are essentially optimistic. As managers they estimate both the cash inflows and outflows associated with a proposed project they are sponsoring with an overly optimistic outlook. This means they will likely overstate the estimated cash inflows and understate the estimated cash outflows. At the very minimum, this natural optimism limits the effectiveness of any of the evaluation techniques we have discussed in this chapter, because all of them use inflow and outflow estimates as the basis of evaluation.

There is nothing wrong with thinking positively. Optimism is, in fact, a desirable trait. Managers must understand, however, that such optimism can cloud their judgment as they assess potential capital projects. Good managers attempt to be as realistic as possible as they prepare proposals for the evaluation of potential capital projects.

## Capital Budgeting Games

The managers who propose potential capital projects understand that there is usually not enough money available to fund all projects, even if they all promise a return greater than the cost of capital. A manager who proposes a capital project is, in fact, competing with other managers' projects for a limited number of capital investment dollars. For this reason, the capital project evaluation process is sometimes treated like some sort of game with little consideration of the potentially disastrous consequences. Some managers manipulate the estimates of cash inflow and cash outflow to get "pet" projects approved, often at the expense of other, more deserving projects. Do not confuse this idea with the natural optimism we discussed a moment ago. The manipulation we are talking about here is an additional factor that can lead to selecting the wrong capital projects.

For example, consider the Electronics Division of Monolith Enterprises. This division has established a limit of $3 million for capital projects in 2002. Mary and Fred are the only two managers within the division who have potential capital projects to propose to division upper management. Both the potential projects will require an initial investment of $2 million, so only one of them is going to be approved.

Mary is in her office late one night putting the finishing touches on her proposal. She is reviewing the cash inflow and cash outflow estimates she has made for her project. As she goes over the estimates one last time, she is feeling a little guilty because she knows she has purposely overstated the inflows and understated the outflows to make her project look more favorable. She is convinced, however, that if she is totally realistic in her estimates, her project will stand no chance of being approved. Why? Because she knows Fred is in his office down the hall putting the finishing touches on his proposal, and she is sure he has manipulated the inflow and outflow estimates on his project to make it look better. To have any chance of approval, then, Mary must "play the game." The sad part of this situation is that Fred is down the hall in his office thinking exactly the same thing about Mary. He is certain she has manipulated her estimates, so he must also, or his project has no chance of being approved. Now we introduce one more person to our scenario—Bill, the division controller. Bill is the person who will evaluate the proposed projects submitted by Mary and Fred and will decide which of the two projects will be funded. He knows that both Mary and Fred have manipulated their estimates, so when he receives them, he compensates by arbitrarily revising their proposals or by using a higher cost of capital percentage in the NPV and IRR evaluations.

Does this seem to you to be an intelligent way to run a business? No, but this kind of game is played every day in many companies by otherwise bright and honest managers.

## Discussion Question

Assume you have been hired as a consultant by Monolith Enterprises to help the company improve its capital project evaluation process.

**7-16.** What suggestions would you make to help Monolith eliminate the kind of "game" being played by Mary, Fred, and Bill?

How does a company make its capital project evaluation process more cooperative and less competitive? This question is difficult, if not impossible, to answer. What we do know, however, is that the global nature of business as we enter the 21st century will not allow these kinds of budget games to continue. U.S. companies are competing with companies from all over the world, and the kind of behavior we have been discussing does not seem to exist in many of these businesses. If U.S. firms are to compete in this worldwide market, they must eliminate dysfunctional business practices. The stakes are simply too high for managers of these companies to continue this approach to capital budgeting.

In a very short time, you will occupy the positions held by Mary, Fred, or Bill. Not at Monolith, of course, because it is a fictitious company. The company that employs you, however, may approach capital budgeting the same way Monolith does. If so, you must do all you can to help the company find a better, more constructive capital budgeting process.

## SUMMARY

There are four elements in the overall planning process for any organization. These elements include the establishing of goals, the formulation of a strategic plan, the preparation of the capital budget, and the preparation of the operating budget.

The capital budgeting process has been described as the *how* of being in business and doing business, which means that the capital budget outlines how a company will allocate its scarce resources over the next five, 10, or even 20 years.

All capital projects have at least four shared characteristics. Such projects are usually long lived, carry with them high costs, have costs associated with the project that usually become sunk almost immediately, and usually involve a high degree of risk.

In the long run, the capital projects a company undertakes must cover at least the cost of the company's capital. The cost of capital is the cost of obtaining financing from both debt and equity sources. The combination of the cost of debt financing and equity financing is referred to as the blended cost of capital. If the capital project being considered does not at least cover the cost of capital, it makes no sense, from a purely financial standpoint, to undertake it.

Over time, several methods have been developed to evaluate potential capital projects. Among these are the net present value method, the internal rate of return method, the payback period method, and the accounting rate of return. Each of these four methods has certain advantages and disadvantages relative to the other methods. The NPV and IRR methods are generally considered to be superior to the payback and accounting rate of return methods because they incorporate the time value of money in their approach to evaluating potential capital projects.

## APPENDIX: THE TIME VALUE OF MONEY

### The Time Value of Money—The Concept of Interest

> *Interest is an interesting thing—*
> *Those who understand it, get it.*
> *Those who don't, pay it.*
>
> —Anonymous

A dollar received at some point in the future does not have the same value as a dollar received today. If you were asked why this is so, you might think the change in value is due to inflation. Even if inflation did not exist, a dollar received in the future would not have the same value as a dollar received today. The reason for the difference in value is that if cash is available now, it can be invested now and earn a return as time passes. This increase in the value of cash over time, due to investment income, is referred to as the time value of money. The concept of the time value of money is used to determine either the future value of money invested today or the present value of money to be received at some point in the future.

## LEARNING OBJECTIVES

*After completing your work in the appendix to this chapter, you should be able to do the following:*

1. Explain the concept of simple interest and compound interest.
2. Determine the future value of a single amount invested today using a future value table.
3. Determine the present value of a single amount to be received at some point in the future using a present value table.
4. Describe the concept of an annuity.
5. Determine the future value of an annuity using a future value table.
6. Determine the present value of an annuity using a present value table.

## Future Value

**future value** The value of a payment, or series of payments, at some future point in time calculated at some interest rate.

**Future value** is the value of a payment, or series of payments, at some future point in time calculated at some interest rate. For example, if you were to invest $2,000 at an annual interest rate of 10 percent, your investment would grow to $2,200 in one year. How? The amount of the increase is calculated by multiplying the principal—the original investment—by the interest rate. In our case the principal is $2,000, the interest rate is 10 percent, so the total return on your investment is $200. The $200 is added to the $2,000 investment for a total of $2,200. So far, so good. But suppose you left the investment untouched for three years. What would be its total value at the end of the three years? The answer depends on whether the interest is calculated as simple interest or compound interest.

**simple interest** Interest calculated on the original principal amount invested only

**Simple interest** is interest calculated only on the original principal. A calculation of interest earned at 10 percent per year for three years on a $2,000 principal using simple interest is presented in Exhibit A7–1.

## Exhibit A7–1
Simple Interest Calculation

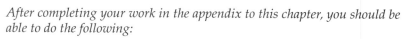

|  | Year 1 | Year 2 | Year 3 |
|---|---|---|---|
| Principal | $2,000 | $2,000 | $2,000 |
| Times the interest rate | × 10% | × 10% | × 10% |
| Equals interest earned | $ 200 | $ 200 | $ 200 |

Note in Exhibit A7–1 that interest for each of the three years is calculated only on the original investment of $2,000. At the end of three years you would receive your $2,000 (return of your principal) and $600 interest (return on your investment).

**compound interest** Interest calculated on the original principal amount invested plus all previously earned interest.

**Compound interest** is interest calculated on the investment principal *plus* all previously earned interest. Continuing with our example, a principal of $2,000 that

**Exhibit A7–2**
Compound Interest
Calculations

|  | Year 1 | Year 2 | Year 3 |
|---|---|---|---|
| Principal + Previously earned interest | $2,000 | $2,200* | $2,420** |
| Times the interest rate | × 10% | × 10% | × 10% |
| Equals interest earned | $ 200 | $ 220 | $ 242 |

* Principal ($2,000) plus the interest earned in year 1 ($200) becomes the amount earning interest in year 2.

** Principal ($2,000) plus the interest earned in year 1 ($200) and the interest earned in year 2 ($220) becomes the amount earning interest in year 3.

earns a compounded rate of 10 percent interest per year for three years is shown in Exhibit A7–2.

Note in Exhibit A7–2 that interest for each of the three years is calculated not only on the original investment of $2,000, but also on the interest earned in previous years. At the end of three years you would receive your $2,000 back (return of principal) and $662 interest (return on your investment). The difference of $62 between the interest earned using compound interest ($662) and the interest earned using simple interest ($600) is interest earned on your previously earned interest.

The power of compounding is tremendous. To demonstrate, let us extend our example of the $2,000 investment. Suppose Dick Gustufson invests $2,000 at 10 percent annual interest when he is 18 years old and leaves it untouched until he is 38 years old. Using the simple interest calculation, Dick's investment will earn interest of $4,000 ($2,000 × 10% × 20 years). If, however, the interest over that same 20 years is compounded, the total interest earned would be $11,454. The $7,454 difference in interest earned is due entirely to interest earning interest on previously earned interest.

We could calculate the amount of compound interest on Dick's investment by extending the three-year example presented in Exhibit A7–2 for another 17 years. This, however, would be cumbersome, time consuming, and tiresome. Fortunately, future value tables greatly simplify the calculation of compound interest.

Future value tables are previously calculated values of $1 at various rates of interest and time periods. The tables are used to determine either the future value of a single payment or the future value of an annuity—that is, a stream of equal payments made at equal intervals.

The *Future Value of $1 Table* (Exhibit A7–3) is used to determine the future value of a single amount deposited today. With this information, we can quickly determine the future value of Dick Gustufson's $2,000 investment at a 10 percent interest rate compounded annually.

As we see in Exhibit A7–3, by moving across the interest rate column headings to the 10 percent column, and then down the time period row to the 20 time periods row, we find a number on the table at the point where the row and column intersect, at a value of 6.727. This number is called a future value factor. Because we are using the *Future Value of $1 Table,* the 6.727 factor tells us that the value of a single dollar 20 years into the future is $6.727, or about $6.73. That is to say that if $1 is invested today at 10 percent, it will be worth $6.73 in 20 years.

But Dick invested $2,000, not $1. To determine the future value of $2,000, we multiply $2,000 by the factor of 6.727 to determine that $2,000 invested today at 10 percent will be worth $13,454 after 20 years ($2,000 × 6.727 = $13,454). If you subtract his initial investment of $2,000, the amount of interest he will earn is $11,454.

A *Future Value of an Annuity of $1 Table,* presented as Exhibit A7–4, is used to determine the future value of a stream of cash flows when the stream of cash flows constitutes an annuity. An **annuity** is a stream of cash flows where the dollar amount of each payment and the time interval between each payment are uniform.

**annuity** A stream of equal periodic cash flows.

## Exhibit A7–3
Future Value of $1 Table

**Future Value of $1**

| Period | 4% | 5% | 6% | 7% | 8% | 9% | 10% | 12% | 14% | 16% |
|--------|------|------|------|------|------|------|------|------|------|------|
| 1 | 1.040 | 1.050 | 1.060 | 1.070 | 1.080 | 1.090 | 1.100 | 1.120 | 1.140 | 1.160 |
| 2 | 1.082 | 1.103 | 1.124 | 1.145 | 1.166 | 1.188 | 1.210 | 1.254 | 1.300 | 1.346 |
| 3 | 1.125 | 1.158 | 1.191 | 1.225 | 1.260 | 1.295 | 1.331 | 1.405 | 1.482 | 1.561 |
| 4 | 1.170 | 1.216 | 1.262 | 1.311 | 1.360 | 1.412 | 1.464 | 1.574 | 1.689 | 1.811 |
| 5 | 1.217 | 1.276 | 1.338 | 1.403 | 1.469 | 1.539 | 1.611 | 1.762 | 1.925 | 2.100 |
| 6 | 1.265 | 1.340 | 1.419 | 1.501 | 1.587 | 1.677 | 1.772 | 1.974 | 2.195 | 2.436 |
| 7 | 1.316 | 1.407 | 1.501 | 1.606 | 1.714 | 1.828 | 1.949 | 2.211 | 2.502 | 2.826 |
| 8 | 1.369 | 1.477 | 1.594 | 1.718 | 1.851 | 1.993 | 2.144 | 2.476 | 2.853 | 3.278 |
| 9 | 1.423 | 1.551 | 1.689 | 1.838 | 1.999 | 2.172 | 2.358 | 2.773 | 3.252 | 3.803 |
| 10 | 1.480 | 1.629 | 1.791 | 1.967 | 2.159 | 2.367 | 2.594 | 3.106 | 3.707 | 4.411 |
| 11 | 1.539 | 1.710 | 1.898 | 2.105 | 2.332 | 2.580 | 2.853 | 3.479 | 4.226 | 5.117 |
| 12 | 1.601 | 1.796 | 2.012 | 2.252 | 2.518 | 2.813 | 3.138 | 3.896 | 4.818 | 5.936 |
| 13 | 1.665 | 1.886 | 2.113 | 2.410 | 2.720 | 3.066 | 3.452 | 4.363 | 5.492 | 6.886 |
| 14 | 1.732 | 1.980 | 2.261 | 2.579 | 2.937 | 3.342 | 3.797 | 4.887 | 6.261 | 7.988 |
| 15 | 1.801 | 2.079 | 2.397 | 2.759 | 3.172 | 3.642 | 4.177 | 5.474 | 7.138 | 9.266 |
| 16 | 1.873 | 2.183 | 2.540 | 2.952 | 3.426 | 3.970 | 4.595 | 6.130 | 8.137 | 10.748 |
| 17 | 1.948 | 2.292 | 2.693 | 3.159 | 3.700 | 4.328 | 5.054 | 6.866 | 9.276 | 12.468 |
| 18 | 2.026 | 2.407 | 2.854 | 3.380 | 3.996 | 4.717 | 5.560 | 7.690 | 10.575 | 14.463 |
| 19 | 2.107 | 2.527 | 3.026 | 3.617 | 4.316 | 5.142 | 6.116 | 8.613 | 12.056 | 16.777 |
| 20 | 2.191 | 2.653 | 3.207 | 3.870 | 4.661 | 5.604 | 6.727 | 9.646 | 13.743 | 19.461 |

## Exhibit A7–4
Future Value of an Annuity of $1 Table

**Future Value of Annuity of $1**

| Period | 4% | 5% | 6% | 7% | 8% | 9% | 10% | 12% | 14% | 16% |
|--------|------|------|------|------|------|------|------|------|------|------|
| 1 | 1.000 | 1.000 | 1.000 | 1.000 | 1.000 | 1.000 | 1.000 | 1.000 | 1.000 | 1.000 |
| 2 | 2.040 | 2.050 | 2.060 | 2.070 | 2.080 | 2.090 | 2.100 | 2.120 | 2.140 | 2.160 |
| 3 | 3.122 | 3.153 | 3.184 | 3.215 | 3.246 | 3.278 | 3.310 | 3.374 | 3.440 | 3.506 |
| 4 | 4.246 | 4.310 | 4.375 | 4.440 | 4.506 | 4.573 | 4.641 | 4.779 | 4.921 | 5.006 |
| 5 | 5.416 | 5.526 | 5.637 | 5.751 | 5.867 | 5.985 | 6.105 | 6.353 | 6.610 | 6.877 |
| 6 | 6.633 | 6.802 | 6.975 | 7.153 | 7.336 | 7.523 | 7.716 | 8.115 | 8.536 | 8.977 |
| 7 | 7.898 | 8.142 | 8.394 | 8.654 | 8.923 | 9.200 | 9.487 | 10.089 | 10.730 | 11.414 |
| 8 | 9.214 | 9.549 | 9.897 | 10.260 | 10.637 | 11.028 | 11.436 | 12.300 | 13.233 | 14.240 |
| 9 | 10.583 | 11.027 | 11.491 | 11.978 | 12.488 | 13.021 | 13.579 | 14.776 | 16.085 | 17.519 |
| 10 | 12.006 | 12.578 | 13.181 | 13.816 | 14.487 | 15.193 | 15.937 | 17.549 | 19.337 | 21.321 |
| 11 | 13.486 | 14.207 | 14.972 | 15.784 | 16.645 | 17.560 | 18.531 | 20.665 | 23.045 | 25.733 |
| 12 | 15.026 | 15.917 | 16.870 | 17.888 | 18.977 | 20.141 | 21.384 | 24.133 | 27.271 | 30.850 |
| 13 | 16.627 | 17.713 | 18.882 | 20.141 | 21.495 | 22.953 | 24.523 | 28.029 | 32.089 | 36.786 |
| 14 | 18.292 | 19.599 | 21.015 | 22.550 | 24.215 | 26.019 | 27.975 | 32.393 | 37.581 | 43.672 |
| 15 | 20.024 | 21.579 | 23.276 | 25.129 | 27.152 | 29.361 | 31.772 | 37.280 | 43.842 | 51.660 |
| 16 | 21.825 | 23.657 | 25.673 | 27.888 | 30.324 | 33.003 | 35.950 | 42.753 | 50.980 | 60.925 |
| 17 | 23.698 | 25.840 | 28.213 | 30.840 | 33.750 | 36.974 | 40.545 | 48.884 | 59.118 | 71.673 |
| 18 | 25.645 | 28.132 | 30.906 | 33.999 | 37.450 | 41.301 | 45.599 | 55.750 | 68.394 | 84.141 |
| 19 | 27.671 | 30.539 | 33.760 | 37.379 | 41.446 | 46.018 | 51.159 | 63.440 | 78.969 | 98.603 |
| 20 | 29.778 | 33.066 | 36.786 | 40.995 | 45.762 | 51.160 | 57.275 | 72.052 | 91.025 | 115.380 |

To see how the table in Exhibit A7–4 is used, assume Susan King intends to deposit $2,000 in an account at the end of each year for four years at a compound interest rate of 12 percent per year. Using the *Future Value of an Annuity of $1 Table* we determine that the factor for 4 years at 12 percent is 4.779. Accordingly, if Susan deposits $2,000 at the end of each year for four years at 12 percent, the account balance will be approximately $9,558 ($2,000 × 4.779).

## Present Value (Discounting)

The basic premise of the present value of money is that it is more valuable to receive cash today (so it can be invested to receive interest) than to receive the cash later. The question is, just *how* valuable is it to receive cash sooner rather than later?

If we know the expected rate of return, it is possible to actually calculate the value of receiving cash sooner rather than later. For example, if you are offered the option of receiving $1,000 today or $1,000 one year from now, how much more valuable is it to receive the $1,000 today? If the $1,000 received today can be invested in a savings account earning six percent interest, then it will grow by $60 during the year. At the end of one year, it will be worth $1,060 and you would be $60 richer than if you had opted to receive the $1,000 one year from now. The $60 growth in value over time exemplifies the time value of money. Clearly, if money is available and invested, it grows as time passes.

If cash can be invested at six percent, $1,000 received today is equivalent to receiving $1,060 one year from now. The amount a future cash flow or stream of cash flows is worth today evaluated at the appropriate interest rate is the cash flow's **present value.** Determining the present value of an amount of cash to be received in the future is called *discounting*.

**present value** The amount future cash flows are worth today based on an appropriate interest rate.

Present value tables greatly simplify the calculation of discounting to find the present value of a single amount or an annuity. Present value tables are previously calculated values of $1 at various interest rates and time periods. The tables are used to determine either the present value of a single amount or the present value of an annuity.

A *Present Value of $1 Table,* presented as Exhibit A7–5, is used to determine the present value of a single amount to be received at some point in the future.

To see how we use the *Present Value of $1 Table,* suppose you visited your rich Aunt Hattie and helped her wash her dog. Your aunt was so touched by your kindness, she offers to give you a gift of $1,000. You are excited and hold out your hand for the money, but she informs you that she is not going to give you the money now. Rather she intends to give you the money one year from now. Her only request is that you tell her how much to deposit in a six percent savings account today so that the account will equal $1,000 one year from now.

In this case, you know that the future value of the amount is $1,000 one year from now. The amount your Aunt Hattie wants to know is the present value, the amount that must be deposited today at six percent so that the account will be worth $1,000 in one year. To find out how much Aunt Hattie must deposit, we use the *Present Value of $1 Table* in Exhibit A7–5. We quickly scan the table to find the point of intersection between the six percent interest rate column and the number of time periods row which is 1. The point of intersection, the present value factor, is 0.943. This factor indicates that the present value of one dollar discounted at six percent is $0.943, or about 94 cents. Thus, if $0.943 is invested today at six percent, it will be worth $1 one year from now.

But Aunt Hattie is going to give you $1,000, not $1. To determine the present value of $1,000, we simply multiply $1,000 by the factor of 0.943 to determine that $943 invested today at six percent will be worth $1,000 in one year, as shown by the time line presentation in Exhibit A7–6.

**Exhibit A7–5**

Present Value of $1 Table

## Present Value of $1

| Period | 4% | 5% | 6% | 7% | 8% | 10% | 12% | 14% | 16% |
|--------|------|------|------|------|------|------|------|------|------|
| 1 | 0.962 | 0.952 | 0.943 | 0.935 | 0.926 | 0.909 | 0.893 | 0.877 | 0.862 |
| 2 | 0.925 | 0.907 | 0.890 | 0.873 | 0.857 | 0.826 | 0.797 | 0.769 | 0.743 |
| 3 | 0.889 | 0.864 | 0.840 | 0.816 | 0.794 | 0.751 | 0.712 | 0.675 | 0.641 |
| 4 | 0.855 | 0.823 | 0.792 | 0.763 | 0.735 | 0.683 | 0.636 | 0.592 | 0.552 |
| 5 | 0.882 | 0.784 | 0.747 | 0.713 | 0.681 | 0.621 | 0.567 | 0.519 | 0.476 |
| 6 | 0.790 | 0.746 | 0.705 | 0.666 | 0.630 | 0.564 | 0.507 | 0.456 | 0.410 |
| 7 | 0.760 | 0.711 | 0.665 | 0.623 | 0.583 | 0.513 | 0.452 | 0.400 | 0.354 |
| 8 | 0.731 | 0.677 | 0.627 | 0.582 | 0.540 | 0.467 | 0.404 | 0.351 | 0.305 |
| 9 | 0.703 | 0.645 | 0.592 | 0.544 | 0.500 | 0.424 | 0.361 | 0.308 | 0.263 |
| 10 | 0.676 | 0.614 | 0.558 | 0.508 | 0.463 | 0.386 | 0.322 | 0.270 | 0.227 |
| 11 | 0.650 | 0.585 | 0.527 | 0.475 | 0.429 | 0.350 | 0.287 | 0.237 | 0.195 |
| 12 | 0.625 | 0.557 | 0.497 | 0.444 | 0.397 | 0.319 | 0.257 | 0.208 | 0.168 |
| 13 | 0.601 | 0.530 | 0.469 | 0.415 | 0.368 | 0.290 | 0.229 | 0.182 | 0.145 |
| 14 | 0.557 | 0.505 | 0.442 | 0.388 | 0.340 | 0.263 | 0.205 | 0.160 | 0.125 |
| 15 | 0.555 | 0.481 | 0.417 | 0.362 | 0.315 | 0.239 | 0.183 | 0.140 | 0.108 |
| 16 | 0.534 | 0.458 | 0.394 | 0.339 | 0.292 | 0.218 | 0.163 | 0.123 | 0.093 |
| 17 | 0.513 | 0.436 | 0.371 | 0.317 | 0.270 | 0.198 | 0.146 | 0.108 | 0.080 |
| 18 | 0.494 | 0.416 | 0.350 | 0.296 | 0.250 | 0.180 | 0.130 | 0.095 | 0.069 |
| 19 | 0.475 | 0.396 | 0.331 | 0.277 | 0.232 | 0.164 | 0.116 | 0.083 | 0.060 |
| 20 | 0.456 | 0.377 | 0.312 | 0.258 | 0.215 | 0.149 | 0.104 | 0.073 | 0.051 |

**Exhibit A7–6**

Time Line Presentation
of Present Value of $1

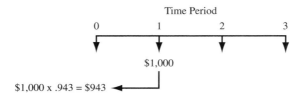

Exhibit A7–6 shows that to earn $1,000 a year from now, given an expected rate of interest of six percent per year, Aunt Hattie must deposit $943. So, the present value of $1,000 to be received one year from now at six percent is $943. The $943 will grow in value as it accumulates interest. This growth is the time value of money. You immediately inform your aunt Hattie that she must deposit $943 today at six percent to have the $1,000 gift ready for you one year from now.

Aunt Hattie is so happy with your quick response that she offers you an additional $1,000 gift. The second $1,000 gift, however, will be given two years from now, which means you will receive the first $1,000 gift at the end of year 1, and the second $1,000 gift at the end of year 2. You are thrilled, but again, your Aunt Hattie requests that you tell her exactly how much she must deposit today at six percent to have the additional $1,000 in two years. We use the *Present Value of $1 Table* in Exhibit A7–5 to find that the present value factor for a time period of two and an interest rate of six percent is 0.890. Accordingly, the present value of $1,000 to be received two years from now is $890 ($1,000 × 0.890). You quickly inform your aunt that she must deposit a total of $1,833 ($943 + $890) today to pay both the $1,000 at the end of year 1, and the $1,000 at the end of year 2. The time line and calculations are shown in Exhibit A7–7.

**Exhibit A7–7**
Time Line Presentation

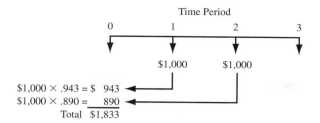

Now suppose your Aunt Hattie planned to give you a gift of $1,000 per year for the next three years. We could rely on the *Present Value of $1 Table* and add the totals for each year as shown in Exhibit A7–8.

**Exhibit A7–8**
Time Line Presentation

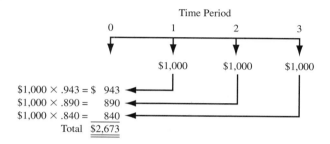

We can simplify the calculations, however, by multiplying the $1,000 by the sum of the three present value factors, which is 2.673. Accordingly, instead of multiplying $1,000 by 0.943, then $1,000 by 0.890, then $1,000 by 0.840, and summing the total, we simply multiply the $1,000 by the sum of the factors as shown in Exhibit A7–9.

**Exhibit A7–9**
Time Line Presentation

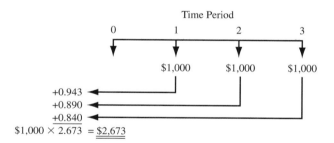

Because the stream of cash flows in our example is an annuity—three equal payments made at regular intervals of one year—we can use the *Present Value of an Annuity of $1 Table,* presented as Exhibit A7–10.

By examining the table in Exhibit A7–10, we find that the present value factor of an annuity for three periods at six percent is 2.673. Notice that the 2.673 equals the sum of the individual present value of $1 factors for each of the three years in Exhibit A7–9. Next, we multiply the $1,000 by the 2.673 factor to find that the present value of Aunt Hattie's $1,000, three-year annuity paid yearly is $2,673.

As you use the future value and present value tables provided in this book, note that the number of interest rates and time periods is limited. Although these smaller tables are useful for learning the basics, in business practice future value and present value tables include a much larger number of interest rates and time periods. If needed, comprehensive tables are available at bookstores and office supply stores.

## Exhibit A7–10
Present Value of an Annuity of $1 Table

### Present Value of Annuity of $1

| Period | 4% | 5% | 6% | 7% | 8% | 10% | 12% | 14% | 16% |
|--------|--------|--------|--------|--------|-------|-------|-------|-------|-------|
| 1 | 0.962 | 0.952 | 0.943 | 0.935 | 0.926 | 0.909 | 0.893 | 0.877 | 0.862 |
| 2 | 1.886 | 1.859 | 1.833 | 1.808 | 1.783 | 1.736 | 1.690 | 1.647 | 1.605 |
| 3 | 2.775 | 2.723 | 2.673 | 2.624 | 2.577 | 2.487 | 2.402 | 2.322 | 2.246 |
| 4 | 3.630 | 3.546 | 3.465 | 3.387 | 3.312 | 3.170 | 3.037 | 2.914 | 2.798 |
| 5 | 4.452 | 4.629 | 4.212 | 4.100 | 3.993 | 3.791 | 3.605 | 3.433 | 3.274 |
| 6 | 5.242 | 5.076 | 4.917 | 4.767 | 4.623 | 4.355 | 4.111 | 3.889 | 3.685 |
| 7 | 6.002 | 5.786 | 5.582 | 5.389 | 5.206 | 4.868 | 4.564 | 4.288 | 4.039 |
| 8 | 6.733 | 6.463 | 6.210 | 5.971 | 5.747 | 5.335 | 4.968 | 4.639 | 4.344 |
| 9 | 7.435 | 7.108 | 6.802 | 6.515 | 6.247 | 5.759 | 5.328 | 4.946 | 4.607 |
| 10 | 8.111 | 7.722 | 7.360 | 7.024 | 6.710 | 6.145 | 5.650 | 5.216 | 4.833 |
| 11 | 8.760 | 8.306 | 7.877 | 7.499 | 7.139 | 6.495 | 5.938 | 5.453 | 5.029 |
| 12 | 9.382 | 8.863 | 8.384 | 7.943 | 7.536 | 6.814 | 6.194 | 5.660 | 5.179 |
| 13 | 9.986 | 9.394 | 8.853 | 8.358 | 7.904 | 7.103 | 6.424 | 5.842 | 5.342 |
| 14 | 10.563 | 9.899 | 9.295 | 8.745 | 8.244 | 7.367 | 6.628 | 6.002 | 5.468 |
| 15 | 11.118 | 10.380 | 9.712 | 9.108 | 8.559 | 7.606 | 6.811 | 6.142 | 5.575 |
| 16 | 11.652 | 10.838 | 10.106 | 9.447 | 8.851 | 7.824 | 6.974 | 6.265 | 5.669 |
| 17 | 12.166 | 11.274 | 10.477 | 9.763 | 9.122 | 8.022 | 7.120 | 6.373 | 5.749 |
| 18 | 12.659 | 11.690 | 10.828 | 10.059 | 9.372 | 8.201 | 7.250 | 6.467 | 5.818 |
| 19 | 13.134 | 12.085 | 11.158 | 10.336 | 9.604 | 8.365 | 7.366 | 6.550 | 5.877 |
| 20 | 13.590 | 12.462 | 11.470 | 10.594 | 9.818 | 8.514 | 7.469 | 6.623 | 5.929 |

As an alternative to using future and present value tables, we can compute future value and present value using nothing more than a somewhat sophisticated business handheld calculator. (It must be a business calculator. Engineering and scientific calculators generally do not have present value and future value functions.) In the business world, most managers rely on calculators and computers to calculate future and present values.

Most computers can also be used to solve present value and future value problems. Many software packages now include modules that can handle simple and advanced calculations dealing with the time value of money.

A working knowledge of present and future value concepts will be extremely important to you not only in your college course work but also in your professional career. Whether the task is the evaluation of potential capital projects, as in this chapter, or any of its many other applications, you will find these concepts invaluable throughout your life.

## KEY TERMS

accounting rate of return   M-236
annuity   M-241
blended cost of capital   M-223
capital assets   M-220
capital budget   M-219
capital budgeting   M-216
capital investments   M-216
capital projects   M-216

compound interest   M-240
cost of capital   M-222
cost of capital rate   M-222
cost of debt capital   M-223
cost of equity capital   M-223
discounting cash flows   M-229
future value   M-240
hurdle rate   M-222

## REVIEW THE FACTS

A. What constitutes a firm's goals?

B. What is a mission statement and how does it relate to a company's goals?

C. What is a strategic plan and how does it relate to a company's goals?

D. What is the purpose of a capital budget and how does it relate to the strategic plan and a company's goals?

E. What is the purpose of an operating budget and how does it relate to the capital budget, the strategic plan, and a company's goals?

F. What are capital investments?

G. What is the difference between a capital investment and a capital project?

H. What is the focus of the capital budget?

I. What does it mean when the cost of a purchased item is capitalized?

J. What does it mean when the cost of a purchased item is expensed?

K. What are the four shared characteristics of virtually all capital projects?

L. What are some other terms used to describe the cost of capital?

M. Describe what is meant by the net present value of an investment.

N. With respect to net present value calculations, what is the advantage of calculating the profitability index?

O. What is determined by the internal rate of return?

P. What is determined by the payback method?

Q. What is the accounting rate of return?

R. What are two factors that can lead to poor capital project selection?

S. What is the basic difference between simple interest and compound interest? (Appendix)

T. What is an annuity? (Appendix)

## APPLY WHAT YOU HAVE LEARNED

### LO 1:   Match Elements of Planning to Characteristics

7–17. Following are the elements of the planning process as discussed in this chapter, with some characteristics pertaining to those elements.

a. Goals
b. Strategic plan
c. Capital budget
d. Operating budget

1. __d__ Pertains to day-to-day activities
2. __c__ Pertains to the allocation of scarce resources
3. __b__ Consists of both financial and nonfinancial considerations
4. __a__ Stated in terms that are not easily quantified
5. __c__ Stated in terms that are easily quantified
6. __d__ Constitutes the *who* of business planning

7. __a__ Constitutes the *why* of business planning
8. __c__ Constitutes the *how* of business planning
9. __b__ Constitutes the *what* of business planning
10. __c__ Relates to long-lived, expensive assets

## REQUIRED:
Match each element of the planning process with the appropriate characteristics. Each letter may be used more than once.

## LO 4: Discuss and Calculate the Cost of Capital

**7–18.** The Marcus Company is in the process of determining a return rate to use for its cost of capital.

Upon review of the financial statements it was determined that the total interest bearing debt is $1,400,000 and total stockholders equity is $1,000,000. In addition, it was determined that the cost of debt financing is 8%, and the cost of equity financing is 18%.

## REQUIRED:
a. What proportion of the Marcus Company's total financing comes from debt?
b. What proportion of the Marcus Company's total financing comes from equity?
c. Calculate the Marcus Company's blended cost of capital rate.

## LO 4: Discuss and Calculate the Cost of Capital

**7–19.** The Byrne Company is in the process of determining a return rate to use for its cost of capital.

Upon review of the financial statements it was determined that the total interest bearing debt is $4,800,000 and total stockholders' equity is $14,400,000. In addition, it was determined that the cost of debt financing is 7%, and the cost of equity financing is 22%.

## REQUIRED:
a. What proportion of The Byrne Company's total financing comes from debt?
b. What proportion of The Byrne Company's total financing comes from equity?
c. Calculate The Byrne Company's blended cost of capital rate.

## LO 4: Discuss and Calculate the Cost of Capital

**7–20.** The Cunningham Company is in the process of determining a return rate to use for its cost of capital.

Upon review of the financial statements it was determined that the total interest bearing debt is $800,000 and total stockholders' equity is $1,700,000. In addition, it was determined that the cost of debt financing is 9%, and the cost of equity financing is 20%.

## REQUIRED:
a. What proportion of The Cunningham Company's total financing comes from debt?
b. What proportion of The Cunningham Company's total financing comes from equity?
c. Calculate The Cunningham Company's blended cost of capital rate.

16.48

## LO 2:  Determine the Sequence of Evaluating Capital Expenditures

**7–21.** Following in random order are the five steps for evaluating a capital expenditure.

a. _____ Identify alternative capital projects.
b. _____ Identify the need for a capital expenditure.
c. _____ Select a method for evaluating the alternatives.
d. _____ Evaluate the alternatives and select the project or projects to be funded.
e. _____ Determine relevant cash inflow and cash outflow information.

**REQUIRED:**

In the space provided, indicate a logical sequence of the steps for evaluating a capital expenditure.

## LO 6 & 7:  Determine Net Present Value, No Residual Value

**7–22.** Florence Kundrat owns Discount Fashions. She is contemplating the purchase of a soda machine which would be used to sell soft drinks to customers for $0.75 each. The following estimates are available:

| | |
|---|---|
| Initial outlay | $3,500 |
| Annual cash inflow | $1,000 |
| Cost of capital | 10% |
| Estimated life of the soda machine | 5 years |
| Estimated residual value of the soda machine | $   -0- |

**REQUIRED:**

Determine the net present value of the soda machine purchase.

## LO 6 & 7:  Determine Net Present Value, No Residual Value

**7–23.** Brianna Garcia is contemplating the purchase of an ice cream vending machine which would be used to sell ice cream to customers for $2 each. The following estimates are available.

| | |
|---|---|
| Initial outlay | $4,000 |
| Annual cash inflow | $1,200 |
| Cost of capital | 12% |
| Estimated life of the ice cream machine | 5 years |
| Estimated residual value of the ice cream machine | $   -0- |

**REQUIRED:**

Determine the net present value of the ice cream machine purchase.

## LO 6 & 7:  Determine Net Present Value, No Residual Value

**7–24.** Javier Cruz is contemplating the purchase of a machine which will automate the production of baseball bats in his factory. The following estimates are available.

| | |
|---|---|
| Initial outlay | $97,000 |
| Annual reduction in manufacturing labor cost | $22,500 |
| Cost of capital | 14% |
| Estimated life of the baseball bat machine | 8 years |
| Estimated residual value of the bat machine | $   -0- |

**REQUIRED:**

Determine the net present value of the baseball bat machine purchase.

## LO 6 & 7:  Determine Net Present Value, No Residual Value

**7–25.** Dahlia Garcia is contemplating the purchase of a machine which will automate the production of hosiery in her factory. The following estimates are available.

| | |
|---|---|
| Initial outlay | $112,000 |
| Annual reduction in manufacturing labor cost | $ 22,500 |
| Cost of capital | 12% |
| Estimated life of the hosiery machine | 8 years |
| Estimated residual value of the hosiery machine | $     -0- |

**REQUIRED:**

Determine the net present value of the hosiery machine purchase.

## LO 6 & 7:  Determine Net Present Value and Profitability Index, Various Rates, No Residual Value

**7–26.** Michael Diaz Sporting Goods is considering the purchase of a machine that is used to cut material to make baseball gloves. The cost of the machine is $265,000. The machine has an estimated useful life of eight years, with no residual value. Currently, the company leases a similar machine for $50,000 per year. If the new machine is purchased, the company's cost of labor would be reduced by $12,000 per year.

**REQUIRED:**

a. Determine the net present value of the machine under each of the following assumptions.
   1. The cost of capital is 12%
   2. The cost of capital is 14%
   3. The cost of capital is 16%
b. Determine the profitability index under each of the following assumptions.
   1. The cost of capital is 12%
   2. The cost of capital is 14%
   3. The cost of capital is 16%

## LO 6 & 7:  Determine Net Present Value and Profitability Index, Various Rates, No Residual Value

**7–27.** Carlos Urriola Manufacturing is considering the purchase of a computer-controlled manufacturing machine that is used in its factory. The cost of the machine $3,600,000. The machine has an estimated useful life of 10 years, with no residual value. If the new machine is purchased, the company's cost of labor would be reduced by $650,000 per year.

**REQUIRED:**

a. Determine the net present value of the machine under each of the following assumptions.
   1. The cost of capital is 10%
   2. The cost of capital is 12%
   3. The cost of capital is 14%

b. Determine the profitability index under each of the following assumptions.
1. The cost of capital is 10%
2. The cost of capital is 12%
3. The cost of capital is 14%

## LO 6 & 7:   Determine Net Present Value, No Residual Value

**7–28.** Frank Eiroa is considering the purchase of an engine lift for use in his marine repair business. He has determined that a used lift is available for $5,500. The engine lift has an estimated useful life of eight years and a residual value of zero. Currently, Frank rents engine lifts as needed. If the lift is purchased, annual rental payment of $1,400 would be saved. The cost of capital is 16%.

**REQUIRED:**
Calculate the net present value of the engine lift purchase.

## LO 6 & 7:   Determine Net Present Value, No Residual Value

**7–29.** Alfredo Lomando is considering the purchase of an industrial glass-cutting machine for use in his business. He has determined that a used glass cutter is available for $25,800. The cutter has an estimated useful life of 10 years and a residual value of zero. Currently, Alfredo rents an industrial cutter for $4,400 annually. The cost of capital is 14%.

**REQUIRED:**
Calculate the net present value of the industrial glass cutter.

## LO 6 & 7:   Determine Net Present Value, with Residual Value

**7–30.** The owner of Wynn Sports Cards is contemplating the purchase of a machine which will automate the production of baseball cards in her factory. The following estimates are available.

| | |
|---|---|
| Initial outlay | $35,000 |
| Annual reduction in manufacturing labor cost | $ 8,500 |
| Cost of capital | 14% |
| Estimated life of the card machine | 5 years |
| Estimated residual value of the card machine | $ 2,000 |

**REQUIRED:**
Determine the net present value of the baseball card machine purchase.

## LO 6 & 7:   Determine Net Present Value, with Residual Value

**7–31.** Kevin Petty owns Discount Auto Parts. He is contemplating the purchase of a brake lathe that could be used to refurbish brake parts for customers. The following estimates are available.

| | |
|---|---|
| Initial outlay | $6,500 |
| Annual cash inflow | $1,500 |
| Cost of capital | 16% |
| Estimated life of the brake lathe | 6 years |
| Estimated residual value of the brake lathe | $1,000 |

**REQUIRED:**
Determine the net present value of the brake lathe purchase.

## LO 6 & 7:  Determine Net Present Value, with Residual Value

**7–32.** Paola Grillon owns Grillon Skin Care Products. She is contemplating the purchase of an industrial mixer that would be used to mix cosmetics in her factory. The following estimates are available.

| | |
|---|---|
| Initial outlay | $78,500 |
| Annual cash inflow | $19,500 |
| Cost of capital | 16% |
| Estimated life of the mixer | 7 years |
| Estimated residual value of the mixer | $ 4,000 |

**REQUIRED:**

Determine the net present value of the industrial mixer purchase.

## LO 6 & 7:  Determine Net Present Value, with Residual Value

**7–33.** Elianne Vinas owns Vinas Shoe Company. She is contemplating the purchase of a cutting machine that would be used to make shoes in her factory. The following estimates are available.

| | |
|---|---|
| Initial outlay | $58,000 |
| Annual cash inflow from reduced labor cost | $11,500 |
| Cost of capital | 12% |
| Estimated life of the cutter | 8 years |
| Estimated residual value of the cutter | $ 2,000 |

**REQUIRED:**

Determine the net present value of the cutting machine purchase.

## LO 6 & 7:  Determine Net Present Value and Profitability Index, Various Rates, with Residual Value

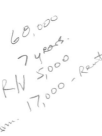

**7–34.** George Gonzalez Construction Company is considering the purchase of a new road grader. The cost of the road grader is $68,000. The road grader has an estimated useful life of seven years and an estimated residual value of $5,000. Currently, the company rents road graders as needed. If the road grader is purchased, annual rental payments of $17,000 would be saved.

**REQUIRED:**

a. Determine the net present value of the grader purchase under each of the following assumptions.
  1. The cost of capital is 12%
  2. The cost of capital is 14%
  3. The cost of capital is 16%
b. Determine the profitability index under each of the following assumptions.
  1. The cost of capital is 12%
  2. The cost of capital is 14%
  3. The cost of capital is 16%

## LO 6 & 7:  Determine Net Present Value and Profitability Index, Various Rates, with Residual Value

**7–35.** Wesley Parks Pencil Company is considering the purchase of a new machine to make pencils. The cost of the machine is $248,000. The pencil machine has an estimated useful life of 10 years and an estimated residual value of $25,000. Currently, the company leases a similar machine for $45,000 per year.

**REQUIRED:**

a. Determine the net present value of the pencil machine purchase under each of the following assumptions.
  1. The cost of capital is 10%
  2. The cost of capital is 12%
  3. The cost of capital is 14%
b. Determine the profitability index under each of the following assumptions.
  1. The cost of capital is 10%
  2. The cost of capital is 12%
  3. The cost of capital is 14%

## LO 6 & 7: Determine Net Present Value and Profitability Index, Various Rates, with Residual Value

**7–36.** Sylvia Heain's Catering Service is considering the purchase of new energy-efficient cooking equipment. The cost of the new equipment is $78,000. The equipment has a estimated useful life of eight years and an estimated residual value of $5,000. Currently, the company leases similar cooking equipment for $10,000 per year. If the new cooking equipment is purchased, the company's cost of electricity would be reduced by $8,000 per year.

**REQUIRED:**

a. Determine the net present value of the cooking equipment under each of the following assumptions.
  1. The cost of capital is 12%
  2. The cost of capital is 14%
  3. The cost of capital is 16%
b. Determine the profitability index under each of the following assumptions.
  1. The cost of capital is 12%
  2. The cost of capital is 14%
  3. The cost of capital is 16%

## LO 6 & 7: Determine Internal Rate of Return, Various Rates, No Residual Value

**7–37.** Penny Williams is contemplating the purchase of a new computer system for her company, Williams Manufacturing. She has made the following estimates.

| | |
|---|---|
| Initial outlay | $18,023.88 |
| Annual cash savings | $ 5,000.00 |
| Estimated life of the computer | 5 years |
| Estimated residual value of the computer | $ -0- |

**REQUIRED:**

a. Determine the internal rate of return for the computer purchase.
b. Indicate whether the computer purchase should be accepted under each of the following assumptions.
  1. The cost of capital is 9%
  2. The cost of capital is 11%
  3. The cost of capital is 13%
  4. The cost of capital is 15%

## LO 6 & 7: Determine Internal Rate of Return, Various Rates, No Residual Value

**7–38.** Valdez Moving and Storage is contemplating the purchase of a new delivery truck. The following estimates are available.

| | |
|---|---|
| Initial outlay | $ 51,590 |
| Annual cash flow from the new truck | $14,000.00 |
| Estimated life of the truck | 6 years |
| Estimated residual value of the truck | $ -0- |

**REQUIRED:**
a. Determine the internal rate of return for the truck purchase.
b. Indicate whether the truck purchase should be accepted under each of the following assumptions.
   1. The cost of capital is 14%
   2. The cost of capital is 16%
   3. The cost of capital is 18%

## LO 6 & 7: Determine Internal Rate of Return for Three Projects, Select Project, No Residual Value

**7–39.** Hank Maupin & Company is in the process of replacing its existing computer system. The following three proposals are being considered.

| | System A | System B | System C |
|---|---|---|---|
| Initial outlay | $18,023.88 | $22,744.72 | $24,031.57 |
| Annual cash savings | $ 5,000.00 | $ 6,000.00 | $ 7,000.00 |
| Estimated useful life | 5 years | 5 years | 5 years |

The estimated residual value of all computer systems under consideration is zero.

**REQUIRED:**
a. Determine the internal rate of return for each of the proposed computer systems.
b. Which computer system would you recommend? Explain your reasoning.

## LO 6 & 7: Determine Internal Rate of Return for Three Projects, Select Project, No Residual Value

**7–40.** David Wilson Equipment Company is in the process of selecting some new manufacturing equipment. The following three proposals are being considered.

| | Equipment A | Equipment B | Equipment C |
|---|---|---|---|
| Initial outlay | $14,902.92 | $18,555.46 | $26,674.63 |
| Annual cash savings | $ 3,000.00 | $ 4,000.00 | $ 5,000.00 |
| Estimated useful life | 8 years | 8 years | 8 years |

The estimated residual value of all equipment under consideration is zero.

**REQUIRED:**
a. Determine the internal rate of return for each of the proposed pieces of equipment.
b. Which piece of equipment would you recommend? Explain your reasoning.

## LO 6 & 7: Determine Net Present Value, Profitability Index, and Internal Rate of Return, Various Rates, No Residual Value

**7–41.** Dunn Manufacturing Company is considering the purchase of a factory that makes valves. These valves would be used by Dunn to manufacture water pumps. The purchase would require an initial outlay of $1,564,800. The factory would have an estimated life of 10 years and no residual value. Currently, the company buys 500,000 valves per year at a cost of $1.50 each. If the factory were purchased, the valves could be manufactured for $0.90 each.

**REQUIRED:**
a. Determine the net present value of the proposed project and whether it should be accepted under each of the following assumptions.
  1. The cost of capital is 12%
  2. The cost of capital is 14%
  3. The cost of capital is 16%
b. Determine the profitability index under each of the following assumptions.
  1. The cost of capital is 12%
  2. The cost of capital is 14%
  3. The cost of capital is 16%
c. Determine the internal rate of return of the proposed project and indicate whether it should be accepted under each of the following assumptions.
  1. The cost of capital is 12%
  2. The cost of capital is 14%
  3. The cost of capital is 16%

## LO 6: Determine Payback Period, Even Cash Flows

**7–42.** Tom Robinson owns Discount Hardware. He is contemplating the purchase of a copy machine which would be used to make copies to sell to customers for five cents each. The following estimates are available.

| | |
|---|---|
| Initial outlay | $4,500 |
| Annual cash inflow | $1,800 |

**REQUIRED:**
Determine the payback period for the copy machine purchase.

## LO 6: Determine Payback Period, Even Cash Flows

**7–43.** Rebecca Pons owns Magic Makers Manufacturing. She is contemplating the purchase of a machine that would be used to manufacture various products that would be sold to magic shops. The following estimates are available.

| | |
|---|---|
| Initial outlay | $23,539.20 |
| Annual cash inflow | $ 7,356.00 |

3.2 years

**REQUIRED:**
Determine the payback period for the machine purchase.

## LO 6: Determine Payback Period, Even Cash Flows

**7–44.** Claudia Vargas is contemplating the purchase of a machine that would be used in her business. The following estimates are available.

| Initial outlay | $5,826.50 |
| Annual cash inflow | $1,355.00 |

**REQUIRED:**
Determine the payback period for the machine purchase.

## LO 6: Determine Payback Period, Even Cash Flows

**7–45.** Cesar Nieto is contemplating the purchase of a machine that would be used in his business. The following estimates are available.

| Initial outlay | $323,400.00 |
| Annual cash inflow | $ 33,000.00 |

**REQUIRED:**
Determine the payback period for the machine purchase.

## LO 6: Determine Payback Period, Uneven Cash Flows

**7–46.** Junior Gonzales is considering the purchase of a fuel truck that he would use to sell gasoline at motor sport racing events in Puerto Rico. He has determined that a used truck is available for $11,000. He believes that the cash inflows would grow each year as he is able to sign fuel supply contracts at more and more events. He has made the following cash inflow estimates.

| First year | $3,000 |
| Second year | $4,500 |
| Third and subsequent years | $5,000 |

**REQUIRED:**
Determine the payback period for the purchase of the fuel truck.

## LO 6: Determine Payback Period, Uneven Cash Flows

**7–47.** Veronica Torres is considering opening a ceramic studio. She has determined that it would require an investment of $14,000 to open the store. She believes that the cash inflows would grow each year as more and more people learn of the store. She has made the following cash inflow estimates.

| First year | $2,000 |
| Second year | $4,000 |
| Third and subsequent years | $5,000 |

**REQUIRED:**
Determine the payback period for the ceramic studio.

## LO 6: Determine Payback Period, Uneven Cash Flows

**7–48.** Karen Calloway is considering adding a new style of gym shorts to her product line. She has determined that it would require an investment of $22,000 to add the new style shorts. She believes that the cash inflows would grow each year as the new style becomes more popular. She has made the following cash inflow estimates.

| First year | $ 4,000 |
| Second year | $ 6,000 |
| Third and subsequent years | $10,000 |

**REQUIRED:**

Determine the payback period for the new style of gym shorts.

## LO 6: Determine Accounting Rate of Return

**7–49.** BRV Construction Company is contemplating the purchase of scaffolding at the cost of $32,000. Currently, the company rents similar scaffolding for use at each of its construction sites. The scaffolding has an estimated useful life of five years and an estimated residual value of $2,000. By purchasing the scaffolding, BRV could save rental fees of $11,760 per year.

**REQUIRED:**

Determine the accounting rate of return for BRV's investment in the scaffolding.

## LO 6: Determine Accounting Rate of Return

**7–50.** Smith and Smith & Associates is contemplating the purchase of equipment that would cost $196,600. Currently, the company rents similar equipment for $45,076 per year. The proposed new equipment has an estimated useful life of eight years and an estimated residual value of $9,000.

**REQUIRED:**

Determine the accounting rate of return for the Smith and Smith & Associates investment in the new equipment. *11 %*

## LO 6: Determine Accounting Rate of Return

**7–51.** Condore & Company is contemplating the purchase of a machine that would cost $142,790. The machine would provide an annual contribution margin of $47,262.55 each year. The proposed new machine has an estimated useful life of five years and an estimated residual value of $10,000.

**REQUIRED:**

Determine the accounting rate of return for Condore & Company's investment in the new machine.

## LO 5, 6, & 7: Determine Relevant Information, Net Present Value, Screen Project, with Residual Value

**7–52.** Frank's Marine Service purchased a forklift five years ago for $16,000. When it was purchased, the forklift had an estimated useful life of 10 years and a salvage value of $4,000. The forklift can be sold now for $6,000. The operating cost for the forklift is $4,500 per year.

Frank is thinking about buying a newer forklift for $17,000. The newer forklift would have an estimated useful life of five years and a salvage value of $7,000. The operating cost for the newer forklift would be 3,000 per year.

The company's cost of capital is 10%.

**REQUIRED:**

a. Prepare a relevant cost schedule showing the benefits of buying the new forklift. (For this requirement, ignore the time value of money.)
b. How much must the company invest today to replace the old forklift?

c. If the company replaces the old forklift, what is the increase in the company's annual contribution margin?

d. If the company sells the old forklift now to make room for the new one, it will not receive the $4,000 salvage value at the end of its useful life. Instead, the company will receive the $7,000 salvage value from the new forklift. With this in mind, if the company buys the forklift, what is the change in the salvage value the company is to receive at the end of the five-year life of the equipment?

e. Calculate the net present value of replacing the old forklift.

f. Do you think the company should replace the old forklift?

## LO 5, 6, & 7: Determine Relevant Information, Net Present Value, Screen Project, with Residual Value

**7–53.** Al Hart of Hart Engineering is considering the purchase of a new copy machine. He purchased the old machine two years ago for $8,500. When it was purchased the old machine had an estimated useful life of eight years and a salvage value of $500. The operating cost of the old machine is $3,000 per year. The old machine can be sold today for $2,000. A new machine can be bought today for $10,000 and would have an estimated useful life of six years with a salvage value of $1,000. The operating cost of the new copy machine is expected to be $1,500 per year.

The company's cost of capital is 8%.

### REQUIRED:

a. Prepare a relevant cost schedule showing the benefit of buying the new copy machine. (For this requirement, ignore the time value of money.)

b. How much must the company invest today to replace the old copy machine?

c. If the company replaces the old copy machine, what is the increase in the company's annual contribution margin?

d. If the company sells the old copy machine now to make room for the new one, it will not receive the $500 salvage value at the end of its useful life. Instead, the company will receive the $1,000 salvage value from the new copy machine. With this in mind, if the company buys the copy machine, what is the change in the salvage value the company is to receive at the end of the six-year life of the equipment?

e. Calculate the net present value of replacing the old copy machine.

f. Do you think the company should replace the old copy machine?

## LO 5, 6, & 7: Determine Relevant Information, Net Present Value, Screen Project, No Residual Value

**7–54.** The managers at AAA Manufacturing Company are considering replacing an industrial mixer used in the company's factory. The company's cost of capital is 10%.

### Information about the old mixer:

| | |
|---|---|
| Cost | $28,000 |
| Estimated useful life | 10 years |
| Estimated salvage value | $ 0 |
| Current age | 5 years |
| Estimated current fair value | $ 8,000 |
| Annual operating cost | $18,000 |

### Information about the new mixer:

| | |
|---|---|
| Cost | $34,000 |
| Estimated useful life | 5 years |
| Estimated salvage value | $ 0 |
| Annual operating cost | $12,000 |

**REQUIRED:**

a. Prepare a relevant cost schedule showing the benefit of buying the new mixer.

b. How much must the company invest today to replace the industrial mixer?

c. If the new mixer is purchased, how much would be saved in operating costs each year?

d. How much would the company receive at the end of the five-year useful life of the new mixer?

e. Calculate the net present value of replacing the old mixer.

f. Do you think the company should replace the old mixer?

## LO 5, 6, & 7: Determine Relevant Information, Net Present Value, Screen Project, No Residual Value

**7–55.** The managers at General Manufacturing Company are considering replacing the industrial lathe used in the company's factory. The company's cost of capital is 12%.

### Information about the old lathe:

| | |
|---|---|
| Cost | $57,000 |
| Estimated useful life | 8 years |
| Estimated salvage value | $ 0 |
| Current age | 2 years |
| Estimated current fair value | $32,000 |
| Annual operating cost | $32,000 |

### Information about the new lathe:

| | |
|---|---|
| Cost | $61,000 |
| Estimated useful life | 6 years |
| Estimated salvage value | $ 0 |
| Annual operating cost | $24,000 |

**REQUIRED:**

a. Prepare a relevant cost schedule showing the benefit of buying the new lathe. (For this requirement, ignore the time value of money.)

b. How much must the company invest today to replace the old lathe?

c. If the company replaces the old lathe, how much will be saved in operating costs each year?

d. Calculate the net present value of replacing the old lathe.

e. Do you think the company should replace the old lathe?

## LO 5, 6, & 7: Determine Relevant Information, Net Present Value, Screen Project, with Residual Value

**7–56.** John Paul Hudik, president of J.P. Hudik Boat Hauling, is considering replacing the company's industrial lift used to haul boats. The new lift would allow the company to lift larger boats out of the water. The company's cost of capital is 14%.

### Information about the old lift:

| | |
|---|---|
| Cost | $94,000 |
| Estimated useful life | 12 years |
| Estimated salvage value | $10,000 |
| Current age | 4 years |
| Estimated current fair value | $48,000 |
| Annual contribution margin | $50,000 |

### Information about the new lift:

| | |
|---|---|
| Cost | $128,000 |
| Estimated useful life | 8 years |
| Estimated salvage value | $ 25,000 |
| Annual contribution margin | $ 65,000 |

**REQUIRED:**

a. Prepare a relevant cost schedule showing the benefit of buying the new lift. (For this requirement, ignore the time value of money.)

b. How much must the company invest today to replace the old lift?

c. If the company replaces the old lift, what is the increase in the company's annual contribution margin?

d. If the company sells the old lift now to make room for the new one, it will not receive the $10,000 salvage value at the end of its useful life. Instead, the company will receive the $25,000 salvage value from the new lift. With this in mind, if the company buys the new lift, what is the change in the salvage value the company is to receive at the end of the eight-year life of the equipment?

e. Calculate the net present value of replacing the old lift.

f. Do you think the company should replace the old lift?

## LO 5, 6, & 7: Determine Relevant Information, Net Present Value, Screen Project, with Residual Value

**7–57.** The managers at Wilma Manufacturing are considering replacing a printing press with a new, high-speed model. The company's cost of capital is 12%.

### Information about the old printing press:

| | |
|---|---|
| Cost | $255,000 |
| Estimated useful life | 10 years |
| Estimated salvage value | $ 25,000 |
| Annual depreciation | $ 23,000 |
| Current age | 3 years |
| Accumulated depreciation to date | $184,000 |
| Estimated current fair value | $150,000 |
| Annual contribution margin | $110,000 |

### Information about the new printing press:

| | |
|---|---|
| Cost | $535,000 |
| Estimated useful life | 7 years |
| Estimated salvage value | $ 45,000 |
| Annual depreciation | $ 70,000 |
| Annual contribution margin | $150,000 |

**REQUIRED:**

a. Prepare a relevant cost schedule showing the benefit of buying the new printing press. (For this requirement, ignore the time value of money.)

b. How much must the company invest today to replace the old printing press?

c. If the company replaces the old printing press, what is the increase in the company's annual contribution margin?

d. If the company sells the old printing press now to make room for the new one, it will not receive the $25,000 salvage value at the end of its useful life. Instead, the company will receive the $45,000 salvage value from the new printing press. With this in mind, if the company buys the printing press, what is the change in the salvage value the company is to receive at the end of the seven-year life of the equipment?

e. Calculate the net present value of replacing the old printing press.

f. Do you think the company should replace the old printing press?

## APPENDIX

### LO 7: Calculate Simple, Compound Interest, Full Years

**7–58.** Greg Gluck Marine borrowed $5,000 from National Bank on January 1, 2000.

**REQUIRED:**

a. Assuming 9% simple interest is charged, calculate interest for 2000, 2001, and 2002.    *450 × 3 yrs = 1350*

b. Assuming 9% compound interest is charged, calculate interest for 2000, 2001, and 2002.    *6475    (1475)*

### LO 7: Calculate Simple, Compound Interest, Full Years

**7–59.** Gary borrowed $8,000 from Orlando National Bank on January 1, 2000.

**REQUIRED:**

a. Assuming 8% simple interest is charged, calculate interest for 2000, 2001, and 2002.

b. Assuming 8% compound interest is charged, calculate interest for 2000, 2001, and 2002.

### LO 7: Calculate Simple, Compound Interest, Full Years

**7–60.** Cam borrowed $2,000 from Miami National Bank on January 1, 2000.

**REQUIRED:**

a. Assuming 6% simple interest is charged, calculate interest for 2000, 2001, and 2002.

b. Assuming 6% compound interest is charged, calculate interest for 2000, 2001, and 2002.

### LO 7: Calculate Future Value, Single Cash Flow, Various Rates and Maturities

**7–61.** Susan Jones made the following investments on January 1, 2000:
   1. $ 2,000 at 10% for 5 years
   2. $12,000 at 4% for 8 years
   3. $ 9,000 at 14% for 15 years

Assume the interest on each investment is compounded annually.

**REQUIRED:**
Calculate the future value of each of the investments listed above at their maturity.

## LO 7: Calculate Future Value, Single Cash Flow, Various Rates and Maturities

**7–62.** Ivan Zhang made the following investments on January 1, 2000:
1. $3,000 at 8% for 6 years
2. $4,000 at 6% for 8 years
3. $5,000 at 10% for 5 years

Assume the interest on each investment is compounded annually.

**REQUIRED:**
Calculate the future value of each of the investments listed above at their maturity.

## LO 7: Calculate Future Value, Single Cash Flow, Various Rates and Maturities

**7–63.** Orlando Gonzalez made the following investments on January 1, 2000:
1. $1,000 at 14% for 3 years
2. $2,000 at 10% for 5 years
3. $4,000 at 8% for 8 years

Assume the interest on each investment is compounded annually.

**REQUIRED:**
Calculate the future value of each of the investments listed above at their maturity.

## LO 7: Calculate Future Value, Yearly Cash Flows, Various Rates and Maturities

**7–64.** Consider the following investments:
1. $2,000 at the end of each of the next five years at 10% interest compounded annually.
2. $12,000 at the end of each of the next eight years at 4% interest compounded annually.
3. $9,000 at the end of each of the next 15 years at 14% interest compounded annually.

**REQUIRED:**
Calculate the future value of each of the investments listed above at their maturity.

## LO 7: Calculate Future Value, Yearly Cash Flows, Various Rates and Maturities

**7–65.** Consider the following investments.
1. $12,000 at the end of each of the next three years at 12% interest compounded annually.
2. $16,000 at the end of each of the next five years at 10% interest compounded annually.
3. $20,000 at the end of each of the next 10 years at 8% interest compounded annually.

**REQUIRED:**
Calculate the future value of each of the investments listed above at their maturity.

## LO 7: Calculate Future Value, Yearly Cash Flows, Various Rates and Maturities

**7–66.** Consider the following investments.
1. $1,000 at the end of each of the next five years at 6% interest compounded annually.
2. $1,000 at the end of each of the next five years at 8% interest compounded annually.
3. $1,000 at the end of each of the next five years at 10% interest compounded annually.

**REQUIRED:**
Calculate the future value of each of the investments listed above at their maturity.

## LO 7: Calculate Present Value, Single Cash Flow, Single Rate

**7–67.** Jim Johnson is planning to buy a new car when he graduates from college in three years. He would like to invest a single amount now, in order to have the $24,000 he estimates the car will cost.

**REQUIRED:**
Calculate the amount Jim must invest today, to have enough to buy the new car assuming his investment will earn 4% compounded annually for the three-year investment.

## LO 7: Calculate Present Value, Single Cash Flow, Single Rate

**7–68.** Lowell Pitman needs to have $50,000 at the end of five years. Lowell would like to invest a single amount now, to have the $50,000 in five years.

**REQUIRED:**
Calculate the amount Lowell must invest today, to have the amount of money he needs assuming his investment will earn 8% compounded annually for the five-year investment.

## LO 7: Calculate Present Value, Single Cash Flow, Single Rate

**7–69.** Lauren Elsea is planning to buy a house when she graduates from college. She would like to have $20,000 for the down payment. Lauren would like to invest a single amount now, to have the $20,000 at the end of three years.

**REQUIRED:**
Calculate the amount Lauren must invest today, to have the amount of money she needs assuming her investment will earn 6% compounded annually for the three-year investment.

## LO 7: Calculate Present Value, Yearly Cash Flows, Single Rate

**7–70.** Linda Chidister is planning to send her son, Edward, to college. While he is in college, Linda intends to give him $3,000 at the end of each year.

**REQUIRED:**
How much must Linda invest today so she will have enough to give Edward $3,000 at the end of each of the next four years assuming the investment will earn 6% interest.

## LO 7:   Calculate Present Value, Yearly Cash Flows, Single Rate

**7–71.** Alex Malpin is planning to spend the next three years doing research in China. An Asian studies research institute has agreed to pay Alex $20,000 at the end of each of the three years he is in China.

**REQUIRED:**

How much must be invested today to have enough to pay Alex $20,000 at the end of each of the next three years assuming the investment will earn 10% interest.

## LO 7:   Calculate Present Value, Yearly Cash Flows, Single Rate

**7–72.** Photo Factory is planning to purchase some photo processing equipment from Ace Equipment Company. The equipment will provide cash flow of $15,000 at the end of each of the next eight years.

**REQUIRED:**

How much should Photo Factory pay for the equipment assuming it will provide $15,000 at the end of each of the next eight years and Ace has promised that it will earn a return of exactly 14%?

# Chapter 8

## The Operating Budget

*I*magine for a moment that midway through your accounting class you and three of your classmates decide to go to Europe. You stand up, excuse yourself from class, and the four of you head for the airport. At the airport you discover that the next flight to Europe departs in four hours and there are only three seats available. You buy three tickets, send one friend back to class, and begin the long wait until boarding. After what seems like an eternity, you board the flight and are on your way.

When you arrive in Paris, your friends ask, "Well, we're here. What now?" You respond, "I don't know, this is a spontaneous thing. We have the freedom to do whatever we want." Your friends have many questions: "Where will we stay? Did you bring any money? Who has a French/English dictionary? Are the clothes we are wearing adequate for the weather in Paris? By the way, what *is* the weather in Paris? Now that we're here, how long will we stay? What will we do? Is there anything other than the Eiffel Tower here? Why did we go to Paris and not some other place? How will we get back home?"

What's wrong with this Paris trip? The obvious answer is a complete lack of planning. Thoughtful planning increases the possibility of success in almost anything we might do, whether business related or not.

Careful planning is in fact a key element of business success. Without such planning, business activities founder and a company almost certainly loses direction. In Chapter 7 we described planning as the *why,* the *what,* the *how,* and the *who* of being in business. Recall that the *why* is the process of setting company goals. The *what* is the development of a strategic plan to implement those goals in the long term. These two planning elements were discussed in some detail in Chapter 7. The *how* is the process of capital budgeting to allocate scarce resources and was the major topic of Chapter 7.

**operating budget** A budget for a specific period, usually one to five years, that establishes who is responsible for the day-to-day operation of a business during that time.

**master operating budget** Another name for *operating budget*.

**master budget** Another name for *operating budget*.

The *who* is the final step—the preparation of the operating budget. The **operating budget** is a budget for a specific time, usually one to five years, that establishes who is responsible for the day-to-day operation of the business during that time. This budget is also sometimes called the **master operating budget** or simply the **master budget**. For the sake of consistency, we will use the term *operating budget* throughout our discussions of this topic.

The operating budget will be an important part of your business life, regardless of your occupation or the type of company for which you choose to work. Whether the organization is profit or not for profit, and whether it is a service, merchandising, or manufacturing firm, budgeting has become increasingly more important in charting the success of today's organizations. Gone are the days when companies could succeed on simple luck and optimism. Gone, too, are the days when a select group of top managers prepared operating budgets with little input from others in the organization. Many companies today involve all managers and employees in the budgeting process. Fortune 500 companies such as Motorola, Honeywell, General Motors, and others have recognized that better budgeting is achieved when they involve those who actually work in the area or function for which the budget is being prepared. As you read the pages that follow, we hope you remember that budgets will be an important ingredient in your personal business success, and that you will very likely be involved in the budgeting process much earlier in your career than you may have expected.

The chapter is divided into two main parts. Part One contains an overview of the operating budget, its purpose, and where it fits into the overall management process. Part Two contains a detailed presentation of how the operating budget is actually prepared and how it should and should not be used by managers. ■

## LEARNING OBJECTIVES

*After completing your work on this chapter, you should be able to do the following:*

1. Describe some of the benefits of the operating budget.
2. Describe the three budgeted financial statements contained in the operating budget and the other budgets that support the budgeted financial statements.
3. Compare and contrast various approaches to the preparation and use of the operating budget.
4. Describe the role of the sales forecast in the budgeting process.
5. Prepare the budgets included in the operating budget.
6. Describe the appropriate use of the operating budget in the overall management process.

## The Operating Budget: What Is It?

What exactly *is* an operating budget? We know it is the plan for a company's operating activities for some period of time, but what is in that plan? The operating budget includes a set of estimated financial statements.

Recall that the three main financial statements are the balance sheet, the income statement, and the statement of cash flows. Businesses prepare these statements at the end of a given time period to show the effects of past transactions and events. An operating budget contains those same three financial statements, except they are estimates—or forecasts—of future transactions and events. The forecasted financial statements in the operating budget are sometimes called pro forma financial statements. *Pro forma* is a Latin phrase meaning "provided in advance."

Because the operating budget is a set of estimated financial statements, much of what we will cover in this chapter will at least be familiar to you. The only difference between the financial statements businesses use to show the effects of past events and transactions, and the ones you will explore in this chapter, is that the budgeted financial statements are used to predict future events.

# BENEFITS OF BUDGETING

A well-prepared operating budget can create many benefits for the company. In this section, we will explore four of them. First, budgeting serves as a guide. Second, it helps organizations allocate resources. Third, it encourages communication and coordination. Fourth, it sets performance standards, or *benchmarks*.

## Serves as a Guide

The operating budget should serve as a guide for a company to follow during the budgeted period. Recall the hypothetical trip to Paris we described in the chapter opener. Suppose that while touring France, our travelers heard about a fantastic side trip (a terrific art show in Nice) not included in their original itinerary. Based on this new information, our travelers would probably adjust their original plan to allow for this side trip. And so it should be with a budget, because companies should adjust their budgets when desirable or necessary.

To illustrate, suppose the budget for Pam's Flower Shop forecasted sales revenue of $310,000 for the first three months of 2002. Business was better than expected and the flower shop had sales of $310,000 by the end of February. Should Pam close the flower shop until April 1 because she attained her budgeted sales figure for the quarter? Of course not. Or suppose Pam has the opportunity to purchase 20 dozen roses just before Valentine's Day at a bargain basement price. She can probably sell all of them for a whopping profit, but she didn't budget for this special purchase. What should she do? It may seem obvious that she should take advantage of this terrific opportunity, but a surprising number of businesses view the budget as "set in stone," so to speak, and meeting the budget becomes the primary business objective. An unwillingness to adjust a budget based on new information can be detrimental to a company because opportunities are missed and poor decisions made.

## Assists in Resource Allocation

As discussed in Chapter 7, all organizations have scarce resources. No company can afford to do everything it desires, or even everything it needs to do within a given time period. A budget can help management decide where to allocate its limited resources.

The budgeting process may uncover potential bottlenecks and allow managers to address these issues in advance as the budget is being prepared, rather than as problems occur during the year. An example of a bottleneck in a manufacturing environment is presented for Montrose Manufacturing Company in Exhibit 8–1.

**Exhibit 8–1**
Example of Production Bottleneck at Montrose Manufacturing

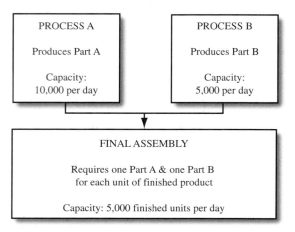

As you can see from Exhibit 8–1, each unit of finished product Montrose manufactures requires one Part A and one Part B. The maximum number of finished units of product the company can produce per day is 5,000. The limiting factor is Process B, which can produce only 5,000 parts per day. Montrose could increase the capacity of Process A from 10,000 parts per day to 100,000 parts per day and the company *still* could produce only 5,000 finished units per day because of the restriction caused by Process B. Process B is the bottleneck in this company's production process.

Assume Montrose Manufacturing Company moved some production machinery from Process A to Process B. This change reduces the capacity of Process A by 2,500 units per day, but the capacity of Process B was increased by 2,500 units per day as reflected in Exhibit 8–2.

**Exhibit 8–2**
Elimination of Production Bottleneck at Montrose Manufacturing

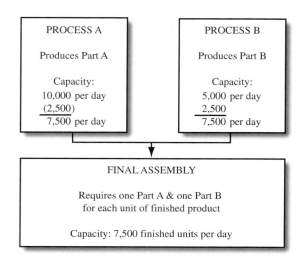

As you can see by looking at Exhibit 8–2, Montrose has increased its capacity to produce finished units by 50 percent (from 5,000 units to 7,500 units) without adding any additional machinery to its operation, which is a significant factor if you recall our discussion of capital expenditures in Chapter 7.

The issue of resource allocation is also important for a merchandising business. For example, February may be so busy for a Pam's Flower Shop that she will need extra workers. If Pam knows this in advance, she will have time to hire the needed workers at the least cost so she can offer quality service and sell more flowers. In contrast, if Pam did not plan for the February rush, she would find herself under-staffed and unable to provide quality, timely service. She might lose customers be-fore she could hire more workers, and sales could drop. Budgeting, then, helps Pam make good decisions about how to allocate her resources.

## Fosters Communication and Coordination

As managers from different functional areas in an organization work together to prepare the budget, they gain a better understanding of the entire business. When managers from all areas learn of difficulties facing others and spot duplication of effort, the firm can then solve problems and coordinate efforts more effectively. Our previous example of Montrose Manufacturing Company and its production bottleneck points out the possibilities of increased communication and coordina-tion through the budgeting process. In working to solve this production problem, the managers of Process A, Process B, and Final Assembly had the opportunity to view the production process from a broader perspective. Rather than concentrat-ing only on their own part of the process, they were better able to understand the problems facing managers in other areas of the company's operations. They were forced to communicate with one another and to better coordinate their efforts.

Even for a small company like Pam's Flower Shop, success can depend on co-ordinating many activities. For example, Pam expects sales to increase in February because of Valentine's Day. She anticipates she will need more flowers to sell, and more labor to sell them. The number of extra workers, however, may depend on the amount of additional flowers ordered. When she prepares the budget, Pam speaks to the inventory manager and the personnel manager about the February rush to better coordinate their activities. Then the managers will know in advance exactly what needs to be done.

## Establishes Performance Standards

The operating budget also sets performance standards for an organization. As managers prepare budgets for their companies, they must estimate performance levels they both want and can attain. If a company's actual sales, for example, are less than its budgeted sales for a particular period, the sales manager will review the deficit and ask why. Once she has learned why, she will probably budget more effectively next time. Without a budget she might not notice the sales shortfall and therefore would not learn from it.

These performance standards become benchmarks against which firms can compare the actual results. Differences between the actual results and the budget can be explored and improvements made. The improvements may focus on per-formance, the budgeting process, or both.

## Discussion Question

8-1. In what other ways do you think a company might benefit from preparing an operating budget?

Many of us have had to prepare a personal cash budget, in which we compare the amount of cash coming in to the amount of cash going out. Because of this personal experience with budgeting, many people think that business budgeting focuses only on budgeting for cash inflows and outflows. This view, however, is far too narrow. Remember, the operating budget is a set of estimated financial statements that includes the balance sheet, income statement, and statement of cash flows, regardless of whether the business preparing the budget is a manufacturer, a merchandiser, or a service company.

Technically, the operating budget consists of only these three pro forma financial statements. In preparing the budget, however, several supporting schedules are included that, when completed, provide the information necessary to complete the three financial statements contained in the budget. These supporting schedules are also usually referred to as budgets, and we will refer to them as such in all our discussions.

## Sales Budget

**sales budget** Details the expected sales revenue from a company's primary operating activities during a certain time period.

The sales budget is the first budget prepared and is based on a sales forecast. As the name implies, the **sales budget** details the expected sales revenue from a company's primary operating activities during a certain time period. Because manufacturers and merchandisers sell tangible, physical product, the sales budget is based on the number of units the firm expects to sell. The sales budget of a service business is based on the amount of services the firm expects to render.

Because sales revenue is an income statement item, the information provided by the sales budget is used to construct the budgeted income statement.

## Production or Purchases Budget

**production budget** Details the cost and number of units that must be produced by a manufacturer to meet the sales forecast and the desired ending inventory.

**purchases budget** Details the cost and number of units that must be purchased by a merchandiser to meet the sales forecast and the desired ending inventory.

For manufacturers, the budget that plans for the cost and number of units that must be manufactured to meet the sales forecast and the desired quantity of ending finished goods inventory is known as the **production budget.** Although merchandisers call this budget the **purchases budget,** the two are functionally equivalent. Their names reflect the source of the item sold: Manufacturers produce the products they sell, and merchandisers purchase the products they sell.

The production budget and the purchases budget are simply pro forma versions of the cost of goods manufactured schedule and the cost of purchases schedule, as discussed in Chapter 2. A production budget is usually more complicated than a purchases budget because, as discussed in Chapter 2, costing manufactured product is more complicated than costing purchased product. A production budget includes schedules for materials, labor, and manufacturing overhead. An operating budget for a service business does not include a production budget or purchases budget because a service company does not sell tangible, physical product.

Only some of the product scheduled to be produced by a manufacturer or purchased by a merchandiser is intended to be sold during the period covered by the budget. The product not projected to be sold is called *ending finished goods inventory* for a manufacturer and *ending merchandise inventory* for a merchandiser. In either case, this projected ending inventory is classified as an asset. Therefore, some of the information provided by the production budget or purchases budget is used to construct the budgeted balance sheet.

The product that is projected to be sold during the period covered by the budget is classified as an expense item and will be shown on the budgeted income statement. As you recall, this expense item is called cost of goods sold. The cost of goods sold information needed to construct the budgeted income statement comes from the cost of goods sold budget.

## Cost of Goods Sold or Cost of Services Budget

**cost of goods sold budget**
Calculates the total cost of all the product a manufacturing or merchandising company estimates it will sell during the period covered by the budget.

**cost of services budget**
Calculates the total cost of all the services a service type business estimates it will provide during the period covered by the budget.

A **cost of goods sold budget** calculates the total cost of all the product a company estimates it will sell during the period covered by the operating budget. This budget differs from the production (purchases) budget because of inventory requirements. Under accrual accounting, the cost of product is not recognized as an expense (cost of goods sold) on the income statement until it is sold. Until then, it is recorded as an asset (inventory) and is shown as such on the balance sheet. For a service type business, this budget is called the **cost of services budget.**

Whether we are talking about the cost of goods sold budget or the cost of services budget, they are similar to the schedules in Chapter 2 regarding the costing of products and services. The only difference is that the budgets discussed in this chapter pertain to the future.

Because cost of goods sold or cost of services is an income statement item, the information provided by the cost of goods sold budget or cost of services budget is used to construct the budgeted income statement.

## Selling and Administrative Expense Budget

**selling and administrative expense budget** Calculates all costs other than the cost of product or services required to support a company's forecasted sales.

After a company makes its sales forecast and estimates its product (or service) cost, it can estimate all other costs needed to support that level of sales. A **selling and administrative expense budget** calculates all costs other than the cost of product or services required to support a company's forecasted sales. The kinds of items included in this budget are identical to those included in the income statements, as discussed throughout this text. They are what we described as period costs in Chapter 2 and include such items as advertising, administrative salaries, rent, and utilities.

## Budgeted Income Statement

**budgeted income statement**
Shows the expected net income for the period covered by the operating budget.

A **budgeted income statement** shows the expected net income for the period covered by the operating budget. It subtracts all estimated product (or service) cost and period cost from estimated sales revenue. This budget is prepared using information from the sales budget, the cost of goods sold (or cost of services) budget, and the selling and administrative expense budget.

## Cash Budget

**cash budget** Shows whether the expected amount of cash generated by operating activities will be sufficient to pay anticipated expenses during the period covered by the operating budget.

A **cash budget** shows whether the expected amount of cash generated by operating activities will be sufficient to pay anticipated expenses during the period covered by the operating budget. It also reveals whether a company should expect a need for short-term external financing during the budget period. Be careful not to confuse the cash budget with the budgeted statement of cash flows, as discussed later in the chapter. The budgeted statement of cash flows is more comprehensive than a simple cash budget.

## Budgeted Balance Sheet

**budgeted balance sheet**
A presentation of estimated assets, liabilities, and owners' equity at the end of the budgeted period.

A **budgeted balance sheet** is a presentation of estimated assets, liabilities, and owners' equity at the end of the budgeted period. It is created exactly the way a balance sheet based on actual historical results is prepared. At the start of the period being budgeted, a company has a balance sheet that presents its assets, liabilities, and owners' equity. Most (if not all) of the company's asset, liability, and equity items will be changed by the estimated results of operations (budgeted income statement). The result is an estimated balance sheet at the end of the budget period.

The budgeted balance sheet for a manufacturer or a merchandiser is prepared using information from the actual balance sheet at the beginning of the period covered by the budget, the production (purchases) budget, and the budgeted income statement. A service type company has no production or purchases budget, so the budgeted balance sheet is prepared using information from the actual balance sheet at the beginning of the budget period and the budgeted income statement.

## Budgeted Statement of Cash Flows

**budgeted statement of cash flows** A statement of a company's expected sources and uses of cash during the period covered by the operating budget.

A **budgeted statement of cash flows** is a statement of a company's expected sources and uses of cash during the period covered by the operating budget. Manufacturers, merchandisers, and service companies create the budgeted statement of cash flows in a manner similar to the way they create the budgeted balance sheet. At the start of the period being budgeted, they report their cash balance. Based on the estimated results of operations (budgeted income statement) and other business activities that either generate or use cash, they estimate the cash balance at the end of the budget period. The purpose of the budgeted statement of cash flows is to explain how that change in cash is to happen.

## Discussion Question

8-2. In what ways do you think the cash budget described earlier differs from the budgeted statement of cash flows?

## Interrelationship among the Budgets

The budgets we have discussed are closely interrelated. A change in any one of them will cause a ripple effect throughout all the others. Exhibit 8–3 shows the extent of this interrelationship.

To demonstrate the interrelationship among the budgets, we return to Pam's Flower Shop for a moment. Because Pam's company is a merchandiser, the operating budget she prepares will include a sales budget, a purchases budget, a cost of goods sold budget, a selling and administrative expense budget, a cash budget, a budgeted income statement, a budgeted balance sheet, and a budgeted statement of cash flows.

Pam prepared the various budgets described for the first three months of 2002 based on the following sales forecast.

### PAM'S FLOWER SHOP
#### Sales Forecast
#### For the Three Months Ended March 31, 2002

|  | January | February | March | Total |
|---|---|---|---|---|
| Sales | $90,000 | $120,000 | $100,000 | $310,000 |

**Exhibit 8–3**
Interrelationship
among the Budgets

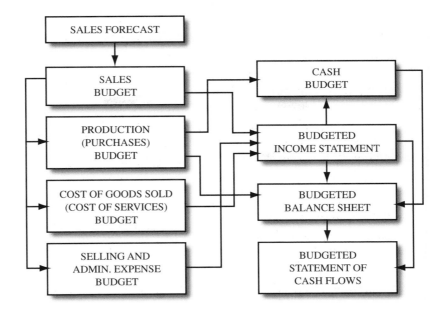

## Discussion Question

**8-3.** From what you have learned so far about the operating budget, which of the budgets for Pam's Flower Shop will be affected by the amounts in this sales forecast? Explain how each is affected.

Now assume that a new flower shop opened just down the street from Pam's after she had prepared her operating budget. Pam believes that to be realistic in her planning, she needs to revise her sales forecast as follows:

**PAM'S FLOWER SHOP**
**Revised Sales Forecast**
**For the Three Months Ended March 31, 2002**

|  | January | February | March | Total |
|---|---|---|---|---|
| Sales | $75,000 | $100,000 | $90,000 | $265,000 |

## Discussion Question

**8-4.** Which of the budgets for Pam's Flower Shop will be affected by the changes in her sales forecast? Explain how each is affected.

Because sales revenue is changed in Pam's revised sales forecast, the sales budget will be different. Even without any information about purchases, you should intuitively recognize that lower sales probably means fewer flowers sold; therefore, fewer flowers will need to be purchased, meaning that the purchases budget must be revised. The same holds true for the cost of goods sold budget. The selling and administrative expense budget may need to be revised based on the new forecast, because lower sales probably means fewer sales clerks, at least. The cash budget will need to be revised because lower sales means less cash collected and lower purchases means less cash spent. The budgeted income statement must surely be revised, because the sales budget, the cost of goods sold budget, and the selling and administrative expense budget are used to construct the budgeted income statement. If those budgets must be revised, the budgeted income statement must also be revised. If the budgeted income statement is affected, the budgeted balance sheet must be revised because the results from the income statement are reflected in the balance sheet. If cash is affected in any way (and we already determined it would be), the budgeted statement of cash flows must be revised.

As you can see, a change in any of the budgets has a ripple effect throughout all the other budgets. Because the various budgets contained in the operating budget are so closely tied together, the preparation of the operating budget in most organizations is extremely time consuming and complicated. Depending on the size of the company, it may take several months to prepare the operating budget. For example, a manufacturer or merchandiser prepares a sales budget for each product the company sells. If the company sells 80 products, then 80 sales budgets must be prepared. If the company also has 80 sales territories, a whopping 6,400 sales budgets must be prepared (80 products $\times$ 80 sales territories). Companies must begin the budgeting process early enough to allow sufficient time for completion. If the budgeted period begins on January 1, 2002, for example, the budgeting process may begin in August or September 2001, or even earlier.

For some large, multinational companies, the process never ends. They work on the 2002 budget from January through December 2001. Then they turn right around in January 2002 and begin work on the 2003 budget, and so on. It takes so long to complete the process that by they time they finish one year, it is time to start again for the next year.

# DIFFERENT APPROACHES TO BUDGETING

We now know what an operating budget is, but exactly how do businesses prepare one? The answer depends on the needs of the business and the approach it takes to the budgeting process. Next we investigate seven budgeting approaches: perpetual, incremental, zero-based, top-down, bottom-up, imposed, and participative approaches.

Firms may vary as to the maximum duration for the operating budget period. Because virtually all prepare it for at least one year, we focus on a one-year budget period in the following discussion.

## Perpetual Budgeting

**perpetual budgeting**
The budgeting approach of updating the budget every month.

**continual budgeting**
Another name for *perpetual budgeting*.

Some companies continually update their operating budgets. As one month ends, another month's budget is added to the end of the budget. Therefore, at any given time, the budget projects 12 months into the future. This budgeting approach is called **perpetual budgeting,** or **continual budgeting.** Companies that use perpetual budgeting always budget 12 months in advance. At any given time, these companies have an operating budget that forecasts 12 months into the future.

The main advantage of perpetual budgeting is that it spreads the workload for budget preparation evenly over the year, which allows employees to incorporate the work required to prepare the budget into their routine work schedule. Another advantage of a perpetual budget is that the budget always extends 12 months into the future. In contrast, when perpetual budgeting is *not* used, the new operating budget is typically prepared when only a couple of months are left on the old budget. One disadvantage of perpetual budgeting may be that the budget preparation process becomes so routine that employees lose the motivation and creativity required to prepare an inovative operating budget. An important aspect of solid budgeting is looking for better ways to do things. Think back to the example we used earlier for Montrose Manufacturing Company, which was able to restructure its production process because its managers were serious about looking for a better way. If the preparation of the budget becomes routine (just another bunch of forms to fill out), managers may stop this critical evaluation and become satisfied with the status quo. Another disadvantage is that many managers believe they do not have sufficient time to do all that is asked of them in their regular day-to-day responsibilities. Adding the responsibility of preparing a perpetual budget to a heavy workload can lead to sloppy budgeting.

## Incremental Budgeting

**incremental budgeting**
The process of using the prior year's budget or the company's actual results to build the new operating budget.

The process of using the prior year's budget or the company's actual results to build the new operating budget is called **incremental budgeting.** If, for example, a company's 2001 budget included $200,000 for maintenance and repairs on the machinery and equipment in its production facility, $200,000 becomes the starting point for this item in preparing the 2002 budget. The only question to be answered is whether the company needs to include more than $200,000 for repairs and maintenance in 2002. This budgeting approach is used by governmental entities such as the federal government and by many companies.

The trouble with the incremental budgeting approach is that if the prior year's budget includes unnecessary costs, or items that do not optimize performance, this waste may be simply rolled over into the next year's budget. The advantage to this approach is its simplicity. Some practitioners and many experts believe the disadvantages greatly outweigh the advantages.

## Discussion Question

**8–5.** In what ways, if any, do you think the federal government's use of incremental budgeting contributes to the national debt?

## Zero-Based Budgeting

**zero-based budgeting**
A process of budgeting in which managers start from scratch, or zero, when preparing a new budget.

An alternative to the incremental budgeting approach is zero-based budgeting. In **zero-based budgeting,** managers start from scratch, or zero, when preparing a new budget. Each item on the budget must be justified every year as though it were a new budget item. Zero-based budgeting is much more difficult and time consuming than incremental budgeting, but many organizations believe the results are worth that time and effort because managers are forced to reexamine the items included in the budget and justify their continuation.

## Top-Down versus Bottom-Up Budgeting

Budgeted information can flow either from the upper levels of management in a company down to managers and employees at lower levels, or vice versa. For fairly obvious reasons, the former approach is known as the top-down approach and the latter as the bottom-up approach. Each has distinct advantages and disadvantages.

### Top-Down Budgeting

**top-down budgeting** A budget prepared by top managers in a company.

*Top-Down Budgeting* When a budget is prepared by top managers in the company, the process is called **top-down budgeting.** The top executives prepare the budget, and lower-level managers and employees work to meet that budget.

The top-down approach has several advantages. First, a company's upper management is usually most knowledgeable about the company's overall operation. It makes sense (on the surface, at least) that upper managers be responsible for the information contained in the operating budget because they are the most experienced and knowledgeable individuals in the company. Second, top management is keenly aware of company goals, so they will prepare the budget with these goals in mind. Finally, the top-down budgeting approach involves fewer people, so it causes fewer disruptions, is more efficient, and is less time consuming than the bottom-up approach.

The top-down approach to budgeting has two major disadvantages. First, lower-level managers and employees are usually less accepting of budgets when they have no part in setting the standards. Second, top managers may be keenly aware of the big picture, but they do not have the working knowledge of daily activities needed to prepare the detailed budgets for all company activities.

Most large, publicly traded companies in the United States use some form of top-down budgeting. Why? If you recall our discussion of the cost of equity capital in Chapter 7, you know that a firm's top management fully understands the need to maximize returns for stockholders. Most of that return is in the form of stock appreciation (increase in the market price of the stock), rather than dividends. The greatest influence on the selling price of a company's stock price is company profits. So, to ensure maximum stock appreciation, a company must be as profitable as possible. The top management of these publicly traded companies generally have a better sense than lower-level managers and employees of how much profit the company must have in a given year to maintain (or attain) a high return for stockholders. In top-down budgeting, the target profit figures become the starting point of the budgeting process.

**imposed budget** A budget in which upper management sets figures for all operating activities that the rest of the company rarely, if ever, can negotiate.

Traditionally, most firms that used top-down budgeting also used an imposed budgeting process. An **imposed budget** is a budget in which upper management sets figures for all operating activities that the rest of the company rarely, if ever, can negotiate. No matter how unreasonable the budget numbers, top management expects all other managers to "do whatever it takes to make it happen." This type of budgeting process can do more harm than good, because it can lead to business practices that conflict with the company's stated goals. Today, however, not all top-down budgets are imposed budgets, as we will see shortly.

### Bottom-Up Budgeting

**bottom-up budgeting** A budget initially prepared by lower-level managers and employees.

*Bottom-Up Budgeting* In **bottom-up budgeting,** the budget is initially prepared by lower-level managers and employees. For example, members of the sales force prepare the sales schedule for their own sales territories. The sales manager then reviews these sales schedules, makes any necessary changes, and combines them to form the overall company sales schedule. Likewise, employees in the production facility prepare schedules for production, including schedules for direct material, direct labor, and manufacturing overhead.

Bottom-up budgeting has three main advantages. First, the budget may be more realistic. Those who work in a functional area are usually better informed about what should be included in the budget than upper managers. If lower-level managers and employees take the budgeting process seriously, they are likely to create an operating budget based on accurate, realistic information. Second, lower-level managers and employees are more likely to work toward budgeted performance standards because they helped to set those standards. Third, as employees prepare the budget, they learn to think about the company's goals, how various activities can affect the future, and how they personally will participate. In short, they begin to think about the work they will need to do in the coming year.

Bottom-up budgeting has two disadvantages. First, employees at every level must take time from their day-to-day responsibilities to work on the budget as it is prepared, reviewed, revised, and approved—all of which adds up to substantial time and effort. Second, some employees may be tempted to prepare a budget that is so generous they can effortlessly outperform it. For example, sales representatives may budget sales of $300,000, when they can achieve sales of $350,000 with little effort. Thus, their actual sales performance looks great compared with budgeted sales. Manipulating the budget to make certain that the actual performance exceeds budgeted performance is one example of a budget game. A *budget game* is the game of using the budget to do things it was never intended to do, such as ensuring a strong performance appraisal.

Bottom-up budgeting is always a participative budgeting process. A **participative budget** is one in which managers and employees at many levels of the company are involved in setting the performance standards and preparing the budget. Recent developments have expanded the use of participative budgeting to top-down budgeting, so it is beneficial to discuss imposed and participative budget philosophies a little further.

**participative budget** A budget in which managers and employees at many levels of the company are involved in setting the performance standards and preparing the budget.

## Imposed versus Participative Budgets

A bottom-up budget will always be a participative budget. Managers and employees at all levels of the company participate in the preparation of a bottom-up budget. A top-down budget, however, can be either imposed or participative.

In recent years, companies have discovered that by allowing more participation, they empower their employees. To empower employees means to give employees the authority to make decisions concerning their job responsibilities, including decisions about items in the operating budget.

A company committed to both top-down budgeting and empowered employees must combine the top-down and bottom-up approaches to budgeting. Rather than having all budget information flow from the top of the company downward to lower levels, upper management provides profit targets to managers at lower levels. These lower level managers then prepare the operating budget for their functional areas, given the profit targets provided by upper management.

# Discussion Questions

**8-6.** What possible positive results do you think can come from more empowerment:

    **a.** for the company? Explain your reasoning.
    **b.** for managers and employees? Explain your reasoning.

**8-7.** What possible negative results do you think can come from more empowerment:

    **a.** for the company? Explain your reasoning.
    **b.** for managers and employees? Explain your reasoning.

As an example of combining the top-down and bottom-up approaches to budgeting, we look at Preston Nydegger Company. Nydegger is a publicly traded company that wants to be one of the top-performing companies (in terms of dividends and stock appreciation) in the stock market. Upper management has determined that the company must earn a profit of $1 million in the upcoming year to reach that goal. The company has three divisions (A, B, & C), and each must earn some part of the targeted $1 million profit. Division C is the smallest of the three, and corporate headquarters has assigned this division a target profit of $150,000 for the next year.

Now that Division C has received its target profit (this is the top-down part), the division manager, Joenne Moss, and her managers and employees set about to prepare the operating budget for the year (this is the participative part). When they have completed their budgeting process, the result in summary form is as follows:

| | |
|---|---|
| Sales | $500,000 |
| Expenses | (450,000) |
| Net Income | $150,000 |

Wait a minute! Something's wrong. The numbers just don't add up. Well, what we see is a conflict between the top-down target profit ($150,000) and what Joenne and her people at Division C think they can accomplish in the upcoming year ($500,000 in sales and $450,000 in expenses). What happens next will determine whether this budget is imposed or participative.

If the upper management of Nydegger Company refuses to negotiate and compromise with Division C, the budget becomes imposed. Remember, there is little room for negotiation between upper management and the rest of the company as to the amounts included in an imposed operating budget. If, however, upper management is willing to yield somewhat on its profit targets, the budget becomes participative.

It is unrealistic to think Nydegger will simply adjust its target from $150,000 to $50,000, which would certainly make the arithmetic in the budgeted income statement work. More than likely, Nydegger's upper management will meet with Joenne and her staff to negotiate a compromise target profit. Let us say they did just that, and the negotiations led to a revised target profit of $90,000 for the division. The revised summary budgeted income statement, then, would be as follows:

| | |
|---|---|
| Sales | $500,000 |
| Expenses | (450,000) |
| Net Income | $ 90,000 |

The math still doesn't work! Management at the division level must now either forecast more sales or find some way to reduce expected expenses (or some combination of the two) to project an additional $40,000 in profit for the year.

The key to making a top-down budget a participative budget is the ability and willingness on the part of upper management to negotiate and compromise.

## Discussion Questions

**8-8.** If you were the chief executive officer of your company, would you prefer a top-down or bottom-up budgeting process? Why?

**8-9.** If you were in middle management, would you prefer a top-down or bottom-up budgeting process? Why?

**8-10.** If you were the company CEO, do you think it would be wise for you to spend time tending to the details of the various budgets, given all your other responsibilities?

The overall approach a company takes to preparing its operating budget may actually be a combination of several of the approaches we have discussed here. For example, one company may have a top-down, participative, zero-based budgeting approach. Another company may be committed to an incremental, participative, bottom-up, perpetual budgeting philosophy. The object is not to select a particular approach from a laundry list. Rather, managers must approach the preparation of the operating budget in a way that makes sense in the circumstances.

# THE SALES FORECAST

*After analyzing all available data, the certified meteorologists at the U.S. Weather Service predicted sunny and warm weather for the next five days, with only a 10 percent chance of rain. It rained every day for the next five days.*

What is true for predicting future weather conditions is also true for predicting the future sales performance of a business. Although technological advances over the past 30 years have improved financial forecasting methods, predicting future sales still remains largely an educated guess. The prediction of sales for the period covered by the operating budget is called the **sales forecast.**

**sales forecast** The prediction of sales for the period covered by the operating budget.

## Cornerstone and Keystone of Budgeting

A solid, realistic sales forecast is perhaps the most critical feature of a solid, realistic operating budget. Why? Once the sales forecast has been developed, the business can prepare the sales budget, the production or purchases budget, the cost of goods or cost of services budget, the selling and administrative expense budget, the cash budget, and the three budgeted financial statements (income statement, balance sheet, and statement of cash flows).

The sales forecast is often called the cornerstone of budgeting. In the construction of a building, the first brick or stone laid is called the cornerstone. The remainder of the entire building is built off this cornerstone. In the construction of the operating budget, the sales forecast is the first step; all the budgets are built from the sales forecast. The sales forecast, then, is the cornerstone of the budgeting process, as depicted in Exhibit 8–4.

**Exhibit 8–4**
The Sales Forecast as the Cornerstone of Budgeting

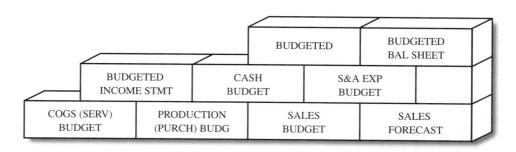

**Exhibit 8–5**
The Sales Forecast as the Keystone of Budgeting

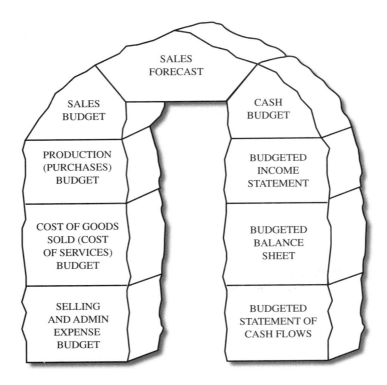

The sales forecast has also been called the keystone of budgeting. This description clearly reflects the importance of the forecast. In the building of a stone archway, the keystone is the stone placed at the exact center at the top of the arch. If this stone is strong and placed properly, the arch will last. In fact, some arches built without mortar in the Middle Ages are still standing. They are held together solely from the strength of the keystone. If the keystone is weak, however, or is improperly set, the arch will collapse; and so it is with budgeting. The quality of the entire master budget depends on the quality and accuracy of the sales forecast as depicted in Exhibit 8–5.

As an archway made of stones depends on the keystone for its strength, the reliability of the operating budget depends on the strength of the sales forecast. If the sales forecast does not reasonably reflect the actual sales during the operating budget period, the budget will not reasonably estimate the actual results for the period. Thus, there will be differences between the actual income statement, balance sheet, and statement of cash flows and the budgeted income statement, balance sheet, and statement of cash flows.

## Factors Affecting the Accuracy of the Sales Forecast

Many factors influence the accuracy of the sales forecast. We have chosen four to discuss here: the economy, industry conditions, the competition, and technology.

***General Economy***   If the economy goes into a recession, consumer saving and spending patterns change. Sales forecasts are usually affected as a result. The problem is, most economists estimate that the economy can be entering or moving out of a recession for at least six to nine months before we realize it. Thus, when a firm creates its sales forecast for the next year's budget, it may be unaware of what the actual state of the economy will be throughout the period covered by the operating budget.

***Industry Conditions***   It is possible for the general economy to be healthy and a particular industry to be in a recession or for the economy to be unhealthy and the industry quite healthy.

***Actions of Competitors***   All companies take great pains to keep information about their plans from their competitors. Therefore, all companies make their sales forecasts without information that has a tremendous impact on the accuracy of the forecast. For example, imagine Intel is about to launch a revolutionary product that could absolutely blow its competitors away. Motorola does not know this, so it creates a sales forecast that is inaccurate because it is unaware of Intel's planned actions.

***Technological Developments***   Technological developments can greatly influence the quality of the sales forecast. It is possible that the market for a particular product may not be as strong—or may not even exist—when the time the period being budgeted for arrives. When Microsoft introduced its Windows 95 program, the need for products compatible with Microsoft's old operating system sharply declined. Sales forecasts for software companies that did not expect the drop in demand for their products were rendered unreliable.

## Discussion Question

**8-11.** What other factors can you think of that would influence the accuracy of a company's sales forecast?

We cannot overemphasize the importance of the sales forecast in the budgeting process, despite the difficulty of being completely accurate. It is worth the time and effort. Managers, however, must prepare and use the operating budget with a solid understanding of its limitations.

## PART TWO: PREPARING AND USING THE OPERATING BUDGET

### Preparing a Master Operating Budget

Marcy's Surf Shop is a retail store that sells only one product (surfboards) and deals in only one product model. The company's fiscal year ends June 30. At Marcy's request, we will prepare the operating budget for the first quarter of the fiscal year ending June 30, 2003. Thus, we will be budgeting for the quarter ending September 30, 2002.

We start with Marcy's budgeted income statement and the budgets that provide information used to construct that budgeted financial statement. We will then prepare the budgeted balance sheet along with all other budgets required to prepare the budgeted balance sheet. Finally, we will prepare the budgeted statement of cash flows.

Because we focus on a merchandising company rather than a manufacturer, we will work with a purchases budget rather than a production budget.

### Budgeted Income Statement

To prepare the budgeted income statement, we need information about sales, cost of goods sold, and selling and administrative expenses for the period covered by the budget. Therefore, we must prepare a budget for each of those items before we can construct the budgeted income statement.

***Sales Budget*** The first information we need to build the budgeted income statement is found in the sales budget. Our first task, then, is to request that Marcy's marketing and sales personnel provide a sales forecast. They tell us that they will be happy to do so, but are not sure how. Should we suggest they take last year's sales numbers and increase them by, say, five percent? This would be incremental budgeting, and—without a critical look at market factors that affect sales—it is a poor approach to budgeting. If simply increasing last year's amounts by a constant percentage were adequate, a computer could easily be programmed to do the job.

Before Marcy's Surf Shop can forecast its sales realistically, sales management and the sales personnel must first consider the factors that influence market conditions. After much discussion, Marcy's staff decided to research the following items:

- Current customer spending patterns
- The ability to attract new customers through market promotions
- The introduction of any new products
- The discontinuation of any products
- The competition
- Price changes        *Cost changes*
- The general economy
- Technological changes

The sales department's recent customer satisfaction survey shows, for example, that 60 percent of all current customers plan to buy another product in the next quarter and that price is the number one consideration in surfboard purchases. Any increase in price is therefore likely to have a negative impact on repeat business. The market research done by the company indicates that thanks to planned market promotions, Marcy's can expect a 20 percent growth in first-time customer purchases.

You see, then, that each of the items chosen for evaluation by the company is researched and the results examined in an attempt to make the forecasting of sales something more than just a guessing game.

Once the sales team considers all its research, it develops a forecast of unit sales for each month in the quarter. The sales team forecasts sales for Marcy's Surf Shop of 30 units in July, 50 units in August, and 40 units in September, shown as Exhibit 8–6.

**Exhibit 8–6**
Sales Forecast for
Marcy's Surf Shop

| | | MARCY'S SURF SHOP | | | |
| | | Sales Forecast | | | |
| | | For the Quarter Ended September 30, 2002 | | | |
| | **July** | **August** | **September** | **Total** |
|---|---|---|---|---|
| Forecasted Sales in Units | 30 | 50 | 40 | 120 |

Based on this forecast, we can prepare Marcy's sales budget for the quarter, as shown in Exhibit 8–7.

We simply used the sales forecast of unit sales and the projected selling price of $200 per surfboard to develop the sales budget.

A real sales budget for an actual company is no more complicated than this one. Of course, in our example, Marcy's sells only one product. Remember from our earlier discussion that if Marcy's sold 80 different products, the company would need to prepare 80 of these sales budgets. If Marcy's sold 80 different products in 80 different locations, the company would need to prepare 6,400 of these sales budgets (80 products × 80 locations).

**Exhibit 8–7**
Sales Budget for
Marcy's Surf Shop

**MARCY'S SURF SHOP**
**Sales Budget**
**For the Quarter Ended September 30, 2002**

|  | July | August | September | Total |
|---|---|---|---|---|
| Forecasted Unit Sales | 30 | 50 | 40 | 120 |
| × Forecasted Sales Price | $ 200 | $ 200 | $ 200 | $ 200 |
| = Budgeted Sales Dollars | $6,000 | $10,000 | $8,000 | $24,000 |

## Discussion Question

**8–12.** What factors should Marcy's management consider when setting the $200 budgeted selling price for its surfboards?

***Cost of Goods Sold Budget*** Once we know how many units Marcy's Surf Shop plans to sell, and the cost per unit, we can prepare a cost of goods sold budget. As its name implies, this budget is used to determine how much cost of goods sold should be based on forecasted sales. Preparing the cost of goods sold budget consists of multiplying forecasted unit sales by the cost per unit. The cost of goods sold budget for Marcy's Surf Shop is presented in Exhibit 8–8.

**Exhibit 8–8**
Cost of Goods Sold
Budget for Marcy's
Surf Shop

**MARCY'S SURF SHOP**
**Cost of Goods Sold Budget**
**For the Quarter Ended September 30, 2002**

|  | July | August | September | Total |
|---|---|---|---|---|
| Forecasted Unit Sales | 30 | 50 | 40 | 120 |
| × Forecasted Unit Cost | $ 120 | $ 120 | $ 120 | $ 120 |
| = Budgeted COGS | $3,600 | $6,000 | $4,800 | $14,400 |

Exhibit 8–8 shows that Marcy's forecasted cost of goods sold for the quarter is $14,400 ($3,600 + $6,000 + $4,800 = $14,400). The cost of goods sold budget provides the forecasted product cost information that is used to prepare the budgeted income statement. This product cost information helps Marcy's management determine whether the company will be profitable based on its budget, or whether changes should be planned now to ensure profits in the budget period.

## Discussion Questions

Compare the sales budget in Exhibit 8–7 with the cost of goods sold budget in Exhibit 8–8.

**8–13.** What are the similarities?
**8–14.** What are the differences?

Realistically, Marcy's will need to purchase more units of product than just the ones it expects to sell in July, August, and September. Thus, in addition to the budgets required to prepare the budgeted income statement, Marcy's will need to prepare a purchases budget. For our demonstration purposes, however, we will wait until after we have prepared the budgeted income statement to present the purchases budget. The only additional budget we need to prepare before we can prepare the budgeted income statement is the selling and administrative expense budget.

***Selling and Administrative Expense Budget*** The various expenses associated with the selling and administrative functions are estimated and used to prepare this budget. Selling and administrative expenses include salaries, advertising, rent, utilities, etc. The selling and administrative expense budget for Marcy's Surf Shop is presented in Exhibit 8–9.

**Exhibit 8–9**
Selling and Administrative Expense Budget for Marcy's Surf Shop

| MARCY'S SURF SHOP | | | | |
|---|---|---|---|---|
| Selling and Administrative Expense Budget | | | | |
| For the Quarter Ended September 30, 2002 | | | | |
| | July | August | September | Total |
| Salaries and Wages | $1,600 | $2,000 | $1,800 | $5,400 |
| Rent | 200 | 200 | 200 | 600 |
| Depreciation | 100 | 100 | 104 | 304 |
| Others | 800 | 1,000 | 900 | 2,700 |
| Total | $2,700 | $3,300 | $3,004 | $9,004 |

The types of items and the amounts included in the selling and administrative expense budget vary from company to company. As we said earlier, the items included in this budget are determined by what is required to support the level of sales in the sales budget.

# Discussion Questions

**8-15.** If you were preparing a selling and administrative expense budget, what are some of the things you would consider as you mapped out strategies to increase sales?

**8-16.** Besides those included in Exhibit 8-9, what are some other administrative costs you think would normally be included in a selling and administrative expense budget?

**8-17.** What do you think might explain the increase in anticipated depreciation expense in September from $100 to $104?

## Building the Budgeted Income Statement

To prepare the budgeted income statement, we use information from the sales, cost of goods sold, and selling and administrative expense budgets. The budgeted income statement depicts the amount of profit or loss a business can expect from its budgeted operating activities. First, we take the total forecasted sales revenue from the sales budget and subtract the forecasted cost of goods sold from the cost of goods sold budget. The result is a forecasted gross profit. We then subtract the total selling and administrative expense which we get from the selling and administrative expense budget. The result is the company's budgeted net income for the period covered by the budget. The budgeted income statement for Marcy's Surf Shop is presented in Exhibit 8–10.

**Exhibit 8–10**
Budgeted Income
Statement for
Marcy's Surf Shop

### MARCY'S SURF SHOP
**Budgeted Income Statement**
**For the Quarter Ended September 30, 2002**

|  | July | August | September | Total |
|---|---|---|---|---|
| Sales | $6,000 | $10,000 | $8,000 | $24,000 |
| − Cost of Goods Sold | 3,600 | 6,000 | 4,800 | 14,400 |
| = Gross Profit | 2,400 | 4,000 | 3,200 | 9,600 |
| − Selling and Admin. Expense | (2,700) | (3,300) | (3,004) | (9,004) |
| = Net Income | $( 300) | $ 700 | $ 196 | $ 596 |

We see from Exhibit 8–10 that Marcy's Surf Shop is projecting a $300 net loss for July. In August Marcy's is projecting a net income of $700 and in September it is $196. The total net income for the quarter, then, is $596.

After the budgeted income statement has been prepared, Marcy's management team may want to change its plans so that it meets its profit goals more effectively. For instance, management may look at the budgeted income statement in Exhibit 8–10 and find the $300 loss in July unacceptable. If so, it would review all the information used to build the budgeted income statement and either adjust its expectations or adjust the assumptions used to prepare the budget.

Whatever the outcome of this evaluation, Marcy's Surf Shop has a better chance of planning for a successful future if management takes the budgeting process seriously. If budgets are used properly, managers will have an opportunity to see trouble spots in advance and make the required adjustments before it is too late.

## Budgeted Balance Sheet

Now that we have prepared the budgeted income statement, we have much of the information we need to prepare the budgeted balance sheet. First, however, we must prepare two more budgets: the purchases budget, as mentioned when we were preparing the budgeted income statement, and the cash budget.

## Purchases Budget

The cost of goods sold budget we prepared accounts only for the units projected to be sold during the period covered by the budget. If Marcy's planned to begin and end the period covered by the budget with no inventory on hand and planned to purchase only the amount of inventory during the budgeted period sufficient to support the level of projected sales, there would be no need for a separate purchases budget. Rather, the company could just use the information from the cost of goods sold budget. This plan is unrealistic, however, because a company like Marcy's must begin and end each period with a certain amount of merchandise on hand. These inventory requirements create the need for the purchases budget. Marcy's purchases budget for the three months ended September 30, 2002, is presented as Exhibit 8–11.

**Exhibit 8–11**
Purchases Budget for
Marcy's Surf Shop

**MARCY'S SURF SHOP**
**Purchases Budget**
**For the Quarter Ended September 30, 2002**

|  | July | August | September | Total |  |
|---|---|---|---|---|---|
| Forecasted Unit Sales | 30 | 50 | 40 | 120 | (a) |
| + Desired Ending Inventory* | 20 | 16 | 24 | 24 | (b) |
| = Total Units Needed | 50 | 66 | 64 | 144 | (c) |
| − Beginning Inventory | ( 8) | ( 20) | ( 16) | ( 8) | (d) |
| = Units to Be Purchased | 42 | 46 | 48 | 136 | (e) |
| × Cost Per Unit | $ 120 | $ 120 | $ 120 | $ 120 | (f) |
| = Cost of Purchases | $5,040 | $ 5,520 | $5,760 | $16,320 | (g) |

*40% of the next month's sales requirements

As you can see by looking at Exhibit 8–11, the purchases budget, even for a small company like Marcy's Surf Shop, can seem rather complicated. A line-by-line analysis of this budget, however, reveals that much of the information it contains is already known, and the new information is basically straightforward.

**(a)** *Forecasted Unit Sales.* These numbers should look familiar to you because you have seen them three times already. They come directly from the sales forecast presented in Exhibit 8–6 and were used to construct the sales budget in Exhibit 8–7 and the cost of goods sold budget in Exhibit 8–8.

**(b)** *Desired Ending Inventory.* These numbers represent the number of units of product the company believes it needs on hand at the end of a given period to support sales in the early days of the next period. As the asterisk note in Exhibit 8–11 explains, Marcy's has decided it should have inventory of product on hand at the end of any given month equal to 40 percent of the next month's sales requirements. At the end of July, for example, Marcy's desires an ending inventory of 20 units, which is 40 percent of August's sales of 50 units (50 × 40% = 20 units).

The amount of desired ending inventory is determined by at least two factors. First, the company must consider how long it usually takes to get product from the company's supplier. This information is obtained from the purchasing records and discussions with the purchasing department. Second, the company must estimate the number of units of product it will sell in the early days of each month. This information comes from historical sales records and discussions with sales personnel.

The desired ending inventory amounts for July, August, and September will be important to us when we construct the budgeted balance sheet, but we will defer our discussion of how they are used until we actually prepare that budget.

## Discussion Question

**8–18.** Can you tell by looking at the purchases budget in Exhibit 8–11 how many surfboards Marcy's has forecasted it will sell in October? Explain your reasoning.

**(c)** *Total Units Needed.* This figure is the sum of (a) and (b).

**(d)** *Beginning Inventory.* Because the purpose of the purchases budget is to determine how many units of inventory must be purchased during each of the months included in the budget period, any inventory forecasted to be on hand at the beginning of each month must be subtracted from the total units needed to determine how many units must be purchased during the month.

The beginning inventory for any period is the ending inventory for the previous period. You will note in the purchases budget in Exhibit 8–11 that the beginning inventory for August (20 units) is the same as the desired ending inventory for July, and the beginning inventory for September (16 units) is the same as the desired ending inventory for August. You should also note that the beginning inventory in the total column (eight units) is the same as the beginning inventory for July, because the total column is for the entire quarter and the quarter begins in July.

## Discussion Question

**8-19.** The purchases budget in Exhibit 8–11 indicates that Marcy's desires ending inventory equal to 40% of the next month's sales requirements. Because sales in July are expected to be 30 surfboards, the beginning inventory in July (which is the ending inventory for June) should be 12 units (30 × 40%). Why do you think the beginning inventory in July is only eight surfboards?

**(e)** *Units to Be Purchased.* This figure is simply (c) minus (d) and tells us the number of surfboards that must be purchased in each of the three months of the budget period and the total for the quarter.

**(f)** *Cost Per Unit.* The cost per unit is what Marcy's must pay for each surfboard it purchases. Note that this cost is the same as the cost per unit used when we prepared the cost of goods sold budget presented in Exhibit 8–8.

**(g)** *Cost of Purchases.* This figure is simply (e) multiplied by (f) and tells us what the purchase of surfboards will cost Marcy's in each of the three months of the budget period and the total for the quarter.

## Cash Budget

When a company uses accrual accounting, revenue is recognized when it is earned rather than when the cash associated with that revenue is collected, and expenses are recognized when the benefit is received rather than when the cash associated with the expenses is paid. Meaning of course, that while the budgeted income statement (including the sales budget, cost of goods sold budget, and the selling and administrative expense budget) provides information about Marcy's projected earnings activities for the budget period, it does not provide direct information about what is projected to happen during that period in terms of cash. Also, unless Marcy's pays cash for its purchase of surfboards, the purchases budget suffers from the same limitation.

Before we can prepare the budgeted balance sheet, we must determine the effect on cash of the budgets we have prepared so far. We do that by preparing a cash budget, which is composed of a cash receipts schedule and a cash payments schedule.

*Cash Receipts Schedule*   The **cash receipts schedule** presents the amount of cash a company expects to collect during the budget period from the sales of its product. Before we can prepare Marcy's cash receipts schedule, we must make certain estimates about the composition of the company's sales (cash or credit) and the pattern of collecting the accounts receivable created by the credit sales. We estimate that 25 percent of Marcy's sales are for cash and the remaining 75 percent are on account (credit sales). Of the sales on account, we estimate that 30 percent are collected in the month of the sale, 60 percent in the month following the sale, and 10 percent in the second month following the sale. Because of the lag between the time a credit sale is made and the time cash is collected, some of the cash for credit sales made in May and June will not have been collected by the end of June, which means that those amounts will be collected during the three months included in our budget period. Therefore, we need to know May credit sales were $4,500, and June credit sales were $6,000.

Using the credit sales figures from May and June, and our assumptions about when cash is collected, we can prepare Marcy's cash receipts schedule for the three months ended September 30, 2002 as shown in Exhibit 8–12.

**Exhibit 8–12**
Cash Receipts Schedule for Marcy's Surf Shop

**MARCY'S SURF SHOP**
**Cash Receipts Schedule**
**For the Quarter Ended September 30, 2002**

| | Jul | Aug | Sep | Total | |
|---|---|---|---|---|---|
| Credit Sales Collected: | | | | | |
| From Accounts Receivable at 6/30/02: | | | | | |
| May Credit Sales ($4,500) | | | | | |
| Collected in July (10%) | $ 450 | | | $ 450 | |
| June Credit Sales ($6,000) | | | | | (a) |
| Collected in July (60%) | 3,600 | | | 3,600 | |
| Collected in August (10%) | | $ 600 | | 600 | |
| | | | | | |
| From New Credit Sales: | | | | | |
| July Credit Sales ($4,500) | | | | | |
| Collected in July (30%) | 1,350 | | | 1,350 | |
| Collected in August (60%) | | 2,700 | | 2,700 | |
| Collected in September (10%) | | | $ 450 | 450 | |
| August Credit Sales ($7,500) | | | | | (b) |
| Collected in August (30%) | | 2,250 | | 2,250 | |
| Collected in September (60%) | | | 4,500 | 4,500 | |
| September Credit Sales ($6,000) | | | | | |
| Collected in September (30%) | | | 1,800 | 1,800 | |
| Budgeted Receipts from Credit Sales | $5,400 | $5,550 | $6,750 | $17,700 | (c) |
| Cash Sales: | | | | | |
| July Cash Sales | 1,500 | | | 1,500 | |
| August Cash Sales | | 2,500 | | 2,500 | (d) |
| September Cash Sales | | | 2,000 | 2,000 | |
| Budgeted Cash Receipts | $6,900 | $8,050 | $8,750 | $23,700 | (e) |

Although the cash receipts schedule presented in Exhibit 8–12 seems quite complex, it is more straightforward than it first appears. It is broken into two major parts. The first presents the amount of cash collected from credit sales during the period covered by the schedule (a through c) and the second part presents the amount of cash collected from cash sales during the budget period (d).

Let us take a few minutes to examine this schedule and see where the numbers came from and what they mean.

**(a)** *From Accounts Receivable at 6/30/02.* The accounts receivable balance at 6/30/02 is composed of receivables arising from sales in May and June. May's credit sales were $4,500. Based on our collection assumption, 30 percent of that amount was collected in May and 60 percent in June. If 90 percent had been collected by the end of June, the remaining $450 ($4,500 × 10%) had not and was included in the balance of accounts receivable at 6/30/02. Since July is the second month following the credit sales in May, the $450 balance is shown as a collection in July ($4,500 × 10%).

Credit sales in June totaled $6,000. Only $1,800 of that amount was collected in June ($6,000 × 30%). If 30 percent had been collected by the end of June, $4,200 ($6,000 × 70%) had not and was included in the balance of accounts receivable at 6/30/02. Since July is the month following the credit sales in June, $3,600 is shown as a collection in July ($6,000 × 60%); and because August is the second month following the credit sales in June, the remaining $600 balance is shown as a collection in August ($6,000 × 10%).

**(b)** *From New Sales.* Recall from the sales budget in Exhibit 8–7 that budgeted sales for the three months covered by our budget example were $6,000 in July, $10,000 in August, and $8,000 in September. One of the assumptions we made as we began our discussion of the cash receipts schedule was that 75 percent of Marcy's sales were credit sales. Therefore, the amounts we are dealing with in this section of the schedule are $4,500 for July ($6,000 × 75%), $7,500 for August ($10,000 × 75%), and $6,000 for September ($8,000 × 75%).

The collection pattern for each of the three months is the same: 30 percent of credit sales are collected in the month of sale, 60 percent in the month following the sale, and 10 percent in the second month following the sale. So for July's credit sales, for example, the schedule shows $1,350 will be collected in July ($4,500 × 30%), $2,700 will be collected in August ($4,500 × 60%), and $450 ($4,500 × 10%) in September. The amounts projected to be collected for August and September credit sales are calculated exactly the same way.

**(c)** *Budgeted Receipts from Credit Sales.* This figure is simply the sum of (a) and (b). It presents the total amount of cash Marcy's expects to collect during the period covered by the schedule from credit sales.

**(d)** *Cash Sales.* This section is the least complicated of the schedule. For the three months included in the schedule it presents the portion of sales that will be cash sales. If 75 percent of the sales made in a given month are credit sales, then 25 percent will be cash sales. Therefore, in July the cash sales will be $1,500 ($6,000 × 25%) and that amount is shown as a cash receipt in July. The amount for August is $2,500 ($10,000 × 25%), and for September $2,000 ($8,000 × 25%).

**(e)** *Budgeted Cash Receipts.* This figure is simply the sum of (c) and (d). As the description indicates, it presents the total amount of cash Marcy's plans to collect from the accounts receivable balance at 6/30/02, the credit sales it will have during the period covered by the schedule, and the cash sales made during the period.

***Cash Payments Schedule*** The **cash payments schedule** presents the amount of cash a company expects to pay out during the budget period. Before we can prepare Marcy's cash payments schedule, we must make certain assumptions about the company's pattern of cash payments. We assume that payment for the purchase of surfboards is made in the month following the purchase. Because of the lag time between the time a purchase is made and the time cash is paid, the purchases made in June will not have been paid by the end of June, which means that this amount will be paid in July, one of the months included in our budget period. Therefore, we need to know that purchases of merchandise in June totaled $5,200. All cash selling and administrative expenses are paid in the month incurred.

Using these assumptions about when cash is paid and the purchases figure from June, we can prepare Marcy's cash payments schedule for the three months ended September 30, 2002, as shown in Exhibit 8–13.

**Exhibit 8–13**
Cash Payments Schedule for Marcy's Surf Shop

**MARCY'S SURF SHOP**
**Cash Payments Schedule**
**For the Quarter Ended September 30, 2002**

|  | July | August | September | Total |  |
|---|---|---|---|---|---|
| Purchases | $5,200 | $5,040 | $5,520 | $15,760 | (a) |
| Selling and Admin. Expense: |  |  |  |  |  |
| Salaries and Wages | 1,600 | 2,000 | 1,800 | 5,400⎤ |  |
| Rent | 200 | 200 | 200 | 600 ⎬(b) |
| Other Selling and Admin. Expense | 800 | 1,000 | 900 | 2,700⎦ |  |
| Purchase of Display Case |  | 240 |  | 240 | (c) |
| Budgeted Cash Payments | $7,800 | $8,480 | $8,420 | $24,700 | (d) |

As you can see from Exhibit 8–13, the cash payments schedule is not nearly as complex as either the purchases budget or the cash receipts schedule. There are a couple of tricky parts, however, so let us examine the items included.

**(a)** *Purchases.* These are payments for the purchase of surfboards. Recall our assumption that payment for the purchase of merchandise is made in the month following purchase. The projected payment of $5,200 in July, then, is for purchases made in June, the payment of $5,040 in August will be for July purchases, and the $5,520 payment in September will be for August purchases.

## Discussion Question

**8–20.** In our assumptions about cash payments, we said that June purchases of merchandise totaled $5,200 so it is easy to see where the July payment originated. Where do you suppose the payment amounts ($5,040 and $5,520) originated for August and September?

**(b)** *Selling and Administrative Expense.* These are payments for the support costs Marcy's anticipates for each month of the budget period. The amounts come directly from the selling and administrative expense budget in Exhibit 8–9.

# Discussion Question

**8-21.** Look back at the selling and administrative expense budget in Exhibit 8-9. All the expense items included in that budget are included in the cash payments schedule *except* depreciation. Why do you think depreciation expense was included in the selling and administrative expense budget but excluded from the cash payments schedule?

---

**(c)** *Purchase of Display Case.* Evidently, Marcy's is planning to purchase a new display case for the showroom during the month of August. This purchase will be addition to Marcy's property, plant, and equipment and will be important to us when we prepare the budgeted balance sheet and the budgeted statement of cash flows. Incidently, the planned purchase of this display case is what caused depreciation expense in Exhibit 8-9 to increase by $4 in September.

**(d)** *Budgeted Cash Payments.* This figure is simply the sum of (a), (b), and (c). As the description indicates, it presents the total amount of cash Marcy's plans to pay out during the period covered by the schedule.

## Building the Cash Budget

Now that we have prepared the cash receipts schedule and the cash payments schedule, we can prepare Marcy's cash budget for the quarter ended September 30, 2002. As was the case with the schedules, we must make some assumptions for the cash budget. First, we estimate that Marcy's Surf Shop will have a cash balance of $2,170 on June 30, 2002. Second, Marcy's desires to maintain a cash balance of at least $1,900 at all times. If cash falls below $1,900, the company will borrow from a local bank. Finally, we ignore the interest Marcy's would be required to pay on any borrowings from the bank.

Using the assumption about Marcy's desired minimum cash balance, and the information from the cash receipts schedule and the cash payments schedule, we can prepare the company's cash budget for the quarter ending September 30, 2002, as shown in Exhibit 8-14.

**Exhibit 8-14**
Cash Budget for
Marcy's Surf Shop

**MARCY'S SURF SHOP**

**Cash Budget**

**For the Quarter Ended September 30, 2002**

|  |  | July | August | September | Total |  |
|---|---|---|---|---|---|---|
|  | Beginning Cash Balance | $2,170 | $ 1,900 | $ 1,900 | $ 2,170 | (a) |
| + | Cash Receipts | 6,900 | 8,050 | 8,750 | = 23,700 | +(b) |
| = | Cash Available | $9,070 | $ 9,950 | $10,650 | $25,870 | (c) |
| − | Cash Payments | (7,800) | (8,480) | (8,420) | = (24,700) | −(d) |
| = | Balance before Borrowing | $1,270 | $ 1,470 | $ 2,230 | $ 1,170 | (e) |
| +/− | Borrowing/(Repayment) | 630 | $ 430 | $ (330) | = $ 730 | +(f) |
| = | Ending Cash Balance | $1,900 | $ 1,900 | $ 1,900 | $ 1,900 | (g) |

The cash budget itself is not as seemingly complicated as the purchases budget, the cash receipts schedule, or the cash payments schedule. There are, however, some potential pitfalls in your understanding of the way this budget is constructed, so we will take a few minutes and discuss the items included.

(a) *Beginning Cash Balance.* Like all balance sheet items, the beginning cash balance for any period is the ending cash balance for the previous period. As mentioned earlier, the ending cash balance for June will be $2,170. Therefore, July's beginning cash balance will be June's ending cash balance. The same pattern holds true for the other months presented. August's beginning balance is July's ending balance and September's beginning balance is August's ending balance. Note, however, that the beginning balance in the total column ($2,170) is the same as the beginning balance for July. Likewise, the ending balance in the total column ($1,900) is the same as the ending balance for September, because the total column represents the entire quarter. The beginning balance for the quarter is July's beginning balance and the ending balance for the quarter is September's ending balance.

(b) *Cash Receipts.* The cash receipts amounts are taken directly from the budgeted cash receipts line of the cash receipts schedule shown in Exhibit 8–12.

(c) *Cash Available.* This figure is simply the sum of (a) and (b). This amount represents the total cash Marcy's expects to be available before deducting any payments.

(d) *Cash Payments.* The cash payments amounts are taken directly from the budgeted cash payments line of the cash payments schedule shown in Exhibit 8–13.

(e) *Balance before Borrowing.* This amount is calculated by simply subtracting (d) from (c). It represents the anticipated ending cash balance before any adjustments for borrowing or loan payments.

(f) *Borrowing/(Repayment).* Marcy's wants to maintain a cash balance of at least $1,900. If the balance before borrowing drops too low, Marcy's will borrow enough money from the bank to bring the balance up to the desired ending cash balance of $1,900. As you can see, July's balance before borrowing is expected to be only $1,270. Therefore, Marcy's can anticipate the need to borrow $630 to bring the balance up to $1,900. So, if the balance before borrowing is less than the desired ending cash balance, as it will be in July and again in August, the amount that must be borrowed to bring the cash balance to the desired amount can be easily calculated. If, on the other hand, the expected balance before borrowing is greater than $1,900, as is the case in September, any amount in excess of the desired ending cash balance will be used to repay the loan ($330 in this instance).

(g) *Ending Cash Balance.* This figure is simply (e) plus the borrowing or less the repayment shown in (f). As we said earlier, this ending cash amount also becomes the next month's beginning cash balance.

Now the information from the cash budget and other budgets can be used to prepare the budgeted balance sheet.

## Building the Budgeted Balance Sheet

We assume that you already know the basics of how a balance sheet is constructed, so, for our presentation of the budgeted balance sheet, we focus on how to determine the various asset, liability, and equity items and dollar amounts for these items.

Although some of the amounts needed to prepare the budgeted balance sheet are taken directly from the budgets already prepared, many amounts are not specifically included in any of those budgets. For example, we have not prepared a budget or schedule that shows the ending balances for accounts receivable, inventory, property, plant, and equipment, accumulated depreciation, accounts payable, notes payable, common stock, additional paid-in capital, or retained earnings. For each of these items, we will present a brief discussion and a schedule to show how to calculate the amounts that should appear on the budgeted balance sheet. You will find as you examine each of these items that the budgeted ending balance is calculated by taking the beginning balance and adding or subtracting the changes that are expected to occur during the budget period. So, for each of these items, the beginning balance is our starting point. As discussed, the *beginning* balance of any balance sheet item is the prior month's *ending* balance. Therefore, all we need is the balance sheet for June 30 to determine the beginning balance for July. The balance sheet of June 30, 2002, for Marcy's Surf Shop is shown in Exhibit 8–15.

**Exhibit 8–15**
Balance Sheet as of
June 30, 2002, for
Marcy's Surf Shop

| MARCY'S SURF SHOP Balance Sheet June 30, 2002 | | |
|---|---:|---:|
| Assets | | |
| Current Assets | | |
| Cash | | $ 2,170 |
| Accounts Receivable | | 4,650 |
| Inventory | | 960 |
| Total Current Assets | | $ 7,780 |
| Property, Plant, and Equipment | | |
| Equipment | | 6,000 |
| Less Accumulated Depreciation | | (1,200) |
| Equipment, Net | | $ 4,800 |
| Total Assets | | $12,580 |
| Liabilities | | |
| Current Liabilities | | |
| Accounts Payable | | $ 5,200 |
| Total Liabilities | | $ 5,200 |
| Owner's Equity | | |
| Paid-in Capital | | |
| Common Stock | | $ 1,000 |
| Additional Paid-in Capital | | 5,475 |
| Total Paid-in Capital | | $ 6,475 |
| Retained Earnings | | $ 905 |
| Total Equity | | $ 7,380 |
| Total Liabilities and Equity | | $12,580 |

Using the June 30, 2002, balance sheet in Exhibit 8–15 and information from the other budgets we have prepared so far, we can prepare a budgeted balance sheet for each of the three months included in our budget period, as shown in Exhibit 8–16.

The balance sheets presented in Exhibit 8–16 are much like the other balance sheets you have seen throughout your studies. The essential difference is not the format, but rather, the time frame. These are projected balance sheets whereas the others have presented past results. There is no total column for this budget, because the balance sheet is a financial snapshot of a business taken at the end of a period. Therefore, in a very real sense, the snapshot taken at the end of September is the total column.

**Exhibit 8–16**
Budgeted Balance
Sheets for Marcy's
Surf Shop

### MARCY'S SURF SHOP
#### Budgeted Balance Sheet
#### For the Quarter Ended September 30, 2002

|  | July | August | September |  |
|---|---|---|---|---|
| Assets |  |  |  |  |
| Current Assets |  |  |  |  |
| Cash | $ 1,900 | $ 1,900 | $ 1,900 | (a) |
| Accounts Receivable, Net | 3,750 | 5,700 | 4,950 | (b) |
| Inventory | 2,400 | 1,920 | 2,880 | (c) |
| Total Current Assets | $ 8,050 | $ 9,520 | $ 9,730 |  |
| Property, Plant, and Equipment |  |  |  |  |
| Equipment | $ 6,000 | $ 6,240 | $ 6,240 | (d) |
| Less Accumulated Depreciation | (1,300) | (1,400) | (1,504) | (e) |
| Equipment, Net | $ 4,700 | $ 4,840 | $ 4,736 |  |
| Total Assets | $12,750 | $14,360 | $14,466 |  |
| Liabilities |  |  |  |  |
| Current Liabilities |  |  |  |  |
| Accounts Payable | $ 5,040 | $ 5,520 | $ 5,760 | (f) |
| Bank Loan Payable | 630 | 1,060 | 730 | (g) |
| Total Liabilities | $ 5,670 | $ 6,580 | $ 6,490 |  |
| Owner's Equity |  |  |  |  |
| Paid-in Capital |  |  |  |  |
| Common Stock | $ 1,000 | $ 1,000 | $ 1,000 |  |
| Additional Paid-in Capital | 5,475 | 5,475 | 5,475 | (h) |
| Total Paid-in Capital | $ 6,475 | $ 6,475 | $ 6,475 |  |
| Retained Earnings | $ 605 | $ 1,305 | $ 1,501 | (i) |
| Total Equity | $ 7,080 | $ 7,780 | $ 7,976 |  |
| Total Liabilities and Equity | $12,750 | $14,360 | $14,466 |  |

As we have done with the other budgets prepared in this chapter, we will now take a few minutes and explain how the items on the budgeted balance sheet were determined.

(a) *Cash.* This amount is taken directly from the ending cash balance line of the cash budget shown in Exhibit 8–14. For example, the amount shown as the ending cash balance of $1,900 in the July column of the cash budget is shown as cash in the July column of the budgeted balance sheet.

(b) *Accounts Receivable.* To determine the ending accounts receivable balance for each month shown in Exhibit 8–16, we simply take the beginning accounts receivable balance, add budgeted credit sales for that month, and subtract budgeted collections for that month.

|  | Jul | Aug | Sep |
|---|---|---|---|
| Beginning Balance | $4,650 | $3,750 | $5,700 |
| + Credit sales | 4,500 | 7,500 | 6,000 |
| − Collections | (5,400) | (5,550) | (6,750) |
| Ending Balance | $3,750 | $5,700 | $4,950 |

The beginning accounts receivable balance of $4,650 for July is taken from the June 30, 2002, balance sheet shown in Exhibit 8–15. The cash receipts budget provides the rest of the information we need. The cash receipts budget shows the projected credit sales, and the total expected to be collected from credit sales. For July, the cash receipts budget shows credit sales of $4,500 and a total of $5,400 collected from credit sales. After adding the credit sales of $4,500 to the beginning balance of $4,650, we subtract the collections of $5,400 to arrive at the ending accounts receivable balance of $3,750. This amount is shown on the budgeted balance sheet for July. The ending accounts receivable amounts for other months are calculated the same way.

(c) *Inventory*. To determine the ending inventory balance for each month shown in Exhibit 8–16, we simply take the beginning inventory balance, add purchases made during the month, and subtract that month's cost of goods sold.

|  | Jul | Aug | Sep |
|---|---|---|---|
| Beginning Balance | $ 960 | $2,400 | $1,920 |
| + Purchases | 5,040 | 5,520 | 5,760 |
| − Cost of goods sold | ( 3,600) | ( 6,000) | ( 4,800) |
| Ending Balance | $2,400 | $1,920 | $2,880 |

The beginning inventory balance for July of $960 is taken from the June 30, 2002, balance sheet shown in Exhibit 8–15. By looking at the purchases budget in Exhibit 8–11 and the cost of goods sold budget in Exhibit 8–8, we find that expected purchases for July are $5,040 and cost of goods sold are expected be $3,600. After adding the purchases of $5,040 to the beginning balance of $960, we subtract the cost of goods sold of $3,600 to arrive at the ending inventory balance of $2,400. This amount is shown on the budgeted balance sheet for July. The ending inventory amounts for other months are calculated the same way.

(d) *Equipment*. To determine the ending balance in the equipment, we adjust the beginning balance by adding the cost of equipment purchased and subtracting the cost of any equipment sold. In our example, the only change in equipment is the $240 for the showcase the company is planning to buy in August. We add $240 to the $6,000 beginning balance to arrive at the budgeted ending balance of $6,240.

(e) *Accumulated Depreciation*. To determine the ending balance for accumulated depreciation, we adjust the beginning balance by adding the depreciation for the period and subtracting the accumulated depreciation associated with any assets that have been sold or scrapped. In our example, the company does not expect to sell or otherwise dispose of any equipment, so the only changes to accumulated depreciation are increases relating to the budgeted monthly depreciation. You might notice that the amount added to accumulated depreciation in September is slightly higher than that for July and August. This is so because of the added depreciation for the showcase the company expects to buy in August.

(f) *Accounts Payable*. To determine the ending accounts payable balance for each month shown in Exhibit 8–16, we simply take the beginning accounts payable balance, add budgeted purchases for that month, and subtract budgeted payments for that month.

|  | Jul | Aug | Sep |
|---|---|---|---|
| Beginning Balance | $5,200 | $5,040 | $5,520 |
| + Purchases | 5,040 | 5,520 | 5,760 |
| − Payments | ( 5,200) | ( 5,040) | ( 5,520) |
| Ending Balance | $5,040 | $5,520 | $5,760 |

The beginning accounts payable balance for July of $5,200 is taken from the June 30, 2002, balance sheet shown in Exhibit 8–15. By looking at the purchases budget in Exhibit 8–11 and the cash payments budget in Exhibit 8–13, we find that expected purchases for July are $5,040 and cash payments are expected be $5,200. After adding the purchases of $5,040 to the beginning balance of $5,200, we subtract the cash payments of $5,200 to arrive at the ending accounts payable balance of $5,040. This amount is shown on the budgeted balance sheet for July. The ending accounts payable amounts for other months are calculated the same way.

**(g)** *Bank Loan Payable.* To determine the ending notes payable balance for each month shown in Exhibit 8–16, we simply take the beginning notes payable balance, add the budgeted borrowing for that month, and subtract budgeted payments for that month.

|  | Jul | Aug | Sep |
|---|---|---|---|
| Beginning Balance | $ -0- | $ 630 | $1,060 |
| + Borrowing | 630 | 430 | -0- |
| − Repayments | -0- | -0- | (330) |
| Ending Balance | $630 | $1,060 | $ 730 |

The beginning notes payable balance for July would normally come from the June 30, 2002, balance sheet shown in Exhibit 8–15; however, in this example the beginning balance for notes payable on June 30, 2002, is zero, so notes payable does not appear. By looking at the cash budget in Exhibit 8–14, we find that borrowing of $630 is expected in July, borrowing of $430 is expected in August, and a repayment of $330 is expected in September.

**(h)** *Common Stock and Additional Paid-in Capital.* In this example, no common stock or additional paid in capital transactions are expected during the budget period. Therefore, the beginning July balance for these items found on the June 30, 2002, balance sheet in Exhibit 8–15 remains unchanged during the budget period.

**(i)** *Retained Earnings.* To determine the ending retained earnings balance, we add the income for the period or, if the company has a loss, subtract the loss and deduct dividends, if they exist, from the beginning retained earnings balance.

|  | Jul | Aug | Sep |
|---|---|---|---|
| Beginning Balance | $ 905 | $ 605 | $1,305 |
| + Income/Loss | ( 300) | 700 | 196 |
| − Dividends | -0- | -0- | -0- |
| Ending Balance | $ 605 | $1,305 | $1,501 |

In our example, the $905 beginning balance of retained earnings is found on the June 30, 2002, balance sheet shown in Exhibit 8–15. To find the ending retained earnings that should appear on the budgeted balance sheet for July, we deduct the budgeted loss for that month of $300 from the beginning retained earnings balance of $905. That figure becomes the beginning balance in August. To determine the August ending balance of retained earnings we simply add August's budgeted net income. September's ending balance would be calculated the same way. There are no dividends in our example so the dividend amount is zero for each month presented.

## Budgeted Statement of Cash Flows

Now that we have prepared all the other budgets, we can now prepare the budgeted statement of cash flows (SCF). This statement must be the final budget prepared because, as you recall from your earlier study of this financial statement, it is a form of financial statement analysis. An SCF prepared on historical results analyzes the income statement and the balance sheet to explain what caused cash to change from the beginning of a period to the end of the period. The budgeted statement of cash flows does exactly the same thing, except that it analyzes the budgeted income statement and the budgeted balance sheet to explain what will cause the projected change in cash from the start to the end of the budget period.

A budgeted statement of cash flows for Marcy's Surf Shop is presented as Exhibit 8–17.

**Exhibit 8–17**
Budgeted Statement
of Cash Flows for
Marcy's Surf Shop

## MARCY'S SURF SHOP
### Budgeted Statement of Cash Flows
### For the Quarter Ended September 30, 2002

|  | July | August | September | Total |
|---|---|---|---|---|
| Cash Flows from |  |  |  |  |
| Operating Activities: |  |  |  |  |
| Net Income | ($ 300) | $ 700 | $ 196 | $ 596 |
| Add: Depreciation | 100 | 100 | 104 | 304 |
| Changes in CA & CL: |  |  |  |  |
| Accounts Receivable | 900 | (1,950) | 750 | (300) |
| Inventory | (1,440) | 480 | (960) | (1,920) |
| Accounts Payable | (160) | 480 | 240 | 560 |
| Net Cash Flow from Op Act | ($ 900) | ($ 190) | 330 | ($ 760) |
| Cash Flow From |  |  |  |  |
| Investing Activities: |  |  |  |  |
| Cash Paid for Showcase |  | (240) |  | (240) |
| Net Cash Flow from Inv Act |  | (240) |  | (240) |
| Cash Flow From |  |  |  |  |
| Financing Activities: |  |  |  |  |
| Borrowing | $ 630 | $ 430 |  | $1,060 |
| Loan Payments |  |  | ($ 330) | ( 330) |
| Net Cash Flow from Fin Act | $ 630 | $ 430 | ($ 330) | $ 730 |
| Increase/(Decrease) in Cash | ($ 270) | $ -0- | $ 0 | ($ 270) |
| Budgeted Beginning Cash Balance | 2,170 | 1,900 | 1,900 | 2,170 |
| Budgeted Ending Cash Balance | $1,900 | $1,900 | $1,900 | $1,900 |

We will not do a line-by-line analysis of the presentation in Exhibit 8–17 because we have explained all the items elsewhere in this chapter as we have constructed the other budgets. It is worthwhile, however, for us to discuss what this budget reveals in overall terms.

In the normal course of business, a company can obtain cash from only three sources: borrowing, owner contributions, and profitable operations. Ultimately, the only source of cash for any company, including Marcy's Surf Shop, is the profitable operation of the business. If a company does not generate enough cash from operations to run the business, it must seek outside financing (borrowing and owner contributions).

The budgeted statement of cash flows in Exhibit 8–17 reveals that for the three months covered by the budget, at least, Marcy's does not anticipate generating enough cash through operations to run the business and must, therefore, borrow the money. Three months is not a very long time, and all companies must obtain outside financing from time to time, but Marcy may not like what she sees when she looks at this budget. If she finds the prospects unacceptable, she may want to continue the budgeting process and make adjustments in how she plans to go about operating her business.

You will be delighted to know we are not going to do that for Marcy. We hope, however, that you have learned what a powerful tool the operating budget can be by going through the steps required to prepare one.

We have seen that the operating budget can serve as a guide for the company to follow, assist a company in allocating its scarce resources, and foster communication and coordination among managers from different functional areas within the company. It can also establish performance standards, or benchmarks, against which the company can compare the actual results. This fourth application presents some serious challenges to managers, however. Misunderstanding how to set and use performance standards can lead to behavior that is actually detrimental to the organization.

Once upon a time, in the United States at least, someone figured out that the operating budget could be used as a means of controlling a company's activities. It is really a pretty simple concept. Once the operating budget is established for the year, you keep one eye on the budget and one eye on the actual results. The idea is that if you prepare a solid budget and then perform to meet that budget, you will naturally keep control of your operation. Before long, this way of using the operating budget had become quite common among U.S. companies. As this practice became more popular, firms began evaluating the performance of their managers based on how they performed against the budget as well. This practice is known as the **performance to budget** evaluation. Salary increases, year-end bonuses, and promotions to senior management began to be dependent on a manager's ability to "meet or beat" the budget. By now, the operating budget had become the principal means used to control costs. It was felt that if managers performed well against the budget, they were doing a good job of controlling the operations they managed, which makes sense, right? Wrong! Unfortunately, that is not what happens when the budget is used as the primary control device in a company. What happens is that using the budget for this purpose actually encourages managers to make bad decisions and discourages them from making good decisions.

**performance to budget**
A process of evaluating managers and employees based on how they perform against the budget.

## The Budget Performance Report

*If I get bigger pants,
does that mean I've lost weight?*

—Paul Valenzuela

**budget performance report**
The evaluation instrument used to evaluate a manager's performance to budget.

As performance to budget became a popular way of measuring management performance, an instrument known as the **budget performance report** was developed to capture the information management thought was needed to perform the evaluation. A typical budget performance report has four columns as shown in Exhibit 8–18.

**Exhibit 8–18**
Budget Performance Report

| (a) | (b) | (c) | (d) |
|---|---|---|---|
| **Description** | **Budget** | **Actual** | **Variance** |
| Salaries and Wages | $25,000 | $23,000 | $2,000 F |
| Office Rent | 10,000 | 10,000 | -0- |
| Office Supplies | 1,000 | 1,200 | 200 U |

As you can see, the report is not terribly complicated. In the description column (a), the items for which the manager being evaluated is responsible are listed. In the budget column (b), the budgeted amount for each of those items is listed. In the actual column (c), the amount actually spent during the period covered by the

**variance** The difference between the amount budgeted and the actual amount

budget is listed. The difference between the amount bedgeted and the actual amount is called a **variance.** The variances in our example appear in column (d). The letter *F* indicates a favorable variance and the letter *U* indicates an unfavorable variance.

# Discussion Question

**8–22.** What do the words *favorable* and *unfavorable* mean to you?

The major problem with the budget performance report is not the report itself but rather the way it is used. As an example, say that Brian Sedgwick is the sales manager at Pepperwood Furniture Company. Among other things, Brian is responsible for gas and oil expenditures for the fleet of delivery trucks his company owns. These trucks are used to deliver products to customers. Say further that Brian is responsible for establishing the budget for this item and he budgeted $50,000 for 2002. Now say that 2002 has ended and he spent $90,000 on gas and oil. Brian's budget performance report for this item would be as follows:

| Description | Budget | Actual | Variance |
| --- | --- | --- | --- |
| Gas & Oil | $50,000 | $90,000 | $40,000 U |

Now, what do you think might have caused this variance? Well, of the several possibilities, we will mention four.

1. Perhaps gas prices went through the roof. The budget was established based on what Brian *thought* gas and oil prices would be during the year. Maybe there was another gulf war in 2002 like there was in 1991. You may not remember but, during the Gulf War, gas prices went sky high.
2. Perhaps the budget Brian established was poorly done. Do not confuse this idea with the first possible explanation. In the first one, Brian did the best he could with the information he had—the information just turned out not to be reliable. This possibility comes from not taking the budgeting process seriously. Thus, for Brian, budgeting may mean filling out forms rather than being part of a real planning process.
3. Perhaps Brian was inefficient and wasted a lot of money. We would never want to forget this possibility. If he did waste money, he should be held accountable for his actions.
4. Perhaps business picked up significantly and the company had to make many more deliveries. This surely would have caused Brian to spend more money on gas and oil. Remember, the support costs in the budget are based on what is forecast to be sold.

Let us expand on the fourth possibility. Brian had an unfavorable variance caused by a good thing (greatly increased sales). This fact should help you understand that *unfavorable* in this context does not mean "bad," but rather "over budget."

Brian Sedgwick's performance evaluation will depend on his company's attitude about what performance to budget means. Unfortunately, in all too many companies in the United States today, the evaluation begins with the variance column. If there are unfavorable variances, regardless of cause, Brian's performance evaluation will not be good. He may not get his bonus, he may not get that raise he was anticipating, and he may not be promoted.

Before we talk about how to overcome the problem we just described, let us look at another example using the same essential facts. Brian budgeted $50,000 for gas and oil expenditures for 2002, but only spent $30,000. His budget performance report would be as follows:

| Description | Budget | Actual | Variance |
|---|---|---|---|
| Gas & Oil | $50,000 | $30,000 | $20,000 F |

We will not discuss what might have caused this variance, but with the exception of the poor budgeting possibility (which is the same in either case), the reasons are just the opposite of what caused the $40,000 unfavorable variance in our first example. If you think about the fourth possibility, then, this favorable variance could have been caused by a decline in the company's business. In other words, Brian has a favorable variance caused by a bad thing. That should help you understand that favorable in this context does not mean "good." It simply means "under budget."

What about Brian's performance evaluation? Once again, it depends greatly on how his company management views the performance to budget. In all too many companies, he would be rewarded in two ways. First, he would receive congratulations from everyone involved in the evaluation on what a great job he did of controlling gas and oil costs for the year. Second, his gas and oil budget for next year will be cut by $20,000. The reasoning is that if that's all he needed for this year, that's all he will need for next year, as well. This is called "use it or lose it" and is a practice that flourishes in many companies in the United States today.

If this is how Brian's company views the evaluation process, it is in his best interest to make sure he does not have actual expenditures that are too far under budget. If Brian is smart, he will make certain that his performance report on gas and oil costs looks something like the following:

| Description | Budget | Actual | Variance |
|---|---|---|---|
| Gas & Oil | $50,000 | $50,000 | -0- |

This item will probably not be examined in any great detail during Brian's performance review, because the usual practice is to concentrate on the variance column. If no variance exists, it is assumed that the amount spent on the item was what should have been spent. This interpretation indicates efficient management, which is what Paul Valenzuela meant in the quotation that opened this section. Buying bigger clothes makes it appear you have lost weight, when in fact you may not have lost any. The way this translates into the topic we are discussing is that if managers are able to secure a large budget for a particular item, they will appear to be efficient simply by spending less than, or exactly, the amount budgeted.

In many companies, then, the focus is only on items with large variances. Further, when these variances are investigated, the analysis usually focuses on the actual performance column of the performance report. If a large, unfavorable variance exists, managers are called on the carpet to explain why they spent more than the budget allowed. If a large, favorable variance exists, the item becomes a target for reducing costs next year, so the budget is cut.

What is bizarre about this method of using the budget performance report is that everybody knows budgets are established for the future. Everybody also knows that the future is to a great extent unknown to us. Yet, once the budget is established it becomes set in stone, so to speak, and any variance (favorable or unfavorable) between the budgeted cost and the actual cost is assumed to be because of the actual.

Are we suggesting that managers should be free to spend whatever amount they see fit on the cost items for which they are responsible? Absolutely not! This idea makes no sense, and it runs counter to everything we have said throughout this chapter, and indeed, throughout this book. Managers should be working every day to control costs and run their operations more efficiently. What we are saying is that this has very little to do with the operating budget. Cost control is an ongoing management process, of which the operating budget is only a part. Using the budget as the primary cost control device in a business is done in place of real control. Perhaps worse than that, using performance to budget as the evaluation instrument for managers encourages them to focus on the elimination of variances as their primary goal. As stated, because the budget is often considered to be set in stone, the only way to eliminate variances is to manipulate the actual performance to match the budget. This is what leads to silly budget games, such as the "use it or lose it" phenomenon we mentioned earlier.

If we lived in a perfect world where we could predict the future accurately, there would be no problem with the performance to budget evaluation technique. Unfortunately, we do not live in such a perfect world, and the future is largely unknown to us. When we prepare the operating budget we are attempting to predict the future. Differences are bound to exist between what we predict and what actually happens.

Earlier in the chapter we presented an exhibit that showed the interrelationship among all the budgets. We have reproduced that presentation as Exhibit 8–19.

**Exhibit 8–19**
Interrelationship among the Budgets

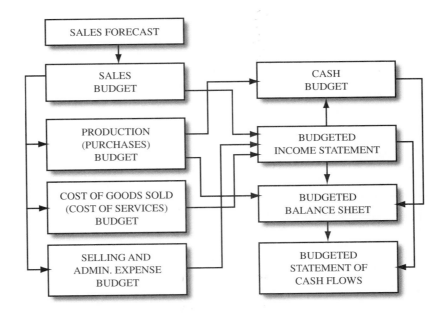

As discussed during this interrelationship topic earlier in the chapter, a change in any one of the budgets has a ripple effect throughout all the other budgets. A little logic tells us that if there are variances in any one of the budgets there will also be a ripple effect throughout all the other budgets.

Perhaps more important as a cause of variances than the interrelationship among the budgets is the role of the sales forecast in the budgeting process. Note in Exhibit 8–19 that all the budgets included in the operating budget are dependent upon the sales forecast, which explains why we described the sales forecast as both the cornerstone and the keystone of the operating budget in our earlier discussions.

The sales forecast is so critical in the budgeting process that we will end this section by sharing three truths with you about the sales forecast and the operating budget:

**Truth 1:** If the sales forecast is inaccurate, the operating budget will be inaccurate. Do not confuse *inaccurate* with *bad*. A bad sales forecast comes from lack of effort and attention. An inaccurate sales forecast comes about when the actual results are different from the operating budget because the future did not turn out the way company management predicted.

**Truth 2:** The sales forecast will be inaccurate. Recall the items we discussed earlier in the chapter that affect a company's ability to forecast sales. The state of the general economy, actions of competitors, technological developments, and many other factors make an accurate sales forecast literally impossible.

**Truth 3:** The operating budget will be inaccurate. Once again, do not confuse inaccurate with bad. Inaccurate simply means that the actual results are going to be different from what was budgeted, meaning, of course, that variances will always exist.

Some approaches to the budget performance report help overcome the variances caused by actual sales being different from budgeted sales. The most popular of these is the flexible budget performance report, which is covered in more advanced accounting courses. Note, however, that it does not eliminate the problem of using the budget in a way that was never intended, that is, as the primary control device in a business.

So, how do managers overcome the problems we have been discussing in this section? Well, they do it by using the budget as it was intended to be used—as a guide for the business. Just as prudent travelers would not hesitate to alter their plans during a trip as updated information becomes available, businesses should not hesitate to adjust their budgets when desirable or necessary. Further, when the period covered by the operating budget is over, an analysis should be performed to compare the actual results to the budget. The focus of this analysis, however, should be on how to improve the budgeting process rather than on the inevitable variances that have occurred.

## SUMMARY

The operating budget is an integral part of the overall planning process for any company. Besides serving as a guide for the business throughout the period covered by the budget, the operating budget can assist management in the allocation of resources, foster communication and coordination among various segments of the company, and establish performance standards.

The operating budget is a set of estimated financial statements. These are the budgeted income statement, the budgeted balance sheet, and the budgeted statement of cash flows. Besides the budgeted financial statements, the operating budget includes several other budgets prepared to support the budgeted financial statements. These are the sales budget, the production (or purchases) budget, the cost of goods sold (or cost of services) budget, the selling and administrative expense budget, and the cash budget (including the cash receipts schedule and the cash payments schedule).

There are several different approaches to the preparation of the operating budget. Perpetual, incremental, zero-based, top-down, bottom-up, imposed, and participative approaches to budgeting are just some that have developed over time. Each approach has certain advantages and certain disadvantages relative to the other approaches.

All the budgets included in the operating budget are dependent on the sales forecast. Indeed, the accuracy of the entire budget is dependent on the accuracy of the forecast. Many factors, including the state of the general economy, the condition of the company's industry, the actions of competitors, and technological developments all influence a company's ability to forecast its sales reasonably.

The operating budget was never meant to be used as the principal cost control device in business. Using the budget for this purpose actually encourages managers to make decisions that are detrimental to the business. If used properly, however, as a guide and coordination instrument, the operating budget can be of tremendous benefit for any company.

## KEY TERMS

bottom-up budgeting   M-276
budget performance report   M-298
budgeted balance sheet   M-271
budgeted income statement   M-271
budgeted statement of cash flows   M-272
cash budget   M-271
cash payments schedule   M-290
cash receipts schedule   M-288
continual budgeting   M-274
cost of goods sold budget   M-271
cost of services budget   M-271
imposed budget   M-276
incremental budgeting   M-275
master budget   M-266

master operating budget   M-266
operating budget   M-266
participative budget   M-277
performance to budget   M-298
perpetual budgeting   M-274
production budget   M-270
purchases budget   M-270
sales budget   M-270
sales forecast   M-279
selling and administrative
    expense budget   M-271
top-down budgeting   M-276
variance   M-299
zero-based budgeting   M-275

## REVIEW THE FACTS

A. What is the operating budget?
B. What is the master budget?
C. Which financial statements are part of the operating budget?
D. What is the difference between the financial statements included in the operating budget and other financial statements you have learned about in this course?
E. List the main benefits of budgeting.
F. What is the basic difference between the production budget and the purchases budget?
G. What are two advantages of perpetual budgeting?
H. What is a disadvantage of perpetual budgeting?
I. What is incremental budgeting?
J. What problem is associated with incremental budgeting?
K. What is zero-based budgeting?
L. Describe the differences between top-down and bottom-up budgeting.
M. Describe the differences between an imposed budget and a participative budget.
N. Why is the sales forecast often called the cornerstone of budgeting?
O. Why is the sales forecast often called the keystone of budgeting?
P. List three factors that should be considered when preparing the sales forecast.
Q. Why does the number of units budgeted to be purchased differ from the number of units budgeted to be sold?
R. When preparing the purchases budget, what two factors should be considered when determining the budgeted ending inventory?
S. What is presented on the cash receipts schedule?

**T.** For a particular budget period, why doesn't the budgeted cash collections from customers equal budgeted sales?

**U.** What is the basic difference between a budgeted balance sheet and an historical balance sheet?

**V.** In the normal course of business, what are the three sources from which a company can obtain cash?

**W.** What is a *performance to budget* evaluation?

## APPLY WHAT YOU HAVE LEARNED

### LO 3 & 4: Determine Order of Operating Budget Preparation

**8–23.** During the budgeting process, not all budgets are prepared at the same time. Following are several operating budgets.

1. _6_ Cash budget
2. _5_ Budgeted financial statements
3. _2_ Purchases budget
4. _1_ Sales budget
5. _4_ Administrative expense budget
6. _3_ Selling expense budget

**REQUIRED:**
Indicate a logical sequence for the preparation of the master budget.

### LO 3: Indicate Advantages and Disadvantages of Top-Down, Bottom-Up Approaches

**8–24.** The master budget can be prepared using either the top-down or bottom-up approach. Following in random order are several advantages and disadvantages of each approach.

| Top-down Bottom-up | Advantage Disadvantage | |
|---|---|---|
| 1. _B_ | _A_ | Budgeting process forces managers at various levels to think about future activities. |
| 2. _T_ | _A_ | Top manager is more knowledgeable. |
| 3. _B_ | _D_ | Employees at various levels must take time from their schedules to work on the budget. |
| 4. _B_ | _A_ | Employees will be more eager to work toward goals they helped set. |
| 5. _B_ | _A_ | Employees feel more like part of the company team. |
| 6. _T_ | _A_ | Top manager is more aware of company goals. |
| 7. _B_ | _D_ | Employees may try to pad the budget. |
| 8. _T_ | _D_ | Employees are less accepting of budgeted goals if they had no part in setting them. |
| 9. _T_ | _D_ | Top manager lacks detailed knowledge required to prepare budgets. |

**REQUIRED:**
For each of these items, indicate whether it is associated with top-down (T) or bottom-up (B), and whether it is an advantage (A) or disadvantage (D).

## LO 3:  Indicate Budgeting Approaches

**8–25.** Following are approaches to budgeting, with a partial definition of those items in scrambled order.

    **a.** Perpetual budgeting         **d.** Top-down budgeting
    **b.** Incremental budgeting     **e.** Bottom-up budgeting
    **c.** Zero-based budgeting

    **1.** _e_ Lower-level managers and employees initially prepare the budget.
    **2.** _c_ Each item on the budget must be justified each year.
    **3.** _a_ The budget is updated every month.
    **4.** _d_ Lower-level managers generally do not participate in budget preparation.
    **5.** _b_ Uses the prior year's budget to build the new budget.

**REQUIRED:**
For each partial definition, identify the budgeting approach to which it refers.

## LO 5:  Prepare a Sales Budget

**8–26.** For 2003, David's Computer Game Company expects to sell 6,000 games in the first quarter, 7,000 games in the second quarter, 9,000 games in the third quarter, and 12,000 games in the fourth quarter. Each game sells for $11.

**REQUIRED:**
Prepare the 2003 sales budget for David's Computer Game Company.

## LO 5:  Prepare a Sales Budget

**8–27.** For 2003, Paul Elsea's Barber Supply Company expects to sell 100 hair dryers in the first quarter, 90 hair dryers in the second quarter, 130 hair dryers in the third quarter, and 150 hair dryers in the fourth quarter. Each hair dryer sells for $67.

**REQUIRED:**
Prepare the 2003 sales budget for hair dryers for Paul Elsea's Barber Supply Company.

## LO 5:  Prepare a Sales Budget

**8–28.** For 2003, Taub Yo Yo Company expects to sell 20,000 units in January, 25,000 units in February, and 30,000 units in March. Each unit sells for $1.20.

**REQUIRED:**
Prepare the sales budget for Taub Yo Yo Company for the first quarter of 2003.

## LO 5:  Prepare a Sales Budget

**8–29.** The Golden Bird Cage Company intends to sell 11,500 bird cages during 2003. The budgeted selling price per cage is $88. The following sales forecast is available:

|                | Units |
|----------------|-------|
| First quarter  | 2,500 |
| Second quarter | 2,100 |
| Third quarter  | 3,800 |
| Fourth quarter | 3,100 |

**REQUIRED:**

Prepare the 2003 sales budget for Golden Bird Cage Company.

## LO 5: Prepare a Sales Budget

**8–30.** Easy-Glide Strollers intends to sell 73,000 baby strollers in the first quarter of 2000. The budgeted selling price per stroller is $59. The following sales forecast is available:

|  | Units |
|---|---|
| January | 22,500 |
| February | 22,500 |
| March | 28,000 |

**REQUIRED:**

Prepare the sales budget for Easy-Glide Strollers for the first quarter of 2000.

## LO 5: Prepare a Purchases Budget

**8–31.** Florence Marie's Hat Shop plans to sell the following quantity of hats during the first four months of 2003.

|  | Units |
|---|---|
| January | 200 |
| February | 250 |
| March | 300 |
| April | 320 |

Florence pays $6 for each hat which she sells for $15.

At the beginning of January, Florence plans to have 40 hats on hand, and hopes to maintain an ending inventory equal to 20% of next month's sales.

**REQUIRED:**

Prepare a purchases budget for the first quarter of 2003 for Florence Marie's Hat Shop. Remember, the first quarter is January, February, and March. April sales are only provided to help compute the ending inventory for March.

## LO 5: Prepare a Sales Budget and Cost of Goods Sold Budget

**8–32.** Refer to the information in problem 8–31.

**REQUIRED:**

a. Prepare a sales budget for the first quarter of 2003 for Florence Marie's Hat Shop.
b. Prepare a cost of goods sold budget for the first quarter of 2003 for Florence Marie's Hat Shop.

## LO 5: Prepare a Purchases Budget

**8–33.** Anahi's Art Supplies plans to sell the following quantity of model AB222 airbrush during the first four months of 2000.

|  | Units |
|---|---|
| January | 400 |
| February | 26 |
| March | 22 |
| April | 20 |

Anahi's pays $44 for each airbrush and sells them for $65.

At the beginning of January, Anahi's Art Supplies plans to have six airbrushes on hand, and hopes to maintain an ending inventory equal to 15% of next month's sales.

**REQUIRED:**

Prepare a purchases budget for the first quarter of 2000 for Anahi's Art Supplies. Remember, the first quarter is January, February, and March. April sales are only provided to help compute the ending inventory for March.

## LO 5:   Prepare a Sales Budget and Cost of Goods Sold Budget

**8–34.** Refer to the information in problem 8–33.

**REQUIRED:**

a. Prepare a sales budget for the first quarter of 2000 for Anahi's Art Supplies.
b. Prepare a cost of goods sold budget for the first quarter of 2000 for Anahi's Art Supplies.

## LO 5:   Prepare a Sales Budget, Cost of Goods Sold Budget, and Purchases Budget

**8–35.** Diaz Lumber plans to sell the following quantity of BC Grade 1/2-inch plywood during the first four months of 2000.

| | |
|---|---|
| January | 220 sheets |
| February | 250 sheets |
| March | 200 sheets |
| April | 300 sheets |

Diaz pays $7 for each sheet of plywood and sells them for $12.

At the beginning of January, Diaz plans to have 66 sheets of plywood on hand, and hopes to maintain an ending inventory equal to 30% of next month's sales.

**REQUIRED:**

a. Prepare a sales budget for the first quarter of 2000 for Diaz Lumber.
b. Prepare a cost of goods sold budget for the first quarter of 2000 for Diaz Lumber.
c. Prepare a purchases budget for the first quarter of 2000 for Diaz Lumber.

## LO 5:   Prepare a Budgeted Income Statement Using Information Provided in Other Budgets

**8–36.** Smith Manufacturing has prepared the following budgeted information for January 2000.

### SMITH MANUFACTURING
#### Sales Budget
#### For January 31, 2000

| | |
|---|---|
| Forecasted Sales in Units | 3,300 |
| × Forecasted Sales Price | $    200 |
| = Budgeted Sales Dollars | $660,000 |

## SMITH MANUFACTURING
### Cost of Goods Sold Budget
### For January 31, 2000

| | |
|---|---|
| Forecasted Sales in Units | 3,300 |
| × Forecasted Cost Per Unit | $ 110 |
| = Budgeted COGS | $363,000 |

## SMITH MANUFACTURING
### Selling and Administrative Expense Budget
### For January 31, 2000

| | |
|---|---|
| Salaries and Wages | $101,500 |
| Rent | 64,000 |
| Depreciation | 53,200 |
| Other | 2,300 |
| Budgeted S & A Expense | $221,000 |

**REQUIRED:**

Prepare a budgeted income statement for January 2000 for Smith Manufacturing.

## LO 5: Prepare a Budgeted Income Statement Using Information Provided in Other Budgets

**8–37.** Gomez Sales Company has prepared the following budgeted information for March 2000.

## GOMEZ SALES COMPANY
### Sales Budget
### For March 31, 2000

| | |
|---|---|
| Forecasted Sales in Units | 110,000 |
| × Forecasted Sales Price | $ 4.95 |
| = Budgeted Sales Dollars | $544,500 |

## GOMEZ SALES COMPANY
### Cost of Goods Sold Budget
### For March 31, 2000

| | |
|---|---|
| Forecasted Sales in Units | 110,000 |
| × Forecasted Cost Per Unit | $ 3.35 |
| = Budgeted COGS | $368,500 |

## GOMEZ SALES COMPANY
### Selling and Administrative Expense Budget
### For March 31, 2000

| | |
|---|---|
| Sales Salaries | $ 51,500 |
| Sales Commission | 11,000 |
| Other Salaries and Wages | 35,000 |
| Store Rent | 24,000 |
| Other Expenses | 10,500 |
| Budgeted S & A Expense | 132,000 |

**REQUIRED:**

Prepare a budgeted income statement for March 2000 for Gomez Sales Company.

## LO 5: Prepare a Budgeted Income Statement Using Information Provided in Other Budgets

**8–38.** Copas Company has prepared the following budgeted information for December 2000.

### COPAS COMPANY
#### Sales Budget
#### For December 31, 2000

| | |
|---|---:|
| Forecasted Sales in Units | 10,000 |
| × Forecasted Sales Price | $ 1,200 |
| = Budgeted Sales Dollars | $120,000 |

### COPAS COMPANY
#### Cost of Goods Sold Budget
#### For December 31, 2000

| | |
|---|---:|
| Forecasted Sales in Units | 10,000 |
| × Forecasted Cost Per Unit | $ 800 |
| = Budgeted COGS | $80,000 |

### COPAS COMPANY
#### Selling and Administrative Expense Budget
#### For December 31, 2000

| | |
|---|---:|
| Sales Salaries | $18,500 |
| Sales Commission | 3,000 |
| Store Rent | 9,000 |
| Other Expenses | 1,500 |
| Budgeted S & A Expense | 32,000 |

**REQUIRED:**
Prepare a budgeted income statement for December 2000 for Copas Company.

## LO 5: Prepare a Budgeted Income Statement

**8–39.** For the first quarter of 2000, Philip's Sales Corporation has budgeted sales of $390,000 and budgeted cost of goods sold of $280,000. In addition, the budget for the first quarter of 2000 includes wages and salaries of $42,000, rent of $9,000, utilities of $2,000, maintenance of $1,000, and other expenses of $3,000.

**REQUIRED:**
Prepare a budgeted income statement for the first quarter of 2000 for Philip's Sales Corporation.

## LO 5: Prepare a Budgeted Income Statement

**8–40.** For January 2000, Edwardo Manufacturing has budgeted sales of $1,200,000 and budgeted cost of goods sold of $980,000. In addition, the budget for January 2000 includes sales salaries of $98,000, administrative salaries of $54,000, rent of $24,000, utilities of $8,000, and other expenses of $9,000.

**REQUIRED:**
Prepare a budgeted income statement for January 2000 for Edwardo Manufacturing.

## LO 5:   Prepare a Budgeted Income Statement

**8–41.** For the year 2000, Martin Sales Corporation has budgeted sales of $3,500,000 and budgeted cost of goods sold of $2,800,000. In addition, the budget for 2000 includes sales salaries of $220,000, administrative salaries of $130,000, depreciation of $180,000, utilities of $38,000, and other expenses of $22,000.

**REQUIRED:**
Prepare a budgeted income statement for 2000 for Martin Sales Corporation.

## LO 5:   Prepare a Budgeted Income Statement for One Quarter

**8–42.** The following budgets were prepared for Gary's Jean Store.

**GARY'S JEAN STORE**
**Sales Budget**
**For the Quarter Ended June 30, 2003**

|  | Apr | May | Jun | Total |
|---|---|---|---|---|
| Forecasted Sales in Units | 300 | 350 | 400 | 1,050 |
| × Forecasted Sales Price | $ 27 | $ 27 | $ 27 | $ 27 |
| = Budgeted Sales Dollars | $8,100 | $9,450 | $10,800 | $28,350 |

**GARY'S JEAN STORE**
**Cost of Goods Sold Budget**
**For the Quarter Ended June 30, 2003**

|  | Apr | May | Jun | Total |
|---|---|---|---|---|
| Forecasted Sales in Units | 300 | 350 | 400 | 1,050 |
| × Forecasted Cost Per Unit | $ 14 | $ 14 | $ 14 | $ 14 |
| = Budgeted Cost of Goods Sold | $4,200 | $ 4,900 | $5,600 | $14,700 |

**GARY'S JEAN STORE**
**Selling and Administrative Expense Budget**
**For the Quarter Ended June 30, 2003**

|  | Apr | May | Jun | Total |
|---|---|---|---|---|
| Salaries and Wages | $1,800 | $2,200 | $1,900 | $ 5,900 |
| Rent | 500 | 500 | 500 | 1,500 |
| Depreciation | 100 | 100 | 100 | 300 |
| Other | 600 | 900 | 800 | 2,300 |
| Budgeted Sales Dollars | $3,000 | $3,700 | $3,300 | $10,000 |

**REQUIRED:**
Prepare a budgeted income statement for the second quarter of 2003 for Gary's Jean Store.

## LO 5:   Prepare a Budgeted Income Statement for One Quarter

**8–43.** Franco's Cart Company manufactures small carts that are designed to be pulled behind a small tractor or riding lawn mower. The following budgets were prepared for Franco's Cart Company.

### FRANCO'S CART COMPANY
### Sales Budget
### For the Quarter Ended March 31, 2003

|  | Jan | Feb | Mar | Total |
|---|---|---|---|---|
| Forecasted Sales in Units | 1,300 | 1,450 | 1,700 | 4,450 |
| × Forecasted Sales Price | $ 186 | $ 186 | $ 186 | $ 186 |
| = Budgeted Sales Dollars | $241,800 | $269,700 | $316,200 | $827,700 |

### FRANCO'S CART COMPANY
### Cost of Goods Sold Budget
### For the Quarter Ended March 31, 2003

|  | Jan | Feb | Mar | Total |
|---|---|---|---|---|
| Forecasted Sales in Units | 1,300 | 1,450 | 1,700 | 4,450 |
| × Forecasted Cost Per Unit | $ 154 | $ 154 | $ 154 | $ 154 |
| = Budgeted COGS | $200,200 | $223,300 | $261,800 | $685,300 |

### FRANCO'S CART COMPANY
### Selling and Administrative Expense Budget
### For the Quarter Ended March 31, 2003

|  | Jan | Feb | Mar | Total |
|---|---|---|---|---|
| Salaries and Wages | $21,950 | $22,200 | $23,600 | $67,750 |
| Rent | 4,000 | 4,500 | 4,500 | 13,000 |
| Depreciation | 3,200 | 3,200 | 3,200 | 9,600 |
| Other | 2,300 | 2,500 | 2,800 | 7,600 |
| Budgeted S & A Expense | $31,450 | $32,400 | $34,100 | $97,950 |

## REQUIRED:

Prepare a budgeted income statement for the first quarter of 2003 for Franco's Cart Company.

## LO 5:   Prepare a Budgeted Income Statement for One Quarter

**8–44.** The following budgets were prepared for Byrne Manufacturing.

### BYRNE MANUFACTURING
### Sales Budget
### For the Quarter Ended September 30, 2000

|  | Jul | Aug | Sep | Total |
|---|---|---|---|---|
| Forecasted Unit Sales | 900 | 1,100 | 1,300 | 3,300 |
| × Forecasted Sales Price | $ 225 | $ 225 | $ 225 | $ 225 |
| = Budgeted Sales Dollars | $202,500 | $247,500 | $292,500 | $742,500 |

### BYRNE MANUFACTURING
### Cost of Goods Sold Budget
### For the Quarter Ended September 30, 2000

|  | Jul | Aug | Sep | Total |
|---|---|---|---|---|
| Forecasted Unit Sales | 900 | 1,100 | 1,300 | 3,300 |
| × Forecasted Cost Per Unit | $ 204 | $ 204 | $ 204 | $ 204 |
| = Budgeted COGS | $183,600 | $224,400 | $265,200 | $673,200 |

**BYRNE MANUFACTURING**
**Selling and Administrative Expense Budget**
**For the Quarter Ended September 30, 2000**

|  | Jul | Aug | Sep | Total |
|---|---|---|---|---|
| Salaries and Wages | $ 4,800 | $ 5,200 | $ 5,800 | $15,800 |
| Rent | 2,400 | 2,400 | 2,400 | 7,200 |
| Depreciation | 1,150 | 1,150 | 1,150 | 3,450 |
| Other | 1,800 | 2,000 | 2,200 | 6,000 |
| Budgeted S & A Expense | $10,150 | $10,750 | $11,550 | $32,450 |

**REQUIRED:**

Prepare a budgeted income statement for the third quarter of 2000 for Byrne Manufacturing.

## LO 5: Prepare a Cash Receipts Schedule for One Quarter

**8–45.** The Deacon Company is preparing a cash receipts schedule for the first quarter of 2003. Sales for November and December of 2002 are expected to be $180,000 and $200,000, respectively. Budgeted sales for the first quarter of 2003 are presented here.

**THE DEACON COMPANY**
**Sales Budget**
**For the Quarter Ended March 31, 2003**

|  | Jan | Feb | Mar | Total |
|---|---|---|---|---|
| Budgeted Sales | $220,000 | $240,000 | $260,000 | $720,000 |

Twenty percent of sales are for cash, the remaining 80% are on account. Ten percent of the sales on account are collected in the month of the sale, 60% in the month following the sale, and the remaining 30% in the second month following the sale. There are no uncollectible accounts receivable.

**REQUIRED:**

Prepare a cash receipts schedule for the first quarter of 2003.

## LO 5: Prepare a Cash Receipts Schedule for One Quarter

**8–46.** The V & A Velez Company is preparing a cash receipts schedule for the first quarter of 2003. Sales for November and December of 2002 are expected to be $300,000 and $310,000, respectively. Budgeted sales for the first quarter of 2003 are presented here.

**THE V & A VELEZ COMPANY**
**Sales Budget**
**For the Quarter Ended March 31, 2003**

|  | Jan | Feb | Mar | Total |
|---|---|---|---|---|
| Budgeted Sales | $220,000 | $290,000 | $340,000 | $850,000 |

Ten percent of sales are for cash, the remaining 90% are on account. Twenty percent of the sales on account are collected in the month of the sale, 70% in the month following the sale, and the remaining 10% in the second month following the sale. There are no uncollectible accounts receivable.

**REQUIRED:**
Prepare a cash receipts schedule for the first quarter of 2003.

## LO 5:   Prepare a Cash Receipts Schedule for One Quarter

**8–47.** The Arauz Company is preparing a cash receipts schedule for the first quarter of 2000. Sales for November and December of 1999 are expected to be $30,000 and $50,000, respectively. Budgeted sales for the first quarter of 2000 are presented here.

**THE ARAUZ COMPANY**
**Sales Budget**
**For the Quarter Ended March 31, 2000**

|  | Jan | Feb | Mar | Total |
|---|---|---|---|---|
| Budgeted Sales | $20,000 | $25,000 | $40,000 | $85,000 |

Fifteen percent of sales are for cash, the remaining 85% are on account. Twenty percent of the sales on account are collected in the month of the sale, 50% in the month following the sale, and the remaining 30% in the second month following the sale. There are no uncollectible accounts receivable.

**REQUIRED:**
Prepare a cash receipts schedule for the first quarter of 2000.

## LO 5:   Prepare a Cash Receipts Schedule for One Quarter

**8–48.** The Phillips Company is preparing a cash receipts schedule for the first quarter of 2000. Sales for November and December of 1999 are expected to be $33,000 and $55,000, respectively. Budgeted sales for the first quarter of 2000 are presented here.

**THE PHILLIPS COMPANY**
**Sales Budget**
**For the Quarter Ended March 31, 2000**

|  | Jan | Feb | Mar | Total |
|---|---|---|---|---|
| Budgeted Sales | $20,000 | $30,000 | $45,000 | $95,000 |

Fifteen percent of sales are for cash, the remaining 85% are on account. Twenty percent of the sales on account are collected in the month of the sale, 50% in the month following the sale, 30% in the second month following the sale. There are no uncollectible accounts receivable.

**REQUIRED:**
Prepare a cash receipts schedule for the first quarter of 2000.

## LO 5:   Prepare a Cash Receipts Schedule for One Quarter

**8–49.** The Aimin Company is preparing a cash receipts schedule for the first quarter of 2000. Sales for November and December of 1999 are expected to be $40,000 and $80,000, respectively. Budgeted sales for the first quarter of 2000 are presented here.

## THE AIMIN COMPANY
### Sales Budget
### For the Quarter Ended March 31, 2000

|  | Jan | Feb | Mar | Total |
|---|---|---|---|---|
| Budgeted Sales | $30,000 | $40,000 | $50,000 | $120,000 |

Ten percent of sales are for cash, the remaining 90% are on account. Fifteen percent of the sales on account are collected in the month of the sale, 60% in the month following the sale, 25% in the second month following the sale. There are no uncollectible accounts receivable.

**REQUIRED:**
Prepare a cash receipts schedule for the first quarter of 2000.

## LO 5:   Prepare a Cash Receipts Schedule for One Quarter

**8–50.** The Gabriel Diaz Company is preparing a cash receipts schedule for the first quarter of 2003. Sales on account for November and December of 2002 are expected to be $500,000 and $750,000, respectively. Budgeted sales for the first quarter of 2003 are presented here.

### THE GABRIEL DIAZ COMPANY
### Sales Budget
### For the Quarter Ended March 31, 2003

|  | Jan | Feb | Mar | Total |
|---|---|---|---|---|
| Budgeted Cash Sales | $ 40,000 | $ 45,000 | $ 55,000 | $ 140,000 |
| Budgeted Sales on Account | $400,000 | $450,000 | $550,000 | $1,400,000 |
| Total Sales | $440,000 | $495,000 | $605,000 | $1,540,000 |

Expected collection pattern for sales on account:
  15% in the month of sale
  60% in the month following the sale
  25% in the second month following the sale
  0% uncollectible

**REQUIRED:**
Prepare a cash receipts schedule for the first quarter of 2003.

## LO 5:   Prepare a Cash Receipts Schedule for One Quarter

**8–51.** The Lila Steinman Company is preparing a cash receipts schedule for the first quarter of 2000. Sales on account for November and December of 1999 are expected to be $200,000 and $400,000, respectively. Budgeted sales for the first quarter of 2000 are presented here.

### The Lila Steinman Company
### Sales Budget
### For the Quarter Ended March 31, 2000

|  | Jan | Feb | Mar | Total |
|---|---|---|---|---|
| Budgeted Cash Sales | $ 20,000 | $ 25,000 | $ 27,000 | $ 72,000 |
| Budgeted Sales on Account | $180,000 | $210,000 | $250,000 | $640,000 |
| Total Sales | $200,000 | $235,000 | $277,000 | $712,000 |

Expected collection pattern for sales on account:
  10% in the month of sale
  70% in the month following the sale
  20% in the second month following the sale
  0% uncollectible

**REQUIRED:**

Prepare a cash receipts schedule for the first quarter of 2000.

## LO 5:   Prepare a Cash Receipts Schedule for One Quarter

**8–52.** The Lowensohn Company is preparing a cash receipts schedule for the first quarter of 2000. Sales on account for November and December of 1999 are expected to be $320,000 and $550,000, respectively. Budgeted sales for the first quarter of 2000 are presented here.

**THE LOWENSOHN COMPANY**
**Sales Budget**
**For the Quarter Ended March 31, 2000**

|  | Jan | Feb | Mar | Total |
|---|---|---|---|---|
| Budgeted Cash Sales | $120,000 | $150,000 | $125,000 | $395,000 |
| Budgeted Sales on | | | | |
|   Account | $180,000 | $225,000 | $190,000 | $595,000 |
| Total Sales | $300,000 | $375,000 | $315,000 | $990,000 |

Expected collection pattern for sales on account:
  30% in the month of sale
  50% in the month following the sale
  20% in the second month following the sale
  0% uncollectible

**REQUIRED:**

Prepare a cash receipts schedule for the first quarter of 2000.

## LO 5:   Prepare a Cash Receipts Schedule for One Quarter

**8–53.** The S.R. Jackson Company is preparing a cash receipts schedule for the second quarter of 2003. Sales on account for February and March of 2003 are expected to be $50,000 and $60,000, respectively. Budgeted sales for the second quarter of 2003 are presented here.

**THE S.R. JACKSON COMPANY**
**Sales Budget**
**For the Quarter Ended June 30, 2003**

|  | Apr | May | Jun | Total |
|---|---|---|---|---|
| Budgeted Cash Sales | $15,000 | $20,000 | $25,000 | $ 60,000 |
| Budgeted Sales on | | | | |
|   Account | $30,000 | $40,000 | $50,000 | $120,000 |
| Total Sales | $45,000 | $60,000 | $75,000 | $180,000 |

Expected collection pattern for sales on account:
25% in the month of sale
50% in the month following the sale
25% in the second month following the sale
0% uncollectible

**REQUIRED:**

Prepare a cash receipts schedule for the second quarter of 2003.

## LO 5: Prepare a Cash Receipts Schedule for One Quarter

**8–54.** The Hodson Company is preparing a cash receipts schedule for the third quarter of 2003. Sales on account for May and June of 2003 are expected to be $100,000 and $120,000, respectively. Budgeted sales for the third quarter of 2003 are presented here.

**THE HODSON COMPANY**
**Sales Budget**
**For the Quarter Ended September 30, 2003**

|  | Jul | Aug | Sep | Total |
|---|---|---|---|---|
| Budgeted Cash Sales | $ 8,000 | $ 9,000 | $ 11,000 | $ 28,000 |
| Budgeted Sales on Account | $80,000 | $90,000 | $110,000 | $280,000 |
| Total Sales | $88,000 | $99,000 | $121,000 | $308,000 |

Expected collection pattern for sales on account:
  10% in the month of sale
  60% in the month following the sale
  30% in the second month following the sale
  0% uncollectible

**REQUIRED:**

Prepare a cash receipts schedule for the third quarter of 2003.

## LO 5: Prepare a Cash Receipts Schedule for One Quarter

**8–55.** The A.R. Oddo Company is preparing a cash receipts schedule for the fourth quarter of 2003. Sales on account for August and September of 2003 are expected to be $200,000 and $220,000, respectively. Budgeted sales for the fourth quarter of 2003 are presented here.

**THE A.R. ODDO COMPANY**
**Sales Budget**
**For the Quarter Ended December 31, 2003**

|  | Oct | Nov | Dec | Total |
|---|---|---|---|---|
| Budgeted Cash Sales | $ 42,000 | $ 46,000 | $ 60,000 | $148,000 |
| Budgeted Sales on Account | $210,000 | $230,000 | $300,000 | $740,000 |
| Total Sales | $252,000 | $276,000 | $360,000 | $888,000 |

Expected collection pattern for sales on account:
  20% in the month of sale
  70% in the month following the sale
  10% in the second month following the sale
  0% uncollectible

**REQUIRED:**

Prepare a cash receipts schedule for the fourth quarter of 2003.

## LO 5 Prepare a Cash Receipts Schedule for One Quarter

**8–56.** The law firm of Hendricks & Hendricks is preparing a cash receipts schedule for the first quarter of 2003. Service revenue for November and

December of 2002 are expected to be $90,000 and $50,000, respectively. All billings are on account. There are no "cash sales." Budgeted service revenue for the first quarter of 2003 is presented here.

### HENDRICKS & HENDRICKS
#### Service Revenue Budget
#### For the Quarter Ended March 31, 2003

|  | Jan | Feb | Mar | Total |
|---|---|---|---|---|
| Budgeted Service Revenue | $40,000 | $50,000 | $65,000 | $155,000 |

Expected collection pattern:
- 30% in the month of sale
- 60% in the month following the sale
- 10% in the second month following the sale
- 0% uncollectible

**REQUIRED:**

Prepare a cash receipts schedule for the first quarter of 2003.

## LO 5:   Prepare a Cash Receipts Schedule for One Quarter

**8–57.** The medical practice of Healit & Quick is preparing a cash receipts schedule for the first quarter of 2000. Service revenue for November and December of 1999 are expected to be $120,000 and $110,000, respectively. All billings are on account. There are no "cash sales." Budgeted service revenue for the first quarter of 2000 is presented here.

### HEALIT & QUICK
#### Service Revenue Budget
#### For the Quarter Ended March 31, 2000

|  | Jan | Feb | Mar | Total |
|---|---|---|---|---|
| Budgeted Service Revenue | $120,000 | $130,000 | $140,000 | $155,000 |

Expected collection pattern:
- 20% in the month of sale
- 60% in the month following the sale
- 20% in the second month following the sale
- 0% uncollectible

**REQUIRED:**

Prepare a cash receipts schedule for the first quarter of 2000.

## LO 5:   Prepare a Cash Payments Schedule for One Quarter

**8–58.** Marcy Steinmann and Company has prepared the following budgets for the first quarter of 2000.

### MARCY STEINMANN AND COMPANY
#### Selling and Administrative Expense Budget
#### For the Quarter Ended March 31, 2000

|  | Jan | Feb | Mar | Total |
|---|---|---|---|---|
| Salaries and Wages | $1,700 | $2,200 | $1,900 | $ 5,800 |
| Rent | 300 | 300 | 300 | 900 |
| Depreciation | 200 | 200 | 200 | 600 |
| Other | 900 | 1,200 | 1,000 | 3,100 |
| Total | $3,100 | $3,900 | $3,400 | $10,400 |

## MARCY STEINMANN AND COMPANY
### Purchases Budget
### For the Quarter Ended March 31, 2000

|  | Jan | Feb | Mar | Total |
|---|---|---|---|---|
| Forecasted Unit Sales | 50 | 60 | 70 | 180 |
| + Desired Ending Inventory | 12 | 14 | 16 | 16 |
| = Total Units Needed | 62 | 74 | 86 | 196 |
| − Beginning Inventory | ( 10) | ( 12) | ( 14) | (10) |
| = Units to Be Purchased | 52 | 62 | 72 | 186 |
| × Cost Per Unit | $ 220 | $ 220 | $ 220 | $ 220 |
| = Cost of Purchases | $11,440 | $13,640 | $15,840 | $40,920 |

Selling and administrative expenses are paid in the month incurred and purchases are paid in the month following the purchase. Purchases for December 1999 are $10,500. No equipment purchases or additional expenditures are made during the quarter.

### REQUIRED:
Prepare a cash payment schedule for the first quarter of 2000.

## LO 5: Prepare a Cash Payments Schedule for One Quarter

**8–59.** Jackson Sales Company has prepared the following budgets for the second quarter of 2000.

## JACKSON SALES COMPANY
### Selling and Administrative Expense Budget
### For the Quarter Ended June 30, 2000

|  | Apr | May | Jun | Total |
|---|---|---|---|---|
| Salaries | $1,000 | $1,200 | $1,300 | $3,500 |
| Rent | 200 | 200 | 200 | 600 |
| Utilities | 120 | 180 | 220 | 520 |
| Depreciation | 80 | 80 | 80 | 240 |
| Other | 500 | 600 | 650 | 1,750 |
| Total | $1,900 | $2,260 | $2,450 | $6,610 |

## JACKSON SALES COMPANY
### Purchases Budget
### For the Quarter Ended June 30, 2000

|  | Apr | May | Jun | Total |
|---|---|---|---|---|
| Forecasted Unit Sales | 70 | 80 | 90 | 240 |
| + Desired Ending Inventory | 16 | 18 | 19 | 19 |
| = Total Units Needed | 86 | 98 | 109 | 259 |
| − Beginning Inventory | ( 15) | ( 16) | ( 18) | (15) |
| = Units to Be Purchased | 71 | 82 | 91 | 244 |
| × Cost Per Unit | $ 100 | $ 100 | $ 100 | $ 100 |
| = Cost of Purchases | $ 7,100 | $ 8,200 | $ 9,100 | $24,400 |

Selling and administrative expenses are paid in the month incurred and purchases are paid in the month following the purchase. Purchases for March 2000 are $6,800. No equipment purchases or additional expenditures are made during the quarter.

### REQUIRED:
Prepare a cash payment schedule for the second quarter of 2000.

## LO 5:   Prepare a Cash Payments Schedule for One Month

**8–60.** The following budgeted information is available for the Top Coat Clothing Company for January 2000.

| | |
|---|---|
| Salaries | $120,000 |
| Rent | 9,000 |
| Utilities | 1,200 |
| Depreciation | 3,200 |
| Others Expenses | 1,500 |
| Purchases | 380,000 |

Selling and administrative expenses are paid in the month incurred and purchases are paid in the month following the purchase. Purchases for December 1999 are $350,000. No equipment purchases or additional expenditures are made during the month.

**REQUIRED:**
Prepare a cash payment schedule for January 2000.

## LO 5:   Prepare a Cash Payments Schedule for One Month

**8–61.** The following budgeted information is available for Jack's Feed Store in June 2000.

| | |
|---|---|
| Salaries | $12,000 |
| Rent | 600 |
| Electricity | 140 |
| Depreciation | 800 |
| Others Expenses | 700 |
| Purchases | 80,000 |

Selling and administrative expenses are paid in the month incurred and purchases are paid in the month following the purchase. Purchases for May 2000 are $75,000. No equipment purchases or additional expenditures are made during the month.

**REQUIRED:**
Prepare a cash payment schedule for June 2000.

## LO 5:   Prepare a Cash Budget for One Quarter

**8–62.** The following information is available for the Art Kriner Company for the first quarter of 2000.

| | Jan | Feb | Mar |
|---|---|---|---|
| Budgeted Receipts from Credit Sales | $5,000 | $5,500 | $5,800 |
| Budgeted Cash Sales | 1,200 | 1,250 | 1.300 |
| Budgeted Cash Payments | 6,300 | 7,185 | 6,520 |

Beginning cash balance for January 2000 is expected to be $1,500. The company intends to maintain a cash balance of at least $1,000. The company has made arrangements to borrow from a local bank if necessary.

**REQUIRED:**
Prepare a cash budget for the first quarter of 2000.

## LO 5: Prepare a Cash Budget for One Quarter

**8–63.** The following information is available for the Dixon Company for the second quarter of 2000.

|  | Apr | May | Jun |
|---|---|---|---|
| Budgeted Receipts from Credit Sales | $500,000 | $520,000 | $550,000 |
| Budgeted Cash Sales | 100,000 | 105,000 | 112,000 |
| Budgeted Cash Payments | 670,000 | 615,000 | 627,000 |

Beginning cash balance for April 2000 is expected to be $90,000. The company intends to maintain a cash balance of at least $50,000. The company has made arrangements to borrow from a local bank if necessary.

### REQUIRED:
Prepare a cash budget for the second quarter of 2000.

## LO 5: Prepare a Cash Budget for One Quarter

**8–64.** The following information is available for the Ortega Company for the first quarter of 2000.

|  | Jan | Feb | Mar |
|---|---|---|---|
| Budgeted Receipts from Credit Sales | $100,000 | $110,000 | $115,000 |
| Budgeted Cash Sales | 80,000 | 95,000 | 98,000 |
| Budgeted Cash Payments | 178,000 | 215,000 | 206,000 |

Beginning cash balance for January 2000 is expected to be $20,000. The company intends to maintain a cash balance of at least $15,000. The company has made arrangements to borrow from a local bank if necessary.

### REQUIRED:
Prepare a cash budget for the first quarter of 2000.

## LO 5: Prepare a Cash Budget for One Month

**8–65.** The following information is available for November 2000.

| Budgeted Receipts from Credit Sales | $25,100 |
|---|---|
| Budgeted Cash Sales | 5,900 |
| Budgeted Cash Payments | 32,600 |

Beginning cash balance for November is expected to be $5,800. The company intends to maintain a cash balance of at least $5,000. The company has made arrangements to borrow from a local bank if necessary.

### REQUIRED:
Prepare a cash budget for November 2000.

## LO 5: Prepare a Cash Budget for One Month

**8–66.** The following information is available for October 2000.

| Budgeted Receipts from Credit Sales | $300,000 |
|---|---|
| Budgeted Cash Sales | 80,000 |
| Budgeted Cash Payments | 410,000 |

Beginning cash balance for October is expected to be $60,000. The company intends to maintain a cash balance of at least $50,000. The company has made arrangements to borrow from a local bank if necessary.

**REQUIRED:**
Prepare a cash budget for October 2000.

## LO 5: Prepare a Cash Budget for One Month

**8–67.** The following information is available for July 2000.

| | |
|---|---|
| Budgeted Receipts from Credit Sales | $500,000 |
| Budgeted Cash Sales | 40,000 |
| Budgeted Cash Payments | 577,000 |

Beginning cash balance for July is expected to be $95,000. The company intends to maintain a cash balance of at least $75,000. The company has made arrangements to borrow from a local bank if necessary.

**REQUIRED:**
Prepare a cash budget for July 2000.

## LO 5: Prepare a Budgeted Balance Sheet and Budgeted Statement of Cash Flows for Three Months

**8–68.** The following information is available for the Perlmuter Printing Supply Company.

**PERLMUTER PRINTING SUPPLY COMPANY**
**Sales Budget**
**For the Quarter Ended September 30, 2002**

| | July | August | September |
|---|---|---|---|
| Budgeted Sales Dollars | $90,000 | $80,000 | $70,000 |

**PERLMUTER PRINTING SUPPLY COMPANY**
**Cost of Goods Sold Budget**
**For the Quarter Ended September 30, 2002**

| | July | August | September |
|---|---|---|---|
| Budgeted COGS | $54,000 | $48,000 | $42,000 |

**PERLMUTER PRINTING SUPPLY COMPANY**
**Selling and Administrative Expense Budget**
**For the Quarter Ended September 30, 2002**

| | July | August | September |
|---|---|---|---|
| Salaries and Wages | $12,600 | $12,000 | $11,800 |
| Rent | 1,000 | 1,000 | 1,000 |
| Depreciation | 1,800 | 1,800 | 1,800 |
| Other | 3,800 | 3,000 | 2,900 |
| Total | $19,200 | $17,800 | $17,500 |

## PERLMUTER PRINTING SUPPLY COMPANY
### Budgeted Income Statement
### For the Quarter Ended September 30, 2002

|  | July | August | September |
|---|---|---|---|
| Sales | $90,000 | $80,000 | $70,000 |
| Cost of Goods Sold | 54,000 | 48,000 | 42,000 |
| Gross Profit | 36,000 | 32,000 | 28,000 |
| Selling and Admin. Expense | 19,200 | 17,800 | 17,500 |
| Net Income | $16,800 | $14,200 | $10,500 |

## PERLMUTER PRINTING SUPPLY COMPANY
### Purchases Budget
### For the Quarter Ended September 30, 2002

|  | July | August | September |
|---|---|---|---|
| Cost of Purchases | $52,000 | $46,000 | $41,000 |

## PERLMUTER PRINTING SUPPLY COMPANY
### Cash Receipts Schedule
### For the Quarter Ended September 30, 2002

|  | July | August | September |
|---|---|---|---|
| Budgeted Receipts from Credit Sales | $78,000 | $76,000 | $68,000 |
| Budgeted Cash Sales | 9,000 | 8,000 | 7,000 |
| Total Cash Receipts | $87,000 | $84,000 | $75,000 |

## PERLMUTER PRINTING SUPPLY COMPANY
### Cash Payments Schedule
### For the Quarter Ended September 30, 2002

|  | July | August | September |
|---|---|---|---|
| Purchases | $56,000 | $52,000 | $46,000 |
| Selling and Admin. Expense: |  |  |  |
| Salaries and Wages | $12,600 | $12,000 | $11,800 |
| Rent | 1,000 | 1,000 | 1,000 |
| Other | 3,800 | 3,000 | 2,900 |
| Budgeted Cash Payments | $73,400 | $68,000 | $61,700 |

## PERLMUTER PRINTING SUPPLY COMPANY
### Cash Budget
### For the Quarter Ended September 30, 2002

|  |  | July | August | September |
|---|---|---|---|---|
|  | Beginning Cash Balance | $ 18,500 | $ 32,100 | $ 48,100 |
| + | Cash Receipts | 87,000 | 84,000 | 75,000 |
| = | Cash Available | $105,500 | $116,100 | $123,100 |
| − | Cash Payments | ( 73,400) | ( 68,000) | ( 61,700) |
| = | Balance before Borrowing | $ 32,100 | $ 48,100 | $ 61,400 |
| +/− | Borrowing/(Repayment) | -0- | $ -0- | $ -0- |
| = | Ending Cash Balance | $ 32,100 | $ 48,100 | $ 61,400 |

## PERLMUTER PRINTING SUPPLY COMPANY
### Balance Sheet
### June 30, 2002

| | |
|---|---:|
| Assets | |
| Current Assets | |
| Cash | $ 18,500 |
| Accounts Receivable | 20,000 |
| Inventory | 16,000 |
| Total Current Assets | $ 54,500 |
| Property, Plant, and Equipment | |
| Equipment | 108,000 |
| Less Accumulated Depreciation | ( 43,200) |
| Equipment, Net | $ 64,800 |
| Total Assets | $119,300 |
| Liabilities | |
| Current Liabilities | |
| Accounts Payable | $ 56,000 |
| Total Liabilities | $ 56,000 |
| Owner's Equity | |
| Paid-in Capital | |
| Common Stock | $ 1,000 |
| Additional Paid-in Capital | 10,000 |
| Total Paid-in Capital | $ 11,000 |
| Retained Earnings | $ 52,300 |
| Total Equity | $ 63,300 |
| Total Liabilities and Equity | $119,300 |

## REQUIRED:

**a.** Prepare budgeted balance sheets for July, August, and September of 2002.

**b.** Prepare budgeted statements of cash flows for July, August, and September of 2002.

## LO 5: Determine Missing Budget Information

**8–69.** Following is a partial performance report.

| Description | Budget | Actual | Variance |
|---|---|---|---|
| Wages | $5,000 | $ 5,200 | $ ? 200 U |
| Store Rent | 6,000 | ? 5800 | 200 F |
| Utilities Expense | 1150 ? | 1,200 | 50 U |

## REQUIRED:
Provide the missing information.

## LO 5: Determine Budget Variances

**8–70.** Following is a partial performance report.

| Description | Budget | Actual | Variance |
|---|---|---|---|
| Sales | $25,000 | $22,000 | 3000 $? U |
| Cost of Goods Sold | 20,000 | 17,600 | 2400 ? F |
| Gross Profit | 5,000 | 4,400 | 600 ? U |

## REQUIRED:
Calculate the variances for this information and indicate whether they are favorable (F) or unfavorable (U).

## LO 5: Determine Budget Variances

**8–71.** Following is a partial performance report.

| Description | Budget | Actual | Variance |
|---|---|---|---|
| Rent Revenue | $15,000 | $14,000 | $? |
| Interest Expense | 15,000 | 14,000 | ? |

### REQUIRED:
Calculate the variances for this information and indicate whether they are favorable (F) or unfavorable (U).

## LO 6: Discuss Variances

**8–72.** Robin Wince owns a small chain of frame shops. All the frames and other merchandise the company sells is purchased by the company's central purchasing department. A partial performance report showing the direct costs for one of Robin's stores appears as follows:.

| | Budget | Actual | Variance |
|---|---|---|---|
| Sales | $200,000 | $200,000 | $ 0 |
| Cost of Goods Sold | 120,000 | 110,000 | 10,000 F |
| Selling and Admin. Expense | 40,000 | 50,000 | 10,000 U |
| Income | $ 40,000 | $ 40,000 | $ 0 |

### REQUIRED:
Robin is concerned even though the variance in income is zero. Because the total variance is zero, the store manager believes that there is no problem. Do you agree with the manager? Why?

## LO 6: Prepare a Memo Regarding Variances

**8–73.** Matt Lehti owns the Zap Record Shop. He is in the process of examining the following performance report.

| | Budget | Actual | Variance |
|---|---|---|---|
| Sales | $100,000 | $120,000 | $20,000 F |
| Cost of Goods Sold | 60,000 | 72,000 | 12,000 U |
| Selling and Admin. Expense | 10,000 | 9,000 | 1,000 F |
| Income | $ 30,000 | $ 39,000 | $ 9,000 F |

Matt is very pleased that the company had favorable variances for sales and income. However, he finds the sizable unfavorable variance for cost of goods sold very disturbing. He is preparing himself for a serious discussion with the purchasing agent who is responsible for purchasing the merchandise sold.

### REQUIRED:
Assume that Matt Lehti has asked you for assistance in preparing for the meeting with the purchasing agent. Prepare a memo to Matt that provides him with any information you think would be helpful.

# Chapter 9

## Standard Costing

$H$ow do managers know which problems are the most pressing ones? How do they know how much time to spend on such problems? Suppose, for example, that you are the production manager for Inline Skate Company. Your responsibilities include making sure that the plant produces high-quality skates at a relatively low cost. If the actual production cost for a pair of skates is $12.87, how would you know whether this amount is acceptable? In addition, how would you know which specific costs are too high, too low, or just right? You could focus on a selected cost area such as direct material, but you might be spending valuable time trying to control costs that are already under control.

Fortunately, standard costing can help overcome some of the guesswork inherent to operating a business. **Standard costing** is the process of setting cost performance goals that benchmark desirable performance and then using these cost goals to evaluate performance.

Under standard costing, employees work to establish performance goals that can be used as benchmarks for good performance. As these goals are being set, employees are planning how factory resources will be acquired and used. Then, once operations begin, employees strive to control costs so the goals can be met.

The goals also provide management with a basis for performance evaluation when actual results are compared to goals to help find areas of weakness.

If the Inline Skate Company used standard costing, you could evaluate the $12.87 cost per pair of skates by comparing it to the amount budgeted. In fact, standard costing would allow you to review each component of production cost. You

**standard costing** The process of setting cost performance goals that benchmark acceptable performance and then using these cost goals to evaluate performance.

would be able to detect cost overruns for direct material, direct labor, variable manufacturing overhead, or fixed manufacturing overhead. In short, standard costing provides managers with a means to quickly focus their attention on problem areas. ■

## LEARNING OBJECTIVES

*After completing your work on this chapter, you should be able to do the following:*

1. Describe standard costing and indicate why standard costing is important.
2. Explain the concept of management by exception.
3. Contrast ideal and practical standards.
4. Identify and discuss the weaknesses of standard costing.
5. Compare standard costing, actual costing, and normal costing.
6. Determine standards for a manufacturing company.
7. Calculate standard cost variances for direct material, direct labor, variable manufacturing overhead, and fixed manufacturing overhead.
8. Describe the meaning of standard cost variances for direct material, direct labor, variable manufacturing overhead, and fixed manufacturing overhead.

# WHY IS STANDARD COSTING USED?

**standard** A preestablished benchmark for desirable performance.

**standard cost system** A system in which cost standards are set after careful analysis and then used to evaluate actual performance.

In today's competitive environment, business success depends in large part on good planning, as discussed in Chapter 8. Standard costing is often a key planning tool. When a company uses standard costing, it establishes performance standards for the coming year. A **standard** is a preestablished benchmark for desirable performance. A **standard cost system** is one in which a company, after careful analysis, sets cost standards and then uses them to evaluate actual performance.

Standard costing is used to bolster business success. In general, the use of standard costing encourages planning, establishes performance targets, and provides a basis for evaluating actual performance.

Planning is a critical part of any standard cost system. Managers and other employees work to gather information and investigate ways of achieving acceptable performance at the lowest cost. With this information, standards are established. For example, standards are created for the amount and cost of direct material, and for the number of direct labor hours and their cost. The process of planning provides benefits to the company because, once employees have established standards during the planning process, they know what needs to be done and how to do it most efficiently.

Once standards have been set, they can be used as performance targets. Managers and employees are encouraged to act so that actual results meet the expectations established by the standards. For example, if the production cost standard (the cost goal) for a pair of skates made by the Inline Skate Company is $13, employees are encouraged to make the skates for $13 or less. In an ideal situation, every employee would work to make the highest-quality skates for less than the $13 standard cost.

**variance** The difference between actual performance and the standard.

To determine whether and where problems exist, managers compare actual results to the standards. A **variance** is the difference between actual performance and

**unfavorable variance** The difference between actual performance and standard performance when the actual performance falls below the standard.

**favorable variance** The difference between actual performance and standard performance when the actual performance exceeds the standard.

**management by exception** The process of focusing management attention on areas where actual performance deviates from the preestablished standards.

the standard. Variances can be used to help determine where managers should focus their attention.

Actual performance that falls below standard results in an **unfavorable variance.** Essentially, an unfavorable variance reflects a situation in which the cost of actual performance is higher than planned performance. For example, if the standard direct labor time to manufacture a desk is 12 minutes and it actually takes 15 minutes, the three-minute difference constitutes an unfavorable variance of three minutes. Because it is more costly to the company when three minutes of additional labor is used than was planned, an unfavorable variance is an indication that a problem may exist and management attention is needed.

When actual performance exceeds the expectations established by the standard, a **favorable variance** results. In our desk example, if it actually takes 11 minutes to make the desk instead of the standard 12 minutes, the difference constitutes a favorable variance of one minute because cost to the company is reduced if labor time is one minute less than planned.

It might seem that a favorable variance indicates that management attention is not needed, but such is not always the case. Managers should review all variances, favorable and unfavorable, and use judgment and additional information to prioritize problem-solving efforts. For example, if a purchasing agent is able to buy direct material for less than the standard price, a favorable variance will occur. If the lower price is the result of purchasing substandard material, the "favorable" variance may not actually be to the company's benefit at all. Another reason to look into the cause of favorable variances is to learn how performance was improved. If the favorable variance is the result of improved performance, management may be able to learn how to make similar performance improvements in other areas of the company.

Items that have no variance should also be investigated. As discussed in Chapter 8, the absence of a variance should not be construed as meaning that everything is as it should be with that particular item. Managers must also remember that the cause of a variance may be the standard and not the performance. Standard setting is not an exact science. Standards must be reviewed often and changed as circumstances warrant.

It is most helpful if managers are able to review related standard cost variances together. For this purpose, a performance report is often prepared that summarizes variances for a particular operation of the company and shows where attention is needed. The process of focusing management attention on areas where actual performance deviates from the preestablished standards is called **management by exception.**

Under management by exception, managers first tend to problems associated with large variances. Then, once the large problems have been addressed, managers can turn to areas associated with lesser variances. Finally, as time permits, items where no variances exist are examined.

## STANDARDS—A CLOSER LOOK

Most companies set cost standards once each year. Even if variances occur, it is generally unwise to casually adjust standards during the year, because managers might be too quick to adjust them to eliminate unfavorable variance instead of working to improve performance. Also, if standards are often adjusted, performance becomes difficult to track. Performance that resulted in an unfavorable variance one month might result in a favorable variance the next month once the standard has been changed. Standards should be altered only if conditions change so significantly that the established standards lose their effectiveness as performance targets.

## Cost and Quantity Standards

Performance standards can be set for almost any business activity. For example, standards can be set for the number of product returns, or for the amount of employee turnover. In practice, however, standards are used most often to help control costs.

Two things can cause cost to increase: the quantity used and the price paid. It is better to establish both a quantity standard and a separate price standard for each material used in production. For example, to say the direct material for product X should cost $3 per unit is not as helpful in controlling cost as saying that it should take 1.5 pounds of material at $2 per pound to make product X. Establishing a quantity and price standard provides performance targets for the amount of material used in production and a separate target for finding the material at the best purchase price.

Although it is also helpful to establish quantity and price standards for direct labor, we generally do not refer to labor in terms of "quantity" and "price." Instead we use the equivalent terms "hours" and "rate." The quantity standard for labor is the number of hours, and the price standard is the rate.

## Ideal versus Practical Standards

During the planning process, managers and other employees work to set standards that will both help provide performance targets and provide a basis for performance evaluation. If we were setting a price standard for the purchase of gasoline, for example, we could set a cost goal of $0.50 per gallon, $5 per gallon, or any price in between. The object would be to select a standard that would challenge employees to find gasoline at the best price. If the standard is set at $0.50 per gallon, it is unlikely that employees will even try to achieve this impossible standard. On the other hand, if the standard is set at $5 per gallon, employees will be able to achieve the standard so easily that it will offer no incentive to find low-cost gasoline. Generally it is best to select a standard that offers a challenging, yet achievable, performance goal.

**ideal standard**  A standard that is attainable only under perfect conditions.

*Ideal Standards*   A standard that is attainable only under perfect conditions is called an **ideal standard.** Under ideal standards, there is no room for substandard performance of any kind. In a manufacturing setting, for instance, ideal standards assume that the plant operates in a perfect world with no machine breakdowns, no waste of direct material for any reason, and no employee rest breaks. In the real world, ideal standards are nearly impossible to achieve. Such standards may frustrate employees because, no matter how hard they try, they will never be able to meet them. In time, employees may throw up their hands and stop trying to meet the standards altogether.

**practical standard**
A standard that allows for normal, recurring inefficiencies.

*Practical Standards*   A standard that allows for normal, recurring inefficiencies is called a **practical standard.** For example, in manufacturing, a practical standard for the quantity of direct material would allow for waste due to expected defects in the material. For labor, a practical standard would provide for employees working at a normal pace with adequate rest periods. When compared to ideal standards, practical standards are more realistic and less likely to result in unreasonable unfavorable variances. In addition, when practical standards are used, an unfavorable variance indicates that a true problem exists. Accordingly, most companies use practical standards.

## Setting Standards

Often, standards are based on past performance. For example, if material Y was purchased for $4.45 per pound last year, it is likely it can be purchased for about $4.45 the next year; but using last year's actual amounts as next year's standards is overly simplistic. When setting standards, it is best to use historical information, and then incorporate any anticipated changes in efficiency or price.

Often, it is best to use a team approach to evaluate each standard. Whether formal or informal, a team approach for gathering input from various knowledgeable employees will result in better, more appropriate standards. For example, when setting direct material standards for a manufacturer, a team approach would likely be better than a single employee setting the standards based solely on his or her own limited knowledge. The team might include an accountant, production-line workers, production supervisors, purchasing agents, and others who are knowledgeable about the quality, use, sources, and prices of direct material. Then, the historical information provided by the accountants, information about usage and quality requirements provided by production personnel, and information about sourcing and pricing from the purchasing agent can be analyzed. Once the team has examined all this information, appropriate direct material standards can be set.

Once reasonable standards have been established, actual performance has been measured and compared to the standards, and a system to provide performance reports has been put in place, standard costing can be a valuable management tool. A flowchart of how standard costing works is shown in Exhibit 9–1. Managers can then encourage employees to strive to meet the performance goals established by the standards, and can use performance reports and management by exception to help direct their attention to troubled areas. Unfortunately, standard costing is not the answer to all management's problems. When managers rely too heavily on standard costing, serious problems occur.

**Exhibit 9–1**
The Standard-Costing Process

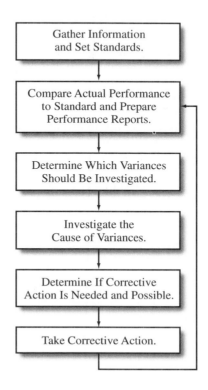

Gather Information and Set Standards.

Compare Actual Performance to Standard and Prepare Performance Reports.

Determine Which Variances Should Be Investigated.

Investigate the Cause of Variances.

Determine If Corrective Action Is Needed and Possible.

Take Corrective Action.

## Problems with Standard Costing

To use standard costing as an effective management tool, managers must be aware of its drawbacks. The first problems may occur when standards are being set. Employees with expertise are often consulted to help establish an appropriate standard. Most of these employees are keenly aware that the standard will be used later to evaluate their performance. With lax standards, employees will not have to work as hard to meet the goals set by the standard, and unfavorable variances will be less likely. With stringent standards, employees will have to work much harder to meet targeted goals. Accordingly, employees often try to ensure that the standards adopted by the company are lax, resulting in suboptimal performance goals.

Another problem with standard costing stems from relying on historical information to set standards. If past performance was less than optimal, the new standards will call for performance that is less than optimal. The inefficiency of the past may be built into the new standards. Sometimes employees and lower-level managers deliberately manipulate actual performance so it appears that less stringent standards should be maintained. This way, employees are less likely to face the consequences of unfavorable performance variances in the future.

Still another serious problem associated with standard costing is that managers tend to manage everything "by the numbers." When a standard cost system is well established, managers often focus almost entirely on significant, unfavorable variances and overlook serious problems that do not give rise to unfavorable variances. For example, a manager may try desperately to reduce an unfavorable direct material variance while completely overlooking a significant product quality problem. Why? The product quality problem does not result in a variance; therefore, a manager whose attention is directed solely by management by exception would have no "exception" to direct him or her to the quality problem. Managers may get so engrossed in chasing down problems associated with unfavorable variance that they waste company time and resources as they try to rectify insignificant unfavorable variances.

In addition, managers who use management by exception may spend so much time on unfavorable variances that they fail to recognize employees who are responsible for favorable variances. By failing to recognize employees who do a good job, managers lose the benefit of positive reinforcement as a management tool.

Still another problem is that managers lose sight of the overall business operation as they focus on the multitude of details which have resulted in unfavorable variances. In time, managers focus so much on unfavorable variance details that they cannot see the forest for the trees. The overall performance of the company may suffer because managers are managing details while ignoring the big picture.

A summary of the problems associated with standard costing is presented in Exhibit 9–2. Take some time to become familiar with these problems.

**Exhibit 9–2**
Summary of Standard
Costing Problems

---

### Problems with Standard Costing

1. Employees who help set standards try to avoid unfavorable variances by setting lax standards.
2. Reliance on historical information may perpetuate past inefficiencies in current standards.
3. Managers manage "by the numbers" and overlook significant problems that do not result in an unfavorable variance or waste time on insignificant unfavorable variances.
4. Managers focus so much on unfavorable variances that they fail to recognize employees who are doing a good job.
5. Managers focus so much on variances that they fail to see the big picture.

## Who Uses Standard Costing?

Almost any business entity can use standard costing regardless of whether it is a for-profit or a not-for-profit organization. Service, merchandising, and manufacturing firms may use standard costing, although it is most often used by manufacturers. When it is appropriate to establish standards of performance for purposes of planning and control, standard costing can be used. For example, a tire store might establish a standard for the amount of time it should take to change a set of tires. An oil change center might establish a standard for the amount of time it should take to change the oil and service an automobile. An airline catering company could develop standards for the quantity and price of each food item, the labor hours and labor rate to prepare each item, and a standard for the amount of overhead cost associated with the preparation of each item it sells.

In a manufacturing environment, a standard cost system is used to budget the cost of producing each individual unit of product. In effect, standard costing is like preparing a budget for a single unit of production. Managers estimate the cost of direct material, direct labor, variable manufacturing overhead, and fixed manufacturing overhead required to produce each item.

In Chapter 3 we discussed two types of cost systems. In an *actual cost system* we compute actual direct material, direct labor, and manufacturing overhead costs. In a *normal cost system* we compute actual direct material and actual direct labor costs, and use a predetermined rate for manufacturing overhead. Standard costing goes one step further. In a standard cost system, estimated amounts are used for direct material, direct labor, and manufacturing overhead. Exhibit 9–3 compares the three cost systems.

In the sections that follow, we discuss the details of how standard costing is used in manufacturing.

**Exhibit 9–3**
Comparison of Actual, Normal, and Standard Cost Systems

| Cost Classification | Actual Cost System | Normal Cost System | Standard Cost System |
|---|---|---|---|
| Direct Material | Actual | Actual | Estimated |
| Direct Labor | Actual | Actual | Estimated |
| Manufacturing Overhead | Actual | Estimated | Estimated |

# BASIC STANDARD COSTING FOR A MANUFACTURER

Standard costing is often used by manufacturing companies. Standards are set for direct material, direct labor, variable manufacturing overhead, and fixed manufacturing overhead. We will walk through the most commonly used standards and variances using the Tree Top Mail Box Company as an example. Tree Top is a small company that makes a single product.

Tree Top Mail Box Company was founded by three college sophomores, Ali, Maria, and Bill. They started the company to earn spending money while they attended college. The trio had done some market research and determined that they could sell decorative wooden mail boxes for $10 each. They each planned to work about 60 hours per month for $10 per hour. Any remaining profits would be left in the company to be divided equally at the end of their venture.

The three entrepreneurs rented a garage to house the small company for $200 per month plus utilities. They purchased equipment, a table saw and drill press, for $900. The estimated useful life of the equipment is three years.

**Exhibit 9–4**
Tree Top's October 2001
Income Statement

---

**TREE TOP MAIL BOX COMPANY**
**Income Statement**
**For the Month Ended October 31, 2001**

| | | |
|---|---:|---:|
| Sales (300 mail boxes at $10 each) | | $3,000 |
| Less Expenses | | |
|     Direct Material | $ 600 | |
|     Direct Labor (180 hours at $10 per hour) | 1,800 | |
|     Rent | 200 | |
|     Utilities (all variable) | 40 | |
|     Miscellaneous Variable Cost | 30 | |
|     Depreciation | 25 | 2,695 |
| Net Income | | $ 305 |

---

In October, Tree Top's first month of operation, the company was able to sell every mail box produced. By the end of October, they had made and sold 300 boxes. As shown on the income statement in Exhibit 9–4, the company's profits for October totaled $305.

## Discussion Questions

**9–1.** How did Ali, Maria, and Bill calculate the depreciation expense of $25 per month?

**9–2.** Can you tell from Exhibit 9–4 whether the three Tree Top employees met their business goals in the month of October? Why or why not?

---

Ali, Maria, and Bill were thrilled that their equity in the company had grown by $305 in the first month. They felt that information for October's business activity could be used to develop a standard cost system to help manage their company.

## SETTING DIRECT MATERIAL STANDARDS

As stated, setting direct material standards involves two important considerations: the quantity of material and the price paid. We now discuss each of these in some detail.

### Direct Material Quantity Standard

**direct material quantity standard** The amount of direct material it should take to manufacture a single unit of product.

**bill of materials** A listing of the quantity and description of each item of direct material used to manufacture an individual product.

The amount of direct material it should take to make a single unit of production is called the **direct material quantity standard.** A bill of materials is often used to help establish the direct material quantity standard. A **bill of materials** is a listing of the quantity and description of each item of direct material used to manufacture an individual product. The bill of material for the 7ULTRA-A CB radio made by Cobra Electronics Corporation included just under 300 items, as shown in Exhibit 9–5.

Each item of direct material, from the speaker to the smallest resistor, is listed. With input from engineering, production, and other personnel, a bill of materials can be prepared and direct material quantity standards can be set. For the Tree Top

## Exhibit 9–5

Bill of Materials for Cobra 7ULTRA-A CB Radio. © Cobra Electronics Corporation, Chicago, IL. Reprinted by permission.

### BILL OF MATERIAL FOR 7ULTRA-A

| | |
|---|---|
| COVER ASS'Y | |
| SPEAKER 8 OHM 0.3W 66MM P-250 | |
| (+)TAPPING SCREW(BH)T3X6-2S (+)BH ZN-PLAT | SPK MTG:3 |
| (+)TAPTITE SCREW(BH)T3X6 (+)BH BLK | UPPER.BOTTOM+ MAIN BODY:8 |
| COVER UPPER ABS 94HB BLK | |
| COVER BOTTOM ABS 94HB BLK | |
| HOLDER(SPK)SPC 16X8XT1.2 | SPK MTG:3 |
| CUSHION 25X25XT5 RUBB.SP0.BLK STIC | |
| FELT &65XT0.3 FELT BLK | |
| FELT 10X110XT0.3 FELT STIC | |
| FELT 10X100XT0.3 FELT BLK | AIR VENT |
| ESCUTCHEON ASS'Y | |
| (+)MACHINE SCREW(FH)M2.6X4 (+)FH ZN-PLAT | |
| NUT M7 BSBM | |
| E.S.C ABS94 L153-S9001 BLK(7ULTRA-A) | |
| LENS ACRYL CLEAR | |
| KNOB(VOL.SQ) ABS 94HB BLK | 95/08/18 |
| KNOB(DOWN) ABS 94HB BLACK | 95/08/18 |
| KNOB(UP)ABS 94HB BLACK | |
| SPRING(COIL) SWP-3 &0.2 | |
| FRONT BODY ASS'Y | |
| TRANSISTOR KTC2078(TO-220AB) | Q704 |
| I.C KIA7217AP | IC401 |
| P.C.B SUB 54X27X1.6 | |
| JACK EARPHONE DHJ-3T | |
| CONNECTOR CH-239(A) SW-1229 | |
| CONNECTOR SCN-16-4 PCB(R) | |
| MICA (FOR T.R 2SC2078) | |
| BUSHING(FOR T.R 2SC2078) | |
| VR10KB:15SK 161V | VR2 |
| VR 50KA:RK16311116B153A | VR1 |
| POWER CORD ASS'Y | |
| (+)MACHINE SCREW(BH)M3X10 (+)BH ZN-PLAT | TR:2 |
| (+)TAPPING SCREW(BH)T3X6-2S (+)BH ZN-PLAT | M.P+MAIN BODY:4 HEAT SINK:1 |
| NUT M3-1S SS41 ZN-PLAT | |
| WASHER SPRING M3 ZN-PLAT | TR:2 |
| RIVET BLIND &3.2 ALB | NAME PLATE MTG:2 |
| BODY MAIN EGI T1.0 US COATING | |
| HOLDER(ANT MTG)SPTE 29X35XT0.3 NI-PLAT | |
| CORD STOPPER P.P BLK | |
| ESD PROTECTOR CUP T0.05 (TRC-499) | |
| HEAT SINK ALP3 T2 | IC MTG |
| HEAT SINK ALP3 T2 | |
| SHIELD HOUSHING SPTE T0.3 | |
| NAME PLATE ALP3 40X20XT0.4 (7ULTRA-A) | |
| MIC ASS'Y | |
| DISK CERAMIC 0.001UF DD330F102Z 50V | C959 |
| MIC CONDENSER KUC4023-010010 | |
| CURD CURLED 3CON 1SH 300MM BLK(KSK-23059) | |
| CONNECTOR PLUG SW-1461 | |
| WIRE 1007 AWG 24 11/0.16 WHT | MIC(-)---SW |
| SW PUSH SPS-9522 | |
| (-)SECURING SCREW M6X8 (P:1) ABS BLK | ACCESSORY |
| (+)TAPPING SCREW(PH)T3X8-2S (+)PH ZN-PLAT | ACCESSORY |
| (+)TAPPING SCREW(TH)T5X12-1S (+)TH ZN-PLAT | ACCESSORY |
| (+)WOOD SCREW (R+FH)2.7X18-1S (+)R+FH NI-PLAT | COVER MTG:3 |
| WASHER 7X25X1.5T BLK RUBBER | ACCESSORY |
| WASHER(LOCK"B"TYPE) M3 "B"ZN-PLAT | ACCESSORY |
| ZN-PLAT | ACCESSORY |
| (+)PLUS SCREW(PH)3X10(+)PH ZN-PLAT | HOLDER MTG |
| COVER BOTTOM ABS 94HB BLK | |
| COVER UPPER(MIC)ABS 94HB BLK | |
| BRACKET (MIC)SPC 58X41XT1 CR-PLAT | |
| BRACKET(SET)SPC T1.5 BLK-SPRAY PICA | |
| HOLDER(MIC)PC BLK | |
| PLATE WEIGHT SPC 36X24XT3 ZN-PLAT | |
| KNOB(LEVER)ABS 94HB GRAY | |
| WIRE CLAMP (CORD)NYLON | |
| HOLDER(MIC) RUBB.(UL)BLK | |
| BOX MIC SW1S 222(W)X70(D)X52(H) | |
| POLYBAG P.P 100X100XT0.05 | ACCESSORY |
| POLYBAG P.P 100X200XT0.05 | |
| MAIN PCB AUTO ASS'Y | |
| FILM RESISTOR 100 1/ 8W 5% ST | R410.513.707.709 |
| FILM RESISTOR 1K 1/ 8W 5% ST | R413.414.901 |
| FILM RESISTOR 10K 1/ 8W 5% ST | R399.411.431. 502.508.515.964 |
| FILM RESISTOR 100K 1/ 8W 5% ST | R404 |
| FILM RESISTOR 1.2K 1/ 8W 5% ST | R518 |
| FILM RESISTOR 150 1/ 8W 5% ST | R951-957 |
| FILM RESISTOR 150K 1/ 8W 5% ST | R701 |
| FILM RESISTOR 180 1/ 8W 5% ST | R962 |
| FILM RESISTOR 1.8K 1/ 8W 5% ST | R420 |
| FILM RESISTOR 22 1/ 8W 5% ST | R511 |
| FILM RESISTOR 2.2K 1/ 8W 5% ST | R401.402.403.408.963 |
| FILM RESISTOR 22K 1/ 8W 5% ST | R967 |
| FILM RESISTOR 2.2 1/ 8W 5% ST | R711 |
| FILM RESISTOR 270 1/ 8W 5% ST | R501 |
| FILM RESISTOR 2.7K 1/ 8W 5% ST | R426.959 |
| FILM RESISTOR 27K 1/ 8W 5% ST | R430 |
| FILM RESISTOR 270K 1/ 8W 5% ST | R428.516 |
| FILM RESISTOR 3.3K 1/ 8W 5% ST | R407.708 |
| FILM RESISTOR 390 1/ 8W 5% ST | R510.702 |
| FILM RESISTOR 3.9K 1/ 8W 5% ST | R406 |
| FILM RESISTOR 47 1/ 8W 5% ST | R425.902 |
| FILM RESISTOR 470 1/ 8W 5% ST | R512 |
| FILM RESISTOR 4.7K 1/ 8W 5% ST | R503.703.704. 705.960 |
| FILM RESISTOR 47K 1/ 8W 5% ST | R961 |
| FILM RESISTOR 470K 1/ 8W 5% ST | R400 |
| FILM RESISTOR 560 1/ 8W 5% ST | R504 |
| FILM RESISTOR 5.6K 1/ 8W 5% ST | R405.409 |
| FILM RESISTOR 68 1/ 8W 5% ST | R706 |
| FILM RESISTOR 6.8K 1/ 8W 5% ST | R517 |
| FILM RESISTOR 15K 1/ 8W 2% ST | R412 |
| AXIAL CERAMIC 0.001UF UP050B102MK 50V | C404.426.427. 950.953.954 |
| AXIAL CERAMIC 0.01UF EP050Y103MN 16V | C402.425.501. 504.508.518.520. |
| AXIAL CERAMIC 0.0022UF EP050X222MN 16V | C410 |
| AXIAL CERAMIC 0.022UF RH050F 223Z 50V | C406.408.521.705.905 |
| AXIAL CERAMIC 220PF UP050B221K 50V | C413.716 |
| DIODE ZENER 1N5239B 9.1V 0.5W (DO-35) | D504 |
| DIODE ZENER 1N5231B 5.1V 0.5W (DO-35) | D501 |
| DIODE 1N4148(R.L) | D405.502.503.902.903 |
| DIODE RECTIFIER 1N4004T/R 400V 1A (DO-41) | D404.701 |
| COIL AXIAL 2.2UH:LAL03TB2R2M | RFC704 |
| COIL AXIAL 6.8UH:LAL03TB6R8K | RFC509.706 |
| COIL AXIAL 0.39UH:LAL02TBR39K | RFC701 |
| MAIN PCB MANUAL ASSY | |
| METAL OXIDE RESISTOR15 2W 5% ST | R427 |
| FILM RESISTOR 10 1/ 2W 5% ST MINI | R999 |
| FILM RESISTOR 4.7K 1/ 2W 5% ST MINI | R712 |
| RESISTOR SEMIFIXED 10KB RVM083H H 8DIA | RV1 |
| RESISTOR SEMIFIXED 2K RVM083H | RV2 |
| ELECT CAPACITOR 0.1UF 50V 20% 5X11 | C403.956 |
| ELECT CAPACITOR 10UF 16V 20% 5X11 | C417.503.902 |
| ELECT CAPACITOR 100UF 16V 20% 8X11 | C424 |
| ELECT CAPACITOR 10UF 16V 20% 4X7 | C411 |
| ELECT CAPACITOR 1000UF 16V 20% 12X16 | C423 |
| ELECT CAPACITOR 2.2UF 50V 20% 5X11 | C707 |
| ELECT CAPACITOR 220UF 16V 20% 10X12 | C422.514 |
| ELECT CAPACITOR 3.3UF 50V 20% 5X11 | C416.421 |
| ELECT CAPACITOR 33UF 16V 20% 5X11 | C407.412.415 |
| ELECT CAPACITOR 47UF 16V 20% 6X11 | C430.515 |
| ELECT CAPACITOR 470UF 16V 20% 10X12 | C502.510 |
| DISK CERAMIC 0.01UF HIK(B)F 103 50V | C721.722.723 |
| DISK CERAMIC 0.022UF F 223Z 50V | C711.714 |
| DISK CERAMIC 0.047UF X 473M 50V | C414.418 |
| AXIAL CERAMIC 0.047UF SA105E473MAA 50V | C405 |
| NPO100D 50V | |
| DISK CERAMIC 100PF NPO101K 50V | C712.718.999 |
| DISK CERAMIC 12PF NPO120K 50V | C513.903 |
| DISK CERAMIC 150PF SL 151K 50V | C715 |
| DISK CERAMIC 270PF SL 271K 50V | C420 |
| DISK CERAMIC 330PF SL 331K 50V | C717 |
| DISK CERAMIC 39PF NPO390K 50V | C704 |
| DISK CERAMIC 4PF NPO040D 50V | C706 |
| DISK CERAMIC 470PF SL 471K 50V | C713 |
| DISK CERAMIC 5PF NPO050D 50V | C506 |
| DISK CERAMIC 82PF NPO820K 50V | C708 |
| DIP TANTALUM 1UF 489D105X0025A125V | C957.958 |
| DIP TRIMMER 20PF 6DIA CVN | CT1 |
| TRANSISTOR KTC3194(O) | Q701.702 |
| TRANSISTOR KTC3198(GR) | Q400.401.505.507 |
| TRANSISTOR KTA1266(GR) | Q402.501.502. 503.506 |
| TRANSISTOR KTC1006 (TO-92L) | Q703 |
| I.C C5122A1P | IC501 |
| DIODE GE 1N60 | D402.403 |
| CRYSTAL HC18U 10.240M 30PM | X1 |
| FILTER CERAMIC LTU455HT | CF2 |
| FILTER CERAMIC SK107M4-AC-20 | CF1 |
| TRASNFORMER CHOKE EI-19 | CH1 |
| TRANSFORMER POWER EI-24 | T1 |
| COIL RF CHOKE 0.8UH SPRING | RFC401 |
| COIL SPRING 5X0.6X13.5T:R | RFC709 |
| COIL SPRING 3.4X0.55X8.5T:R | RFC705 |
| COIL RF CHOKE 10UH 10% | RFC707 |
| COIL IFT 455KHZ-A | L902 |
| COIL IFT 455KHZ-B | L903 |
| COIL 27MHZ RX ANT | L901 |
| COIL VCO | L501 |
| COIL RF PRE AMP A TX27MHZ | L701.702 |
| P.C.B MAIN 150 X121.5X1.6 94HB1/0 | |
| MAIN PCB SMD ASS'Y | |
| F AMP MODULE ASS'Y | |
| CHIP RESISTOR 0 1/10W 5% T 2012 | R200.219 |
| CHIP RESISTOR 100 1/10W 5% T 2012 | R203 |
| CHIP RESISTOR 1K 1/10W 5% T 2012 | R209 |
| CHIP RESISTOR 10K 1/10W 5% T 2012 | R207 |
| CHIP RESISTOR 12K 1/10W 5% T 2012 | R211 |
| CHIP RESISTOR 15K 1/10W 5% T 2012 | R218 |
| CHIP RESISTOR 150K 1/10W 5% T 2012 | R205 |
| CHIP RESISTOR 1.8K 1/10W 5% T 2012 | R206 |
| CHIP RESISTOR 220 1/10W 5% T 2012 | R212 |
| CHIP RESISTOR 22K 1/10W 5% T 2012 | R213 |
| CHIP RESISTOR 3.3K 1/10W 5% T 2012 | R210 |
| CHIP RESISTOR 33K 1/10W 5% T 2012 | R217 |
| CHIP RESISTOR 3.9K 1/10W 5% T 2012 | R202 |
| CHIP RESISTOR 470 1/10W 5% T 2012 | R204.208 |
| CHIP RESISTOR 47K 1/10W 5% T 2012 | R214.216 |
| CHIP RESISTOR 560 1/10W 5% T 2012 | R201 |
| CHIP RESISTOR 82K 1/10W 5% T 2012 | R215 |
| ELECT CAPACITOR 1UF 50V 20% 4X7 | C209 |
| ELECT CAPACITOR 10UF 16V 20% 4X7 | C204 |
| CHIP CERAMIC 0.001UF CM21 X7R102K 50V AT | C206 |
| CHIP CERAMIC 0.01UF CM21 X7R103K 50V AT | C201.203 |
| CHIP CERAMIC 0.047UF CM21 X7R473K 50V AT | C202.205.207.208 |
| TRANSISTOR KTA1504SY(SOT-23) | Q204 |
| TRANSISTOR KTC3880SY(SOT-23) | Q201.202.203 |
| DIODE GE 1N60 | D201 |
| P.C.B IF MODULE 44X16.88X1.6 94HB1/1 | |
| VCO MODULE ASS'Y | |
| CHIP RESISTOR 0 1/10W 5% T 2012 | R600.609 |
| CHIP RESISTOR 10K 1/10W 5% T 2012 | R606.607 |
| CHIP RESISTOR 120K 1/10W 5% T 2012 | R603 |
| CHIP RESISTOR 22K 1/10W 5% T 2012 | R608 |
| CHIP RESISTOR 220K 1/10W 5% T 2012 | R604 |
| CHIP RESISTOR 2.7K 1/10W 5% T 2012 | R605 |
| CHIP RESISTOR 47 1/10W 5% T 2012 | R601 |
| CHIP RESISTOR 820 1/10W 5% T 2012 | R602 |
| CHIP CERAMIC 0.01UF CM21 X7R103K 50V AT | C601.610.611 |
| CHIP CERAMIC 120PF CM21 CG 121J 50V AT | C608 |
| CHIP CERAMIC 18PF CM21 CG 180J 50V AT | C602 |
| CHIP CERAMIC 22PF CM21 CG 220J 50V AT | C603 |
| CHIP CERAMIC 220PF CM21 CG 221J 50V AT | C607 |
| CHIP CERAMIC 27PF CM21CG 270J 50V AT | C609 |
| CHIP CERAMIC 33PF CM21 CG 330J 50V AT | C606 |
| CHIP CERAMIC 47PF CM21 CG 470J 50V AT | C605 |
| TRANSISTOR KTC3875SY | Q602 |
| TRANSISTOR KTC3880SY(SOT-23) | Q601.603 |
| DIODE VARICAP LV2209 | D601 |
| P.C.B VCO MODULE 30.7 X16.88X1.6 94HB1/1 | |
| LOW PASS FILTER MODU | |
| CHIP CERAMIC 220PF CM21 CG 221J 50V AT | C801.805 |
| CHIP CERAMIC 470PF CM21 CG 471J 50V AT | C802.803 |
| COIL SPRING 3.4X0.55X6.5T:R | L802 |
| COIL SPRING 3.4X0.55X7.5T:R | L803 |
| COIL SPRING 3.4X0.55X8.5T:R | L804 |
| P.C.B LPF MODULE 15.39X40.5 X1.6 94HB1/1 | |
| 4.5T SPRIN.COIL ASSY | L801 |
| COIL SPRING 3.4X0.55X4.5T:R | |
| CORE 1108-KA-058 M9DTH3.7X6 | |
| RF AMP H/H MODULE | |
| CHIP RESISTOR 0 1/10W 5% T 2012 | |
| CHIP RESISTOR 100 1/10W 5% T 2012 | R107 |
| CHIP RESISTOR 10K 1/10W 5% T 2012 | R106.108 |
| CHIP RESISTOR 18 1/10W 5% T 2012 | R104 |
| CHIP RESISTOR 330 1/10W 5% T 2012 | R103 |
| CHIP RESISTOR 33K 1/10W 5% T 2012 | R105 |
| CHIP RESISTOR 470 1/10W 5% T 2012 | R109.110 |
| CHIP CERAMIC 0.01UF CM21 X7R103K 50V AT | C112 |
| CHIP CERAMIC 150PF CM21 CG 151J 50V AT | C109 |
| CHIP CERAMIC 220PF CM21 CG 221J 50V AT | C108 |
| CHIP CERAMIC 33PF CM21 CG 330J 50V AT | C102 |
| CHIP CERAMIC 47PF CM21 CG 470J 50V AT | C104 |
| CHIP CERAMIC 680PF CM21 CG 681J 50V AT | C114 |
| TRANSISTOR KTC3880SY (SOT-23) | Q102.103 |
| DIODE SI CHIP KDS226 (SOT-23) | D101 |
| P.C.B RF MODULE 39.25X16.88X1.6 94HB1/1 | |
| 6.5T SPRIN.COIL ASSY | L102.104 |
| COIL SPRING 3.4X0.55X6.5T:R | |
| CORE 1108-KA-058 M9DTH3.7X6 | |
| PACKING ASS'Y | |
| BOX TRAY SW1S 222(W)X127(D)X52(H) | |
| BOX INNER SW1S 224(W)X220(D)X54(H) | |
| BOX OUT DW1E 355(W)X238(D)X206(H) | |
| POLYBAG P.P 200X300XT0.05 | SET:1 MANUAL:1 |
| MANUAL OWNER'S MANUAL OWNER'S | |
| CARD REGISTRATION ARTPAPER 158X342 | |
| CARD BOARD | |
| CB RULE | |
| SCHEMATIC DIAGRAM WOODFREEPAPER 420X297 | |
| CARD INFORMATION WOODFREEPAPER 98.5X150 | |
| LABEL CAUTION | |
| LABEL FCC POLYESTER 67X10XT0.05 | |
| SUB PCB ASS'Y | |
| FILM RESISTOR 10K 1/ 8W 5% ST | R950 |
| LED LAMP SLB55VR3 RED 3 V 60MW | LED1 |
| LED DISPLAY UL-G233G-13 GRN | |
| SW TACT SAT-1102-2 | SW3.4 |
| SUB MATERIAL ASS'Y | |
| TUBE UL/CSA KEIT-30 AWG 12 (2&) CLEAR VINYL | |
| TUBE UL/CSA KEIT-30 AWG 2 (6.5&) CLEAR VINYL | |
| TUBE HIS 11M/M | |
| TUBE EMPIRE 1& | |
| PE SCOTCH 15M/M (0.015X20M) | |
| TAPE PACKING OPP (0.05X50M) | |
| TAPE PACKING O.P.P.(0.05X25M) IVORY | |
| SOLDER BAR 63:37 | |
| SOLDER ROSIN CO.WIRE60:40 0.04"-0.05" | |
| FLUX ROSIN | |
| THINNER FOR FLUX | |
| SILICON GREASE YG-6111 OR XG-6111 | |
| STAVILIZER MATERIAL | |
| BOND #201 | |
| COMPOUND #1200 500GR | |

Mail Box Company, the bill of materials would be quite simple. Basically it involves only one direct material—wood.

To determine the direct material quantity standard for the Tree Top Mail Box Company using practical standards, Ali measured the wood included in a single mail box. He determined that each mail box was made of 16 feet of $1/4 \times 2$ inch pine. Then he examined the scrap wood from the prior week's production and estimated that the amount of wood to make a single mail box should be increased by 35 percent to allow for scrap due to knots and other expected defects in the wood. Accordingly, Tree Top adopted a practical direct material quantity standard of 21.6 feet (16 feet $\times$ 1.35% = 21.6 feet) per mail box.

## Direct Material Price Standard

**direct material price standard** The anticipated cost for each item of direct material used in the manufacture of a product.

In addition to the amount of direct material used, the price per measure of direct material will affect the total cost of direct material. The **direct material price standard** is the anticipated cost for each item of direct material used in the manufacture of a product. For the plastic used to make golf balls, the direct material price standard would be the cost per pound of plastic. For wire used in a CD player, the direct material price standard would be the cost per foot of wire. Notice that the direct material price standard reflects a price per measure of direct material (that is, per foot of wire), *not* per unit of production (such as, per CD player).

Because purchasing agents are generally knowledgeable about the price paid for direct material, they are likely to be key players in determining direct material price standards. Purchasing agents would also gather historical direct material price information, making necessary adjustments for any anticipated price changes.

As indicated, Tree Top uses wood that measures $1/4 \times 2$ inches. The direct material price standard is expressed as an amount per foot of this wood. The Tree Top Mail Box Company has no purchasing agent, so Ali shopped around and found that good-quality pine wood could be purchased for $0.70 per 8 foot length. Also, Ali determined that no price increases were expected during the year. Accordingly, Tree Top established a standard price per foot of wood of $0.0875 ($0.70 / 8 feet = $0.0875) per foot.

Although only a single direct material is used to make Tree Top's mail boxes, most products require the use of many different raw materials. Separate standards must be established for each direct material used in production. If production required the use of material A, material B, and material C, separate quantity and price standards must be prepared for each.

Once a manufacturer knows the direct material quantity standard and the direct material price standard, the standard cost for direct material per unit of production can be determined. For Tree Top, the standard cost for direct material of $1.89 is calculated by multiplying the standard quantity of 21.60 feet by the standard price of $0.0875, as shown.

| Standard Quantity | | Standard Price | | Standard Direct Material Cost Per Unit |
|---|---|---|---|---|
| 21.60 Feet | $\times$ | $0.0875 | = | $1.89 |

# SETTING DIRECT LABOR STANDARDS

As with direct material, setting direct labor standards involves two important considerations: the number of direct labor hours and the wage rate per hour.

## Direct Labor Efficiency Standard

**direct labor efficiency standard** The estimated number of direct labor hours required to produce a single unit of product.

The estimated number of direct labor hours required to produce a single unit of product is called the **direct labor efficiency standard.** When the direct labor force works efficiently, labor hours are kept to a minimum. Conversely, too many hours of direct labor relative to production would indicate labor inefficiency. The standard for the number of direct labor hours could be called the direct labor quantity standard, or the direct labor hours standard, but neither of these terms sounds quite right, which explains why this standard has come to be known as the direct labor efficiency standard.

The production supervisors and other production employees are often key players in establishing direct labor efficiency standards. Historical information about direct labor and production volumes are used to help establish an appropriate standard for the number of direct labor hours per unit of production. Also, information from industrial engineers, such as the results of time-and-motion studies, may be helpful in determining the amount of direct labor time it should take to efficiently produce a unit of product.

Tree Top's founders wanted to select a standard that would help encourage them to make as many mail boxes as possible, but allow them to work at a quick, yet reasonable pace. After reviewing their activities for October, the three agreed that the standard hours allowed for a single unit of production should be 0.6 hours (36 minutes). This time, then, became Tree Top's labor efficiency standard.

## Direct Labor Rate Standard

**direct labor rate standard**
The planned hourly wage paid to production workers.

The **direct labor rate standard** is the planned hourly wage paid to production workers. The personnel manager is often a key player in determining the direct labor rate standard. Sometimes direct labor rates are established through collective bargaining or other employment agreements. Other times a less formal procedure is used to set hourly pay rates. In either case, historical information coupled with information regarding anticipated pay rate changes establishes the direct labor rate standard. Often, companies compute an expected average hourly direct labor rate, which is used as the plant-wide direct labor rate standard. For Tree Top, Ali, Maria, and Bill agreed that, based on their original plan, the direct labor rate standard of $10 per hour should be used.

Once a company knows the direct labor efficiency standard and the direct labor rate standard, the standard labor cost per unit of production can be determined. In the case of Tree Top, based on the direct labor efficiency standard of 0.6 hours and the direct labor rate standard of $10 per direct labor hour, the standard labor cost to make a single mail box is $6, shown as follows:

| Direct Labor Efficiency Standard | × | Direct Labor Rate Standard (Per Hour) | = | Standard Direct Labor Cost Per Unit |
|---|---|---|---|---|
| 0.6 Hours | × | $10 Per Hour | = | $6 |

## Setting Variable Manufacturing Overhead Standards

Recall that manufacturing overhead includes all production costs that are not part of direct materials or direct labor. Manufacturing overhead includes costs of operating the factory such as the cost of rent, insurance, depreciation, supplies, taxes, raw materials handling, and so forth. Recall also that costs can be classified as either fixed or variable. Fixed costs are those that remain constant in total, even as activity changes. Variable costs, in contrast, increase in total as activity changes. Therefore, variable manufacturing overhead would include those manufacturing overhead costs that increase in total as production increases.

In Chapter 3, we saw that manufacturing overhead was often allocated to production based on direct labor hours, direct labor cost, machine hours, or some other allocation base. In this section, we illustrate how a standard cost system works when manufacturing overhead is allocated using direct labor hours as the allocation base. Although the specific calculations would be somewhat different, standard costing can be used for other allocation bases as well.

To set standards for variable manufacturing overhead, managers must first estimate variable manufacturing overhead costs. Once they estimate total variable manufacturing overhead, they can then determine a cost per direct labor hour, or per unit of some other allocation base.

For Tree Top Mail Box Company, variable manufacturing overhead cost includes utilities and miscellaneous variable cost, as shown on October's income statement presented in Exhibit 9–4. The miscellaneous variable cost includes the cost of indirect material such as glue, small nails, and wood stain. Based on October's results, Ali, Maria, and Bill estimated that variable manufacturing overhead cost would be about $63. The $63 includes $33 for utilities and $30 for miscellaneous variable cost. Tree Top planned to allocate this variable overhead cost to production based on direct labor hours.

## The Standard Variable Manufacturing Overhead Rate

**standard variable manufacturing overhead rate** The rate used to apply variable manufacturing overhead to units of manufactured product.

The rate used to apply variable manufacturing overhead to units of product is known as the **standard variable manufacturing overhead rate.** As stated, Ali, Maria, and Bill expected to work about 60 hours each, or a total of 180 direct labor hours per month. Based on the planned variable manufacturing overhead cost of $63 and 180 estimated direct labor hours, we compute a standard variable overhead rate of $0.35 by dividing the $63 budgeted variable manufacturing overhead by the 180 estimated direct labor hours, as follows:

| Budgeted Variable Manufacturing Overhead | ÷ | Budgeted Direct Labor Hours | = | Standard Variable Manufacturing Overhead Rate |
|---|---|---|---|---|
| $63 | ÷ | 180 Hours | = | $0.35 Per Hour |

When the variable manufacturing overhead allocation is based on direct labor hours, once the direct labor efficiency standard and the standard variable manufacturing overhead rate per direct labor hour have been determined, the standard variable manufacturing overhead cost per unit can be determined. The standard variable manufacturing overhead cost to build a single unit of production is calculated by multiplying the direct labor efficiency standard (the estimated direct labor hours per unit) by the standard variable manufacturing overhead rate. For Tree Top, standard cost per unit for variable manufacturing overhead is $0.21, determined as follows:

| Standard Direct Labor Hours Allowed | × | Standard Variable Manufacturing Overhead Rate | = | Standard Variable Mfg Overhead Cost Per Unit |
|---|---|---|---|---|
| 0.6 Hours | × | $0.35 Per Hour | = | $0.21 |

## Fixed Manufacturing Overhead Standards

Unlike variable manufacturing overhead cost, which changes in total as production increases or decreases, fixed manufacturing overhead cost remains constant in total regardless of how many units are produced.

To set the fixed manufacturing overhead standards, manufacturers must first estimate the total cost of fixed manufacturing overhead. For Tree Top Mail Box Company, this amount consists of rent of $200 per month and monthly depreciation of $25 for the equipment used to make the mail boxes. Fixed manufacturing overhead then totals $225 per month ($200 + $25 = $225).

## Standard Fixed Manufacturing Overhead Rate

**standard fixed manufacturing overhead rate** The rate used to apply fixed manufacturing overhead to units of manufactured product.

As with variable manufacturing overhead, fixed manufacturing overhead can be allocated to production based on units of production, direct labor hours, direct labor dollars, machine hours, or some other allocation base. The rate used to apply fixed manufacturing overhead to units of product is known as the **standard fixed manufacturing overhead rate.**

Our illustration assumes that fixed manufacturing overhead is allocated to production based on direct labor hours. In such a case, the standard fixed manufacturing overhead rate is determined by dividing the total estimated fixed manufacturing overhead cost by the total estimated direct labor hours. In the case of Tree Top Mail Box Company, the standard fixed manufacturing overhead rate of $1.25 per direct labor hour is calculated by dividing the budgeted fixed manufacturing overhead cost of $225 by the budgeted direct labor hours of 180 as shown here:

| Budgeted Fixed Mfg Overhead | ÷ | Budgeted Direct Labor Hours | = | Standard Fixed Mfg Overhead Rate |
|---|---|---|---|---|
| $225 | ÷ | 180 Hours | = | $1.25 |

We calculate the standard fixed manufacturing overhead cost to build a single unit of product by multiplying the direct labor efficiency standard per unit by the standard fixed manufacturing overhead rate. For Tree Top, standard cost per unit for fixed manufacturing overhead is $0.75, determined as follows:

| Standard Direct Labor Hours Allowed | × | Standard Fixed Mfg Overhead Rate | = | Standard Fixed Mfg Overhead Cost Per Unit |
|---|---|---|---|---|
| 0.6 Hours | × | $1.25 Per Hour | = | $0.75 |

**Total Standard Cost Per Unit** Once standards have been set for direct material, direct labor, variable manufacturing overhead, and fixed manufacturing overhead, the total standard cost per unit can be calculated. This amount reflects how much it *should* cost to produce a unit of product. The standard cost per unit represents a useful estimate that can be helpful for planning and setting selling prices. For Tree Top, the total standard cost per mail box is $8.85 as shown in Exhibit 9–6.

**Exhibit 9–6**
Total Standard Cost Per Mail Box Built

| | |
|---|---|
| Standard Direct Material Cost Per Mail Box | $1.89 |
| Standard Direct Labor Cost Per Mail Box | 6.00 |
| Standard Variable Manufacturing Overhead Cost Per Mail Box | .21 |
| Standard Fixed Manufacturing Overhead Cost Per Mail Box | .75 |
| Total Standard Cost Per Mail Box | $8.85 |

As you might imagine, the *actual* cost of producing an item is almost never exactly the same as the *standard* cost. When actual cost exceeds standard cost, management should take steps to determine the cause of the variance, and, if necessary, take corrective action.

Actual total production cost that exceeds the standard may indicate that a general problem exists, but it provides almost no information that can help managers focus on the true cause of the problem. Managers need access to information that can be used to isolate and address specific cost problems.

The next sections show how managers use standard costing to isolate specific problems for each production cost category.

# VARIANCE ANALYSIS

Standard costs can help control costs by serving as benchmarks to compare with actual production costs. To use standard costing as a control device, managers compare *standard costs* to *actual costs* to see whether a variance exists. Instead of calculating a single variance for total production cost, they make variances specific enough to isolate a particular production process problem. In this section we examine how detailed standard costs variances are calculated for direct material, direct labor, variable manufacturing overhead, and fixed manufacturing overhead. We will walk through the calculations for each standard cost variance using Tree Top Mail Box Company as an example.

Unfortunately for Tree Top, November was not nearly as successful as October. The company produced and sold only 225 mail boxes in spite of demand for many more. The income statement for the month of November appears in Exhibit 9–7.

**Exhibit 9–7**
Tree Top's November 2001 Income Statement

| TREE TOP MAIL BOX COMPANY | | |
|---|---:|---:|
| **Income Statement** | | |
| **For the Month Ended November 30, 2001** | | |
| Sales (225 mail boxes at $10 each) | | $2,250 |
| Less Expenses | | |
| Direct Material (6,000 feet of wood) | $ 477 | |
| Direct Labor (162 hours at $10.50 per hr) | 1,701 | |
| Rent | 200 | |
| Utilities (all variable) | 50 | |
| Miscellaneous Variable Costs | 90 | |
| Depreciation | 25 | 2,543 |
| Net Income | | $ (293) |

November's loss disturbed Ali, Maria, and Bill because they had spent nearly as much time at the shop as in October, but produced far fewer mail boxes. The question is, what changes should Tree Top make to get the company back on track? We can answer this question once we have calculated the variances and examined their causes.

To calculate standard cost variances, we use the standard costs discussed in the preceding sections, and compare them with Tree Top's actual performance. Actual performance data are obtained from various sources, including company reports and files. In our Tree Top Mail Box Company example, we have included the key details in November's income statement, presented in Exhibit 9–7.

## Direct Materials Variances

Direct material variances can be used to answer three important questions. (1) Did the company use more or less direct material than it should have, based on the standards set? (2) Did the company pay more or less than it should have when the direct material was purchased from the supplier based on the standards set? (3) What was the cost impact of these quantity and price differences?

**direct material quantity variance** A measure of the over- or underconsumption of direct material for the number of units actually manufactured.

**direct material usage variance** Another name for the *direct material quantity variance.*

## Direct Material Quantity Variance

The **direct material quantity variance,** sometimes called the **direct material usage variance,** is a measure of the overconsumption or underconsumption of direct material for the number of units actually manufactured. It informs management whether too much or too little direct material is used in the manufacturing process based on the standards. The direct material quantity variance is the difference between the standard quantity and the actual quantity of direct materials used. We follow three steps to calculate the direct material quantity variances. First, we calculate the standard quantity of direct material allowed for actual production. Second, we calculate the variance in units of direct material. Finally, we calculate the variance in dollars.

*Step 1:* Calculate the standard quantity of direct material allowed for actual production.

The standard quantity of direct material allowed is the amount needed for actual production, according to the standard. It is the amount *allowed* for *actual* production. To calculate this amount, we determine how much direct material should have been used according to the standard to make the units actually produced.

Recall that Tree Top produced 225 mail boxes in November. To determine the quantity of the wood that *should* have been used to make 225 mail boxes, we multiply the direct material quantity standard (21.60 feet per unit) by the number of mail boxes produced (225). For Tree Top, the standard quantity of direct material allowed for the actual production of 225 mail boxes is 4,860 feet, as shown here:

| Standard Quantity Per Unit | | Number of Units Produced | | Standard Quantity of Direct Material Allowed |
|---|---|---|---|---|
| 21.60 Feet | × | 225 Units | = | 4,860 Feet |

We see from the calculations that 4,860 feet of wood is the standard direct material quantity allowed for the units produced—the direct material quantity that *should* have been used based on the number of units *actually* produced.

*Step 2:* Calculate the direct material quantity variance in units of direct material.

We calculate the direct material quantity variance in units of direct material by subtracting the actual quantity of direct material used from the standard quantity of direct material allowed. For Tree Top Mail Box Company, the direct material quantity variance in feet is determined by comparing the quantity of wood it *should* have taken to make the 225 mail boxes (determined in step 1) to the quantity of wood it *actually* took to make the mail boxes (the actual quantity).

## Discussion Question

**9-3.** If the actual amount of wood used was more than the standard quantity of wood, do you think the direct material quantity variance would be favorable or unfavorable? Explain your reasoning.

To use standard costing, a manufacturer must maintain a record of the quantity of direct material used in production. In the case of Tree Top, this information is found in the income statement as presented in Exhibit 9–7. A review of that income statement shows that the actual quantity of direct material Tree Top used to make the 225 mail boxes in November was 6,000 feet of wood. Often the quantity of material used in production differs from the quantity of material purchased. For this calculation it is important to remember to use the quantity of material used, not the quantity purchased.

Tree Top's direct material quantity variance is calculated by finding the difference between the standard quantity of direct material allowed and the quantity of direct material used in production. In this case the variance is 1,140 unfavorable, as calculated here:

| Standard Quantity Allowed for Production | − | Actual Quantity Used | = | Quantity Variance in Feet |
|---|---|---|---|---|
| 4,860 Feet | − | 6,000 Feet | = | 1,140 Unfavorable |

We can see from the presentation that Ali, Maria, and Bill used 1,140 more feet of wood than the standard allowed to make the 225 mail boxes. Does this overuse of direct material really matter? Even if the direct material quantity variance in feet is 1,140 unfavorable, it *may* represent an insignificant dollar amount. To evaluate whether this variance is worthy of attention, we need to assign a dollar amount.

*Step 3:* Calculate the direct material quantity variance in dollars.

To avoid contaminating the quantity variance with problems relating to the actual price paid for material, the dollar amount assigned to the direct material quantity variance is based on the standard direct material price, not the actual price. Tree Top's direct material quantity variance in dollars is $99.75. This amount is calculated by multiplying the direct material quantity variance (1,140 feet) by the direct material standard price of $0.0875, as follows:

| Quantity Variance in Units of Direct Material (Feet) | × | Standard Price Per Unit of Direct Material (Feet) | = | Quantity Variance in Dollars |
|---|---|---|---|---|
| 1,140 Unfavorable | × | $0.0875 | = | $99.75 Unfavorable |

The direct materials quantity variance in dollars provides valuable information about the cost of using too much direct material to make the mail boxes. Now that a dollar amount has been assigned to the variance, we can evaluate its importance and devote the amount of management attention that is appropriate.

## Discussion Questions

9–4. Based on Tree Top Mail Box Company's quantity variance, do you think that Ali, Maria, and Bill need to examine reasons for using so much wood? Explain your reasoning.

9–5. If the dollar amount of a variance is insignificant, does the variance information help Tree Top's management team determine where it should focus attention? Explain.

9–6. If there had been no variance, would this mean Tree Top used the appropriate amount of wood to build its mail boxes in November? Explain your reasoning.

We assume that only one direct material is used to make the mail boxes for Tree Top. In practice most products require several different direct materials, ranging from one to thousands, and a separate material quantity variance is computed for each direct material used. The logic and computations, however, are similar to those presented here.

Once the direct material quantity variance has been calculated, management can assess the situation and, if necessary, take corrective action. Generally, a quantity variance should be discussed with the individuals who are responsible for the amount of direct material used. The focus of the discussion should be on finding and eliminating the cause of the variance. In many companies, the person responsible for direct material consumption is the production supervisor, who would attempt to determine the cause of the variance and take steps to eliminate it.

## Direct Material Price Variance

The **direct material price variance** is a measure of the difference between the amount the company *planned* to pay for direct material and the amount it *actually* paid. This variance provides an indication of whether the price paid to suppliers for direct material compares favorably to the standard price. To find the direct material price variance we use a two-step process. First, we determine the amount that should have been paid for the direct material. Second, we calculate the dollar amount of the direct material variance.

*Step 1:* Determine the amount that should have been paid for the direct material purchased according to the standard price.

According to the detailed information on November's income statement, Tree Top Mail Box Company purchased 6,000 feet of wood. How much should the company have paid for the 6,000 feet of wood if it had been able to purchase it at the standard price? We determine this amount by multiplying the actual quantity of direct material purchased by the standard price. Often the quantity of material purchased differs from the quantity of material used in production. Which amount should we use? For this calculation remember to use the quantity of material purchased, not the quantity used in production.

| Actual Quantity Purchased | × | Direct Material Standard Price | = | Quantity Purchased Priced at Standard |
|---|---|---|---|---|
| 6,000 Feet | × | $0.0875 | = | $525 |

Our calculations show that, based on the standard price of $0.0875 per foot, the 6,000 feet of wood purchased should have cost $525.

*Step 2:* Calculate the dollar amount of the direct material price variance.

We calculate the dollar amount of the direct material price variance by subtracting the actual cost of direct material from the standard cost of the direct material purchased (determined in step 1). According to the detailed information on November's income statement, Tree Top purchased the 6,000 feet of wood for $477. By comparing the standard cost of $525 to the actual cost of $477, we determine that the price variance is $48 favorable.

| Quantity Purchased Priced at Standard | − | Actual Direct Material Cost | = | Direct Material Price Variance |
|---|---|---|---|---|
| $525 | − | $477 | = | $48 Favorable |

To review the calculations for the direct material price variance in dollars, we compare the amount the wood purchased *should* have cost, $525, to what the wood *actually* cost, $477, to determine the direct material price variance.

When a product requires the use of multiple direct materials, a separate material price variance is computed for each direct material used. The logic and computations, however, are similar to those presented here.

Once the direct material price variance has been calculated, management can assess the situation and, if necessary, take corrective action. In most manufacturing companies, direct material is purchased by purchasing agents working in the company's purchasing department. Therefore, direct material price variances are brought to the attention of the purchasing agent responsible for buying the particular direct material so that the price can be evaluated and corrective action taken when necessary.

In the case of Tree Top, the actual price paid for the wood was lower than the standard price, resulting in a favorable direct material price variance. It may seem that a favorable variance would not warrant investigation, but this is not always the case.

A significant favorable variance is worth examining for several reasons. First, repeated favorable variances may be an indication that the standard is too lax. Second, management should investigate the variance to see whether the techniques used to achieve the favorable variance can be used by other areas of the company to help reduce cost. Third, a favorable variance may have occurred because of a trade-off of some other value. For example, it might be achieved by purchasing direct material of a substandard quality.

Bill purchased the wood for Tree Top from the lumber company at a discounted price. The lumber company was able to offer the discount because another customer had refused the wood and the lumber company was overstocked. As it turned out, the wood had an unusually high number of knots and other blemishes. The substandard wood, then, may have caused the use of more direct material and direct labor than would have otherwise been required for production.

## Discussion Questions

**9-7.** How might the purchase of wood at a discount affect the direct material quantity variance?

**9-8.** If there had been no variance, would this mean Tree Top paid what it should have for the wood used to build its mail boxes in November? Explain your reasoning.

## Direct Labor Variances

Direct labor variances help managers answer three key questions. (1) Did it take more or fewer direct labor hours than it should have taken for the company to manufacture its products based on the standards set? (2) Was the company's hourly direct labor rate more or less than it should have been based on the standards set? (3) What was the cost impact of these differences in the number of direct labor hours and the hourly labor rate?

It may be helpful to consider some parallels between direct material and direct labor. Instead of using "quantities" and "prices" terms as for direct material, we use "hours" and "rates" with direct labor. In reality, only the descriptive words change, the meanings stay the same. The "quantity" of direct material is similar to the "hours" of direct labor. Likewise, the "price" per measure of direct material is similar to the "rate" per hour of direct labor. Because of these similarities, the steps and calculations of standard cost variances for direct labor are comparable to direct material variances.

**direct labor efficiency variance** A measure of the difference between the planned number of direct labor hours and the actual number of direct labor hours for the units actually manufactured.

## Direct Labor Efficiency Variance

The **direct labor efficiency variance** is a measure of the over- or underconsumption of direct labor for the number of units actually manufactured. In other words, the direct labor efficiency variance informs management whether too much or too little direct labor is used in the manufacturing process based on the standards. This variance is comparable to the direct material quantity variance. Both are used to evaluate the quantity of something used. In the case of the direct material quantity variance, the focus is on the quantity of direct material used. In the case of the direct labor efficiency variance, the focus is on the quantity of direct labor hours used.

We use three steps to calculate this variance. First, we find the standard number of direct labor hours allowed for production. Second, we determine the variance in hours. Finally, we calculate the variance in dollars.

*Step 1:* Calculate the standard number of direct labor hours allowed for actual production.

In this first step we determine the amount of direct labor time it *should* have taken to make all the units that were *actually* made during the period. According to the direct labor efficiency standard for Tree Top, it should have taken 0.6 hours (36 minutes) to make each mail box. Because 225 mail boxes were made in November, the total amount of direct labor hours should have been 135 hours (225 × 0.6 = 135).

*Step 2:* Calculate the direct labor efficiency variance in hours.

We compute the direct labor efficiency variance in hours by subtracting the standard direct labor hours allowed from the actual number of direct labor hours worked. According to information taken from Tree Top's November income statement presented in Exhibit 9–7, the actual number of direct labor hours used in November was 162. By comparing the standard hours allowed for the 225 mail boxes, 135 hours, to the actual direct labor hours, 162 hours, we see that the direct labor efficiency variance in hours is 27 hours unfavorable.

| Standard Direct Labor Hours Allowed | − | Actual Direct Labor Hours | = | Efficiency Variance in Hours |
|---|---|---|---|---|
| 135 Hours | − | 162 Hours | = | 27 Hours Unfavorable |

The variance between the standard and actual number of hours worked indicates that Tree Top's employees did not work very efficiently. If they had, they would have completed the 225 mail boxes in 135 hours, or maybe even less.

To grasp the true magnitude of the 27-hour unfavorable variance, we must assign a dollar amount.

*Step 3:* Calculate the direct labor efficiency variance in dollars.

To avoid contaminating the efficiency variance with problems relating to the actual labor rate, we calculate the direct labor efficiency variance in dollars by multiplying the variance in hours by the standard direct labor rate, not the actual labor rate. In the case of Tree Top, we multiply the 27 hour unfavorable direct labor efficiency variance by the standard direct labor rate of $10, shown as follows:

| Direct Labor Efficiency Variance in Hours | × | Standard Direct Labor Rate | = | Direct Labor Efficiency Variance in Dollars |
|---|---|---|---|---|
| 27 Hours | × | $10 | = | $270 Unfavorable |

Once the direct labor efficiency variance has been calculated, management can assess the variance and, if necessary, take corrective action. The plant manager would probably ask the production supervisor or production-line employees to help determine why the unfavorable variance occurred. Once the cause of the problem is found, corrective action can be taken.

Tree Top determined that substandard wood caused the unfavorable direct labor efficiency variance. To make mail boxes of sufficient quality, Ali, Maria, and Bill needed extra time to cut the knots and other blemishes from the wood. The solution to the variance problem is to purchase only good-quality wood in the future.

## Direct Labor Rate Variance

**direct labor rate variance**
A measure of the difference between the actual wage rate paid to employees and the direct labor rate standard.

The **direct labor rate variance** is a measure of the difference between the actual wage rate paid to employees and the direct labor rate standard. This variance shows the effect of unanticipated wage rate changes. The direct labor rate standard for the company is $10 per hour. As you will note by looking at the November income statement in Exhibit 9–7, each of the three owners received a 50 cent raise during November. So, for Tree Top, the direct labor rate variance will indicate added cost caused by the pay raises. We use a two-step process to calculate the direct labor rate variance. First, we find the amount the company should have paid for direct labor for the hours worked. Second, we determine the dollar amount of the direct labor rate variance.

*Step 1:* Determine the amount that should have been paid for the actual direct labor hours worked according to the direct labor rate standard.

In this step we determine how much the company should have paid for the direct labor hours actually worked, based on the direct labor rate standard. For Tree Top, the actual direct labor hours totaled 162 for November. By multiplying the 162 actual direct labor hours by the direct labor rate standard of $10, we determine that the company should have paid $1,620.

| Actual Direct Labor Hours | × | Direct Labor Rate Standard | = | Actual Direct Labor Hours at the Standard Rate |
|---|---|---|---|---|
| 162 Hours | × | $10 | = | $1,620 |

Once we determine what the company should have paid according to the standard, we can compare it to the amount actually paid to determine the direct labor rate variance.

*Step 2:* Calculate the dollar amount of the direct labor rate variance.

We compute the dollar amount of the direct labor rate variance by subtracting the actual cost of direct labor from the standard cost of the direct labor actually worked. The direct labor rate variance compares the amount the actual direct labor hours should have cost to the actual cost. In the case of Tree Top, we find that the actual direct labor cost for November was $1,701, as shown on the November income statement in Exhibit 9–7. Tree Top's labor hours at standard should have cost $1,620. When we compare actual labor cost ($1,701) to standard cost ($1,620), we find an unfavorable direct labor rate variance of $81, calculated as follows:

| Actual Direct Labor Hours at the Standard Rate | − | Actual Direct Labor Cost | = | Direct Labor Rate Variance |
|---|---|---|---|---|
| $1,620 | − | $1,701 | = | $81 Unfavorable |

The calculated variance is unfavorable because the actual labor cost is higher than the cost based on the standard rate. This $81 unfavorable variance provides useful information to Ali, Maria, and Bill about the effect of their $0.50 per hour raise.

# Discussion Questions

**9-9.** What effect did the $0.50 per hour pay raise have on November's profits?

**9-10.** In light of the financial problems that occurred in November, do you think Tree Top's owners should roll back the wage rate to $10 per hour? Explain your reasoning.

As with other variances, once the direct labor rate variance has been calculated, management can assess the variance and, if necessary, take corrective action. Direct labor rate variances are caused by labor rate changes that are unanticipated. Generally, when labor rates are contractually set or a result of collective bargaining with labor unions, labor rate changes are not unexpected. Accordingly, these labor rates are factored into the labor rate standard. A labor rate variance can be caused by an unexpected rate change of some kind, or perhaps an unanticipated change in the makeup of the labor force. For example, if the company retains more experienced workers and has fewer new workers, an unfavorable rate variance is likely because new employees generally begin their employment at a lower hourly wage than experienced employees.

In the case of Tree Top Mail Box Company, the November income statement shows that Ali, Maria, and Bill gave themselves an unplanned 50 cent per hour raise. Although no corrective action will likely be taken, the trio now knows how the raise affected profits.

The direct labor variances reveal that Ali, Maria, and Bill had two important problems in November regarding direct labor cost. First, it took 27 extra hours to make the 225 mail boxes. The extra 27 hours increased labor cost by $270. Second, the hourly wage paid to Ali, Maria, and Bill was higher than the planned $10 standard wage rate. This higher wage rate increased labor cost by $81. The total effect of these two direct labor problems is $351 unfavorable.

## Manufacturing Overhead Variances

Manufacturing overhead variances help managers answer two vital questions. (1) Did the company spend more or less on overhead items than it should have, based on the standards that were set? (2) Did the company utilize its production facility efficiently?

In this section we look at four different manufacturing overhead variances, two that deal with variable manufacturing overhead and two with fixed manufacturing overhead.

## Variable Manufacturing Overhead Efficiency Variance

**variable manufacturing overhead efficiency variance** A measure of the variable manufacturing overhead cost attributable to the difference between the planned and actual direct labor hours worked.

The **variable manufacturing overhead efficiency variance** is a measure of the variable manufacturing overhead cost attributable to the difference between the planned and actual direct labor hours worked. Surprisingly, this variance relates more to the efficiency of direct labor than anything else. While production workers work in the factory, they consume electricity as they use lights and air conditioning and operate machinery. They also use supplies and other factory resources that all are part of manufacturing overhead. So, as workers work longer, they use more factory resources. How much more? The variable factory overhead efficiency variance helps answer this question.

An unfavorable variable manufacturing overhead efficiency variance is a measure of the variable manufacturing overhead cost associated with the extra hours worked by direct labor. A direct relationship exists between the direct labor efficiency variance and the variable manufacturing overhead efficiency variance. Accordingly, if the direct labor efficiency variance is unfavorable, the variable manufacturing overhead efficiency variance will also be unfavorable. Likewise, if the direct labor efficiency variance is favorable, the variable manufacturing overhead efficiency variance will also be favorable.

The first two steps for calculating the variable manufacturing overhead efficiency variance are the same as those for determining the direct labor efficiency variance. These steps are to find the standard number of direct labor hours allowed for actual production and then to calculate the direct labor efficiency variance in hours.

Assuming the direct labor efficiency variance has been calculated, we review the information learned from those calculations before moving to the third step of the calculations, which is determining the variable manufacturing overhead efficiency variance in dollars.

Recall that our calculation showed that Tree Top used an extra 27 direct labor hours to make the 225 mail boxes in November. The extra 27 direct labor hours not only increased direct labor cost, but it also increased other costs. While Ali, Maria, and Bill worked the extra 27 hours, they consumed electricity, supplies, and other factory resources. In sum, the inefficiency of the workforce increased variable manufacturing overhead cost. Had they not worked the extra 27 hours, Tree Top's owners would have saved not only the labor cost, but also the factory resources they consumed as they worked the extra time.

*Step 3:* Calculate the variable manufacturing overhead efficiency variance in dollars.

To calculate the variable manufacturing overhead efficiency variance in dollars, multiply the direct labor efficiency variance in hours by the standard variable manufacturing overhead rate.

For Tree Top, the direct labor efficiency variance in hours we calculated earlier is 27 hours. We multiply this amount by the standard variable manufacturing overhead rate we calculated earlier of $0.35. This results in an unfavorable variable manufacturing overhead efficiency variance of $9.45 as shown here:

| Direct Labor Efficiency Variance in Hours | | Standard Variable Mfg Overhead Rate | | Variable Mfg Overhead Efficiency Variance |
|---|---|---|---|---|
| 27 Hours | × | $0.35 | = | $9.45 Unfavorable |

Now that the $9.45 variance has been calculated, management can assess the variance and take corrective action if necessary. Because the variable manufacturing overhead efficiency variance is based on direct labor efficiency, improving the direct labor efficiency variance will solve the variable overhead efficiency variance problem.

Tree Top's variable manufacturing overhead efficiency variance is so small that it may warrant no management attention. Even so, as Ali, Maria, and Bill work to bring the direct labor efficiency variance under control, the variable manufacturing overhead variance will also improve.

# Discussion Questions

**9–11.** If variable manufacturing overhead is allocated to production based on direct labor hours, will an unfavorable variable manufacturing overhead efficiency variance always accompany an unfavorable direct labor efficiency variance? Explain your reasoning.

**9–12.** If the direct labor efficiency variance is zero, will the variable manufacturing overhead efficiency variance also be zero? Explain your reasoning.

## Variable Manufacturing Overhead Spending Variance

**variable manufacturing overhead spending variance** The difference between how much was actually spent on variable manufacturing overhead and the amount that should have been spent based on the actual direct labor hours worked.

The **variable manufacturing overhead spending variance** is the difference between what was actually spent on variable manufacturing overhead and what should have been spent, based on the actual direct labor hours worked. The question this variance answers is, based on the actual number of direct labor hours worked, is variable manufacturing overhead cost in line? In the case of Tree Top, given that production took 162 direct labor hours, was variable manufacturing overhead more or less than it should have been for that many direct labor hours? To find the answer, we must first determine the standard variable manufacturing overhead for the actual number of hours worked and then calculate the overhead spending variance in dollars. Let us look at the first step in this process.

*Step 1:* Determine the standard variable manufacturing overhead for the actual number of hours worked.

To determine the standard variable manufacturing overhead for the actual hours worked, we multiply the standard variable manufacturing overhead rate by the actual number of direct labor hours. This calculation shows us the amount that should have been spent for variable manufacturing overhead based on the actual labor hours worked. Based on Tree Top's standard variable manufacturing overhead rate of $0.35 per hour, the standard variable manufacturing overhead cost for the 162 actual direct labor hours is $56.70 as shown here:

| Actual Direct Labor Hours | | Standard Variable Mfg Overhead Rate | | Standard Variable Mfg Overhead for Actual Direct Labor Hours |
|---|---|---|---|---|
| | × | | = | |
| 162 Hours | × | $0.35 | = | $56.70 |

Now that we know how much Tree Top's variable manufacturing overhead should have been, we can compare it to the actual variable manufacturing overhead amount to determine the amount of the variance.

*Step 2:* Calculate the variable manufacturing overhead spending variance.

We calculate the variable manufacturing overhead spending variance by comparing standard variable manufacturing overhead for the actual number of hours worked (determined in step 1) to the amount actually spent for variable manufacturing overhead. This calculation compares *actual* variable manufacturing overhead cost to what it *should* have been for the actual hours worked. In the case of

Tree Top, the actual amount spent for variable manufacturing overhead in November was $140. By comparing this amount to the standard of $56.70, we determine that the variable manufacturing overhead spending variance is $83.30 unfavorable as shown here:

| Standard Variable Mfg Overhead Cost for Actual Direct Labor Hours | | Actual Variable Mfg Overhead Cost | | Variable Mfg Overhead Spending Variance |
|---|---|---|---|---|
| $56.70 | – | $140.00 | = | $83.30 Unfavorable |

## Discussion Questions

9-13. What are some possible reasons why Tree Top Mail Box Company's variable manufacturing overhead spending was much higher than it should have been based on the standards?

9-14. If there had been no variance, would this mean Tree Top paid what it should have for variable manufacturing overhead in November? Explain your reasoning.

As managers assess the variable manufacturing overhead spending variance, they should keep in mind that it is a result of many different overhead expenditures. In practice, most companies break down the variable manufacturing overhead spending variance into separate variances for each variable manufacturing overhead item. For example, a manufacturer would have separate variance calculations for electricity, water, telephone, cleaning supplies, maintenance supplies, and so forth. The logic and calculations for each variance, however, would be similar to what we have presented here.

For Tree Top Mail Box Company, the trouble with variable manufacturing overhead cost is a combination of an unfavorable efficiency variance of $9.45 and an unfavorable spending variance of $83.30. Although the unfavorable efficiency variance will require little or no attention, the spending variance is sizeable and should be investigated. Each component of variable manufacturing overhead should be reviewed to see whether overhead spending can be reduced.

### Fixed Manufacturing Overhead Budget Variance

**fixed manufacturing overhead budget variance** The difference between the actual amount of total fixed manufacturing overhead cost and the budgeted fixed manufacturing overhead cost.

The **fixed manufacturing overhead budget variance** is a measure of how actual total fixed manufacturing overhead compares to budgeted fixed manufacturing overhead. For example, if a company expects fixed manufacturing overhead cost to be $200,000 per month, the budget variance indicates whether the actual fixed manufacturing overhead is more or less than the $200,000.

We take only one step to compute the fixed manufacturing overhead budget variance. The dollar amount is calculated simply by subtracting actual fixed manufacturing overhead cost from the budgeted fixed manufacturing overhead. For Tree Top, the fixed manufacturing overhead budget variance for November is zero, because actual fixed manufacturing overhead cost exactly equals the amount budgeted, shown as follows:

| Budget Fixed Mfg Overhead Cost | | Actual Fixed Mfg Overhead Cost | | Fixed Mfg Overhead Budget Variance |
|---|---|---|---|---|
| $225 | – | $225 | = | $0 |

The company has only two fixed overhead items, rent and depreciation, so the fact that actual cost equaled budgeted cost is not surprising. If Tree Top purchased additional production equipment resulting in higher depreciation cost, an unfavorable variance could occur.

Fixed manufacturing overhead costs are generally associated with long-term commitments for specific factory resources. Examples of fixed overhead include the cost of depreciation on factory equipment, factory rent, insurance, and property taxes. Unlike other factory costs, fixed overhead is less likely to be affected by the routine decisions that managers and employees make daily. Therefore, the variation between the amount budgeted and the actual fixed factory overhead incurred is just as likely to be caused by a flawed budget as it is by spending decisions made during the budgeted period. For example, if a company budgets $50,000 for property taxes but the taxes are actually $51,000, the $1,000 variance that results is caused by a flawed budget, not by uncontrolled spending. Accordingly, fixed manufacturing overhead budget variances should be closely scrutinized to determine whether the required corrective action is to improve the budgeting process or to modify spending during the period.

Like variable manufacturing overhead, fixed manufacturing overhead comprises many different items. In practice, separate budget variances are calculated for each fixed manufacturing overhead item.

## Fixed Manufacturing Overhead Volume Variance

**fixed manufacturing overhead volume variance**
A measure of the utilization of plant capacity. This variance is caused by manufacturing more or less product during a particular production period than planned.

The last standard cost variance we discuss is the **fixed manufacturing overhead volume variance,** which measures utilization of plant capacity. A variance is caused by the manufacture of more or less product during a particular production period than planned. When a manufacturer invests in expensive production machinery, it does so in anticipation of producing a given amount of product. If the company expects to produce only a small amount of product, it invests in inexpensive, low-volume equipment. If, however, the company expects to produce a large volume of product, it usually acquires more costly, high-volume equipment. If expensive, high-volume equipment is purchased but actual production is low, then it is likely that the company spent too much on production capacity. The fixed manufacturing overhead volume variance focuses on this relationship between production capacity and the actual volume produced.

When Ali, Maria, and Bill formed their manufacturing company, they could have set up shop to produce a very small number of mail boxes using hand tools; or they could have chosen to invest heavily in a building and automated equipment, thereby greatly increasing their plant capacity. They chose to rent a small garage and invest a small amount in power tools that gave them a capacity to produce about 300 mail boxes per month. If they produce more than 300 mail boxes, that's great, but if they produce fewer, they are underutilizing their capacity to produce. In November, they produced only 225 mail boxes. Tree Top Mail Box Company, then, underutilized its capacity to produce by 75 mail boxes. Is this a big problem? To evaluate the magnitude of the problem we need to assign a dollar amount to the underutilization.

In the case of Tree Top Mail Box Company, the monthly fixed cost of $225 provides a capacity to produce 300 mail boxes. We follow three steps to calculate the fixed manufacturing overhead volume variance. First, we find the difference between expected and actual production. Second, we determine the standard number of direct labor hours associated with the production. Finally, we calculate the dollar amount of the fixed manufacturing overhead volume variance. We examine these steps in detail next.

*Step 1:* Calculate the difference between expected (budgeted) production and actual production.

The budgeted production for Tree Top is 300 mail boxes per month. Tree Top's actual production was less than its budgeted production by 75 mail boxes, shown as follows:

| Plant Production Capacity | | Actual Number of Units Produced | | Under- Or Overproduction in Units |
|---|---|---|---|---|
| 300 Units | – | 225 Units | = | 75 Units Under |

As you will see, when fixed manufacturing overhead is allocated to production based on direct labor hours, the direct labor efficiency standard, with the standard fixed manufacturing overhead rate per direct labor hour, is used to calculate the dollar amount of the fixed manufacturing overhead volume variance.

*Step 2:* Determine the standard number of direct labor hours associated with the under- or overproduction.

We determine the standard number of direct labor hours associated with the under- or overproduction by multiplying the under- or overproduction by the direct labor efficiency standard. In the case of Tree Top, the direct labor efficiency standard is 0.6 hours per unit. Accordingly, the standard direct labor hours associated with the underproduction of 75 mail boxes is 45 hours (75 units × 0.6 hours per unit), shown as follows:

| Amount of Under- or Overproduction | | Direct Labor Efficiency Standard | | Standard Number of Hours Associated with Production |
|---|---|---|---|---|
| 75 Units | × | 0.6 Hours Per Unit | = | 45 Hours |

Now that we know the number of standard hours associated with the over- or underproduction, we can assign a dollar amount based on the standard fixed manufacturing overhead rate per hour.

*Step 3:* Calculate the dollar amount of the fixed manufacturing overhead volume variance.

The dollar amount of the fixed manufacturing volume variance is calculated by multiplying the standard number of direct labor hours associated with the under- or overproduction by the standard fixed manufacturing overhead rate per direct labor hour. In the case of Tree Top, the fixed manufacturing overhead volume variance is $56.25, calculated as follows:

| Standard Direct Labor Hours for Under- or Overproduction | | Standard Fixed Mfg Overhead Rate | | Fixed Mfg Overhead Volume Variance |
|---|---|---|---|---|
| 45 Hours | × | $1.25 | = | $56.25 Unfavorable |

Once the fixed manufacturing overhead volume variance has been calculated, management can attempt to determine what caused it. In the case of Tree Top, the variance resulted primarily from inefficiencies caused by substandard direct material. Surprisingly, however, fixed manufacturing overhead volume variances are often caused by marketing and sales activities, rather than by the production department. In general, production occurs in response to sales demand. If the product is selling poorly, production volume will be low because little product is needed to fulfill demand. Conversely, if sales demand is high, production volume is likely to be large to meet demand.

# Using Standard Cost Variances to Manage by Exception

Once all the standard cost variances have been calculated, the accounting department prepares a performance report that lists each variance. Then managers can use management by exception to address the problems associated with the unfavorable variances, beginning with the largest. A performance report is presented in Exhibit 9–8 for Tree Top Mail Box Company.

As the Tree Top Mail Box Company example shows, sometimes relationships among standard cost variances can occur that help explain the cause of some variances. Also, managers must develop the skill to review the variances and then seek out their causes and possible remedies. Even though managers can use standard costing to spot pressing issues, they must be careful of its shortcomings. Standard costing is one management tool, but not the only tool.

**Exhibit 9–8**
Tree Top's November
Performance Report

### TREE TOP MAIL BOX COMPANY
**Performance Report**
**For November 2001**

| Variance | Amount | Favorable/ Unfavorable |
|---|---|---|
| Direct material quantity variance | $ 99.75 | Unfavorable |
| Direct material price variance | 48.00 | Favorable |
| Direct labor efficiency variance | 270.00 | Unfavorable |
| Direct labor rate variance | 81.00 | Unfavorable |
| Variable mfg overhead efficiency variance | 9.45 | Unfavorable |
| Variable mfg overhead spending variance | 83.30 | Unfavorable |
| Fixed mfg overhead budget variance | 0 | —— |
| Fixed mfg overhead volume variance | 56.25 | Unfavorable |
| Total | $551.75 | Unfavorable |

# Summary

In the process of operating businesses, managers must focus their valuable time on areas that need to be improved. One area that requires constant attention is controlling the costs of operations. A process designed to help managers focus on cost items that need attention is standard costing, which sets cost performance goals and then uses these cost goals to evaluate performance.

Differences between the costs incurred by actual performance and what the costs should have been, based on the standards, are called variances. A favorable variance results when the cost of actual performance is lower than planned performance. An unfavorable variance results when the cost of actual performance is higher than planned performance. Managers can investigate all variances from standard, or they can focus their attention only on significant variances. Focusing only on significant variances is known as management by exception.

In establishing performance standards, managers can use either ideal standards, which can be attained only under perfect conditions, or practical standards, which allow for normal working conditions.

Although a standard costing system can be extremely helpful to managers, it has several potential problems. These include employees setting lax standards to avoid unfavorable variances, relying on historical information that may perpetuate past inefficiencies, and managing "by the numbers" thus overlooking significant problems that do not result in variances.

A standard cost system in a manufacturing environment uses estimates for the cost of direct materials, direct labor, and manufacturing overhead. This system is in contrast to both an actual cost system, which uses the actual cost for direct materials, direct labor, and manufacturing overhead, and a normal cost system, which uses actual costs for direct materials and direct labor, and estimates for manufacturing overhead.

The standards used in a manufacturing type company generally include a direct material quantity standard, a direct material price standard, a direct labor efficiency standard, a direct labor rate standard, a standard variable manufacturing overhead rate, and a standard fixed manufacturing overhead rate.

To use standard costing as a control device, managers compare standard costs to actual costs to see whether a variance exists. Then they investigate variances, as appropriate, which is known as variance analysis. The variances most commonly used are the direct material quantity variance, the direct material price variance, the direct labor efficiency variance, the direct labor rate variance, the variable manufacturing overhead efficiency variance, the variable manufacturing overhead spending variance, the fixed manufacturing overhead budget variance, and the fixed manufacturing overhead volume variance.

# APPENDIX—RECORDING PRODUCT COST USING STANDARD COSTING

This appendix is intended to provide an overview of the accounting entries to record product costs using standard costing.

**LEARNING OBJECTIVES**

*After completing your work in this appendix, you should be able to do the following:*

1. Record the purchase of direct material and the direct material price variance.
2. Record the use of direct material and the direct material quantity variance.
3. Record the use of direct labor and the direct labor rate and efficiency variances.
4. Record actual variable manufacturing overhead cost incurred.
5. Record the application of variable manufacturing overhead to production.
6. Close the variable manufacturing overhead accounts and record the variable overhead variances.
7. Record actual fixed manufacturing overhead cost incurred.
8. Record the application of fixed manufacturing overhead to production.
9. Close the fixed manufacturing overhead accounts and record the variable overhead variances.
10. Close the standard cost variances to cost of goods sold.

The following accounts will be used for the entries in this appendix:

1. Cash
2. Raw materials inventory

3. Work-in-process inventory
4. Direct materials price variance
5. Direct materials quantity variance
6. Direct labor efficiency variance
7. Direct labor rate variance
8. Variable manufacturing overhead efficiency variance
9. Variable manufacturing overhead spending variance
10. Fixed manufacturing overhead budget variance
11. Fixed manufacturing overhead volume variance
12. Variable manufacturing overhead incurred
13. Variable manufacturing overhead applied
14. Fixed manufacturing overhead incurred
15. Fixed manufacturing overhead applied
16. Accumulated depreciation
17. Accounts payable
18. Cost of goods sold

Recall that debits increase assets, expenses, and losses, while credits increase liabilities, equity, revenues, and gains. Also, you will learn that if a variance is favorable, the variance account is credited and if a variance is unfavorable, the variance account is debit.

When standard costing is used, direct materials, work-in-process, and finished goods inventories are maintained at standard cost. The standard cost variances account for the difference between the standard cost maintained in inventory and actual costs.

## Purchase of Direct Material

The following table presents the information needed to make the direct materials purchases entry for Tree Top Mail Box Company:

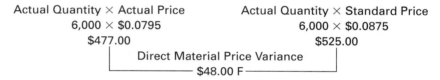

| Actual Quantity × Actual Price | Actual Quantity × Standard Price |
|---|---|
| 6,000 × $0.0795 | 6,000 × $0.0875 |
| $477.00 | $525.00 |

Direct Material Price Variance
$48.00 F

To record the purchase of raw material, raw materials inventory is debited for the actual quantity multiplied by the standard price. For Tree Top, the amount is $525. The amount credited to accounts payable or cash is the actual purchase price of the material. For Tree Top, the amount is $477. The difference between the amount debited to direct material and the amount credited to accounts payable is taken to the direct materials price variance account. If a credit to the variance account is required to balance the entry, the variance is favorable. Conversely, if a debit is required the variance is unfavorable. For Tree Top, the variance is $48 favorable so the direct material price variance account will be credited.

The entry for Tree Top appears as follows:

| | | |
|---|---|---|
| Raw Materials | 525.00 | |
| Accounts Payable | | 477.00 |
| Direct Materials Price Variance | | 48.00 |

## Use of Direct Material

The following table presents the information needed to make the entry for the direct materials used by Tree Top Mail Box Company:

Actual Quantity × Standard Price
6,000 × $0,0875
$525.00

Standard Quantity × Standard Price
225 × 21.6 Feet × $0.0875
4860 Feet × $.0875
$425.25

Quantity Variance
$99.75 U

To record the use of direct material, work-in-process inventory is debited for the standard quantity of material allowed for production multiplied by the standard price. For Tree Top, the amount is $425.25. The amount credited to raw materials is the actual quantity of material multiplied by the standard price. For Tree Top, the amount is $477. The difference between the amount debited to work in process and the amount credited to raw materials is taken to the direct material quantity variance account. If a credit to the variance account is required to balance the entry, the variance is favorable. Conversely, if a debit is required, the variance is unfavorable. For Tree Top, the variance is $99.75 unfavorable so the direct material quantity variance account will be debited.

The entry for Tree Top appears as follows:

| | | |
|---|---|---|
| Work-in-Process Inventory | 425.25 | |
| Direct Materials Quantity Variance | 99.75 | |
|     Raw Materials Inventory | | 525.00 |

### Recording Direct Labor

The following tables present the information needed to make the entry to record direct labor for Tree Top Mail Box Company:

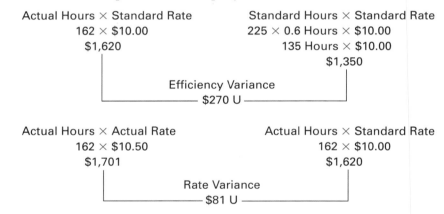

Actual Hours × Standard Rate
162 × $10.00
$1,620

Standard Hours × Standard Rate
225 × 0.6 Hours × $10.00
135 Hours × $10.00
$1,350

Efficiency Variance
$270 U

Actual Hours × Actual Rate
162 × $10.50
$1,701

Actual Hours × Standard Rate
162 × $10.00
$1,620

Rate Variance
$81 U

To record direct labor cost, work-in-process inventory is debited for the standard hours allowed for production multiplied by the standard direct labor rate. For Tree Top, the amount is $1,350. Cash or wages payable is credited for the actual amount of wages paid to employees. For Tree Top, the amount is $1,701. The difference between the amount debited to work in process and the amount credited to cash is equal to the direct labor efficiency and rate variances. If the variance is favorable, the variance account is credited. Conversely, if the variance is unfavorable, the variance account is debited. For Tree Top, the efficiency variance and the rate variance are unfavorable so both of these variance accounts will be debited.

The entry for Tree Top appears as follows:

| | | |
|---|---|---|
| Work-In-Process Inventory | 1,350.00 | |
| Direct Labor Efficiency Variance | 270.00 | |
| Direct Labor Rate Variance | 81.00 | |
|     Cash | | 1,701.00 |

## Recording Variable Manufacturing Overhead

The following tables present the information needed to make the entries for variable manufacturing overhead for Tree Top Mail Box Company:

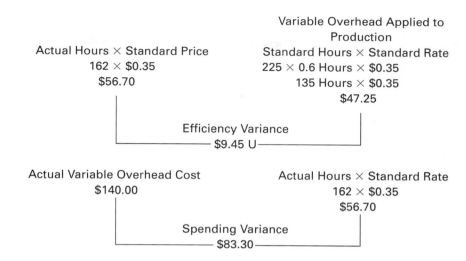

The variable manufacturing overhead incurred account is debited for the actual cost of variable manufacturing overhead. For Tree Top, the amount is $140. Depending on whether the item was purchased on account or for cash, accounts payable or cash would be credited. We assume the items were purchased for cash.

The entry for Tree Top appears as follows:

Variable Manufacturing Overhead Incurred  140.00
    Cash                                  140.00

Work-in-process inventory is debited and variable manufacturing overhead applied is credited for the standard direct labor hours allowed for production multiplied by the standard variable overhead application rate. For Tree Top, the amount is $47.25.

The entry for Tree Top appears as follows:

Work-In-Process Inventory                  47.25
    Variable Manufacturing Overhead Applied        47.25

The difference between the balance of the variable manufacturing overhead incurred account and the variable manufacturing overhead applied account is equal to the variable overhead efficiency and spending variances. These variance accounts are established when the variable manufacturing overhead incurred and the variable manufacturing overhead applied accounts are closed. This closing procedure is generally done only at year end. For demonstration purposes, we will assume that Tree Top has elected to close the overhead accounts to establish the variable overhead efficiency and spending variances at the end of November. As with the variance previously discussed, if the variance is favorable, the variance account is credited. Conversely, if the variance is unfavorable, the variance account is debited. For Tree Top, both the efficiency variance and the spending variance are unfavorable so the variance accounts will be debited as shown in the following entry.

Variable Manufacturing Overhead Applied            47.25
Variable Manufacturing Overhead Efficiency Variance    9.45
Variable Manufacturing Overhead Spending Variance    83.30
    Variable Manufacturing Overhead Incurred            140.00

### Recording Fixed Manufacturing Overhead

The following tables present the information needed to make the entries for fixed manufacturing overhead for Tree Top Mail Box Company:

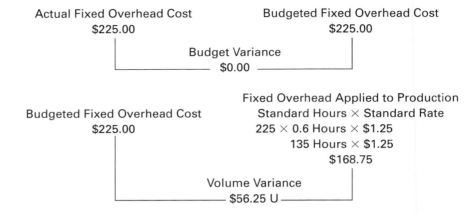

| Actual Fixed Overhead Cost | Budgeted Fixed Overhead Cost |
|---|---|
| $225.00 | $225.00 |

Budget Variance
$0.00

| Budgeted Fixed Overhead Cost | Fixed Overhead Applied to Production<br>Standard Hours × Standard Rate |
|---|---|
| $225.00 | 225 × 0.6 Hours × $1.25 |
| | 135 Hours × $1.25 |
| | $168.75 |

Volume Variance
$56.25 U

The fixed manufacturing overhead incurred account is debited for the actual cost of fixed manufacturing overhead. For Tree Top, the $225 actual fixed manufacturing overhead consists of $200 for rent and $25 for depreciation. Cash should be credited for the amount of rent paid and accumulated depreciation should be credited for the depreciation.

The entry for Tree Top appears as follows:

| | | |
|---|---|---|
| Fixed Manufacturing Overhead Incurred | 225.00 | |
|   Cash | | 200.00 |
|   Accumulated Depreciation | | 25.00 |

Work-in-process inventory is debited and fixed manufacturing overhead applied is credited for the standard direct labor hours allowed for production multiplied by the standard fixed overhead application rate. For Tree Top, the amount is $168.75.

The entry for Tree Top appears as follows:

| | | |
|---|---|---|
| Work-In-Process Inventory | 168.75 | |
|   Fixed Manufacturing Overhead Applied | | 168.75 |

The difference between the balance of the fixed manufacturing overhead incurred account and the fixed manufacturing overhead applied account is equal to the fixed overhead budget and volume spending variances. These variance accounts are established when the fixed manufacturing overhead incurred and the fixed manufacturing overhead applied accounts are closed. As with variable overhead, this closing procedure is generally done only at year end. For demonstration purposes, we will assume that Tree Top has elected to close the fixed manufacturing overhead accounts at the end of November. Once more, if the variance is favorable, the variance account is credited. Conversely, if the variance is unfavorable, the variance account is debited. Although entries for zero variances are not generally made in practice, we will show an entry for the budget variance for this demonstration. The volume variance will appear as a debit because it is an unfavorable variance.

The entry for Tree Top appears as follows:

| | | |
|---|---|---|
| Fixed Manufacturing Overhead Applied | 168.75 | |
| Fixed Manufacturing Overhead Budget Variance | 0 | |
| Fixed Manufacturing Overhead Volume Variance | 56.25 | |
|   Fixed Manufacturing Overhead Incurred | | 225.00 |

### Closing the Variance Accounts

The variance accounts are monitored during the year but generally no accounting entries are made to dispense with the amounts until the end of the year. For demonstration purposes, we will assume that Tree Top has elected to close the variance accounts at the end of November.

In most cases an accounting entry is made to close the standard cost variances to cost of goods sold. Because the amount of the variances is generally relatively small and most product cost ends up in cost of goods sold by year end, closing the variance accounts to cost of goods sold is adequate for most companies.

Tree Top's entry to close the standard cost variances to cost of goods sold follows:

| | | |
|---|---|---|
| Cost of Goods Sold | 551.75 | |
| Direct Material Price Variance | 48.00 | |
| Direct Material Quantity Variance | | 99.75 |
| Direct Labor Efficiency Variance | | 270.00 |
| Direct Labor Rate Variance | | 81.00 |
| Variable Manufacturing Overhead Efficiency Variance | | 9.45 |
| Variable Manufacturing Overhead Spending Variance | | 83.30 |
| Fixed Manufacturing Overhead Budget Variance | | 0 |
| Fixed Manufacturing Overhead Volume Variance | | 56.25 |

## APPENDIX SUMMARY

When standard costing is used, direct materials, work-in-process, and finished goods inventories are maintained at standard cost. The standard cost variances account for the difference between the standard cost maintained in inventory and actual costs. If a variance is favorable, the variance account is credited. Conversely, if a variance is unfavorable, the variance account is debited.

To record the purchase of raw material, raw materials inventory is debited for the actual quantity multiplied by the standard price. The amount credited to accounts payable or cash is the actual purchase price of the material. The difference between the amount debited to direct material and the amount credited to accounts payable is taken to the direct materials price variance account.

To record the use of direct material, work-in-process inventory is debited for the standard quantity of material allowed for production multiplied by the standard price. The amount credited to raw materials is the actual quantity of material multiplied by the standard price. The difference between the amount debited to work in process and the amount credited to raw materials is taken to the direct material quantity variance account.

Work-in-process inventory is debited for the standard hours allowed for production multiplied by the standard direct labor rate. Cash or wages payable is credited for the actual amount of wages paid to employees. The difference between the amount debited to work in process and the amount credited to cash is equal to the direct labor efficiency and rate variances.

The variable manufacturing overhead incurred account is debited for the actual cost of variable manufacturing overhead. Work-in-process inventory is debited and variable manufacturing overhead applied is credited for the standard direct labor hours allowed for production multiplied by the standard variable overhead application rate. The difference between the balance of the variable manufacturing overhead incurred account and the variable manufacturing overhead applied account is equal to the variable overhead efficiency and spending variances. At year end, these variance accounts are established when the variable manufacturing overhead incurred and the variable manufacturing overhead applied accounts are closed.

The fixed manufacturing overhead incurred account is debited for the actual cost of fixed manufacturing overhead. Work-in-process inventory is debited and fixed manufacturing overhead applied is credited for the standard direct labor hours allowed for production multiplied by the standard fixed overhead application rate. The difference between the balance of the fixed manufacturing overhead incurred account and the fixed manufacturing overhead applied account is equal to the fixed overhead budget and volume spending variances. At year end, these variance accounts are established when the fixed manufacturing overhead incurred and the fixed manufacturing overhead applied accounts are closed.

The variance accounts are generally closed to cost of goods sold at year end. Because the amount of variances is generally relatively small and most product cost ends up in cost of goods sold by year end, closing the variance accounts to cost of goods sold is adequate for most companies.

## KEY TERMS

bill of materials   M-332
direct labor efficiency standard   M-334
direct labor efficiency variance   M-342
direct labor rate standard   M-335
direct labor rate variance   M-344
direct material price standard   M-333
direct material price variance   M-341
direct material quantity standard   M-332
direct material quantity variance   M-338
direct material usage variance   M-338
favorable variance   M-327
fixed manufacturing overhead
  budget variance   M-348
fixed manufacturing overhead
  volume variance   M-349
ideal standard   M-328

management by exception   M-327
practical standard   M-328
standard   M-326
standard costing   M-326
standard cost system   M-326
standard fixed manufacturing
  overhead rate   M-336
standard variable manufacturing
  overhead rate   M-336
unfavorable variance   M-327
variable manufacturing overhead
  efficiency variance   M-345
variable manufacturing overhead
  spending variance   M-347
variance   M-326

## REVIEW THE FACTS

A. What is standard costing?
B. What is a standard?
C. What is a variance?
D. Describe management by exception.
E. How often do most companies set cost standards?
F. What are the two things that can cause cost to increase?
G. What is the difference between an ideal standard and a practical standard?
H. Briefly describe five problems with standard costing.
I. What is a bill of material?
J. What are the two direct material standards?
K. What are the two direct labor standards?
L. How can standard costs be used to control cost?
M. What is measured by the direct material quantity variance?
N. What is measured by the direct material price variance?
O. What is measured by the direct labor efficiency variance?
P. What is measured by the direct labor rate variance?
Q. What is measured by the variable manufacturing overhead efficiency variance?

R. What is measured by the variable manufacturing overhead spending variance?
S. What is measured by the fixed manufacturing overhead budget variance?
T. What is measured by the fixed manufacturing overhead volume variance?

# APPLY WHAT YOU HAVE LEARNED

## LO 7: Determine Direct Material Variances

**9–15.** The Zhang Manufacturing Company purchased 4,000 pounds of direct material at $5.20 per pound. It used 2,700 pounds to make 5,000 finished units. The standard cost for direct material is $5.00 per pound and the quantity standard is 0.5 (one-half) pound per finished unit.

**REQUIRED:**
a. According to the appropriate standard, how much should the company have paid for the 4,000 pounds of direct material purchased?
b. Determine the direct material price variance based on the amount of direct material purchased.
c. According to the appropriate standard, how many pounds of direct material should have been used to make the 5,000 finished units?
d. Determine the direct material quantity variance in pounds of direct material.
e. Determine the direct material quantity variance in dollars.
f. Appendix: Prepare the following journal entries:
   (1) Record the purchase of direct material.
   (2) Record the use of direct material.

## LO 7: Determine Direct Material Variances

**9–16.** The Carbonnell Manufacturing Company purchased 15,000 pounds of direct material at $1.30 per pound. It used 14,700 pounds to make 5,000 finished units. The standard cost for direct material is $1.35 per pound and the quantity standard is three pounds per finished unit.

**REQUIRED:**
a. According to the appropriate standard, how much should the company have paid for the 15,000 pounds of direct material purchased?
b. Determine the direct material price variance based on the amount of direct material purchased.
c. According to the appropriate standard, how many pounds of direct material should have been used to make the 5,000 finished units?
d. Determine the direct material quantity variance in pounds of direct material.
e. Determine the direct material quantity variance in dollars.
f. Appendix: Prepare the following journal entries:
   (1) Record the purchase of direct material.
   (2) Record the use of direct material.

## LO 7: Determine Direct Material Variances

**9–17.** The Smithstone Company purchased 2,500 square feet of direct material at $6.30 per square foot. It used 2,055 square feet of material to make 500 finished units. The standard cost for direct material is $6.15 per square foot and the quantity standard is four pounds per finished unit.

**REQUIRED:**

a. According to the appropriate standard, how much should the company have paid for the 2,500 square feet of direct material purchased?

b. Determine the direct material price variance based on the amount of direct material purchased.

c. According to the appropriate standard, how many square feet of direct material should have been used to make the 500 finished units?

d. Determine the direct material quantity variance in square feet of direct material.

e. Determine the direct material quantity variance in dollars.

f. Appendix: Prepare the following journal entries:
   (1) Record the purchase of direct material.
   (2) Record the use of direct material.

## LO 7:   Determine Direct Material Variances

**9–18.** Econo Manufacturing purchased 20,000 square feet of direct material at $0.54 per square foot. It used 12,625 square feet to make 1,250 finished units. The standard cost for direct material is $0.55 per square foot and the quantity standard is 10 square feet per finished unit.

**REQUIRED:**

a. According to the appropriate standard, how much should the company have paid for the 20,000 square feet of direct material purchased?

b. Determine the direct material price variance based on the amount of direct material purchased.

c. According to the appropriate standard, how many square feet of direct material should have been used to make the 1,250 finished units?

d. Determine the direct material quantity variance in square feet of direct material.

e. Determine the direct material quantity variance in dollars.

## LO 7:   Determine Direct Material Variances

**9–19.** The following information is presented for the Scout Manufacturing Company.
   - Direct material price standard is $1.55 per gallon.
   - Direct material quantity standard is 2.5 gallons per finished unit.
   - Budgeted production is 1,000 finished units.
   - 4,000 gallons of direct material were purchased for $6,000.
   - 2,800 gallons of direct material were used in production.
   - 1,100 finished units of product were produced.

**REQUIRED:**

a. Determine the direct material price variance.

b. Determine the direct material quantity variance in dollars.

## LO 7:   Determine Direct Material Variances

**9–20.** The following information is presented for the Flowvalve Manufacturing Company.
   - Direct material price standard is $15 per pound.
   - Direct material quantity standard is 1/4 pound per finished unit.
   - Budgeted production is 20,000 finished units.

- 6,000 pounds of direct material were purchased for $91,320.
- 4,650 pounds of direct material were used in production.
- 18,000 finished units of product were produced.

**REQUIRED:**
a. Determine the direct material price variance.
b. Determine the direct material quantity variance in dollars.

## LO 7: Determine Direct Material Variances

**9–21.** The following information is presented for the Munter Manufacturing Company.

- Direct material price standard is $3.25 per pound.
- Direct material quantity standardis  six pounds per finished unit.
- Budgeted production is 25,000 finished units.
- 175,000 pounds of direct material were purchased for $559,650.
- 155,200 pounds of direct material were used in production.
- 25,600 finished units of product were produced.

**REQUIRED:**
a. Determine the direct material price variance.
b. Determine the direct material quantity variance in dollars.

## LO 7: Determine Direct Material Variances

**9–22.** Information from the Quincy Company is as follows:

| | |
|---|---|
| Actual cost of 33,000 lbs of direct material purchased | $97,350 |
| Direct material used in production | 30,575 lbs |
| Actual production | 2,980 units |
| Direct material price standard | $3.00 per lb |
| Direct material quantity standard per finished unit of production | 10 lbs |
| Budgeted production | 3,000 units |

**REQUIRED:**
a. Determine the direct material price variance.
b. Determine the direct material quantity variance in dollars.

## LO 7: Determine Direct Material Variances

**9–23.** Information from the Wayne Manufacturing is as follows:

| | |
|---|---|
| Actual cost of 10,000 lbs of direct material purchased | $2,400 |
| Direct material used in production | 9,177 lbs |
| Actual production | 980 units |
| Direct material price standard | $0.25 per lb |
| Direct material quantity standard per finished unit of production | 9 lbs |
| Budgeted production | 1,000 units |

**REQUIRED:**
a. Determine the direct material price variance.
b. Determine the direct material quantity variance in dollars.

## LO 7:  Determine Direct Material Variances

**9–24.** Information from the Myco Manufacturing Company is as follows:

| | |
|---|---|
| Actual cost of 120,000 feet of<br>    direct material purchased | $427,200 |
| Direct material used in production | 111,100 feet |
| Actual production | 3,200 units |
| Direct material price standard | $3.50 per foot |
| Direct material quantity standard<br>    per finished unit of production | 35 feet |
| Budgeted production | 3,500 units |

### REQUIRED:
a. Determine the direct material price variance.
b. Determine the direct material quantity variance in dollars.

## LO 7:  Determine Direct Labor Variances

**9–25.** The direct labor rate standard for Amy Manufacturing is $12 per direct labor hour. The direct labor efficiency standard is two hours per finished unit. Last month, the company completed 8,000 units of product using 16,350 direct labor hours at an actual cost of $194,565.

### REQUIRED:
a. According to the appropriate standard, how much should the company have paid for the 16,350 actual direct labor hours?
b. Determine the direct labor rate variance.
c. According to the appropriate standard, how many hours of direct labor should it have taken to produce the 8,000 units?
d. Determine the direct labor efficiency variance in hours.
e. Determine the direct labor efficiency variance in dollars.
f. Appendix: Prepare a journal entry to record the direct labor and the direct labor rate and efficiency variances.

## LO 7:  Determine Direct Labor Variances

**9–26.** The direct labor rate standard for Calspan Manufacturing is $18.50 per direct labor hour. The direct labor efficiency standard is six minutes or 1/10 of an hour per finished unit. Last month, the company completed 105,650 units of product using 10,400 direct labor hours at an actual cost of $191,360.

### REQUIRED:
a. According to the appropriate standard, how much should the company have paid for the 10,400 actual direct labor hours?
b. Determine the direct labor rate variance.
c. According to the appropriate standard, how many hours of direct labor should it have taken to produce the 105,650 units?
d. Determine the direct labor efficiency variance in hours.
e. Determine the direct labor efficiency variance in dollars.
f. Appendix: Prepare a journal entry to record the direct labor and the direct labor rate and efficiency variances.

## LO 7: Determine Direct Labor Variances

**9–27.** The direct labor rate standard for Key Largo Manufacturing is $10 per direct labor hour. The direct labor efficiency standard is three hours per finished unit. Last month, the company completed 2,800 units of product using 8,620 direct labor hours at an actual cost of $88,355.

**REQUIRED:**

a. According to the appropriate standard, how much should the company have paid for the 8,620 actual direct labor hours?
b. Determine the direct labor rate variance.
c. According to the appropriate standard, how many hours of direct labor should it have taken to produce the 2,800 units?
d. Determine the direct labor efficiency variance in hours.
e. Determine the direct labor efficiency variance in dollars.

## LO 7: Determine Direct Labor Variances

**9–28.** The direct labor rate standard for Sakura Manufacturing is $15.25 per direct labor hour. The direct labor efficiency standard is 30 minutes or 1/2 of an hour per finished unit. Last month, the company completed 27,800 units of product using 14,050 direct labor hours at an actual cost of $215,246.

**REQUIRED:**

a. Determine the direct labor rate variance.
b. Determine the direct labor efficiency variance in dollars.
c. Appendix: Prepare a journal entry to record the direct labor and the direct labor rate and efficiency variances.

## LO 7: Determine Direct Labor Variances

**9–29.** The direct labor rate standard for Melissa Valdez Manufacturing is $10 per direct labor hour. The direct labor efficiency standard is 0.25 (one-quarter) hour per finished unit. Last month, the company completed 38,000 units of product using 9,280 direct labor hours at an actual cost of $97,904.

**REQUIRED:**

a. Determine the direct labor rate variance.
b. Determine the direct labor efficiency variance in dollars.
c. Appendix: Prepare a journal entry to record the direct labor and the direct labor rate and efficiency variances.

## LO 7: Determine Direct Labor Variances

**9–30.** The following information is presented for the Marathon Manufacturing Company.
- Direct labor rate standard is $11.55.
- Direct labor efficiency standard is 2.5 hours per finished unit.
- Budgeted production is 1,200 finished units.
- Production required 2,910 direct labor hours at a cost of $33,174.
- 1,150 finished units of product were produced.

## REQUIRED:

**a.** Determine the direct labor rate variance.

**b.** Determine the direct labor efficiency variance in dollars.

## LO 7: Determine Direct Labor Variances

✳ **9–31.** The following information is presented for the Picos Manufacturing Company.
- Direct labor rate standard is $12.
- Direct labor efficiency standard is two hours per finished unit.
- Budgeted production is 2,200 finished units.
- Production required 4,560 direct labor hours at a cost of $54,036.
- 2,250 finished units of product were produced.

## REQUIRED:

**a.** Determine the direct labor rate variance.

**b.** Determine the direct labor efficiency variance in dollars.

## LO 7: Determine Direct Labor Variances

**9–32.** The following information is presented for the Lew Green Manufacturing Company.
- Direct labor rate standard is $24.
- Direct labor efficiency standard is three hours per finished unit.
- Budgeted production is 775 finished units.
- Production required 2,375 direct labor hours at a cost of $57,475.
- 810 finished units of product were produced.

## REQUIRED:

**a.** Determine the direct labor rate variance.

**b.** Determine the direct labor efficiency variance in dollars.

## LO 7: Determine Direct Labor Variances

**9–33.** Information from the Spin Manufacturing Company is presented as follows:

| | |
|---|---|
| Actual number of direct labor hours | 275 |
| Actual direct labor cost | $4,620 |
| Actual number of units produced | 800 units |
| Direct labor rate standard | $16.10 |
| Direct labor efficiency standard | .3 hours per unit |
| Budgeted production | 850 units |

## REQUIRED:

**a.** Determine the direct labor rate variance.

**b.** Determine the direct labor efficiency variance in dollars.

## LO 7: Determine Direct Labor Variances

**9–34.** Information from the Popular Manufacturing Company is as follows:

| | |
|---|---|
| Actual number of direct labor hours | 1,275 |
| Actual direct labor cost | $16,065 |
| Actual number of units produced | 1,255 units |
| Direct labor rate standard | $12 |
| Direct labor efficiency standard | 1 hour per unit |
| Budgeted production | 1,200 units |

**REQUIRED:**

**a.** Determine the direct labor rate variance.

**b.** Determine the direct labor efficiency variance in dollars.

## LO 7: Determine Direct Labor Variances

**9–35.** Information from the Electronic Manufacturing Company is as follows:

| | |
|---|---|
| Actual number of direct labor hours | 12,830 |
| Actual direct labor cost | $292,524 |
| Actual number of units produced | 2,040 units |
| Direct labor rate standard | $23.10 |
| Direct labor efficiency standard | 6 hour per unit |
| Budgeted production | 2,000 units |

**REQUIRED:**

**a.** Determine the direct labor rate variance.

**b.** Determine the direct labor efficiency variance in dollars.

## LO 7: Determine Direct Material and Direct Labor Variances

**9–36.** Information from the Atlantic Company is presented as follows:

| | |
|---|---|
| Actual cost of 30,000 lbs of direct material purchased | $97,500 |
| Direct material used in production | 28,100 lbs |
| Actual number of direct labor hours | 12,850 |
| Actual direct labor cost | $165,765 |
| Actual production | 2,500 units |
| Direct material price standard | $3.30 per lb |
| Direct material quantity standard per finished unit of production | 11 lbs |
| Direct labor rate standard | $13 |
| Direct labor efficiency standard | 5 hour per unit |
| Budgeted production | 2,400 units |

**REQUIRED:**

**a.** Determine the direct material price variance.

**b.** Determine the direct material quantity variance in dollars.

**c.** Determine the direct labor rate variance.

**d.** Determine the direct labor efficiency variance in dollars.

## LO 7: Determine Direct Material and Direct Labor Variances

**9–37.** Information from the Progressive Company is presented as follows:

| | |
|---|---|
| Actual cost of 9,000 lbs of direct material purchased | $2,200 |
| Direct material used in production | 7,800 lbs |
| Actual number of direct labor hours | 980 |
| Actual direct labor cost | $14,945 |
| Actual production | 240 units |
| Direct material price standard | $0.25 per lb |
| Direct material quantity standard per finished unit of production | 30 lbs |
| Direct labor rate standard | $15 |
| Direct labor efficiency standard | 4 hour per unit |
| Budgeted production | 250 units |

## REQUIRED:

**a.** Determine the direct material price variance.
**b.** Determine the direct material quantity variance in dollars.
**c.** Determine the direct labor rate variance.
**d.** Determine the direct labor efficiency variance in dollars.

### LO 7: Determine Direct Material and Direct Labor Variances

**9–38.** Information from the Packard Company is presented as follows:

| | |
|---|---|
| Actual cost of 1,000 lbs of direct material purchased | $10,300 |
| Direct material used in production | 830 lbs |
| Actual number of direct labor hours | 1,220 |
| Actual direct labor cost | $13,176 |
| Actual production | 400 units |
| Direct material price standard | $10 per lb |
| Direct material quantity standard per finished unit of production | 2 lbs |
| Direct labor rate standard | $11 |
| Direct labor efficiency standard | 3 hour per unit |
| Budgeted production | 450 units |

## REQUIRED:

**a.** Determine the direct material price variance.
**b.** Determine the direct material quantity variance in dollars.
**c.** Determine the direct labor rate variance.
**d.** Determine the direct labor efficiency variance in dollars.

### LO 7: Determine Variable Manufacturing Overhead Variances

**9–39.** Billy Clifford Manufacturing applies variable manufacturing overhead to production on the basis of $15 per direct labor hour. The labor efficiency standard is five hours per finished unit. Last month the company produced 12,000 units and used 62,000 direct labor hours. Actual variable overhead cost incurred totaled $920,000.

## REQUIRED:

**a.** Determine the variable manufacturing overhead spending variance.
**b.** According to the appropriate standard, how many direct labor hours should it have taken to produce the 12,000 units?
**c.** Determine the direct labor efficiency variance in hours.
**d.** Determine the variable manufacturing overhead efficiency variance in dollars.

### LO 7: Determine Variable Manufacturing Overhead Variances

**9–40.** Clifford Knapp Manufacturing applies variable manufacturing overhead to production on the basis of $5 per direct labor hour. The labor efficiency standard is two hours per finished unit. Last month the company produced 11,000 units and used 22,400 direct labor hours. Actual variable overhead cost incurred totaled $111,700.

## REQUIRED:

**a.** Determine the variable manufacturing overhead spending variance.
**b.** According to the appropriate standard, how many direct labor hours should it have taken to produce the 11,000 units?

c. Determine the direct labor efficiency variance in hours.

d. Determine the variable manufacturing overhead efficiency variance in dollars.

## LO 7: Determine Variable Manufacturing Overhead Variances

**9–41.** Carlos Gonzalez Marine Manufacturing applies variable manufacturing overhead to production on the basis of $6 per direct labor hour. The labor efficiency standard is three hours per finished unit. Last month the company produced 15,000 units and used 45,650 direct labor hours. Actual variable overhead cost incurred totaled $277,800.

### REQUIRED:

a. Determine the variable manufacturing overhead spending variance.

b. According to the appropriate standard, how many direct labor hours should it have taken to produce the 15,000 units?

c. Determine the direct labor efficiency variance in hours.

d. Determine the variable manufacturing overhead efficiency variance in dollars.

e. Appendix: Prepare the following journal entries:

   **(1)** Record the actual variable manufacturing overhead. (Use "various accounts" for the credit side of the entry.)

   **(2)** Record the variable manufacturing overhead applied to production.

   **(3)** Close the variable manufacturing overhead accounts and establish the variable overhead variance accounts.

   **(4)** Close the variance accounts to cost of goods sold.

## LO 7: Determine Variable Manufacturing Overhead Variances

**9–42.** Alpine Manufacturing applies variable manufacturing overhead to production on the basis of $13 per direct labor hour. The labor efficiency standard is four hours per finished unit. Last month the company produced 3,000 units and used 11,700 direct labor hours. Actual variable overhead cost incurred totaled $157,200.

### REQUIRED:

a. Determine the variable manufacturing overhead spending variance.

b. Determine the variable manufacturing overhead efficiency variance in dollars.

c. Appendix: Prepare the following journal entries:

   **(1)** Record the actual variable manufacturing overhead. (Use "various accounts" for the credit side of the entry.)

   **(2)** Record the variable manufacturing overhead applied to production.

   **(3)** Close the variable manufacturing overhead accounts and establish the variable overhead variance accounts.

   **(4)** Close the variance accounts to cost of goods sold.

## LO 7: Determine Variable Manufacturing Overhead Variances

**9–43.** The Adler Manufacturing Company applies variable manufacturing overhead to production on the basis of $22 per direct labor hour. The labor efficiency standard is 0.5 hours per finished unit. Last month the company produced 14,500 units and used 7,300 direct labor hours. Actual variable overhead cost incurred totaled $162,000.

### REQUIRED:

a. Determine the variable manufacturing overhead spending variance.

b. Determine the variable manufacturing overhead efficiency variance in dollars.

## LO 7: Determine Variable Manufacturing Overhead Variances

**9–44.** The following information is presented for the Carol Green Manufacturing Company.

- Standard variable manufacturing overhead rate is $3.50 per direct labor hour.
- Direct labor efficiency standard is three hours per finished unit.
- Budgeted production is 810 finished units.
- Production required 2,370 direct labor hours.
- Variable manufacturing overhead cost was $8,500.
- 775 finished units of product were produced.

### REQUIRED:
a. Determine the variable manufacturing overhead spending variance.
b. Determine the variable manufacturing overhead efficiency variance in dollars.

## LO 7: Determine Variable Manufacturing Overhead Variances

**9–45.** The following information is presented for the Anne Reed Manufacturing Company.

- Standard variable manufacturing overhead rate is $7.00 per direct labor hour.
- Direct labor efficiency standard is six hours per finished unit.
- Budgeted production is 500 finished units.
- Production required 3,400 direct labor hours.
- Variable manufacturing overhead cost was $23,600.
- 550 finished units of product were produced.

### REQUIRED:
a. Determine the variable manufacturing overhead spending variance.
b. Determine the variable manufacturing overhead efficiency variance in dollars.

## LO 7: Determine Variable Manufacturing Overhead Variances

**9–46.** The following information is presented for the Willie Kemp Manufacturing Company.

- Standard variable manufacturing overhead rate is $2 per direct labor hour.
- Direct labor efficiency standard is four hours per finished unit.
- Budgeted production is 1,500 finished units.
- Production required 6,100 direct labor hours.
- Variable manufacturing overhead cost was $12,325.
- 1,550 finished units of product were produced.

### REQUIRED:
a. Determine the variable manufacturing overhead spending variance.
b. Determine the variable manufacturing overhead efficiency variance in dollars.

## LO 7:   Determine Variable Manufacturing Overhead Variances

**9–47.** Information from the Systems Manufacturing Company is as follows:

| | |
|---|---|
| Actual number of direct labor hours | 12,000 |
| Actual variable manufacturing overhead cost | $145,965 |
| Actual number of units produced | 2,440 units |
| Standard variable manufacturing overhead rate | $12.10 per direct labor hour |
| Direct labor efficiency standard | 5 hours |
| Budgeted production | 2,500 units |

### REQUIRED:
a. Determine the variable manufacturing overhead spending variance.
b. Determine the variable manufacturing overhead efficiency variance in dollars.

## LO 7:   Determine Variable Manufacturing Overhead Variances

**9–48.** Information from the Altos Manufacturing Company is as follows:

| | |
|---|---|
| Actual number of direct labor hours | 12,330 |
| Actual variable manufacturing overhead cost | $74,490 |
| Actual number of units produced | 12,540 units |
| Standard variable manufacturing overhead rate | $6 per direct labor hour |
| Direct labor efficiency standard | 1 hour |
| Budgeted production | 12,000 units |

### REQUIRED:
a. Determine the variable manufacturing overhead spending variance.
b. Determine the variable manufacturing overhead efficiency variance in dollars.

## LO 7:   Determine Variable Manufacturing Overhead Variances

**9–49.** Information from the Aspen Manufacturing Company is as follows:

| | |
|---|---|
| Actual number of direct labor hours | 175,000 |
| Actual variable manufacturing overhead cost | $2,400,000 |
| Actual number of units produced | 21,740 units |
| Standard variable manufacturing overhead rate | $14 per direct labor hour |
| Direct labor efficiency standard | 8 hours |
| Budgeted production | 20,000 units |

### REQUIRED:
a. Determine the variable manufacturing overhead spending variance.
b. Determine the variable manufacturing overhead efficiency variance in dollars.

## LO 7:   Determine Fixed Manufacturing Overhead Variances

**9–50.** The Hill Manufacturing Company applies fixed manufacturing overhead at the rate of $5.50 per direct labor hour. Fixed manufacturing overhead is budgeted to be $330,000 per month. The direct labor efficiency standard is five hours per finished unit. Although budgeted production for the month was 12,000, the company only produced 11,800 units. Production required actual direct labor hours of 60,000 and actual fixed manufacturing overhead cost incurred was $325,000.

**REQUIRED:**

a. Determine the fixed overhead budget variance.
b. What is the difference between the planned number of units and the number of units actually produced?
c. Determine the fixed manufacturing overhead volume variance.
d. Appendix: Prepare the following journal entries:
   (1) Record the actual fixed manufacturing overhead. (Use "various accounts" for the credit side of the entry.)
   (2) Record the fixed manufacturing overhead applied to production.
   (3) Close the fixed manufacturing overhead accounts and establish the fixed overhead variance accounts.
   (4) Close the variance accounts to cost of goods sold.

## LO 7: Determine Fixed Manufacturing Overhead Variances

**9–51.** The Johnson Manufacturing Company applies fixed manufacturing overhead at the rate of $4.60 per direct labor hour. Fixed manufacturing overhead is budgeted to be $910,800 per month. The direct labor efficiency standard is three hours per finished unit. Although budgeted production for the month was 66,000, the company produced 67,800 units. Production required actual direct labor hours of 203,000 and actual fixed manufacturing overhead cost incurred was $920,000.

**REQUIRED:**

a. Determine the fixed manufacturing overhead budget variance.
b. What is the difference between the planned number of units and the number of units actually produced?
c. Determine the fixed manufacturing overhead volume variance.
d. Appendix: Prepare the following journal entries:
   (1) Record the actual fixed manufacturing overhead. (Use "various accounts" for the credit side of the entry.)
   (2) Record the fixed manufacturing overhead applied to production.
   (3) Close the fixed manufacturing overhead accounts and establish the fixed overhead variance accounts.
   (4) Close the variance accounts to cost of goods sold.

## LO 7: Determine Fixed Manufacturing Overhead Variances

**9–52.** The Quality Manufacturing Company applies fixed manufacturing overhead at the rate of $7 per direct labor hour. Fixed manufacturing overhead is budgeted to be $336,000 per month. The direct labor efficiency standard is three hours per finished unit. Although budgeted production for the month was 16,000, the company only produced 15,500 units. Production required actual direct labor hours of 60,000 and actual fixed manufacturing overhead cost incurred was $344,000.

**REQUIRED:**

a. Determine the fixed manufacturing overhead budget variance.

b. Did the company produce as many units as it had planned? What is the difference between the planned number of units and the number of units actually produced?

c. Determine the fixed manufacturing overhead volume variance.

## LO 7: Determine Fixed Manufacturing Overhead Variances

**9–53.** The following information is presented for the Oddo Manufacturing Company.

- Standard fixed manufacturing overhead rate is $2 per direct labor hour.
- Direct labor efficiency standard is four hours per finished unit.
- Budgeted production is 2,500 finished units.
- Budgeted fixed manufacturing overhead is $20,000.
- Actual fixed manufacturing overhead cost was $10,750.
- 2,150 finished units of product were produced.

### REQUIRED:

a. Determine the fixed manufacturing overhead budget variance.

b. Determine the fixed manufacturing overhead volume variance in dollars.

## LO 7: Determine Fixed Manufacturing Overhead Variances

**9–54.** The following information is presented for the Alexander Manufacturing Company.

- Standard fixed manufacturing overhead rate is $6.50 per direct labor hour.
- Direct labor efficiency standard is two hours per finished unit.
- Budgeted production is 5,000 finished units.
- Budgeted fixed manufacturing overhead is $65,000.
- Actual fixed manufacturing overhead cost was $66,100.
- 5,150 finished units of product were produced.

### REQUIRED:

a. Determine the fixed manufacturing overhead budget variance.

b. Determine the fixed manufacturing overhead volume variance in dollars.

## LO 7: Determine Fixed Manufacturing Overhead Variances

**9–55.** The following information is presented for the Adcox Manufacturing Company.

- Standard fixed manufacturing overhead rate is $9.50 per direct labor hour.
- Direct labor efficiency standard is nine hours per finished unit.
- Budgeted production is 9,000 finished units.
- Budgeted fixed manufacturing overhead is $769,500.
- Actual fixed manufacturing overhead cost was $755,360.
- 8,500 finished units of product were produced.

### REQUIRED:

a. Determine the fixed manufacturing overhead budget variance.

b. Determine the fixed manufacturing overhead volume variance in dollars.

## LO 7:   Determine Fixed Manufacturing Overhead Variances

**9–56.** Information from the Michael Manufacturing Company is as follows:

| | |
|---|---|
| Actual number of direct labor hours | 12,200 |
| Actual fixed manufacturing overhead cost | $145,900 |
| Actual number of units produced | 2,400 units |
| Standard fixed manufacturing overhead rate | $12 per direct labor hour |
| Direct labor efficiency standard | 5 hours |
| Budgeted production | 2,500 units |
| Budgeted fixed manufacturing overhead | $150,000 |

**REQUIRED:**

a. Determine the fixed manufacturing overhead budget variance.
b. Determine the fixed manufacturing overhead volume variance in dollars.

## LO 7:   Determine Fixed Manufacturing Overhead Variances

**9–57.** Information from the Jennings Manufacturing Company is as follows:

| | |
|---|---|
| Actual number of direct labor hours | 5,130 |
| Actual fixed manufacturing overhead cost | $24,900 |
| Actual number of units produced | 5,400 units |
| Standard fixed manufacturing overhead rate | $5 per direct labor hour |
| Direct labor efficiency standard | 1 hour |
| Budgeted production | 5,000 units |
| Budgeted fixed manufacturing overhead | $25,000 |

**REQUIRED:**

a. Determine the fixed manufacturing overhead budget variance.
b. Determine the fixed manufacturing overhead volume variance in dollars.

## LO 7:   Determine Fixed Manufacturing Overhead Variances

**9–58.** Information from the Cathy Manufacturing Company is as follows:

| | |
|---|---|
| Actual number of direct labor hours | 5,200 |
| Actual fixed manufacturing overhead cost | $88,960 |
| Actual number of units produced | 2,700 units |
| Standard fixed manufacturing overhead rate | $15 per direct labor hour |
| Direct labor efficiency standard | 2 hours |
| Budgeted production | 3,000 units |
| Budgeted fixed manufacturing overhead | $90,000 |

**REQUIRED:**

a. Determine the fixed manufacturing overhead budget variance.
b. Determine the fixed manufacturing overhead volume variance in dollars.

## LO 7:   Determine Fixed Manufacturing Overhead Variances

**9–59.** Todd Manufacturing Company's budgeted production is 200,000 units per month. Budgeted monthly fixed manufacturing overhead is $2,400,000 and is applied to production at a rate of $4 per direct labor hour. The direct labor efficiency standard is three direct labor hours per unit of production. Last month it took 520,000 actual direct labor hours to produce 175,000 units. Actual fixed manufacturing overhead for the month was $2,435,000.

**REQUIRED:**
a. Determine the fixed manufacturing overhead budget variance.
b. Determine the fixed manufacturing overhead volume variance.

## LO 7: Determine Budgeted Production and Fixed Manufacturing Overhead Variances

**9–60.** The E. O. Mast Manufacturing Company applies fixed manufacturing overhead at the rate of $20 per direct labor hour. Fixed manufacturing overhead is budgeted to be $4,000,000 per month. The direct labor efficiency standard is two hours per finished unit. Last month the company produced 89,000 units using 180,000 direct labor hours and incurring fixed manufacturing overhead cost of $4,100,000.

**REQUIRED:**
a. Determine the fixed manufacturing overhead budget variance.
b. Did the company produce as many units as it had planned? What is the difference between the planned number of units and the number of units actually produced?
c. Determine the fixed manufacturing overhead volume variance.

## LO 7: Determine Budgeted Production and Fixed Manufacturing Overhead Variances

**9–61.** The Annie Manufacturing Company applies fixed manufacturing overhead at the rate of $10 per direct labor hour. Fixed manufacturing overhead is budgeted to be $418,000 per month. The direct labor efficiency standard is four hours per finished unit. Last month the company produced 9,800 units using 36,500 direct labor hours and incurring fixed manufacturing overhead cost of $410,000.

**REQUIRED:**
a. Determine the fixed manufacturing overhead budget variance.
b. Did the company produce as many units as it had planned? What is the difference between the planned number of units and the number of units actually produced?
c. Determine the fixed manufacturing overhead volume variance.

## LO 7: Determine Budgeted Production and Fixed Manufacturing Overhead Variances

**9–62.** The St. Hill Manufacturing Company applies fixed manufacturing overhead at the rate of $15 per direct labor hour. Fixed manufacturing overhead is budgeted to be $247,500 per month. The direct labor efficiency standard is six hours per finished unit. Last month the company produced 2,500 units using 15,500 direct labor hours and incurring fixed manufacturing overhead cost of $230,000.

**REQUIRED:**
a. Determine the fixed manufacturing overhead budget variance.

b. Did the company produce as many units as it had planned? What is the difference between the planned number of units and the number of units actually produced?

c. Determine the fixed manufacturing overhead volume variance.

## LO 7:  Determine Budgeted Fixed Factory Overhead and Fixed Manufacturing Overhead Variances

**9–63.** Information from the South Manufacturing Company is as follows:

| | |
|---|---|
| Actual number of direct labor hours | 32,500 |
| Actual fixed manufacturing overhead cost | $428,000 |
| Actual number of units produced | 8,000 units |
| Standard fixed manufacturing overhead rate | $12 per direct labor hour |
| Direct labor efficiency standard | 4 hours |
| Budgeted production | 9,000 units |
| Budgeted fixed manufacturing overhead | $ ? |

### REQUIRED:

a. Determine the fixed manufacturing overhead budget variance.

b. Determine the fixed manufacturing overhead volume variance in dollars.

## LO 7:  Determine Fixed Manufacturing Overhead Variances

**9–64.** Information from the North Manufacturing Company is as follows:

| | |
|---|---|
| Actual number of direct labor hours | 13,000 |
| Actual fixed manufacturing overhead cost | $50,000 |
| Actual number of units produced | 2,120 units |
| Standard fixed manufacturing overhead rate | $4 per direct labor hour |
| Direct labor efficiency standard | 6 hours |
| Budgeted production | 2,000 units |
| Budgeted fixed manufacturing overhead | $ ? |

### REQUIRED:

a. Determine the fixed manufacturing overhead budget variance.

b. Determine the fixed manufacturing overhead volume variance in dollars.

## LO 7:  Determine Fixed Manufacturing Overhead Variances

**9–65.** Information from the West Manufacturing Company is as follows:

| | |
|---|---|
| Actual number of direct labor hours | 27,000 |
| Actual fixed manufacturing overhead cost | $260,000 |
| Actual number of units produced | 3,250 units |
| Standard fixed manufacturing overhead rate | $9 per direct labor hour |
| Direct labor efficiency standard | 8 hours |
| Budgeted production | 3,500 units |
| Budgeted fixed manufacturing overhead | $ ? |

### REQUIRED:

a. Determine the fixed manufacturing overhead budget variance.

b. Determine the fixed manufacturing overhead volume variance in dollars.

## LO 7:  Determine Direct Material, Direct Labor, Variable Manufacturing Overhead and Fixed Manufacturing Overhead Variances

**9–66.** Information from the Quintana Company is as follows:

### Actual costs and amounts:

| | |
|---|---|
| Actual production | 3,800 units |
| Actual cost of 23,000 lbs of direct material purchased | $89,700 |
| Actual amount of direct material used | 22,950 |
| Actual direct labor cost | $23,205 |
| Actual direct labor hours | 1,950 hours |
| Actual variable overhead cost | $12,000 |
| Actual fixed overhead cost | $18,000 |

### Standards and other budgeted amounts:

| | |
|---|---|
| Budgeted production | 4,000 units |
| Direct material price standard | $3.85 |
| Direct material quantity standard | 6 lbs per unit |
| Direct labor rate standard | $11 per hour |
| Direct labor efficiency standard per unit | 0.5 hours |
| Standard variable mfg. overhead rate | $5.50 per direct labor hour |
| Standard fixed mfg. overhead rate | $10 per direct labor hour |
| Budgeted fixed manufacturing overhead | $20,000 |

### REQUIRED:
Determine the following variances:
  a. Direct material price variance
  b. Direct material quantity variance in dollars
  c. Direct labor rate variance
  d. Direct labor efficiency variance in dollars
  e. Variable manufacturing overhead spending variance
  f. Variable manufacturing overhead efficiency variance in dollars
  g. Fixed manufacturing overhead budget variance
  h. Fixed manufacturing overhead volume variance in dollars

## LO 7:  Determine Direct Material, Direct Labor, Variable Manufacturing Overhead and Fixed Manufacturing Overhead Variances

**9–67.** Information from the Holzmann Company is as follows:

### Actual costs and amounts:

| | |
|---|---|
| Actual production | 6,300 units |
| Actual cost of 20,000 lbs of direct material purchased | $40,000 |
| Actual amount of direct material used | 19,100 |
| Actual direct labor cost | $386,100 |
| Actual direct labor hours | 26,000 hours |
| Actual variable overhead cost | $165,000 |
| Actual fixed overhead cost | $310,000 |

**Standards and other budgeted amounts:**

| | | |
|---|---|---|
| Budgeted production | 6,000 | units |
| Direct material price standard | $2.10 | |
| Direct material quantity standard | 3 | lbs per unit |
| Direct labor rate standard | $15 | per hour |
| Direct labor efficiency standard per unit | 4 | hours |
| Standard variable mfg. overhead rate | $6.50 | per direct labor hour |
| Standard fixed mfg. overhead rate | $12.75 | per direct labor hour |
| Budgeted fixed manufacturing overhead | $306,000 | |

## REQUIRED:

Determine the following variances:

a. Direct material price variance
b. Direct material quantity variance in dollars
c. Direct labor rate variance
d. Direct labor efficiency variance in dollars
e. Variable manufacturing overhead spending variance
f. Variable manufacturing overhead efficiency variance in dollars
g. Fixed manufacturing overhead budget variance
h. Fixed manufacturing overhead volume variance in dollars

## LO 7: Determine Direct Material, Direct Labor, Variable Manufacturing Overhead and Fixed Manufacturing Overhead Variances

**9–68.** Information from the Collins Company is as follows:

**Actual costs and amounts:**

| | | |
|---|---|---|
| Actual production | 2,300 | units |
| Actual cost of 16,000 lbs of direct material purchased | $19,360 | |
| Actual amount of direct material used | 12,000 | |
| Actual direct labor cost | $46,410 | |
| Actual direct labor hours | 4,750 | hours |
| Actual variable overhead cost | $29,100 | |
| Actual fixed overhead cost | $50,125 | |

**Standards and other budgeted amounts:**

| | | |
|---|---|---|
| Budgeted production | 3,000 | units |
| Direct material price standard | $1.10 | |
| Direct material quantity standard | 5 | lbs per unit |
| Direct labor rate standard | $12 | per hour |
| Direct labor efficiency standard per unit | 2 | hours |
| Standard variable mfg. overhead rate | $6 | per direct labor hour |
| Standard fixed mfg. overhead rate | $8 | per direct labor hour |
| Budgeted fixed manufacturing overhead | $48,000 | |

## REQUIRED:

Determine the following variances:

a. Direct material price variance
b. Direct material quantity variance in dollars
c. Direct labor rate variance
d. Direct labor efficiency variance in dollars
e. Variable manufacturing overhead spending variance
f. Variable manufacturing overhead efficiency variance in dollars
g. Fixed manufacturing overhead budget variance
h. Fixed manufacturing overhead volume variance in dollars

# Chapter 10

## Evaluating Performance

*I*magine for a moment that you opened a shoe store in a local shopping center. After you have operated the store for some time, its success prompts you to open a second location. So you set up shop in the second location, select a manager, and open for business. The second store too does very well, and in time, your shoe store chain grows to five stores. Needless to say, it was a lot easier to manage the company when there was just a single location and you could oversee the entire operation personally. Unfortunately, it is impossible to give five separate stores the same personal, hands-on management attention. There are practical limits to how much a single manager can manage, especially when there are several different geographic locations. As a business grows, the diversity of knowledge required to effectively manage, combined with time constraints, adds to the inability of a single manager to manage the entire enterprise.

When a manager can no longer manage the whole company singlehandedly, management responsibility must be delegated to subordinate managers, each of whom is responsible for the performance of a part of the company. Evaluating the performance of these managers is the focus of this chapter. ∎

## LEARNING OBJECTIVES

*After completing your work on this chapter, you should be able to do the following:*

1. Describe centralized and decentralized management styles.
2. Describe the different types of business segments and the problems associated with determining segment costs.
3. Prepare a segment income statement.
4. Describe and calculate the return on investment.
5. Describe and calculate residual income.
6. Describe nonfinancial performance measures.

# BUSINESS SEGMENTS

**business segment** A part of a company managed by a particular individual or a part of a company about which separate information is needed.

To help make businesses more manageable, their owners often divide them into parts. A **business segment** represents a part of a company managed by a particular individual, or a part of a company about which separate information is needed, perhaps to evaluate management performance or to help managers make better management decisions.

Companies can be segmented by geographic area or location, business function, product, product line, or department. Examples of business segments include the Latin American Area of the Dow Chemical Company, an individual Sears department store, a Motorola manufacturing plant, and the Department of Accounting at the University of Miami. A segment can be described as a department, a division, an area, a region, a product line, or some other designation.

Obtaining detailed information about business segments is a vital part of the management decision process. Managers need information that relates to their business segment. Reports that provide information pertaining to a particular business segment are called **segment reports.** Segment reports should not be clouded by data that relate to other segments or by general information pertaining to the company as a whole. For example, if you were the manager of the Hard Rock Cafe in Orlando, Florida, and responsible for enhancing the restaurant's profits, you would benefit by having information about your particular restaurant. Although it might be somewhat helpful to know the overall profitability of the entire restaurant chain, specific information about the Orlando Hard Rock would be much more useful. You might want to know detailed sales information by product, by server, and by time of day. You would also want a comprehensive listing of your restaurant's expenses. Reports that include only revenues and expenses for your restaurant would help you to find opportunities to increase profits.

**segment reports** Reports that provide information pertaining to a particular business segment.

## Discussion Question

**10-1.** If you were the manager of the Contemporary Hotel at Disney World, what information would you want to help maximize the performance of the hotel?

## Segment Information

Depending on the needs of management and the availability of information, segment reports may be simple and include little detail, or they may be quite elaborate and include an abundance of detailed segment information. For example, it is possible for segment reports to consist simply of a listing of the segment's sales by product; or, segment reports may include sales, expenses, and other information. The extent of the information included in segment reports depends on management's need to know, balanced with the cost of providing the information.

# THE SEGMENT INCOME STATEMENT

**segment income statement**
An income statement prepared for a business segment.

An income statement prepared for a business segment is called a **segment income statement.** When a segment income statement is prepared, either the functional income statement or the contribution income statement format can be used. Recall from our discussions in Chapter 5 that the functional income statement separates costs into product and period costs. The contribution income statement classifies costs by behavior, either variable or fixed. We know that a variable cost is one that changes in total based on some activity, whereas a fixed cost is one that remains unchanged regardless of the level activity. To be sure you remember these two income statement formats, we reproduce them in Exhibit 10–1.

**Exhibit 10–1**
Functional and Contribution Income Statement Formats

| Functional Format | Contribution Income Format |
|---|---|
| Sales | Sales |
| − Cost of Goods Sold (Product Cost) | − All Variable Costs (Product and Period) |
| = Gross Profit | = Contribution Margin |
| − Selling and Admin. Expense (Period Cost) | − All Fixed Costs (Product and Period) |
| = Net Income | = Net Income |

**segment margin** The amount of income that pertains to a particular segment.

To prepare a segment income statement, we gather revenue and expense information that pertains to the particular segment and then arrange it in the appropriate income statement format. The amount of income that pertains to a particular segment is called the **segment margin.** Because the contribution income format is particularly well-suited for our work in this chapter, we use that format in all our remaining presentations. A segment income statement for the Miami office of the Quintana Company appears in Exhibit 10–2.

It is important that the segment income statement for the Miami office of the Quintana Company include all the appropriate information for the Miami office, and no more. Often, this is easier said than done. Generally, revenue can easily be traced to individual business segments, therefore, obtaining detailed revenue information by segment is not too difficult. Unfortunately, however, the same cannot always be said for cost information.

**Exhibit 10–2**
Segment Income Statement for the Miami Office

**QUINTANA COMPANY MIAMI OFFICE**
**Segment Income Statement**
**For the Year Ended December 31, 2001**

| | |
|---|---|
| Sales | $1,200,000 |
| Variable cost | 800,000 |
| Contribution margin | 400,000 |
| Fixed cost for Miami office | 300,000 |
| Segment margin | $ 100,000 |

It is often difficult (if not impossible) to obtain cost information that includes all the costs for a particular segment and excludes costs associated with other segments. There are several reasons for this. First, it may be difficult to identify all the costs that relate to the segment. For example, say that the Norris Division of the NHL Company has three copiers. Certainly the cost of these copiers should be included in any evaluation of the Norris Division. These three copiers, however, are just three of the 27 copiers owned by the NHL Company (the other 24 copiers are in other segments). The problem is that all 27 copiers were purchased by the central company purchasing department and Norris has no record of the cost of its three copiers.

## Discussion Question

**10–2.** What are three other costs that relate directly to the Norris Division, but for which the division probably does not have information?

The second reason it may be difficult to identify costs to particular segments is that costs are often mixed together in the accounting process. An example of this might be advertising purchased by the NHL Company, which benefits not only the Norris Division, but also the five other divisions of the company. The exact amount that should be charged to the Norris Division is virtually impossible to determine accurately.

## Discussion Question

**10–3.** What are three other costs that benefit the Norris Division but benefit at least one other division as well?

To help manage a business segment, we should include all the costs associated with the segment on cost reports prepared for it. It is equally important that costs that do not pertain to the segment be excluded from the segment's cost reports. In the case of variable costs, this is fairly straightforward. Variable costs can be traced directly to the business segments to which they pertain and then be included on the appropriate segment reports.

Fixed cost are more difficult to trace to individual business segments and therefore present more of a challenge. One problem with tracing fixed costs to business segments is that some fixed costs pertain to a single business segment whereas others benefit several segments or perhaps the company as a whole. Fixed costs that arise to support a single segment are called **direct fixed costs** or **traceable fixed costs.** These fixed costs can be *traced* to an individual business segment. Direct fixed costs should be included on the cost reports for the segment to which they pertain. Fixed costs that arise to support more than one segment or the company as a whole are called **common fixed costs** or **indirect fixed costs.**

This discussion of direct and indirect costs should not seem entirely new. It is a subject we covered in some depth in Chapter 2 when we discussed the concept of a cost object. As you recall, a cost object is any activity or item for which a separate cost measurement is desired. A cost that can be traced directly to a cost object is a direct cost, whereas a cost that is incurred to support multiple cost objects is an indirect cost. In our present discussion, the cost object is the business segment.

**direct fixed cost** Fixed costs incurred to support a single business segment.

**traceable fixed cost** Another name for *direct fixed cost.*

**common fixed cost** Fixed costs incurred to support more than one business segment, or the company as a whole.

**indirect fixed cost** Another name for *common fixed cost.*

Because common fixed costs benefit several segments or the company in general, segment managers often have little control over these costs. A simple question can be asked to determine whether a cost is a common cost or a direct cost:

*Would the cost continue if the segment were to disappear?*

If the cost will continue even if the segment disappeared, the cost is a common fixed cost. If, on the other hand, the cost would disappear if the segment disappears, the cost is a direct fixed cost. There are very few, if any, common variable costs; thus, in virtually all instances, the common costs we must consider are fixed.

For many years there has been debate as to whether cost reports prepared for an individual segment should include some allocated amount of common fixed costs. Proponents of allocation maintain that common fixed costs benefit the entire company and therefore each segment should be charged for its "fair share" of the common cost. Further, they argue that it is impossible to determine true segment profitability if common costs are excluded. Opponents of allocation argue just the opposite. They maintain that because segment managers have little or no authority to exercise control over common fixed costs, these costs should not be included in segment reports. These folks believe it is unfair to charge a manager's department for costs that are out of his or her control. In addition, common fixed costs are generally distributed to various business segments based on an arbitrary allocation scheme and can make a segment appear to be unprofitable when, in fact, that segment is contributing to the overall profitability of the company. Managers may attempt to "control" the common fixed costs allocated to their segment by manipulating the allocation base.

## Discussion Question

10–4. Assume for a moment that you are a segment manager at Motorola. How would you react to a charge made to your department for a portion of the cost of the fleet of corporate aircraft, even though you have never even seen one of the planes?

Both the proponents and opponents of common fixed cost allocation to business segments feel strongly about their positions. There seems to be little question, however, that the practice of including common fixed costs in segment reports is losing popularity. This fact is not surprising when we consider that the main purpose of management accounting is to influence managers to act to benefit the company. It seems clear that including common fixed costs in segment reports can lead managers toward behavior that is counterproductive. Restricting a segment cost report to costs over which a manager has control makes it a more useful tool for supporting sound business decisions.

## PITFALL OF ALLOCATING COMMON FIXED COSTS— A CLOSER LOOK

When common fixed costs are allocated to segments, segment information may be misleading and result in disastrous business decisions. As an example, consider the segmented income statement for Flandro Feed Stores presented in Exhibit 10–3.

**Exhibit 10–3**
Flandro Feed Stores
Segment Income
Statement

**FLANDRO FEED STORES**
**Segment Income Statement**
**For the Year Ended December 31, 2002**

| | Company Total | North Store | South Store | Central Store |
|---|---|---|---|---|
| Sales | $500,000 | $105,000 | $225,000 | $170,000 |
| Variable cost | 332,950 | 73,750 | 141,000 | 118,200 |
| Contribution margin | 167,050 | 31,250 | 84,000 | 51,800 |
| Direct fixed cost | 75,000 | 20,000 | 32,000 | 23,000 |
| Segment margin | 92,050 | 11,250 | 52,000 | 28,800 |
| Common fixed cost | 60,000 | 12,600* | 27,000** | 20,400*** |
| Net income | $ 32,050 | ($ 1,350) | $ 25,000 | $ 8,400 |

\* $105,000/$500,000 = 21% × $60,000 = $12,600
\*\* $225,000/$500,000 = 45% × $60,000 = $27,000
\*\*\*$170,000/$500,000 = 34% × $60,000 = $20,400

As you can see from Exhibit 10–3, the $60,000 common fixed cost has been allocated to the business segments based on relative sales volume, which means that because the South Store provided 45 percent of the company's sales ($225,000/$500,000 = 45%), this store is allocated 45 percent of the common fixed cost ($60,000 × 45% = $27,000). Of the common fixed cost, 34 percent was allocated to the Central Store based on its percentage of sales, and 21 percent was allocated to the North Store. As you can see, it appears that the North Store is unprofitable. Based on the information in Exhibit 10–3, it seems that profits could be increased if the unprofitable North Store is closed. By closing the North Store it appears that the $1,350 loss would be eliminated. Let us look at the results had the North Store been eliminated. The segment income statement for Flandro Feed Stores without the North Store is presented in Exhibit 10–4.

**Exhibit 10–4**
Flandro Feed Stores
Segment Income
Statement with North
Store Eliminated

**FLANDRO FEED STORES**
**Segment Income Statement**
**For the Year Ended December 31, 2002**

| | Company Total | South Store | Central Store |
|---|---|---|---|
| Sales | $395,000 | $225,000 | $170,000 |
| Variable cost | 259,200 | 141,000 | 118,200 |
| Contribution margin | 135,800 | 84,000 | 51,800 |
| Direct fixed cost | 55,000 | 32,000 | 23,000 |
| Segment margin | 80,800 | 52,000 | 28,800 |
| Common fixed cost | 60,000 | 34,200* | 25,800** |
| Net income | $ 20,800 | $ 17,800 | $ 3,000 |

\* $225,000/$395,000 = 57% (rounded) × $60,000 = $34,200
\*\* $170,000/$395,000 = 43% (rounded) × $60,000 = $25,800

M–382   **Introduction to Management Accounting**

As Exhibit 10–4 shows, when the North Store is eliminated, Flandro's net income actually *declines* from $32,050 to $20,800. On the surface this seems to make no sense, because the results in Exhibit 10–3 showed the North Store with a net loss for the year of $1,350. So, how did eliminating the North Store cause profits to drop by $11,250 ($32,050 − $20,800)? The answer lies in the practice of allocating common fixed cost. Notice in Exhibit 10–4 that the common fixed cost of $60,000 did not change when the North Store was removed, because the common fixed cost is for items that are necessary to operate the company even if there are fewer stores. For example, even if the North Store closes, common costs for such items as accounting, finance, and the cost of operating the home office would continue. Therefore, the $60,000 common fixed cost would have to be distributed to the two remaining stores. Again, this configuration is done based on relative sales values.

In truth, the North Store is contributing to Flandro's overall profitability. When the North Store is eliminated, so is its segment margin. It is not a coincidence that the $11,250 decline in profits without the North Store is exactly equal to the North Store's segment margin in Exhibit 10–3. If the North Store is eliminated, its segment margin disappears, but the common fixed cost remains and must be allocated to the remaining segments.

To avoid such misleading information and the poor decisions that can result, many companies have stopped the practice of allocating common fixed costs to segments. The segmented income statement for Flandro Feed Stores without the allocation of common fixed cost is shown in Exhibit 10–5.

**Exhibit 10–5**
Flandro Feed Stores Segment Income Statement without Allocation of Common Fixed Cost

**FLANDRO FEED STORES**

**Segment Income Statement**

**For the Year Ended December 31, 2002**

|  | Company Total | North Store | South Store | Central Store |
|---|---|---|---|---|
| Sales | $500,000 | $105,000 | $225,000 | $170,000 |
| Variable cost | 332,950 | 73,750 | 141,000 | 118,200 |
| Contribution margin | 167,050 | 31,250 | 84,000 | 51,800 |
| Direct fixed cost | 75,000 | 20,000 | 32,000 | 23,000 |
| Segment margin | 92,050 | $ 11,250 | $ 52,000 | $ 28,800 |
| Common fixed cost | 60,000 |  |  |  |
| Net income | $ 32,050 |  |  |  |

As shown in Exhibit 10–5, when common fixed costs are not allocated, the segment margin becomes the "bottom line" for each segment. This amount is a better indicator of segment profit performance because it considers direct costs, costs over which the segment manager has control.

To provide useful information to help evaluate segment performance and to help segment managers make informed decisions, all direct costs that pertain to a particular segment must be included in the management reports for that segment. If a direct cost is excluded, it is unlikely that the segment manager will work to reduce that cost. For example, assume that a leased copy machine is used exclusively by the finance department of a major corporation. Assume further that the rent for the copy machine, plus the rent for all the other copy machines used by the company, is included in a monthly bill from the Acme Copy Machine Company. If the rent cost included on this single bill is not distributed (charged) to user departments, the cost for each department is understated by the amount of the rent. If this happens, the rent for the copy machine would be excluded from the information used to help evaluate the finance department's performance. Therefore, it is unlikely that the finance department manager would work to reduce the rental cost by switching to a less expensive copy machine. In fact, once the manager finds that the cost of the copy machine is not charged to the department, he or she might even upgrade to an overly elaborate copy machine knowing that the department will not be penalized for such an expenditure. Thus, it is important to include all costs associated with a business segment in the segment's cost reports.

## SERVICE DEPARTMENT COST ALLOCATION

**service department** A business segment responsible for secondary (support) functions. Service departments provide service to the main business operations and to other service departments.

The main operation of a merchandiser is selling products. For a manufacturer, the main operation is manufacturing and selling products. For a service business, the main operation is providing services to customers. In addition to any company's main business operation, however, secondary support operations also occur. Most companies, whether merchandisers, manufacturers, or service-type businesses, also have accounting departments, a personnel department, and other departments that provide support to the various functions of the company. Further, telephone service must be provided, and a facility (building) within which to operate. The business segments that handle these and other secondary operations are called **service departments.** These departments provide necessary services to the main business operations and other service departments.

## Discussion Question

**10–5.** Besides the ones listed in the previous paragraph, what are five other service departments you think would be common to most companies?

The cost of operating a service department can be substantial. This cost is allocated to the departments that use the services provided. In other words, if a particular department receives benefit from a service department, that department should be charged for the cost of the service.

Determining the amount of service department cost to charge various user departments is not an exact science. For some kinds of service cost, a direct correlation can be found between the amount of service provided to a department and the cost charged to that department. In these instances, the manager of the user department rarely disputes the charge. For other types of service cost, however, no direct cause and effect can be found. In that event, the cost charged to departments for services is based on an allocation method that may or may not be accurate or even fair. This allocation is much like that of common fixed cost to segments, as discussed earlier. The allocation of service department cost when no correlation can be found between the service and the cost can actually cloud management's vision about the performance of a department.

As was the case with the allocation of fixed common cost to segments, certain managers believe that service department costs should be allocated whereas others believe the practice should be stopped. As usual, both sides hold strongly to their views. Although some companies have stopped allocating service department cost, the majority of companies still maintain this practice. The responsibility of department managers is to be vigilant in making certain that the costs charged to their departments reasonably reflect the amount of service received. Examples of service departments and possible allocation bases are shown in Exhibit 10–6.

**Exhibit 10–6**
Representative Service Departments and Possible Allocation Bases

| Service Department | Allocation Basis |
| --- | --- |
| Personnel Department | • Number of employees |
| Telephone | • Number of phones<br>• Number of lines<br>• Long-distance charges |
| Copy Machine or Copy Center | • Quantity of services used:<br>  • Number of single-sided copies<br>  • Number of double-sided copies<br>  • Number of bindings |
| Employee Cafeteria | • Number of employees<br>• Number of meals served |
| Finance Department | • Amount of capital invested |
| Building Occupancy | • Square footage of building occupied |
| Computer Operations | • Computer mainframe time<br>• Number of personal computers<br>• Number of reports generated |
| Computer Programming | • Hours of programming |
| Office Services | • Square footage of office occupied<br>• Number of offices |
| Engineering Department | • Number of engineering changes<br>• Hours of engineering services |
| Maintenance | • Square footage of building occupied<br>• Hours of maintenance |
| Aircraft Operations | • Number of passenger miles<br>• Number of hours flown<br>• Weight of load and distance flown |

# ACTIVITY-BASED SERVICE DEPARTMENT COST ALLOCATION

Activity-based costing is a topic we covered in Chapter 3 when we discussed alternative ways to allocate manufacturing overhead to units of product produced. Activity-based costing can also be a valuable tool for allocating service department cost to other departments. When possible, the allocation base used to allocate cost should be an activity that causes the cost. As stated in Chapter 3, an activity that causes cost to occur is called a *cost driver.* The two major benefits to using cost drivers to allocate service department cost are (1) this cost allocation method tends to be more fair and accurate, and (2) in attempting to control the cost allocated to their departments, managers will work to reduce the allocation base—the cost driver. Because the cost driver is also the cost cause, reducing the cost driver will actually reduce the amount paid by the company for goods and services. For example, when the cost driver used to allocate basic phone service is the number of phone lines, a reduction in the number of phone lines will not only reduce the allocation of phone cost, but it will also reduce the amount the company spends for phone service. This reduction results in true cost savings for the company.

## Discussion Question

**10-6.** Refer to the list of five service departments you made in response to Discussion Question 10-5. What is a possible allocation base for each of the departments you listed?

It is important to know about service department cost allocation for several reasons. First, as a department manager, you will need to know how to control service department costs allocated to your department. Second, you should be able to discriminate between costs that are arbitrarily allocated to your department and those that are equitable. Third, as a high-level manager, you should be able to recognize when an allocation method should be modified or replaced, because it does not result in information that provides incentives for managers to act in fulfillment of company goals.

Sometimes the allocation method can cause managers to do counterproductive things, especially when activity-based costing is not used to allocate costs. For example, consider what happened to a major corporation when it changed the allocation base it used to distribute the cost of office space. From a charge for all the square footage the departments occupied, the firm changed to a charge for only the square footage of the enclosed office space occupied by the departments. Top managers felt that departments should not be charged for halls, elevator waiting areas, or other common areas but only for the office space dedicated entirely to the department's use. Some managers recognized that their department's allocation for office space could be cut if they were to reduce the square footage used for enclosed offices. Accordingly, they demolished several offices occupied by department secretaries and provided them with desks and work space in the "common" area. The result was an increase in the amount of common space, and a marked decrease in the amount of square footage used for enclosed offices. Because the departments were only charged for enclosed office space, their office space cost allocation was reduced.

The change worked to the detriment of the company as a whole, however, because managers were rewarded for remodeling their offices even though the cost of the remodeling was unnecessary. Interestingly, only managers who had a working knowledge of how service department costs were allocated knew how to take advantage of the situation.

## Discussion Question

**10-7.** Do you think the cost previously described should even be allocated? If not, explain your reasoning. If yes, what would you suggest to the company to overcome the dysfunctional management behavior described?

Reducing the service cost allocated to a particular department is not a difficult task to accomplish. First, the department manager must determine what allocation base is being used. Second, the manager must reduce the amount of the allocation base consumed by the department. If the allocation base used is a cost driver, the actual cost involved will decrease. If the allocation base is arbitrary and unrelated to the actual cost, the amount allocated to the department will decrease, but the actual cost to the company will continue and simply be shifted to some other manager's department.

As an example of how to control service department cost allocation, assume that the cost of photocopies is allocated based on the number of copies made. A reduction in the number of copies made will reduce the copy cost allocated to the user department. An attempt to reduce the number of copies would include a review of department procedures to ensure that only necessary copies are made. It might also include a review of alternate imaging technology to find ways to reduce the need for photocopies. This same logic can be used to control the cost allocation for telephone use, which is often allocated to departments based on the number of phone lines used. To reduce the cost allocation, unnecessary telephones are eliminated.

In each of these two examples, because the allocation base is a cost driver, a reduction in the base would not only cause a reduction in the cost allocated to the department but would also cause a true reduction in cost to the company.

## APPROACHES TO SEGMENT MANAGEMENT

The strategy used to manage business segments varies from company to company. Some companies prefer that top management make all but the most routine decisions, whereas other companies prefer that lower-level managers make most or all of the decisions within their area. When almost all decisions are made by the top managers and little is left to the discretion of lower-level managers, the company is said to have a centralized management style. Conversely, if management decisions are made at the lowest possible management level, the company is said to have a decentralized management style. These management styles have both advantages and disadvantages.

### Centralized Management

**centralized management** A management style in which top managers make most management decisions.

When a **centralized management** style is used, top management makes most management decisions. Middle- and lower-level managers are responsible only for routine decisions and supervisory functions. This management style ensures that the wishes of top management are incorporated into each management decision. Top managers often have the most experience, which could lead to wise business decisions. A centralized management style has certain disadvantages: (1) Top managers must spend their valuable time making routine, low-level business decisions. (2) Top managers may not have an intimate familiarity with the various routine aspects of the business. (3) Lower-level employees have little opportunity to gain experience in decision making.

### Decentralized Management

**decentralized management** A management style in which lower-level managers are responsible for decisions that relate to their segment of the company.

When a **decentralized management** style is used, lower-level managers are responsible for management decisions that relate to their segment of the business. When a highly decentralized management style is used, decisions are made at the lowest possible level in the organization.

A decentralized management style has several advantages. It helps spread the decision-making responsibilities among the various management levels of the company and allows lower-level managers greater control over their business segments. Another benefit is that a decentralized management style provides an opportunity for lower-level managers to sharpen their decision-making skills, thus providing the company with experienced managers to progress through the ranks to top management positions. Decentralization also means that decisions are made by the managers who are most familiar with the problems and opportunities occurring in the routine operations of the company. Top managers may be somewhat removed from the intimacies of the daily routine business operations and therefore would be hard pressed to make well-informed decisions. Another advantage is that it relieves top managers of the responsibility of routine decisions and allows them to focus on strategic decisions and the overall goals of the organization.

A disadvantage of decentralized management is that decisions may not entirely reflect the views of top managers. Also, decisions are made by managers who may be less experienced than the top managers.

## Discussion Questions

**10–8.** If you were the chief executive officer of your company, would you prefer a centralized or decentralized management style? Why?

**10–9.** If you were a lower-level manager in your company, would you prefer a centralized or decentralized management style? Why?

**10–10.** What similarities do you see between our discussion here of centralized and decentralized management and our discussion in Chapter 8 of top-down and bottom-up budgeting?

# EVALUATION OF BUSINESS SEGMENTS

To evaluate the performance of business segments, we must first determine just what constitutes good performance. To establish whether a manager is doing a good job, for example, we must first have some idea of just what a "good job" means. To evaluate segment performance, a standard must be developed that establishes just what constitutes "good performance."

The performance of a business segment can be evaluated based on a number of criteria. The most logical evaluation criteria match the scope of responsibility and authority afforded the segment's manager. That is, if a particular segment's manager has the responsibility and authority only to control costs, the segment performance should be evaluated based on criteria that focus on cost control. Conversely, if the segment manager has the responsibility to generate revenue and also to control costs, the segment's performance should be evaluated based on criteria that focus on profits. Segments may be categorized based on the criteria used for their evaluation. The most popular segment categories are revenue centers, cost centers, profit centers, and investment centers.

## Revenue Centers

**revenue center** A business segment in which the manager has responsibility and authority to act to increase revenues but has little or no control over costs and the amount invested in the segment.

A **revenue center** is a business segment whose manager has responsibility and authority to act to increase revenues but has little control over costs and the amount invested in the segment. The performance of a revenue center is evaluated based on the amount of revenue generated by the segment, and the manager is evaluated based on his or her ability to generate sales revenue.

✳ An example of a business segment properly designated a revenue center is a sales office whose segment manager has little or no control over costs. The results of the manager's actions would affect sales revenue but have minimal effect on cost.

## Cost Centers

**cost center** A business segment where the manager has responsibility and authority to act to decrease or at least control costs but has little or no control over the revenues generated or the amount invested in the segment.

A **cost center** is a business segment whose manager has responsibility and authority to decrease or at least control costs while keeping output high. Generally, cost center managers are not responsible for generating revenue, nor do they have control over the amount invested in the segment. The performance of a cost center is evaluated based on the amount of cost incurred by the segment and the manager is evaluated based on his or her ability to control these costs.

Business segments that provide service to the company or customers but do not contribute directly to revenues are good candidates to be designated as cost centers. Examples of cost centers include the accounting department of a hospital, a repair department that handles warranty repair work, an assembly department, and an inspection facility in a manufacturing plant.

## Profit Centers

**profit center** A business segment in which the manager has the responsibility and authority to act to increase revenue and decrease or at least control costs, but has little or no control over the amount invested in the segment.

A **profit center** is a business segment whose manager has the responsibility and authority to act to increase revenue and decrease or at least control costs but does not have control over the amount invested in the segment. The performance of a profit center is evaluated based on the amount of profits it generates. The manager of a profit center is evaluated based on his or her ability to increase revenue and control expenses, because profits are increased by increasing revenue and/or decreasing expenses.

Examples of profit centers include individual stores in a department store chain, a college bookstore, and a pathology testing center.

### Measuring Performance of Revenue, Cost, and Profit Centers

The most commonly used method of evaluating the performance of revenue centers, cost centers, and profit centers is performance to budget. The sales goals established during the budgeting process can be used as a basis for evaluating the performance of revenue centers. If, for example, actual sales are higher than budgeted sales, this would be a favorable indication. If, on the other hand, actual sales are lower than budgeted sales, this would be an unfavorable indication. For a cost center, the goals established during the budgeting process for output and cost can be used as a basis for evaluating cost center performance. Actual production that exceeds budgeted production, for example, would be a favorable indication. Costs per unit of output that are lower than budgeted would also be a favorable indication. Obviously, favorable performance would be indicated by high output and low cost relative to output volume. For a profit center, the profit goals established during the budgeting process can be compared to actual profits to evaluate profit center performance. Favorable performance would be indicated by actual profits that meet or exceed budgeted profits.

It is often argued that having managers strive to meet budgeted performance targets is so simplistic that it leads to suboptimal performance. Managers may simply strive to meet the expectations established by the budget instead of trying to maximize sales. Another potential problem is that managers who are evaluated based on performance to budget can make themselves look good by negotiating relatively low budgeted sales and relatively high budgeted costs. Then when the actual sales are higher than budget, and the actual costs are lower than budgeted, the manager appears to have performed well. This information may seem familiar to you. Other chapters in the text included brief discussions of the problems associated with performance to budget as a way to measure managers' performance—a subject addressed in Chapter 8 when we presented the operating budget and again in Chapter 9 in the presentation of standard costing. Everything about the potential for counterproductive behavior inherent in the performance to budget evaluation technique applies to measuring the performance of revenue centers, cost centers, and profit centers.

If we move away from performance to budget as a means of evaluating revenue center managers, however, what do we put in its place? This topic has been a topic of debate for some time in management accounting circles. The answer, we suspect, is not to drop performance to budget as a performance measure entirely. Rather, it should be supplemented with other types of measures, some of which are presented near the end of this chapter. For now, just remember that a company runs a real risk of encouraging silly management behavior if it relies too heavily on performance to budget as a means of evaluating its managers.

## Investment Centers

Does earning a profit of $100,000 constitute good performance? Before we can tell just how good it is, we should also consider the amount of investment required. Surely, almost any business segment can be profitable if there is an unlimited amount to invest in assets and technology. In business, the hope is to keep the profit high and the amount invested low.

**investment center** A business segment that is evaluated based on the amount of profit generated relative to the amount invested in the segment.

An **investment center** is a business segment that is evaluated on the amount of profit generated relative to the amount invested in the segment. An investment center manager should strive to maximize profit while minimizing the amount of investment used to earn the profit. Reducing the investment in a given segment allows the freed-up funds to be used by other segments. If the funds are not needed by the company elsewhere, financing can be reduced.

If a segment manager has responsibility and authority for revenues, costs, and capital investment in the segment, it should probably be designated an investment center. Examples of business segments that might be designated investment centers are individual stores in a department store chain, a college bookstore, and a pathology testing center. Note that these examples are the same as those given for segments designated as profit centers in our earlier discussion, because the classification of a business segment as a revenue center, profit center, cost center, or investment center depends not only on the operation of the segment but also, and as importantly, on the responsibility and authority afforded the segment's manager. If a manager's responsibility includes the generation of revenue, cost control, and control of the amount invested in the segment, then the business segment she or he manages should be designated an investment center.

As stated earlier, an investment center should be evaluated not only on the income generated by the segment, but also on the amount of investment required to earn the income. Obviously the higher the net income, the better, and the lower the investment required to generate that net income, the better. To evaluate the performance of an investment center we must be able to quantify the relationship between income earned and the investment required. For example, if you are about to invest in a savings account, it might be beneficial to know that a $5,245 deposit will earn interest of $183.57 in one year's time. Without knowing the percentage interest rate of return, however, the amounts have little meaning when evaluating the performance of the savings account. In business, the percentage return on an amount invested is called the return on investment.

# RETURN ON INVESTMENT

In 1903, Pierre Du Pont and two cousins, Alfred and Coleman, formed the E.I. Du Pont de Nemours Powder Company by combining several gunpowder companies they had purchased from other Du Pont family members. When the cousins purchased the companies, they paid for them by issuing bonds equal in value to the expected future earnings potential of the companies acquired to form the new business. Pierre and his cousins could realize a profit only when the income from the new company exceeded the projected income of the companies they had purchased. Therefore, if income did not increase, there would only be enough profits to pay the bonds, leaving no profit for the cousins. This transaction is an early example of a leveraged buyout.

Knowing only the *amount* of income was not enough to monitor the success of the new organization. Accordingly, Pierre Du Pont devised the return on investment model to calculate the percentage return on the cousins investment. The return on investment could be used to assess whether the returns of the individual segments of the Du Pont Company exceeded the rate used to calculate the purchase price and interest payments on the bonds. Of course, the hope was that each of the segments of the Du Pont Company would have a return on investment that exceeded the rate used to determine the purchase price. The company went on to become the Du Pont Chemical Company we know today.

## Discussion Question

**10–11.** What similarities do you see between our discussion here of return on investment and our discussion in Chapter 7 of capital expenditures?

**return on investment (ROI)**
The percentage return generated by an investment in a business or a business segment.

Since its inception, Du Pont's return on investment model has been a popular method of evaluating investment centers. **Return on investment (ROI)** is the percentage return generated by an investment in a business or business segment. The ROI is calculated by dividing the amount of income by the amount invested. For example, assume that the Eastern Division of the Lisa Company generated a segment margin of $896,750 for 2002 and the amount invested in the division was $10,550,000. This information is interesting, but it is probably more meaningful to know the percentage return that the investment generated. The ROI for the Lisa Company is 8.5 percent, determined as follows:

$$\frac{\text{Segment Income}}{\text{Investment in the Segment}} = \text{Return on Investment}$$

$$\frac{\$896,750}{\$10,550,000} = 8.5\%$$

After we determine the ROI for the division, the next question is, is the ROI adequate? If a company uses ROI as the measurement criterion for evaluating segment performance, it must establish a required rate for the ROI. The required rate of return that companies normally use is the blended cost of capital rate, as discussed in Chapter 7 concerning capital expenditures. Once established, the required ROI rate is used as a benchmark to evaluate the performance of the various investment centers in the company. A segment with an ROI that equals or exceeds the company's required rate will be viewed favorably, whereas a segment with an ROI that is lower than the required rate will be viewed as deficient. If we assume that the required rate for the ROI for the Lisa Company is eight percent, then the Eastern Division's performance is certainly adequate.

# Discussion Question

**10–12.** What similarities do you see between our discussion here of the ROI calculation and our discussion in Chapter 7 of the internal rate of return?

In evaluating segment performance, we can rank segments by their return on investment. For example, if the Western Division of the Lisa Company has income of $857,500 with an investment on $9,800,000, how does the performance of the Western Division compare to that of the Eastern Division? The return on investment of both divisions is presented as Exhibit 10–7.

**Exhibit 10–7**
Return on Investment for Both Divisions of Lisa Company

| Eastern Division | Western Division |
|---|---|
| $\dfrac{\text{Segment Income}}{\text{Investment in the Segment}} = \text{ROI}$ | $\dfrac{\text{Segment Income}}{\text{Investment in the Segment}} = \text{ROI}$ |
| $\dfrac{\$896,750}{\$10,550,00} = 8.5\%$ | $\dfrac{\$857,500}{\$9,800,000} = 8.75\%$ |

Based on the ROI, the performance of the Western Division is superior to that of the Eastern Division because its ROI is greater. In this case, the Western Division's manager may be rewarded because of that division's better performance. As you might imagine, the use of ROI tends to encourage competition among segment managers, who strive to enhance performance evaluation by choosing investments that will work to increase their segment's ROI.

For the ROI to increase, the ROI of any new investment must exceed the segment's current ROI. If a new investment promises an ROI that is equal to the segment's current ROI, the segment's ROI will remain unchanged. However, if the new investment's ROI is less than the segment's current ROI, the segment's ROI will decrease. For example, assume that the manager of the Eastern Division is contemplating a new investment in the hope of improving his or her performance evaluation. An investment opportunity is available that promises additional income of $123,750 and requires an additional investment of $1,500,000. The ROI for this new investment opportunity is 8.25 percent calculated as follows:

$$\frac{\text{New Investment Income}}{\text{Investment in the New Project}} = \text{ROI}$$

$$\frac{\$123,750}{\$1,500,000} = 8.25\%$$

Based on the company's required rate of return of eight percent, it seems that the project should be accepted. Will the manager of the Eastern Division accept the project because it exceeds the company's required ROI and would benefit the company as a whole? Unfortunately, the answer is probably no. The manager of the Eastern Division may not select this project because it would work to reduce the *segment's* current ROI, as shown in Exhibit 10–8.

Although the Eastern Division's ROI would still be well above the required ROI rate of eight percent, the new investment would reduce the division's ROI from 8.5 percent to approximately 8.47 percent.

**Exhibit 10–8**
Effect of New Project on Eastern Division's Segment ROI

| Eastern Division *Without* the New Investment Opportunity | Eastern Division *With* the New Investment Opportunity |
|---|---|
| $$\frac{\text{Segment Income}}{\text{Investment in the Segment}} = \text{ROI}$$ | $$\frac{\text{Segment Income}}{\text{Investment in the Segment}} = \text{ROI}$$ |
| $$\frac{\$896,750}{\$10,550,000} = 8.5\%$$ | $$\frac{\$896,750 + \$123,750}{\$10,550,000 + \$1,500,000} = \text{ROI}$$ |
| | $$\frac{\$1,020,500}{\$12,050,000} = 8.47\%$$ |

When ROI is used as the segment performance measure, the evaluation is usually based not only on how the segment's ROI compares to the company's required rate, but also on how segment's ROI compares to the ROI of other segments. Therefore, managers will only select projects that will enhance their current ROI. Unfortunately this often works to the detriment of the company as a whole, because projects that meet the company's required ROI rate are rejected simply because they will not increase the segment's ROI. Fortunately, another evaluation technique encourages managers to accept projects that have an ROI exceeding the company's required ROI rate. This evaluation technique is called residual income.

# RESIDUAL INCOME

**residual income** The amount by which a segment's actual income exceeds the income needed to meet a company's required rate of return.

**Residual income** is a technique used to evaluate investment centers by focusing on the amount by which a segment's actual income exceeds the income needed to meet the company's required rate of return. As an example, let us take another look at the Lisa Company. Recall that the investment in the Eastern Division of the Lisa Company is $10,550,000 and that the company's required rate of return is eight percent. With that said, the Eastern Division must earn $844,000 ($10,550,000 × 8%) just to equal the eight percent required rate of return. This required earnings amount represents the dollar amount of earnings the segment must earn to equal the required rate of return for the company. Any earnings in excess of the required earnings (in this case $844,000) will constitute the segment's residual income. For the Eastern Division, the $896,750 actual income exceeds the $844,000 required income by $52,750. Therefore, the residual income for the Eastern Division is $52,750, calculated as follows:

| | |
|---|---|
| Actual Income | $896,750 |
| Less Required Income ($10,550,000 × 8%) | ($844,000) |
| Equals Residual Income | $ 52,750 |

This is not to say that the Eastern Division only earned $52,750. Rather, the Eastern Division's income exceeded the company's required earnings by $52,750.

If the division's actual income were less than the income required to meet the company's required rate of return, the residual income amount would be a negative number. In our example, the positive residual income amount indicates that the segment's actual earnings exceed the company's required rate of return. In the unlikely event that residual income is zero, it would indicate that the actual income for the segment exactly equals the company's required rate of return.

# Discussion Question

**10–13.** What similarities do you see between our discussion here of the residual income calculation and our discussion in Chapter 7 of net present value?

We now calculate the residual income for the Western Division so we can evaluate the relative performance of the two divisions. Using the amounts previously presented for the Western Division, we calculate residual income as $73,500:

| | |
|---|---|
| Actual Income | $857,500 |
| Less Required Income ($9,800,000 × 8%) | ($784,000) |
| Equals Residual Income | $ 73,500 |

Notice that the residual income of the Western Division exceeds that of the Eastern Division. Accordingly, the performance of the Western Division would obviously be viewed more favorably than that of the Eastern Division. In an attempt to improve the Eastern Division's relative performance, managers would strive to increase revenue, decrease expenses, or seek new, high-return investment opportunities.

When ROI is used to evaluate potential investment opportunities, managers invest only in projects with an anticipated return that exceeds the segment's current ROI. Projects that exceed the company's required rate of return but did not exceed the segment's current ROI would likely be rejected. Look again at the investment opportunity proposed for the Eastern Division. Recall that the project would require an investment of $1,500,000 with anticipated additional income of $123,750. Therefore, the total investment of the Eastern Division would increase to $12,050,000 ($896,750 + $123,750), while total segment income would increase to $1,020,500 ($896,750 + $123,750).

If residual income were used to evaluate segment performance, management of the Eastern Division would tend to accept the proposed project if it worked to increase residual income. Look again at the residual income for the Eastern Division both with and without the proposed investment opportunity. The data are presented in Exhibit 10–9.

**Exhibit 10–9**
Residual Income for Eastern Division with and without Proposed Investment

| Eastern Division *Without* the New Investment Opportunity | | Eastern Division *With* the New Investment Opportunity | |
|---|---|---|---|
| Actual Income | $896,750 | Actual Income | $1,020,000 |
| Required Income | | Required Income | |
| $10,550,000 × 8% = | $844,000 | $12,050,000 × 8% = | $ 964,000 |
| Residual Income | $ 52,750 | Residual Income | $ 56,000 |

As you can see, the investment opportunity for the Eastern Division would increase residual income. Therefore, management of the Eastern Division would tend to favor the investment. Notice that the residual income method, unlike ROI, prompts managers to accept projects with return rates that exceed the company's required rate of return even if the project's rate of return falls short of the segment's current ROI.

# Nonfinancial Performance Measures

In the past, business in the United States has focused almost exclusively on financial amounts to measure success. Success has been gauged by how much revenue can be generated, how much costs can be reduced, or how much profit can be earned. Recently, however, many companies have begun to also consider nonfinancial performance measures in evaluating business performance. Many managers are finding out that tracking the various flows of dollars and cents alone cannot ensure business success. Intense competition has prompted U.S. businesses to take a second look at nonfinancial performance measures in the hope that better performance on these will ultimately lead to greater financial rewards.

## Quality

Today, many companies are calling for continuous quality improvement in every area of business. Today's quality-conscious companies are not only producing higher-quality products, but also demanding high-quality performance throughout every aspect of business. To remain competitive, U.S. companies must produce the high-quality products their customers have come to expect. Thus, they have begun to monitor product quality in a number of ways. Production reports are no longer limited to data pertaining to numbers of units and unit cost. Information about the number of defective products and the amount of rework is now prepared and used as a basis for measuring segment success. Product quality is also monitored by tabulating the amount and nature of customer complaints. Product warranty repair costs and the number of repairs or service calls are also useful tools in evaluating product quality.

The trend in business today is to establish extremely high goals for quality. For FedEx, 100 percent on-time deliveries is the goal. Imagine, not 90 percent or 95 percent, but 100 percent on-time deliveries. This goal may seem impossible to achieve, but FedEx has mobilized the company to achieve high-quality performance in every aspect of the delivery process. From delivery truck maintenance to the package tracking system, quality is the hallmark of the company.

## Discussion Question

**10–14.** What, if any, are the potentially negative financial effects of focusing on quality?

## Customer Satisfaction

In today's competitive business environment, customer satisfaction is often viewed as the most critical ingredient in achieving and maintaining success. Even if customer satisfaction is important, how can it be evaluated to measure segment performance? There are several ways. First, customer complaints can be monitored. At IBM, for example, detailed records are kept regarding each customer complaint. In addition to a simple count of the number of complaints, IBM records the nature and severity of each and follows up every compliant to ensure that the customer's needs have been reasonably met.

To satisfy customers, you must first know what customers want. Surveys can be used to identify what is important to customers and to help determine whether they are satisfied with products and services. For example, buyers of Infinity automobiles are surveyed each time their cars are serviced. This survey accomplishes at least two important things. First, it provides information that can be used to evaluate the performance of the service facilities. Second, it can alert the company to an unhappy customer so that reasonable action can be taken to remedy each customer complaint.

## Discussion Question

**10–15.** What, if any, are the potentially negative financial effects of focusing on customer satisfaction?

### Employee Morale

An increasing number of companies are targeting company morale as an almost certain road to higher profits. It stands to reason that employees who are happy with their jobs are more likely to work hard to benefit both themselves and the company. Without question, low morale leads to high turnover, which in turn leads to the enormous cost of hiring and training employees. It follows, then, that managers should work to keep employee morale high. Measuring employee morale can be challenging, but some useful indicators of employee morale are the amount of absenteeism, the rate of employee turnover, and recruiting success rates.

## Discussion Question

**10–16.** What, if any, are the potentially negative financial effects of focusing on employee morale?

### Employee Safety

In today's business world, it is critical that employees be provided with a safe work environment. The Dow Chemical Company, for example, has invested a great deal in promoting safety in the workplace. Employees are routinely reminded of the importance of safety through company-provided posters, safety seminars, and safety awareness contests. The information Dow provides to its people is not limited to safety on the job but also extends to automobile and home safety.

Dow Chemical is not alone in its campaign to promote safety. Many companies are using employee safety information to evaluate segment performance. Some measures that indicate the level of employee safety include the number of hours worked between injury accidents, the number of hours worked per injury accident, and the number of employees injured or killed in a given time period. Managers can be evaluated based on the number of safety seminars or other safety programs they hold per year.

## Discussion Question

**10–17.** What, if any, are the potentially negative financial effects of focusing on employee safety?

## Efficiency

In today's competitive environment, customers demand high-quality products at the lowest possible price. Accordingly, efficiency has become one of the cornerstones of success for many companies. Efficiency is the measure of output achieved versus the amount of resources required. To increase production efficiency relative to material, companies are attempting to produce the maximum number of units with the minimum amount of wasted material. This efficiency can be measured by the amount of scrap or the amount of material used per unit produced. For labor, efficiency can be measured by the relationship of production output to the direct labor required.

Many manufacturers are making major commitments to improve general plant efficiency. To be successful, these efforts must be supported by everyone from production-line workers to the chief executive officer. It is particularly important that top management be supportive. Typically, efficiency drives extend far beyond making minor changes and rallying the troops to work a little faster. Rather, they encompass major reorganizations of labor, new plant layouts, and innovative work flow philosophies. Many of the concepts that contribute to increased plant efficiency are part of the just-in-time philosophy.

## Discussion Question

**10–18.** What, if any, are the potentially negative financial effects of focusing on efficiency?

## JUST-IN-TIME PHILOSOPHY

**just-in-time (JIT)** A philosophy that eliminates all unnecessary inventory and limits the use of company resources until they are absolutely needed to fulfill customer demand.

The **just-in-time (JIT)** philosophy involves eliminating all unnecessary inventory and limiting the use of company resources until they are absolutely needed to fulfill customer demand. Expenditures are made only to fulfill the immediate customer demand. Products are "pulled" through the system. That is, products are made in response to the *pull* from customer demand, rather than to a *push* to have inventory to fill orders that may or may not materialize.

Often, JIT is described as a method of eliminating or greatly reducing inventory by delaying the purchase of raw material until it is needed for production. This narrow view is greatly flawed and prompts many managers to reject the whole JIT idea. Limiting the use of company resources until they are needed for production cannot be achieved by simply adopting a mind-set that purchases will be delayed until the last possible minute. Instead, the JIT philosophy focuses on delaying expenditures for inventory and reducing inventory levels to near zero by creating very efficient production processes that require only a minimal amount of inventory to successfully manufacture high-quality products.

One key component of JIT is that manufacturers must be able to depend on their suppliers for 100 percent on-time deliveries of 100 percent defect-free material. For JIT to work, manufacturers must develop close relationships with suppliers who can provide absolutely on-time deliveries and absolutely consistent high quality. When JIT is implemented, manufacturers defer quality inspections to suppliers and insist upon parts and components that are free of defects. **Zero defects** is a term that is often used to describe the concept of products that are completely free of imperfections. In a JIT environment, zero defects becomes the norm.

**zero defects** Describes the concept of products that are completely free of imperfections.

As part of the program to develop close relationships with their suppliers, firms greatly reduce that number of suppliers. By working with a core of carefully selected suppliers, the manufacturer is able to make substantial purchase commitments that help compensate suppliers for the added effort required to meet the manufacturer's demands. Also, the financial benefits they gain from receiving on-time deliveries of consistently high-quality products make it possible for manufacturers to justify paying a premium price for the goods they purchase.

**setup time**   The time it takes to prepare manufacturing equipment for the production of particular products.

In a JIT environment, setup times must be reduced to the lowest possible levels. As mentioned in Chapter 3, **setup time** is the time it takes to prepare manufacturing equipment for the production of a particular product. One major problem with long setup times is that while production equipment is being setup, it cannot be used to produce anything. The trouble does not end there, however. If setup time is substantial, fewer and longer production runs must be made to justify the substantial setup effort. It makes no sense to go through a long setup process to produce only a few units. The result of long production runs is higher inventory levels. This method is in direct conflict with the JIT philosophy. Conversely, if setup time is very short, running a short production run to produce fewer units of product is more feasible. With shorter production runs making fewer units, inventories can be reduced.

In JIT environments, setup time is now measured and average setup times are used to evaluate the performance of segment managers. In factories using just-it-time production, setup time is reduced from hours or days to minutes.

**throughput time**   The time that passes from the time a unit of product enters the production process until it emerges as a finished product.

Another focus of the JIT philosophy is reduced throughput time. **Throughput time** is the time between the entrance of a unit of production into the production process and the time it emerges as a finished product. It is an important measure of plant efficiency because the amount of money invested in work-in-process inventory can be lowered by reducing the time products are in the production process. In addition to reducing inventories, shorter throughput time frees production equipment so it can be used to make other products. Throughput time can thus be measured and used as a basis for evaluating performance.

**lead time**   The time that passes from the time an order is received until the product is complete and ready for shipment.

Another hallmark of the JIT philosophy is reduction in lead time. **Lead time** is the time between the receipt of an order and the completion of a product ready for shipment. Decreasing setup and throughput times can greatly reduce lead time. Many manufacturers that have adopted JIT have reduced lead time from months or years, to days or even hours. Lead time can be measured and used as a basis for evaluating plant performance.

**unscheduled downtime**   The amount of time production equipment is out of service due to unscheduled repairs and maintenance.

In a further effort to increase efficiency, managers are working to reduce unscheduled downtime. **Unscheduled downtime** is the amount of time production equipment is out of service due to unscheduled repairs and maintenance. To keep this factor low, managers implement routine maintenance programs that not only keep unscheduled downtime to a minimum but also keep machinery running at peak performance. Companies are now tracking unscheduled downtime and using the information to evaluate plant performance.

By now, you may be wondering just how these JIT production improvements can be achieved. They do not come cheaply or easily. A great deal of time and money must be spent to achieve the added efficiency that comes with a JIT production environment. Some key factors are improved plant layout and product flow, mechanized procedures for machine setup, convenient storage and labeling of machine parts used in the setup process, and a formal plant maintenance program.

The production plant layout should be designed so that raw materials enter the production process with little or no need to be transported to work stations. For example, when a new Saturn automobile in made, the truck that transports the seats to the factory is literally connected to the production building, and the seats are fed to the production line, in the proper order, through conveyors in the truck to conveyers in the factory. The days of buying a bunch of seats of various colors and styles to be stored in a warehouse are gone at Saturn. Gone too are the days when materials handling personnel picked through massive inventories of seats to find the color and style they needed only to transport the selected seats to the production line. By cooperating with a seat manufacturer and a transportation company, Saturn can depend on the seats not only arriving on time but being received in the correct order by color and style with zero defects. A backup plan for shipment delays is the responsibility of the supplier and transportation company.

In addition to facilitating efficient handling of raw material, a JIT environment should also strive to streamline the movement of material from one production process to the next. For example, the Dunlop Golf Ball Factory in South Carolina has eliminated the use of hopper carts to transport golf balls from the painting process to the packaging process. This decision was achieved by changing the plant layout so that golf balls travel by conveyor from one process to the next. This production improvement saves time and eliminates the need for handling the golf balls between processes. An added feature of this change was the elimination of inspection stations between the painting department and the packaging department, as the golf balls were no longer subject to blemishes caused by rough treatment in the hopper carts. The production change worked to greatly increase plant efficiency and improve product quality.

Each manufacturing environment is unique. Managers and plant workers cooperate to continually reinvent the production environment. Old production techniques and strategies must be set aside in favor of new standards of production excellence, efficiency, and product quality. Company management and production personnel must work together to achieve the world-class production excellence required in today's competitive business environment. It takes a team effort characterized by an innovative spirit and a willingness to invest in grand-scale changes.

## SUMMARY

As companies grow and the products and services they provide become more diversified, it becomes a virtual impossibility for one person to perform all management functions. More managers are required to operate and control the various facets of what we call management. A natural outgrowth of a company's evolution is the creation of business segments. A segment is any part of a company about which separate information is required to evaluate performance.

When a company is segmented, it will employ either a centralized management style or a decentralized management style. In a centralized company, upper management makes most of the important business decisions. In a decentralized company, lower-level managers are responsible for virtually all decisions that relate to their segment of the company.

Determining what costs should be charged to a particular business segment and the amount of those costs is sometimes very difficult. Some costs associated with operating a business segment are directly incurred by that segment. Others, however, are incurred to support more than one segment. These common costs must be allocated in some way to the segments receiving the benefit of the costs.

The four most commonly used designations of business segments are revenue centers, cost centers, profit centers, and investment centers. Revenue centers, cost centers, and profit centers are usually evaluated based on performance to budget.

The performance of investment centers is most often evaluated using the return on investment (ROI) technique or the residual income approach.

Although performance to budget and either return on investment or residual income are still commonly used to evaluate business segment performance, other nonfinancial measures have become popular in recent years. Many companies are now emphasizing such things as product quality, customer satisfaction, employee morale, safety in the workplace, and efficiency as ways to better measure and improve company performance.

## KEY TERMS

business segment  M-378
centralized management  M-387
common fixed cost  M-380
cost center  M-389
decentralized management  M-387
direct fixed cost  M-380
just-in-time (JIT)  M-397
indirect fixed cost  M-380
investment center  M-390
lead time  M-398
profit center  M-389
residual income  M-393

return on investment (ROI)  M-391
revenue center  M-388
segment income statement  M-379
segment margin  M-379
segment reports  M-378
service department  M-384
setup time  M-398
throughput time  M-398
traceable fixed cost  M-380
unscheduled downtime  M-398
zero defects  M-397

## REVIEW THE FACTS

A. Describe a business segment.
B. What is the difference between direct fixed cost and common fixed cost?
C. What is a service department?
D. Why is it important to know about service department cost allocation?
E. Describe the difference between centralized and decentralized management.
F. Describe a revenue center.
G. Describe a cost center.
H. What is the difference between a profit center and an investment center?
I. Why is residual income sometimes preferred to return on investment?
J. List five nonfinancial performance measures.
K. What is meant by the just-in-time philosophy?
L. How can companies achieve the very low inventory levels embraced by the just-in-time philosophy?

## APPLY WHAT YOU HAVE LEARNED

### LO 2 & 3:  Prepare a Segment Income Statement with and without the Allocation of Common Fixed Costs to Segments

10–19.  The Almer Sales Company has two divisions. The following information is available for the year ended December 31, 2000.

The sales for Almer are $300,000 for the Eastern Division and $200,000 for the Western Division. Variable costs for the Eastern Division are $250,000, whereas variable costs for the Western Division are $170,000. Direct fixed costs of the Eastern Division are $20,000 and direct fixed costs of the Western Division are $15,000. The Almer Company allocates common fixed costs to segments based on relative sales. Common fixed costs for the company are $25,000.

**REQUIRED:**

a. Prepare a segment income statement for the company which distributes common fixed costs to segments based on relative sales. Your answer should include a column for the total company and columns for each segment.

b. Do you think it is wise to evaluate the performance of a business segment based on income that includes an allocation for common fixed costs? Why or why not?

c. Prepare a segment income statement for the company which does not distribute common fixed cost to segments. Your answer should include a column for the total company and columns for each segment.

## LO 2 & 3: Prepare a Segment Income Statement with and without the Allocation of Common Fixed Costs to Segments

**10–20.** The Ted Green Sales Company has two divisions. The following information is available for the year ended December 31, 2000.

   The sales for the company are $30,000 for the North Division, and $90,000 for the South Division. Variable costs for the North Division are $18,000, while variable costs for the South Division are $54,000. Direct fixed costs of the North Division are $5,000 and direct fixed costs of the South Division are $15,000. The company allocates common fixed costs to segments based on relative sales. Common fixed costs for the company are $10,000.

**REQUIRED:**

a. Prepare a segment income statement for the company which distributes common fixed costs to segments based on relative sales. Your answer should include a column for the total company and columns for each segment.

b. Do you think it is wise to evaluate the performance of a business segment based on income that includes an allocation for common fixed costs? Why or why not?

c. Prepare a segment income statement for the company which does not distribute common fixed cost to segments. Your answer should include a column for the total company and columns for each segment.

## LO 2 & 3: Prepare a Segment Income Statement with and without the Allocation of Common Fixed Costs to Segments

**10–21.** The Albert Pons Company has two divisions. The following information is available for the year ended December 31, 2000.

   The sales for the company are $200,000 for the Central Division, and $400,000 for the South Division. Variable costs for the Central Division are $150,000, whereas variable costs for the South Division are $300,000. Direct fixed costs of the Central Division are $19,000 and direct fixed costs of the South Division are $54,000. The company allocates common fixed costs to segments based on relative sales. Common fixed costs for the company are $27,000.

**REQUIRED:**

a. Prepare a segment income statement for the company which distributes common fixed costs to segments based on relative sales. Your answer should include a column for the total company and columns for each segment.

b. Do you think it is wise to evaluate the performance of a business segment based on income that includes an allocation for common fixed costs? Why or why not?

c. Prepare a segment income statement for the company which does not distribute common fixed cost to segments. Your answer should include a column for the total company and columns for each segment.

## LO 2 & 3:  Prepare a Segment Income Statement with and without the Allocation of Common Fixed Costs to Segments

10–22. The Peppermill Company has three divisions. The following information is available for the year ended December 31, 2000.

The sales for the company are $200,000 for the Central Division, and $400,000 for the South Division, and $600,000 for the West Division. Variable costs for the Central Division are $150,000, variable costs for the South Division are $300,000, and variable costs for the West Division are 450,000. Direct fixed costs of the Central Division are $20,000, direct fixed costs of the South Division are $54,000, and direct fixed costs of the West Division are $100,000. The company allocates common fixed costs to segments based on relative sales. Common fixed costs for the company are $102,000.

**REQUIRED:**

a. Prepare a segment income statement for the company which distributes common fixed costs to segments based on relative sales. Your answer should include a column for the total company and columns for each segment.

b. Based on your answer for part a, which segment seems to have generated the least profit?

c. Prepare a segment income statement for the company which does not distribute common fixed cost to segments. Your answer should include a column for the total company and columns for each segment.

d. Based on your answer for part c, which segment seems to have generated the most profit?

## LO 2 & 3:  Prepare a Segment Income Statement with and without the Allocation of Common Fixed Costs to Segments

10–23. The Pitman Sales Company has three divisions. The following information is available for the year ended December 31, 2000.

The sales for the company are $100,000 for Division A, and $200,000 for Division B, and $300,000 for Division C. Variable costs for Division A are $50,000, variable costs for Division B are $100,000, and variable costs for Division C are $150,000. Direct fixed costs of Division A are $20,000, direct fixed costs of Division B are $30,000, and direct fixed costs of Division C are $60,000. The company allocates common fixed costs to segments based on relative sales. Common fixed costs for the company are $186,000.

**REQUIRED:**

a. Prepare a segment income statement for the company which distributes common fixed costs to segments based on relative sales. Your answer should include a column for the total company and columns for each segment.

b. Based on your answer for part a, which segment seems to have generated the least profit?
c. Prepare a segment income statement for the company which does not distribute common fixed cost to segments. Your answer should include a column for the total company and columns for each segment.
d. Based on your answer for part c, which segment seems to have generated the most profit?

## LO 2 & 3:   Prepare a Segment Income Statement with and without the Allocation of Common Fixed Costs to Segments

10–24. The Porter Sales Company has three divisions. The following information is available for the year ended December 31, 2000.
The sales for the company are $100,000 for Division 101, and $100,000 for Division 202, and $200,000 for Division 303. Variable costs for Division 101 are $50,000, variable costs for Division 202 are $60,000, and variable costs for Division 303 are $110,000. Direct fixed costs of Division 101 are $20,000, direct fixed costs of Division 202 are $30,000, and direct fixed costs of Division 303 are $50,000. The company allocates common fixed costs to segments based on relative sales. Common fixed costs for the company are $40,000.

**REQUIRED:**
a. Prepare a segment income statement for the company which distributes common fixed costs to segments based on relative sales. Your answer should include a column for the total company and columns for each segment.
b. Based on your answer for part a, does it appear that one of the segments should be closed?
c. Prepare a segment income statement for the company which does not distribute common fixed cost to segments. Your answer should include a column for the total company and columns for each segment.
d. Based on your answer for part c, does it still seem that one of the segments should be closed?

## LO 2:   Analyze Segment Cost and Prepare a Memo

10–25. The following segment income statement has been prepared for the Albertson Sales Company.

### ALBERTSON SALES COMPANY
#### Segment Income Statement
#### For the Year Ended December 31, 2000

|  | Company Total | Medical Division | Industrial Division | Consumer Division |
|---|---|---|---|---|
| Sales | $750,000 | $337,500 | $157,500 | $255,000 |
| Variable cost | 499,425 | 211,500 | 110,625 | 177,300 |
| Contribution margin | 250,575 | 126,000 | 46,875 | 77,700 |
| Direct fixed cost | 112,500 | 48,000 | 30,000 | 34,500 |
| Segment margin | 138,075 | 78,000 | 16,875 | 43,200 |
| Common fixed cost | 90,000 | 40,500* | 18,900** | 30,600*** |
| Net income | $ 48,075 | $ 37,500 | ($ 2,025) | $ 12,600 |

\* $337,500/$750,000 = 45% × $90,000 = $40,500
\*\* $157,500/$750,000 = 21% × $90,000 = $18,900
\*\*\*$255,000/$750,000 = 34% × $90,000 = $30,600

The company President, Bob Albertson, is calling a management meeting to explore the idea of closing or selling the Industrial Division. Many managers are complaining that the division is "dragging the company down."

Assume that, in preparation for the meeting, Mr. Albertson has contacted you and asked that you explore the situation.

**REQUIRED:**
Based on the information presented for the Albertson Sales Company, prepare a memo to Mr. Albertson which includes a brief summary of the problem and a proposed solution.

## LO 2: Identify the Area of Responsibility Associated with Different Types of Business Segments

**10–26.** Following are some popular segment classifications followed by three areas of management responsibility.

**Segment Classification:**

Revenue center    _____    _____    _____
Cost center    _____    _____    _____
Profit center    _____    _____    _____
Investment center    _____    _____    _____

R—Revenue
C—Cost
I—Amount invested

**REQUIRED:**
In the blank spaces provided, match the area or responsibility, revenue (R), cost (C), and amount invested (I) to the appropriate segment classification. Although not all the blank spaces will be used, some segment classifications will have more than one area of responsibility.

## LO 4: Determine Return on Investment

**10–27.** The Chemical Division of CalChem Incorporated generated a segment margin of $220,680 for the year 2000 and the amount invested in the division was $1,226,000.

**REQUIRED:**
Determine the return on investment for the Chemical Division.

## LO 4: Determine Return on Investment

**10–28.** The Southern Division of the Benson Sales Company generated a segment margin of $790,020 for the year 2000 and the amount invested in the division was $4,158,000.

**REQUIRED:**
Determine the return on investment for the Southern Division.

## LO 4: Determine Return on Investment

**10–29.** The Automotive Division of the Bascom Company generated a segment margin of $1,916,800 for the year 2000 and the amount invested in the division was $11,980,000.

**REQUIRED:**
Determine the return on investment for the Automotive Division.

## LO 4:   Determine Return on Investment

**10–30.** The Alcad Farm Products Company generated income of $558,620 for the year 2000 and the amount invested in the division was $3,286,000.

**REQUIRED:**
Determine the return on investment for Alcad.

## LO 2 & 4:   Determine and Interpret Return on Investment

**10–31.** The following information is available for the three divisions of the Pompano Company.

| **Amount invested in each division:** | |
|---|---|
| Division A | $3,255,000 |
| Division B | $2,145,000 |
| Division C | $3,587,000 |

| **Segment margin of each division:** | |
|---|---|
| Division A | $553,350 |
| Division B | $407,550 |
| Division C | $573,920 |

The required rate of return for the company is 16%.

**REQUIRED:**
a. Determine the return on investment for each division.
b. Rank the three divisions assuming they are considered profit centers.
c. Rank the three divisions assuming they are considered investment centers and performance is evaluated based on return on investment.
d. Why do the rankings for parts b and c differ?

## LO 2 & 4:   Determine and Interpret Return on Investment

**10–32.** The following information is available for the three divisions of the Stevens Company.

| **Amount invested in each division:** | |
|---|---|
| Division 101 | $1,225,000 |
| Division 202 | $2,445,000 |
| Division 303 | $3,697,000 |

| **Segment margin of each division:** | |
|---|---|
| Division 101 | $198,450 |
| Division 202 | $371,640 |
| Division 303 | $569,338 |

The required rate of return for the company is 15%.

**REQUIRED:**
a. Determine the return on investment for each division.
b. Rank the three divisions assuming they are considered profit centers.
c. Rank the three divisions assuming they are considered investment centers and performance is evaluated based on return on investment.
d. Why do the rankings for parts b and c differ?

## LO 2 & 4: Determine and Interpret Return on Investment

**10–33.** The following information is available for the three divisions of the Reed Company.

**Amount invested in each division:**

| | |
|---|---|
| North Division | $7,225,000 |
| South Division | $5,105,000 |
| Central Division | $4,322,000 |

**Segment margin of each division:**

| | |
|---|---|
| North Division | $1,336,625 |
| South Division | $ 898,480 |
| Central Division | $ 816,858 |

The required rate of return for the company is 14%.

**REQUIRED:**
 a. Determine the return on investment for each division.
 b. Rank the three divisions assuming they are considered profit centers.
 c. Rank the three divisions assuming they are considered investment centers.
 d. Why do the rankings for parts b and c differ?

## LO 5: Determine Residual Income

**10–34.** The Eastern Division of the Key Largo Company generated a segment margin of $1,836,800 for the year 2000 and the amount invested in the division was $12,780,000.
  The company's required rate of return is 14%.

**REQUIRED:**
Determine the residual income for the Eastern Division.

## LO 5: Determine Residual Income

**10–35.** Division A of the Emry Company generated a segment margin of $522,567 for the year 2000 and the amount invested in the division was $2,778,450.
  The company's required rate of return is 18%.

**REQUIRED:**
Determine the residual income for Division A.

## LO 5: Determine Residual Income

**10–36.** Central Division of the Craft Company generated a segment margin of $244,765 for the year 2000 and the amount invested in the division was $1,335,500.
  The company's required rate of return is 17%.

**REQUIRED:**
Determine the residual income for the Central Division.

## LO 2, 4, & 5: Determine and Interpret Return on Investment and Residual Income

**10–37.** The following information is available for the three divisions of the Top Company.

**Amount invested in each division:**

| | |
|---|---|
| Division D | $7,555,000 |
| Division E | $5,995,000 |
| Division F | $3,082,000 |

**Segment margin of each division:**

| | |
|---|---|
| Division D | $1,133,250 |
| Division E | $ 911,240 |
| Division F | $ 493,120 |

The required rate of return for the company is 14%.

**REQUIRED:**

a. Determine the return on investment for each division.
b. Determine the residual income for each division.
c. Rank the three divisions assuming they are considered profit centers.
d. Rank the three divisions assuming they are considered investment centers and performance is evaluated based on return on investment.
e. Rank the three divisions assuming they are considered investment centers and performance is evaluated based on residual income.
f. Why do some of the rankings for parts c, d, and e differ?

## LO 2, 4, & 5: Determine and Interpret Return on Investment and Residual Income

**10–38.** The following information is available for the three divisions of the Slick Company.

**Amount invested in each division:**

| | |
|---|---|
| Division 1 | $1,155,000 |
| Division 2 | $3,988,000 |
| Division 3 | $3,080,000 |

**Segment margin of each division:**

| | |
|---|---|
| Division 1 | $196,350 |
| Division 2 | $634.092 |
| Division 3 | $492,800 |

The required rate of return for the company is 15%.

**REQUIRED:**

a. Determine the return on investment for each division.
b. Determine the residual income for each division.
c. Rank the three divisions assuming they are considered profit centers.
d. Rank the three divisions assuming they are considered investment centers and performance is evaluated based on return on investment.
e. Rank the three divisions assuming they are considered investment centers and performance is evaluated based on residual income.
f. Why do some of the rankings for parts c, d, and e differ?

## LO 2, 4, & 5: Determine and Interpret Return on Investment and Residual Income

**10–39.** The following information is available for the three divisions of the Kenyon Company.

**Amount invested in each division:**

| | |
|---|---|
| Division H | $5,188,000 |
| Division I | $2,588,000 |
| Division J | $6,386,000 |

**Segment margin of each division:**

| | |
|---|---|
| Division H | $ 933,840 |
| Division I | $ 491,720 |
| Division J | $1,136,708 |

The required rate of return for the company is 16%.

**REQUIRED:**

a. Determine the return on investment for each division.
b. Determine the residual income for each division.
c. Rank the three divisions assuming they are considered profit centers.
d. Rank the three divisions assuming they are considered investment centers and performance is evaluated based on return on investment.
e. Rank the three divisions assuming they are considered investment centers and performance is evaluated based on residual income.
f. Why do some of the rankings for parts c, d, and e differ?

## LO 2 & 4: Determine and Interpret Return on Investment

**10–40.** The following information is available for the three divisions of the Planet Company.

**Amount invested in each division:**

| | |
|---|---|
| Automotive Division | $1,235,000 |
| Industrial Division | $2,005,000 |
| Consumer Division | $6,022,000 |

**Segment margin of each division:**

| | |
|---|---|
| Automotive Division | $202,540 |
| Industrial Division | $332,830 |
| Consumer Division | $963,520 |

The required rate of return for the company is 14%.

The company uses return on investment to evaluate segment performance.

The company is considering acquiring an automotive parts manufacturing company that is expected to provide income of $36,450. The acquisition would require an investment of $225,000. Although the prospective acquisition would fit nicely into the Automotive Division's operation, the Automotive Division's manager has voiced considerable reservations. He believes it would not be in the company's best interest to acquire the new segment.

The manager of the Industrial Division concurs with the Automotive Division manager. Oddly enough, the Consumer Division manager not only thinks the acquisition is a good idea, but has volunteered to accept it in her division.

**REQUIRED:**

  a. Determine the return on investment for each division.
  b. Do you feel that it is in the company's best interest to acquire the automotive parts manufacturer? Explain your answer.
  c. Why are the Automotive and Industrial Division managers reluctant to recommend the acquisition?
  d. Why would the Consumer Division manager volunteer to accept the proposed acquisition into her division?

## LO 2 & 5: Determine and Interpret Residual Income

**10–41.** Refer to the information in problem 10–40.

**REQUIRED:**

Explain how each of the managers' feelings about the acceptability of the proposed acquisition would differ if the company used residual income to evaluate segment performance instead of return on investment.

# Glossary of Accounting Terms in IMA

**accounting rate of return**   The rate of return for a capital project based on the anticipated increase in accounting operating income due to the project, relative to the amount of capital investment required. (p. M-236)

**activity-based costing**   Allocating cost to products based on the activities that caused the cost to happen. (p. M-72)

**administrative cost**   All costs incurred by a company that are not product costs or selling costs. Includes the cost of accounting, finance, employee relations, and executive functions. (p. M-22)

**allocation base**   An amount associated with cost objects that can be used to proportionately distribute manufacturing overhead costs to each cost object. (p. M-71)

**annuity**   A stream of equal periodic cash flows. (p. M-241)

**bill of materials**   A listing of the quantity and description of each item of direct material used to manufacture an individual product. (p. M-332)

**blended cost of capital**   The combined cost of debt financing and equity financing. (p. M-223)

**bottom-up budgeting**   A budget initially prepared by lower-level managers and employees. (p. M-276)

**breakeven**   Occurs when a company generates neither a profit nor a loss. (p. M-155)

**break-even point**   The sales required to achieve breakeven. This can be expressed either in sales dollars or in the number of units sold. (p. M-155)

**budget performance report**   The evaluation instrument used to evaluate a manager's performance to budget. (p. M-298)

**budgeted balance sheet**   A presentation of estimated assets, liabilities, and owners' equity at the end of the budgeted period. (p. M-271)

**budgeted income statement**   Shows the expected net income for the period covered by the operating budget. (p. M-271)

**budgeted statement of cash flows**   A statement of a company's expected sources and uses of cash during the period covered by the operating budget. (p. M-272)

**business segment**   A part of a company managed by a particular individual or a part of a company about which separate information is needed. (p. M-378)

**capital assets**   Long-lived expensive items such as land, buildings, machinery, and equipment. (p. M-220)

**capital budget**   The budget that outlines how a company intends to allocate its scarce resources over a five-year, 10-year, or even longer time period. (p. M-219)

**capital budgeting**   The planning and decision process for making investments in capital projects. (p. M-216)

**capital investments**   Business expenditures in acquiring expensive assets that will be used for more than one year. (p. M-216)

**capital projects**   Another name for *capital expenditures.* (p. M-216)

**cash budget**   Shows whether the expected amount of cash generated by operating activities will be sufficient to pay anticipated expenses during the period covered by the operating budget. (p. M-271)

**cash payments schedule**   Presents the amount of cash a company expects to pay out during the budget period. (p. M-290)

**cash receipts schedule**   Presents the amount of cash a company expects to collect during the budget period. (p. M-288)

**centralized management**   A management style in which top managers make most management decisions. (p. M-387)

**common cost**   Another name for *indirect cost.* (p. M-21)

**common fixed cost**   Fixed costs incurred to support more than one business segment, or the company as a whole. (p. M-380)

**compound interest**   Interest calculated on the original principal amount invested plus all previously earned interest. (p. M-240)

**continual budgeting**   Another name for *perpetual budgeting.* (p. M-274)

**contribution income statement**   An income statement that classifies cost by behavior (fixed cost and variable cost). (p. M-151)

**contribution margin**   The amount remaining after all variable costs have been deducted from sales revenue. (p. M-152)

**contribution margin ratio**   The contribution margin expressed as a percentage of sales. (p. M-154)

**controller**   A company's chief accountant, who is responsible for the preparation of accounting reports for both external and internal decision makers. (p. M-8)

**cost**   The resources forfeited to receive some goods or services. (p. M-20)

**cost accounting**   A narrow application of management accounting dealing specifically with procedures designed to determine how much a particular item (usually a unit of manufactured product) costs. (p. M-5)

**cost behavior**   The reaction of costs to changes in levels of business activity. (p. M-118)

**cost center**   A business segment where the manager has responsibility and authority to act to decrease or at least control costs but has little or no control over the revenues generated or the amount invested in the segment. (p. M-389)

**cost driver**   A cost cause that is used as a cost allocation base. (p. M-73)

**cost object**   Any activity or item for which a separate cost measurement is desired. (p. M-21)

**cost of capital**   The cost of obtaining financing from all available financing sources. (p. M-222)

**cost of capital rate**   Another name for *cost of capital.* (p. M-222)

**cost of debt capital**   The interest a company pays to its creditors. (p. M-223)

**cost of equity capital**   What equity investors give up when they invest in one company rather than another. (p. M-223)

**cost of goods sold budget**   Calculates the total cost of all the product a manufacturing or merchandising company estimates it will sell during the period covered by the budget. (p. M-271)

**cost of services budget**   Calculates the total cost of all the services a service type business estimates it will provide during the period covered by the budget. (p. M-271)

**cost pool**   An accumulation of the costs associated with a specific cost object. (p. M-71)

**cost-volume-profit (CVP) analysis**   The analysis of the relationship between cost and volume and the effect of these relationships on profit. (p. M-154)

**decentralized management**   A management style in which lower-level managers are responsible for decisions that relate to their segment of the company. (p. M-387)

**direct cost**   A cost that can be easily traced to an individual cost object. (p. M-21)

**direct fixed cost**   Fixed costs incurred to support a single business segment. (p. M-380)

**direct labor cost**   The cost of all production labor that can be traced directly to a unit of manufactured product. (p. M-26)

**direct labor efficiency standard**   The estimated number of direct labor hours required to produce a single unit of product. (p. M-332)

**direct labor efficiency variance**   A measure of the difference between the planned number of direct labor hours and the actual number of direct labor hours for the units actually manufactured. (p. M-342)

**direct labor hours**   The time spent by production workers as they transform raw materials into units of finished products. (p. M-28)

**direct labor rate standard**   The planned hourly wage paid to production workers. (p. M-333)

**direct labor rate variance**   A measure of the difference between the actual wage rate paid to employees and the direct labor rate standard. (p. M-344)

**direct material**   The raw material that becomes a part of the final product and can be easily traced to the individual units produced. (p. M-28)

**direct material price standard**   The anticipated cost for each item of direct material used in the manufacture of a product. (p. M-332)

**direct material price variance**   A measure of the difference between the amount the company planned to pay for direct material purchased and the amount it actually paid for the direct material. (p. M-341)

**direct material quantity standard**   The amount of direct material it should take to manufacture a single unit of product. (p. M-332)

**direct material quantity variance**   A measure of the over- or underconsumption of direct material for the number of units actually manufactured. (p. M-338)

**direct material usage variance** Another name for the *direct material quantity variance*. (p. M-338)

**direct materials cost** The cost of all raw materials that can be traced directly to a unit of manufactured product. (p. M-26)

**discounting cash flows** Determining the present value of cash to be received in the future. (p. M-229)

**engineering approach** A method used to separate a mixed cost into its fixed and variable components using experts who are familiar with the technical aspects of the activity and associated cost. (p. M-125)

**equivalent units** The number of units that would have been completed if all production efforts resulted in only completed units. (p. M-91)

**factory burden** Another name for *manufacturing overhead cost*. (p. M-29)

**factory overhead** Another name for *manufacturing overhead cost*. (p. M-29)

**favorable variance** The difference between actual performance and standard performance when the actual performance exceeds standard. (p. M-327)

**finished goods inventory** Products that have been completed and are ready to sell. (p. M-27)

**fixed cost** A cost that remains constant in total regardless of the level of activity. (p. M-118)

**fixed manufacturing overhead budget variance** The difference between the actual amount of total fixed manufacturing overhead cost and the budgeted fixed manufacturing overhead cost. (p. M-348)

**fixed manufacturing overhead volume variance** A measure of the utilization of plant capacity. This variance is caused by manufacturing more or less product during a particular production period than planned. (p. M-349)

**functional income statement** An income statement that classifies cost by function (product cost and period cost). (p. M-151)

**future value** The value of a payment, or series of payments, at some future point in time calculated at some interest rate. (p. M-240)

**high-low method** A method used to separate a mixed cost into its fixed and variable components using the mathematical differences between the highest and lowest levels of activity and cost. (p. M-132)

**hurdle rate** Another name for *cost of capital*. (p. M-222)

**hybrid firms** Companies that generate revenue from providing services and selling products. (p. M-39)

**ideal standard** A standard that is attainable only under perfect conditions. (p. M-328)

**imposed budget** A budget in which upper management sets figures for all operating activities that the rest of the company rarely, if ever, can negotiate. (p. M-276)

**incremental budgeting** The process of using the prior year's budget or the company's actual results to build the new operating budget. (p. M-275)

**indirect cost** A cost that supports more than one cost object. (p. M-21)

**indirect fixed cost** Another name for *common fixed cost*. (p. M-380)

**indirect labor** The labor incurred in support of multiple cost objects. (p. M-29)

**indirect materials** Materials consumed in support of multiple cost objects. (p. M-29)

**Industrial Revolution** A term used to describe the transition in the United States from an agricultural-based economy to a manufacturing-based economy. (p. M-9)

**Institute of Management Accountants (IMA)** A professional association of management accountants comparable to the professional association of financial accountants (American Institute of Certified Public Accountants). (p. M-11)

**internal rate of return (IRR)** The calculated expected percentage return promised by a proposed capital project. (p. M-233)

**inventoriable cost** Another name for *product cost*. (p. M-22)

**investment center** A business segment that is evaluated based on the amount of profit generated relative to the amount invested in the segment. (p. M-390)

**job cost sheet** A document that tracks the costs of products and organizes and summarizes the cost information for each job. (p. M-78)

**job order costing** A costing method that accumulates cost by a single unit, or batch of units. (p. M-76)

**just-in-time (JIT)** A philosophy that eliminates all unnecessary inventory and limits the use of company resources until they are absolutely needed to fulfill customer demand. (p. M-397)

**labor time ticket** A document used to track the amount of time each employee works on a particular production job or a particular task in the factory. (p. M-83)

**lead time**  The time that passes from the time an order is received until the product is complete and ready for shipment. (p. M-398)

**least-squares method**  Another name for *regression analysis.* (p. M-134)

**linear regression analysis**  Another name for *regression analysis.* (p. M-134)

**management accounting**  The branch of accounting designed to provide information to internal economic decision makers (managers). (p. M-5)

**management by exception**  The process of focusing management attention on areas where actual performance deviates from the preestablished standards. (p. M-327)

**managerial accounting**  Another name for management accounting. (p. M-5)

**manufacturing overhead**  All activities involved in the manufacture of products besides direct materials or direct labor. (p. M-29)

**manufacturing overhead allocation**  The process of assigning or allotting an amount of manufacturing overhead cost to each unit of product produced based on some reasonable basis of distribution. (p. M-71)

**manufacturing overhead cost**  All costs associated with the operation of the manu-facturing facility besides direct materials cost and direct labor cost. It is composed entirely of indirect manufacturing cost—that incurred to support multiple cost objects. (p. M-26)

**master budget**  Another name for *operating budget.* (p. M-266)

**master operating budget**  Another name for *operating budget.* (p. M-266)

**materials requisition**  A formal request for material to be transferred from the raw materials storage area to production. (p. M-81)

**material stores**  Another name for *raw materials inventory.* (p. M-26)

**mission statement**  A summary of the main goals of the organization. (p. M-218)

**mixed cost**  An individual cost that has both a fixed cost and a variable cost component. It also describes a company's total cost structure.(p. M-124)

**net cash flows**  Cash inflow less cash outflow. (p. M-228)

**net present value (NPV)**  The present value of all cash inflows associated with a proposed capital project minus the present value of all cash outflows associated with the proposed capital project. (p. M-229)

**normal cost system**  System in which product cost reflects actual direct material cost, actual direct labor cost, and estimated overhead costs. (p. M-87)

**operating budget**  The budget that plans a company's routine day-to-day business activities for one to five years. (p. M-220)

**operating budget**  A budget for a specific period, usually one to five years, that establishes who is responsible for the day-to-day operation of a business during that time. (p. M-266)

**opportunity cost**  The benefit foregone (given up) because one alternative is chosen over another. (p. M-195)

**organizational goals**  The core beliefs and values of the company. They outline why the organization exists and are a combination of financial and nonfinancial goals. (p. M-217)

**outsourcing**  Buying services, products, or components of products instead of producing them. (p. M-192)

**overhead**  In a manufacturing company, another name for manufacturing overhead cost; in a service type business, the indirect service cost. (p. M-29)

**participative budget**  A budget in which managers and employees at many levels of the company are involved in setting the performance standards and preparing the budget. (p. M-277)

**payback period method**  A capital budgeting technique that measures the length of time a capital project must generate positive cash flows that equal the original investment in the project. (p. M-235)

**performance to budget**  A process of evaluating managers and employees based on how they perform against the budget. (p. M-298)

**period cost**  All costs incurred by a company that are not considered product cost. Includes selling and administrative cost. (p. M-22)

**perpetual budgeting**  The budgeting approach of updating the budget every month. (p. M-274)

**practical standard**  A standard that allows for normal, recurring inefficiencies. (p. M-328)

**predetermined overhead application rate**  An overhead allocation rate calculated using estimated annual manufacturing overhead cost and the annual estimated amount for the allocation base. (p. M-87)

**present value**   The amount future cash flows are worth today based on an appropriate interest rate (p. M-243)

**process costing**   A method of allocating manufacturing cost to products to determine an average cost per unit. (p. M-76)

**product cost**   The cost of the various products a company sells. (p. M-22)

**production budget**   Details the cost and number of units that must be produced by a manufacturer to meet the sales forecast and the desired ending inventory. (p. M-270)

**profit center**   A business segment in which the manager has the responsibility and authority to act to increase revenue and decrease or at least control costs, but has little or no control over the amount invested in the segment. (p. M-389)

**profitability index**   A method used to rank acceptable proposed capital projects. (p. M-233)

**purchase order**   A formal document used to order material from a vendor. (p. M-79)

**purchase requisition**   A request form that lists the quantity and description of the materials needed. (p. M-79)

**purchases budget**   Details the cost and number of units that must be purchased by a merchandiser to meet the sales forecast and the desired ending inventory. (p. M-270)

**purchasing department**   A specialized department that purchases all the goods required by a company. (p. M-79)

**qualitative factors**   Factors that cannot be measured by numbers—they must be described in words. (p. M-185)

**raw materials inventory**   Materials that have been purchased but have not yet entered the production process. (p. M-26)

**real rate of return**   Another name for *internal rate of return.* (p. M-233)

**receiving report**   A document that indicates the quantity of each item received. (p. M-80)

**regression analysis**   A method used to separate a mixed cost into its fixed and variable components using complex mathematical formulas. (p. M-134)

**relevant cost**   A dollar inflow or outflow that pertains to a particular management decision in that it has a bearing on which decision alternative is preferable. (p. M-184)

**relevant costing**   The process of determining which dollar inflows and outflows pertain to a particular management decision. (p. M-184)

**relevant net cash flows**   Future net cash flows that differ between or among the alternatives being considered. (p. M-228)

**relevant range**   The range of activity within which cost behavior assumptions are valid. (p. M-122)

**required rate of return**   Another name for *cost of capital.* (p. M-222)

**residual income**   The amount by which a segment's actual income exceeds the income needed to meet a company's required rate of return. (p. M-393)

**return on investment (ROI)**   The percentage return generated by an investment in a business or a business segment. (p. M-391)

**revenue center**   A business segment in which the manager has responsibility and authority to act to increase revenues but has little or no control over costs and the amount invested in the segment. (p. M-388)

**sales budget**   Details the expected sales revenue from a company's primary operating activities during a certain time period. (p. M-270)

**sales forecast**   The prediction of sales for the period covered by the operating budget. (p. M-279)

**scarce resources**   A term describing the limited amount of money a company has to invest in capital projects. (p. M-227)

**scatter graphing**   A method used to separate a mixed cost into its fixed and variable components by plotting historical activity and cost data to see how a cost relates to various levels of activity. (p. M-126)

**scientific management**   A management philosophy based on the notion that factories were run by machines—some mechanical and some human. Scientific management experts believed they could improve production efficiency by establishing standards of performance for workers. (p. M-10)

**segment income statement**   An income statement prepared for a business segment. (p. M-379)

**segment margin**   The amount of income that pertains to a particular segment. (p. M-379)

**segment reports**   Reports that provide information pertaining to a particular business segment. (p. M-378)

**selling and administrative expense budget**   Calculates all costs other than the cost of product or services required to support a company's forecasted sales. (p. M-271)

**selling cost** The cost of locating customers, attracting customers, convincing customers to buy, and the cost of necessary paperwork to document and record sales. (p. M-22)

**sensitivity analysis** A technique used to determine the effect on cost-volume-profit when changes are made in the selling price, cost structure (variable and/or fixed), and volume used in the CVP calculations. Also called "what if" analysis. (p. M-161)

**service department** A business segment responsible for secondary (support) functions. Service departments provide service to the main business operations and to other service departments. (p. M-384)

**setup time** The time it takes to prepare manufacturing equipment for the production of particular products. (p. M-398)

**simple interest** Interest calculated on the original principal amount invested only. (p. M-240)

**special order** An order that is outside a company's normal scope of business activity. (p. M-190)

**standard** A preestablished benchmark for desirable performance. (p. M-326)

**standard cost system** A system in which cost standards are set after careful analysis and then used to evaluate actual performance. (p. M-326)

**standard costing** The process of setting cost performance goals that benchmark acceptable performance and then using these cost goals to evaluate performance. (p. M-326)

**standard fixed manufacturing overhead rate** The rate used to apply fixed manufacturing overhead to units of manufactured product. (p. M-334)

**standard variable manufacturing overhead rate** The rate used to apply variable manufacturing overhead to units of manufactured product. (p. M-334)

**strategic plan** A long-range plan that sets forth the actions a company will take to attain its organizational goals. (p. M-219)

**sunk cost** A past cost that cannot be changed by current or future actions. (p. M-184)

**throughput time** The time that passes from the time a unit of product enters the

production process until it emerges as a finished product. (p. M-398)

**time-adjusted rate of return** Another name for *internal rate of return.* (p. M-233)

**time value of money** The interest earning potential of cash. (p. M-189)

**time value of money** The increase in the value of cash over time due to investment income. (p. M-229)

**top-down budgeting** A budget prepared by top managers in a company. (p. M-276)

**traceable fixed cost** Another name for *direct fixed cost.* (p. M-380)

**treasurer** The corporate officer who is responsible for cash and credit management and for planning activities, such as investment in long-lived property, plant, and equipment. (p. M-7)

**unfavorable variance** The difference between actual performance and standard performance when the actual performance falls below standard. (p. M-324)

**unscheduled down time** The amount of time production equipment is out of service due to unscheduled repairs and maintenance. (p. M-398)

**variable cost** A cost that changes in total proportionately with changes in the level of activity. (p. M-119)

**variable manufacturing overhead efficiency variance** A measure of the variable manufacturing overhead cost attributable to the difference between the planned and actual direct labor hours worked. (p. M-345)

**variable manufacturing overhead spending variance** The difference between how much was actually spent on variable manufacturing overhead and the amount that should have been spent based on the actual direct labor hours worked. (p. M-347)

**variance** The difference between actual performance and the budgeted or standard amount. (p. M-326)

**work-in-process inventory** Products that have entered the production process but have not yet been completed. (p. M-27)

**zero-based budgeting** A process of budgeting in which managers start from scratch, or zero, when preparing a new budget. (p. M-275)

**zero defects** Describes the concept of products that are completely free of imperfections. (p. M-397)

# *Index: Management Accounting*